- 1

1!

THE AGE OF OLIGARCHY

Pre-industrial Britain
1722–1783

Foundations of modern Britain

General editor: *Geoffrey Holmes*

THE AGE OF OLIGARCHY
Pre-industrial Britain 1722–1783

Geoffrey Holmes
and
Daniel Szechi

LONGMAN
LONDON AND NEW YORK

Longman Group UK Limited,
Longman House, Burnt Mill,
Harlow, Essex CM20 2JE, England
and Associated Companies throughout the world

*Published in the United States of America
by Longman Publishing, New York*

First published 1993

ISBN 0582 20956 0 CSD
ISBN 0582 20955 2 PPR

British Library Cataloguing-in-Publication Data

A catalogue record for this book is
available from the British Library

Library of Congress Cataloging in Publication Data
Holmes, Geoffrey S., 1928–
    The age of oligarchy: pre-industrial Britain, 1772–1783 /
Geoffrey Holmes and Daniel Szechi.
        p. cm. – (Foundations of modern Britain)
    Includes bibliographical references and index.
    ISBN 0–582–20956–0 (CSD). – ISBN 0–582–20955–2 (PPR)
    1. Great Britain – Politics and government – 1714–1760. 2. Great
Britain – Politics and government – 1760–1789. I. Szechi, D.
(Daniel) II. Title. III. Series.
DA480.H55 1993
941.07 – dc20   92–21857
                                                                  CIP

Set 9A in 9½/12 Linotron 202 Times
Produced by Longman Singapore Publishers (Pte) Ltd.
Printed in Singapore

Contents

Contents

PART THREE: POWER IMPERIAL: TRIUMPH AND DISASTER, 1746–1783

vi

Contents

List of maps

Editor's foreword

So prodigious has been the output of specialised work on British history during the past twenty years, and so rich its diversity, that scholars and students thirst continually after fresh syntheses. Even those who read for the pure pleasure of informing themselves about the past have become quite reconciled to the fact that little can now be taken for granted. An absorbing interest in local situations, as a way to understanding more general ones; a concern with those processes of social change which accompany economic, educational and cultural development, and which often condition political activity too: these and many other strong currents of modern historiography have washed away some of our more comfortable orthodoxies. Even when we know *what* happened, there is endless scope for debate about *why* things happened and with what consequences.

In such circumstances a new series of general textbooks on British history would not seem to call for elaborate justification. However, the six volumes constituting *Foundations of Modern Britain* do have a distinct rationale and they embody some novel features. For one thing, they make a serious attempt to present a history of Britain from the point at which 'Britain' became first a recognisable entity and then a Great Power, and to trace the foundations of this state in the history of pre-eighteenth-century England. The fact that five of the six authors either have taught or are teaching in Scottish universities, while one has held a chair in the University of Wales, should at least help to remind them that one aim of the series is to avoid excessive Anglo-centricity. The first two volumes, spanning the years 1370–1660, will certainly concentrate primarily on the history of England, emphasising those developments which first prepared the way for, and later confirmed her emergence as an independent 'Commonwealth', free from Continental trammels whether territorial or ecclesiastical. But the reader should also be aware, as he reads them, of England's ultimate rôle as the heart of a wider island kingdom in which men of three nations came to be associated. During the period covered by volumes 3, 4 and 5, 1660–1870, this 'United Kingdom of Great Britain' became not only a domestic reality but the centre of an Empire and the possessor of world-wide influence. Space will allow only limited treatment of Ireland and of Anglo-Irish relations until after the Union of 1801. It is appropriate, however, that in the final volume of the series reasserted nationalism should figure almost as strongly as the erosion of imperial status in the story of Britain's slide down the slippery slope from palmy greatness to anxious mediocrity. The terminal date of volume 6, 1975, is deliberately chosen: the year in which Britain, tortured once again by her Irish inheritance and facing demands for Scottish devolution, or even independence, belatedly recognised that the days of complacent self-sufficiency as regards Europe, too, were past.

As well as paying more than mere lip-service to its own title, the present series adopts an irreverent attitude to time-honoured chronological divisions. Those lines of demarcation between volumes which dominated virtually every English history series conceived before 1960 (and, with a few exceptions, have displayed a remarkable capacity for survival subsequently) are seen as a quite unnecessary obstacle to readers' understanding of the way modern historiography has reshaped whole vistas of our island's history in the past forty years. Years such as 1485, 1603, 1689, 1714, 1760 or 1815 established themselves in textbook lore at a time when they accurately reflected the heavily political and constitutional emphasis of traditional history teaching. Even on those terms they have become of limited utility. But equally seriously, the conventions which such divisions perpetuate often make it extremely difficult for authors to accommodate funda-mental aspects of social and economic development within their allotted compass. The brutal slicing off of 'Tawney's century' (1540–1640) at 1603 is perhaps the worst of these atrocities; but it is not the only one.

All dates are to some extent arbitrary as lines of division, and all present their own difficulties. It is hoped, nonetheless, that those selected in this series to enclose periods which are in any case a good deal longer than average, may prove less inhibiting and confusing than some of their predecessors and much more adaptable to the needs of British history courses in universities and colleges.

In one further important respect the authors have kept in mind the practical requirements of students and teachers. Their approach eschews lengthy narrative wherever possible and concentrates, within chapters short enough to be rapidly absorbed, on the development of themes and the discussion of problems. Yet at the same time they attempt to satisfy their readers' need for basic information in two ways: by providing, at appropriate stages, skeletal 'frameworks' of events, chronologically ordered, within which the subsequent analysis and interplay of argument can be set; and by placing at the end of each volume a 'compendium' of factual data, including statistics, on a scale much greater than that of normal textbook appendices.

These compendia are essential companions to the texts and are designed for ready and constant use. The frequent references to them which punctuate so many chapters in this series will be found within square brackets, e.g. [B]. They should be easily distinguishable from the numerous arabic numbers within round brackets inserted in the text, e.g. (117). These refer readers to the Bibliography, in which most items are thematically arranged and serially numbered. Where necessary, specific page numbers (in italic) follow the main reference in the round brackets. In references to articles page numbers are not usually given. References to statutes, also in round brackets, are by regnal year and chapter. Superior numerals are for the references which appear at the end of the relevant chapter. The place of publication of books is London unless otherwise indicated.

Geoffrey Holmes

Preface

This book has had rather a chequered history. I was originally contracted to write a single volume, on a similar scale to the other volumes in the *Foundations of Modern Britain* series, covering the period 1660–1783, and began work on it in 1981. Unfortunately, a decade of serious and worsening health problems made it look at one stage as if the entire project would have to be abandoned unfinished, leaving a yawning gap in the series.

Two things saved the book from abandonment. One was the agreement of Daniel Szechi, then of St John's College, Oxford, now of Auburn University, Alabama, to take on responsibility for some of the later chapters, especially those in Part Three. I was and am exceedingly grateful to him. Of the 22 chapters in the book, Daniel has been wholly responsible for 6 – chapters 6, 16, 18, 19, 20 and 22, and for several sections of the Compendium; he has also prepared the index, has checked the Frameworks of Events, has given much help with the Bibliography, and has shared the proof-reading with my wife. Chapter 21 Daniel and I wrote between us. The rest of the book is my work.

The other rescue package was the work of Andrew MacLennan, the Humanities Editor of Messrs Longman, to whom I owe an inestimable debt. It was Andrew's idea that I should find a collaborator to undertake the last few chapters, when I no longer felt well enough to write them myself. It was also, crucially, Andrew's suggestion that the single unwieldly pile of typescript which finally arrived on his desk in the summer of 1991 (I didn't dare weigh it, but it must have topped the scales at many pounds avoirdupoids) should be divided into two separate books, with the division falling at the end of my original Part Two, i.e. the early 1720s. I must acknowledge with special warmth the encouragement, understanding and unshakeable forbearance which he has shown me over many years.

Because the original single-volume treatment was organised in a number of substantial but discrete sections, arranged broadly chronologically, dividing it to make two related but independent volumes, each self-sufficient and convincing in its own right, proved less arduous in practice than we might have feared. Nonetheless, a few rough edges remain. The division at 1722, like so many chronological clean cuts, is more justifiable in terms of politics (with the Election of 1722, which ushered in the long period of Whig oligarchy) than economic or social terms. Our treatment of Scotland and Ireland straddles the divide between this book and *The Making of a Great Power*; that book took the aftermath of the Union of 1707 as far as 1727; this one goes back to the 'Fifteen Rebellion. With Ireland, Daniel's chapter 16 begins as far back as the Williamite settlement. I can only plead that a clean cut at either 1714 (the traditional dividing date) or 1722 makes no sort of sense with either country. There has also had to be a rather untidy overlap between the Compendia in the two books, about two-thirds of the original appearing in both. The solutions to my problems which finally emerged may not be wholly satisfactory, but I believe they were the best possible in the circumstances.

There has been another less than satisfactory result of the way the book was written, which applies to my chapters, though not to Daniel's. With a textbook which takes almost a decade in the writing parts are bound to be out of date by the time the book is published. The textbook writer's nightmare, a rush of relevant material published at a late stage in the book's production, has afflicted me not once but several times over the past decade. For all my efforts, I have not been able to incorporate as much recent work as I would have wished in the finished book.

Apart from my debt to Daniel, it is a pleasure to record a number of other personal obligations in the writing of this book. David Hayton's expert advice was invaluable for Daniel in writing the difficult chapter on post-Revolution Ireland. Eric Evans kindly sacrificed time from a period of leave to read through all the chapters in Parts Two and Three; and both authors found his observations of great assistance. I am grateful to the British Academy for awarding me a Small Grant which enabled me to spend time in London looking at some important primary sources; and to the University of Lancaster, for making me a grant from its Research Fund, thanks to which I was able to employ for a few months two part-time research assistants, Stuart Handley and Alan Marshall, who did excellent spadework on the Frameworks of Events and some sections of the Compendium, respectively. Stuart was also a great help in checking references and quotations when I was unable to travel to London myself.

More than ever before, my greatest debt has been to my wife, Ella. Without her scholarly and secretarial assistance, encouragement and nursing care, this book would never have been completed, let alone seen through the press. Any errors, of course, which escaped the net of her and my friends' scrutiny are my responsibility alone.

Geoffrey Holmes
Burton-in-Lonsdale
March 1992

Acknowledgements

The publishers would like to thank the following for permission to reproduce copyright material: Cambridge University Press for tables J.4 and L.1 from W.A. Cole's chapter in *The Economic History of Britain since 1700: I, 1700–1860*, R.C. Floud and D.H. McCloskey, eds, (1981); and Oxford University Press for the figure in M.1 from *Crime and the Courts in England 1660–1800*, J.M. Beattie (1986).

Note on dating and quotations

For the first half of the eighteenth century, England still used the Julian calendar ('Old Style' or O.S.) when much of the rest of Europe used the more accurate Gregorian calendar ('New Style' or N.S.). Old Style dating was 11 days behind New Style, and this discrepancy continued until 1752, when the New Style calendar was finally adopted in England (see p. 240). In this book all dates before 1752, except where otherwise noted, are given in Old Style; the New Year is, however, taken to begin on 1 January, although in England the Julian New Year began on 25 March. In a few cases, both Old Style and New Style dates are given, thus : 15/26 January 1744.

In original quotations, spelling and punctuation have been modernised.

List of abbreviations

The following abbreviations are used in end-notes, compendium and bibliography.

Add.MSS	Additional Manuscripts, British Library
AgHR	*Agricultural History Review*
BIHR	*Bulletin of the Institute of Historical Research*
BL	British Library
CJ	*Journals of the House of Commons*
EcHR	*Economic History Review*, 2nd series
EHR	*English Historical Review*
HJ	*Historical Journal*
HMC	Historical Manuscripts Commission
JBS	*Journal of British Studies*
JEH	*Journal of Ecclesiastical History*
LJ	*Journal of the House of Lords*
Parl. Hist.	*Parliamentary History: A Yearbook* (1982–6) or *Parliamentary History* (1987–)
P & P	*Past and Present*
RO	Record Office
TRHS	*Transactions of the Royal Historical Society*, 5th series

To
Richard and Robyn
GSH
Jessica and Edward
DS

PART ONE

The Age of Walpole, 1722–1746

1722   George I's first Parliament dissolved (Mar). General Election (Mar–Apr): Whigs increase majority over Tories to *c.* 200, even before hearing petitions [E.1]. Dubois reveals Jacobite plot to Walpole; death of Sunderland; Congress of Cambrai, planned to settle outstanding international problems in Western and Southern Europe, begins informal sessions (Apr).

        News of the Jacobite conspiracy ('Atterbury Plot') made public (8 May); arrest of bishop of Rochester's secretary (15th). Patent granted to William Wood for minting a new copper coinage in Ireland (July), sparking off three years of Irish 'Patriot' opposition to 'Wood's Half-Pence'. Bishop Atterbury arrested (Aug); his release under Habeas Corpus refused (Sept).

        Parliament meets (9 Oct). Habeas Corpus Act suspended, after defeat of Opposition amendment – supported by some Whigs – to limit suspension to 6 months (16th). Jacobite Christopher Layer condemned to death for treason (Nov). Emperor grants by charter right to Ostend Company (Austr. Neths.) to trade with East and West Indies – early alarm in Britain and Holland (Dec).

        Duke of Marlborough dies. Defoe's *Moll Flanders* published.

1723   Walpole fails to oust Carteret from the ministry [cf. 1724] (Jan). Bill of Pains and Penalties against Atterbury passes Commons with huge majorities (Apr); Atterbury's stout defence in Lords (11th–13th May), but bill passes there by 83:43 (15th); execution of Layer; Bolingbroke's pardon passes the Great Seal and he returns to England (25th – cf. 1725); Parliament prorogued (28 May) – not to meet again this year, and with Walpole's 'interest so strong that he has nothing to apprehend, unless it be from the too great majority of Whigs in Parliament, for it is impossible to satisfy them all . . .' [George Baillie, MP, Treasury Commissioner, July 1723].

        Bishop Atterbury goes into exile (June). Nationalist agitation in Ireland: Irish Parliament meets (Sept) and votes to address the King that the patent granted to William Wood [cf. 1722] was 'prejudicial to the revenue, destructive of trade, and dangerous to property'. Deaths in France of Dubois (Aug) and Regent Orléans (Nov).

        Workhouse Test Act passed. Trenchard's 'Cato's Letters' in the *London Journal* end, after viciously attacking the Anglican charity school movement for encouraging Jacobitism and social insubordination. Deaths of Sir Christopher Wren and Sir Godfrey Kneller, the painter; birth of Adam Smith.

1724   Second session of George I's second Parliament meets; Congress of Cambrai begins its formal sessions (Apr) after two years delay, but achieves little – Spain's disillusionment with France and Britain over her Mediterranean aspirations grows.

        First of Swift's *Drapier's Letters* published, attacking effects of 'Wood's Half-Pence' on Irish prosperity (Feb); subsequent *Letters* call for Ireland's liberation from slavish dependence on England; Carteret dismissed from his Secretaryship (Mar); despatched to Ireland as Lord Lieutenant with the brief of pacifying the kingdom (Apr); duke of Newcastle, Lord Chamberlain since 1717, begins epic tenure as a Secretary of State – claims of Walpole's old ally, Pulteney, passed over (6 Apr); Parliament prorogued (24th).

        Parliament reassembles; Spanish diplomat, Ripperda, sent on mission of reconciliation to Vienna (Nov – cf. 1725). London aldermen, at Walpole's instigation, petition for reduction of City's privileges; leave given in Commons for introduction of City of London Election Bill; Commons vote to impose duty of 3d. per bushel on Scottish malt – half the English rate (Dec).

Death of Robert Harley, earl of Oxford, statesman (May) and execution of Jonathan Wild, master-thief and fence; Part I of Defoe's *Tour through the Whole Island of Great Britain* and Vol. I of Bishop Burnet's *A History of My Own Time* published.

1725   Lord Chancellor Macclesfield resigns (Jan); impeached for sale of offices, abandoned by Walpole, found guilty and disgraced – fined £30,000 (Feb–May). City Election Bill, affirming Court of Aldermen's right of veto and disfranchising *c*. 3,000 liverymen passes its third reading in Commons – only 83 votes against (19 Mar); William Pulteney [Cofferer of the Household since 1723] 'set[s] himself at the head of the Opposition to the Court' in the Commons (8–9 Apr); Commons, 231:111, order a bill to reverse Bolingbroke's attainder but exclude him from House of Lords (Apr). [First] Treaty of Vienna signed by Spain and the Emperor (Apr O.S.) – arousing anti-Jacobite and commercial fears in Britain, and concern for Balance of Power. Parliament prorogued (May). Shawfield (Malt Tax) riots in Glasgow (June). British diplomacy [Townshend] answers Vienna Treaty with Alliance of Hanover, concluded between Britain, France and Prussia (Aug O.S.).

Government back down before Irish opposition to new coinage – Wood's patent annulled. Duke of Roxburgh, Scottish [Squadrone] Secretary of State since 1716, dismissed for inertia during Malt Tax riots: supremacy of Islay and Argyll in Scottish political management begins (Sept).

Comprehensive review of customs duties undertaken (new Book of Rates). First of 'Wade's roads' built in Scottish Highlands [1725–37]. Alexander Pope translates the *Iliad* and the *Odyssey*. Halley's second edition of Flamsteed's *Historia Coelistis* (which Flamsteed did not endorse) lists 3,000 stars observable from England.

1726   New session of Parliament opens – King's Speech announces war with Spain imminent and seeks supply for increasing Navy; army estimates easily approved, Pulteney and Tory leader Wyndham disagreeing over opposition (Jan); Daniel Pulteney's motion for enquiring into National Debt crushed by 262:89; Opposition (Tory-Pulteneyite) attack on Alliance of Hanover beaten off – support pledged for George I's electorate, if attacked, 285:107 (Feb). Parliament prorogued after 4 months (May). Poor harvest in Ireland leads to onset of famine.

British naval forces sent to Baltic, Spanish and W. Indian waters (summer – autumn); Cardinal Fleury becomes Louis XV's chief minister and supreme influence over French foreign policy (June). Russia adheres to Vienna alliance and the Dutch to that of Hanover (Aug); Prussia withdraws from Hanover Alliance and signs treaty of alliance with Emperor at Wusterhausen (Oct).

First issue of a major new opposition journal, *The Craftsman*, founded by Bolingbroke and the Pulteneys (6 Dec).

Jonathan Swift's *Gulliver's Travels* published.

1727   Beginning of fifth session of Parliament; Henry Pelham's government motion to increase the size of the army by 8,000 carried, 250:85, in committee (Jan). Land Tax doubled to 4s. in the £; Spanish forces lay siege to Gibraltar (Feb). Vote of censure on Walpole defeated, 248:124 (Mar); government proposal to balance the budget by raiding the Sinking Fund agreed (Apr); Parliament prorogued (May).

Preliminaries of Paris signed by Britain, France, United Provinces (UP) and the Emperor: Charles VI agrees not to press Austria's commercial aspirations and to attend a congress [at Soissons] to settle the outstanding disputes and grievances of the powers (May). But Spain still recalcitrant over Gibraltar and Italy.

Death of George I en route for Hanover (11 June): accession of Prince of

Wales as George II; new King attempts to replace Walpole by Spencer Compton. Short parliamentary session (27 June–17 July); Walpole uses Treasury interest to pilot through increase in Civil List and survives the crisis with aplomb (July).

Parliament dissolved (Aug); General Election (Aug–Sept) – Tory strength lowest since 1679 [E.1].

Period of epidemics and heavy mortality in England and Wales begins [1727–9]. London dissenting ministers (Presbyterian, Independent, Baptist) draw together and appoint a General Committee of the Three Denominations. Death of Sir Isaac Newton; his *Principia* (1687) published in English.

1728 George II's first Parliament meets; Arthur Onslow, ministerial candidate, elected Speaker – destined to hold office for 33 years (Jan). Low Tory morale and many absences; Commons vote to employ Hessian mercenary troops by 280:84, but Land Tax lowered to 3s. in the £ (Feb). Poor harvest in Ireland.

Spain ceases hostilities and accepts Paris Preliminaries as confirmed by Convention of Pardo; other outstanding questions referred to a congress (Feb-Mar). Bank of England lends £1.75 million to the government at 4 per cent (May); Walpole's majorities remain enormous and impregnable down to time of prorogation (28th).

Congress of Soissons opens (June [concl. 1729]) – serious Austro-Spanish differences persist. Prince Frederick arrives in Britain (Dec) – created Prince of Wales 9 Jan 1729.

Alexander Pope's *The Dunciad* and John Gay's *Beggar's Opera* performed – Walpole and his regime now the butt of literary-political satire.

1729 Parliament reassembles (21 Jan); King's Speech stresses continuing uncertain prospects of European settlement; Opposition still weak and divided; motion attacking alliance with France attracts only 80 votes (5 Feb). First signs that ministerial majority might prove vulnerable (Mar) – reduced to 35 in a vote on Spanish depredations against British shipping (13th). Parliament prorogued (14 May). Another bad harvest in Ireland leads to famine across the whole country, with Ulster particularly badly hit.

Townshend travels to Hanover with George II – his foreign policy now too hawkish and pro-French for Walpole (May). Treaty of Seville signed with Spain (Oct O.S.) – the outcome of Walpole's personal foreign policy initiative [H(vi)].

Widespread killer epidemics – the worst in the 18th century – sweep England and Wales. John Wesley becomes tutor of Lincoln College and leader of Oxford's tiny 'methodist' society.

1730 Third session of Parliament begins (Jan). 80 Whigs desert the administration in annual vote on Hessian troops; full-scale parliamentary storm over news that the French had refortified Dunkirk; revival of campaign for place legislation – Sandys's pensions bill rallies Country support and passes by 10 votes (but rejected by Lords); abolition of duties on salt moved from back benches and uneasily accepted by Walpole (Feb).

Parliament prorogued (May). Resignation of Townshend (16 May); Carteret dismissed from Lord Lieutenancy of Ireland; Harrington, a diplomat, made Northern Secretary (June), Devonshire Privy Seal, with further extensive reshaping of the ministry. Further European tension as Italian clauses of Seville Treaty are ignored; Walpole decides on secret negotiations with Charles VI with aim of resolving Britain's European problems and defusing parliamentary opposition (Sept). Deist Matthew Tindal publishes *Christianity Old as Creation*.

1731 *The Craftsman* prints details of Vienna negotiations, which were being kept secret from France; its publisher, Francklin, jailed on charge of sedition (Jan); opening of Parliament (21st). Commons vote to re-engage Hessian troops, 249:164; Opposition vote falls by 43 when government's handling of Spanish relations endorsed by Parliament (Feb).

[Second] Treaty of Vienna concluded with Emperor (Mar) – Austria gives vital ground on Spanish claims in Italy in return for British guarantee of Pragmatic Sanction [A; H(vii)]; Vienna Treaty triumphantly revealed to Commons (Apr); end of session (May).

Spain, for time being satisfied, accedes to the Austro-British treaty (July). British mercantile and squirearchical uneasiness with foreign policies of Walpole's government damped down.

Colony of Georgia established. *The Gentleman's Magazine* founded; John Hadley invents his quadrant.

1732   Parliament reassembles and its attention switches to the revenue (Jan); Walpole proposes reduction of land tax to 1s. in the £ to be partly paid for by reimposing salt duties removed in 1730; Opposition campaigns against the duties as unjust to the poor, and Commons vote to accept proposal in principle only by 205:176 (Feb); Salt Bill committed and passed by majorities of 64 and 72 (Mar). Prorogation of Parliament (1 June).

Report of committee on frauds and abuses in the customs presented to Treasury (June) – since Christmas 1723, 6 customs men murdered, 250 assaulted, 250,000 pounds of tea and 650,000 gallons of brandy seized and condemned, massive frauds revealed in tobacco and wine trade. Treasury prepares plans to remove domestically-consumed tobacco and wine from customs net and subject them to excise duties ('Excise Scheme'). *The Craftsman* 'unleashes a press campaign of unparalleled fury' [Plumb] against salt duties and threat of 'general' excise (Oct–Nov).

'The Protestant Dissenting Deputies' formed as parallel lay organisation to the Protestant Dissenting Ministers (cf. 1727) and pressure group. Water-driven threshing machine invented (by Michael Menzies).

1733   Parliament meets for its sixth session. Augustus II of Poland dies (Jan). Many public meetings, popular demonstrations and riots directed against Excise; 54 constituencies, especially trading boroughs, 'instruct' their members to oppose it (Jan–Mar). First part of Walpole's Excise Scheme – for a tobacco excise – presented to the Commons (amid intense lobbying by Londoners) and approved in committee by 265:204 (14 Mar); ministry faced with dwindling majorities on the Excise Bill: motion to print the bill lost by only 16 votes (4–5 Apr); bill postponed until 12 June – effectively anaesthetised (11th).

Dismissal of Excise rebel peers, Chesterfield and Clinton (13 Apr). Tied vote in House of Lords (75:75) on an enquiry into the use of the confiscated estates of the South Sea Company's directors (24 May); by means of the bishops' votes government narrowly survives Opposition attack in Lords on South Sea question (2 June); more Excise rebels, duke of Montrose, earls of Stair and Marchmont, dismissed and duke of Bolton and Lord Cobham deprived of their regiments. Parliament rises (13 June).

French candidate, Stanislas Leszczynski, elected King of Poland (Aug): leading to election of rival Imperialist-backed and pro-Russian candidate, Augustus III [Augustus of Saxony], and to outbreak of the War of the Polish Succession (Oct), when Leszczynski deposed and France declares war on Charles VI. Horatio Walpole's mission to the Hague – Britain joins Dutch in offering mediation between combatants, but her prime minister turns down first Austrian pleas for armed assistance due under terms of second Treaty of Vienna (Oct–Nov).

Treaty of Escorial ('First Bourbon Family Compact') signed, effecting rapprochement between France and Spain: Philip V and Louis XV pledge 'eternal friendship'; Louis agrees to Don Carlos's claims on Parma/Piacenza and to anti-British clauses regarding trade and Gibraltar (29 Oct O.S.).

Molasses Act passed – attempt to protect West Indian sugar planters against harder times. Pope's *Essay on Man* published. John Kay, a Bury weaver (or 'reedmaker') patents his flying shuttle.

1734   Last session of Parliament begins; Walpole easily deflects desultory Opposition calls for intervention on behalf of Austria; Opposition request for papers relating to Treaty of Seville rejected (Jan). Tory motion, 'Patriot'-backed, to repeal Septennial Act lost, but only by 247:184, 77 Whig 'Patriots' voting against the government (Mar). Parliament dissolved (17 Apr).

General Election (Apr–May): emotive and sometimes violent campaign, fought largely on Excise issue, reduces ministerial majority *vis-à-vis* both Tories and Opposition Whigs – the latter rising to 83 – [E.1].

Polish Succession War goes against Leszczynski and the French in Poland but goes badly for Austria in Italy: duchy of Naples won for Don Carlos (Apr–Aug); Sicily then conquered by Spanish general, Montemar. French successes on the Rhine as well as in Lombardy.

Marine chronometer invented by John Harrison. Voltaire publishes his *Lettres Anglaises*, inaugurating the anglophil phase of the Enlightenment.

1735   New Parliament meets; King's Speech asks for increased revenue to build up the armed forces in view of war on Continent; Commons Address promising necessary supplies carried, 265:185 (Jan). Government motions to raise number of seamen to 30,000 and size of army to 25,000 men carried, though against stiff opposition (Feb) – Walpole boasting in the Navy debate of 'not one drop of English blood spilt, or one shilling of English money spent'. Place Bill rejected in Commons by only 26 votes (Apr); Parliament prorogued (May).

Pulteney disheartened by failure of Opposition to break through, threatens to absent himself from Parliament in 1736; Bolingbroke retires to France.

Preliminaries of Vienna, ending hostilities outside Poland, signed by Austria and France (Sept O.S.); Spain, dissatisfied, refuses to sign until 1736.

Hogarth paints and engraves his *Rake's Progress* and sees the passing of 'Hogarth's Act', to protect himself and other engravers and designers from piracy.

1736   Parliament reassembles – thin attendance (Jan). Full-blooded revival of Church issues in politics: threatening to split the bipartisan Opposition (Mar); Opposition Whig proposal to repeal Test Acts in favour of Protestant dissenters defeated, 251:123 – Tories uncomfortably aligned with ministerialists among majority (12th); Quaker Tithe Bill introduced – Walpole decides to support Quaker relief, offending Gibson and the bishops.

Mortmain Bill from Whig back benches, hitting charitable bequests to Anglican Church (see Ch. 8), passes Commons, 176:72 (Apr). Commons approve Quaker Tithe Bill, only 48 Tories present to oppose (3 May); rejected by Lords, after great revolt of Whig bishops (12th); Gibson, ministry's chief ecclesiastical adviser and the leading figure on the bench since 1723, falls from favour. Parliament prorogued (20th).

Porteous Riots in Edinburgh: Porteous, Captain of City Guard, lynched by mob after firing on a threatening crowd at the hanging of a smuggler (7 Sept).

Gin Act passed. William Warburton's *The Alliance between Church and State* published. John Wesley sails for Georgia.

1737   Death of Archbishop Wake (Jan); Gibson passed over and John Potter, bishop of Oxford, made Primate (9 Feb).

Third session of George II's second Parliament begins (1 Feb). Ministry proposes no reduction of standing army (18,000), carries army estimates by 246:177 (18th). Hardwicke appointed Lord Chancellor (21st); Opposition motion to increase the allowance of Prince of Wales to £100,000 p.a. – deeply repugnant to King and opposed by Walpole – gains 204 votes; lost only through absence of 45 Tory MPs (22nd). Bill to punish Edinburgh for the Porteous riots, earlier promoted by Opposition peers as a trouble-making measure, passes a thin Commons at end of session; leads to permanent alienation of part of Scots contingent at Westminster, led by Argyll, from Walpole regime (June). Prorogation of Parliament (21st).

Culmination of long quarrel between King and Prince of Wales (Sept); Frederick expelled from St James's Palace; sets up court at Leicester House and becomes, from now on, permanent focus of opposition to George II's ministers. Death of Queen Caroline (20th Nov).

Act for Licensing Plays passed; many playwrights (e.g. Fielding) turn to writing novels instead.

1738   Parliament reassembles (Jan); Opposition leaders dismayed by refusal of Prince and his followers to support move to reduce standing army (Feb). Merchants petition Commons against Spanish depredations on British shipping, encouraging renewed attacks on ministry: 206 Opposition votes cast against Walpole's conciliatory motion on relations with Spain (Mar). Reporting of MPs' speeches in press declared breach of privilege (Apr); Parliament rises (May).

Birth of future George III (24 May). Agreement reached between British and Spanish governments on outstanding differences (Sept), but nullified by refusal of South Sea Company to cooperate. [3rd] Treaty of Vienna achieves final settlement of Polish Succession War (cf. 1735) – major setback for Emperor Charles VI (Nov).

Bolingbroke writes – in France – *The Idea of a Patriot King*. John Wesley has his Aldersgate conversion experience (May).

1739   New agreement, Convention of El Pardo, signed with Spain (Jan: H (iv)); reported to Parliament in King's Speech (1 Feb); amendment to Commons' address deleting favourable mention of Convention lost, 230:141 – but big attendances, major debates and tense excitement follow (Feb–Mar). Final carrying of address of thanks for Spanish Convention, 260:232 (8 Mar) leads to a large-scale secession of Opposition MPs led by Wyndham, Pulteney and Sandys, 'to destroy this fallacy, that the voice of the House of Commons is the sense of the nation' (see Colley 28a, *224–50*). Prorogation (June).

British fleets sent to patrol Channel and maraud in West Indies (July). After intense Cabinet pressure on Walpole, war ['of Jenkins' Ear'] declared against Spain (19 Oct). Opposition secession abandoned before meeting of Parliament (15 Nov) – first session for 14 years to begin before Christmas. Admiral Vernon captures from Spaniards Puerto Bello in Isthmus of Panama (Nov). Severe frost hits Ireland for 7 weeks; rivers freeze, livestock dies and autumn crops ruined (Dec).

Philosophical Society founded. George Whitefield and John Wesley begin open-air preaching near Bristol.

1740   Attempt to introduce new Place Bill narrowly blocked and Pulteney's call for papers relating to El Pardo defeated by 49 votes (Jan-Feb). End of parliamentary session; appointment of Lord Hervey as Privy Seal, to Newcastle's dismay (29 Apr). Death of Wyndham (June) – blow to idea of 'broad-bottom' opposition/government; dismissal of Argyll from all his posts.

Accession of Frederick II of Prussia (May). Britain's war against Spain languishes in Atlantic and Caribbean theatres. Death of Charles VI (13 Oct O.S.); Maria Theresa succeeds to Habsburg dominions – but with threatening noises from Charles Albert, Elector of Bavaria, her uncle by marriage. Harvest failure in Ireland; onset of most severe nationwide famine before the 1840s.

Treasury Commission remodelled – Bubb Doddington removed; Parliament meets; Hardwicke warns Lords of danger of war with France without a new alliance system (Nov). Prussia invades Silesia (Dec); Maria Theresa appeals for help to guarantors of Pragmatic Sanction, including Britain and France (Dec-Jan).

Samuel Richardson's novel *Pamela* published (1740–2); Arne composes *Rule Britannia*; Captain Thomas Coram establishes the Foundling Hospital in London; Benjamin Martin invents pocket-sized microscope; George Anson begins his voyage round the world.

1741   Place Bill passes Commons – ministerialists, relying on the Lords, acquiescent (Jan); motion calling for Walpole's dismissal secures little Tory support and is lost, 290:106; Place Bill defeated in Upper House (Feb).

Frederick the Great's army defeats Austrians at Mollwitz (Mar O.S.); French envoy, Belleisle's mission to German electors on behalf of Charles Albert of Bavaria's territorial and imperial claims. On Walpole's motion Parliament votes £300,000 subsidy to Maria Theresa and pledges support for Pragmatic Sanction and Balance of Power in Europe (Apr). Parliament dissolved (27th). Drought ruins Irish harvest; mortality due to famine by end of year running at c.15 per cent of Irish population.

General Election (May) – ministry loses vital ground [E.1].

Failure of joint British naval-military attack on Carthagena (Apr); George II goes to Hanover (May); Austria promised aid of 12,000 mercenary troops as well as subsidies (June); King, without consulting English ministers, withholds Hanoverian aid from Maria Theresa (July); Franco-Bavarian forces move on Austria (July-Aug); another French army invades Westphalia (Aug); in view of the latter, George II negotiates *for Hanover* convention of neutrality and commitment to Franco-Bavarian candidate for imperial succession: consternation among British ministers (Sept). Convention of Klein-Schnellendorf secures truce – mediated by British diplomacy – between Austria and Prussia (28th O.S.).

Failure of British attack on Spanish island of Cuba. Opening of fourth Parliament of Walpole's period of supremacy – ministry's notional majority precarious (Dec); government candidate loses chairmanship of Committee of Elections (16th).

David Hume attracts attention with the appearance of his *Essays: Moral and Political*.

1742   Massive attendance in Parliament after Christmas recess; Pulteney's call for secret committee of investigation into negotiations with foreign powers rejected by only 3 votes, 253:250 – 'the greatest number that ever lost a question' [Horace Walpole]; Bavarian Charles Albert elected Emperor, styled Charles VII (Jan).

Resignation of Walpole (2 Feb); his ministerial colleagues open negotiations with Pulteney and Carteret; Argyll's Fountain Tavern speech advocating Broad-Bottom administration (12th) but Newcastle 'prevailed with his Majesty not to countenance the Tory party in the least' (Egmont, 15 Feb). New ministry emerges, with Wilmington (formerly Compton) as First Lord of Treasury, Carteret Northern Secretary, Harrington (transferring to) Lord President, Sandys, Chancellor of Exchequer (12th–16th).

Commons motion to enquire into conduct of ministry for last 10 years carried by 252:245 after narrow failure of attempt to extend it to 20 years; Argyll resigns over King's refusal to appoint a Tory to Admiralty Board; Pulteney and many former opposition Whigs vote against Tory motion to repeal Septennial Act (Mar).

Frederick II's army defeats Austrians at Chotusitz (May); he prepares to look for terms of peace from Austria. With aid of Carteret's diplomacy, Treaty of Breslau – guaranteed by Britain – concluded: Silesia ceded to Prussia (June). Tory leader in Lords, Gower, defects to Whigs, appointed Privy Seal; Pulteney created earl of Bath (July).

Parliament reassembles (Nov). Failure of attempt to revive Commons secret committee investigating Walpole ministry; motion to pay Hanoverian troops carried by 67 (Dec).

First performance of G.F. Handel's *Messiah*; Benjamin Huntsman of Sheffield invents process of making crucible cast steel.

1743   Death of Fleury (Jan) – Louis XV takes over direction of French policy. Six leading Tories: Beaufort, Barrymore, Orrery, Wynn, Cotton and Sir Robert Abdy, send secret invitation to France to invade Britain and restore the Pretender (Apr). Prorogation of Parliament (Apr); Carteret, accompanying King to Hanover, resumes his lofty diplomatic progresses on Continent (May). George II leads the British-financed 'Pragmatic Army' (Hanoverians, Hessians, Austrians, British) to victory over French at Dettingen (June), but then lapses into inactivity unpopular with taxpayers and critics of Hanover at home.

Death of Wilmington (2 July). Henry Pelham succeeds him as First Lord of Treasury (25 Aug) and later displaces Pulteneyite Sandys (Dec) as Chancellor of Exchequer. Treaty of Worms signed – Britain, Austria, Sardinia – enlisting Charles Emmanuel III to assist in expelling French and Spanish forces from Habsburg territory in northern Italy: diplomatic coup for Carteret (Sept). France responds with Treaty of Fontainebleau, 'Second Family Compact', with Spain (Oct) – led France to declare war on Britain and Austria in 1744.

Cabinet votes 9–4 not to ratify Convention of Worms, because of Carteret's open-ended commitments to Maria Theresa (24 Nov); Parliament reassembles (1 Dec). Commons vote, despite anti-Hanover rhetoric of William Pitt, to continue Hanoverian troops in British service; Gower resigns in protest against continued proscription of Tories; Henry Fox appointed to Treasury Commission (Dec).

Fielding's *Jonathan Wild* published; Thomas Boulsover invents Sheffield plate. Rules for conduct of Methodist 'classes' laid down. Archbishop Herring (translated from Bangor, Apr) embarks on his epic primary visitation of diocese of York (Apr).

1744   A crowded Commons Supply Committee approves army estimates for Hanoverian troops, 271:226, but Carteret's position gravely weakened by criticism in the debate (Jan). Indecisive naval battle off Toulon, incompetently fought by Admiral Mathews; Marshal Saxe's French army in Netherlands – George II tells Parliament of French plans to invade Britain but French stores and fleet hit by storms (Feb). France declares war on Britain (Mar). Parliament prorogued (May).

Frederick the Great, alarmed at revival of Habsburg fortunes since 1742, negotiates League of Frankfort to restore territorial possessions and re-affirm imperial status to Elector of Bavaria (May). French invasion threat recedes as Saxe's army is depleted (June–July). Prussia invades Habsburg Bohemia (Aug); Prague capitulates (Sept).

Pelhams and Whig Old Corps start to put pressure on King to force Carteret out of office (Nov); Carteret, now earl of Granville, resigns (24th): succeeded by

Harrington; other Whigs associated with Granville and Bath dismissed. Parliament meets (27th). 'Broad-Bottom' administration constructed, with Gower returning to Privy Seal (26 Dec), three other Tories in non-Cabinet office (Sir J.H. Cotton, J. Pitt and Sir J. Phillips) and former opposition Whigs, Bedford (1st Lord of Admiralty), Sandwich and George Grenville.

Prussians retreat on Silesia with heavy losses, but only because Austrians forced to pull out of Bavaria and Alsace to deal with them (Nov–Dec).

Anson returns to Spithead after circumnavigating the globe. First Methodist conference held. Rules of cricket first codified.

1745   Death of Charles Albert of Bavaria (Emperor Charles VII); Dorset's appointment as Lord President completes the Broad-Bottom ministry in Britain (Jan). Duke of Cumberland, aged 24, appointed Captain-General of the army; death of Robert Walpole, earl of Orford (Mar).

Austria and Bavaria make peace by the Treaty of Fusson; outnumbered allied army under Cumberland, attempting to save Tournai from Marshal Saxe, suffers glorious defeat at Fontenoy (Apr). Fall of Tournai to French (May), followed by most of Flanders (June–Sept). Capture of Louisburg fortress and Cape Breton Island (St Lawrence river) from the French (June).

Parliament prorogued (2 May). Prince Charles Edward Stuart, 'the Young Pretender', lands at Eriskay, Western Isles (23rd July); reaches Scottish mainland (25th); news of his landing reaches London (2nd week Aug); Jacobite standard raised at Glenfinnan (19th). Britain makes peace with Prussia by Convention of Hanover (Aug).

Young Pretender enters Edinburgh; routs Cope's small force at Prestonpans (21 Sept). Cumberland recalled from Netherlands to take command of campaign against Jacobites; Parliament meets (Oct). Pretender's forces capture Carlisle and reach Manchester (Nov). Highlanders reach Derby (4 Dec) but begin retreat north (6th), as Pretender's officers refuse to follow him further; Jacobite army back in Scotland (20th).

Death of Dean Swift; Hogarth completes the six paintings of *Marriage à la Mode*.

1746   Jacobites capture Stirling (8 Jan) but its castle holds out; Lord George Murray defeats government forces at Falkirk (17th). Ministerial and Court crisis in London (10–14 Feb): resignations of Newcastle, Pelham, Harrington, Bedford, Gower; George II's attempt to form a new administration under Bath and Granville immediately collapses; Pelhams return to office. King at last constrained to bring William Pitt into office – appointed Joint-Vice-Treasurer of Ireland (22nd). Commons demonstrate new ministry's strength by a majority of 133 for the Hanoverian troops (Apr).

Jacobite army pursued north by 'Butcher' Cumberland; finally routed at Culloden (16 Apr). Pitt promoted Paymaster-General (May). End of parliamentary session (12 Aug).

La Bourdonnais captures Madras from British East India Company (Sept). Prince Charles Edward taken off from Scotland by French man-of-war (19th). Harrington replaced by Chesterfield as Northern Secretary (29 Oct). Parliament begins new session (Nov).

Repeal of City of London Elections Act of 1725.

CHAPTER 1

The hegemony of Sir Robert Walpole

There were two succession issues in early Hanoverian Britain. One was the succession to the crown: the question of whether the legal Protestant heir, having made good his claim to the Stuart inheritance in August 1714, could translate legality into acceptability and permanence (Ch. 5; *Making of a Great Power*, Ch. 25). The other was the succession to the leadership of the new governing party, the Whigs. The second issue, like the first, helped to perpetuate political instability after Queen Anne's death. Well inside two years of George I's accession three of the lords of the Junto, Halifax, Wharton and Somers, were dead. In 1717, at the time of the great Whig schism, Orford too departed from the Cabinet – in his case voluntarily – breaking in the process with his old colleague, Sunderland; he neither accepted nor sought office again. Now only Sunderland remained of that formidable quintet whose authority in the party had been almost unchallengeable since the closing year of William III's reign. There was a huge vacuum to be filled, and the bizarre quarrel which at this time rent the royal family could only heighten and complicate the competition to fill it.

One indicator of the prevailing uncertainty was the headship of the Treasury, which Godolphin and Oxford had made, under Anne, the dominant position in the state. Between Oxford's dismissal in July 1714 and March 1718 its tenancy changed no fewer than six times [see D.1]. Death was responsible for only one of these changes, the removal of Halifax in 1715; the Tories could claim no credit for any. When the sixth, and thus far most durable incumbent, Charles Spencer, 3rd earl of Sunderland, was in turn replaced on 30 April 1721 by his fiercest rival for the Whig succession, Robert Walpole, few could have been certain that the contest was over. And who would have ventured to prophesy that Walpole would remain First Lord of the Treasury and Chancellor of the Exchequer for a staggering twenty-one years, achieving a degree of dominance over the political world that few ministers had approached before and that no single individual, minister or king, was to equal again? For continuous tenancy of the Treasury Walpole's record stands unchallenged in the past 392 years.

It was not only politically, however, that Walpole's presence through the 1720s and 1730s was so commanding. Historians of the economy, finance, diplomacy and the constitution, of Church and Dissent, even of literature and the press, have also become conditioned to thinking of the years from 1721 to 1742 as the age of Walpole, seeing in his engulfing influence an indispensable frame of reference for their respective studies. Part One of this book deliberately interprets 'the age of Walpole' flexibly. The great man's resignation from office in February

1742, though obviously an event of the first importance in high politics, marked only in one sense the end of an epoch. For the next four years much of the Walpole legacy to Hanoverian Britain was at risk. The one-party oligarchy he had cemented was threatened, and still more the constitutional and political system he had painstakingly and artfully constructed and which he believed could only be preserved by his chosen heirs, the Pelhams, and the 'Old Corps' of the Whig party. But beyond that, the security of the Hanoverian dynasty, the sound health of the public finances and the economic prosperity to which the Walpole regime had sacrificed so much, were all endangered in the 1740s by Britain's involvement in a great European war – her first since 1713. Although out of office, 'kicked upstairs' to the House of Lords and suffering from rapidly degenerating health, Walpole continued for three years after his resignation to operate shrewdly behind the scenes, working to preserve what he saw, rightly or wrongly, as twenty-one years of supremely important achievement. At the time of his death in March 1745 success was not fully assured, but by the spring of 1746 the main uncertainties had been resolved. The months of February – May 1746 saw the triumph of the Old Corps finally secured (above, p. 11); the last lingering threat of a Tory revival snuffed out, and Walpole's disciple, that unobtrusive but first-class administrator Henry Pelham, firmly entrenched at the head of the Treasury. Far to the north, meanwhile, the last hopes of the Jacobites were being blasted on the bloody field of Culloden. In the spring of 1746 a *Nunc Dimittis* could appropriately have been chanted for Walpole's shade.

Prelude to hegemony

Understanding British politics in the age of Walpole must logically begin with an understanding of the hegemony of Walpole himself. Hence the concentration in this present chapter on the one central question, in its twin aspects: how did Robert Walpole first establish and then maintain his unique personal supremacy over both the Whig party and the King's government under the first two Hanoverians? But since this was the hegemony not just of a man but of a system – a system which ultimately proved strong enough to outlive its creator by a further seventeen years – a further and more complex question necessarily follows from the first two. What were the elements from which this political system of the age of Walpole and the Pelhams was constructed? How, in other words, did the politics of oligarchy work in the new, stable, Whig-controlled state of 1722–46, and after? To address this question will be the concern of the two chapters that follow (Chs. 2–3).

Robert Walpole was 44 years old when he returned to the Treasury on 30 April 1721. We are already aware that the foundations on which he was able to build thereafter were in some respects substantial, (*Making of a Great Power*, Ch. 25). And if this was true of the groundwork of political stability, it was equally true of his own position and prospects. Walpole had prepared himself through a tough twenty-year apprenticeship for the responsibility of wearing on his own broad shoulders the political mantle of his old mentors, the Junto. Only four years after his first election to the House of Commons as MP for Castle Rising his ministerial career had begun, as a junior member of the Lord High Admiral's Council. Since then he had served with conspicuous success as Secretary-at-War, Treasurer of the Navy, for two spells as Paymaster-General (the second when he was grudgingly readmitted to office by George I in 1720), and – the most valuable experience of all – for 18 months (1715–17) as First Lord of the Treasury [D.6; D.1]. Well before Queen Anne's death, Walpole was being seen as a man of the future, marked out by his insatiable appetite for work, his pugnacity and dexterity in debate, and most of all by his impressive mastery of the details of public finance. Even when in opposition to the Harley ministry after 1710, he had been dubbed by his fellow Whig, Arthur Mainwaring, 'the greatest figures man in England'. In fact his feats when in opposition between 1702 and 1720 had brought him at least as much kudos as his varied experience in office. In January 1712 his Tory enemies had paid him the compliment of voting him to the Tower. When he resigned from the Cabinet in 1717, in protest against the dismissal of his brother-in-law, Lord Townshend, an impressive group of Whig friends and associates, including the talented Secretary-at-War, William Pulteney, left office with him in a display of solidarity more striking even than the fall of the associates of Robert Harley in 1708 (27a, *49–50*). In the course of the next three years, while turning the parliamentary screws on the Stanhope-Sunderland administration and keeping a high political profile in the eyes of the King, Walpole had at the same time begun to move overtly away from his former ultra-partisan style of Whiggery and towards the consensus attitudes which were to be such a distinctive hallmark of his great ministry of 1721–42. And although there are other explanations of the change, the necessity of his cooperating in opposition not only with Country Whigs but with Tories, over such matters as Oxford's impeachment (where he executed an extraordinary volte-face), the size of the army, the defence of the Test and Occasional Conformity Acts and the defeat of the Peerage Bill, plainly helped it forward.

Nevertheless it was with bad grace that George I had agreed to re-employ Walpole in June 1720. The office of Paymaster, though immensely lucrative, was pointedly not of Cabinet rank, unlike the Presidency of the Council which was (admittedly reluctantly) given to Townshend. How hard Walpole fought to bring the other 1717 rebels back into office with him is not certain, but in any case he clearly lacked the necessary leverage, and his relations with Pulteney suffered serious damage as a result.[1] The door to the Treasury, to the premiership, and ultimately to the undisputed leadership of the Whigs still seemed barred against him in the summer of 1720. It was the South Sea crisis which handed him the key to it, and he found and turned the lock unerringly. It has been a matter of debate whether it was primarily political skill and courage or financial acumen which enabled Walpole to calm the frenzy caused by the bursting of the Bubble (*Making of a Great Power*, Ch. 17; 26a, *301–41*; 69, *Ch. 7*). The most convincing answer is that it was a unique combination of both, but that he also rode his luck. Fortunate chance had postponed his re-entry into the ministry until after the adoption of the South Sea Company's proposals for the settlement of the National Debt, for, whatever his public posture towards it in opposition, there is little doubt that in private he had approved of the greater part of the Company's scheme. What cannot be denied is that the settlement of the crisis in 1720–1 was pre-eminently Walpole's achievement and that his was deservedly the credit for rescuing the Company, restoring public confidence, saving the government from certain collapse and preserving his party. What he could not do was save Stanhope from the stroke which killed him after making a passionate defence of the ministry in the House of Lords, or Sunderland from the necessity of resigning his post at the head of the Treasury Board; though in his self-appointed rôle of 'Skreen-Master-General' – as it was cynically described by Tories and disgruntled Country Whigs – Walpole did procure Commons' votes clearing both the earl and Lord Stanhope's brother, Charles, of charges of corrupt practice.

With Sunderland departed to a decently backstage office, that of Groom of the Stole, Walpole could no longer be denied the First Lordship. There was no other credible candidate, and George I had enough gratitude as well as enough realism to concede the fact. Once in the Treasury again Walpole was poised to take the game which had been played out for the past six and a half years. He now held a hand of winning cards. Much has been made of the fact that King George was strongly averse to Walpole's assuming prime ministerial status. But, as even the First Lord's most talented rival among the younger Whigs in the Cabinet admitted, although the King was 'resolved that Walpole shall not govern', it was 'hard to be prevented'.[2] He commanded the House of Commons; he manipulated, through the Treasury, an infinitely larger share of patronage than any other minister or group of ministers, and it was Walpole and not Sunderland who controlled the invaluable Secret Service Fund (31; for a different view, cf. 26a, *358–80*; 62b). And so, while Sunderland was still influential in the royal closet during the autumn and winter of 1721–2 and was not disposed to give up the struggle for supremacy without a fight, the odds were now weighted too heavily against him. His failure in August 1721 to push Charles Stanhope into the Treasury against Walpole's wishes was a mortifying setback and showed the way the land lay.[3] Sunderland's frantic intrigues with Tories and even Jacobites before and during the 1722 Election are a measure of his desperation. The earl's sudden death from pleurisy in April 1722, therefore, may be seen as another stroke of luck for Walpole, but it was one that merely hastened rather than made possible his final unqualified victory.

That consummation was brought even closer by the treasonable activities of the Atterbury conspirators. Later in 1722 these were efficiently unmasked by the government's spy network and were then brilliantly turned by Walpole to his own, as well as his party's, political advantage (62b). The last realistic opportunity to prevent his supremacy becoming entrenched probably occurred in 1724, when Lord Carteret, a Secretary of State, a Sunderland protégé and a favourite of the King's, made his own challenge and was totally outmanoeuvred (see above, p. 3). It was in the following year that Walpole, having already (to the astonishment of most politicians) refused a peerage, accepted a knighthood and the coveted Order of the Garter. Even at the time many saw this award not just as a signal honour but as a truly symbolic event. Historians can be even more certain of its significance. For although Walpole was not to reach the very highest plateau of his power until 1730, the point at which Townshend resigned from the ministry, after 1725 his hegemony, disturbed (as we shall see) by only the briefest interlude of doubt in 1727 (below, pp. 21–2), had been more or less indisputable. From the mid-1720s, moreover, the Walpole 'system' had begun to operate fully at all political levels, symptomising the smooth transition in British politics from the Augustan age of party to the new order of 'Venetian oligarchy' (22, *xiii–xv*; 14, *186–7*).

The bases of power

No man could have stayed on the pinnacle as long as Sir Robert Walpole did, surviving in the process a change of monarch, the eighteenth century's supreme test of political endurance, without possessing outstanding qualities. But, as one can see even more clearly a century later in the case of Lord Liverpool – a much less gifted prime minister but one with another impressive record of survival – personal attributes in themselves will not be enough unless the political conditions of the time mark up their value. Some of the enduring individual qualities on which Walpole's supremacy was to rest, notably his exceptional grasp of public finance, have been noticed already. By taking a broader view of the bases of his power, however, by considering 'climatic' as well as personal factors, we may not only discover why one remarkable individual contrived to dominate British politics for over twenty years but also capture something of the distinctive ambience of 'the age of Walpole', to which the man himself so closely related.

One important clue to his success lies in his family and personal background. To the great majority of members of Parliament this was traditional and reassuring. Although not born to the purple, Walpole was no *arriviste*. The Walpoles had been squires in Norfolk since Henry II's reign, and to the very end of his life Sir Robert studiously preserved many of the characteristic habits and tastes of this class. In every way he looked the part: from his florid, coarse-featured face to the immense physical bulk which he acquired in early middle age and the belly that was the despair of flattering portrait painters. But as well as looking the part, he played it, and to perfection. Public style was nicely matched with domestic image. He took delight in keeping open table and in harrying the Norfolk fox. He made almost a fetish of his lack of refinement and social polish: few men in politics, for instance, possessed a more bottomless store of bawdy stories or told them with greater relish. The glorious interior of his great house at Houghton and the superb collection of paintings with which he filled it gave the lie to opponents who sneered that he was a complete philistine. Nevertheless, there was an unmistakable earthiness about Walpole; the very ostentation with which he revelled in the trappings of power and its attendant riches served only to underline its grubbier side.

Yet while Walpole could play the squire with conviction, and (unlike the Junto) instinctively understood the prejudices and anxieties of the gentry class, his background was significantly much broader than that of the orthodox country gentleman. Two connections he made in early manhood were of great importance

16

to him on his way up the ladder, and at the top of it. The first was with his boyhood and college friend, Viscount Townshend, talented head of the leading Whig noble house in Norfolk, for this ensured him a very early entrée to the inner circle of the Whig aristocracy in Anne's reign, including membership of the fashionable Kit-Cat Club, then the social and political heart of the party in London. The alliance between two of Whiggery's brightest hopes, cemented in 1713 by Townshend's marriage to Walpole's sister, became a key fact of early Hanoverian politics, and it remained so right down to the late 1720s. The second connection which broadened Walpole's political as well as social horizons was his own marriage to Catherine Shorter, daughter of a Baltic merchant and grand-daughter of a former Lord Mayor of London. Flighty and extravagant, Catherine brought Walpole little enough domestic bliss. But she did bring him, through her relatives and their City friends, close contacts from the very start of his parliamentary career with another of the essential elements in the Whig party of his day, the wealthy London business class; this was another world of which the average country gentleman had minimal knowledge. From the 1720s onwards, the art of government in Britain came to consist, much more than in the age of great party issues, in the ability to mediate and maintain a successful balance between the dominant interests in the victorious oligarchy, and in the political nation [A] at large. Personal and family connections gave Walpole a built-in advantage in the cultivation of this art.

In character, too, as well as in background, Walpole was ideally equipped for the politics of his own age. Again, the *context* of his premiership is all-important, for if ever a politician arrived on his cue, it was he. The age of Walpole was a practical, dispassionate, utilitarian age: one in which great ideals and fiercely conflicting ideologies were of waning importance. One of the prime consequences of this was that politics, especially by George II's reign, became more personal and intimate than at any time since the Tudor period. Political success came most readily to those who were adept at handling individuals and small groups of men, and Walpole had developed this skill to the level of wizardry. Although a shrewd and persuasive debater as well as a supreme 'man of business', he was never ranked with the silver-tongued, emotive orators of his day. He could not rise to the inspirational heights of a Halifax, a St John or a Pulteney. Neither could he play on the heart-strings, as a new and inveterate parliamentary opponent of the 1730s, William Pitt, was to do. Little trace remained, anyway, by 1721 of those streaks of passionate Whiggery which had marked his early political career. Yet at the practical business of cajoling, manipulating and finally dominating men, he was without peer. All the qualities a man needed for this most personal of the political arts were his: a great stock of good humour; patience in abundance; a cool nerve and almost unshakeable self-control; courage, and, when he needed it, ruthlessness. Above all, Walpole possessed a faculty so rare that in the whole century after the Restoration only Shaftesbury and Harley, in the forefront of politics, shared it to a comparable degree: an intuitive perception of human motive, an understanding so nearly infallible in Walpole's case as to amount to genius. None of these gifts would have been so politically effective, however, without the appetite to put them constantly to use. And Sir Robert's appetite for power was insatiable: he gloried in power, and in the wealth and honours it brought him, in a manner so unashamed as to be almost guileless.

Walpole's capacity and achievement as a statesman, administrator and finance minister will be assessed later (Ch. 5). But two of the most distinctive facets of his statesmanship, his realism and his pragmatism, ought to be emphasised here and now, if only to dispel the common notion that, finance apart, he was little more than an adroit and power-hungry political operator. 'In politics, my dear lord', Carteret wrote plaintively to a Cabinet colleague in 1721, 'there is no doing what one will'.[4] Walpole was the eighteenth century's master of the art of the possible. Preconceived theories and ideal considerations troubled him little throughout his career as prime minister; certainly they never threatened – save briefly in 1733 (below, pp. 76, 82) – to destroy the pragmatist's 'clear-headed sense of what was attainable, or of what in political terms was necessary, merely desirable or frankly irrelevant' (5, *176*). As for what *was* attainable, this was always seen by Walpole within the context of the two overriding aims of his administration: security and prosperity. He did not view individual issues simplistically. But because of the essential economy and simplicity of his basic objectives he was able to judge such issues as they arose by two acid tests. Would they help to preserve, or would they endanger, the security of the new dynasty, and the security of Britain at large from Jacobite plots or from deeply divisive political conflicts? Would they promote or retard prosperity – the prosperity of commerce, industry and, not least, the land? The Walpole regime, like that of the Pelhams afterwards, set itself to demonstrate that the new Whiggery was just as capable as the old Toryism of making the world safe for the members of Walpole's own class, the landowners, and it could adduce the rising land prices and falling land taxes of the 1720s and early 1730s in support of its claim.

The hegemony of Sir Robert Walpole, therefore, witnessed the triumph of realism and pragmatism. Whenever they were in conflict with ideology they usually won the day, and there were times, without doubt, when they drove morality, too, from the field. Before 1721 Walpole had already shown his new colours. Both the Septennial Act and the Peerage Bill had been constitutionally dubious measures. But although Walpole had supported the first because it was realistic he had opposed the second because it was unrealistic. So, also, after 1721: Walpole (as will be seen) was harshly realistic throughout in his outlook on social evils and injustices, warily realistic in his attitude to demands for full toleration for those traditional Whig supporters, the Protestant dissenters, and prosaically realistic in his concept of Britain's European and world rôle (Chs. 4, 5). His down-to-earth statesmanship contrasts unromantically with the broad vision of the Elder Pitt, with his sense of Britain's destiny as a great imperial power and his ambition to realise it. Yet the comparison is in a sense beside the point. For the Britain of 1721, or for that matter of 1731, did not need a man of exceptional vision at the helm. In close on a quarter of a century of conflict that had raged from their youth to their early middle age, the men of Walpole's generation had had more than enough opportunity to observe something of the futility and crippling cost, as well as the hard-earned gains, of warfare on the grand scale. They had seen the National Debt soar to frightening heights [G.1] and the resources of thousands of landed families eroded. More recently, this same generation had seen Britain faced with an armed rebellion over the succession and with a horrendous financial scandal which had caused much private devastation and seriously damaged the government's reputation. These were compelling reasons why the Britain of 1721 needed peace, for at least another ten to fifteen years; why she needed to deny the enemies of the Hanoverian dynasty opportunities for subversion, especially the encouragement that war could easily offer them; why she needed a tranquil, healing interlude in domestic politics, and why she needed to rebuild her business confidence, capitalise on her recent overseas gains and consolidate her economic growth without the violent fluctuations which war too often brought (134). In 1721 thoughts of further conquests and imperial glory were for the future, not the present. It was the great virtue of Sir Robert Walpole's statesmanship that he recognised these needs more clearly than any of his contemporaries and that he had the ability to convince others that his ministry's objectives were the reasonable and right ones for the Britain of his day.

The growth of a vigorous and vociferous opposition to him, especially from around 1730 onwards, should not deceive us into believing that throughout the second half of his ministry Walpole grew out of tune with the aspirations of the political nation as a whole. It is important, for example, not to misread the significance of the Excise Crisis of 1733–4, when the hostile public reaction to a thoroughly sound, even imaginative, policy measure was provoked for factious ends by an opposition determined to misrepresent the aims of the policy and to vilify its author. Not until late in the 1730s did Walpole begin genuinely to lose his feel for the pulse of the nation, a pulse which hitherto he had generally managed to detect despite the strident voices of interested pressure-groups such as the 'Patriots' and the City of London trading and financial community (Chs. 4, 5). Only thereafter was his hegemony supported more by the mechanics of the 'system' which he and the Old Corps Whigs had fashioned than by personal stature and by the ability of his regime to identify itself with a broad consensus of national priorities. Until then its basic objectives could usually command a good deal of support, even when its methods could not.

Anatomy of a supremacy

It was suggested earlier that, without discounting the importance of political management and the other techniques associated with 'the politics of oligarchy' (Ch. 2), the longevity of the Walpole regime can be explained largely in terms of the dovetailing of individual genius with favourable circumstances. Thus, no prime minister could have survived for twenty-one years in the intensely personal political atmosphere which prevailed for at least four decades from the 1720s without consummate ability in managing three groups of men: his own ministerial colleagues, the King and the court, and the members of the House of Commons. And in Walpole's relations with these three groups lies much of the secret of his political art.

From most of his colleagues in the ministry after 1721 Walpole could evoke loyalty, not so much by his position and influence as by the sort of person he was. His humanity, his ready sympathy, his spontaneous, gusty warmth were compelling qualities. Plumb has singled out his handling of the young duke of Newcastle as a classic example of his mastery of intra-ministerial relations (26b, *50–1*). By the early 1720s several years in the Cabinet and great territorial influence had not removed the duke's *naïveté* or his painful hesitancy and lack of self-confidence. But Walpole recognised in this former adversary of 1717–20 an invaluable potential asset. Other ministers might scoff at him behind his back, but to Walpole, Newcastle's pocket boroughs, mania for management, tireless capacity for work, and the prodigality with which he lavished his private fortune in the service of 'the public'[5] were no joke. So the First Lord first secured his gratitude by persuading a dubious King to appoint him Southern Secretary of State in Carteret's stead (1724), and then proceeded to treat him with special affection, admit him to his closest confidences and, to all appearances, to place the highest value on his opinions. The duke was completely captivated and for fourteen years Walpole had no more devoted follower.

A very different side to Walpole's relations with his Cabinet and ministerial colleagues was the combination of subtlety and steel with which he dealt with dissidents or potential rivals. It is first seen in his reaction to Bolingbroke's return to England in 1723: he could no longer block or prevent it, and he chose not to obstruct the recovery of the estates which the viscount forfeited when he fled to France in 1715; but he could and did make sure that in the final deal of 1725 Bolingbroke would not recover his seat in the House of Lords.[6] The same deadly combination was next displayed in 1724–5, in the treatment meted out to three former Sunderland allies who, unlike Newcastle, had not taken kindly to Walpole's primacy: Carteret, who was given the choice of demotion to the Lieutenancy of Ireland or dismissal [D.6; above, p. 3]; Roxburgh, the Scottish Secretary of State, who was blandly sacked after the Glasgow Malt Tax riots; and Lord Chancellor Macclesfield, whom Walpole could probably have saved from impeachment on a corruption charge but chose instead, cunningly but effectively, to abandon. His loftiest victim was Townshend. Having for so long before 1722 considered himself, and been considered, the senior partner in the firm of Townshend and Walpole,[7] it was not surprising that he should in time come to resent his old friend's growing dominance, and in particular his intrusion into the conduct of foreign affairs (Ch. 4). For his pains he was in the late 1720s edged first into isolation, then into resignation. The disciplining of Lord Cobham and the other Excise Bill and South Sea rebels in 1733 was significantly more brusque (p. 6 above; Chs. 4, 5, '*Opposition and Decline*'). By the early 1730s, as power increased Walpole's arrogance, he doubtless felt he could afford to be more ruthless; and in the process the old subtlety became less and less in evidence. In Cobham's case, certainly, and possibly also in the cases of two of the Scottish grandees dismissed without ceremony, the prime minister subsequently had some cause to regret the uncompromisingly punitive measures of 1733 (20, *205–6, 209*).

One reason for Walpole's more peremptory approach to ministerial dissidents in the 1730s is that by then he felt much more secure in the favour of his royal master than at any time in the early or late 1720s. Despite all the constitutional changes which had taken place since 1688, the confidence of the ruler was still basic to political success. The general rôle of the Crown in the political system of Walpole and the Pelhams is a subject more proper to the next chapter. In the present context it need only be emphasised that, for all the advances since the Revolution in the influence of the House of Commons and Walpole's unique rapport with that House right down to 1739, he was at all times the *King's* minister. Not even at the unchallengeable peak of his ministerial authority from 1730–7 did he ever forget that power ultimately depended on the favour of the Crown. And in practical terms this meant gaining and keeping the firm support, not only of George I and George II, but of those in the royal entourage whose influence with the two kings counted for most.

In George I's case Walpole was in one respect very fortunate. The baleful influence over domestic politics of the King's two leading German ministers, Bernstorff (unaffectionately referred to as 'the old man') and Bothmer, was already at an end by 1721, undermined by Stanhope and then effectively destroyed by the deal which brought the Walpoleans back into office the previous year.[8] Even so, there was no miraculous conversion of the first Hanoverian. From the South Sea settlement onwards Walpole set out patiently and methodically to earn his total confidence, relying mainly on the demonstration of his mastery of public business and of his utter indispensability in Parliament, but also recruiting the valuable support of the duchess of Kendal. The former countess von der Schulenburg, created an English duchess in 1719 and dubbed 'the maypole' by a malicious court, may have been marginally the uglier of the two unprepossessing German ladies the divorced Elector had brought with him from Hanover in 1714; but as George I's mistress since the 1690s and the mother of three of his daughters, she was secure in the King's affections. She was also cultivated and shrewd. Walpole had early made it his business to establish that her sway 'behind the curtain' was much greater than that of Freiin von Kielmansegg, countess of Darlington, who was also commonly believed to share George's bed but was in fact his morganatic half-sister (24a, *23–4*). He had begun to pay court to the duchess during 1719–20, while still in opposition, and continued to do so after the direction of the Treasury had added considerably to his friendship's appeal. By 1725, helped further by the fact that at this stage he still kept himself as remote as he decently could from foreign affairs (where royal feathers were still most easily ruffled), Walpole could at last regard himself as the trusted as well as the indispensable first servant of the King. In the following year George I underlined his favour in the most signal manner when Sir Robert became the first commoner for generations to receive the coveted Order of the Garter.[9]

When George I died suddenly at Osnabrück in 1727 Walpole had very quickly to adapt himself to an entirely different set of personal relationships at Court. His problems were greatly magnified by the fact that despite the formal reconciliation between the King and the Prince and Princess of Wales in 1720, the subsequent years had seen something less than true harmony within the royal family. Politicians out of favour with the government continued to find a congenial retreat at Leicester House and Walpole knew that he and Townshend were blamed by the Prince for the terms of what the latter saw as a capitulation on his part rather than a pacification. It had long been assumed, in fact, and not least by Walpole himself, that when George II came to the throne it would be with the intention of putting the ministry into fresh hands. When the unexpected happened in 1727, therefore, the First Lord was understandably in a state of acute anxiety. Yet far from deserting him, his political touch had never been so certain as it was in this brief crisis. It was the touch of a political craftsman at the height of his maturity.

It has often been said that it was Walpole's ability to persuade the Commons to grant the new King a Civil List of unprecedented generosity that turned the scales in his favour and against his main rival, Spencer Compton, who was the current Speaker of the House of Commons. Naturally he was fully alive to the value of his Treasury influence, as well as of his unrivalled parliamentary know-how at this ticklish juncture. But if he had misjudged the motives and mainsprings of the new royal circle it is very doubtful whether these assets could still have saved him. In the event his judgement proved faultless. For years he had recognised that it was Princess Caroline and not George Augustus's mistress, Henrietta Howard, who had paramount influence with the Prince, and long before her husband came to the throne he had cultivated Caroline's friendship as assiduously as he had ever cultivated anyone (or as he himself put it, with a characteristically rustic turn of phrase, he 'took the right sow by the ear'). It was largely through her influence that he had been able to persuade a grudging Prince to seek his father's forgiveness in 1720, the event which more than any other persuaded George I that Walpole should be readmitted to office. Now, in 1727, it was Caroline who chivvied the new King into changing his mind about dropping Walpole, and for the next ten years she consistently remained the prime minister's staunchest ally. In the meantime the capture of the volatile George II was not only far swifter than that of the less malleable George I but far more total. Before the end of 1727 he was already talking to Walpole of the bond between them being 'for my life . . . and . . . for your life' (26b, *169*). And there is good reason to believe that right to the end he regarded this as an unbreakable pledge, one that gained in strength year by year, as Walpole inimitably played out his unique double rôle as 'minister for the King in the House of Commons' and 'minister for the House of Commons in the closet'. Even in 1742, when after a disastrous General Election and a succession of lost divisions his parliamentary supremacy had manifestly gone beyond recall, Walpole had literally to beg his royal master to accept his resignation.

Arguably the most significant thing about Walpole's fall, therefore, is that while one of the two central pillars by which the great man's hegemony had been supported for twenty-one years was still standing firm and strong to the last, that was not enough to save his premiership from destruction. It was not enough because the second and equally important pillar, Walpole's command over the Lower House of Parliament, had finally given way under the accumulated strains of the previous three to four years. Whether or not Walpole was 'the first prime minister' may be open to debate (5, *163–5*). What is surely beyond question is that he was the first prime minister who frankly recognised that his authority rested as much on the Commons as on the Crown and who deliberately chose to sit there throughout his entire ministry. As early as 1723 George I offered him a peerage. When, to the amazement of his contemporaries, he turned it down, deflecting the honour to his son instead, he broke totally with convention. In the very recent past, for example, Harley (1711), St John (1712) and Stanhope (1717) had all succumbed to the lure of a title at a time when their stock in the Lower House of Parliament was high. But Walpole doted on the Commons: he cherished it, not only as a vital source of power but almost as the breath of life itself. To Philip Yorke, the son of Walpole's eminent colleague, Lord Chancellor Hardwicke [D.3] Sir Robert was quite simply 'the best House of Commons man we ever had'.[10] What made him so?

It was assuredly not the use of bribery or corruption, although the ceaseless campaign of vilification waged against him for years by his opponents consistently claimed that that was how he had maintained his control for so long. The parliamentary enquiry conducted after his fall failed – to the evident chagrin of its instigators – to dig up any conclusive proof of his guilt. It is true that its work was hampered to some extent by the manoeuvres of Walpole's friends. It is also possible, of course, that both in dispensing the Secret Service money and in other ways Walpole may have been more skilful in covering his tracks than either contemporaries or modern historians have allowed. It is undeniable that he took a fairly cynical view of human nature and that one effect of his lengthy supremacy was to lower the tone of politics in the third and fourth decades of the eighteenth century, in comparison with the first two. But it is also worth recording that it was the considered opinion of Arthur Onslow, Speaker of the House from 1728 to 1761 and a man of unimpeachable probity himself, that the years 1717–21, especially when Sunderland was at the Treasury in the fraught aftermath of the Whig schism, was a more corrupt time than any period in Walpole's primacy (20, *170*). Few members of the opposition in the 1730s were more scathing about Walpole's political morality than Lord Chesterfield. Yet he also readily conceded that Sir Robert was the most consummate *manager* of Parliament who had ever lived.

Walpole's parliamentary management has been closely and convincingly studied (27a, *Ch. 5*; 31; 21). Only the briefest sketch of his methods will be attempted here, especially since it is only possible to appreciate their full efficiency within the context of the political structure of his age (Chs. 2, 3). He by no means neglected the House of Lords, as we shall see, but while casting a superintending eye over it, he was normally content to leave its day-to-day management to Newcastle and other Cabinet colleagues who sat there. The Commons was a different matter. That was his stage. He was well served there by able henchmen such as Henry Pelham and Thomas Winnington, as well as by Speaker Onslow, whom Walpole (who had nominated him for the Chair in 1727) affectionately called his 'Governor'.[11] But the controlling hand was always his.

Walpole's Commons strategy was basically a threefold one: to construct a firm foundation for a reliable majority; to ensure that that foundation cohered; and to seek to supply it at all times with enough reinforcements to thwart the opposition whenever the House divided. His chief instruments, apart from exerting maximum pressure on the electorate on the few occasions that this body was exercised under the Septennial Act,[12] were patronage, discipline and, most of all, communication. From the start of his ministry he grasped the all-important truth that in a political world where the fires of party were already beginning to burn lower, one too in which seven-year Parliaments had imparted more stability to political office-holding, the pursuit of lesser office or official favour was bound to become more of an end in itself for a significant number of politicians. The fund of patronage was certainly more than ample, and unlike his recent predecessors, Godolphin and Harley, Walpole had no scruples about singlemindedly using every scrap of it he could lay his hands on, encroaching far beyond the customary limits of Treasury influence in the process. Nevertheless, there always remained serious limits to what patronage could accomplish in parliamentary terms. In the first place, the proportion of placemen, contractors or pensioners in any given House of Commons of this period was never very large – certainly under 30 per cent of the total membership, and at times less than a quarter (20, *191*); in the second place, although there was normally a strong disposition among the beneficiaries of patronage to support the government of the day, it was by no means a slavish disposition and it required tending with watchful care.

One aspect of Walpole's response to this situation was to impose a tougher discipline on 'the Court and Treasury Party' than any of his predecessors had attempted. Hitherto the more minor placemen had been subject to occasional, limited purges, but rarely to anything consistently drastic. Harley, for example, when Secretary of State under Godolphin had expressed the view that as long as an office-holder supported the ministry on essential financial business, he ought to be allowed latitude on other issues;[13] during his own premiership from 1710 to 1714 he himself had normally interpreted this latitude generously. But after 1733, when for the first time his administration was exposed to a very serious threat in Parliament, Walpole laid down a very different principle: everyone who held office or commission from the Crown, major or minor, must normally vote in accordance with the Treasury line, or invite dismissal. The principle was not always rigorously applied in practice, especially in the tense years from 1738 to 1742, but any office-holder who flouted it did so in full knowledge of the risks.

Even patronage reinforced by discipline, however, could never guarantee Walpole an inbuilt Commons majority in any of the three Parliaments of 1722–41. That remained the case even in the years 1725–37 when the efforts of his Scottish managers, Argyll and Islay, were ensuring him the almost unwavering support of the vast majority of the 45 MPs from 'North Britain'. In the end, what Walpole relied on most of all to deliver the votes when they most mattered were his expert and painstaking techniques of communication. Even on the ministry's most natural supporters he spent both time and care ungrudgingly, explaining government policies and attitudes both in a general way – for example, in the great eve-of-session meetings which he and his Commons' managers staged with Whig clients and placemen and with influential backbenchers – and in the course of sessions, as new issues arose. The more delicate the situation, the more likely it was that there would be 'open' meetings for all potential supporters, including the independent Whig backbenchers. So it was with the Cockpit meeting in 1733 when, with an audience of 250, the First Lord brilliantly picked up the pieces of party unity broken by the Excise affair (20, *204*; see also p. 000 below on the Excise Crisis).

The independent Whigs were arguably the most important factor of all in Walpole's parliamentary calculations, and unquestionably so in the difficult Parliament of 1734–41. In those years the ministry was frequently opposed in the Commons not simply by Tory votes but by those of a very substantial, 'formed' Whig opposition (Ch. 5). Modern scholarship has rightly corrected the older orthodoxy that the Whig backbenchers were 'Independents' in the comprehensive sense of being little affected by party loyalty or by a sense of obligation to give the administration of the day a sympathetic hearing (31, *33–4*; 37a). But these members were electorally independent, having stood for Parliament wholly or largely on their own interests, and they were not tied to the Court's apron-strings by places or pensions. A large body of members who in the final resort could determine the parliamentary fate of every Whig administration between 1721 and 1756 inevitably acquired a very special place in the politics of oligarchy, as it developed under the first two Georges (Ch. 3). And it was in coaxing and convincing these men, especially, that Walpole was called on to display the full range of his parliamentary gifts. The challenge was the stiffer because, being the only commoner in the Cabinet until Sir Charles Wager went to the Admiralty in 1733, the prime minister had to carry the main burden of defending the administration in the Lower House across almost the entire board of policy questions.

Most, though not all, of the independent Whigs were country gentlemen, and Sir Robert's debating talents were tailor-made for them. His style may have lacked the rhetorical flourishes of a Pulteney or a Pitt, but it was incisive and direct: a clear statement of a case usually backed up with a simple but impressive array of facts and figures. Equally important at times was his skill in playing on the sympathies and prejudices of the gentry on the Whig benches, sentiments to which he was instinctively attuned. It was for their benefit that he kept his language plain enough so that, even in a finance debate, the most doltish squire could usually follow his drift; chose his metaphors from the farmyard or the hunting field; munched his Norfolk apples to sustain him during debates, and studiously preserved his East Anglian accent. Nor was it fiscal considerations alone which made him so anxious to keep down the Land Tax. His undeviating and uncompromising refusal to have any truck, in any circumstances, with Tories was a trump card which he could always produce when required. One by one, all his chief opponents, from Sunderland onwards, discarded it; but Walpole, never. First and last, he was adept at pulling together the threads of *party* loyalty, and in appealing, in and out of the House, to the deepest traditions and prejudices of Whiggery. Add to all this the genuine respect with which he invariably treated the Commons, and his astonishingly regular attendance there, in spite of all the pressures of public business upon him, and it is not difficult to understand why even the waspish Chesterfield awarded him the parliamentary accolade.

Thus the hegemony of Sir Robert Walpole rested on a facility to come to terms with a political system very different in some fundamental respects from that in which he had first made his reputation, and on a capacity to achieve the maximum conceivable degree of influence within that system:

> He accepted, and trimmed his sails to meet, all the rough weather which challenged the ambitious politician in early Hanoverian England: the fragmentation of the ruling one-party oligarchy; the uncertain favour of kings and courtiers; above all the crucial fact that . . . the prime minister and his government never controlled an absolute majority of the Commons.

Walpole mastered all the inherent difficulties of the political world in which he lived; not only that, he turned them into positive and long-term assets. No politician can do more (30, *180*).

---

1. Of the Walpoleans, other than Townshend, only Methuen was found a berth in 1720.
2. Add. MSS 32,686, f. 193: Lord Carteret to duke of Newcastle, 27 Aug 1721.
3. Add. MSS 32,686, f. 191: Charles Stanhope to Newcastle, 26 Aug.
4. Add. MSS 32,686, f. 186: Carteret to Newcastle, 22 Aug 1726.
5. See R. A. Welch, *Newcastle: A Duke without Money* (1974), *passim*.
6. H. L. Snyder, 'The Pardon of Lord Bolingbroke', *HJ* **14** (1971).
7. Add. MSS 32,686. f. 193: 27 Aug 1721.
8. Bernstorff, however, back in Hanover, appears to have clung tenaciously to the remaining shreds of his influence over English affairs, especially in foreign policy. R. Hatton (24a), pp. 244–6, 277 and n. 82.
9. He revelled in the honour with his customary uninhibited relish. See Plumb (26b), p. 101, for the antics of 'Sir Blue-String'.
10. [Philip Yorke], *Walpoliana* (1781), p. 17, quoted in Cruickshanks (31), p. 24.
11. For Onslow's political and procedural influence see Thomas (17), Ch. 15 and *passim*.
12. Thanks to the operation of this Act Walpole had to face only three newly elected Parliaments in the 19 years from May 1722 to April 1741.
13. HMC *Bath MSS*, I, 110–11: Harley to Godolphin, 15 Oct 1706.

CHAPTER 2

The politics of oligarchy: I – Monarchy and aristocracy

In the previous chapter we saw that Walpole maintained his supremacy for so long under the first two Georges largely because his talents were ideally suited to the political system of the day. This was a system which he himself helped to fashion, which he handed on in turn to his political heirs, the Pelham brothers, and which has become synonymous with the so-called Whig Oligarchy.

The term 'Whig Oligarchy' is appropriate in at least two senses. In the first place, after the Tory dismissals of 1716 one-party monopoly of all central offices of government and Household and one-party control of the main institutions of county administration remained unbroken until the death of George II. At the height of Walpole's power few appointments of state were made, however minor, that did not meet with his approval; the first criterion applied, whether filling Cabinet posts or the humblest clerkships, was loyalty. Tories were ruthlessly excluded from the reckoning on automatic suspicion of Jacobitism, unless, like Winnington, Henry Legge or the Fox brothers they had already plainly signalled their conversion to Whiggery from the old family creed. In the 1740s, in consequence of the coalition wheeling and dealing of Pulteney and Henry Pelham which followed Walpole's fall (Ch. 4), half a dozen Tories were found places that were 'lucrative and honourable' but 'of no great power', as Hardwicke put it. But only Gower (as Privy Seal), Bathurst and John Pitt survived for any time, and then only because they too changed parties (28a; 38a; 12a, II). Two effects of the prolonged proscription of the Tory party are worth noting. One was the partial erosion of the principle, firmly established in Anne's reign, of a 'non-political' civil service (*Making of a Great Power*, Ch. 16; Ch. 5 '*Achievement*'), not so much by sackings of men already in post but through partisan vetting of new recruits. The other notable effect was on the county commissions of the peace. It had long been recognised that the JPs, as well as providing the vital amateur component in the administrative and judicial system, wielded considerable political influence, especially during elections. Because of the notorious stigma placed on any landowner of substance by his removal from his local bench, pre-1715 party administrations had sought to regulate the commissions in their own favour more by additions than by subtractions. The first two Hanoverian Lord Chancellors, Cowper and Macclesfield, broke sharply with convention by carrying out a series of drastic purges, and by 1727 there was not a county in England, with the possible exception of Herefordshire, and scarcely a division within any county, where the local Whigs were not in a comfortable majority. This status quo Walpole and the Pelhams were thereafter content to preserve, and even Lord Chancellor Hardwicke's well-publicised concessions to local Tory worthies in the 1740s and 1750s were very carefully weighed and selective (78a and b).

There is a second and stricter sense in which the political system managed by Walpole and his successors was not merely Whiggish but intensely oligarchic. For all but a few relatively brief interludes between 1722 and 1760 most of the real political power and decision-making in Britain was concentrated in very few hands, and those hands, apart from the early Hanoverian kings themselves, were predominantly landed and aristocratic as well as partisan. The interludes – of which 1733, 1738–9, 1744 and the later 1750s are the chief examples – (above, pp. 6, 8, 10–11) – are important and instructive; but as recent work has emphasised they were not the only occasions on which the oligarchs were forced to be aware of a wider constituency. In this the city of London was always a prominent factor, supplying along with some leading provincial towns a dimension to politics that was bourgeois, or popular, and not infrequently Tory (55; 54; 53; 33b). But although the political system did from time to time have to accommodate such elements, its controls remained down to 1761 in the hands of a ruling élite in which little over a score of Whig families and the merest handful of ex-Tory converts held nearly all the levers that mattered.[1] A few commoners, for example Doddington and Edgecumbe, might play necessary supporting rôles from the fringe of the favoured inner circle, either as electoral managers or House of Commons 'understrappers'; three or four individuals of obscure birth might rise *via* the law, as did Parker, King and Ryder, and one must not ignore aristocratic magnates, like the Watson Wentworths and Fitzwilliams, just because their influence at this stage was still primarily local. But the fact remains that, under the Crown, early and mid-Georgian Britain was effectively ruled from the centre by a tiny nucleus of the so-called 'governing class'.

Proscriptive and exclusive though it was, the political system of the years 1721 to 1761 proved robust and durable. The pattern of ministerial continuity and change convincingly reflects this. After the end of Sunderland's last challenge to Walpole, in April 1722, there were no more than seven years *in toto* out of the next forty in which the Whig oligarchy failed to provide Britain with strong, stable and on the whole successful government. Even periods when the fabric of ministerial stability was disturbed were not without their achievements, as can be seen from February 1742 to November 1744, when the Pelham brothers and the Old Corps were contesting with Pulteney and Carteret for Sir Robert's inheritance (Ch. 5), or in the 39 months which followed Henry Pelham's death in March 1754 (pp. 240–1 below). The purpose of this chapter and the next is to analyse the politics of oligarchy in the years of the Whig Supremacy: to identify and examine the main components in the system; to see how they functioned; and to seek to explain why, by and large, they continued to do so smoothly until first, some jarring elements in the 1750s, and then George III, along with John Wilkes and the American colonists, started to toss their various spanners into those well-oiled works.

Our first concern, an important one, will be with the rôle of the Crown in the political system of the day. Our second, bringing the present chapter to a close, will be with the influence of the House of Lords: assessing the Lords not just institutionally but as the collective presence of those 190 or so aristocrats (202a, *28–30*) who traditionally stood closer to the monarch than any other subjects and who, despite constitutional disadvantages in Parliament, continued to exercise great power in the eighteenth-century state. In Chapter 4 we shall turn to the Commons and to the rôle of 'party' in the politics of oligarchy, the matter which has fired much of the controversy that has centred on that House since Namier's time. In the end, however, we shall suggest that the tendency to view politics under the first two Georges, between General Elections, almost exclusively in terms of parliamentary, ministerial or palace manoeuvres is distorting. The world of 'high politics' could not and did not remain insulated from extraneous, or even from popular pressures, any more in the age of Walpole and the Pelhams than in the age of Shaftesbury and Wharton.

At the apex of the Walpole-Pelham system, formally at least, stood the monarchy. This prompts two questions. How far was the Whig oligarchy sustained by the presence on the throne for forty-six years of two 'Whig monarchs' and by the political prejudices they harboured? And to what extent did the early Hanoverian kings rather than the politicians themselves manage to control the balance of power and the distribution of favours within that oligarchy?

Linda Colley has urged that George II in 1727, like his father in 1717, 1721 and 1725, hankered (to say the least) after a mixture of Whigs and Tories in his ministry: envisaging not a 'balance', since that would not have been feasible given the parliamentary preponderance of the former, but enough of a representation for the Tory party to allay its fears and neutralise its Jacobite propensities (28a; cf. 6, *intro.*, *5*). It is a difficult hypothesis to sustain. George I had offered an olive branch of sorts in 1714 to Tories who had boldly supported the Protestant Succession in Parliament, but it soon withered (5, *Ch. 6*; 28a, *54–5*). Later he showed himself willing to decoy individual Tories of evident parliamentary talent away from their party. Thus he cemented Lord Carteret's transition from Hanoverian Toryism to Whiggery by making him envoy to Sweden (1719) and a Secretary of State in 1721. He also detached Harcourt, the former Tory Lord Chancellor, with a viscountcy in 1721,[2] and ultimately Lord Trevor with the Cabinet office of Lord Privy Seal. That he teetered more generally in the Tory direction in the crisis of 1717, so soon after the Jacobite rebellion and the fall of the Nottinghamites, is doubtful, and his supposed wavering in 1721 was purely a product of the Tories' own self-delusion.

> The report of the Tories coming in having reached the King's ears [Newcastle recorded at that time], he has been so good as to declare to me and to many other of his servants the concern he has with that report, and has assured us that he neither has or ever had any such thoughts, and is determined to stand by the Whigs and not take in any one single Tory.[3]

George II, like his father, was convinced (and not without some justification) that even those parliamentary Tories who were not positively pro-Stuart were negatively anti-Hanoverian, especially in foreign affairs (6, *Intro, 7*; 31, *29–30*).

He may at times have felt a sneaking admiration for the Tories' ability to preserve their identity and solidarity. But he never really trusted them; and although, at the height of the savage Whig infighting of 1733, when he was afraid that Walpole's ministry might be brought down, he is supposed to have declared to Lord Hervey that he would rather have a Tory administration of his own choice than a coalition forced upon him by the leaders of a mongrel opposition, it is hard to take this seriously (20, *203, 205*). George II's years as King were festooned with splenetic nonsenses, uttered in the heat or strain of the moment by a highly excitable man and swiftly forgotten or ignored thereafter. And certainly while the 'broad-bottom' schemes of 1742–6 were afoot, the King never betrayed the slightest relish at the prospect of having to admit Tories to office in more than barely token numbers.

It seems beyond doubt, therefore, that one very distinctive feature of the political system of 1722–60 was a monarchy not merely reconciled to a single-party monopoly of office but active in promoting it, in a way that would have appalled William III and Anne. The question remains, however: could either George I or George II have resisted a major influx of Tories if the political arithmetic of the House of Commons had created much greater pressure for it? Constitutionally, the Revolution of 1688 and subsequent legislation down to the 1701 Settlement Act had left the monarch still with a great deal of formal power (*Making of a Great Power*, Ch. 13). Yet when it came down to the harsh realities of power, especially in ministry-building or breaking, how much did these formal prerogatives amount to? In domestic politics, at least, many things told against the first two Georges. They were up against not so much the law of the constitution as its now established conventions. The convention of holding lengthy sessions of Parliament annually, of a strengthened Commons' financial stranglehold over Parliament, and therefore over government, and of a Cabinet system, for instance, were inherited from the period 1689–1714. Fresh conventions, such as the custom of formal as well as informal Cabinets meeting independently of the monarch (75; but cf. 24a, *129–30*), developed before the end of George I's reign; and yet more, such as the septennial convention whereby Parliaments were normally allowed to run their maximum 7-year course, became established before the fall of Walpole. There were other handicaps, too, which the early Hanoverians had to struggle against: the financial strait-jacket of the Civil List [*The Making of a Great Power*, F.vi], particularly constricting for George I; the latter's inability or unwillingness to wrestle with the English language; and both monarchs' distracting preoccupation with the affairs of their electorate. All these and other factors for long seemed to most historians to add up to a rôle for the Crown in the political system of 1721–60 which, except at odd crises, was fitful and essentially subsidiary.

How have these assumptions stood up in the face of the detailed attention given to this period since 1957 (38a)? We now know what a deal of time and art even the great Walpole felt bound to lavish on the Court and the royal entourage, especially in the early years of his ministry, and how, right to the end, great House of Commons man though he was, he never forgot where ultimately his authority rested (Ch. 1). It is equally well established that from 1725 onwards, and arguably from earlier, Walpole nearly always got his own way on major issues, when he really wanted it. The question is, was this a measure of his own personal dominance and political genius, or of the basic ineffectuality of the monarchy in the domestic political system? Eighteen months after his resignation, Sir Robert, in his new rôle as *éminence grise*, wrote from the depth of his own experience a most revealing letter to his protégé, Henry Pelham:

> The King must, with tenderness and management, be shown what he may with reason depend upon, and what he will be deceived and lost if he places any confidence and reliance in . . . *Address and management* are the weapons you must fight and defend with: plain truths will not be relished at first, in opposition to prejudices, conceived and infused in favour of his own partialities; and you must dress up all you offer with the appearance of no other view or tendency but to promote his service in his own way, to the utmost of your power. And the more you can make anything *appear* to be his own, . . . the better you will be heard.[4]

'Tenderness', 'address' and 'management', the need to preserve the appearance of the King's autonomy – every word and phrase signals that George II, at least, was much more than a mere cipher or a rubber stamp for the decisions of his politicians. They tell us of a self-important man of decided opinions, a King who could be skilfully led but not driven. And while George I differed much in character and temperament from his son, there is nothing in the best and most up-to-date study of his life and reign (24a) to suggest that his acquiescence in his ministers' policies and schemes could readily be taken for granted. One general deduction that can safely be drawn from Walpole's advice to Pelham in 1743 is that, in a constitutional situation which was still so fluid – in that government had ceased to be fully royal without as yet having become fully parliamentary – the personality, as well as the priorities, of the ruler was likely to be a crucial determinant of the way the system worked every time the constitutional equation had to be resolved.

It is, for example, quite impossible to understand the relations of George I with British politicians after 1714 without being aware of the fact that for almost 40 of his 54 years before coming to England from Hanover he had been closely involved in the military and political affairs of the Continent. Obviously his European status was not on a par with that of William III. Yet he was an experienced soldier, had a close family connection with the rising power of the Hohenzollerns (Ch. 4, p. 58) and a relationship through marriage with both the Habsburgs and the French Regent, Orléans, and he inherited to the full his father's intense concern with the consolidation and extension of his German domains. In foreign affairs, therefore, he was always well-informed and involved; the achievement of his main Hanoverian ambition in 1719, with the acquisition of Bremen and Verden (Ch. 4), did not diminish his involvement. To describe British foreign policy between 1721 and 1727 as 'Townshend's policy' or even as 'Whig policy' may be convenient shorthand, but it is no more than a half-truth (24a, *267–79*; 89a).

In other respects, too, George I has been (as he was at the time) one of the most misunderstood of Britain's kings. His 'image', in modern public relations parlance, was against him, and only belatedly did it receive attention. It was shyness and apprehension, not – as his subjects imagined – distaste for the polite society of his new kingdom, which led him to resort so frequently in the early years of his reign to the privacy of his own palace apartments and to the comfortable company of his Germans and Turks. He had a temperamental dislike of fuss and ceremonial, and in the years since his sensational divorce of his wife, Sophia Dorothea, in 1694, had developed a loathing for publicity. When he was urged out of his protective cocoon by Stanhope and Sunderland in the years 1717–20, and set himself as a matter of policy to outshine the social glitter of the rival court at Leicester House (Ch. 1), he did so with calculation and Germanic thoroughness (see 25). But it was unfortunate, all the same, that for the most part the conviviality and warmth of feeling disguised behind his sombre, deadpan features were revealed only in his domestic circle (24a; 26a; 25). His grasp of affairs, moreover, was not to be underestimated: the 'very sound brain and judgement' which the Dutch diplomat, van der Meer, had observed in him in 1702 came closer to the truth than the 'honest blockhead' preserved for posterity in Lady Mary Wortley Montagu's bitchy aphorism. He kept an especially tenacious hold on his right to take military, as well as foreign policy decisions, and he could be relied on to assert his influence in the political crises of his reign.

On the other hand, it cannot be plausibly argued that George I was *consistently* effective in domestic politics. The main reason for this was not so much lack of ability as lack of application. In autocratic Hanover, with his trusted ministers and bureaucrats on hand, he had never had to work hard at being a ruler; in Britain, with its troublesome parliaments and parties and its multiplicity of interests vying for consideration, he was never prepared to work hard at being a politician. We may take just three illustrations among many. When he arrived in London on 20 September 1714, he had done so little homework in the seven weeks since Anne's death that he was ignorant even of the ranks of the British peerage. Then there was his attitude to Court appointments. His two successors were to guard their Household and Bedchamber prerogatives jealously, some-times to the discomfiture of the Whig chieftains, who rightly regarded them as valuable grist to the patronage mill, but George I rarely exerted himself to make his own choices (25, *140–1*). Lastly, there is the more basic, and politically more damaging, matter of language. The King arrived in England able neither to speak, write nor understand more than a few words of English. Although in the course of time he could not help acquiring a vestigial vocabulary, to the end of his reign the King's Speeches to Parliament had to be read for him by the Lord Chancellor, because (as a foreign observer of one such occasion recorded in astonishment in 1725) 'the present reigning King cannot speak English'.[5] Such negligence over a period of fourteen years would be scarcely credible were it not consistent with almost everything else we know about his complacent attitude to domestic affairs. After two hours giving audiences in his closet and one more dealing with papers at his desk, George I was convinced he had had a very hard day. Queen Anne, despite an inferior intelligence, was conscientious, proud and obstinate enough to preserve for the Crown a rôle of importance in the day-today working of domestic politics (22, *Chs. 6, 12*). This rôle was undoubtedly diminished between 1714 and 1727.

In some ways George II was an obvious improvement on his father. He did master the language; he worked far harder at kingship, indulging a passion for minutiae and capitalising on a photographic memory, and until 1737 he had the valuable support of a queen who had the self-confidence he himself lacked. Caroline's painful death at the age of 54 left him desolated.[6] After the convulsions into which the world of high politics was plunged by his unexpected accession (Ch. 1), there were few who doubted that at certain junctures the new King *could* occupy the pivotal place in the political system to which, in his pipe-dreams, he aspired. Whether he ever did firmly occupy it is more debatable. The same goes for his more continuous influence on policy and patronage. That he wished to be influential is clear. He read through reams of state papers and peppered them with his fussy annotations. Yet the number of fields in which he was able to exert his authority with any consistency seems to have been strictly limited. One of them, foreign policy, was admittedly of the first importance. George II was as well versed in European affairs as his father and no more averse than the latter to seeing British policy, at times, 'distorted for Hanoverian ends'[7] (Ch. 4). Only once between 1727 and the Elder Pitt's advent in 1757 did any British minister fly in the face of the King's opinions in foreign policy – and get away with it; even that celebrated clash (in 1733 over the Polish Succession) and the apparent surrender to Walpole was less clear-cut than used to be thought. There were times, as in the winter of 1727–8, when Townshend was ill, and for much of 1736–8, when George's intervention was so frequent as to amount to virtual direction of foreign policy (89a, *38–45*). Foreign policy apart, one can point to two areas of patronage in which he was both self-assertive and obdurate. Fittingly, for one who had won his soldierly spurs at Oudenarde and who was to take immoderate pride in leading his forces in the field at Dettingen, the King kept an eagle eye on all military appointments, and only rarely, and by sleight of hand, could Walpole manage to slide in his own candidates for army promotion. And when Newcastle in the 1750s tried to rig Household patronage from the Treasury, as Walpole had before 1727, George positively excoriated him (34, *121*).

How can we explain, therefore, why George II became increasingly convinced, as the years went by, that he would never succeed in his ambition to translate prerogative into consistent power in domestic politics? Why was it that in the eighteen years left to him after Sir Robert's fall, self-pitying observations such as 'Ministers are the Kings in this country'[8] fell with growing frequency from his lips and pen? J.B. Owen has suggested that such comments were to some degree ritualised and should not be taken at face value; and in an important revisionist essay developing some of the themes of an earlier book (34; cf. 38a, *passim*) he plausibly argues that not even in the 1730s, and still less after 1742, was George II a mere pawn in the political game. All the same, there is evidence that some, at least, of the King's pessimism was both genuine and justified, and it is not easy to go all the way with Owen to the conclusion that he 'held his own [against the politicians] as well as was possible for any monarch who had to cope with the realities of a period of mixed government' (34, *133*). That he fought hard to preserve the shrunken territory bequeathed him by his father cannot be gainsaid. But against numerous small successes must be set a sequence of clangorous failures. His ultimate capitulations in 1756 and 1757 to Pitt, his scourge for many years, were only the last of many painful and face-losing blows to his pride and prerogative, suffered in the glaring spotlight of the high political arena. Those defeats – of which those of 1727, 1733, 1742 and 1746 were only the most spectacular – no doubt occurred partly because the political system itself, and above all the increasing dominance within it of the Commons, could not readily be moulded to the monarch's prejudices and whims. And yet, in the 1740s and 1750s, especially, the abiding impression is of a ruler whose wounds were largely self-inflicted – whose aspirations were as much a prey to his own flaws of temperament and capacity as to the predator politicians who dominated the Whig Oligarchy.

George II brought both to life and kingship a parade-ground mentality. He enclosed himself in method and routine and was easily disconcerted by the unexpected. His slavery to habit (even his evening visits to his mistress were occasions for courtiers to set watches by) is sometimes seen as a leading clue to the pattern of his relationship with his most successful ministers. It becomes more revealing, however, if we recognise it as the defensive screen which the King put out between himself and the world. Behind it blustered a splenetic and basically unstable man, lacking in fixity of purpose, temperamentally unable to sustain his energy. His epic outbursts of ferocious temper were symptomatic of this. After he quarrelled with the Pelham brothers in 1744, they and all their friends (according to one fellow-sufferer) were forced 'to bear . . . even with such foul language that no one gentleman could take from another'.[9] Yet by 1747, only a year after they had finally demolished the King's attempts to rule through a ministry of his making rather than of theirs, the Pelhams had become one of those comfortable habits which George II found it so hard to break; and thereafter it was their opponents who were the 'fools', 'scoundrels' and 'blockheads', or who became the butt of more scatological royal insults. Such eruptions smack of weakness, not strength. We must not get it out of proportion (42, *63–4*). Even in his old age the King's opinion could never be disregarded. But while in foreign affairs it was normally inescapable, on the domestic front it could be changed, circumvented or even overridden by ministers who appreciated, as Walpole had, the supreme value of 'management'. In the end, what most determined the measure of the Crown's importance in the working of the political system between 1727 and 1760 was that, rightly or wrongly, George II convinced himself of his own ineffectuality. What confidence he did possess in the first half of his reign was largely destroyed when he had written terms virtually imposed on him by the Old Corps in 1746, a crushing blow the like of which not even Queen Anne had ever had to suffer (38a, *298–9*). To his credit, he did – unlike two at least of his Stuart predecessors – have enough political sense to accept this and other defeats, once they became inescapable, and this streak of realism did the political system a very important service. It is understandable, nonetheless, that many historians have been persuaded (as was the young George III, by the time he came to the throne [Ch. 18]) that in the last thirteen years of his reign the old King did, by and large, sell the pass to the great Whig political families; and likewise to the institution he felt he would never get the better of as long as he lived, 'that damned House of Commons'.

Any sketch of the structure of early Hanoverian politics must of necessity place the House of Commons at the heart of the whole system. The House of Lords as an institution lost considerable ground to the Commons in the thirty years which followed the end of its 'golden period', around 1723. The decline was not in formal constitutional powers but in political status. The Upper House no longer occupied a place of consistent centrality in the political process, and at times, especially after 1743, it contrived to appear almost peripheral to that process. In the first place, the Tory party suffered critical losses and defections among the peerage in the first half of George I's reign. Even before the extraordinary mortality among the bishops in the years 1721–4, which enabled Walpole and his 'Pope', Edmund Gibson, to instal prelates of Whiggish sympathies in seventeen sees (Ch. 7), the fairly even balance of parties in the Lords which had existed for much of the period between 1689 and 1714 had been utterly destroyed. By 1723 a muster of forty Tory peers was already exceptional; by 1740, thirty would have been remarkable, and after 1745, little over twenty (21, *93*; 28a, *61–5*; 203a, *14, 26*). Secondly, careful and systematic management of the Upper House by the Walpole-Pelham regime created a more pliant 'party of the Crown' among the Whig majority there than Westminster had ever known before, prompting disenchanted lords of both parties to bestow such uncomplimentary labels as 'acquiescent', 'insignificant' or 'pretty much . . . useless' on their chamber (21, *85–6*). Patronage was of course a key factor, here as elsewhere, in the workings of oligarchy.[10] But in addition, regular leadership of the House (normally by one of the Secretaries of State), sessional meetings, a well-drilled committee routine and a tight control over the recruitment and attendance of the twenty-six bishops all played a significant part; so too did the use of the 'Court List' of Scottish representative peers to ensure that no Scot with a record of persistent dissidence in the Lords had a hope of re-election. Some techniques, for instance the 'list' system, Walpole borrowed from Oxford's Tory administration of 1710–14; in other respects, he and Newcastle were the innovators.

The cumulative effect of all these developments would by themselves have substantially affected the relative standing of the Upper House, and the presence of the First Lord of the Treasury in the Commons for all but six months of the 33 years from 1721–54 inflicted further damage. But although the importance of the Lords was depressed, it was not destroyed. The very care which Walpole, in particular, lavished on the cultivation of a secure majority there indicates how rarely it was left out of his calculations. And in spite of that care, the man who well remembered the vital contribution of the Lords to the downfall of the Tory ministers in 1701 and their narrow failure to bring down the Harley ministry in December 1711 over its peace policy, only just survived himself when the Lords ran amok in the wake of the Excise Crisis, after a drove of Scottish as well as Court peers had defected to the opposition (203a, *101–2*; 32a, *99–100*). The stern disciplinary measures which restored his control of the House in 1733 did not prevent another humiliation there over the Quaker Relief Bill in 1736 (Ch. 7; 109b; 109a). 'And although Sir Robert's resignation in February 1742 is rightly attributed, first and foremost, to his loss of control in the Commons, he cannot have overlooked the fact that in addition the impregnable Lords majority of 50 which his ministry had commanded at the start of 1741 had crumbled away to a mere 12 by the eve of his fall (21, *91*).

Down to 1746 emphatically, and to a lesser extent thereafter, both government and opposition envisaged a far from insignificant rôle for the Upper Chamber. For the administration it was, as Hill has put it, the indispensable 'longstop' (20, *205*): fielding and knocking into shape untidy bills which had escaped from the Lower House in haste, and especially valuable for killing off backbench measures, such as Place and Pensions Bills – measures which were unacceptable to the ministry but so popular with independent members of both parties that it would have been most imprudent to try to crush them in the Commons. Equally important, the Lords was still the focus of much public interest as a debating chamber, which explains why both government and opposition prepared so carefully for the set-piece debates there on the State of the Nation, and also why first the Tories, from the early 1720s, and later Tories and dissident Whigs together, used the right of the minority lords to enter 'Protests' in the Lords' *Journals* as a means of getting their arguments across to the public in print. It also explains why, after breaking with the Excise rebels, Walpole felt it essential to reinforce a now weak ministerial debating team by procuring peerages for Hervey, Talbot and the eloquent lawyer, Philip Yorke, whom the King created Lord Hardwicke. It is only from the mid–1740s onwards that the view of the eighteenth-century House of Lords as a chamber without a major rôle to play, encapsulated in John Cannon's epigrammatic debunking of its members as 'firemen in a town without fires', gets closer to the mark; for those were the years after the defection of their former leader, Lord Gower, to the Whigs, which 'shattered Tory morale and effectively emasculated what was left of concerted Tory activity in the House of Lords' (203a, *125*; 28a, *65*).

Even institutionally, therefore, the decline of the House of Lords must not be exaggerated. And in any event, both collectively and individually the peers who sat there (or at least the Whigs among them) retained immense political influence. Politically, as well as economically, culturally and in terms of the social pre-eminence of the peerage, the eighteenth century merits supremely well Cannon's description of it as the 'aristocratic century' (203a; cf. 289, *Ch. 2*). For one thing, it is clear from what we know of Cabinet membership between the early 1690s and 1760 that the peers significantly increased their hold over the highest posts in the administration after 1720. Under William III it had been quite common for a Cabinet of ten or eleven members to contain three commoners, all in key working offices. The same was true of several periods in Anne's reign and George I's, down to the winter of 1716–17; indeed there would have been four commoners in Harley's Cabinet in 1710–11 if Sir John Leake, the First Lord of the Admiralty, had been called to the table.[11] By the late 1720s, however, Walpole found himself the only commoner in the 'inner' Cabinet (26b, 197), and both the full and inner Cabinets of the years 1742–60 were massively dominated by the *haute noblesse*. By November 1744 there were more dukes in Henry Pelham's Cabinet than had existed in the entire English peerage in 1688, leaving aside the ennobled royal bastards of Charles II. From 1690 down to 1721, except when the earl of Nottingham was sole Secretary in 1692–3, at least one of the two English Secretaries of State was invariably a commoner, and members of the House of Commons had occupied both Secretaryships from 1700–02, 1704–06 and 1716–17. From 1721 onwards, however, until Sir Thomas Robinson's appointment as Southern Secretary after Henry Pelham's death, even these posts became aristocratic monopolies.

During the same period there was a parallel and equally striking rise in the aristocratic content of the House of Commons. Except in 1708, the number of peers' sons returned to the Commons changed relatively little between the General Election of 1690 and that of 1715, when it stood at thirty-four. Thereafter the increase was dramatic, reaching fifty-nine by 1727 and seventy-eight by 1747 (203b). But that increase was only one facet of the much wider ability of peers, both English and Scottish, to control or influence the election of their nominees and clients to parliamentary seats. As late as 1710, when the fiercest of all eighteenth-century elections was fought, there were still only thirteen true proprietory boroughs in England, returning twenty-five MPs, plus possibly ten other single seats, which were *firmly* under the control of lay members of the House of Lords.[12] A Wharton nominee at Aylesbury, a Booth in Cheshire and a Cavendish at Derby were among the many well-established Whigs who perished in that never-to-be-forgotten holocaust. The change that came over the scene subsequently was momentous. It is hazardous to put firm figures on the numbers of MPs in any Parliament who 'owed their seats' to aristocratic influence. But Professor Cannon's estimate of a rise from 105 to 167 between 1715 and 1747 in the number of seats in which English *and Scottish* peers had a commanding interest is an accurate reflection of the prevailing trend under the first two Hanoverians, and it was a trend which was to continue (203a, *106–7*).

It was the unreformed electoral system combined with the Septennial Act which, at bottom, made this remarkable change possible. During the first great age of Party that system, for all its inequalities and anomalies, had not obstructed the broad expression of 'the sense of the people' (*Making of a Great Power*, Ch. 21). From the 1720s to the 1750s it unquestionably did do so.[13] If General Elections under the first two Georges had been decided by the votes of the counties and of those cities and boroughs with over 500 voters, or had they even been determined, under the prevailing system, by total votes cast, the Tories would have won not only the 1722 Election but those of 1734 and 1741 as well. Yet only once between 1727 and 1761 did Tory candidates capture as many as a quarter of the seats in the House of Commons (28a, *122, 296*; E.1). The reason, quite simply, was that in the mass of smaller boroughs, in many of which magnate influence or venality (or both) were pronounced, the Tory party was totally crushed. By the supreme political irony of the eighteenth century, Walpole's masterly management of the House of Commons over two decades was set at nought in 1741, after an election in which he and his supporters actually increased their popular support, but suffered mortally from having previously alienated too many 'great men', those grandees whose borough patronage and capacity to influence the composition of the House was a vital ingredient in the political system which Walpole shaped and the Pelhams inherited.

In the next chapter we must enquire, first, how that system worked inside the House of Commons, and secondly, how its working was affected by the different parties, groups and forces which composed that House, or which could bring pressure from without to bear upon it.

---

1. If this should seem a wild exaggeration, it is worth remembering the influence wielded and the offices accumulated by the following fifteen families alone: the Walpoles, Townshends, Pelhams and Stanhopes; the Yorkes, Cavendishes, Russells, Campbells and Darcys; the Onslows, the Temple-Grenville clan, the Pitts and the Foxes. Only the two latter were non-landed in their recent origins.
2. Not with the Privy Seal in 1720, as Colley states (28a, p. 197): that office went to a Pierrepont, the staunchly Whig duke of Kingston.
3. Add. MSS 32686, f. 175: Newcastle to Dr Jordan, 18 July 1721.
4. W. Coxe, *Memoirs of the Administration of the Right Honourable Henry Pelham*, 2 vols (1829), I, pp. 104–5: Walpole to Pelham, 20 Oct 1743 (my italics).
5. Madame Van Muyden, ed., *The Letters of . . . César de Saussure: a Foreign View of England in the Reign of George I and George II* (1902), p. 62. Ragnhild Hatton's attempted rehabilitation of George in this respect founders on a misinterpretation of one crucial document: (24a), pp. 130–2, 339, n. 61; cf. G.C. Gibbs's review in *Welsh Hist. Rev.*, **10** (1980–1), pp. 248–51.
6. See Plumb (26b), pp. 159–61 for a brilliant cameo of Queen Caroline of Ansbach.
7. J. Black (89a), p. 29. See also G.C. Gibbs, 'English Attitudes towards Hanover and the Hanoverian Succession', in A.M. Birke and K. Kluxen, eds, *England and Hanover* (1986), pp. 43–4, 49; J.B. Owen, (34), pp. 122–6.
8. P.C. Yorke. *The Life and Correspondence of Philip Yorke, Lord Chancellor Hardwicke* (Cambridge, 1913) I, p. 383: 'Notes of Audience' [by Hardwicke], 5 Jan 1744.
9. Add. MSS 32705, f. 187: duke of Richmond to Newcastle, 16 Sept 1745.
10. 69 members of the House of Lords held pensions or offices from the Crown in 1714; roughly 100 (out of a total of 183) by 1740. G. Holmes (22), pp. 435–9; C. Jones (21), p. 96.
11. Lord Dartmouth's Cabinet and Committee minutes, 18 June 1710–17 June 1711: William Salt Library, Stafford, Dartmouth MSS.
12. In addition, the four members jointly sent to Westminster by East and West Looe were nominated by the then bishop of Winchester, Sir Jonathan Trelawney, bart., and four more English boroughs were under the joint control of a peer and a commoner acting in concert. G.S. Holmes, 'The Influence of the Peerage in English Parliamentary Elections, 1702–1713', Oxford B. Litt. thesis, 1952, Chs. 2, 3 and App. A and C.
13. G. Holmes (57). Dr Clark, in his criticism of a whole 'received interpretation' of the character and influence of the late 17th- and early 18th-century English electorate does not – if I understand him aright – challenge this, the most central of my arguments. J.C.D. Clark (289), pp. 20–1 and cf. pp. 15–23 *passim*.

CHAPTER 3

The politics of oligarchy: II – Commons, parties and people

The structure of the House of Commons under Walpole and the Pelhams has been the subject of a prolonged debate among historians. This debate has gone on for sixty years, and with particular liveliness since 1970, and it is still unresolved. In sustaining it the most fundamental disagreement has been over the importance of the part played in parliamentary politics by 'party', in the pre–1722 sense of that term. Broadly speaking, three interpretations have had most influence on the scholarship and writing of the last generation: an influence complicated in the case of the third school, at least, by profound internal differences of emphasis.

Down to the mid–1960s the 'Namierite' interpretation held almost complete sway. Its foundation was the famous premise, first enunciated with olympian authority by Sir Lewis Namier in 1929–30, that 'the political life of the period could be fully described without ever using a party denomination' (43a, *xi*). Although 'the period' to which Namier originally referred was a brief one, spanning only the few years either side of 1760, it was later much expanded – in both directions – by the author himself and by other scholars who had been deeply influenced by his thinking and methods (43a; 43b; 35a; 38a and b; 39). Namier and the Namierites did not deny that the old party labels 'Whig' and 'Tory' continued to be regularly used under the first two Georges,[1] or that in the constituencies they still retained some emotional appeal; but they maintained that as a key to the way politics actually worked at Westminster they had become irrelevant by George II's reign, if not before. Instead historians were asked to envisage the members of the House of Commons all falling into 'three broad divisions, based on type and not on party' (35a, *21*). These divisions were not always described in precisely the same terms; but in general they were held to correspond to (1) courtiers and placemen, (2) 'independents' – by definition, overwhelmingly country gentlemen, and (3) the politicians or political factions competing for the spoils of office.

In place of pure Namierism, which has been in slow retreat for the past twenty-five years, two alternative models have been suggested since the 1960s to enable us to comprehend what went on in the early Georgian House of Commons. One of them sees the basic polarity in the House, ideologically as well as structurally, as a Court-Country one, with most office-holders and 'expectants' finding a congenial home at the former pole, and most backbenchers at the latter, but with some pulling-power still exercised from time to time by the old Whig and Tory loyalties. *How* strong their pull was, however, is a matter on which the advocates of this interpretation are not agreed. The instincts of the former Namierite, J.B. Owen, prompt him to dismiss it, in his later writings, as very slight (10, *105ff, esp. 112–14*). In the work of W.A. Speck and H.T. Dickinson it emerges rather more strongly (35c and *Colloquy*; 284, *Pt. 2, esp. 167–9*; 27a and b). In the second favoured interpretation of recent years, however, there are far fewer inhibitions about accepting the survival of Whiggery and Toryism far into the reign of George II: not merely as distinctive creeds but as the rallying standards of major parliamentary forces. These forces were unarguably subject to schisms, prolonged and serious at times in the case of the Whigs; yet it is stressed that there were also lengthy periods – and many other briefer interludes – of substantial unanimity. And whatever disagreements divide this third school (notably over the strength of Jacobitism among the Tories of 1723–46) (cf. 12a, *I [Cruickshanks, 'The Tories']*, *62–78*; 65a, *Ch. 1*; 289, *26–37 & Ch. 3*; 29, with 20; 28a), there is consensus on two fundamentals: first, that such patterns of behaviour can only be explained by the hypothesis that politics down to the 1740s at least was as much concerned with issues as with tactics, and second, that no matter what cross-currents Court and Country principles produced – 'the flurries of a day', as the Whig MP Samuel Sandys preferred to call them[2] – the mainstream of political activity ran firmly along Whig and Tory channels (see also 37a; 16; 31; 36, *Chs. 3, 4, 5*).

In the remaining two sections of this chapter we shall explore the significant areas of common ground as well as the main points of difference between these diverse interpretations. In the process a picture of parliamentary politics, taking in both the structure and the behaviour of the House of Commons, can be pieced together which is a good deal more coherent and intelligible than the wrangles of twentieth-century historiography might lead us to expect. What is more, it is a picture that enables us to explain how the so-called 'Old Corps' of the Whigs, those who were more or less consistently associated with Walpole and the Pelhams right through George II's reign, were able to use the Commons as the most essential vehicle for their long stay in the sun.

The structure of the House of Commons

The early Georgian House of Commons may be compared to a roughly cubic structure made up of a variety of movable blocks, each block painted in one or the other of the two primary party colours, Whig or Tory. At any time the blocks could fall together into the most coherent and symmetrical pattern they were capable of adopting, up to three quarters of them presenting a great splash of Whig colour on one side (the 'government' side) of the structure, and the remainder, sharply contrasted in their Tory colours, on the other (or 'opposition') side. When Lord Dupplin drew up a list of the members elected to the House of Commons in 1754, he affixed the label 'Whig' or 'Tory' to every one, just as previous analysts had done over thirty years earlier, after the results of the 1722 Election had come in. He was sensibly returning to base – re-stating the conventional bottom line of every new Parliament in this period; and both before

1730 and after 1747, especially, convention and reality coincided frequently. At the same time, the fact that Dupplin also listed the members in alternative groupings reminds us that our symbolic blocks were adaptable: capable of being reassembled to form more complex and variegated structures, though many of them in practice rarely, if ever, left their natural location.

One thing which every ministry down to 1757 could take for granted was that, except in the most unusual circumstances, the overwhelming majority of Tory members would be in opposition to it; indeed there were times (for example, from 1723–5 and to a lesser extent from 1747–9) when they virtually *were* 'the Opposition'. There were still 178 Tories in the Commons after the 1722 election. After the first General Election of George II's reign, in 1727, Tory strength dwindled away to a mere 130. But for the rest of the reign there were no more catastrophic slumps from that level: a significant rise after the 'Excise' election of 1734, a fall in 1747, but never a presence that could be totally ignored [E.1]. On the extremely rare occasions, until the advent of the Pitt-Newcastle administration in 1757, when Tory members created a structural upheaval by voting on the same side as Whig ministers, or at least abstaining rather than vote against them, there could be one of two explanations. Such actions were sometimes a response to their traditional instincts as monarchists or supporters of constitutional propriety, as in the factious vote on the Prince of Wales's allowance in 1737, or in the infamous division forced by Whig rivals in February 1741 to try to remove Sir Robert from the King's councils 'for ever' (see above, pp. 8, 9). At other times they occurred when Whig ministers – as they not infrequently did in the 1730s (Ch. 7) – found themselves occupying the old 'Tory' position of propping up the Church of England against fierce assaults from their party's own backbenchers.

Another important element of stability in the structure of the Commons, in addition to the almost unwavering disposition of the Tory 'blocks', was provided by the regular adhesion of a distinctive set of non-Tory 'blocks' to the opposing side. Namier categorised these members as 'the followers of Court and Administration, the "placemen", *par excellence* a group of permanent "ins"'; Owen, more concisely, as 'the Court and Treasury Party' (35a, *22*; 38b, *5*). If the term 'party' is to retain genuine meaning, however, as a body of men bound together by certain common principles and by interests *other than self-interest*, it is best avoided in this context, and the members in question would be better described as 'the Dependants'. As the recipients of official favour, in one form or another, their common bond of loyalty was primarily a self-interested one. Most held paid offices of one kind or another. A minority had been granted pensions or government contracts. A much larger minority held commissions in the armed forces (in all, 236 army and navy officers sat in the House at some time between 1715 and 1754, around 70 on average in each Parliament) (12a, *I, 141–5*); while in addition members from any one of these categories, plus a handful outside them, might be 'dependants' in the further sense that their very presence in the House of Commons was the result of their nomination and election for one of the small number of 'government boroughs'.[3] In numbers 'the Dependants' began, in the 1720s, by being rather fewer than the Tories on the other side of the basic divide in the House, but the fall in Tory numbers over the next three decades was matched by a growth in the size of the army of Dependants. The most careful and reliable gauge to that growth (12a, *I, 81–105*), though it omits pensioners and those MPs with a non-financial (usually electoral) obligation to the Court, shows the numbers creeping up from 157 in 1716 to 185 in 1734 and 194 in 1746. So even if we discount more inflated estimates, as it would be prudent to do (e.g. 20, *191–210*), it is not difficult to appreciate why, as time went by, the Whig oligarchs came to attach more and more importance to patronage as the safest cement of their parliamentary majorities. It was not only a matter of numbers; office-holders were also the most easily organised voters in the House.

But to whom, or to what, did these 'Dependants' feel they owed dependance? The high command of the Old Corps, after controlling so much patronage for so long, naturally liked to regard them as *their* men. But the very rare occasions between 1722 and 1760 when placemen's loyalties were put under severe strain plainly suggests, like the much more clear-cut evidence of the 1760s and 1770s (Chs. 18, 20), that in the last resort they themselves recognised an overriding loyalty to the King, and to themselves (not necessarily in that order), rather than to any set of politicians. The main exceptions were the members of the Prince of Wales's household – core of the so-called 'reversionary interest' [A] – whose main obligation was to the heir to the throne; significantly they accounted for roughly half the defections of placemen in the last few years of Walpole's ministry, after the Prince had thrown in his lot with the Opposition (Ch. 5). All the same, to find over twenty Dependants voting against the administration in a major division, as happened in 1739 over the Spanish Convention, or immediately after the 1741 Election in the key vote on the chairmanship of the Committee of Elections, was quite exceptional. So while it is true that 'patronage, of itself, was never enough to control the Lower House' (20, *191*), it is clear that it did provide the indispensable core of the government's majorities under Walpole and the Pelhams, even in times of acute stress such as the Excise crisis (31).

Most of the civilians among the Dependants were involved only with the smaller change of politics: they were men who saw the House of Commons mostly as a vehicle for the achievement of profit rather than power. But there were also of course many members in the House at all times in this period who were playing for much higher stakes, being, in a real sense, *power*-politicians. And there were even more members, most of them elected on their own interests or 'bottoms', whose presence there was a matter of inclination, duty or prestige. They had no need to seek material advancement or to pursue politics as a profession, and not a few of them lacked the capacity, as well as the desire, to cut a figure 'in Court or Council'. Their attendance at Westminster was at best spasmodic. Yet these members, usually referred to as the Independents or as 'the country gentlemen', could rarely be left out of the professionals' calculations. In fact we have already seen (Ch. 1) how cultivating them was an outstanding feature of Walpole's art as a House of Commons man.

It has indeed become universally accepted by historians of eighteenth-century Britain that in the system of politics under the Whig Oligarchy, and thereafter down to the time of the Younger Pitt, these 'independent' members were an essential working component. Yet the precise nature and importance of their rôle has become a deeply confusing matter for students. Even their numbers in the period 1722–54 have been the subject of prodigious disagreements among the most reputable authorities, with estimates ranging from 300–350 at the top of the scale (35b, *60*; 38a, *42*; 21, *107*) down to 'about one hundred' (26a, *65*) or, on one count, as low as 80–90 by 1754 for those 'who lived up to the Patriot ideal of complete independence',[4] at the other end. The prevalent labels have been responsible for at least part of the difficulty. 'Country gentlemen' is a generic term useful enough for social analysis but less satisfactory for political analysis, if by using it we squeeze out of the reckoning merchants and lawyers, who on some issues had very different priorities from those of the county squires. 'Independents' can be even more misleading. It can easily conjure up visions of a St Stephen's Chapel[5] thickly populated by men whose votes were normally cast on the basis of the arguments advanced in debate, and therefore rarely predictable in advance; likewise it can tempt us to play down the party commitments of a very large segment of the House of Commons to the point where they may seem of little relevance. Nothing could be further from the reality. Many of the most strongly committed Whigs as well as Tories in the Commons were backbenchers who (in Owen's helpful phrase [10, *107*]) were 'non-dependants', men not directly obligated either to the Court or to any private professional politician or patron. Evidence of their voting patterns shows that the normal predilection of the Whigs among them was to support the Whig administration of the day against all comers, giving it at least the benefit of the doubt on all major public issues and on recognised votes of confidence – the same divisions, in fact, on which their Tory counterparts could usually be found in opposition. This norm has prompted some historians recently to argue, as Eveline Cruickshanks does, that 'there were few real "independents" on the Whig side' (31, *33*). Yet this would seem too strong a reaction against the Namierite view. For the numerous votes of the Whig non-dependants – and they were at least as numerous in the Parliament of 1747–54 as those of the Tories – *could* be lost to the administration in special circumstances. Such members would often desert when 'Country' legislation or motions were before the House, for on such measures they regarded themselves as the true keepers of the Whig conscience; or on those less frequent but much more critical occasions when confidence began to fade in a ministry's competence or its capacity to interpret the public interest. Desertions were never on a spectacular scale, but they were as crucial as the abstentions of the placemen in similar circumstances and they, as in 1720–1, 1733 and 1741, were a prospect which any government ignored at its peril.

Not for nothing, therefore, did Walpole and Henry Pelham lavish time and care upon winning the hearts and minds of the non-dependant Whigs; by the same token, those Whigs of front-bench standing who entered into permanent opposition periodically addressed themselves to the same purpose. That the latter's blandishments succeeded so infrequently partly reflects the extent to which 'formed opposition' was still frowned upon, as something constitutionally improper. But it is also an indicator of the fact that the proportion of truly volatile backbenchers among the non-dependants in the House was a good deal smaller than used to be thought. Had it not been so, the political world of Westminster would have been much more readily destabilised than in practice it was by the intrigues and manoeuvres of the one major segment of the Commons we have still to examine, the power-politicians.

There were by the 1730s and 1740s never more than a quarter of the 558 members of the House of Commons, and usually less, who were actively engaged in struggling for the bigger prizes of Hanoverian politics – such goodies as might fall from the over-loaded table of the Whig peers (Ch. 2). These were the political blocks whose activities and rivalries caught most of the attention of observers at the time, as they have of historians since. They were composed, firstly, of protagonists of the front rank: notably Walpole, Henry Pelham and William Pulteney (until he became earl of Bath in 1742), and the stars of a rising generation, such as Henry Fox, William Pitt and the Grenville brothers, Richard and George. A more numerous and still important second rank was made up largely of men connected by friendship or alliance with one or more of the front-liners, as Edgecumbe, Falmouth, Winnington and Horace Walpole were with Sir Robert, or Sandys and Gybbon with Pulteney, or George Lyttleton with Pitt and the Grenvilles. But there were also a few free-wheelers (and dealers) at this level, much the most prominent being George Bubb Dodington, a man of no mean talent as well as the possessor of a formidable interest in parliamentary boroughs. Thirdly, there were the kinsmen, clients and electoral nominees of the Whig grandees whose own ambitions and careers were inseparable from the politics of oligarchy: the 'connexions' of such as Newcastle, Devonshire, Bedford and Argyll, and a variety of smaller clusters.

Because one party monopolised the Crown and dominated the Commons throughout the period the quintessential 'professional' or power-politician was a Whig. Namier misled almost two generations of students, however, by his insistence that Toryism in mid-Hanoverian England was synonymous with a backbench mentality. Admittedly most Tory commoners, from vociferous spokesmen like Will Shippen[6] down to the serried but often silent ranks of knights of the shire, were reconciled by the 1730s to a lifetime in opposition. But a few front-bench leaders, for instance Sir William Wyndham, Sir John Hynde Cotton, and later Sir Watkin Williams Wynn, were able and ambitious enough to continue to cherish some hopes of office, as Tories in a coalition ministry, without having to turn their coats; while clients of Gower, Bathurst and other Tory peers would not have turned down the chance of office if their patrons' rosier dreams had been realised in 1727 or 1742 (but cf. Ch. 5). Although the power-politicians active in House of Commons politics from 1722 to 1754 did incorporate some personal followings, like the ones just mentioned, they were never dominated by great proprietary 'parties'. Only the dozen or so members whom the Pelham brothers could normally call their own, most of them electoral nominees of Newcastle, formed a 'connexion' which combined stability with moderate size. How far personal parties existed at all before the late 1750s is, to say the least, highly doubtful, and most historians of the 1980s would probably agree in considering them a feature peculiar, though not entirely unique, to the 1760s (36,

15–17; below, Ch. 18). Down to the mid–1750s, and arguably rather later, small blocks of personal adherents fitted in much the same way into the political structure as they had since Anne's reign (22), as components of the Whig and Tory parliamentary parties, deriving importance more from their coherence, frail though that sometimes proved to be, than from their numbers, though none of them remotely approached the dominant rôle of the Junto Whigs of the early eighteenth century in either respect.

The most striking difference between these blocks in George II's reign and their counterparts under Anne is that the former rarely moved monolithically between the government and opposition sides. Yet although most families of any political significance, except the Walpoles and Pelhams, 'were too divided among themselves to follow any very coherent pattern of behaviour' (38a, *84*), there is no doubt that greater mobility across the government-opposition frontier charac-terised Commons' professionals as a whole in this period. For the Whigs, at least, this became an inevitable fact of life, given a finite amount of patronage, a Britain firmly in the groove of single-party government, and that party dominated for so long by one man and those who carried the mark of his approval. Lasting movements into opposition were for many years small-scale (Ch. 5), and it was not until the period 1733–6 that they became substantial, and ultimately damaging to Walpole. A further haemorrhage of career Whigs began in 1737, following the outbreak of a new vendetta in the Royal Household; while the fall of the Great Man allowed many of the deserters to drift back to the ministerial camp again, and some to pick up their prizes on the way, the world of the professionals remained subject to sudden motion, at least down to 1751 – the year of Prince Frederick's death. Meanwhile the more ambitious Tories had begun to add their own trickle in the 1740s to the two-way flow across the border (Ch. 5).

Patterns and springs of behaviour in the commons

Court and Country?

Because some non-dependants as well as many professional scalp-hunters on the Whig side opposed the Walpole regime after 1733, and in doing so frequently voted with Tories against it, some historians have been drawn to the conclusion that the basic polarities of parliamentary politics changed soon after 1720, from Whig-Tory to Court-Country (see above, pp. 39–40). It would seem fair to say that they have not convincingly made out their case. Part of that case has rested on surviving division-lists (e.g. 35c, *60–2, 74–5*), but it has been objected that these are neither conclusive in themselves (when compared, say, with many of the lists on 1701–16) nor properly representative of the public issues which formed the diet of the House of Commons in the Walpole-Pelham era. Divisions in 1730–4 on the Hessian troops, the Standing Army, the Excise bill and the repeal of the Septennial Act may seem to invite the deduction that an almost ritualised bipartisan Opposition had by then emerged, forged on old 'Country' principles, but on closer scrutiny they reveal dozens of Whig backbenchers continuing to support the Court. The second reservation is even weightier. For such lists as these have come down to us principally as the result of hand-picking and printing by an Opposition leadership which (especially in the case of the Whigs) had a strong vested interest in presenting itself in Country or 'Patriot' colours. If, for example, the Tories had thought fit to record and print some of the Commons' divisions on the string of anti-clerical bills introduced into the House (mostly against Walpole's wishes) between 1730 and 1737 (Ch. 7), they would have left us evidence of a very different voting pattern, especially on the Whig side (35c; 31, *32–3*; 289, *31*). Ideological arguments have also been advanced to justify a Court-Country interpretation of the pattern of political behaviour from the 1720s, arguments which appeal beyond the evidence as to how MPs voted to the language of debate and the literature of polemic. But this too proves to be selective ground, drawing much on the rhetoric of *The Craftsman* or of Pulteneyite set-pieces in the chamber, but paying much less attention to the extensive ideological substructure beneath the deep differences on religious principles or dynastic issues which, even in George II's reign, were still priority matters with a majority of members (284; cf. 289, *Chs. 3, 5*; 28a, *Ch. 4*).[7]

It is only when we recognise how pervasive these old Whig/Tory distinctions could still be that we can understand why there was never any realistic chance of Bolingbroke's dream of a New Country Party or Patriot alliance being realised in Walpole's lifetime, or indeed for some time after (20, *210–11*; 14, *128*). The best efforts of Pulteney and Wyndham never produced even a marriage of convenience between dissident Whigs and Tories, but at best a series of intermittent and uneasy liaisons, during which the two sides eyed each other with intense wariness (Ch. 5). Just as 'the survival of distinctly Tory attitudes prevented the party's amalgamation with dissident Whiggery' (28a, *101*), so the Whigs, professionals and independents alike, remained overwhelmingly convinced that Divine Right ideologies were still so deeply rooted among the Tories as to make their admission to office and power in any number an unacceptable risk. The acid test came in 1742 (Ch. 5), when following Walpole's fall the Pulteneyites accepted the Pelhams' lures with indecent haste to ensure that the Tories, whose votes had been vital in procuring the prime minister's resignation, were kept firmly on the outside, looking in.

Tory and Whig

As late as the Parliament of 1727–34 there were still in the House of Commons 139 English and Welsh Whigs alone whose careers had been forged, like those of Walpole and Pulteney, in the party furnace of 1701–16. The fact that this old generation of Whigs, of whom the duke of Newcastle was to be the last survivor, would never, even in their private exchanges, discount the possibility of a Tory revival always made it difficult to swallow the assumption that traditional party labels lost all genuine meaning in the Britain of Walpole and the Pelhams. This was so even when it was still widely believed that although 'Toryism' persisted into the middle of the eighteenth century, a Tory *party* did not. Over twenty years of reappraisal has now left no room for doubt that in Parliament, as in the country at large, the Tories survived the Great Proscription of the first two Georges as very much a party in reality as well as in name (12a, *I*; 20; 37a; 28a). Indeed, Linda Colley's full-scale study of the Tories from 1714–60, which more than anything turned this growing conviction into certainty, stresses both the remarkable cohesion and sense of identity which they retained over thirty years after the Hanoverian Succession and the effectiveness of their Westminster, as well as their local, party organisation. In the Commons their solidarity was especially displayed over foreign policy issues, where they were vociferous in condemning Hanoverian influence on British policy (Ch. 4), over 'Church in danger' issues, and at all times over classic Country measures, such as Place bills and pressure for shorter Parliaments.[8] Their opponents were never allowed to forget that those 130–150 recalcitrants in the Commons, and not least those who represented popular boroughs, were just the tip of a large iceberg in the electorate. Indeed the Whigs were convinced, and rightly so, that this was an iceberg which would surface and might even capsize the ship of oligarchy if ever the Tories got back into office in large enough numbers to regain what they had lost in 1714, control over Crown patronage. And among government and opposition Whigs alike there was almost as much agreement (though with less justification) that what above all kept this iceberg intact and formidably dangerous was the stubborn refusal of the majority of Tories to accept the permanency of the Hanoverian dynasty.

The lively debate in recent years about whether the Tories were a Jacobite party under the first two Georges has been stimulating but in the end frustrating. This is partly because the matter can never be definitely resolved, much of the evidence tending by its very nature more towards obfuscation than towards clear-cut conclusions. But equally to the point, it is now no longer necessary to prove the ideological purity of English Tories on the succession issue in order to demonstrate that Toryism maintained a high and pugnacious profile in parliamentary politics down to the 1750s. Serious question-marks remain against both of the more extreme positions advanced in the debate: that the Great Proscription forced Tories who had previously been open-minded or downright sceptical about the Stuart cause, to embrace it in desperation; alternatively, that realistic hopes from time to time of sharing power with Whigs in a coalition ministry gave the Tories every incentive to reconcile themselves to the Hanoverians. The most confusing argument deployed has been that based on the demonstrable unwillingness of Tory parliamentarians to involve themselves in Jacobite conspiracies and rebellions (Ch. 6); so chilling were the deterrents against involvement that those who stood aloof cannot be confidently credited even with pragmatic loyalty to the ruling dynasty let alone an emotional or rational commitment to it (6, *intro*; 29). After all, as crusted a Jacobite as Thomas Rowney, the veteran MP for Oxford who had 'drunk the Pretender's health 500 times', was reported 'frightened out of his wits, and ordered his chaplain to pray for King George' when Bonnie Prince Charlie landed in 1745.[9] B.W. Hill is persuaded by his reading of the evidence that 'the great majority of the Tory party [under George II] was

47

Hanoverian by conviction or caution' (20, *193*), but it would probably be nearer to the truth to say that the majority, though remaining Jacobites by conviction, were *de facto* Hanoverians by caution. The hard core of unapologetic supporters of the Stuarts, led at first by Shippen and later by Hynde Cotton and Sir Watkin Williams Wynn, and the equally select group of unblemished upholders of the Protestant Succession, who down to 1740 rallied round Wyndham, were permanent features of the Commons scene. But the characteristic Tory MP, under Walpole and the Pelhams as in the last year of Queen Anne, was a fence-sitter.

Much the most significant aspect of Tory behaviour, however, is that disagreements and uncertainties over the succession never threatened to split the party, either in elections or in the House of Commons; ironically, this made the Tories more rather than less vulnerable to the everlasting Whig charge that, given half a chance, the bulk of the party would reveal its true colours – those of 'the King over the water'. Whether or not the charge was just is far less important than that it was widely believed, and that it weighed decisively with both George I and George II in cold-shouldering a sequence of Tory bids to regain royal favour, particularly in the ministerial crises of 1717, 1727 and 1742.

Equally important in understanding patterns and springs of parliamentary behaviour in the age of oligarchy is a recognition of the continued existence of a Whig party, albeit a divided one. Naturally the fact that Whig MPs were split in their attitude to the Walpole regime, especially after 1733, led to a good deal of calculated opportunistic voting by the 'outs', doing their utmost to discomfit the 'ins', and this continued to a lesser degree under the Pelhams. But it would be very mistaken to assume from this that there was no principled political conduct on the Whig side, and misguided to imagine that no common values or attitudes persisted after the early 1720s on which the great body of Whigs could find common ground. The common denominators of eighteenth-century Whiggery have been lucidly discussed by H.T. Dickinson (27b). Some of them, it is true, were negative emotions. Speaker Onslow once said of Sir Robert Walpole's invariable recipe for rallying the Whig troops at crisis times: 'he always aimed at the uniting of the Whigs against the Tories as Jacobites, . . . and making therefore combinations between them and any body of Whigs to be impracticable.'[10] But there were also more positive convictions which demarcated Whigs from Tories in the early Georgian House of Commons: convictions rooted in the post-1688 traditions of the party and professed as resolutely by the quintessential 'ins' of the Old Corps, with their steadfast personal loyalty to Walpole and his heirs, as by the most detached Whig backbencher.

Loyalty to the Protestant Succession, for example, was not just a convenient passport to office for Whigs; it was total and instinctive. The few aberrants of the early 1720s – Cowper, Sunderland and the first duke of Wharton – were the tiny handful of exceptions that proved the oldest rule in the Whig book. All Whigs continued to espouse toleration for Protestant dissenters, even if they were less than unanimous about the methods by which, and the extent to which, further relief should be pursued; all took an erastian, if not a downright anti-clerical view of the Established Church, poles apart from the attitude of the High Tories. Every Whig stood firm on the fundamentals of the Revolution constitution, as it had evolved between 1689 and 1716 – its centrepiece a sovereign Parliament within the framework of a mixed monarchy. The duration of Parliaments may have been a matter for dispute among Whigs, but the ultimate supremacy of Parliament (a Whig Parliament, of course), as against prerogative and closet, was as much a part of the ark of the covenant in the 1740s as it had been in 1680.

The issues which split the Whigs, especially in the disturbed 1730s and the early 1740s, are sometimes as revealing as those which periodically united them. They were not all matters of tactical manoeuvre or perceived with an eye to the main chance. It was natural and legitimate that over half a century after the Exclusion Crisis, and more than three decades on from the outbreak of the Spanish Succession War, there should have been genuine differences over how the Whig Bible ought to be re-interpreted in the very different climate of George II's reign. It is in this light that we should see Whig divisions over religious policy (even Walpole's Cabinet was occasionally split by these [Ch. 7]); or disagreements over relations with Europe, and particularly the tension in the 1730s between the militant Whig instinct to fight for Britain's trade and colonies and the cautious instinct to do nothing that might jeopardise the succession (Ch. 4). There were still backbenchers enough who clung stubbornly to the Country traditions of the Old Whigs: whose dislike for a standing army, for instance, prompted them to oppose the army estimates even in the highly nervous aftermath of the Atterbury Plot. Yet it is striking that, except for time-honoured Country issues of this kind, none of the divergent views which caused Whigs to vote in substantial numbers against fellow Whigs brought the dissidents in the party ideologically closer to the Tories. Any explanation of why a 'broad-bottom' approach to *government*, as opposed to opposition, attracted virtually no Whig support until the late 1730s, and even thereafter remarkably little, must take this factor, as well as blunt self-interest, into account.

Pressure groups: parliamentary and extra-parliamentary

Any account of British eighteenth-century politics would be seriously incomplete without taking note of two further elements, namely, the parliamentary interest-groups and the extra-parliamentary pressure-groups which were active in every main phase. The years of oligarchy from the 1720s to the 1750s were no exception. Whether linked or unlinked to each other, and no matter how diverse their activities, these groups had one feature in common. Their members, often drawn from across the spectrum of parties, or from 'ins' and 'outs' alike, combined together on certain issues dear to their hearts or close to their pockets, with the prime aim of influencing the decisions of the legislature or the government. The interest-groups in the Commons, made up of MPs alone but frequently responsive to a corresponding lobby 'out of doors', could be of considerable importance at times in the structure and working of the House: and both types of group supplied a series of sub-themes to the subject-matter of political life.

No ministry in this period could afford to ignore the views of the two biggest commercial pressure-groups in the Commons, the East India and West India interests. Although the situation was to change decisively under George III, in the 1730s and 1740s it was the West India interest, made up of sugar planters or ex-planters, merchants trading with the Caribbean and wealthy absentee landowners such as the Lascelleses and Stapeltons, which was the more influential of the two.[11] These members had the ear of the House and were the driving force behind several major economic or fiscal measures, including some that were unpalatable to Walpole and Henry Pelham. The most notable was the Molasses Act, passed at the third attempt in 1733 – a vintage year for well-organised groups ready to trade their votes in return for ministerial support (31, *34*; 33b, *53*. See also above, pp. 6–7 and J.1.(i)). The interests of London were rarely so coherent or so readily definable as those of the sugar barons. But when a broad consensus did appear in the City for or against a controversial line of policy, as over the Tobacco Excise bill in 1733 or Spanish trade in 1738–9 (Ch. 4), the capital could rely not only on its own four members but on the most formidable back-up forces. Within the House there would usually be at least thirty Bank or Company directors, aldermen, and other London merchants or wealthy tradesmen occupying provincial borough seats, and from outside a supporting barrage of petitions, addresses and 'instructions' could be orchestrated by the City corporations in conjunction with sympathetic MPs. Even Walpole found such a combination, fully mobilised, very difficult to resist.[12]

Of a different nature was the anti-clerical and dissenting Whig alliance whose campaign in the 1730s for a common programme on religious issues was conducted in conjunction with two permanent extra-parliamentary associations. One of these, the Quaker Meeting for Sufferings, had the limited objective of securing measures of relief for Friends. Although no MPs were directly involved in it, its organisation and lobbying techniques were so skilful that, after scoring an early success in 1722, it embarked in the next decade on a campaign to excuse Quakers from payment of tithes; after recruiting William Glanville to sponsor the Tithes Bill in the Commons, and scores of other Whigs, including Walpole, to promise support for it, they saw it passed there – only to fail in the Lords, with seismic results (Chs. 2, 7). The second and ostensibly far more powerful association, the Committee of Protestant Dissenting Deputies, represented the numerous body of Presbyterians, Congregationalists and Baptists. Founded in 1732 in emulation of the Quakers' organisation, it brought together several MPs, led by Samuel Holden, and a variety of lay nonconformist worthies for the more sweeping purpose of securing the outright repeal of the Test and Corporation Acts. Three motions to that end, in 1732, 1736 and 1739, failed, however, to get Commons' approval, not only because Walpoleans were unwilling to alienate their Low Church clerical allies but because Pulteney and his opposition Whigs were equally scared of damaging their relations with the Tories. Nevertheless, the best-prepared effort, in 1736, did secure 123 good Whig votes in a full House of 378, and as well as causing embarrassment to their front benchers, the Deputies' activities highlighted the deep divisions which the Toleration issue could still cause, on grounds of principle as well as of expediency, within a party traditionally committed to the ideal (109c; 33b, *53–4*; 109a).

Even by the modest standards of the pre-industrial age the Walpole-Pelham period was not a notable one for output of important public legislation. It contrasts sharply in this respect with the years 1689–1720. But the fact is that at no time between 1660 and 1783 do major public issues, either on or off the statute-book, offer an exclusive key to the day-by-day working of politics. The same can be said, even more forcefully, of those intricate moves on the Court and ministerial chess-board, which historians are prone to scrutinise lovingly. Whether at parliamentary level, in the constituencies, or in what Brewer has called the 'alternative' political world of the unrepresented towns and of popular participation – a world which had surprising vitality even in George II's reign and was to acquire still more later (44; 33a and b) – it was *local* concerns that were often paramount, and the degree of awareness and excitement they created could well disturb, now and again, the calm control of the provincial landed oligarchs.

These local concerns are most clearly reflected in the great volume of local and private bills and petitions which came before Parliament every session[13] and in the pressure-groups which came together for the purpose of advancing or opposing them.[14] The total content of such bills and petitions displays infinite variety, but under Walpole and the Pelhams turnpikes, enclosures, river navigation and harbour schemes, church-building and poor relief were their most prominent, recurrent themes. Bills proposing action on such measures were printed, widely circulated, and often keenly debated; the interests which promoted them could be as impressive in their way as the better known City or dissenting groups, and the opposition to them, to be successful, had to be at least equally effective in organisation, publicity and lobbying. Enclosures and turnpikes could easily foment popular unrest (Ch. 11); river improvements, workhouse-schemes, and so forth, could become foci for local partisanship, and the majority interests involved were ignored at their peril by local MPs and landed magnates. The most powerful families, such as the Grosvenors in Cheshire and the Leveson Gowers in Staffordshire, could be damaged by such issues (33b, *49–50*). Even central government itself had to tread warily if a sensitive local issue took on emotive parliamentary overtones: hence Walpole's decision to abandon the cause of the local Whigs in the turbulent affair of the Manchester Board of Guardians of the Poor in 1731, after the Opposition had successfully portrayed this issue as one of restrictive, self-perpetuating Whig political control versus 'popular liberties'.[15]

'Popular liberties' were a favourite rallying-cry in the organisation of any extra-parliamentary cause, most effectively as the warhead of missiles intended to make impact on Westminster, but sometimes as the thrust behind purely local pressures, exerted for instance through the provincial press or public meetings. The classic example of the former was the near country-wide campaign against Walpole's Excise scheme. This was a campaign which, though obviously directed and manipulated to some extent by the parliamentary politicians, also took on a spontaneous life of its own. It produced a deluge of petitions, including at least eight from non-parliamentary boroughs, most of them laying stress on the un-English and anti-libertarian character of 'the exciseman'; it also encouraged a vigorous and effective revival of the once-popular ploy of constituents 'instructing' their members to vote in a specific way (32a). Petitions to the Commons were the more flexible instrument, however, for they could be employed in bids to secure economic as well as political ends. They were not always successful, but if they were so numerous as to assume virtually the character of a protest from a whole industry, and especially if the industry was well-championed, there was always a fair chance that they would extract the required legislation from governments ever sensitive to the views of cudgel-carrying backbenchers. The act of 1721 forbidding the wearing of printed or dyed East India calicoes (see *Making of a Great Power*, Ch. 19 and p. 210) was the product of just such pressure from manufacturing and weaving interests, powerfully articulated in the House.

From time to time local unrest over industrial grievances or trade disputes, as over enclosures or turnpikes, broke through the accepted peaceful pipelines to Parliament and spilled over into violent disorders of a traditional kind (Ch. 12). The fact remains, however, that the new urban political culture of both London and the English provinces was already developing fast by the 1730s. Such a culture directly foreshadowed the bourgeois-popular politics of the Wilkite era (Ch. 22), taking in not just social and occupational groups which were never, or almost never, reflected in the membership of the House of Commons (such as attorneys, shopkeepers and small manufacturers), but elements which had no direct representation of any kind at Westminster. Occasionally it was propagated by political clubs, like the Standfast Society in Bristol or the Charter Club in Colchester, or through Chambers of Commerce and Guilds, like the Sheffield Master Cutlers,[16] but it was also generated by coffee-house and tavern debate, and owed much to the spread of urban literacy and to a provincial press which was increasingly vocal in unrepresented towns, such as Manchester and Leeds, as well as in parliamentary boroughs (Ch. 13).

Strangely, as it may now seem, the one glaring lacuna in the popular, extra-parliamentary political activity of the Walpole era was a truly radical campaign for political reform itself. Despite the patchy evidence that can be accumulated of plebeian dislike for the Whig oligarchy, one can only endorse Professor Dickinson's conclusion that the lower and lower-middling orders of society, though ready enough to appeal to a libertarian heritage and mouth 'Country' slogans to redress material grievances, were still inhibited by limited political consciousness and inbred social assumptions 'from developing a radical pro-gramme aimed at transforming their own position in society' (33b, *61*; cf. 57). Among the urban bourgeoisie we can detect in the 1740s the first scattered signs that a modest movement for a reform of parliamentary representation, as distinct from earlier calls for more frequent Parliaments, was beginning to be cooked up. But even here the suspicion is that it was not so much the groundlings themselves as their Tory MPs, backed by some well-primed opposition newspapers and journals, who were stoking up the oven.

Although it was never quite as 'adamantine' as Sir John Plumb memorably portrayed it (14, *xviii*), the political system of the age of Walpole and the Pelhams which we have been examining undoubtedly became over time both secure and stable. The fact that there was lively opposition, in and out of Parliament, to the administrations of 1727–57, and no lack of issues at times for opponents to seize upon, does not in itself constitute an argument for instability (*Making of a Great Power*, Ch. 25). On the contrary, a system which allows opposition healthy outlets, as by and large it did in this period, is likelier to encourage stability than one which does not. We must also remember that while many Whigs in the 1730s and for part of the 1740s wanted to change the ministers, very few indeed wanted fundamentally to change the system. The Tories and Jacobites who did seek to change it, by ending proscription, shortening Parliaments and possibly even widening the franchise, proved powerless to do so (60; 33a). The politics of oligarchy in early- and mid-Georgian Britain did foster a climate of stability, but not, as the last two chapters have tried to show, because they were predictable or mechanistic. If politics in the long reign of George II had really been as one-dimensional, as desiccated and as stultifying as Namierite historians were inclined at one time to suggest, the oligarchy of the Whig ruling élite would have crumbled away with dry rot long before it finally subsided through old age.

---

1. Having proclaimed that politics could be 'fully described without ever using a party denomination', Namier himself proceeded to use these denominations, especially 'Tory', to an embarrassing degree in (43b).
2. Quoted in R. Sedgwick (12a), II, p. 407.
3. In such boroughs as Portsmouth, Harwich and Rochester, and in several of the Cinque Ports, government departments (mainly the Admiralty, Post Office, Treasury and Customs) had a decisive grip, via local patronage, over one or both seats.
4. D. Jarrett, 'The Myth of "Patriotism" in Eighteenth-Century English Politics', in Bromley and Kossman, eds, *Britain and the Netherlands*, V (1975), pp. 129, 135–6.
5. The meeting place of the House of Commons in the Palace of Westminster throughout the period covered by this book.
6. Jacobite MP for Newton (Lancs), 1715–43.
7. And see also (for the ideological-linguistic argument), I. Kramnick, *Bolingbroke and his Circle* (Oxford, 1968).
8. Note that Tory proposals in 1739 and 1740 to repeal the Septennial Act failed to attract the support of any leading Whig dissidents. Pulteney was adamant that he would not buy Tory votes in the Commons at the cost of destroying what he rightly saw as the foundation of Whig electoral dominance since 1715. See Colley (28a), pp. 95, 216.
9. Lord Egmont in 1750, quoted in Owen (10), p. 114.
10. HMC 14th Report, IX, p. 462: Arthur Onslow's 'Anecdotes'.
11. 27 'West Indians' sat in Parliament between 1715 and 1754 (compared with 41 'Nabobs' and directors of the East India Company); Sedgwick, ed., (12a), I, pp. 10, 152–3; J. Brooke (39), pp. 230–40.
12. See, in general, L.S. Sutherland (55); A.J. Henderson, *London and the National Government, 1721–1742* (Durham, N.C., 1945). As Walpole told the Attorney-General in 1739: 'If the City of London showed their inclinations against him in this public manner, . . . he should think himself bound to yield.' Diary of Sir Dudley Ryder, 6 Oct 1739, quoted in Sedgwick, ed. (12a), II, p. 282.
13. Of the 2,779 Acts passed between 1714 and 1754, 2,009 originated in petitions to Parliament and were therefore technically 'private' bills, even though a substantial proportion (mostly local measures) ended up officially as 'public Acts'. See Sedgwick, ed., (12a), I, pp. 6–10.
14. S. Lambert, *Bills and Acts: Legislative Procedure in Eighteenth-Century England* (Cambridge, 1981); P.D.G. Thomas (17), Chs. 3, 9.

15. S. Handley, 'Local Legislative Initiatives for Economic and Social Development in Lancashire, 1689–1731', *Parl. Hist.*, **9** (1990); L. Colley (28a), p. 163.
16. HMC, *Portland MSS*, VI, p. 145, for the promotion by the Master Cutlers of the contentious Don Navigation scheme. In general, see Colley (28a), pp. 163–8.

CHAPTER 4

Foreign policy in the age of Walpole: trade, the succession and the balance of power, 1714–1748

Some of the most furiously debated and divisive issues in British politics during the 1730s and early 1740s were questions of foreign policy. The issue of Britain's relations with Spain did more to shake Sir Robert Walpole's tentacular grip on power than any domestic matter, and differences over the Continental diplomacy of Lord Carteret caused severe tensions within the Whig Oligarchy in the two years following Walpole's resignation. This was no novel trend. It had been set as far back as the last years of William III, when the controversies over the Standing Army, the Partition Treaties and the Spanish Succession crisis of 1701 helped to wreck first a Whig administration, and then a Tory one. During Anne's reign the Whigs had remained to a great extent united over foreign affairs (see *Making of a Great Power*, Ch. 15). But after the Hanoverian Succession rifts were not long in appearing. It was the opposition of the Walpole-Townshend Whigs to the 'Northern Design' of Stanhope and the King which did most to precipitate the schism of 1716–17, and it was the incompatibility of their attitudes to relations with Spain, Austria and France which from 1727–30 finally destroyed the long partnership between Walpole and Townshend.

These periodic disputes between rival factions of the Whigs under the first two Georges were not, however, over the basic objectives of British foreign policy; rather it was the methods by which these objectives were to be pursued or the establishment of priorities that caused disagreement. From 1714 through to the late 1740s the same three overriding national interests, which had become their prime concerns after the Glorious Revolution, continued to dominate the Whigs' thinking on Britain's relations with her European neighbours. The three themes impart a measure of consistency to foreign policy during the entire period from 1689 to 1748, despite many short-term shifts and sudden turns. The Whig-controlled House of Lords underlined all of them in 1717 when it congratulated George I on the conclusion of the Triple Alliance with Holland and Regency France: 'an alliance which opens to us so fair a prospect of an undisturbed succession, an equal balance of power, and a flourishing commerce' (2, *VII, 421*). Purely as aims the second and third of these had even created common ground between Whigs and Tories in the years before 1714, and whatever the private reservations of many of the latter about the House of Hanover, defence of its legal rights to the throne had been the official policy of a Tory ministry down to the time of Oxford's fall (*Making of a Great Power*, Ch. 15, pp. 253–4). After the unhappy breakdown of the old alliances in 1712–13 the three selfsame interests pointed inexorably away from a drift back into isolation and towards the maintenance of the post-Revolution interdependence between Britain and

Europe. To what extent, and by what means, however, was still uncertain at the accession of George I.

I

This chapter will try to establish how effectively under the Whig Oligarchy successive British ministries pursued the new foreign policy inaugurated by William III after 1689; how they sought to preserve a power equilibrium in those Continental theatres where Britain had interests; and how successfully foreign policy was used to complement domestic measures for both securing the new Protestant dynasty and advancing the commercial and colonial interests of the state between 1714 and the end of the Austrian Succession War in 1748. First, however, it must be emphasised that although the aims of Whig policy remained broadly constant, the context within which it was formulated became much changed as time went by, as many new pieces were inevitably brought into the mosaic of international relations. And such changes complicated and intensified the debates about how British aims could best be achieved.

By far the most persistent and disturbing of these novel factors was Hanover. The tension that was created after 1714 between interests which were regarded as essentially national and the Hanoverian interests of the first two Georges was present almost from the start and remained well beyond 1748. The fundamental dilemma posed for every Whig statesman involved in the making of British foreign policy was that the conduct of foreign relations still lay within the formal prerogatives of two kings who were also the ambitious rulers of a north German electorate. This had various disturbing implications. There were, for example, many problems caused by the personal diplomacy of the two Georges (the first especially) during their regular, lengthy visits to the Continent. They conducted negotiations with the advice of one accompanying English Secretary of State and of their own German officials, but not infrequently without either the authorisation or knowledge of the other Secretary or the rest of the Cabinet. In theory they were supposed to wear two separate hats while abroad, but the practice was different. Even when they entered into engagements purely in their electoral capacity, these could cause appalling discomfiture in Whitehall, as George II's humiliating neutrality convention of 1741 did to Walpole's ailing administration (89b, *155*; above, p. 9). An associated problem was the pro-Hanoverian bias which George I's German ministers in London were able to impart to British policies between 1714 and 1720. The influence of Bernstorff caused particular dismay until he was eventually checkmated by Stanhope.

Yet even if they had not been embarrassed by royal initiatives or German intrusions, British ministers would still have found it impossible to ignore the natural North European and German preoccupations of the kings they served. In the first half of George I's reign the most obsessive of these were the territorial ambitions of Hanover which the King expected British diplomatic and, if necessary, naval muscle to further. In particular he was determined to profit from the crumbling of Swedish power in the North after 1709 by annexing Bremen and

Verden (*Making of a Great Power*, pp. 250–1). These were not the 'insignificant' duchies which both Whig and Tory critics of the government's Baltic policies were fond of depicting. On the contrary, they were strategically and economically important, controlling the mouths of two of Germany's great rivers, and in Bremen's case, offering a major commercial outlet which Hanover had not hitherto possessed. In the event, British naval squadrons under Hopson and Norris, despatched to the Baltic from 1715, did contribute materially to the final cession of Bremen and Verden to Hanover in 1719, doing some violence in the process to one of the key clauses of the Act of Settlement. [*Making of a Great Power*, F. vii (3)]. By that time greed for territory had given way in Hanover to fear of further Russian expansion along the Baltic coast. George I did not hide his alarm at Russian designs on Mecklenburg, Schleswig Holstein and even Sweden. The death of Peter the Great in 1725 lessened such fears, but did not remove them, as an agitated letter written by Townshend to Horace Walpole in the summer of 1728 plainly shows: 'I never saw the King [George II] more displeased in his life than he was upon reading what was said in this project [of Mecklenburg and Schleswig] and your despatches upon those two articles . . . For God's sake, dear Horace, do your best. Both your reputation and mine are at stake.'[1]

After 1725, however, the overriding concern of the two Georges as Electors of Hanover was the defence of their electorate in time of war or threat of war. This was a potent factor in the years 1725–9, from 1733 to 1735, when George II, as King of England, stayed out of the Polish Succession War but, as Elector of Hanover, was cautiously engaged in it (89a, *40–3*) and from 1740–8, as it was to be subsequently from 1748 to 1763; and except in the 1730s it was a consideration which British ministers found it virtually impossible to ignore. It thus became a source of embarrassment in the House of Commons, when it led to the hiring of Continental mercenary troops at the British taxpayer's expense to protect Hanover, a state so vulnerable militarily that the Prussians regarded it as 'only a breakfast' for their generals. In fact the recurring affair of the Hessian troops (1725–30) eventually became one of the few issues before 1733 seriously to dent Walpole's majority, while the issue of Hanoverian troops themselves brought members out in near-record numbers in 1742 and 1744 (89b, *155;* 82, *98*).[2]

On the other hand there was a greater measure of common ground between Hanoverian and British interests than the critics of the former normally acknowledged, and there were also occasions when the Hanover connection facilitated rather than hampered British diplomatic initiatives. Britain did, after all, have her own national interest in trying to preserve the Balance of Power in the North (*Making of a Great Power*, Ch. 15). Whig statesmen such as Stanhope and Townshend were as concerned as the Hanoverians in the 1710s and 1720s that Russia should not fill too much of the vacuum left by the collapse of Swedish power after Pultawa (1709). Moreover, keeping a British fleet in the Baltic, as Stanhope and his colleagues did from 1715–19 and Townshend from 1726–7, could be justified on the grounds of protecting national commercial interests, even if its presence also gratified the Elector of Hanover.[3] Parliament voted money for such a fleet on each occasion on these very grounds. It is clear too that

57

British intelligence benefited materially from the Hanover connection, especially for counter-Jacobite information, and that George I's knowledge of German and North European problems and personalities was potentially useful if harnessed to British diplomatic expertise and power.[4] The main problem for the Whigs lay in keeping a fair balance between the two countries' interests. They did not always succeed, especially between 1716 and 1719, when the protests of the Townshend-Walpole group were not without substance, and again after the renewal of major warfare in 1740, but it is arguable that though frequently wrong-footed by the Hanover connection, British policy-makers were only rarely pulled right off the track by it.

Hanover apart, British foreign policy had to be periodically reformulated after 1714 within a changing European power structure. The objective of preserving the Balance of Power remained one of the highest priorities. And although for form's sake many Whigs continued to denounce the Treaty of Utrecht, as Walpole did as late as 1739, as 'the source of all the divisions and distractions in Europe ever since' (1, *XI, 232*), the defence of the equilibrium achieved in 1713–14, except in Southern Europe, quickly became as great a shibboleth to the Whigs, in practice, as to the Tories whose controversial handiwork it had been. But the *distribution* of Continental power was very different by the 1740s from the heyday of Louis XIV. Briefly we might notice three distinct shifts of scene: the movement of new states into, or close to, the ranks of the Great Powers; the loss of front-rank status by other states; and special circumstances affecting the dispositions of the two inveterate dynastic Houses of Habsburg and Bourbon.

The most significant newcomers to the centre stage of European diplomacy in the course of the years 1714–48 were Prussia and Russia. Their influence and importance, unlike that of Savoy, who exchanged her Utrecht acquisition of Sicily for Sardinia after the Mediterranean crisis of 1718–19, no longer remained localised. The rise of Prussia had been foreshadowed during the Spanish Succession War. But even while her growing military strength, built up under the spartan regime of her barrack-square king, Frederick William I (1713–40), was making her a welcome recruit to major confederations like the Alliance of Hanover of 1725 [H.v], most British politicians continued to assume that Prussia's chief ambitions would remain focused on the North, and that in a future crisis she would again align with Britain, as she had in the past.[5] Frederick the Great dealt a rude shock to these assumptions in 1740 with his ruthless predatory strike against the province of Silesia, the richest jewel in the Austrian crown lands, for as well as launching the biggest Continental war since 1713, he ensured at a stroke that neither the physical nor the diplomatic map of Europe would ever be the same again. Russia's rise followed a different pattern. In her case the death of Peter the Great in 1725 damped down for a while the apprehensions felt in the West during the previous quarter of a century, when Russia's aggression had culminated in the Tsar's extensive gains from Sweden at Nystad (1721): Ingria, Karelia, Esthonia and Livonia. The long period of petticoat or minority rule in Russia from 1725 to 1762[6] helped to relieve tension. Nevertheless, the diplomatic relations broken off between Russia and Britain in 1719 were not restored until 1728, and it was not until Walpole's conclusion of an Austro-

Russian commercial treaty in 1734 that British statesmen could begin to make Russia a substantive factor in their calculations. Her great potential as a force in Central and West European wars was recognised in the Russo-British defensive alliance of 1742 and by the British subsidies which brought Russian troops to the Rhine in 1748. Russia's military intervention in the Austrian Succession War, however, was never wholehearted. It was in the Seven Years' War, when Russian troops inflicted severe defeats on Frederick the Great's armies (below, pp. 241–2), that vague threat was first unquestionably translated into formidable reality (83, *205–11*; 89b, *156*).

While Prussia and Russia were becoming far larger counters in the European power game, the United Provinces were drifting steadily into second-class status. For those responsible for reorientating British foreign policy, this was a change as difficult to come to terms with as any in the years 1715–48. The Dutch, whose seventeenth-century greatness was founded mainly on commercial pre-eminence, had been a core unit of the two great alliances which William III had constructed against France – an integral part, with Austria and Great Britain, of that 'Old System' which the Whigs of Anne's reign had inherited and cherished and which the peacemaking of Harley and the Tories had undermined (*Making of a Great Power*, Ch. 15). Their position of commercial leadership had been lost in the 1680s, and their rôle in world trade continued steadily to diminish from 1700–63 (125, *271–2*). In addition, by 1713 twenty years of exhausting war had depleted their financial strength and seriously reduced their naval and military capability. More than that, it had begun to sap their political will. The neglect of the Dutch navy after 1713 was symptomatic of the deep reluctance of those mercantile oligarchies which effectively ruled the United Provinces until the Orange revival of the 1740s to commit themselves to any European engagement which threatened to draw the States into a major war. Though ready to involve themselves in the early post-Utrecht years in renewed Whig initiatives for collective security, the Dutch significantly refused to confirm their initial participation in the Quadruple Alliance of 1718 [H.iv] because there was a risk it might provoke a full-scale war with Spain. Subsequently they were tepid and tardy in associating themselves with the Alliance of Hanover, and they almost outdid Walpole himself in shunning the combatants in the War of the Polish Succession. Even so, it took their utter failure to budge the Dutch from neutrality in the Austrian Succession War after 1740 to complete the conviction of Whig ministers that they were no longer dealing with a front-line Continental force across the southern North Sea.[7]

However, the principal threat to 'the balance of Europe' right through from 1713 to 1748 was not the rise of two new powers in the North and East, nor the decline of one of the two maritime powers of the West, but the continuing dynastic rivalry between Habsburgs and Bourbons. All the sharpest divergences after 1714 from foreign policy patterns established under William III and Anne can be related, above all, to the altered dispositions or ambitions of Habsburg Austria or of Bourbon France and Spain.

From 1715 to 1723, for instance, the minority of Louis XV of France affected

European relations profoundly. For over half a century his great-grandfather's ambition and pride had overshadowed a whole continent. But in 1715 Louis XIV died and was succeeded by a boy of five, and by a Regent, the duke of Orléans, whose policies were always conducted with at least one eye on establishing his own claims to the succession.[8] Both Orléans and his supple foreign minister, Dubois, accepted that the maintenance of peace in Europe on the basis of the Utrecht and Rastadt treaties was the best guarantee of the Regent's domestic stability. They reasoned that such a peace was unlikely to be achieved unless Britain, who had her own succession preoccupations, could be convinced not only that France was no longer a threat but that she was prepared to become a most valuable friend. Their pledge of good faith was to renounce France's support of the Pretender and to promise her help in curbing the Mediterranean ambition of Orléans's rival, Philip V of Spain. Both Stanhope, the Secretary of State who accompanied the King on his long visit to the Continent in 1716–17, and George I himself, whose influence on foreign affairs was at its peak at this time (24a, *216–7*), quickly seized the olive branch. Indeed, it ideally complemented the 'peace plan for the south' which had begun to crystallise in their own minds (24a, *184*). The result was the Anglo-French Treaty of 1716, the *rapprochement* which led in turn to the Triple Alliance the next year [H.iii] and to France's subsequent involvement in every Britain-centred defensive alliance and peace-keeping initiative thereafter, until the Congress of Soissons in the late 1720s. By then Orléans and Dubois had both died and had given way (1723–6) to the duke of Bourbon, who maintained their policies if not their diplomatic acumen, and he in turn to Cardinal Fleury, who worked for some years longer in apparent amity with Walpole. 'France was never our enemy but under Lewis the Fourteenth', argued the pro-government *British Journal* in 1728; '. . . she has done signal benefits to us since the regency of the late duke of Orleans'.[9] By about 1730, however, as Louis XV began to assert himself and as traditional anti-Habsburg feeling at Versailles grew more intense, Fleury became more ambivalent towards Britain, while other new ministers, notably the Foreign Secretary, Chauvelin, grew positively hostile. Walpole thus found another changing situation on his hands as the Treaty of the Escorial – the Bourbon 'Family Compact' of 1733 – emphatically underlined (above, p. 7). The next ten years were to be a prelude to the resumption by the two powers of the full-blooded hostility which had marked their relations from 1689 to 1713.

Of the two Bourbon kingdoms it was Spain which had been perceived down to 1729 as the greater threat to the hard-won peace of Europe. This was one more notable change of diplomatic context to which Whig foreign policy had to adapt itself from quite early in George I's reign. One reason for it was Spain's resuscitation as a colonial and naval power under Philip V (below, p. 65). Another was the refusal of Philip, abetted by his crafty minister, Alberoni, to accept that the loss of some Spanish territories surrendered at Utrecht was final. The annexation of Sicily by Sardinia, Naples by Austria and Gibraltar by England were especially obnoxious. The third reason was Philip's second marriage (1714) to a redoubtable Italian princess, Elizabeth Farnese. Her consuming ambition to establish her sons in Italian principalities, if necessary at the expense of the

Habsburgs, was to be a source of periodic destabilisation in Europe for much of the 1720s and 1730s.

What of the Habsburgs themselves, hereditary rulers of Austria and its many subject kingdoms and provinces, and down to the death of Charles VI in 1740, holders of the German Imperial Crown? For most of the thirty-five years between the Treaties of Utrecht and Aix-la-Chapelle the House of Habsburg was a source of uncertainty and concern to its old allies, without ever permanently appeasing the jealous hostility of its former enemies. The reasons for this state of affairs were many. The Habsburg lands had always been a polyglot empire, embracing a diversity of races, tongues and cultures, but this characteristic was magnified to a bizarre degree by the territorial accretions of 1713–14. These brought the far-flung Flemings of the former Spanish Netherlands and the Italians of the Milanese and Naples, along with the Sardinians (soon to be replaced by the Sicilians) into a vast stewpot which already included Germans, Bohemians, Magyars, Croats, Serbs and a number of other lesser ingredients. Problems of government, always severe, were still further aggravated; there were some European powers, understandably, who came to regard Charles VI's dominions as virtually ungovernable. Other reasons for the tensions caused by the Habsburg factor are directly traceable to Charles VI himself. For a decade after Rastadt he mulishly refused to concede Philip V's title to the Spanish throne, continuing to call himself King of Spain, and he bore a standing grudge against his former Grand Alliance partners who, in his view, had disgracefully abandoned his cause in the years 1711–13. Furthermore, the chief object of his resentment, Britain, soon became further tarred in his eyes because of a marked deterioration (1716–20) in his relations with Hanover (83, *115–17*; 24a).

In addition, there was the Ottoman threat to the Habsburg lands and the consequent instability in south-eastern Europe, remaining a major sub-theme in relations between the Great Powers (cf. *Making of a Great Power*, Ch. 15). It is often forgotten how fearsome the Turkish army still was in the first half of the eighteenth century. As recently as 1711 it had inflicted on Peter the Great a humiliating defeat which forced Russia to disgorge her coveted Black Sea base at Azov. This feat throws into high relief the brilliant victories won over numerically superior Ottoman forces by the great Imperial general, Prince Eugene, in the renewed Austro-Turkish War of 1716–18, culminating in the battle of Belgrade, leading to the Emperor's gains at the Peace of Passarowitz. There he secured a further clutch of Turkey's European provinces to add to the reconquests made by Leopold I at Carlowitz in 1697 (ibid., Ch. 15, p. 249). Sadly for the Habsburgs, Charles VI allowed himself to be drawn into a new Russo-Turkish conflict in the late 1730s, with his armies already weakened and demoralised by their disastrous experiences in the Polish Succession War, and in the Peace of 1739 about two-thirds of the gains of 1718 had to be surrendered. It is worth noting in this context that, except for Walpole's notorious inactivity in the 1730s (see below, pp. 66–8), British foreign ministers after 1718, as earlier, remained concerned with the Balance of Power in the South East; just as Townshend in the 1720s tried to encourage the Ottomans to engage the Russians on the Caspian to divert Peter the Great from fresh adventures along the Black Sea littoral, so in the 1740s Carteret and Newcastle gained a diplomatic victory by dissuading the Turks from exploiting the Austrian Succession conflict to make further depredations on the dominions of Britain's hapless ally, Maria Theresa. Contrary to what is often said, British ambassadors at Constantinople were not invariably outgunned by those of Bourbon France (83, *365–6*).

The plight of Maria Theresa in the war of 1740–8 highlights what was by far the most important of the new factors governing the policy of Britain and many other states towards Austria after 1714. By 1720 Charles VI had recognised that there was little chance of his having a son to succeed to his dominions. An abiding preoccupation of his over the next two decades, therefore, was to secure the full right of inheritance of his daughter, Maria Theresa (aged only three in 1720), first by internal agreements, then by international guarantees. From 1724 onwards the so-called 'Pragmatic Sanction' [A] became a vital counter in every treaty or settlement which the Emperor made with a foreign power. Britain's guarantee of the Sanction was finally given in the Second Treaty of Vienna in 1731, a treaty which, through Walpole's initiative, marked a brief rapprochement between the two former allies after a long period of strained relations. But six years before that, in 1725, the Emperor had demonstrated, by making a dramatic deal with his hitherto-inveterate foe, Philip V of Spain (thereby effecting the second of the three 'Diplomatic Revolutions' of the years 1714–56),[10] just how far he was prepared to go to preserve the territorial integrity of his heartlands. The price Charles paid to Spain for a pledge of support for Maria Theresa was a recognition in principle of the Italian rights of Elizabeth Farnese's son, Don Carlos. The price which Europe paid for the Habsburg *volte face* of 1725 (First Treaty of Vienna) was a serious threat to its peace which lasted for several years (above, pp. 4–6).

The weakness caused to Austria's bargaining position by the Pragmatic Sanction issue and the unstable eccentricities of her policies gave powerful ammunition to those Whig politicians in Britain who argued that in the post-Utrecht era the interests of Protestant Britain (and Hanover) and the Catholic Habsburgs were becoming incompatible. The argument between these Austrophobes, headed until 1730 by Lord Townshend, and fellow Whigs, like Newcastle, who continued to cling to the 'Old System' as the linchpin of any Balance of Power policy, seemed to have settled itself by 1738, after the five years of frigidity between London and Vienna which had ensued from Walpole's refusal to assist Austria in the Polish Succession War. But the new wars which began in 1739 and 1740, especially the War of the Austrian Succession, led to the ailing alliance reviving – as Carteret had forecast it would.[11] At a time when most of Charles VI's desperately-sought guarantees of the Pragmatic Sanction were proving worthless, Britain belatedly filled in the blank cheque of 1731 with a heavy outlay of men and money. In the event, it was not until 1756 that the Old System finally collapsed under the accumulated weight of its own irrelevance. It was not to be easily replaced (Ch. 21).

Walpole's chief reward from Charles VI for committing his country to support Maria Theresa's rights in 1731 had been a commercial one – the Emperor's abandonment of the Ostend East India Company. The emergence of Austria as a potential trade rival to the Maritime Powers was a further development of the 1720s which added to European tensions and fuelled the anger of the anti-Habsburg faction in Britain. It came about partly through the Emperor's Italian acquisitions of 1714 but mainly because of the privileges he granted to a new trading company founded in the Austrian Netherlands. The suspicions of Townshend and Walpole reached their height when, by the Austro-Spanish treaty of 1725, the Ostend Company received special privileges in Spanish ports on top of its Caribbean and Far Eastern interest, and the temporary suspension of the Company's operations in 1726 only partially allayed alarm. Thirteen years later Walpole could still rake up the Emperor's 'strenuous' persistence with his inimical Ostend scheme, with its 'fatal' implications for British trading interests, as a major justification for not having supported him when the Polish War exploded (1, *XI, 231–2*).

The brief eruption of Flemish competition in the 1720s was, however, only one relatively minor respect in which the commercial and colonial conditions governing British foreign policy, like its Balance of Power context, changed fundamentally after Utrecht. The Whig ministries of George I and George II, along with the parliamentary majorities on which they relied, were just as committed as any late Stuart regime had been to promoting the advance of British trade, and possibly more committed than any previous administration had been to using foreign policy to this end. But in three major ways the nature and extent of that commitment changed between 1714 and 1748. The most striking change was delayed until the closing years of the period, when in addition to defending the commercial supremacy she had enjoyed since the late seventeenth century, Britain embarked on a struggle with France for colonial mastery. The other two changes came earlier: the first being the recognition of France by the late 1720s as a more dangerous trade rival than hitherto; the second being the naval and commercial revival of Spain under Philip V, adding a fresh dimension to the threat which that kingdom and empire posed to the balance of dynastic power in Southern Europe.

The armed contest for empire between Britain and France did not begin until about 1744, and between then and the end of the Austrian Succession War its scale was still very limited. Yet some, at least, of the features which were to characterise it down to its decisive culmination in the Treaty of Paris (Ch. 17) are detectable from the outset. Thus even by 1748 the contest had already taken in parts of three continents. In the struggle against Louis XIV only North America and the Caribbean islands had been a war theatre, but in the 1740s Anglo-French hostilities spread to West Africa and, more significantly, to the sub-continent of India. What made the eighteenth-century contest for empire so notably different in character from the 'scrambles' of the later nineteenth century was the fact that although much overseas territory was eventually to change hands in Britain's favour, the contest with France was not primarily about territory, for its own sake. Basically it was about trade. The prizes at stake, most of them evident by the 1740s, were *commodities*: the cottons and spices of India; the sugar of the West Indian islands; the tobacco and rice of the southern colonies of North America; the furs and fish of the northern colonies and of Canada; and the slaves of Africa (unhappily, very much regarded as commodities).

In retrospect the struggle must strike us as unavoidable, if only because of the sheer scale of the colonial and Indian contributions to the economies of both the contesting powers. Britain's 'Commercial Revolution' had owed a great deal of its late seventeenth-century impetus to colonial sugar and tobacco and to East Indian fabrics (*Making of a Great Power*, Ch. 3). But if the economic rôle of her overseas territories had been valuable to her then, it had become utterly indispensable by the 1750s. Between 1698 and 1714 the colonial trade of England alone expanded remarkably [see J.3] and in addition, the increase of Scotland's transatlantic imports under the Union became dramatic after 1740. Despite the huge individual fortunes made by such West India tycoons as the Beckfords, the principal growth-points after 1714 were not so much sugar as tobacco, the slave trade and – most vital of all in the long run – the market value of the North American colonies to English manufacturers. Without the great and constantly growing demand generated across the North Atlantic by a colonial population which increased perhaps ten-fold between 1700 and 1775, some British industries, facing prohibitive tariffs on the Continent, would have been hard pressed to survive. By the 1730s it had become imperative that the French should not erode or capture this critical market.

This was no hypothetical danger, because for the French, too, imperial territories and overseas trading factories became of unforeseen economic importance over the years 1713–50. Although Colbert had laid the foundations of an overseas empire in the 1660s and 1670s, by constituting the first French *Compagnie des Indes Orientales*, establishing the Senegal Company for slaving, organising the settlement of Canada, and trying to bring some state control to the earlier free-enterprise plantations in the West Indies, these early landmarks were arguably less important from the British point of view than France's acquisition from Spain in the settlement of 1697 of the western part of the large Caribbean island of Hispaniola. French planters already controlled two of the most valuable West Indian sugar islands in Guadeloupe and Martinique. With their new acquisition, renamed St Dominique, they were able inside twenty to thirty years to take over the sugar king's crown from their British rivals.

Far to the north of the American continent France made important cessions to Britain in the Utrecht Settlement (*Making of a Great Power*, Ch. 19; H.i.a [4]), but on the credit side in 1713 she did retain two assets off French Canada of the greatest potential importance. One was her right to share in the richest source of fish known in the world, the Newfoundland Banks; the other was the continued possession of Cape Breton Island off Nova Scotia, on which she proceeded to build the most powerful military and naval base in the whole of North America, at Louisburg. Louisburg not only protected the approaches to Canada via the St Lawrence river but menaced the British colonists of New England. Also undisturbed in 1713 was French control over Louisiana, her tobacco colony in the south with its port of New Orleans. The final turning-point for France, essential to her great maritime and colonial challenge in the middle third of the eighteenth century, came in 1723 with the reconstitution of the French East India Company.

As a result of its subsequent dramatic progress, the trade between the French stations in South India and the Company's home port of Lorient was able to play a major part in the unprecedented level of activity and prosperity which French overseas trade as a whole had reached by 1740. This French Commercial Revolution of the first half of the eighteenth century and the essential part played by her colonies in it was reflected in the spectacular growth not only of Lorient and of Nantes, but most of all of the port of Bordeaux, the focal point for the French West Indies trade and the eventual handler of a quarter of the country's entire maritime traffic.

The mid-eighteenth-century struggle for trade and empire was something more, however, than a contest between the Western world's two greatest powers set on a collision course, and this fact was of great importance to British foreign policy. The Dutch, after their prolonged ordeal of the period 1672–1713, no longer possessed the resources at one and the same time to protect a vulnerable land frontier and to maintain a great navy. But the revival of Spanish colonial and commercial dreams under Philip V was more substantially based. Spain continued to enjoy the annual gold and silver harvest from the mines of Mexico and Peru; she still dominated South America, and also controlled great harbours and markets in Central America, such as Vera Cruz, Puerto Bello and Carthagena. The Spanish flag still flew over some Caribbean islands, including the biggest of all, Cuba, and on the mainland to the north, over Florida. A successful naval programme was carried through in the 1730s, at the end of which Spain had thirty-four good ships of the line.

Indeed, it was a naval and trade war between Britain and Spain, breaking out in 1739, which triggered off the far bigger Franco-British contest for empire. For after the great uneasiness which had prevailed between the Bourbon powers in the 1720s, especially after the First Treaty of Vienna (p. 4 above), a close alliance, as we have seen, had been forged between Spain and France in 1733; it was this 'Family Compact', as much as Britain's obligations to Maria Theresa, which ensured that the war of 1739 would become swallowed up in the early 1740s in the far wider War of the Austrian Succession and would serve as a prelude to the outbreak of the first open hostilities between France and Britain for thirty-one years.

The root cause of the Anglo-Spanish War was the mounting friction engendered over many years by illicit British trading on a vast scale with Spanish Central America, and the draconian measures taken by Madrid to try to discourage it. Although some of the smuggling activity was carried on by the South Sea Company, exploiting the *Assiento* and, more especially, its 'annual ship' concessions (*Making of a Great Power*, Ch. 19; H.i.b), in accordance with certain generally understood conventions, the bulk was the work of private interlopers, making use of British West Indian harbours as bases and recognising no rule books. And it was their activities which drove Spanish colonial governors to develop a system of licensed *guarda costas* – private enterprise coastguard vessels which, not surprisingly (since they were often manned by ex-pirates or other thugs), inflicted on British crews and ships both heavy losses and some well-authenticated atrocities. It was one such atrocity, the peculiar question of

Captain Robert Jenkins's Ear,[12] which was joyfully seized on in 1738 as the heaven-sent climax to a lurid campaign of English hatred against Spain. For some years this had been busily promoted in the press, supported in the Commons by the West India interest (Ch. 3) and by the Patriot opposition, and most eloquently articulated by the fieriest young member of 'Cobham's Cubs', William Pitt. The subsequent storm was enough to frighten some of Walpole's closest colleagues, such as Newcastle and Harrington, to split the inner cabinet seriously for the first time since 1730, and to wreck the chances of the Convention of El Pardo [H.viii], in spite of the fact that not only Walpole but also the Spanish government and the South Sea Company were all anxious to come to a negotiated settlement of mutual grievances.[13] To the prime minister's undisguised and justified disgust (89a, *112–13*), and to the dismay of the court of Madrid, war inexorably followed in October 1739.

II

Walpole's failure to persuade either his colleagues and supporters or his opponents that another negotiated settlement with Madrid was fair and politic brought to an end a decade of Walpolean peace and neutrality,which had begun when the First Lord of the Treasury, elbowing aside the King's principal Secretary of State, Lord Townshend, had concluded a vital earlier settlement with Spain, the Treaty of Seville in 1729 (above, p. 5). But the outbreak of the War of Jenkins's Ear also marked the end of a much lengthier period, starting at Utrecht, when, despite numerous alarms, British policy succeeded either in preserving the peace in Western and Central Europe or, when other states did come to blows in Italy and the Rhineland from 1733–5, in keeping Britain herself uninvolved. For the future of Britain's relations with Europe this is arguably the most significant interlude in the entire century after 1660. For a whole generation after 1689 it had seemed that treading the stony Williamist track of close commitment to the affairs of the Continent (*Making of a Great Power*, Ch. 15) involved the constant risk of war. Indeed, Britons looking back on the Revolution at the time of the Treaty of Paris in 1763 could reflect on three-quarters of a century in which there were four major European wars, three of them involving the heavy engagement of British troops on the continental mainland, and on thirty-eight years out of seventy-four – not including the year of the first Jacobite rebellion – when British troops were under arms and the country's finances on a war footing. And yet amid these bellicose statistics stood the unarguable fact that right in the middle of that period the second post-Revolution generation had grown to manhood knowing virtually nothing of foreign war. The distant rumblings of one or two naval operations, like Byng's victory at Cape Passaro (1718) or an abortive Spanish attack on Gibraltar (1727) might briefly disturb their tranquillity. Yet in the end, a sequence of Whig administrations found it possible for twenty-six years after 1713 to avoid the ultimate penalty of European commitment, large-scale warfare, and to do this without (until 1733, at least) significantly reducing the depth of that commitment. Three times they slithered on the edge of the precipice

– first in 1718, then in the mid–1720s, and finally over the Polish Succession question in 1733; but each time they kept their footing.

On the first two occasions they did so mainly through hectic diplomatic activity; and it should be stressed that the feverish diplomacy of the years 1714–39, which students of the age of Walpole often find arid and perplexing, is just as revealing about the impact on Britain of the new foreign policy as are the later statistics of war. In the first place, it reminds us that few people who had lived through the trauma of the Spanish Succession War had any desire to repeat the experience (ibid., Ch. 15, p. 254). The very same man who in 1711 had led the attack of the Whig opposition in the Commons on the peace policy of Harley's ministry told a packed House 28 years later:

> I have lived, Sir, long enough in the world to see the effects of war on this nation. I have seen how destructive the effects, even of a successful war, have been; and shall I, who have seen this, when I am admitted to the honour to bear a share in His Majesty's councils, advise him to enter upon a war while peace may be had? No, Sir . . . (1, *XI, 232*: 21 Nov 1739).

The warmonger of 1711, and the peace advocate of 1739 was Robert Walpole, and we may be sure that there was no hypocrisy about his highly instructive conversion.

Secondly, the intensive diplomacy of the years 1714–39 enables us to understand why, under the early Hanoverians, British public opinion (even the bulk of responsible Tory opinion) came to accept that a collective security system for the protection of national interests was a legitimate priority of every ministry in conducting foreign policy. For over a long trial period it proved its efficacy in maintaining 'the Balance of Europe'. It was not only the concept of a Balance of Power (85) which became entrenched in the thinking of every Whig regime from 1714 down to the ministry of the Pelhams, just as before 1714 it had taken root in the mentality of the Junto. In addition, the Williamist *means* of achieving that end was increasingly taken for granted: namely, the involvement of Britain at the very heart of major Continental alliance systems. That this aspect of the revolution in foreign policy took a long time after 1689 to win widespread support (*Making of a Great Power*, Ch. 15) was mainly because for a quarter of a century such a policy had inevitably been equated with containing the power of France, and events proved that this could only be done by Britain becoming the cornerstone and paymaster of great war coalitions. In the eyes of the first generation after 1688, totally unprepared for it by any past experience, such a rôle was bound to appear controversial, however commonplace it was to become by 1815.

It was in resolving reasonable doubts about the commitments of the new foreign policy, and in tempering the xenophobia that lay behind the less rational hostility of the backwoodsmen (chiefly Tory) that the period from 1714 to 1739 was to prove of such lasting importance. It was then that three Whig statesmen of great ability, Stanhope, Townshend and Walpole, were able to demonstrate for the first time that alliance systems, backed up by prototype 'Congresses' for the settlement of European differences (Cambrai, 1722–4; Soissons, 1728–9 – see above, pp. 3, 5), could be used *peacefully* to preserve the delicate dynastic balance between Habsburg and Bourbon so painfully contrived at Utrecht, and to resolve other problems at the same time. Thus by skilful negotiations, mixed (in the cases of Stanhope and Townshend) with occasional sabre-rattling,[14] the Balance of Power was substantially preserved down to 1735,[15] and at no great financial cost. By 1733 public opinion had been so far converted to the new world of Great Power concert and alliance-centred diplomacy that Walpole's evasion of his obligations at that time to aid Austria militarily was criticised not only by members of his own party but even by some Tories.

For the Whigs it had been a very satisfying feather in their caps that they were able to cajole the Dutch again into a new alliance system as early as 1717, only five years after the bitter recriminations which followed the disaster of Denain (ibid., Ch. 14). The way for that Triple Alliance [H.iii] had in fact been carefully prepared, not only by the Anglo-French treaty of 1716 (ibid., p. 208) but by an even earlier Barrier Treaty between the Habsburgs and the United Provinces, which settled outstanding matters in the Austrian Netherlands. The faithful performance by the Dutch of their military obligations to Britain at the time of the 'Fifteen Rebellion had also played its part in the genesis of the Triple Alliance (82, *16–17*). In the following year came the Quadruple Alliance, associating the Emperor Charles VI with the Triple Alliance powers, with a view to imposing on Philip V a negotiated settlement of the crisis in Southern Europe provoked initially by the Spanish capture of Sardinia in 1717 (ibid., pp. 208–9); this was remarkable as much for the ease with which Parliament was persuaded to approve it and endorse the subsequent declaration of war against Spain, as for Stanhope's success in bringing the recalcitrant Austrians, for the time being, back into 'the Old System' (88a).[16] As with the Triple Alliance, however, the spadework had been done earlier, by the covert negotiation of the Treaty of Westminster between Britain and the Emperor in 1716 (88a, *288, n. 4*).

When the Quadruple Alliance was suddenly blown apart in 1725 by the First Treaty of Vienna between Spain and Austria, and the peaceful equilibrium of Europe once again threatened, a new security 'system' was urgently called for. That Townshend was able to respond so promptly and decisively with the Alliance of Hanover, the greatest *coup* of his career as Secretary of State from 1721–30, can also be attributed to careful preliminary tilling of the ground as well as to a receptive domestic climate. Prussia, the new member of the original trio in this Alliance [H.v], had already been wooed by Britain in the Treaty of Charlottenburg in 1723 (88b; 87). Only Carteret's alliance-making in the Austrian Succession War, following Walpole's near-isolationism of the 1730s, had to be conducted almost from scratch, and even then, not entirely so. In the extraordinary years 1742–3, when Carteret's fitful genius seemed to carry all before it in European diplomacy (above, pp. 9–10; H. ix), he did profit somewhat from Sir Robert's belated attempts to build a new confederacy against France from 1739 to 1741 (89b, *154–5*).

In a famous speech to the Commons in November 1739 justifying his ministry's recent conduct of foreign affairs, Walpole defended himself against the charge that he had allowed the Balance of Power to be disturbed by the War of Polish

Succession by claiming that his policies had served two ends even more fundamental to national well-being: they had furthered British commerce and they had
neutralised the threat from the Jacobites. 'The general interest of a trading
people', as he put it on this occasion (1, *xi*, *231–2*), was something that every
British ministry since 1701, Whig or Tory, had claimed to be pursuing and which
every subsequent administration down to 1763 explicitly espoused; how justifiably
may be judged from the presence of commercial or colonial terms in a majority
of the alliance treaties and in every peace treaty which Britain concluded in this
period. Whether in all circumstances Whig governments pursued commercial
interests *consistently* after 1714 is a matter for some doubt, as Jeremy Black
plausibly suggests (89a, *Ch. 5*). But at least all parties in the Commons professed
to agree they 'ought to be principally in the eye of every gentleman in this
House'[17] and were aware that their perceived neglect was political dynamite.
What Britons could not always agree on was how these interests could best be
fostered: whether by war, as the Whigs of Anne's reign, and after 1737 William
Pitt, maintained (and as the great colonial gains or commercial concessions of the
Treaties of Utrecht and Paris appeared to demonstrate), or by peace, as the
Harley Tories insisted from 1711–12 and as Walpole so strongly urged. The death
of the Ostend Company (above, pp. 62–3) and the relative prosperity of British
overseas commerce and shipping during and after the Polish Succession hostilities
have seemed to some historians to vindicate Walpole's view (Ch. 5). But they
certainly did not convince those London merchants and Whig 'Patriots' who
applauded Pitt when he denounced the Pardo Convention (above, p. 66; H.viii]
as 'a stipulation for national ignominy' and thundered for war with Spain on the
ground that 'when trade is at stake, it is your last retrenchment; you must defend
it or perish' (1, *x*, *1280, 1283*).

III

Pitt was unquestionably right to argue that further *colonial* acquisitions – in his
opinion the only secure guarantee of lasting commercial supremacy – could only
be secured by fighting Spain, and ultimately France. Yet the early years of the
War of Jenkins's Ear appeared to vindicate Walpole's more pacific and cautious
approach, for they were unsuccessful and disillusioning ones for Britain, and
disastrous in the short term for her trade (89a, *112–13*). They make an oddly
unimpressive prelude to a sequence of hostilities which were to culminate during
the Seven Years' War in the resounding naval and colonial triumphs of 1759–60.
Quite apart from the apathetic control of war policy by Walpole, the Royal Navy,
though in better shape in 1739 than is generally believed, had inevitably suffered
some damage from the long years of peace and frugal government since 1718,
and most of its commanders (and even more of its men) had little battle
experience. The Spanish, for their part, proved to be far from the pushovers that
the Opposition of the late 1730s had recklessly predicted. Admiral Vernon's
initial success in capturing Puerto Bello was never followed up and the Spanish
admirals in the Caribbean succeeded not only in protecting their other bases,

such as Havana, but in convoying four great treasure fleets safely to Spain between 1741 and 1749. Indeed, the expected 'war of plunder' might quite possibly have turned into a humiliation for Britain, if the death of Charles VI in 1740 had not distracted France with a full-scale Continental war when she had already made plans to throw her navy into the scales on the side of her Spanish ally in the West Indies theatre. In fact, these plans might already have been implemented if the decisiveness of Fleury's orders to the French fleet had been matched by the latter's logistical competence (81, *201–2*).

However, a naval and colonial war between the world's two greatest maritime powers could not be long delayed, and it became an inevitability after Britain began to contribute with troops, as well as ships, money and diplomatic effort, to support the Habsburg Continental cause (above, pp. 10–11). Compared with the Seven Years' War, the Franco-British struggle of 1743–8 beyond the Continental mainland was much more a maritime and trade war and a series of local struggles between rival commercial companies and colonists than a full-blown conflict for imperial dominion. Even the official declaration of war was delayed until 1744, and British regiments were so comprehensively tied up in Flanders with the 'Pragmatic army' that it was not until 1747–8 that any military contingent was sent across the Atlantic. The Royal Navy could spare only small squadrons for distant waters because of pressing commitments in the Channel and the Mediterranean. In the West Indies, consequently, no islands were gained or lost, though in a fierce commerce war the British ultimately gained the upper hand. In North America the war hinged almost entirely on possession of the vital French base of Louisburg, from which they commanded the St Lawrence, victualled their Newfoundland fishing fleets and threatened Nova Scotia and Massachusetts. It fell in June 1745 and resisted recapture. In India the rival East India Companies, with only marginal support at first from their respective governments, focused their attention on each other's trading posts (though the *Compagnie des Indes* did hint at future developments by concluding alliances with some of the native princes of South India). Whereas in North America it was the British who enjoyed a critical advantage in the possession of a fleet on permanent station (in the West Indies), in India it was the French who could summon similar reinforcements from Mauritius. And when in 1746 Jean-François Dupleix, the talented 'Commandant Géneral' who had taken charge four years earlier, captured Madras, the chief British trading post in the South, he did so with the decisive assistance of ships and European troops from France's island base in the Indian Ocean (258, *157–9*).

The general Peace of Aix-la-Chapelle in 1748 [H.x] left all the most serious Franco-British colonial problems unsolved. The French had had striking success in the Netherlands since the spring of 1745, with their great victory at the battle of Fontenoy, followed by the capture of Brussels, recalling the great years of *la gloire* under Louis XIV; these triumphs, together with their Indian bargaining counter, enabled their negotiators to insist on the exchange of Louisburg for Madras. The protests of the British public and press, however, (not to mention the anger of the Newfoundlanders and New Englanders) at the surrender of 'the people's darling acquisition' suggested that from now on the future of North

America would be the most sensitive issue in British foreign policy. The Aix-la-Chapelle treaty is often seen, like Ryswick in 1697, as a typical compromise of exhaustion. It is certain that France would not have negotiated seriously at all had not her ships been swept from the seas by a revivified British Navy, and her own people ravaged by famine, in 1747. Not surprisingly, there was much in the settlement, in addition to overseas issues, that was inconclusive. While imperial and trading ambitions on both sides were unrequited, Frederick the Great's retention of Silesia left Central Europe still dangerously destabilised and therefore a source of continuing anxiety to George II both as King of Great Britain and as Elector of Hanover. Diplomatically, too, the powers were in disarray: the Old System was finally crumbling, with the Dutch effaced and the Austrians disgusted by both Hanoverian and Pelhamite policies; the Franco-Spanish Compact was under strain; and Russia, like Prussia, had become an increasingly dangerous 'floater' in the European power table. And yet some things *were* settled in 1748. The commercial differences between Britain and Spain were patched up, more or less to the British government's satisfaction. A power equilibrium was achieved in Italy which was to last until the 1790s; and the Pragmatic cause was stronger in Germany since the death of the Bavarian Emperor Charles VII.

In some ways the most significant among the provisions of the 1748 treaty [H.x (2),(3)] were those in which Louis XV agreed to respect the Hanoverian Succession, expel the Pretender and demolish the Dunkirk fortifications. These entailed much more than a formal re-run of Utrecht; they were a true watershed in Britain's foreign relations. During the period of Britain's emergence as a Great Power between 1689 and 1714, the establishment and defence of the Protestant Succession had become a keystone of her foreign policy (*Making of a Great Power*, Ch. 15). The Rebellion of 1715 and the plots of the next seven years guaranteed that the Jacobite threat would remain, at least until the mid–1720s, the single most important consideration affecting the calculations of George I's Whig ministers in their attitude to European affairs. Fresh guarantees of the succession were secured in the treaties with both France and Austria in 1716 and in the Triple and Quadruple Alliances; after the Austro-Spanish *volte face* of 1725 the same factor was the Walpole ministry's chief selling-point when rallying Parliament round the Alliance of Hanover and its subsequent ramifications. When in the 1730s Walpole clung on to the hollow remnants of the entente with France and kept the kingdom on a pacific course he did so in the belief that neutrality would pay political as well as economic dividends. Ever since he had become reluctantly reconciled to Stanhope's adventurous policies of 1717–18, Walpole had consistently regarded war with France as the one unthinkable scenario. Playing fast and loose with the French alliance, as he did when he secretly negotiated with Austria in 1730–1, was one thing, but war was a totally different matter. That, he never doubted, would inexorably lead to a French invasion in support of the Jacobites, and quite probably to new civil war at home, and the near-coincidence in 1733–4 of the Polish Succession crisis abroad with unrest over the Excise bill at home weighed especially heavily in his foreign policy calculations.[18] His opponents charged him with scaremongering to hypnotise a gullible public into prolonging the life of his own regime. Yet ultimately a French invasion force under the formidable Saxe was only deterred in 1744 by bad weather. This fact, plus the outbreak of a serious Jacobite rebellion even without French help in the following year, when Britain had large forces committed on Continental soil, must surely acquit Walpole both of misjudgement and deception.

Only with the crushing of that rebellion in 1746 and the subsequent measures against the Highland clans (Ch. 6) did the Jacobite danger recede for good and all. What the relevant clauses of the Aix-la-Chapelle treaty signalled, therefore, was the effective removal of support for the Stuart cause from the agenda of practical statecraft in the rest of Europe; and with that the safety of the Protestant Succession ceased to represent, for the first time in fifty-nine years, a basic priority of Whig foreign policy.

1. Norwich RO Bradfer-Lawrence MSS (31 July 1728): quoted in J. Black (89b), p. 168.
2. G.C. Gibbs, 'English Attitudes towards Hanover and the Hanoverian Succession in the First Half of the Seventeenth Century', in A.M. Birke and K. Kluxen, eds, *England and Hanover* (Oxford, 1986).
3. See government instructions to Carteret, 1719, *Diplomatic Instructions (Sweden), 1689–1727*, p. 109, quoted in C. Wilson (125), p. 283.
4. R. M. Hatton (24a); id., *The Anglo-Hanoverian Connection, 1714–1760* (Creighton Lecture, 1982), p. 9.
5. For example Carteret, in the debate on the King's Speech, 15 Nov 1739: 'The King of Prussia likewise is a power we may always depend on . . .' (1), XI, p. 20.
6. Russia was ruled in these years by one sickly adolescent, Peter II (1727–30) and by three Tsarinas – Catherine I (1725–7), Anna (1730–40) and Elizabeth (1740–62).
7. The Dutch succeeded in preserving their neutrality in European wars until 1780, when they entered the American War *against* their old British allies (Ch. 19).
8. Add. MSS. 32686, f. 206: Carteret to Newcastle, 28 Sept 1721.
9. *The British Journal*, 10 Aug 1728, quoted in J. Black (89a), p. 176.
10. The first was the Anglo-French entente of 1716–17, and the third was sealed by the Austro-French alliance of 1756 (Ch. 16).
11. To the House of Lords, 15 Nov 1739, (1), XI, p. 20.
12. H.W.V. Temperley, 'The Causes of the War of Jenkins' Ear', *TRHS*, 3rd series (1907), pp. 197–236.
13. Add. MSS. 32692, ff.21–235 *passim*, letters of Lord Chancellor Hardwicke to duke of Newcastle, 2 March–13 Aug 1739.
14. For example White Kennett to Samuel Blackwell, 6 Apr 1718: 'Though we are sending fleets into the Mediterranean and Baltic, yet we hope they are rather to preserve peace than to engage in any action'. BL Lansdowne MSS. 1013, f. 238.
15. On paper, until the third Treaty of Vienna (1738).
16. The final settlement was achieved in 1720, after Alberoni's dismissal, when Spain adhered to the Quadruple Alliance in the Treaty of London.
17. Walpole, in the debate on the SpanishConvention, 8 Mar 1739, (1), X, 1291–2.
18. Most of all in the summer of 1733, when the Pretender was vaunting his optimism and the French had a large naval squadron ready for sea. In general see Black (89a), pp. 150–2 and nn. 87–8.

CHAPTER 5

The Walpole regime and Britain

When a statesman dominates the political life of his country, and much else, for two decades it is both natural and right that historians should wish to scrutinise his achievements searchingly. In the case of Sir Robert Walpole the process of assessment, and the historiographical debate over whether the legacy of his regime was or was not a fortunate one for Britain, mirror fairly closely the fierce argument between that regime's supporters and its opponents and detractors at the time. Not until the 1980s has a British prime minister attracted such extremes of adulation and obloquy as Walpole did at the pinnacle of his influence in the 1730s. Historiographically the process of revision still goes on. The first purpose of this chapter is to draw up a balance sheet of the regime's achievements and failures in the light of contemporary criticism and of present-day reflective analysis.

With Walpole's foreign policy (Ch. 4), the swing of the pendulum seems currently to be moving more in his favour than in the past. Little more than a decade ago it was fairly generally assumed that for some ten years before the outbreak of war with Spain in 1739 Walpole dictated the main course of Britain's relations with Europe as much as he dominated almost every other field of policy, imparting to them a distinctively conciliatory and pacific bias that could, it seemed, be set in marked contrast to the more positive attitudes, impetuosity and occasional brinkmanship of Stanhope and Townshend. It was also commonly argued that, although successful for a while in the negotiations at Seville (1729) and Vienna (1731), the ultimate effect of Walpole's disengagement from a warring Continent in the mid-1730s was to leave Britain isolated: her entente with France as much in ruins as the old Habsburg alliance, and even Spain prepared to tweak the British nose in the Americas in the conviction that Walpole would not resort to force in retaliation (27a, *Ch. 7*; 30, *35–7*). The only solid short-term advantage usually credited to his isolationism was the spur which Britain's neutrality gave to a flagging economy, although in denying the Jacobites an opportunity to rebel or invade during the Polish Succession war, it is conceded that Walpole's judgement has been vindicated far more in retrospect than the scorn of his opponents would allow at the time (30, *37*; cf. above, *Ch. 4*).

Recently, however, we have been cautioned not to exaggerate Walpole's ability to mould foreign policy after 1729 entirely in accordance with his own wishes. The two Secretaries, Newcastle and Harrington, were not ciphers and neither they nor Walpole himself could easily shake off the royal watchdog, George II. Even the decision to ignore the Emperor's appeal for assistance in 1733 begins to look more like a consensus policy when the scanty surviving evidence is carefully reassessed (89b). As for the benefits of Whig peace-keeping diplomacy as a whole from 1721 to 1739, whether the prime movers were Townshend or, subsequently, Walpole and George II, the modern verdict tends towards cautious approval. 'An expensive and lengthy war in the mid-thirties', wrote Paul Langford in 1976, 'in a cause which did not directly affect either Britain or Hanover, would not necessarily [as Newcastle was later to claim] have made a further conflict on the death of Charles VI impossible'. Such a war, largely unforeseen, would have been very unpopular and would have seriously weakened the ministry's standing, as well as probably provoking a Jacobite invasion at a far more sensitive time than in 1745. Looked at with this perspective, the defeat of Walpole's Spanish policy in the later 1730s, by minority vested interests and ill-informed popular prejudice, can be seen as bringing to a premature and rather wretched end a phase of foreign policy since the Treaty of Seville 'which was in many ways more coherent, more sensible and more fundamentally in Britain's interest than that of most eighteenth-century ministers' (89b, *169*; see also 82, *109–10, 115*). Jeremy Black has gone still further in redressing the balance of traditional interpretations, taking a cool view of the flamboyant, risky initiatives of Stanhope, and concluding that 'British foreign policy in the age of Walpole . . . in many respects, *particularly in the period 1732–8*, . . . was better matched to Britain's capabilities and to the international situation than in other periods of the century' (89b, *169* [my italics]). Walpole's main gamble during the Polish Succession crisis – on Austria emerging from it painfully wounded by the Bourbon states but far from totally crippled – was in the end proved by the events of the 1740–48 war to have been a successful one.

One key to locating the mainspring of Walpole's personal involvement in the foreign policies of his ministry is his position as First Lord of the Treasury. This is particularly true of the years from 1729 to 1734, when those policies carry the unmistakable imprint of financial imperatives. These were years which began with agitation in Parliament over the high cost of Lord Townshend's muscular diplomacy of 1725–8, which saw in the early '30s the Land Tax briefly reduced to its lowest level of the eighteenth century, and which culminated in the upheaval of the Excise Crisis. The prime minister's unwavering response to the critics of his administration's conduct of external relations in the 1730s was that it delivered the goods, in terms of peace and a secure succession, and that it did so at low cost and with tangible benefits to the economy. How far, in other ways, did his twenty-one-year stewardship of the Treasury promote the financial health and economic well-being of Great Britain?

Sir Robert Walpole was very much a pioneer in attempting to integrate fiscal measures with what (with strict reservations) might be termed an 'economic strategy' for encouraging overseas trade and stimulating deserving or hard-pressed domestic manufactures. As a landed gentleman in one of the most progressive farming counties in England, he also felt a continuing concern for the prosperity of agriculture and a determination that the difficulties of landowners and tenants alike must not be aggravated by an unnecessary burden of direct taxation. Indeed, the grain farmers of East Anglia, Lincolnshire and East

Yorkshire had particular cause to be grateful in the hard years of the 1730s (Ch. 9) for the upsurge in corn exports which neutrality in the Polish Succession War made possible, as well as for the fact that the Land Tax was kept at an average of 1.8 shillings in the pound for ten years from 1730 to 1739. The grain boom alone, Dr Black has pointed out, produced 'a benefit for the economy far greater . . . than the losses suffered when a few British merchantmen in the West Indies were seized by Spain', though Walpole was vilified on account of the latter while the former passed unsung (6, *17 [Intro]*). We should remember, nevertheless, that he himself, ever the pragmatist, was thoroughly realistic about the impossibility of *sustaining* an effective economic overlordship from the Treasury, and that some of the policies which historians have solemnly attributed to far-sighted planning were, as often as not, *ad hoc* responses to particular circumstances and pressures (30, *40*).

Public finance was always his overriding preoccupation. The scope of financial policy, of course, was greater in early Georgian Britain than it had been before the Financial Revolution of the 1690s. For instance, a vital part of Walpole's brief at the Treasury was to preserve a fruitful and as far as possible trouble-free relationship between the government and the great financial institutions, as well as the many large private investors on whose goodwill the creditworthiness of the regime largely depended. And although his administration's relations with the corporation of London were often stormy,[1] the City *per se* believed in him. Walpole had good cause, by 1739 at least, to be satisfied with his stewardship of the Treasury, and the situation he left to his successors when he resigned had not been greatly impaired by the early years of the Spanish war. He had had three main, interlinked aims: to reduce and rationalise the National Debt, to restore and maintain complete confidence in the financial solidity of the Whig-Hanoverian regime, and to keep the general level of taxation low, while improving the efficiency of the tax system inherited from Montagu and Godolphin (*Making of a Great Power*, Ch. 17) and shifting its centre of gravity away from the direct and much closer to the indirect side. Apart from one stunning setback, he lived to see all these objectives substantially realised. This was not wholly, however, a post-1721 achievement. Both his earlier spell as Chancellor of the Exchequer and First Lord (1715–17) and the political and financial measures for the settlement of the Bubble Crisis which he urged through Parliament in 1721, when initially still Paymaster General (69, *160–176*; cf. 26a, *339–58*), laid essential foundations for the policies that followed.

The year 1717, for example, had seen two measures that were arguably of greater long-term value than any others in dealing with the Debt problem, namely, the first step in the consolidation of interest rates, and the introduction of the 'Sinking Fund'. One was a purely Walpole initiative; the other was devised by him as a means of gradually paying off the capital of the long-term war debt of 1689–1713, but launched by Stanhope after the resignation of the Walpoleans from office.[2] The funded loans of William III's reign and Anne's had been raised at many different rates from 14 per cent down to 6.25; to service them was not only very expensive but an administrative nightmare. The 1717 scheme to consolidate the whole debt in the first instance at 5 per cent was thus of major importance, and it paved the way for a further conversion operation, down to 4 per cent, over the years 1727–30. That the Treasury was able to achieve the latter at a time of international tension speaks volumes for its success in keeping interest rates on new borrowing down to levels that before 1714 would have been unimaginable, with the going rate down to 3 per cent by the 1730s. During the 1730s not even the Dutch government, long the byword for prudent housekeeping in Europe, could borrow money more easily or cheaply than Walpole's ministry. And since private interest rates after 1725 tended to take their lead from the yields of government stock, the indirect benefit to the economy as a whole will also be obvious. Confidence and credit, however, also depended on resorting to borrowing only as an emergency device, not as a standard one, and on reducing the existing debt burden at the same time. Here the rôle of the Sinking Fund was important, especially after the collapse of the South Sea scheme in 1720. Within a decade of its inception the British public had come to regard this fund as a popular talisman, as yet another proof that in the hands of a thoroughly reliable and financially competent administration, investment in government bonds and short-dated securities was impregnably safe. Between 1721 and 1739 £12.8 million worth of the pre-1722 debt was discharged, and it is clear that a good deal more could have been paid off if the First Lord had thought it essential to do so. Walpole, however, had assured himself by the late 1720s that anxiety about the size of Britain's National Debt was a thing of the past, and at that point he made a conscious decision to cream off most of the Fund's handsome surplus into the ordinary revenue in order to keep taxation low and to deal with other pressing problems (69, *206–10, 470–2, 526–7*; 27a, *99–101*).

In the 1690s and under Queen Anne England had been taxed at levels beyond all experience and precedent, and by 1713 the landed interest was so intent on relief that the Commons overrode the advice of the Treasury, under Oxford, and in the session after the Peace of Utrecht insisted on a two shillings rather than a three shillings in the pound rate of Land Tax. In the same period customs revenue had also risen significantly (*Making of a Great Power*, Chs. 17, 19), but not as fast as income from excise duties [G.2(iii)], which at the peak of the Spanish Succession War were bringing in over 30 per cent of the government's total income, though even that was some 10 per cent less than the yield of the land and window taxes in the same years. Walpole's administration of the Treasury down to 1740 brought about a sea change. By the quinquennium 1731–5, years of undisturbed peace for Britain, government revenue was up *in toto* by some £2 million on that for the war years 1706–10. And yet in the mid–1730s the Land Tax now yielded less than half of what it had brought during the middle years of Anne's reign;[3] while customs revenue made up part of the difference, its rise was small beer compared with the startling growth in the produce of excise duties, for instance, from £8.23 million (1706–10) to £14.29 million (1731–5) [for alternative figures illuminating the same trends, see G.2(iii)].

It is easy to be misled by the collapse of Walpole's celebrated Excise Scheme in 1733–4 into thinking that his fiscal strategy ultimately failed. Certainly the characteristic phlegm – the 'sort of unpleased smile'[4] – with which he accepted his defeat, in the face of an unscrupulously-orchestrated parliamentary and popular clamour, masked deep disappointment at having to abandon the boldest and most imaginative stroke of policy of his entire ministry (32a; cf. 32b). The plan to relieve first colonial tobacco, then wine from all but nominal customs, and to subject them instead to a bonded warehouse system and to an excise duty if retained for domestic consumption, recommended itself to the Treasury on just about every financial and economic ground. If effected it would have given a boost to re-exporters and dealt a massive blow to customs evasion, with the Tobacco Bill alone expected to transfer up to £500,000 a year from smugglers' pockets to the Exchequer. Above all it represented for Walpole the culmination of a process, begun in 1723 with imported tea, coffee and cocoa [G.2(ii)], designed to reduce the Land Tax burden on landowners and farmers to negligible, or even nil, proportions in peacetime. The whole thrust of the tax system would have been moved decisively towards consumable commodities, on which (in theory) every subject paid according to requirements and means. However, the great Excise storm, in which the Whig regime was shaken close to its foundations by false opposition claims that the government was bent on a General Excise and on the bureaucratic subversion of English 'liberties', must not obscure the great progress made, even without the proposed 1733 duties, towards Walpole's central fiscal objective. Over two decades he still brought about a remarkable shift in the incidence of taxation, with vital social and political as well as financial implications. Throughout the decade 1731–40, including two years of war at the end, existing excises, including the restored salt duty (see above, pp. 5–6) regularly brought in 50 per cent of government income, while barely 18 per cent came from the Land Tax [cf. G.2(iii)]. A further significant achievement that can be set to Walpole's credit was that he was able to increase customs revenue [ibid.] in spite of having freed the vast majority of still-dutiable British manufactured goods from export duties altogether, and having abolished, or much reduced, many import duties on raw materials essential to home industries [see G.2(ii) (1721)]. That the consequent losses were far more than recouped was due in part to increased levels of trade but in the main to a series of measures in the 1720s designed to improve customs administration and reduce fraud.[5]

Although duties continued to be reviewed and adjusted later, by far the most sweeping changes made in the first half of the eighteenth century were carried through at one fell swoop in the great customs reform of 1721–2.[6] Although it can be argued that this was primarily an administrative exercise, aimed at restoring order to confusion (70, *311–13*), its priorities were entirely in line with the economic thinking of its architect. England had become a semi-protectionist state under the last two Stuarts, as we have seen, far more by accident than design (*Making of a Great Power*, Ch. 19). Walpole did not therefore *invent* state protectionism in Britain; but he was more responsible than any other eighteenth-century statesman for systematising and rationalising it. He was an unabashed mercantilist. The pledge given in the King's Speech of October 1721, 'to make the exportation of our own manufactures and the importation of the commodities used in the manufacturing of them as practicable and easy as may be',[7] was conspicuously honoured by the Treasury over the next twenty years. Walpole never doubted that the selective manipulation of duties was the best way to protect native industries, such as silk (especially), linen and white paper, which now found themselves exposed to the full blast of peacetime Continental competition; or to encourage both manufacturers and merchants who were anxious about raw material prices and were facing ever-rising tariff walls in Western and Central Europe and increasingly stiff competition from the French in the newer southern markets. If other European governments could take a leaf out of Colbert's interventionist book by enforcing an outright prohibition of some imports and by granting state bounties to certain industries, so could Walpole; among the beneficiaries were the light woollen, silk, linen and fustian industries, as a result of the 1721 Act against the use of painted calicoes, and the manufacture of sailcloth, cossetted by the Acts of 1731 and 1736.[8] Nor did the prime minister need any persuading by mercantile or colonial pressure groups that the preservation of the Navigation System (ibid., Ch. 13) fundamentally intact, in the interests both of transatlantic commerce and of the re-export and entrepôt trades, was a *sine qua non* of economic prosperity.

When we go on to ask, however, how trade and industry actually fared between 1721 and 1742, the picture is less easy to delineate, for there are a variety of obfuscating circumstances. In the first place these were testing years for many branches of British industry, both for those newer industries, deprived, as we have seen, of their protective wartime cocoon against foreign competition, and textile areas, struggling with a mixture of adverse market conditions and declining demand for some once-popular export lines, such as Devonshire serges, Essex and Suffolk bays and West Country broadcloths. Another serious problem was the declining competitiveness of the West Indian sugar plantations in this period. Thirdly, the domestic situation was far from uniformly favourable. The great epidemics of the years 1728–41 seriously affected domestic demand for home products: it was fortunate indeed that a phase of low agricultural prices, yielding much surplus spending power and boosting demand for cheap consumables (137a), began in the 1730s and more than redressed the balance (*Making of a Great Power*, Chs. 2, 19; this volume, Chs. 9–11). In addition to circumstances over which no ministry could have exercised control, even Walpole had to accept that there were limits to the willingness of Parliament to implement economic measures which the government itself thought useful and desirable (138, *127*; 30, *40–1*). And finally the historian, for his part, must grapple with the thorny problems of statistical evidence bearing on the state of the economy in this period, the most obvious of which are the frailties of the official trade figures (Ch. 10).

Thus it is hardly surprising if historians disagree over the extent of economic progress under the Walpole regime. But some of these differences can be ironed out if we make a distinction between the 1720s, when by most pointers growth seems to have been sluggish, and the 1730s, when it was clearly lively. One of the most carefully compiled and weighted indices of the 'real output' of industry and commerce combined in eighteenth-century Britain[9] suggests an overall rate of progress for 1720–40 not emphatically slower than that of 1700–20 or (more surprisingly, at first sight) that of 1760–80, and sluggish only by comparison with the exceptional ebullience of the 'pre-industrial' economy in the two decades

1740–60. In the case of the industries engaged in the export trade, the area for which Walpole (as a good mercantilist) expressed most concern, their performance during his ministry was, on the same evidence, almost identical with that of 1760–80. A.H. John has in fact argued (137a) that although England's total exports, at an average annual value of £5 million, were only about 5 per cent higher in the 1720s than they had been throughout the first two decades of the century, in the years 1731–40 they rose to an average of £5.84 million, with re-exports (average £3.20 million) even more ebullient.[10] In view of the manifold problems outlined above, such figures do appear to lend substance to Walpole's claim that his policies, including his foreign policy from 1729–39, had gradually created the right climate for economic regeneration and steady growth, and a firm platform for more rapid expansion when circumstances would conspire more favourably (Chs. 10–11).

Some of the contemporary criticisms levelled at Walpole on the economic front should be treated with reserve. For instance, the complaints of merchants in Liverpool, Bristol or London about the tobacco trade partly reflect a market saturated after 1725 by increased productivity in Virginia, and partly the extent to which the full benefits of that still vital branch of transatlantic commerce were being largely creamed off, not always legally, by Glasgow merchants (32b, *271–2, 289–99*). Petitions to Parliament from old woollen regions which had reigned supreme in the years 1660–1700 – from Essex, Devonshire, Wiltshire and even proud Norfolk – may suggest that they found *themselves* on a downward slope; and yet, by the 1730s woollen exports *in toto* were up strongly compared with the first decade after the French wars. Other regions, notably the West Riding of Yorkshire, were in fact usurping the textile crowns formerly worn by East Anglia and the West Country. In the same fashion the manufacture and export of alternative fabrics, especially fustians, calicoes and linens, were performing healthily, despite a new upsurge of textile imports from the East in the 1730s. Iron and steel production too was rising again in the 1730s, partly because of a strong North American demand for South Yorkshire and Midlands metalware. These are important pointers to the future. Prosperity is always relative, and with living standards continuing to rise [M.1-M.2], Walpole's Britain was clearly prosperous enough by the late 1730s to provide the essential springboard for the economy's more dramatic advances over the next two decades (Ch. 10–11). And, it cannot be overstressed, peace, greater social cohesion and pragmatic religious tolerance played their part in this achievement at least as much as financial reforms and economic legislation. That said, something more than Walpole's cautious and consensual policies was needed by 1740 to switch the engine room of the British economy over the last fifty to sixty years of the century from steady to full-steam ahead.

Although the mounting opposition to 'the Robinocracy' exploited whatever chinks could be found in the foreign, fiscal and economic policies of the government, most of the vitriol which splashed from opponents' speeches and pens in the 1730s had the more predictable object of disfiguring the political record of the ruling oligarchy. A perpetually recurring theme was the abuse by the regime, and above all by Sir Robert Walpole personally, of political power.

Dissident Whigs and Tories alike accused him and his allies of undermining the constitution, debasing politics and corrupting both the great and small who were involved in politics, down to the voters of the meanest parliamentary borough. By the Tories specifically, they were charged with prostituting the Church of England and the cause of religion itself for their own political gain. Interestingly enough, the neglect of grave social abuses in early Hanoverian Britain was seldom laid to their account; although this may be a sin in the eyes of some modern historians, 'social engineering' in a twentieth- or even a nineteenth-century sense was a concept foreign to most eighteenth-century political minds. When Walpole remarked complacently, 'I am no Saint, no Spartan, no reformer', he was doing little more than reiterate the common assumption of both his class and his age, that poverty, oppressive or discriminatory laws inherited from earlier generations (such as the game laws), urban squalor, the gin mania and much else were not proper matters for legislation. They called for private Christian charity, or corporate Church action or civic initiative, perhaps, but not for state intervention. Partial exceptions were made from time to time, as with Workhouse Acts, but very few (185a; 185b; 30, *43–4*).

Nevertheless it is undeniable that Walpole's unique period of dominance touched the society and institutions of the day, for good or ill, in many ways other than the ones which have absorbed this chapter so far. The effects on religion of government policies in the years 1720–40 will be dealt with more closely later (Chs. 7–8). Only two main points will be made here. One is that however much Protestant dissenters grumbled about the penal acts which successive Whig ministries chose to leave on the statute book, they were able to prosper quietly under Walpole and the Pelhams, with little practical curb on their freedom to worship, to educate their children and to involve themselves in local government much as they pleased. Although the Sacheverell affair of 1709–10 had taught Walpole a lesson he never forgot about the folly of goading the Anglican clergy too far – a lesson whose implications he had plainly spelled out to his party in opposition to Stanhope and Sunderland (*Making of a Great Power*, Ch. 23) – he remained to the end of his career a pragmatic tolerationist. Adamant that the nonconformists must not come into full civil rights by the front door, through outright repeal of the Test and Corporation Acts, he was happy enough to open yet another side door for them to sneak through, in the shape of the Indemnity Acts, first passed in 1728. Thereby they might move more than halfway to what, he conceded, was 'in itself desirable, and right' without offering 'the Church party . . . any occasion to inflame the nation'. Events were to justify his prudence.[11] As for the state Church itself, beyond the formal retention of the Tests it had little cause to thank the Walpole regime. In return for the political support from the Anglican hierarchy which he expected and for the most part received (Chs 2, 7), Walpole offered no *quid pro quo* in terms of official backing for the far-reaching programme of Church reform and revitalisation which his clerical ally, Edmund Gibson, devised in the 1720s, and without the much-needed countenance from the politicians and legislators the bishop's plans withered on the vine. Anglican leaders also felt, and probably rightly, that the government could have tried harder than it did to stem the anti-clerical assaults from the Whig benches in the 1730s (108a; 97; cf. Ch. 7, p. 105).

We saw earlier that 'corruption', in the crude sense imputed to him by opposition polemicists, was a relatively minor contributor to the maintenance of Walpole's hegemony and of the Whig political system (Ch. 1, p. 23). He himself loftily dismissed that 'stale argument . . . the common refuge of the disappointed and disaffected ever since government had a being' (1, *XI, 90*: 15 Nov 1739). But this is not to say that Walpole's legacy to the constitutional and political development of the eighteenth-century state was a wholesome one. In some respects he did leave behind him for the benefit of the next generation a polity far stabler than the one he himself took over (but cf. Ch. 1). Yet at the same time he fed rather than discouraged the appetite of the political termites which from the 1760s were to gnaw away at this very structure he had completed; through, for instance, his total indifference to the serious flaws in the electoral system, which began to come under desultory scrutiny in the 1740s, and through his shameless perversion of 'the influence of the Crown' to partisan ends. Likewise the cynicism with which he exploited the frailties of the lesser pawns in the game of politics and his brazen manipulation of its rules, of which his attitude to the Scots and their government is a prime example (250c; 232b), lowered the tone of the political process in a way that *ultimately* did his Whig political heirs no good.

Finally, there is a constitutional legacy to be weighed. Walpole's neglect of the full Cabinet in favour of an inner *conciliabulum* of trusted colleagues stunted one of the more important developments of the early eighteenth century, while his demand for the total loyalty of everyone engaged in the government service, at whatever level, led between 1721 and 1742 to some erosion of that non-partisan, professional stratum in the civil service which had been another vital bequest of his predecessors, Godolphin and Harley (cf. *Making of a Great Power*, Ch. 16). Both steps, along with his establishment after the 1733 crisis of the principle that every member of the Commons or Lords who held civil or military office, however petty, 'was expected politically to dance to the tune of the First Lord of the Treasury, or risk dismissal' (30, *42*) arguably led in the long run to more disciplined and controlled government; so, without doubt, did Walpole's further elevation of the supremacy of the Treasury. Yet all these developments also helped to build up suspicion, and to expose his regime to charges of unscrupulousness in the arrogation and abuse of power and of showing a contempt for constitutional proprieties. Such strictures were rejected by Walpole, who saw himself, as we know, as a respecter of the constitution, in his relations both with the monarchy and the House of Commons. Yet it is not difficult to understand why jealous and infuriated political enemies saw things altogether differently.

Opposition and decline

In this and earlier chapters frequent mention has been made of 'the opposition' to Sir Robert Walpole, and to its growth. After well over a decade of striving this opposition eventually grew strong enough in February 1742 to bring down the Titan by a series of parliamentary votes. How and why did this come about?

Until 1726, the year that the disenchanted Whig William Pulteney (p. 4 above) forged an alliance with Lord Bolingbroke, the ex-Tory leader recently returned from exile, to found *The Craftsman*, 'opposition' meant, almost wholly, Tory opposition. And although the parliamentary Tory party was generally consistent in its anti-government stance, its morale was not high enough in the mid-1720s nor the attendance of its members regular enough to disturb the equanimity of a massive ministerial majority. Bolingbroke, who had long since severed the last of his Jacobite links, was excluded from the House of Lords and poured much of his great talent into the new journal. By combining literary quality with its parade of a 'Patriot' Country platform, and by advocating a coalition of parties to supplant the old, supposedly worn-out alignment of Whigs and Tories, *The Craftsman* swiftly became the most effective organ of opposition propaganda British politics had seen. The effects of this on the parliamentary situation, however, were slow to be felt. The ministry was as yet quite popular, with Whigs at least, and no great emotive issue had arisen to provide the focus of widespread discontent. Finance and foreign policy periodically divided the House of Commons but without threatening any serious convulsion. In the last session of George I's reign in 1727 Pulteney could carry with him only ten firm supporters from the Whig side, and after the election later that year, in which Tory numbers were further reduced [E.1], the tally of *regular* Whig dissidents rarely exceeded fifteen down to 1730 (20, *196, 199*; 31, *32*). The 1730 session caused Walpole discomfort in the Commons, with far more Whigs now behaving truculently and either close votes or heated debates on such issues as the retention of the Hessian troops in the King's pay and the French re-fortification of Dunkirk. Yet except on odd occasions, for example when Walpole proposed to reintroduce the salt duty in 1732, the momentum of 'the Opposition' – as it can now reasonably be called – could not be maintained during 1731–2. Effective cooperation and mutual trust between its Whig and Tory components proved far more difficult to attain in practice than for *The Craftsman* to preach in theory.

It was the Excise Crisis which transformed the situation, providing the ideal issue for fusing together, for a period at least, Whig 'Countrymen' and 'Patriots' with Tories of all hues. It was made-to-measure, too, as a platform for carrying the question of the Whig regime's reputation and survival beyond Parliament and the London press into and throughout the provinces, and there making it a burning cause down to the most popular levels of politics, and ultimately at the hustings (Ch. 3). The years 1733–6 saw by far the biggest migration so far of the Whig party's alienated 'professionals' in Parliament (Ch. 3, p. 45), as the original Pulteneyite defectors were joined first by the Excise rebels[12] and then, after the 1734 Election, by 'Cobham's Cubs' and other new arrivals in Parliament. The most startling of the latter, for audacity and blazing eloquence, was a young man of 36, a cornet in Lord Cobham's regiment of Horse named William Pitt, who adhered to the 'Cubs' after his election for Old Sarum in February 1735.[13] From January 1735, when the first session of the new Parliament met, the 'formed' Whig opposition in the Commons rose to around eighty, and since the

Tories had improved their own position at the 1743 Election [E.1] the ruling party was rarely free from some degree of pressure throughout the remaining seven years of Walpole's primacy. None the less, its *working* majority for business in the early years of the 1734–41 Parliament remained as large as 100 votes or so in normal circumstances. Although the ministry had a few hairy moments in 1736, and again in the session of February–June 1737, most of them stemming from the Porteous Riots in Edinburgh (above, pp. 7–8; also Ch. 12) and a bitter dispute over the allowance to be voted for Frederick, Prince of Wales and his Household, it was still reasonably buoyant, generally supported by many Whig backbenchers, and able to profit from continuing distrust and conflict of aims between the dissident Whigs and the Tories.[14] Outside Parliament, moreover, it was noted that by the end of 1735 the government had succeeded, through lavish subsidies to its own propaganda organs, in drawing the sting of *The Craftsman* and other Opposition papers, such as the *London Evening Post*. The conclusion of a Commons' Committee after Sir Robert's fall that the Treasury had disbursed over £50,000 on the production and circulation of newspapers and pamphlets in the decade prior to February 1741 tells less than the full story, and the peak of that effort was probably reached between 1732 and 1736 (280b, *197–202*; 28a, *222*). Bolingbroke's retirement to France in May 1735 was largely the result of despair – the conviction that he could neither fight 'the system' indefinitely nor change the fundamental attitudes of the Tories. Even Pulteney, 'dead-hearted', spent much of 1736 in Holland (23, *244–7*; 28a, *219*).

The true beginning of Walpole's slide down the slippery slope can be clearly traced to the summer and autumn of 1737. First, it became apparent during the summer that the anger of many Scots over a ham-handed bill to punish the City of Edinburgh for its magistrates' failure to prevent the Porteous Riots was no storm in a teacup, like the Malt Tax furore of 1725; it permanently alienated from Walpole a substantial minority of the normally docile Scottish Whig contingent at Westminster and made an implacable enemy of the greatest Whig magnate in Scotland, the imperious duke of Argyll. In spite of the fact that Argyll's Campbell brother, Islay – the ministry's artful 'fixer' north of the border (Ch. 15) – stayed loyal to the Old Corps, the outcome was to be a disaster for the ministry in Scotland at the 1741 Election, at which the Opposition was to capture over half the forty-five seats. A second numerous batch of chickens which escaped from the government's run in 1737 and came back to roost, with the Opposition, in 1741 were the adherents of the 'reversionary interest' [A]. In late summer 1737 the Prince of Wales at last declared total war on his father, and on Walpole, and took with him most of the MPs who were attached to him through his Leicester House and Duchy of Cornwall patronage (31, *32, 41–2*). The Cornish boroughs, like Scotland, were to be a disaster area for the ministry at Walpole's last General Election, returning fifteen Opposition members. Any chance of Walpole repeating his success of 1720 in patching up a reconciliation between the King and the heir to the throne was conclusively destroyed in November 1737 with the death of Queen Caroline, the prime minister's greatest ally in the closet (Ch. 1). It is sometimes said that his assurance, especially the easy confidence with which he had sustained his dominance over his own government colleagues, was never the same again after this, 'the worst blow that befell him in a very bad year' (27a, *180*; but cf. 28a, *222*).

Outside Parliament and the Court London posed an increasingly intractable problem. Here again 1737 was a dismal year for Walpole. The corporation of London, whose Common Council had been anti-Court since the end of Anne's reign, slipped finally away from him in this year when the ministry lost its majority in the Court of Aldermen. This had been on the cards ever since the Excise Crisis, which had united Tories and 'Patriot' Whigs in the City in ferocious opposition to the tobacco bill; but from another standpoint the loss of London merely reflected the logic of the government's declining fortunes in the parliamentary elections there held in 1722, 1727 and 1734 (53; 12a, *I, 280–2*). The London electorate was to utter a resounding anti-Walpole voice in 1741, but in the meantime the capital had already contributed more than any other centre of opposition to the undermining of Walpole's authority after 1737 by its strident rôle in the Anglo-Spanish crisis of 1738–9 (Chs. 3, 4). By June 1739 Sir Robert had been reduced to such 'a strain of melancholy and complaints' by the evident disaffection of several of his chief colleagues, notably Newcastle and Hardwicke, that it is possible that the ministry would have collapsed from its own internal strains in the winter of 1739–40 if the premier had not bowed to the prevailing clamour in the City and the pressure of his own supporters and glumly accepted the necessity for the War of Jenkins's Ear.[15]

However, that war, with its half-hearted direction and its deeply disappointing course, offered him no more than short-term security. In the long run, it only made his own position seem less and less credible, to foes and colleagues alike. Yet George II remained stubbornly loyal, and the Tories, for the first eighteen months or so of the war, almost as reluctant as they had ever been to help to deliver a parliamentary *coup de grâce*, as long as Pulteney, Carteret and the Patriots seemed likely to be the only beneficiaries of a change of tack. But although in disarray at the time of the ill-judged vote of censure in February 1741, the Opposition forces had re-grouped again before Parliament's dissolution in April (partly owing to an instruction from the Pretender to his sympathisers among Tory MPs to concert with the Whigs to bring Walpole down). The Election that followed left the Robinocracy with a majority so slender over the 135 Tories and over 130 committed anti-ministerial Whigs [E.1], that, as Dodington admitted, it 'exceeded my most sanguine expectations'.[16] When the new Parliament met in December 1741 the prime minister's friends still hoped for gains in disputed election cases to restore a manageable majority, but these conspicuously failed to materialise as placemen with an eye to the weathervane faded away (Ch. 3); after suffering seven narrow defeats in Commons' divisions during December and January, and resisting an Opposition demand for an enquiry into the conduct of the war by a hair-raising three votes, Walpole finally decided to call it a day on losing the Chippenham election vote on 2 February 1742 (38a, *16–35*). Even so, it took a long (and on George II's side, tearful) interview to convince the King of the logic of both the political and constitutional situation, namely, that as long as his 'great man' continued at the helm, the ministry which he had commanded and so skilfully steered for twenty-one years could no longer guarantee to 'do the King's business' in Parliament.

Oligarchy preserved, 1742–6

When on the day of his resignation Sir Robert announced to one of his few unwavering friends in the Cabinet that he would go immediately to the Lords as earl of Orford, his first thoughts – despite his disillusionment at the recent behaviour of his colleagues – were for the party he had devotedly served for forty years and for the Whig oligarchy he had fashioned and sustained since 1716. 'I am of opinion [he wrote to Devonshire] that the Whig party must be kept together, which may be done with this Parliament if a Whig administration be formed.'[17] The next four years were to justify Walpole's optimism and shrewd judgement of the scene. They were also to demonstrate how, even out of office, he himself was actively involved both in safeguarding the Whig system and in ensuring, so far as he could, the continuing control over it of his own political heirs of the Old Corps. A fitting epilogue, therefore, to these chapters on the Walpole regime must seek to explain why the Old Corps, nudged along by the old master, finally succeeded in preserving simultaneously a one-party supremacy and their own pre-eminence within it.

In the first place it was crucial that in February 1742 only the one great sacrificial victim was offered to the Opposition. In total contrast with the general slaughter that marked such years as 1710, 1714 and 1762, all the main supports of the old system except the great central pillar, including Newcastle, Hardwicke, Devonshire and, most significantly of all, Henry Pelham, remained in place. The stability of the building required careful attention for a while, but the danger of collapse was much reduced once Walpole had so contrived his own departure as to keep the initial damage to a minimum. That the structure survived, arguably stronger than ever by 1746, to overshadow the British political arena for a further sixteen years is largely attributable to the extreme difficulty of replacing it with anything that looked remotely as viable, and the overriding factor here was the heterogeneous nature and disunity of the Opposition which had brought Walpole down. During the prime minister's lengthy holding operation from 1733–41, his appeals to the rooted anti-Toryism of the non-dependent Whig backbenchers had usually been successful. From the start of his last four years 'behind the curtain', therefore, Walpole's strategy was to encourage his friends to exploit these old divisions whenever possible, and further than that, to play off the Pulteney-Carteret following among the Whigs against the younger 'Patriot' element, when necessary appealing to the loyalty of the Independents against both. In that as in other respects, the broadening out of the war from 1743 helped the Old Corps considerably.

The position of the Tories was an unenviable one from the start. They were gravely handicapped in any case because of the death in 1740 of Sir William

Wyndham: he had been the only Tory leader qualified, both by his Hanoverianism and his many years spent coaxing his troops into the same battle-line as the Opposition Whigs, to fight the Tory corner for a share in the spoils of a decisive victory over 'the Minister'. There was some show of support from a tiny minority of the Whig dissidents for what Argyll, in an initiative whose importance may have been exaggerated, described as a government 'without distinction of parties' which would 'restore affairs upon so broad a bottom that the nation might be satisfied' (20, *225*). But a 'broad-bottom' approach never held any appeal for the vast bulk of Whigs, least of all for those in the Pulteney-Carteret camp; and with one notable exception (28a; cf. Ch. 2 above) few historians have been convinced that it seriously commended itself to the King either. George II may have contemplated one or two gestures to the Tories in the immediate aftermath of Walpole's fall, though it is equally possible that he allowed rumours of impending Tory appointments, such as that of Sir John Hynde Cotton, to circulate as a ploy to draw the Whigs together again. In the event, although Lord Gower was made Lord Privy Seal after Parliament had been prorogued, not a single Tory commoner in 1742 received a morsel at the centre of government. Even local concessions, in the commissions of the peace, were few until April 1745, when the 'Broad-Bottomed Treaty' between the Pelhamites and the Tory leadership promised, and to some extent produced, even-handedness in the appointment of JPs 'to gentlemen of figure and fortune . . . without distinction of parties'.[18] This treaty followed the admission to Court and ministerial office some months earlier of several front-line Tories (38a, *258–64*; 36, *63–5*; cf. Ch. 3), but the few Tories who did achieve central office in 1744–5 (above, pp. 10–11) were unable to deliver the *quid pro quo* which the Old Corps had required of them, consistent support for the administration – past habits simply died too hard with them (78a, *109*). Gower, having earlier left the ministry in 1743 for the same reason, decided this time, almost alone, to stay on, accepting the label of 'Whig' in doing so. But for nearly all the rest resignation was inevitable, even before the '45 Rebellion destroyed the last outside chance for many years of Tories effecting even a minor dent in the armour of the Whig oligarchy.

Like the Tories, the dissident Whigs contributed to their own frustration in the years following their seeming victory in February 1742, as well as allowing themselves to be outjockeyed by the Pelhams. For the Pulteneyites the two key questions in 1742 were: could they gain the confidence of the King? And could they capture the chief citadel of influence and patronage, the Treasury? The first skirmishes yielded no more than a limited success. Sandys and other disciples of Pulteney took non-Cabinet office, while Carteret's fluent German and formidable command of European affairs, having earned George II's admiration in the past, now secured him a Secretaryship of State. But Pulteney himself, wrong-footed by his frequent past avowals of disinterestedness in opposition, did not press his claims for the succession to Sir Robert Walpole, accepting a seat in the Cabinet without office; while the headship of the Treasury went in 1742 to the anodyne earl of Wilmington (above, p. 9). Later in the year, on Walpole's shrewd advice, Pulteney was offered in compensation the earldom of Bath, which he promptly accepted. His political standing never recovered. As for Pitt and the

Patriots, they were shut out of the original distribution of rewards in 1742, and, no less disillusioned than the Tories with the evident self-interest of the Pulteneyites and with their cynicism in helping to protect Walpole from impeachment, went into opposition to the new ministry on the same ostensibly Country platform from which they had lambasted the old. They themselves subsequently split over support for the war in 1743–4, with Cobham and the Grenvilles favouring peace while Pitt, by backing the Pelhams in their moves to extend Britain's war commitments, paved the way for his eventual appointment to office in 1746 (10, *58*; 12a, *II, 355–6*).

When Wilmington died in August 1743 it was Henry Pelham who staked out his claim to the Treasury with a conviction that Bath had so evidently lacked the year before. Pelham, who had achieved 'a very high rank in the House of Commons' in the 1730s,[19] had been marked out by Walpole as his preferred heir and again had the advantage of being prompted by him at this important juncture. Such was his capacity as an administrator that apart from one brief convulsion in February 1746, his position as First Lord and Chancellor of the Exchequer was not relinquished until he died in 1754, and command over the Treasury eventually gave him secure authority over the whole administration. This outcome was not pre-ordained, however. George II's attitude to Henry Pelham before 1746 was no more enthusiastic than his father's initial attitude to Walpole had been in 1721. In addition, Pelham had to defend the government in the Commons during the most unpopular period of the Austrian Succession War, frequently left exposed by Carteret's high-handed solo act in control of foreign affairs. 1743–5 were not easy years for the Old Corps, in spite of a comfortable ministerial majority in most divisions (28a, *243*). An ultimatum to the King in the autumn of 1744, forcing him to choose between them and the imperious and maverick Carteret and compelling the latter's resignation (above, pp. 10–11)[20] earned them a brief respite, but the fact that the Pelhams in December embarked on their Broad-Bottom experiment (36, *63–5*) illustrates how much less than secure they still felt. As well as bringing some Tory commoners into the ministry, with no lasting parliamentary benefit, and then proceeding to negotiate the 'treaty' with the Tories on concessions in the localities, referred to earlier, efforts were also made to embrace in the coalition the so-called New Allies, including 'Patriots' such as the Grenvilles and Chesterfield. Yet with Carteret (now earl of Granville) able to intrigue with the King backstairs, royal favour remained elusive in 1745 and in the course of the Jacobite rebellion seemed likely to be withdrawn altogether. Fortunately for Pelham and the Old Corps George II showed his customary ill-judgement in choosing when and how to act on his instincts. Delaying his strike until the Scottish rebels were in final retreat, he found to his chagrin that by then the ministry's prestige and morale had recovered while Bath and Granville had lost much of their once-powerful parliamentary following. The Bath-Granville ministry of February 1746, therefore, proved three days less than a seven days' wonder. The Pelhams returned, on their own brutally clear terms (36, *67*), and although Walpole was no longer alive to see it, the final victory of his 'system' and of the men in whose charge he had left it was henceforward assured.

1. A.J. Henderson, *London and the National Government 1721–1742* (Durham, N. Carolina, 1945); N. Rogers, 'Resistance to Oligarchy: The City Opposition to Walpole and his Successors', in J. Stevenson, ed., *London in the Age of Reform* (Oxford, 1977); H. Horwitz (53).
2. For the working of the Sinking Fund, see Dickson (69), pp. 85–6.
3. These calculations are based on a 5-year average centred on the years 1710 and 1735 (see G.2(iii): *Changing Levels and Incidence of Taxation*).
4. John, Lord Hervey, *Some Materials towards Memoirs of the Reign of King George II*, ed. R. Sedgwick (1931), I, p. 162.
5. See E.E. Hoon, *The Organization of the English Customs System, 1696–1786* (1968 edn.), p. 30, for the revised Book of Rates, 1725 (11 Geo. I, c.7); P.W.J. Riley (250c), pp. 279–82, for consolidation of English and Scottish Customs Boards; H.T. Dickinson (27a), pp. 102–3.
6. 8 Geo. I cap.15, 16. See G.2(ii) and R. Davis (70); A. Kennedy, *English Taxation 1640–1799* (1913), p. 98.
7. *CJ* XIX, 646: 19 Oct 1721.
8. M. Jubb (138), pp. 127–8; Dickson (69), p. 202. The 1721 Calicoes Act was, however, the culmination of two years of struggle, notably against the vested interests of the East India Company. A.P. Wadsworth and J. de L. Mann (145b), pp. 134–48.
9. P. Deane and W.A. Cole (128a), p. 78, but cf. the critical reassessment of this and other tables in this work in N.F.R. Crafts, (130b). Because Crafts finds it impracticable, for the purpose of his thesis, to subdivide the years 1700–60 statistically, his revisions are not very helpful for present purposes. However, cf. Chs. 9, 10 and J.4(i) and (ii) [Tables].
10. Calculations based on E. B. Schumpeter, *English Overseas Trade Statistics, 1697–1808* (Oxford, 1960). These statistics, it should be noted, have not gone entirely unchallenged.
11. Horace Walpole to N. Thompson, 12 Dec 1751, quoted in J. Black (6) p. 15. For the very similar attitude of his colleague, Newcastle, a far more devout Anglican, Add. MSS 32690, ff. 115–16. For the effect of the Indemnity Acts, spasmodic until 1758, annual thereafter, see J.S. Watson, 'Dissent and Toleration', in A. Natan, ed., *Silver Renaissance* (1961); M. Watts (95), Ch. 4 and pp. 478–90.
12. The Excise storm weakened the ministry in the Lords as well as in the Commons. See above, p. 6.
13. Although sharp-tongued in debate, the 'Cubs' were not a large pack: they scarcely exceeded half a dozen in numbers, even after George Grenville had entered the House in 1741. There were two Pitts (William and Thomas) and three Grenvilles, as well as George Lyttleton, who like the Grenvilles was a nephew of Cobham.
14. See B.W. Hill (20), p. 214; L. Colley (28a), p. 221, for the critical Tory abstentions which robbed the Opposition of victory in the Prince's allowance vote, 1737.
15. Add. MSS. 32692, ff. 64–5: Hardwicke to Newcastle, 2 June 1739; also, *inter alia*, ibid. f. 152: Walpole to Newcastle, 17 July; f. 370: Godolphin to Newcastle, 12 Oct; f. 377–80: Newcastle to Hardwicke, 14 Oct.
16. Bubb Dodington to Argyll, 18 June 1741: W. Coxe, *Memoirs of Sir Robert Walpole* (1798), III, p. 566.
17. Walpole to duke of Devonshire, 2 Feb 1742: Coxe, *Walpole*, III, p. 592.
18. Add. MSS. 35602, f. 57: 'copy of a paper delivered to my Lord Gower by Mr Pelham, April 7th, 1745'. See also ibid, f. 46: 20 Mar 1744[5]; Add. MSS. 32993, f. 308.
19. Add. MSS. 32692, f. 379.
20. The terms of the ultimatum are in Add. MSS. 32993, f. 282: Memo. 20 Sept 1744; a barbed account of the power struggle and of Carteret's fall, in *The Correspondence of Horace Walpole* (Yale edn., ed. W. S. Lewis), XVIII, pp. 535–7.

CHAPTER 6

Catholicism and Jacobitism, 1689–1746

The second great Jacobite rising of the eighteenth century, which did so much to make the regime of the Pelhams impregnable for the next eight years, had many features which distinguished it from the rebellion thirty years earlier, but one of the most notable was undoubtedly the almost non-existent contribution made to it by the English Roman Catholics. Against all the odds the Catholics had survived the shock of 1688–9 relatively successfully. Many must have feared the worst after their champion, James II, fled the country. Popular hostility towards Catholics was then running as high as it had ten years before – or so it seemed during the destructive outburst of mob violence against Catholics and Catholic property of December 1688. Some of the very Whigs associated with the witch-hunt after the Popish plot had returned in triumph with William of Orange, expecting to see their friends, if not themselves, dominate the first post-Revolution ministry. The prospect, soon realised, of war between militantly Protestant England and Catholic France had seemed certain to make things worse, especially after James had gone to Ireland to commit what for English recusants, mindful of the past, was a supreme indiscretion – fomenting a great Catholic rebellion across the water with the declared purpose of securing a base for a counter-revolutionary attempt on Britain.

I

Of course, the Catholic community did not escape the Revolution and its aftermath unscathed, and it was compromised by its involvement in Jacobitism for at least the next thirty-five years. After the passing of the Bill of Rights there could be no reasonable expectation of another Catholic King, or even a Catholic consort, without first braving the perils of invasion and armed insurrection. All the ground gained from 1685 to 1688 was lost, while the array of old penal laws on the statute book were supplemented with harsher measures. The Toleration Act of 1689 explicitly ruled out, 'any ease, benefit or advantage to any papist or popish recusant whatsoever'. The Tests continued to exclude Catholics from public office and both Houses of Parliament until 1829. New acts prohibited Catholic possession of arms, cavalry-sized horses, and residence within the bounds of London and Westminster, as well as making it more difficult for Catholics to own land or pursue careers in the professions. The double land tax imposed on recusants in every Land Tax Act after 1692 was a heavy burden for a community containing (and reliant on) a disproportionate number of landed gentry. Eight shillings in the pound off landed rents in wartime, even where assessments were favourable, was no laughing matter if the law was upheld, and there is convincing evidence it was. There was no empty rhetoric in Sir Edward Southcote's lament to his son in 1720 that, since his return to Staffordshire from the Continent in 1689, he had, 'lived . . . in an iron cage of double taxes', and there is no ignoring the evidence of the Northumberland land registers that 'there was scarcely a Roman Catholic gentleman in the county whose estates were not heavily mortgaged before 1715' or that by 1800 the ancient Catholic gentry of that county had suffered 'almost total elimination'.[1]

Nevertheless, doubt has recently been cast on the old interpretation which saw England's northern Catholics driven into rebellion in 1715 by desperation at the crippling level of taxation.[2] Because, in general, they were not involved in politics or in the expensive urban pleasures of English society, most Catholic gentry had a lower cost of living than their Protestant counterparts as well as more time to devote to their estates. The mountain of debt the Catholic élite as a whole appears to have been groaning under, if petitions to the Forfeited Estates Commission set up in 1716 are taken at face value, was partially artificial. By a variety of bookkeeping and presentational contrivances the forfeited Catholic rebels and their families sought to checkmate the Commission. According to their returns their estates had been afflicted for generations with tenants who never paid their rents, debts that were never met and mines that employed hundreds but never showed a profit, notwithstanding which many owners somehow managed to enjoy a comfortable standard of living. Double taxation and the costs of evasion must have hit the Catholic community in the pocket, but it is very difficult to know how hard.

In the wake of extensive northern Catholic involvement in the 1715 Jacobite rebellion, the community was hit by a fresh wave of penal legislation and attempted expropriation, which necessitated elaborate, and therefore expensive, legal defences. The earl of Derwentwater lost his head and a number of other Catholic gentry were executed or imprisoned; Lord Widdrington was only saved by George I's exercise of royal clemency. But it could have been far worse. One recent estimate[3] of Catholic involvement in the Jacobite army that surrendered at Preston puts it as high as a third, or about 1,500 of the 4,500 or so rebels thought to have been there. There was therefore some justification in the regime's imposition of swingeing penalties on Catholic landownership and other forms of property wherever they could make them stick – particularly in Lancashire, the main source of this 'horde' of popish rebels, where one quarter of the land (by value) was owned by Catholics. The Catholic community was forced into quietism to protect itself, and between 1716 and 1745 this insidiously enervated their opposition to the established order. It is true that only a handful supported the accommodation between the Catholic community and Hanoverian dynasty proposed by the Duke of Norfolk and Lord Waldegrave in 1716.[4] On the other hand, after 1715 Catholic involvement in Jacobite plots and rebellions was minimal. Money and homage continued to flow from the English Catholics to the Jacobite court until the 1760s, but the dwindling Catholic élite was no longer prepared to risk what it had left by rebelling.

In spite of its tribulations post-Revolution Catholicism in England and Wales did more than merely survive. Noble and gentry support for it shrank for the reasons outlined above and because of the drawing power of Anglican high society. Recruitment for the English Catholic mission on the Continent quietly fell off. But the mission itself, though it contained fewer priests in 1750 than in 1700, was far from declining in vigour, and lay adherence to the old faith not only maintained its pre-Revolution level, but actually increased after 1700, at a rate of around half a percent per annum (96). It was a situation which owed something to James II: directly, in that James was responsible for instituting a system of ecclesiastical government for English Catholics under his four Vicars-Apostolic, which revitalised the mission; and indirectly, in that his failure (and theirs in 1715) eventually prompted old recusancy in England to shed its damning association with 'Popery'. By the mid-eighteenth century England's ruling élite was sufficiently reassured by Catholic quietism to allow its paranoia about the threat posed by the Catholic community to die away. Hence in 1778 Sir George Saville could propose a Catholic Relief Bill which would have been unthinkable to any but a few enlightened Whigs, such as Stanhope, sixty years earlier, and succeed in carrying it through both Houses of Parliament with very few voices raised in opposition.

Significantly, however, one of those voices was that of John Wilkes, and he was a symptom of a larger phenomenon. England's ruling classes no longer considered English Catholicism a threat; the nation at large was not so enlightened. Demagogues like Wilkes opposed Catholic relief because it pleased their constituency. The old-fashioned anti-popery of the early Methodists was one of their most effective crowd-pullers. And the Gordon riots demonstrated in terrible fashion how out of touch with popular prejudice the élites were (Ch. 12). The ingrained anti-popery of England's lower orders, painfully instilled over nearly three centuries, was not easily swept away. There were to be ugly No-Popery riots at Stockport in 1852; militant Protestant lecturers in the Midlands and the North fuelled numerous other mob disorders between 1859 and 1868 (220, *279–82*), and in 1909 in Liverpool there was burning, looting and pitched battles in the streets between Protestant and Catholic communities.[5] Nevertheless, by the 1780s English Catholicism was no longer officially persecuted even if it was still denied any access to power. In that respect at least it had emerged from the dark trough it had been in since the 1580s.

II

The assumption that Catholicism was coterminous with Jacobitism had been one factor keeping English Catholicism beyond the pale. The conjunction between the squalid demise of the Jacobite cause in the late 1750s, when it was finally killed by Charles Edward Stuart's brutality and alcoholism, and the growth of élite tolerance of English Catholicism is not coincidental. In the eyes of the English governing class, if Jacobitism was gone then Catholicism was no longer a threat. Jacobitism, however, was a more complex phenomenon than such a simplistic analysis, directly traceable to official propaganda, allows.[6] The paragraphs that follow will investigate the motives of late seventeenth- and early eighteenth-century Jacobites, examine their background and finally attempt a brief account and assessment of the Jacobite rebellions of 1715–16 and 1745–6.

The roots of Jacobitism lay in the civil wars and interregnum of the mid-seventeenth century. Cavalier heroism and perseverance were the touchstones of late seventeenth-century Toryism. An ancestor killed fighting for the King at Marston Moor or Naseby; a family decimated by Cromwell's Major-Generals, was a common source of pride uniting Tories across the country, and from 1681 to 1688 put the seal of honourable tradition on the Tories' unswerving monarchism. James II's behaviour in 1687–8 alienated the majority of Tories, but to the very end he could still count on a handful of ultra-loyalists like the earl of Ailesbury, Lord Griffin, the earl of Middleton, Viscount Preston and Sir John Fenwick. These (and, initially, Catholics everywhere in the British Isles) were the bedrock of Jacobitism. The Jacobites' motivation in the 1690s was correspondingly straightforward: they were loyalists after the model of their revered Cavalier ancestors (e.g. 63, *21–4*).

Groups hostile to the political status quo often start out with only one clearly understood grievance. Soon, however, that initial alienation accrues extra layers and elaborations; the movement becomes a sink for all discontents with the powers that be. Jacobitism was no exception. It retained a strong loyalist-monarchist tendency to the very end, but it also became a vehicle for more disparate and often less elevated grudges. In 1707 Anglo-Scottish Union was bulldozed through the Scottish Parliament by very dubious means, against the express wishes of the majority of the Scottish people (*Making of a Great Power*, Ch. 20). Thereafter, its repeal became a constant theme in Jacobite propaganda in Scotland and the mainstay of Jacobitism's appeal there (232b, *256–8*). In 1715 most English Tories feared that the Hanoverian dynasty's Whig bias heralded an attack on the Church's privileges. For some the Tories' proscription from office confirmed this belief and precipitated their involvement in Jacobite conspiracy. Uncompromising support for the established Church duly became a standard refrain in Jacobite propaganda (106, *186–96*). Between 1716 and 1745 the Whig oligarchy's predeliction for curtailing popular, customary rights precipitated many confrontations with the lower orders in London and elsewhere. Legislation bolstering Aldermanic authority in London and reducing the power of the Common Council created enduring, radical opposition, expressed through Common Council and organisations like the Independent Electors of Westminster, which tended to shade into Jacobitism (52, *177–212*; 65a, *139–47*). Likewise, enforcement of the Game Laws to the detriment of common rights in Windsor forest provoked clashes with 'Blacks' determined to maintain them. The government responded with the Black Acts of 1723–4, reinforcing the game laws and disarming most of the rural population (*Making of a Great Power*, Ch. 18). Jacobites like Sir Henry Goring abetted the Blacks' attacks on wardens and game parks, and a promise to repeal the notorious Acts duly became entrenched in Jacobite propaganda.[7]

By the mid–1740s Jacobitism had accumulated so many of these social-cum-constitutional grievances on top of its original, dynastic premise, that it had insensibly become a neo-radical movement. At the time of the '45 Rebellion the Jacobites promised to: hold a free Parliament (excluding all placemen); abolish the standing army; repeal the Union; repeal the Septennial Act; repeal the Black Acts; do away with the National Debt; withdraw Britain from Europe's great-power confrontations; and restore Common Council's former authority in London. Wilkes and his successors would have had few problems identifying with such a manifesto (Ch. 22), and indeed there is evidence of a continuity in personnel between the last dying throes of the Jacobite movement and the early stages of late eighteenth-century radicalism (66, *87*; 146, *184–5*).

What prevented Jacobitism becoming simply a façade for pre-Wilkesite radicalism were its abiding religious undercurrents. Although its ideology absorbed a variety of popular grievances, the aristocrats and landed gentlemen who supplied its crucial mobilising force acted, and suffered, for the Jacobite cause out of religious conviction. Every 10 June (the Old Pretender's birthday) from 1711 to 1714 crowds in Edinburgh demonstrated against the Union, broke the Provost's windows, lit bonfires and drank the Pretender's health, but in 1715 the arrest of well-known Jacobite leaders such as George Lockhart of Carnwath ensured that the city remained quiet. The social elite that mobilised Jacobite armies were men like Lockhart and Lord Forbes of Pitsligo, whose prayer before setting out on his second rebellion in 1745 was 'Oh Lord, Thou knowest our cause is just. Gentlemen, march' summarises the man. Their ideals stemmed from Nonjuring/High Church theology and the austere morality inseparable from it. This put paramount emphasis on the social order's divine sanction and the concomitant responsibilities of those chosen to rule. Correspondingly the Jacobite elite expected exemplary standards of morality to be observed by their royal family (65b, *36–47*). And the exiled court usually met their expectations. In the 1690s it became renowned for its piety. James II spent a good deal of time in his final years in a Trappist monastery. Mary of Modena ended her days in a convent. The Old Pretender was a devout Catholic who tried to have his father canonised. When, however, the court failed to meet their moral requirements it plunged the whole movement into crisis. 'Queen' Clementina's desertion of 'King' James III in 1724 after quarrels at court upset so many Jacobites that it paralysed the movement for nearly four years. Likewise Charles Edward's drunkenness, profligacy and insistence on living openly with his mistress, Clementina Walkinshaw, scandalised his erstwhile supporters and accelerated its eclipse.

This is not to say that all Jacobites were moral paragons. There was always an element to whom the movement's loyalist traditions, accumulated ideological hostility to the established order and deep religious commitment meant nothing. Underground organisations always attract dubious characters out for excitement and gain, and the Jacobites had their share. They ranged from hitherto successful men driven out of conventional politics, like Bolingbroke and the earl of Mar, through such shady double-agents as Robert Ferguson and James Plunkett, to the simply destitute, like the earl of Kilmarnock, who confided before his execution: 'for the two Kings and their rights, I cared not a farthing which prevailed; but I was starving, and, by God, if Mahommed had set up his standard in the Highlands I had been a good Mussulman for bread'. Because they tended to be energetic, such men also tended to be disproportionately important in Jacobite conspiracies. Jacobite religious idealism had many positive aspects, generating fidelity, commitment and perseverance. It also often generated a distinctly unhelpful fatalism. To take only one example, Harry Straton, the Old Pretender's agent in Edinburgh in 1715, when asked if he knew of anything that might encourage the uncommitted to join the uprising, simply observed: 'We had a just cause and there was a just God.'[8] Men of action were required to get things going, and once they had done so they tended to assume command. Thus Bolingbroke and Mar both gained the top Jacobite ministerial office, that of Secretary of State, and each eventually sold the movement's secrets to the government in hopes of a pardon. Lower down, the duke of Ormonde's secretary, one Maclean, betrayed plans for a rising in south-western England in 1715, and Charles Edward's secretary, John Murray of Broughton, stole the Jacobite army's remaining funds after Culloden and then turned King's evidence against his former comrades.

So much for the Jacobites' motivation. Turning to their background, three features stand out. The movement's religious composition bears directly on its contemporary image and hence on its successes and failures; its regional peculiarities go a long way to explain the course of the various rebellions; and its social composition indicates how it survived so long under severe, albeit intermittent, government pressure.

Protestant, Anglican-episcopalian involvement in Jacobitism increased steadily from 1689 to 1746. By 1745 Protestants were overwhelmingly predominant. The process gathered way as the prospect of support from the Catholic powers of Europe dwindled. In 1689 James II was distinctly unconciliatory towards his Protestant subjects. Because he expected a French invasion, backed by an Irish Catholic rebellion, to restore him, he did not see any need to make concessions. Consequently, in England only Protestant ultra-loyalists like Ailesbury were prepared to work for his restoration, and in Scotland support for viscount Dundee's rebellion suffered. The Jacobites' defeat in Ireland marked the beginning of the end of this Catholic ascendancy at the exiled court. Preparing the way for a projected French invasion of England in 1692, James was already taking a more accommodating line in his pronouncements on the Church of England's prospects under his government. His reasoning is easily inferred, and underlay all future Jacobite plans: since the support of an invading army could not henceforward be relied upon, and since the experience of the years 1689–91 had shown England to be the key to winning all three kingdoms, he needed to gain substantial Protestant support. England was overwhelmingly Protestant, so he had to woo Protestants.

James's passionate Catholicism intensified with age. Nonetheless the Protestant faction at his exiled court was already well entrenched by 1693 when its leader Middleton was appointed Secretary of State, and despite some setbacks between 1702 and 1714, when Queen Anne's manifestly popular accession undermined the exiled Protestants' position and the War of Spanish Succession increased hopes of a serious French invasion of England, the Protestant ascendancy at the Stuart court and in the movement was never disturbed (64, *19–26*). From 1716 it became almost total; Catholics held only offices without power. This reflected the Jacobites' situation in Britain after 1716. The English Catholics were neutralised by fines and taxation, the Irish Catholics could not be used because to do so was sure to antagonise the English, and the Scottish Catholics were a tiny minority. A Jacobite restoration could only be achieved by Protestant risings in England and Scotland. It is ironic that because James II, the Old Pretender, and Charles Edward (to a lesser extent) all remained steadfastly Catholic, the positive image this Protestant ascendancy otherwise might have created in England was almost wholly negated.

Almost as important as the Jacobites' religious divisions were their conflicting national aspirations. Scottish and Irish Jacobites resented the Stuart court's anglocentricity, but they usually recognised the logic behind it. Jacobite support was surest in Ireland – despite James II's conduct in 1689–90,which earned him the nickname *Seamus an chaca* ('James the beshitten') from the Gaelic poets. Until they developed an autonomous republican ideology of their own in the 1790s the Catholic Irish had nowhere else to go, and support for the Jacobite cause was correspondingly widespread. Irish Catholic rebels were anathema in Britain, however, and the only time another Irish uprising was even considered after 1691 was in 1759, when the French were too desperate and the Jacobite court too moribund to be concerned about the likely outcome.

Scotland was the best prospect after Ireland, and support for the exiled Stuarts was hugely boosted by two events: the loss by the Scottish Episcopalians of established clerical status after the Revolution (*Making of a Great Power*, Ch. 13) and the Union with England. Because it inescapably conflicted with the re-established Presbyterian order in Scotland, the Episcopalian church rapidly became the mainstay of Scottish Jacobitism. In north-eastern and Highland Scotland it remained the dominant church, and for three generations influenced the gentry and aristocracy there through the regular promulgation of its beliefs in their households and its indoctrination of their children.[9] The Union boosted Jacobite support in Scotland by making a Stuart restoration a precondition for the recovery of Scotland's independent national sovereignty. The Union arose from English concern about the security of the Hanoverian succession. If there was no Hanoverian succession to protect, Scotland could be released from its fetters. Correspondingly, after 1707 there was a growing identification of Jacobite and nationalist elements in the Scottish political nation. Only a Jacobite victory could deliver repeal of the Union, therefore militant nationalists took up the Stuart cause and many ordinary Scots who could not bring themselves to fight for a Catholic pretender were unwilling to oppose those who could (63, *55–71*). Nevertheless, the Scottish Jacobites by and large recognised that they could not succeed on their own. Albeit reluctantly (and in both 1715 and 1745 optimism overcame experience), they wanted the English Jacobites to lead any rebellion.

Jacobite support in England was always dependent on how well the Tory party was doing in English politics. This is not to say the Tories were all, or even mostly, Jacobite in sympathy. The adage 'all Jacobites were Tories but not all Tories were Jacobites', has a good deal of truth in it. There were always Jacobites in the Tory party after 1689, and they always portrayed their fellow-Tories as

Jacobites under the skin. Except for the years 1715–22 and 1743–5 however, it seems unlikely that this was the case. For most of the period 1689–1746 the Tories aimed at achieving power (or hanging on to it) within the parameters set by the Revolution Settlement. English Tories turned to Jacobitism only when they despaired of achieving their ends by constitutional means.

Between 1715 and 1722 the Whig regime was proscribing Tories from every conceivable office of honour or authority, impeaching their leaders Oxford, Bolingbroke, Ormonde and the Earl of Strafford, and threatening the Church's privileges. No one knew where it would end. Many Tories consequently turned to the Jacobite option, if only to the extent of giving money to Jacobite agents collecting funds in 1716–17 to finance a projected Swedish invasion. Virtually the entire Tory leadership, with the single exception of Sir Thomas Hanmer, was involved in one or other of the plots hatched during these years (106, *206–41*; cf. 28a, *29–33*), and if the distinctly Jacobitical sentiments expressed in riots by erstwhile Tories from the lower orders are anything to go by, their inclination towards the Jacobite cause was matched by their constituency.[10] In 1743–4, the Tories were again in despair, having, as they saw it, been cheated of the fruits of victory over Walpole by the defection of the Pulteneyites and the solidarity of the Old Corps. A significant section of the Tory leadership, Sir John Hynde Cotton, the duke of Beaufort, the earl of Barrymore, the earl of Orrery, Sir Watkin Williams Wynn and Sir Robert Abdy, approached the French with a request for an invasion which they would support with a rebellion. Up to half the parliamentary Tory party may have been directly or indirectly involved. The French (who were nobody's dupes) sent over several spies, made their own assessment, and agreed to invade with 10,000 men commanded by their best general, Maurice de Saxe. But the plot was discovered, French preparations were wrecked by a terrific storm, and the invasion had to be abandoned. By 1745 the Tories were engrossed in constitutional politics again, and were as surprised as the government by Charles Edward's landing at Moidart (65a, *38–78*).

The upshot of all this is that the English Tory party contained a latent Jacobite tendency which occasionally predominated. They were not normally or necessarily Jacobite, but could become so under certain conditions. Except during those periods when the Tory party, more or less unwillingly, embraced the Jacobite option, die-hard English Jacobites were a small minority. Even when the English Tories did incline in some numbers towards Jacobitism they were very cautious. The bitter experiences of 1715–22 taught them two lessons: that rebel amateurs stood little chance against professional soldiers, no matter what the odds in their favour, and that the exiled court was full of spies. Thus in 1743–4 they made the landing of a large invasion force a precondition of rebellion, and demanded that the Stuart court be kept in the dark until the last minute. Neither criterion shows much zeal or confidence in the outcome of the rebellion. Without the rest of the Tories the English Jacobites were insignificant, and most Tories usually had too much to lose to commit themselves so irrevocably to the Stuart cause.

In their social composition the Jacobites were a cross-section of British society. We know most, naturally, about élite involvement because they were the ones who raised money, visited the exiled court and led the rebellions. Nevertheless there is sufficient evidence from seditious words cases, indictments for riot, and so on, to indicate that some of the bourgeoisie, and an indefinable (but substantial) number of the lower orders were also sympathetic. In England Jacobitism was probably most prevalent amongst northern, West Country and Welsh squires and the middle orders of Bristol, London and Manchester.[11] In Scotland in 1715 it may have touched a majority of the lairds and nobility of the North and Highlands and the patriciates of Edinburgh and the east-coast burghs. By 1745 it probably commanded majority allegiance only in the Highlands. In Ireland it offered the only prospect of immediate salvation for the Catholic majority and probably enjoyed their support at all levels of society. In mainland Britain Jacobite support was overwhelmingly Anglican/Scottish Episcopalian, though at various times a few Dissenters (notably some Quakers), and even a solitary Jew were apprehended for their involvement. Economically, nothing distinguishes the Jacobites from their Whig peers. They were as likely to be improving landowners, investors in new industries or enterprising merchants as anyone else.

It is indeed the Jacobites' economic and social typicality that explains the paranoia the Whig regime suffered on their account. Most Jacobites were Tories, and almost anyone *could* become a Tory. Catholic Irish gentry were obvious suspects, but who could have predicted that the duke of Wharton (the son of 'Honest Tom' of Junto fame), with his impeccable Whig background and credentials, would turn that way? Few Jacobites were as obliging as 'Honest Will Shippen', MP for Newton, who wore his Jacobitism on his sleeve. With hindsight we know the Jacobites only occasionally posed a real threat to the Revolution Settlement, but contemporaries – even ministers with the best available information at their disposal – could never be sure of that. 'I am not ashamed to say I am in fear of the Pretender', Walpole told the House of Commons in 1738 (65a, *15*). It is easy to see why.[12]

III

Once the Irish and Highland wars of 1689–91 were over (*Making of a Great Power*, Chs. 13, 14), only two full-scale Jacobite risings took place: the 1715–16 rebellion in England and Scotland, and that of 1745–6 in Scotland. Yet these were only the major episodes in a continuous series of conspiracies, negotiations and revolts punctuating the history of Britain between 1689 and 1760. Plots were hatched, exploded or investigated in 1689–90, 1692, 1695–6, 1704, 1706–8, 1709–10, 1713–14, 1714–15, 1716–17, 1720–22, 1725–7, 1730–2, 1743-4, 1750–2 and 1758–9. Foreign invasions inspired by the Jacobites were foiled by the elements and the Royal Navy (in almost equal parts) in 1692, 1696, 1708, 1719, 1744, 1746 and 1759. Some historians are still disinclined to take the Jacobites seriously as a threat to the established order after 1689, but none can deny their impact on Britain's domestic politics and international relations. This was true most of all, of course, of the 'Fifteen and the 'Forty-five. We must briefly look in conclusion at their prospects and the reasons for their failure.

The 1715 rebellion was the most serious mainland uprising the Jacobites ever launched. It could have precipitated a prolonged civil war had the rebels not conducted themselves so incompetently. There was an organised conspiracy underlying the revolt, which envisaged the major rising in England (supported, it was hoped, by French troops) and an auxiliary one in Scotland. Before the conspirators' preparations were complete, however, George I's Whig ministry learned what was going on and ordered the arrest of most of the English plotters, including two important members of Queen Anne's last ministry, Lord Lansdowne and Sir William Wyndham. A few, like Thomas Forster, MP for Northumberland, and the earl of Mar, escaped and in desperation started the rebellion.

In Scotland Whig support in the North-East and Highlands was initially overwhelmed by the response to Mar's rebellion (63, *133–54*). Between 12,000 and 20,000 joined the rebels. Given a Scottish population of roughly one million, the Jacobites thus managed to mobilise between 5 and 10 per cent of the adult male population. Mar, however, was no soldier. Lacking both flair and sense of urgency, he sat at Perth for two months accumulating troops and supplies. Meanwhile the duke of Argyll, with forces less than a third of Mar's, held down most of southern Scotland and nipped in the bud a rising in Edinburgh planned by Lockhart of Carnwath. When in November Mar's officers forced him to advance on Edinburgh with a 10,000-strong army, Argyll met him head-on at Sherrifmuir with barely 3,000, of whom only half were regulars. Against all the odds Mar snatched defeat from the jaws of victory, and the Jacobites retreated back to Perth. After that it was all downhill for the Scottish rebels, despite the Old Pretender's arrival at Peterhead on 22 December. Argyll's army, reinforced by 6,000 Dutch troops, went over to the offensive in January 1716 and steadily pushed the Jacobites north. On 4 February the Old Pretender and Mar embarked for France, and by 8 February the Jacobite army had dispersed.

In England the rebels' conduct was even more inept. Forster and a handful of friends and neighbours, including the earl of Derwentwater, raised about 300 men and proclaimed the Old Pretender as 'King James III' at Warkworth on 9 October 1715. After wandering about Northumberland for a while, they crossed into Scotland to join up with Viscount Kenmuir's southern Scottish rising at Rothbury. Reinforced by a detachment of Mar's army under Brigadier Mackintosh the rebels then turned south into Cumberland, and after bloodlessly putting to flight 10,000 men of the *posse comitatus* gathered by the Bishop of Carlisle, marched into Lancashire and took Preston on 10 November. When his army was attacked there on 13 November by an inferior force of regulars under Wills and Carpenter, 'General Tom Foster' panicked and for no good reason, surrendered. Meanwhile a muster at a race-meeting near Bath in September saw a good number of West Country Tory gentlemen turn up, mill about, and go home when nobody appeared to take command.

The 1745 rebellion, by contrast, completely surprised both the government and the Jacobites in Britain. On the Jacobites' part it was a masterpiece of improvisation and boldness. By the same token it was doomed as soon as the government could recover its balance and mobilise its resources.

Having languished impotently in France for over a year after the 1744 French invasion plan was abandoned, the Old Pretender's son, Charles Edward, concocted in sheer frustration a scheme whereby some Irish emigré merchants would convey him secretly to Scotland, where he landed on 25 July 1745. Despite considerable discouragement from the first chieftains he consulted, Charles refused to give up, and sheer perseverance, backed by lying assurances of an imminent French invasion (the French, in fact, had known nothing of his plans)[12] eventually won some of them over. By mid-August he had gathered a small army of about 1,300. With considerable dash, and outstanding generalship from Lord George Murray, the Jacobites captured Perth and Edinburgh while Sir John Cope's army was blundering around the Highlands, and then, when Cope caught up with them, defeated him at the battle of Prestonpans.

Immediately the Prince started agitating for an invasion of England, and promised an English rising, of which he had no assurance whatsoever, in order to get his way. By now about 4,500 strong, the Jacobite army crossed into England in early November and by 4 December had advanced as far as Derby, sidestepping two Hanoverian armies, Wade's and Cumberland's, on the way. At Derby, however, Charles's mendacity came home to roost. Confronted by his officers with a demand for proof of his claims that the French were about to invade and the English Tories to rise if the army only advanced a little further, he could only prevaricate, and his commanders promptly demanded that the army withdraw to Scotland.[13] Ironically, it seems there was by this time, unbeknownst to him, some truth in his claims – the French were finally about to launch an invasion in support of the Jacobite army and *some* English Tories appear to have been so bedazzled by Charles's success that they were toying with the idea of joining him. Nonetheless the army retreated and thanks to Murray's generalship reached Scotland without mishap on 20 December.

Thus far the Jacobites had always held the strategic initiative and had used it very effectively. Henceforth, however, they were forced on to the defensive, trying to hang on to the area under their control against steadily worsening odds. The Royal Navy and winter storms thwarted the Duc de Richelieu's plans for a sudden French invasion, and the English Tories were busy defusing Whig accusations of disloyalty by parading their zeal for the Hanoverians. All the Jacobites had to oppose the full might of the English state was that part of Scotland's meagre resources which was under their control. The outcome may fairly be called inevitable. After a last, defiant victory at Falkirk the Jacobites were slowly and inexorably driven north. Finally Charles, by now estranged from Murray, decreed that the army should stand and fight, and on 16 April it did so at Culloden. The Jacobites had less than 5,000 half-starved, exhausted men, and the Whig army under Cumberland 9,000 well-fed, fresh regulars, more than half of them Scotsmen. The outcome was a bloody rout, made worse by Charles's crass ineptitude in his conduct of the battle. Even so 4,000 stragglers and detachments rallied at Ruthven prepared to carry on the war – only to find that Charles, despairing, had already fled, leaving them no alternative but to disperse.[14]

The Jacobite rebellions of 1715–1746, like those of 1689–91, ultimately shared two characteristics. Neither was supported by a large-scale rising in England, and neither enjoyed serious reinforcement from abroad. When they were contemplating how best to restore the Stuarts both the Jacobite court and the Jacobites in Britain and Ireland were agreed that these were the two prerequisites of success. Either of these two necessary events *could* have occurred, particularly in 1715. As things turned out, however, all the rebellions did was underline England's economic and demographic dominance in the British Isles, and demonstrate the power and resilience of the English state.

---

1. M. Rowlands, 'The Iron Cage of Double Taxes', *Staffordshire Catholic History*, III (1963), p. 45; E. Hughes (149), pp. xvii–xviii
2. P. Monod, *Jacobitism and the English People, 1688–1788* (Cambridge, 1989). pp. 325–6; cf. Hughes (149).
3. Monod, op. cit., pp. 320–2.
4. See J.C.D. Clark, ed., *The Memoirs and Speeches of James, 2nd Earl Waldegrave, 1742–1763* (1988).
5. P.J. Waller, *Democracy and Sectarianism. A Political and Social History of Liverpool* (Liverpool, 1981), pp. 237–41.
6. R.C. Jarvis, *Collected Papers on the Jacobite Risings*, 2 vols, (Manchester, 1972), II, pp. 121–37.
7. E.P. Thompson (223a); E. Cruickshanks and H. Erskine-Hill, 'The Waltham Black Act and Jacobitism', *JBS*, **24** (1985) Auburn Univ. Library, Stuart Papers microfilm 254/92.
8. A. Aufrere (ed.), *The Lockhart Papers* (1817), I, p. 494.
9. B. Lenman, 'The Scottish Episcopal Clergy and the Ideology of Jacobitism', in Cruickshanks, ed. (65b).
10. N. Rogers, 'Riot and Popular Jacobitism in Early Hanoverian England', in Cruickshanks, ed. (65b), pp. 70–85.
11. F.J. McLynn, *The Jacobite Army in England, 1745* (Edinburgh, 1983), pp. 92–101; N. Rogers, 'Popular Jacobitism in a Provincial Context: Eighteenth-Century Bristol and Norwich', in E. Cruickshanks and J. Black, eds., *The Jacobite Challenge* (1988).
12. Ibid., pp. 117–42; McLynn, *Jacobite Army*, pp. 124–32.
13. F.J. McLynn, *France and the Jacobite Rising of 1745* (Edinburgh, 1981), pp. 29–34.
14. Nonetheless we should take note of self-confessedly 'pusillanimous' Archbishop Herring's observation five years after the failure of the 'Forty-five, that 'at the Revolution, . . . in my conscience, I believe it, there was less danger of popery than there is now'. G.H. (Add. MSS 35,599, ff. 14–15: Herring to Hardwicke, 28 July 1750.)
15. W.A. Speck, *The Butcher: The Duke of Cumberland and the Suppression of the '45* (Oxford, 1981); K. Tomasson and F. Buist, *Battles of the '45* (1962), pp. 88–180.

CHAPTER 7

Erastianism and reason:
the Church in the age of Walpole and the Pelhams

By the late 1730s, about the time Walpole's grip on the tiller began to weaken, those Whiggish divines who now virtually monopolised the ruling establishment of the Church of England were experiencing a deep sense of betrayal. A quarter of a century after the succession of the Protestant House of Hanover they felt little reason to be grateful for what they had received, as a Church, from either the new dynasty or the Whig Oligarchy in return for their staunch support of both. True, they had been protected, so far, from the horrors of a Roman Catholic restoration. But in recent years they had been exposed to the worst anti-clerical onslaught since the 1530s [N.3.B], had suffered a grievous legislative blow to their charitable revenues (ibid. and p. 110 below), and had seen the greatest champion of their cause, Bishop Edmund Gibson, disgraced and his far-reaching reform plans largely disregarded by the ministry and by Parliament. The prevailing mood in 1738–9, as two young clergymen named John Wesley and George Whitefield were just beginning to make a stir in London and the West Country, was defensive and despondent rather than – as time-hallowed tradition would have it – 'complacent'.

'Complacency', it is true, is a quality which fits neatly into the stereotype picture of the eighteenth-century Church of England, the image which the corrective work of Norman Sykes (108a; 97) and his heirs took such a long time to dispel, and which still lingers on in a few widely-read books (e.g. 115b). This stereotype embraced the Anglican clergy of the age of Walpole and the Pelhams, and indeed of the generation beyond, in a series of sweeping general charges. Among these some of the most damaging were widespread inertia; among the higher clergy, worldliness and time-serving, (epitomised by the obsequiously pro-government voting of the bishops in the House of Lords); and an equal lack of spirituality among the vast majority of the parish clergy who, having finally abandoned their lost Tory political cause (*Making of a Great Power*, Ch. 23), were concerned in the main with currying the favour of lay patrons, clinging to a dubious social status, or scraping a livelihood. In churches that became year by year emptier and emptier,[1] (the stereotype continues), the parsons, many of them pluralists, went on preaching conventional morality and obedience, leaving the vital spark of the Faith, the Gospel message of salvation, camouflaged almost out of existence. Until it began to acquire a modest leaven of evangelicalism in the closing decades of the century (so the old orthodoxy concluded), such a Church was wholly incapable of taking up the torch which the first Methodists raised as the Walpole era drew to a close.

The main purpose of this chapter is to enquire why the Hanoverian Church of England has had such an appallingly bad press, and, at more length, how justified the standard criticisms made of it still appear to be in the light of twentieth-century research. And if, as has been suggested already, the Anglican clergy as a whole were better-intentioned, as well as more conscious of their Church's deficiencies, than they are often given credit for, we must also ask in conclusion: why was it that intention was only rarely translated into achievement? And why had the Church's physical and spiritual contact with at least a third of the adult population of England and Wales become either tenuous or non-existent by the time Methodism burst on the scene?

To the first question two partial answers may be suggested at the outset. In the first place, the Anglican Church at this period suffered a severe mauling at the hands of its own contemporaries, and well into the present century many historians were apt to take at face value highly-coloured contemporary criticisms, despite the fact that these were often far from objective. Especially damaging were those which fell too readily from the lips of the early evangelical preachers, swept along on the tide of their own rhetoric by the fierce conviction that all who had not experienced the New Birth, as they had, were spiritually unregenerate. Thus Whitefield poured bitter scorn on the much-revered Archbishop Tillotson as one who 'knew no more of true Christianity than Mahomet' and savaged 'our clergy' as men 'only seeking after preferment . . . to spend on the pleasures of life' (113a, *149*; 113b, *17*). Other evangelicals in Anglican orders, as Whitefield was, flayed their brethren in similar terms, Henry Piers denouncing the 'Godly Unrenewed . . . who are content with such a faith as neither purifies the heart nor works by love' as enemies to the Church who were as dangerous as 'infidels professed', and Jacob Rogers preaching a vehemently anti-clerical sermon in Yorkshire in 1739 on the text 'Beware of Dogs'.[2] The hostility to the clergy, their motives and their morals, voiced from outside the profession was not only coarser and more pungent than the criticism from within; it was also frequently tinged with savage ridicule:

> First, as a rule I'll lay it down
> That in this giddy, busy town
> The clergy least religion have
> Of all the folks this side the grave.
> For now the black-coat greedy dons
> Are almost like old Eli's sons,
> Keep up the priesthood for a cloak
> Though most believe it all a joke.

So ran a fairly typical offering of a London scribbler of Walpole's day. As for the speeches which assailed the Church from the Whig back-benches in the House of Commons year after year in the 1730s, though more seemly than the outpourings of Grub Street, they were even more withering in their rancour. But these were far from being impartial witnesses. Their animosity was rooted in the past, and above all it had more relevance to past politics than to present religion.

This leads us to a second and more direct reason why historians have often taken a bleak view of the eighteenth-century Church of England. There was for long a widespread tendency to regard it in isolation, with little reference to what had gone on before 1714 in England or what was taking place contemporaneously on the Continent. Yet we have seen ourselves how the Church had found itself in serious difficulties since the closing years of the seventeenth century, partly as a result of the Revolution, partly because of the intellectual climate of the age, and partly because long-standing economic weaknesses were aggravated by heavy taxation. That post-Revolution Church had not lacked ability or vigour. Its greatest tragedy lay less in the existence of its many problems, most of which it was prepared to confront and some of which it might well have overcome in time, than in the fact that Anglicans were so sharply divided about how to tackle them, and in the process got so involved in the distractions of lay politics. Since these activities discredited the bulk of the clergy in the eyes of the Whigs, it is particularly important to bear in mind, as we come to assess the state of health of the Anglican Church from the 1720s to the 1760s, that this was a Church which had to function within an erastian and largely inimical Whig polity.

The present posture of scholarship on the eighteenth-century Church, though still handicapped by the scarcity of those local studies which can throw so much light on the national picture (104a and b),[3] seems to be pointing the way to a picture far more subtle and complex than that of our stereotype: in some ways more favourable to the Church, yet still quite full of features that were very disturbing to those who at the time were genuinely concerned themselves at the direction in which the Church, and the Faith, appeared to be going. What follows should be seen as an 'interim report', appropriate to the current state of knowledge. We know enough about most aspects of the Church to put us on our guard against caricature and to heighten our awareness of elements of light and shade in many parts of the picture, but rarely enough to indulge with great confidence in firm, well-ordered and clearly-tabulated conclusions.

At least one of the basic weaknesses of the Hanoverian Church most commonly identified, the excessive erastianism [A.] which pervaded and inhibited it, can certainly be confirmed in general terms. It was a more debilitating malaise in the age of Walpole and the Pelhams than at any time since the Reformation, and while one can sympathise with a state church forced to accommodate itself to a Whig Oligarchy determined to depress clerical pretensions as never before, the feeling remains that the clergy could have struggled harder to resist the muzzle. That said, there are important aspects of Church-State relations in this period which have frequently been misunderstood. It is clear that after 1720 there was a deliberate attempt to subject the Church to the Whig patronage machine. It is also clear that in this process two men played a key rôle: on the government side, the duke of Newcastle (102), and on the Church side, from 1723 (when he succeeded John Robinson as Bishop of London) until 1736, Edmund Gibson. Gibson was selected by Walpole as the chief ecclesiastical arm of Whig policy because William Wake, Archbishop Tenison's successor at Canterbury [N.1], was distrusted by the ruling party for his supposed 'softness' towards Tories and High Churchmen and for a less than accommodating attitude to the dissenters. And so, where appointments were concerned, Wake's authority was by-passed by Gibson, very much as Tenison's had been earlier, by Archbishop Sharp and Queen Anne.[4] This was a situation fraught with strain at first, for despite a weak appetite for politics Wake was a fine churchman and a respected Primate. But it became of little account after 1730, when he relapsed into a state of virtual vegetation in which (as Gibson himself rather cruelly remarked) he 'had nothing to do but to make two dinners a week and to sign dispensations' (108b, *II, 149, 253–5*).

But what were the hard implications of the Walpole-Gibson pact? And just how much could patronage and political control over the Church achieve in practice? Certainly it meant that from 1723 the door to the bishops' bench and to the other plums of preferment in the state-controlled larder, notably the twenty-seven deaneries in England and Wales,[5] was effectively slammed in the faces of almost all who were suspected of Toryism and of many whose only obvious offence was their High Churchmanship. With 'nineteen Whig bishops out of the 26' (on Sunderland's computation) already in place by September 1721,[6] the nine further episcopal appointments and promotions of the years 1723–4, the first two years of Gibson's 'pontificate', had a decisive effect in shaping the Church hierarchy of the next quarter of a century. And undoubtedly the government reaped rich benefits in the House of Lords as a result (Ch. 2). All the same, one can easily exaggerate both the comprehensiveness of political patronage and the subservience of bishops to the state. The first reservation to note is that while the Crown could nominate to the highest positions in the Church (except archdeaconries) when vacancies occurred, it could not *create* ecclesiastical vacancies, there or anywhere. It is true that Atterbury was deprived of the see of Rochester in 1723 by a parliamentary bill of pains and penalties, but this was a wholly exceptional case (*Making of a Great Power*, Ch. 25). Once a key appointment had been made, therefore, the government, like the Church, was stuck with it. Furthermore, in its attempts to mould the character of the lower clergy the government, as such, only had at its direct disposal the Lord Chancellor's patronage over 1,050-odd livings, including chapelries. Some of those livings, admittedly, were valuable, and the Walpole ministry successfully resisted Gibson's strenuous efforts to persuade the then Lord Chancellor, Lord King, to surrender the nominations to him in the interests of the Church. All the same, they represented only a small fraction of the total of well over 11,000 livings, a far smaller proportion than the advowsons in the hands of the Church Establishment itself (26 per cent) and private patrons (53.5 per cent) (102).

Indeed, in the early decades of the Hanoverian period many of the Anglican livings in the gift of private landowners (a reasonable guess would be over 2,000 of them) were still controlled by Tory squires – by men whose own conversion to the regime was a slow process, at best.[7] In Yorkshire, the only county in which the voting patterns of the parish clergy over the first half of the eighteenth century have been closely studied, a substantial defection of parsons from the Tory cause is not detectable before 1734. Eight years later, however, a great change had occurred: little more than a quarter of the 346 Yorkshire parsons who travelled to York to poll at the county by-election of 1742 cast their votes for the candidate of 'the Church Party' (cf. *Making of a Great Power*, Ch. 23, p. 363).[8] A political shift of this magnitude serves to remind us that the Walpole-Gibson alliance and the egregious Newcastle were not solely dependent on the disposal of Crown livings to combat High Church Toryism and disaffection among the lower clergy. Conciliatory religious policies could play an important part; the extensive private patronage of the Whig magnates was pressed into service; and, as Hirschberg has shown, not only in the Gibson era but for long after it, there was far more mutual and genuine cooperation between the politicians and the bishops over the exercise of the Church's own patronage (and indeed Crown patronage, too) than historians have hitherto realised (102). Even together these weapons could not work miracles overnight. But there is reason to believe that by the time of Walpole's fall they had already wrought a profound change in the character of the clerical rank and file.

Even when we turn to the bench of bishops itself it becomes clear that the broader generalisations about the efficacy of political control must be tempered in a number of ways. Gibson's policy from 1723 to 1736 was to elevate to and promote within the episcopate only those sound Whigs and politically moderate, doctrinally orthodox and spiritually worthy churchmen who, he considered, would best serve the joint interests of both Church and Crown. In general Walpole and Newcastle agreed with him. Yet Gibson was not invariably successful in getting the King to accept his nominees. One thorn in his flesh after 1727 was Queen Caroline, a keen amateur theologian with a penchant for extremes of churchmanship. Although Gibson sometimes thwarted her, he had to accept at least three bishops he disapproved of over the years 1727–33;[9] he was also forced reluctantly to agree to the promotion of the controversial Ben Hoadly to the golden prize of Winchester in 1734. Furthermore the parliamentary record of the bishops, even of the Whig bishops, is not quite so straightforward as one is usually led to believe. From 1723–30 all but the tiny handful of Tory survivors on the bench found little to strain their sense of duty to the Court. Not so in the 1730s. The years 1730–6 were a time of mounting Whig anticlericalism in Parliament, a delayed backlash from all the conflicts and resentments of Anne's reign and the impulse behind a spate of hostile backbench bills in the House of Commons which caused the bishops, as well as their clergy, grave anxiety (Ch. 2). Despite their conviction that Walpole's ministry could have done more to deter these attacks, the bishops did remain loyal to the administration up to and through the Excise Crisis and the 1734 Election. But there were limits to what they would stand, and after the Mortmain Bill of 1735 (below, p. 110), a measure which threatened clerical charities and was covertly favoured by the ministry, had caused much disaffection among Church leaders, there was an open breach with the government the following year over the Quaker Relief (or Tithes) Bill, which Walpole and his colleagues openly espoused. As a result the Bill was defeated in the Lords, with fourteen of the twenty-six bishops voting against it and eleven abstaining (108b; 108a).

Under the shock of this rebellion the Walpole-Gibson entente collapsed completely. The wrath of the government was considerable, even George II joining in and (as Lord Hervey put it) 'with his usual softness in speaking of any people he disliked, called the bishops, whenever he mentioned them in private . . . a parcel of black, canting, hypocritical rascals'.[10] Once Gibson resigned as ecclesiastical adviser to the government, most of the other bishops, deprived of his forceful leadership, came back into line. But a dissident group of four or five, of whom Reynolds, Smallbrooke and Secker of Bristol (a future Primate) were the most notorious, asserted their independence on several critical occasions in the years of Walpole's decline, 1739–41. Indeed, on the eve of the premier's fall Newcastle could feel certain of only sixteen of the twenty-six votes of the lords spiritual (21). As late as 1743 the entire bench revolted again, opposing a government finance measure, the proposal to reduce the duties on spirits, on the grounds of its undesirable social effects. It was not until the 1750s, in fact, that the uniform docility of the bishops in the Upper House could be taken more or less for granted.

The triumph of erastianism in the last years of George II is encapsulated in the sad case of Matthew Hutton, whose brief career at Canterbury, 1757–8, came to an untimely end when he was too conscientious in obeying a ministerial summons in bleak midwinter to attend a Navy debate in the Lords, contracted pneumonia, and died. It was the nearest any eighteenth-century prelate came to martyrdom. The same decade also saw Newcastle's influence over patronage reach its peak, during the feeble primacy of Hutton's predecessor, Thomas Herring [N.1]. It was in 1755 that Thomas Jones, chaplain of St Saviour's Southwark, challenged his fellow clergy with the question:

> are we half so eager to hunt for souls as we are to hunt after preferment? And here what a mean and scandalous thing it is for those who are honoured with a commission from God . . . to be dangling at the heels of a man in power for a little paltry promotion.

Even so, Newcastle's influence never remotely approached the 'absolute dominance' with which he has often been credited. He was scrupulous in respecting Lord Chancellor Hardwicke's rights in the field of parochial advowsons, and he continued to seek advice from his ecclesiastical friends over the bishoprics, deaneries and prebends which fell within his own field, as when, for instance, he consulted Bishop Secker of Oxford over the 'troublesome' case of the deanery of Christ Church in 1755, professing himself 'always . . . proud to show my regard to your Lordship personally, and to your recommendations.'[11] Although he increasingly urged on bishops and chapters his own or other lay-sponsored candidates when livings or prebends in the Church's own gift fell vacant, his excellent relations with the Church hierarchy were no more impaired by their many refusals than by their acceptances. It is surely significant that when Newcastle fell in 1762, the bishops were desolated (102).

What has been said about the relations of the episcopate with the state must in itself cast some doubt on the facile view that the Hanoverian Church suffered a prolonged crisis of leadership, lasting many decades. That doubt increases when we examine other articles of the common indictment against the bishops, for example, the charge of absenteeism and/or gross dereliction of diocesan duty. Much of the evidence brought in support of this charge has been highly selective.

That hardiest of textbook annuals, the episcopal career of Benjamin Hoadly, is a classic case in point. Hoadly was made bishop of Bangor soon after George I's accession in too-obvious recognition of his outstanding services as the leading controversialist in the Whig-Low Church cause during Anne's reign. The mistake the Whigs made was not to reward him, but to do so with a bishopric; the appointment undoubtedly became an embarrassment to the Church, compounded when, as one of the sharpest political 'pens' at Walpole's disposal, he was subsequently promoted to Hereford and Salisbury, and ultimately to Winchester. Hoadly was no mere political hack. Pope's jibe that he was one of 'Heaven's Swiss, who fight for any god, or man'[12] was nonsense. He was a sincere devotee of the causes he espoused, with a razor-sharp, if acerbic, intellect and a genuine concern with the theological and spiritual problems facing the Christian churches of his day, as his Visitation charges and works such as the *Plain Account of the . . . Lord's Supper* (1735) clearly reveal (97, *168*). What should have disqualified him from episcopal office was not the unpopularity of his extreme erastianism and theological views but the fact that he was a cripple, who could not mount a horse and who even had to preach on his knees. That said, it throws a most distorting light on the quality of the Georgian bench as a whole to recount, *ad nauseam* (and incorrectly), that in six years as bishop of Bangor Hoadly never once set foot (or chaise) in his poor, remote and mountainous see: in the first place, because in view of Hoadly's disabilities his fellow prelates formed a sort of syndicate to see that essential diocesan work that was beyond him, especially confirmations, was done on his behalf (101, *135–6, 362*); secondly, because Bangor from 1715–21 presents us with the only spectacular case of non-residence in a bishop between 1714 and 1782, when Richard Watson embarked on his extraordinary career at Llandaff, much of which he spent ruralising on the shores of Lake Windermere, mixing vigorous agricultural improvements with writing 'doughty defences of the Christian faith' (99, *509*).

In complete contrast, Sykes's definitive life of Bishop Gibson (108a) reveals a man of exceptional ability and drive, as well as scholarship; a political animal, admittedly, but above all a devoted churchman with ambitious reforming schemes, the failure of most of which was due principally to inadequate interest and support from the party he served so well (97, *192–202*). Most early- or mid-Georgian bishops who have been the subject of modern biographies emerge with credit, pastorally at least. Bennett's study of White Kennett, who was bishop of Peterborough until 1728, concludes, for instance, that 'it is difficult to see what more a bishop . . . could have done for the spiritual welfare of his diocese.'[13] Certainly, as long as Gibson reigned the Church of England could still boast its fair stock of able and energetic prelates, and not all the dedicated ones were men, like George Hooper of Bath and Wells, whose careers had been formed in an earlier and more exacting environment.[14] What is more, it was still possible in the Walpole era for a very poor man of ability to rise high within the Church. Several of the divines who achieved lawn sleeves under George I had been 'servitors' or 'poor boys' as undergraduates, among them Gibson himself and Potter. It was thanks to Gibson's personal patronage that Isaac Maddox, a former charity-school orphan, was made a bishop in 1736. It has to be said that the demands of parliamentary attendance, sometimes taking them away from their dioceses for six months in the year [E.2], put the bishops' consciences under severe strain; and there were some, inevitably, whose consciences became dulled by the political grind as well as by advancing age: Lancelot Blackburne's last ten years as archbishop of York (1733–43) were undoubtedly scandalous, especially in his neglect of ordinations (104b); but by then he was well into his eighties. Unfortunately the eighteenth-century Church had no retiring age. William Talbot had been a reasonably vigorous prelate at Oxford in Queen Anne's reign. But his nine years at Durham, to which he was promoted in his sixties, in 1721, were a disaster for some parts of his diocese – the growing port of Sunderland, for example (149).

By and large, however, the picture of the episcopate which comes across before 1740 is far from disgraceful. During the next decade it becomes more tarnished. Two ineffectual archbishops of Canterbury in succession, Potter and Herring, in the twenty years from 1737 to 1757, were less than ruinous [N.1], but not much less. Gibson had seemed for so long the obvious heir apparent to Canterbury that his abrupt removal from the fray, to devote himself to purely pastoral duties 'after a life of labour and difficulty',[15] left a huge vacuum. The credit for the promotion of Potter, after thirty humdrum years at Oxford as an academic and a bishop, was claimed (perhaps unwisely, in the event) by Lord Hervey. Months before Wake's death he had put to Walpole the pragmatic, erastian case for the elevation of a scholarly nonentity: 'Sure, Sir, . . . you have had enough of great geniuses. Why can you not take some Greek or Hebrew blockhead, that has learning enough to justify the preferment, and not sense enough to make you repent of it?'[16] Herring had at least laboured for some years before his elevation in the stony vineyard of York, and he had the qualities of an earnest and good-natured diocesan bishop. But he seems to have recommended himself largely by his success in raising large sums for the government during the 'Forty-five, and his natural timorousness and horror of innovation ('these are no times for stirs in the Church', he remarked in the calm of 1754)[17] made him even more poorly equipped than Potter for true leadership in an age of crisis for religion.

Yet Newcastle did pick some winners for the bench, even in the 1740s, '50s and early '60s. He himself, it should be remembered, was a model of piety by the standards of the eighteenth-century aristocracy and, in contrast with the vocal anti-clerical minority in his party, his intentions towards the Anglican Church were strictly honourable. His nominees included a number of men of remarkable stamina, such as Drummond of St Asaph, Salisbury and York, whose stomping of their dioceses in the summer months to confirm and ordain rivalled the feats of the most vigorous bishops of the Tillotson-Tenison era. Other Newcastle bishops, notably Trevor and Keene, proved to be munificent church builders. The mid-eighteenth-century Church never lacked its ornaments of learning, such as William Warburton, and – more to its honour – prelates who combined their erudition with true piety. Such was certainly the case with John Hume (Newcastle's spiritual mentor for many years), with Joseph Butler, and not least with

Thomas Secker, whose promotion to Canterbury in 1758, after many years in the episcopal dog-house, was as successful as it was surprising.

Two of the longest-standing misconceptions about the higher clergy of the Hanoverian Church are that most bishoprics yielded lush financial rewards, and that increasingly, as the eighteenth century wore on, the scions of wealthy families scooped most of the richest prizes in the Church hierarchy – aristocratic connection, we are told, being more important than merit in the scramble up the highest rungs of preferment. These have been shown to be half-truths, at best. Seven or eight sees were, in fact, so miserably endowed that but for the deaneries or rectories which, by convention, became attached to them *in commendam* during the eighteenth century, they would have ruined their holders [N.2]. A few sees, notably Durham, Winchester and Ely, could be made to yield great profits, but in many of the rest nominally attractive incomes were often almost wiped out by heavy and unavoidable expenses. Even at Canterbury a primate with any conscience was lucky to clear 10 per cent of his income in an average year. A mitre carried with it professional eminence and local prestige, but such was the pastoral labour involved and so heavy the outlays, not least on hospitality and charity, that financially a fat deanery was a better proposition than the average bishopric. One can only feel a pang of sympathy for the 'terrible apprehensions' experienced by George Smalridge, only recently established in the rich deanery of Christ Church, when he heard of his intended 'promotion' to Bristol, then the most beggarly of English sees.[18] As for the advantages of high social rank, it is undeniable that sprigs of the aristocracy and wealthy squirearchy were attracted into the profession in growing numbers as the century went on. But there are scores of cases to disprove the assumption that the higher the birth, the lower the sense of clerical responsibility; neither is it true that the well-born regularly leapfrogged to the highest preferment over the heads of a host of worthier men. 'The dunces of great families', as I have remarked elsewhere, 'had to be satisfied with a prosperous country living, and perhaps with a cathedral sinecure thrown in for good measure'. And even among those who were thought worthy of bishoprics, some of the best born (as Hirschberg reminds us) 'toiled till the end of their days in middling sees for (to their minds) lamentable profits' (187a, *Ch. 4, esp. p. 90*; 98, *224*).

If it is unsafe to generalise about the dignitaries of the Church, it is obviously still more difficult to do so about the parish clergy (99, *494–504*; 112, *265ff*). It would seem inherently probable that there was more negligence here, away from the spotlight, and possibly more worldliness too – if (and it was a big 'if') such a sin was affordable. Yet enough is known from those individual cases which have been chronicled[19] to persuade modern scholars that in every generation there must have been, at worst, a substantial minority of parochial clergymen whose ministries were models of conscientious duty. Well before the early Evangelical Awakening of the 1740s there were many hundreds of vigorous and caring pastors – particularly identifiable in market towns – well capable of repelling within their own parishes the national plague of falling congregations. When a visiting divine attended morning service at Thirsk in 1725 he was much struck by the very large and attentive congregation, 'much owing [he found] to the diligent and exemplary conduct of the former curate there, which seems to be well followed by the present minister, [who] . . . came hither about two years since'.[20] The inhabitants of the Pennine village of Ingleton went so far as to petition the bishop of Chester to secure a better stipend for their curate, whom the bishop himself acknowledged was 'more than ordinarily diligent in preaching and catechising and all other offices of his ministry', and of a 'life . . . so exemplary that he has won many dissenters to the Church.'[21] In some respects the tarnished image of the eighteenth-century Church of England was a reflection of the rising expectations of its early Georgian laity, encouraged by the work of the reforming prelates of the later Stuart period (187a, *Ch. 4*). Communions are a case in point. Before the Revolution monthly celebrations had been quite rare outside the fashionable parishes of London. By the 1730s they were becoming increasingly conventional in provincial towns of over 2,000 inhabitants. By mid-century that practice had in places spread wider still, as the well-documented case of East Hoathley, a small Sussex town with a rector of no very startling zeal, illustrates.[22] Negligent parsons were now, in fact, in danger of being pilloried for omitting to perform duties which would have been considered exceptional in Charles II's reign; facts sometimes cited by historians as evidence of declining clerical standards (e.g. 132, *185*) may more accurately reflect a shift in consumer priorities.

One aspect of the Church of England at the grassroots on which enough work has been done to permit some modest generalisations is the economic condition of the parish clergy, a matter which vitally affected the efficacy of their pastoral and mission work. After the early years of the century that condition improved perceptibly as a result of the distribution of 'Queen Anne's Bounty'[A]. By 1736 well over 1,100 vicarages and perpetual curacies had received payments from this fund, and they in turn triggered off many hundreds of private benefactions. The return made by the Governors of the Bounty to Parliament in 1736 still showed 5,600 out of 11,000 churches and chapels of ease with an income of under £50 a year; but because so many of the poorer livings were combined, and also because the incumbents of others augmented their incomes from various sources, ecclesiastical and non-ecclesiastical, the figure of 5,600 is a very imperfect yardstick of clerical poverty. The improvement attributable to the Bounty was important to the Church, not only in attracting better candidates into the ministry but because *some* change for the better in parochial provision was essential to clerical morale; for no bishop would have disagreed with the comment of the author of *The London Tradesman* that 'there is not a more helpless thing in nature than a poor clergyman'.[23] It has usually been argued that the passing of the Mortmain Act dealt a hard blow to this recovery. Certainly, the primary target of this mean-spirited Whig measure of 1736 was the Church's income from bequests, but Ian Green has argued that, after a short-term setback, 'the work of the Bounty was not greatly affected' (111b, *249*; cf. ibid. *231, 241–9*; 187a, *86–7*; 111a, *93–110*). Nevertheless, it was not until the parsons' tithe and glebe incomes began to profit, like landowners' incomes in general, from the growing agrarian prosperity of the second half of the century (Ch. 9) that the improvement in the economic status of the parish clergy became widespread and emphatic, at all levels except that of the clerical proletariat (110, *ch. 1*).

The exception, however, is vital. For, in spite of the Bounty, this 'proletariat' was a large and worrying one and the economic gap between it and the rest of the parish clergy widened, rather than narrowed, as time went by. The greatest bane of the Church was the position of its stipendiary curates. Thanks to the vigilance of reforming bishops such as Tenison, Burnet, Wake and Kennett, that position did improve in many dioceses, mainly in the South, between 1680 and 1730, but that was little comfort to those serving in remote and economically backward regions such as Wales and North Yorkshire, or in north-west Lancashire, where 'only six cures out of 44 were worth as much as the £20 optimistically selected by the last Parliament of Queen Anne's reign as the minimum stipend' (104b, *229*). Locked in their poverty-trap through lack of family connections, many were condemned to lurch indefinitely from one ill-rewarded post to another, picking up what scraps they could, usually village schoolmasterships, on the way, and finding even poor incumbencies always unattainable (104a, *65*; 187a, *106*). Other problems were only slightly less intractable than that of the stipendiary curates. The number of incumbencies, whether vicarages or perpetual curacies, which remained too ill-endowed to be regarded as a reasonable livelihood by themselves still ran into several thousands by 1750, despite the best efforts of the Bounty Commissioners. So pluralism remained an economic imperative for numerous parish clergy in George II's reign, as it had been at every period since the Reformation, and nowhere more so than in large tracts of the north of England where, for a variety of reasons, the average incumbent's situation was more than usually bleak. Of the 711 clergy identified in the diocese of York at the time of Herring's primary visitation in 1743, nearly half were pluralists, and only 443 of the 836 Yorkshire and Nottinghamshire parishes which submitted returns had a resident parson.[24] It would be quite wrong to assume that the unlucky parishes, here or elsewhere, were always neglected. Many were served by a full-time curate; many more, usually the smaller, contiguous livings, by vicars or curates doubling up; few, except the sparsely-populated dale or hill-country parishes, had to do without a service on a Sunday. But unquestionably, 'poverty-stricken pluralists were a poor advertisement for the Church of England' (104b, *223*); the service they were able to give their cures must often have been little more than formally adequate, and here and there the Church stood justly accused of inexcusable pastoral neglect.

The state church in Hanoverian England was not alone in having serious problems and shortcomings. The experience of the mainstream English Protestant nonconformists after 1720 – of the 'Old Dissent', as we must now begin to call it, to distinguish it from the new phenomenon of Methodism (but see also p. 123 below) – was hardly trouble-free either. The Presbyterians, the most numerous and prosperous of the sects of the post-Toleration generation, were split wide open in the next two decades by the Unitarian schism. The Quakers and the Baptists, too, began to decline in active numbers (95). Likewise the dissenters' social appeal, fairly broad-based below gentry level at the beginning of the eighteenth century, was contracting. By the 1740s the tendency for the Old Dissent to become increasingly the preserve of a comfortably-off urban middle class and of modestly-prosperous lower-middling social groups was becoming marked. Fading in many rural areas where it had once been strong, its urban redoubts were being undermined more insidiously by a failure – just as marked as that of the Established Church – to reach out to the lower orders of the growing mid-Hanoverian towns. Anglican and nonconformist ministers alike *did* succeed in keeping alive among the middle ranks – among tradesmen, professional families, urban gentry and substantial farmers – both a sense of moral rectitude (and that in an age whose standards of behaviour at times shocked even the worldly-wise) and a faith which went deeper than formal piety. Such genuine devotion, owing little to the Evangelical Revival but a good deal to middle-class women, finds no place in the stereotype accounts of eighteenth-century religion. Nevertheless, the impression persists that by 1740 or thereabouts such manifestations were in danger of becoming spiritual oases in an increasingly pagan land. In the lives of the poor, indeed in the lives of most labouring folk and artisans, in the towns at least, it is difficult to find any *general* evidence that the Christian religion was playing more than a tangential part, at best.

The Church of England was not blind to this crisis. In the three decades following the Revolution, when the Church's social conscience was at its most acute – and long before the Wesleys and Whitefield came on the scene – various long-term solutions had been explored by both clergy and laymen. One was through the setting up of charity schools, financed partly by public subscriptions and designed both to educate in basics, and to christianise, children of the poor. By 1712 lists of over 600 such schools (117 of them in London) were being published and by 1725 it was claimed the total had risen to 1,356, educating in that year alone nearly 33,000 boys and girls.[25]. By 1730 the movement was losing impetus in England (though not in Wales) but its contribution both to the wider spread of literacy and self-education and to the later success of popular evangelism has been badly underestimated (274a; 187a, *Ch. 3*). A second approach to the problem of re-christianisation had been through the setting up of one of the two great Anglican voluntary societies, founded at the turn of the century as a counterweight to the standard High Church prescription of political action as the panacea of reform (*Making of a Great Power*, Ch. 23). Whereas the Society for the Propagation of the Gospel (SPG, 1702) was formed to promote overseas missions, the Society for Promoting Christian Knowledge (SPCK, 1699) had the two-fold domestic purpose of sponsoring and coordinating the charity school movement, on the one hand, and providing and disseminating religious literature, on the other. Thirdly, Church leaders were not indifferent to social conditions, especially in the appallingly overcrowded poorer districts of London. Eighteenth-century Anglican teaching on the Christian obligation of relieving poverty, as Daniel Baugh has stressed, was unwavering (185a, *69–75*). There was also deep concern with the collapse of public morality, that 'degeneracy of manners' which was a matter of general complaint throughout George II's reign. In general the early Hanoverian bishops and City clergy favoured the Low Churchmen's voluntary approach, lending their backing, for example, to the many lay Societies for the Reformation of Manners which attempted, through private prosecutions in the civil courts, to wage war on misdemeanours ranging from prostitution to Sabbath-breaking. But they were not averse to working through Parliament if a suitable opportunity arose, as with the evil of gin-drinking which caused such alarm, especially from the 1730s.[26]

In their different ways these various endeavours did something to crack the surface of the problem, but little more than that. By 1740 the Church of England was only fractionally nearer bringing religion to the people; in fact, in some respects it was farther away from that goal than it had ever been. Its ministers may have continued to baptise, marry and bury the lower orders of English society, but only from a small minority could it claim to evoke any genuine Christian commitment. The reasons were manifold, and among them were factors not touched on so far in this chapter. For instance, the grave administrative difficulties alluded to with regard to the post-Revolution Church (*Making of a Great Power*, Ch. 23) continued to hamper an effective urban ministry. Eighteenth-century Anglicans were far more active in church building than their Stuart predecessors.[27] Yet the response to population growth was uneven and too often inadequate. In Sheffield, for instance, during the eighteenth century, while the population rose from around 5,000 to over 40,000, only two new Anglican churches were built to supplement the original parish church of Holy Trinity. One, the magnificent building of St Paul's, incredibly stood empty from 1721 to 1740, because of a dispute over the right of presentation, while the second advertised the establishment's middle-class bias by guaranteeing each of the sixty subscribers who built it both a private pew and a private burial vault as their freehold inheritance. Nevertheless, it can be strongly argued that it was more a general climate of clerical opinion than any specific weakness or abuse which placed the biggest obstacle in the path of a broader Anglican appeal.

The eighteenth-century Church of England was a church of its time: it was a church of Reason. In their conduct of services its clergy were probably 'higher', by and large, than most historians have assumed – at least under the first two Georges (112). In their *message*, however, they were exceedingly low-key. We have noted in an earlier chapter the crisis of confidence in their own mission which was induced in Anglican divines in the late seventeenth and early eighteenth centuries by the rationalist intellectual challenge (*Making of a Great Power*, Ch. 23; cf. Ch. 10). Powerful streams of thought that were essentially non-Christian or positively anti-Christian, notably the Deist stream, propelled by such bold spirits as John Toland and given renewed impetus later by Matthew Tindal, and the Unitarian stream, associated with ordained Anglicans of intellectual distinction like Whiston and Clarke [N.5], were both fed plentifully from two common sources, Sir Isaac Newton's *Principia* and John Locke's *The Reasonableness of Christianity*. So, too, were the intellectual roots of the deadliest apostle of post-Deist unbelief, David Hume, that arch-empiricist whose essay 'Of Miracles' (1748) concluded mockingly 'that the Christian religion not only was at first attended with miracles, but even at this day cannot be believed by any *reasonable* person without one.'[28] Deists and Unitarian heretics alike asserted, as Newton and Locke had done, the capacity of the human reason to comprehend all religious truths, however profound, no less than to comprehend the facts of the physical universe. Reason was thus enrolled to undermine or reject outright the established tenets of Christianity. But it was just as natural for Anglicans, like other Christians, to harness those same claims to the defence of their beliefs; for after all, Newton and Locke, as well as being intellectual giants, always regarded themselves as good Church of England men. What is more, the enormous influence which the cult of Reason came to exert over the Church long outlasted the post-Revolution generation, extending over two or even three more generations and fundamentally affecting not only Anglican theology but, increasingly, much of the practice of the established religion far into George III's reign (282; 287; 289, *279–89*; cf. 112).

Two of the earliest converts to a more rational approach to religious orthodoxy had been John Tillotson and Thomas Tenison, the first two Primates of the post-Revolution Church. Tenison personally selected most of the early Boyle Lecturers (*Making of a Great Power*, Ch. 24). But Tillotson's influence was far more lasting, because he was one of the finest preachers of the day and his sermons – which cascaded from his pen in a never-ending torrent – established themselves as models, first for the Low Church clergy of Anne's reign and later for thousands of clergy in the Hanoverian Church. Tillotson's message has often been misunderstood by historians, as it was by many of his successors, Hoadly among them.[29] He never, as is commonly averred, preached 'mere morality': he constantly stressed the all-embracing love of God, was wholly orthodox in his insistence on the Christian doctrine of salvation and advocated a 'sanctified life' as a natural fruit of Faith, never as an end in itself or even as means to a higher reward in a future life. Neither is it true that he made Reason the sole arbiter of Faith; there was, on the contrary, much that was traditional in his theology, which found room for 'revealed' as well as 'natural' religion. What stamped Tillotson as a true disciple of Newton and made him the most influential of the latitudinarians was his lack of dogmatism. In his calm and measured prose, he carefully skirted round the niceties of dogma, leaving as much latitude as possible to private judgement, trading (it has been rightly said) in reasonable probabilities rather than in certainties, advocating a Faith that would bring 'peace and tranquillity' of mind in this life as well as salvation at the end of it (287, *20–1*).

Thus it was that the Church that took Tillotson for its model, and for which Locke became almost a second Bible, came to insist in its practice as well as in its preaching on rationality and restraint, on a basic decency and seemliness. The dirtiest word in the vocabulary of orthodox eighteenth-century Anglican churchmen, the churchmen of Reason, became the word 'enthusiasm'. The Puritan radicals of the 1640s and 1650s had been 'enthusiasts'; so in their very different way had been the Sacheverells of the early 1700s, and both seemed equally repellent. It could well be argued that the prevailing rationalism which permeated so much of eighteenth-century religion, and the standard of values which it encouraged, were not without their desirable consequences for the Church – and even for the nation. They contributed to the stifling of that High Church *political* activism which had been so damaging before 1720 (*Making of a Great Power*,

Ch. 23). They equipped the Church admirably to deal with its *intellectual* critics; just how effectively was best shown during that otherwise troubled decade, the 1730s, when a broadside of theological masterpieces delivered by Butler, Berkeley and Law put the English Deists comprehensively to rout [N.5]. And they contributed also to the steady advance of practical – if not always legislative – religious tolerance under the Whig-Low Church alliance. But tragically they achieved all this at a great price. For they were equally responsible for depriving the Church at large of the main weapons in its armoury with which it could successfully have attacked mass indifference or mass unbelief. A restrained and seemly Church of Reason would never get across to the man- or woman-in-the-street, still less to the man- or woman-in-the-gutter, because they were not very reasonable beings. If they were ever to be convinced of the reality and relevance of the Christian faith for them, it could not be within the formal practice of a Church whose services – at least if they were town-dwellers – they rarely, or never, attended; nor could it be through offering them the rational expectation of being ensured, by Faith, a measure of happiness and well-being in this life which instinct and experience alike told them they could not anticipate.

What the hungry and lost sheep needed was a message of salvation, rooted in hope and directed at the heart. They might never have received that message, and indeed Christianity might conceivably have lost its hold on the bulk of Englishmen and women almost entirely before the end of the eighteenth century, but for the beginning, in the 1730s, of what we now know as 'the Evangelical Revival'.

---

1. 'Many people rarely went through a church porch between being christened and being buried', in Porter's view, though he is quick to add: 'Yet practically everyone, in his own fashion, had faith' (132), p. 184.
2. Henry Piers, *A Sermon Preached . . . at Sevenoaks* (1742), p. vii; (for Rogers), *The Weekly Miscellany*, 26 July 1740, quoted in J.D. Walsh (113b), p. 17.
3. An important study of religion in Lancashire in the late seventeenth and eighteenth centuries by Dr J. Albers awaits publication.
4. N. Sykes, 'Queen Anne and the Episcopate', *EHR*, **50** (1935).
5. Plus 49 cathedral canonries or prebends in the Crown's gift. Sir J. Fortescue, ed., *The Correspondence of King George III* (1927), I, pp. 33–44. Cf. N.4 *note*.
6. Add. MSS. 32686, f. 204: Sunderland to Newcastle, 21 Sept 1721.
7. Tory MPs alone nominated to 210 benefices during the 1740s. Colley (28a), p. 107.
8. J.P. Quinn, *et al.*, 'Yorkshiremen Go to the Polls: County Contests in the Early Eighteenth Century', *Northern History*, **21** (1985), p. 173.
9. Francis Hare, bishop of St Asaph, 1727 (transl. to Chichester, 1731) and Thomas Sherlock, bishop of Bangor, 1728 (Salisbury, 1734) were High Churchmen; Robert Butts, bishop of Norwich, 1733 (Ely, 1738), a Latitudinarian.
10. R. Sedgwick, ed., *Hervey's Memoirs* (1931), II, p. 535.
11. *The Works of the Rev. Thomas Jones* (2nd edn. 1763), p. 367; Add. MSS. 32858, f. 67: Newcastle to Secker, 6 Aug 1755; cf. ibid., ff. 108–9: Secker to Newcastle, 11 Aug.
12. J. Butt, ed., *The Poems of Alexander Pope* (1963), p. 749, quoted by J.A. Downie in J. Black (6), p. 174.
13. G. V. Bennett, *White Kennett, Bishop of Peterborough* (1957), p. 245.
14. For Hooper (d. 1727), 'ruthlessly conscientious in the spiritual functions of his office',

see W.M. Marshall, *George Hooper 1640–1727: Bishop of Bath and Wells* (Sherborne, 1976).

15. Add. MSS. 32692, f. 268: Gibson to Newcastle, 3 Sept 1739.
16. R. Sedgwick, ed., *Hervey's Memoirs*, II, p. 546 [1736].
17. Add. MSS. 35599, f. 217: Herring to Lord Hardwicke, 10 Oct 1754. 'Our present Establishment and liturgy', he added, 'is good enough for me'.
18. HMC *Portland MSS.*, V, p. 321. Smalridge would never have accepted had he known that his Tory convictions would anchor him there from 1713 until his death. Of one of his successors, Conybeare (1750–55), Secker wrote: 'I fear [he] . . . was a loser by his bishopric and hath by no means made a competent provision for his two children'. Add. MSS. 32858, f. 108.
19. For a good recent example, see *A Parson in the Vale of White Horse: George Woodward's Letters from East Hendred, 1753–1761*, ed. D. Gibson (Gloucester, 1982).
20. HMC *Portland MSS.*, VI, p. 97.
21. Bodl. Lib. MS. Tanner 152, ff. 41–2. I owe this reference to Dr. R.I. Clark.
22. HMC *Portland MSS.*, VI, p. 97; Pruett (104a), pp. 121–2, for Leicestershire in 1718; Thomas Turner, *The Diary of a Georgian Shopkeeper*, ed. G.H. Jennings (Oxford, 1979). F.C. Mather, in a most valuable study (112), has stressed the great regional variations in sacramental practice, from diocese to diocese and archdeaconry to archdeaconry, and concludes that in this respect at least there is no firm evidence of a *general* decline after 1750 (pp. 270–5).
23. R. Campbell, *The London Tradesman* (1747), p. 36.
24. Herring's visitation returns of 1743, a unique and much-quarried source, are printed in *Yorks. Arch. Soc. Trans.*, vols 71–9 *passim* (1928–31).
25. These statistics raise many problems of definition, as local studies by Joan Simon and D.H. Webster have shown, but on balance they may under-estimate the progress of the movement, as a whole, while over-estimating the part in it of the SPCK subscription schools. On this point see Holmes (187a), pp. 53–4.
26. D.W. Bahlman, *The Moral Revolution of 1688* (Yale, 1957); P. Clark, 'The "Mother Gin" Controversy in Early 18th-Century England', *TRHS* 5th ser., **38** (1988) (this interesting re-examination unfortunately ignores the House of Lords). See also above, p. 106 [on bishops' voting 1743].
27. See the valuable essay by C.W. Chalklin, 'The Financing of Church Building in the Provincial Towns of Eighteenth-Century England', in P. Clark, ed. (210), pp. 284ff.
28. D. Hume, *Enquiries concerning Human Understanding*, ed. L.A. Selby-Bigge, revised P.H. Nidditch (3rd edn., Oxford, 1975), p. 131 [my italics].
29. For a valuable reappraisal, on which what follows is largely based, see R.R.L. Emerson, 'Latitudinarianism and the English Deists' in J.A.L. Lemay, ed., *Deism, Masonry and the Enlightenment. Essays honoring Alfred Owen Aldridge* (Newark, Delaware, 1987) pp. 19–48.

CHAPTER 8

Methodism and evangelicalism: the first phase

For John Wesley, unarguably the most towering figure in Britain's eighteenth-century religious revival and not a man to sell himself short, there was never any doubt that 'God began His great work in England' on a May evening in 1738.[1] That was the evening on which he himself walked unenthusiastically along London's Aldersgate Street to attend a meeting of a Church of England religious society founded a few weeks earlier, one of many such small groups which had come together in recent years. The societies were mostly made up of young laymen, of good schooling, trying to fit themselves for discipleship in a land where Christianity had begun to seem increasingly beleaguered. Their origins can be traced back at least sixty years to the London of the 1670s and to the influence of Anthony Horneck (99, *290–3*). Originally composed mainly of superior artisans and tradesmen, with a smattering of men of professional background, they had increased in the 1680s and enjoyed a vogue in the 1690s, under the inspiration of Josiah Woodward, so that by 1701 there were already around forty of them in London and its environs, and a few others in the provinces, mainly in Oxford, Cambridge and Bristol. With their emphasis on sick- and prison-visiting, their members became noted for their social conscience as well as for self-discipline, for regular church attendance, and for their insistence on the power of private prayer and on group discussion (113a, *144–8*). Another characteristic they shared was their strict Anglicanism, with a distinct tendency towards high churchmanship; and all these features they still retained in the 1730s, when, after a period of marking time, the societies revived and began to multiply and to fan out further into the provinces in response to the bleak religious and moral climate of that decade (119, *427*; 99, *327*).

Their importance to a student of the Evangelical Revival, therefore (Methodist hagiography notwithstanding), goes well beyond the immediate and accidental context in which a Church of England clergyman had an experience in Aldersgate of profound significance for the future. Thanks in particular to John Walsh (113a), we can now see them in their own right as an important link in a complex causal chain which led to 'the Awakening'. Whatever the individual 'conversion' experiences of those involved in it, the Awakening as a national and collective phenomenon did not just happen, in a flash. It came about relatively slowly, as a result of many different impulses, and not the least of them was the influence of these little cells of young Anglicans, seeking a worthier and holier life in the 1730s with the recent publication of such works of stern piety as William Law's *Serious Call* to provide them with inspiration.[2] These society members were not only after self-improvement; they were searching for some release for pent-up aspirations and a wider battlefield than their own lives and circles on which to

117

combat evil. It was Methodism in the end that pointed most of them to that battlefield, and recruits from the Anglican religious societies, a youthful, dedicated élite already mentally committed to 'innovations in the Church',[3] proved ideal for the purpose of holding together and educating the converts captured by the emotional appeal of the popular evangelists (113a, *147–8*). When Chandler, bishop of Durham, peevishly reviled the early Methodists as a pack of 'insolent boys' (113b, *19*), he was unconsciously complimenting them on two of their greatest assets as evangelisers and critics of the existing order. George Whitefield, the most audacious of all and (like Wesley) a devotee of 'societies', was 'converted' at 20 and was a mere 22 when he first began to electrify congregations, in 1737.

In later life John Wesley looked back to Aldersgate and to 24 May 1738 as the time of his own conversion. And yet on the face of things that seems an extraordinary word to apply to Wesley. The son of the rector of Epworth, an Anglican clergyman well known in Anne's day, and bred up in a strict High Church tradition, Wesley had for 12 years prior to 1738 lived to all appearances a life of austere, selfless service: first as a Lincolnshire curate, then as an Oxford don, and finally as a New World missionary. At Oxford, for instance, when he became a tutor of Lincoln College in November 1729, he at once lent his support to a tiny group which came to be called the 'Holy Club', recently formed by his undergraduate brother, Charles. Over fifty years later he was to write[4] that 'the first rise of Methodism . . . was in November 1729, when four of us met together at Oxford'. The very word came into Oxford currency soon afterwards, applied to these young men who observed such uncharacteristic discipline or *method* in their studies, as well as in their Christian lives, and who set themselves apart by prison visiting, a spartan diet and even long hair styles. Of course, they had many mockers and critics. Yet they gained recruits, and the anonymous author of *The Oxford Methodists*, a tract published in London in 1733, ventured to suggest that these young gentlemen might in time 'be the means of reforming a vicious world; and may rejoice in the good they have done perhaps half a century after most of their social opponents, the gay scoffers of the present generation, are laid low and forgotten.' A truly remarkable prophecy!

The Holy Club, more select and rigorous than the standard religious society, provides us with a second link in the Revival chain: Whitefield and the great Yorkshire evangelist Benjamin Ingham were among its fifteen members by 1735, as well as the two Wesleys and others later to make their mark. But for John Wesley, at least, something vital was still missing. 'God deliver me from a half Christian', he wrote to his father in 1734 (119, *432*), and in his frequent moments of despondent self-examination, that is what he felt himself to be. He sought to fill the gap early in 1736 by going to Georgia as a missionary, with the 'chief motive, to which all the rest were subordinate [he frankly wrote] . . . the hope of securing my own soul'. But his two years there were, from his point of view, a failure. Despite working inhumanly hard, he only became increasingly frustrated: 'I, who went to America to convert others, was never myself converted to God'.[5] By the time he returned home in February 1738, however, another link in the chain leading to the Awakening had already been forged. The name of 'methodist' had begun to be bruited further afield through the eloquent preaching of George Whitefield.

Since leaving Oxford Whitefield had been ordained by Bishop Benson, had embraced the evangelical doctrine of justification by faith and had been taken under the wing of the most remarkable religious patroness of the century, the countess of Huntingdon.[6] Indeed he had already made a considerable stir in London, south and south-western England before he too had set out, just after Wesley had left, for America. The Gloucester innkeeper's son, drawn into the Wesley circle while a servitor at Pembroke College, Oxford (1733–6), was a speaker of such histrionic power that the greatest actor of the day, David Garrick, once told a friend he would give £1,000 to be able to utter the word 'Oh!' like Mr Whitefield. Even in 1737, Whitefield was awestruck by the huge congregation who packed London churches to hear him. 'One might, as it were, walk upon the people's heads', he wrote.[7] It was to be George Whitefield, too, as we shall see, who on his return from Georgia first brought the techniques of *popular* evangelism to England; it is as near certain as any historical speculation can be that, even if Wesley had never come back, Whitefield's dynamism would still have ensured an Evangelical Revival in eighteenth-century England. Because he was not much interested in organisation, such a revival would have lacked some of the distinguishing features of Wesleyan Methodism. Yet it is significant that a shrewd foreign observer of the volatile English religious scene in August 1739, some months after Wesley had begun field preaching, concentrates exclusively on Whitefield as the inspiration of the new phenomenon, 'Methodism'.[8]

That situation was changing dramatically, even as that observer wrote – though hardly as dramatically as the man who was then dictating events had himself changed. The eighteen months since February 1738 had transformed the disconsolate, unfulfilled John Wesley who had returned from America into a man utterly certain of his own faith and totally convinced of his destiny to set tens of thousands of others on the path to salvation. The miracle for him had begun on that May evening in Aldersgate Street, as one of the society's members was reading aloud Martin Luther's preface to the *Epistle to the Romans*. In words which even today are immensely moving in their simplicity, Wesley records how

> about a quarter before nine, while he was describing the change which God works in the heart through faith in Christ, I felt my heart strangely warmed. I felt I did trust in Christ, Christ alone for salvation; and an assurance was given me that he had taken away my sins, even *mine* . . .[9]

There is a sense in which the whole future of the Evangelical Awakening in England hinged on those words 'I felt my heart strangely warmed'. For the rest of his life, throughout a mission lasting over fifty years, Wesley, once the austere intellectual, consistently taught that true faith was a thing of the heart not of the head; that it had to be 'felt', not demonstrated to oneself or anyone else by learning, argument and logic. Rational argument could lead a man, as it had led Tillotson and hundreds of subsequent Anglican divines who inherited the legacy of Newton and Locke, to theological probabilities, but only the heart could lead him to the certainties which, as Wesley knew, every human being in his bones craves for. In a remarkable sermon on Salvation by Faith Wesley later proclaimed that the faith which brought the assurance of salvation was 'not barely a speculative, rational thing, . . . a train of ideas in the head; but also a disposition of the heart,' a disturbing message, it goes without saying, for a Church of England whose religion – as Archbishop Herring sadly conceded in 1748 – had 'lost its power over the heart' (113a, *149*; 99, *427*).

But while John Wesley had found certainty and joy himself by May 1738, it was to be almost a year before he discovered the best means of bringing the same comfort to others. Forming his own Church of England society in Fetter Lane, wrestling with the souls of condemned prisoners behind the walls of Newgate, preaching a series of passionate, uncompromising sermons from the pulpits of London churches – none of these provided the answer. The sermons only seemed to antagonise the well-to-do in the congregations he addressed. By contrast, clergymen complained, 'the people crowd so, that they block up the church';[10] and his preaching thus closed door after door behind him. After Aldersgate by far the most important step forward in 1738, for Wesley himself and for the Revival, was a visit he paid in the summer to Germany. There he learned at first hand something of the methods of that 'lovely people' (as he called them), the Moravians. They had already made their reputation overseas as the greatest Protestant missionaries of their time, and specialised in a disciplined group organisation to further their main objective nearer home, which was to revitalise the existing Protestant churches from within (95, *395–6*). Although Wesley was later to claim that there was no more to Methodism than 'Church of Englandism felt' and came before long to distrust the mystical, pietist element among the Yorkshire 'Brethren', in particular (99, *337–8*), it is impossible not to be struck by the extent of Moravian influence in the early stages of the Revival. One can detect it not merely in common methods but in the absolute commitment of the Brethren to the first of all distinguishing Protestant doctrines, that of Justification by Faith Alone. It was a doctrine still embedded, uncompromisingly enough, in the Thirty-Nine Articles, but which the Church of England, in the eyes of the early evangelicals, seemed to have long since lost sight of.

If Moravianism provides a fourth link in the chain, the fifth was undoubtedly the habit of open-air preaching, recently popularised by a small group of evangelists in Wales. Back from Germany, Wesley still clung even in the early months of 1739 to his innate sense of 'decency and order' – those quintessential virtues of the eighteenth-century Anglican clergy – and 'should have thought the saving of souls almost a sin if it had not been done in a church'.[11] It was the last obstacle to a clear sight of the way ahead, and it was removed at the end of March 1739 when he arrived in Bristol and watched Whitefield preaching with startling effect to thousands of West-Country colliers and other poor people in the open fields outside that city. After a few days of characteristic soul-searching, Wesley remembered the Sermon on the Mount and on 2 April 1739 entered in his Journal: 'at four in the afternoon, I submitted to be more vile and proclaimed in the highways the glad tidings of salvation'. Years afterwards the greatest Welsh revivalist of the day, Howell Harris, was sternly to rebuke John Wesley for monopolising the credit for the Awakening, 'whereas all know Mr Whitefield was the first field-preacher in England, and *the work was in the fields in Wales long before.'*[12] In fact, the Awakening in Wales can be traced back well before Harris himself to the itinerant, open-air preaching of the Reverend Griffith Jones in Pembrokeshire and Carmarthenshire in 1714. Although this was nipped in the bud by his bishop, and Jones went on to become more famous as the founding father of the Welsh charity school movement (274a; cf. Ch. 7 above), it pointed the way to Harris when, along with Daniel Rowland and Howell Davies, he launched the true Welsh revival in 1736–8. This revival was to lead to the foundation of 433 religious societies in Wales and the Welsh border counties before the middle of the century (95, *397*), but it was both initiated and largely sustained by itinerant preaching, and it may well be very significant, though not necessarily conclusive that George Whitefield had begun to correspond with Harris a few weeks before he himself first preached to the Kingswood miners on 17 February 1739 (113a, *135*; cf. 113b, *9*).

In the ten weeks which followed his own 'initiation' on 2 April John Wesley preached 150 open-air sermons to West-Country audiences crammed into every foot of ground, and this experience revealed a power latent in him which he had never dreamed he possessed. He found he could captivate even hard-bitten and seemingly godless colliers or weavers. He saw his prayers visibly heal and tranquillise the tormented. When he returned to London, briefly, that summer his reputation had gone before him: 12,000 flocked to hear him at Blackheath, another 15,000 on Kennington Common – gatherings surpassed only by those which had recently surged to Moorfields and elsewhere to listen to Whitefield.[13] It has been noted that throughout England the years 1738–40 saw a rash of popular disorders that was exceptional in the first half of the eighteenth century: turnpike riots, food riots, gin riots, and industrial disorders, too, especially among coal-miners and weavers (Ch. 11). They focused the attention of thinking and devout men both on the plight of the poor and on the fact that the urban poor, in particular, seemed impervious to Christian teachings concerning order and the humble acceptance of man's earthly lot. It would be stretching the evidence, perhaps, to see these disorders as yet another cause of the Evangelical Awakening, but they do offer some clue as to why, with so many diverse elements that were religious and individual in its heredity, the Revival was catalysed at this particular time. Certainly, the early sermons of both Whitefield and Wesley reflect an acute concern with the problem of poverty itself as well as the challenge of bringing salvation to the unchurched masses, and both evangelists were overjoyed when their field-preaching reached out to 'outcasts of men' and revealed what Walsh calls 'an almost untapped, apparently limitless market for the Gospel' (113b, *13–15*).

Nevertheless, as 1739 gave way to 1740, with Whitefield back in America on the second of thirteen indefatigable visits, and Wesley already a magnetic and controversial figure over much of southern England and South Wales, the latter was unequivocal in proclaiming himself no more or less than a priest of the Church of England doing his duty as he saw it. Not only then but down to the 1760s, at least, he honestly could not see that anything he was doing or preaching was inconsistent with his obligations as an ordained Anglican minister. And while of course only a minority of his fellow clergy came to agree with him, this remained his official line to the end of his life in 1791. Yet as early as 1739–40 he was already sowing the seeds of a distinctive 'Methodist' organisation; for wherever he preached and taught, he left behind him 'societies', subsequently divided into 'classes'. The classes were organised usually by lay people and financed by small subscriptions, and their vital rôle was to act both as focal points for the converts Wesley and others had gathered in and as the bases for a continuing mission in the places he had visited (115b, *65–7*).

From 1740 onwards it would be perverse not to see the Wesleys and *Wesleyan* Methodism as the spearhead of the Evangelical Revival in eighteenth-century England (though not in Wales, where there was to be another story). Things could not possibly have been the same without, for example, the incomparable hymns of Charles Wesley, 'in the first decade of the Revival . . . not a whit behind his brother and George Whitefield as an untiring evangelist' (99, *408*), but subsequently making many more converts through his genius in carrying the work forward on a tide of joyful sound.[14] Clearly, things would have been very different, too, without brother John's passion for organisation, of which the 'classes' were to be only the first revelation; without his inspired use of lay preachers; and above all without the stupendous physical energy with which, over fifty-two years, he *in person* brought Christianity to the people of England, his 250,000 miles on horseback – never less, he claimed, than 4,500 in any one year; and his 40,000 sermons. But all this and much else granted, it would be even more misleading to consider either the Wesleys or Methodism as a whole as either the beginning or the end of the Revival.

The central argument of the first half of this chapter has been that John Wesley's personal 'conversion' in 1738 and his adoption of field-preaching and group organisation was only one of the many links in a chain which led to the Revival. There were the mainstream religious societies, with their late Stuart background and High Church pedigree, and the more radical groups with which the Wesleys themselves had been associated, the Oxford 'Holy Club' and the Fetter Lane Society. There was the precedent of an indigenous Welsh revivalism, based on field-preaching, in the mid- to late-1730s, which for many years ran a criss-crossing course with the movements of Wesley and Whitefield but which produced a Calvinist brand of Methodism which the Wesleys found increasingly distasteful. There was, of course, Whitefield himself, possibly influenced by Harris, and much encouraged by Lady Huntingdon, yet contributing something that was truly innovatory, heroic and distinctive of his own. There was the very influential example of the Moravians, both in Germany and in London. Nor can we explain wholly satisfactorily how a chain became a chain reaction if we leave secular circumstances out of account – the popular unrest in the last years of the Walpole order, and the mounting concern over the irreligion of the poor.

Was there also a Puritan link in the chain? The question has much exercised students of eighteenth-century religion in England. Reference is often made to Philip Doddridge, the distinguished nonconformist minister at Northampton (1730–51) and master of the famous Northampton Academy, whose message was strongly evangelical even if his methods were traditional and socially respectable in their orientation. Through his teaching, his writing and his hymns he became a source of inspiration to many, including several Anglican bishops whom he counted among his friends (117). There are strands of evidence, however, which would seem to indicate a rather more substantial link than the influence of a few individual dissenting preachers. The early Methodist societies, especially those influenced by the Calvinistic theology of Whitefield, are known to have absorbed many migrants from dissenting congregations, for example in Newcastle on Tyne and in London, where there were complaints from the Independents, especially, that Methodism had 'devoured' some meetings almost whole.[15] Nor is it difficult to discern those qualities in the teaching and practice of Whitefield[16] and of Harris, and even of the Arminian Wesleys, that struck a responsive chord in the hearts of men and women who stood in the Puritan tradition but found the ossification and squabbling of Old Dissent in the 1730s and 1740s desperately unsatisfying.

Overwhelmingly, however, the Revival was an Anglican phenomenon. Howell Harris, like Wesley and Whitefield, remained an Anglican to his dying day. Almost from the start, moreover (though this essential point is too often lost sight of) it is possible to make a firm distinction between Methodists, of all hues, and 'Church Evangelicals'. One can identify over a score of Church of England ministers from 1740 to 1760 who raised the torch of religious revival in their own neighbourhoods quite independently of the Methodists and who never became entangled with them. Among the most influential were William Grimshaw, vicar of Haworth, Samuel Walker, rector of Truro, Thomas Jones (St Saviour's, Southwark), Henry Venn (Clapham) and William Romaine, the most dazzling Anglican preacher in London, of whom it was said that people came to town 'to see Garrick act and Romaine preach', yet that 'he never was corrupted from the simplicity which is in Christ'.[17] But there were increasing numbers of others, too, less prominent nationally but figures of consequence locally: clergymen such as Francis Okeley, Martin Madan, John Berridge in Bedfordshire, George Thompson in Cornwall, and Thomas Haweis at Oxford (99, *472–82*). Although there were one or two exceptions, notably Thompson of St Gennys, most of these divines had never even met the great itinerant evangelists when they began their own missions. Of Grimshaw it was later said (by Venn) that at the time of his conversion in 1742, he was 'an entire stranger to the people called Methodists', while John Wesley himself wrote of Romaine, an Oxford contemporary who began preaching in 1738, 'he owed me nothing . . . he was not my son in the Gospel' (113a, *137*). By 1760 it had become possible to identify, not a party, but a distinctive evangelical connexion, among the clergy of the Church of England, though this is not to say there were not some cross-currents running between them and the Methodists, for example, the squadron of private chaplains financed by the countess of Huntingdon, with their numerous chapels in which they preached the message of salvation to the well-to-do.[18]

There are three points about these early 'Church Evangelicals' which merit particular emphasis. Firstly, with only a tiny handful of exceptions, they were not itinerants but outstanding parish priests who regarded their mission as local and often went out of their way to emphasise their obedience to the existing Church order. Secondly, 'the men of note amongst them received the treasure, not from hand to hand, but by the independent study of God's word, often after years of struggle . . .'[19] Finally, until the second decade, at least, of George III's reign the Church Evangelicals constituted a tiny group numerically (even by the very end of the century, Gladstone later estimated, it was barely to account for five per cent of the entire Anglican ministry). But influence and numbers are two very different things; the conversion of John Thornton, a wealthy London merchant, in 1754 (11b [R. W. Greaves, 'Religion']) foreshadowed the vital development in the last quarter of the century, when the Church Evangelicals drew into their orbit many devotees among the educated laity, as well as among the poor and uneducated, thereby ensuring that the Revival would eventually have consequences of the utmost importance in terms of social reform and political action.

Even in the first phase of the Revival, therefore, it is clear that there were many important differences, of method and doctrine, among the evangelicals. At the same time, certain common threads did run across and through the whole Revival in its early decades. One was that it was preponderantly Anglican in origin, however orthodox or unorthodox the forms it came to take. A second was that it drew inspiration from certain common intellectual sources, in particular the works of Law. Thirdly, all evangelicals came to place their trust in the Light Within rather than in a search for truth that was rational, philosophical or historical. Many clever, learned men who had tried the latter path, the path of the Age of Reason, and found no lasting spiritual home, came to feel in the end, with the great William Law himself, confounder of the Deists, that 'the debate was equally vain on both sides' and that the only secure resting place for true faith was in the heart. Lastly, for all the revivalists, religion had to be at all costs a vital thing, speaking directly to all men and women, reclaiming them for Christ and involving them in a personal relationship with a personal Redeemer; in the words of a French observer, they spoke in their sermons 'perpetuellement de régénération intérieure, de nouvelle naissance en Jésus Christ, de mouvement de l'esprit . . .'[20] Indeed all the preaching and teaching of the evangelicals, resting as it did, first and last, on *the Gospel*, was a conscious reaction against the accepted conventions of their time; against the cold formalism of so much contemporary practice; and not least against the preaching of 'mere morality', for, as Thomas Jones of Southwark unforgettably put it in 1755, 'we have all solemnly engaged [in the 39 Articles] to preach free salvation by Jesus Christ, without man's merits or deservings . . . [yet] have preached morality so long that we have hardly any morality left'.[21]

The two final questions to be considered in this chapter relate to Methodism alone and to its relationship with the Church of England. How, in the first place, can we measure the impact of the early Methodist movement? Plotting its influence geographically and in terms of the social order is easier by far than gauging the extent of its religious and spiritual effects on the laity. Equating numbers of converts with formal membership of Methodist classes is a highly imperfect yardstick, because of what Knox called 'the constant and violent leakage in the movement' (119, *461*), and above all because of John Wesley's periodic purges of the dross (as he saw it) from his own societies.[22] The point must be made, nevertheless, that on the evidence of early membership figures it would be hard to understand how the movement came to attract all the publicity and opposition it did [N.4.]. It would seem that only a very small proportion of the masses who heard Wesley and Whitefield preach in the first years of the Awakening, let alone those who went into the fields and barns to listen to their lieutenants, subsequently committed themselves to joining a Methodist society; this is true even of the first glorious battlefield of the Revival, the West Country (113b, *11–12*). Yorkshire, too, despite the fervent activity of Benjamin Ingham, had provided Methodism with only 3,000 firm members by 1751. However, there is no doubt that Yorkshire and other parts of Northern England, especially Tyneside, together with the west and south-west of England, from Gloucestershire to Cornwall, Wales and of course London provided the most fertile ground for the Revival; conversely, Calvinist Scotland proved largely deaf to the Methodists' appeal and some large regions of England, for instance East Anglia, strangely recalcitrant. There is little question also that town-dwellers proved more susceptible than village communities (no surprise, considering the influence of the rural parish church), or that Wesleyan Methodism, apart from the initial intake of young bourgeois intellectuals and petty bourgeois (above, pp. 117–18), did have a far stronger impact on certain social and occupational groups (such as colliers, clothworkers, seamen, tinminers and their families) than on others. Maldwyn Edwards's analysis of Wesley's own mission reveals very strikingly just how much it was a mission to the poor and more particularly to the non-agricultural poor (113b, *11–12*; 114, *I, 57–9*). Its overall impact on a country much of whose population, outside London, was still domiciled in agricultural communities, even by 1750–80, was necessarily limited by this fact. It is in the light of such organisational, geographical and social circumstances that we should judge the official total membership of the Wesleyan (Arminian) Methodists, which at the first English count in 1767 was given as 25,911, and also the total for the whole of Britain in 1791 (only 72,000) [see N.4 for further comments on these figures]. 'Official' membership totals for the Wesleyan Methodists also reflected theological differences. Profound disagreements over salvation doctrine between the Whitefield-Harris stream of Calvinistic evangelicalism (and many of the Church Evangelicals, too, for that matter) and that of the Wesleys had surfaced almost from the start, though it was not until 1768–70 that the prospect of a permanent rift between the main branches of the Methodists became stark.

How did the orthodox Church of England, its bishops, its clergy and its laymen at all levels, react to the rise of Methodism? John Wesley's wish that *his* Methodists should remain within the Church of England was clear enough from his actions as well as his words. One can illustrate this in many ways: from the absolute determination of the Wesleys to keep their societies theologically in line with the accepted views of the overwhelming majority of eighteenth-century Anglican parsons and to avoid the 'excesses' of the old Calvinist doctrine of predestination (118, *41ff*); from the first set of rules which Wesley drew up for his societies in 1743, which explicitly urged attendance at parish churches, or from Wesley's extreme care, in his endless journeyings, to fix the times of his meetings so that as far as possible they would not clash with local church services. This was equally true of Whitefield. And yet the fact that by the time of John's death in 1791 the Methodists were virtually a separate body, and that well before then they had had their own ordinations, was by no means entirely the fault of the Established Church. Although most of Wesley's fellow clergy, even to begin with, may have been dubious or uneasy, they were far from uniformly hostile. Indeed, the most formidable prelate of his day, Edmund Gibson (Ch. 7), was for some years favourably disposed towards Wesley, and in the belief that he and his movement might work a great power for good in the Church, was inclined to reprove their irregularities only mildly or overlook them altogether. What made the ultimate schism so hard to avoid was not just the increasingly entrenched attitudes of the establishment but the extreme courses which Methodism was prone to follow and the unfortunate associations it took on, especially in its first decade.

So it was with the characteristic Methodist organisation: first, the societies and classes, with the encouragement they gave to lay preaching, or something close to it, by class leaders; then the annual conferences of ministers and lay preachers, starting in 1744, and finally the grouping of societies into 'circuits', initially (in 1747) only seven of them, but by 1791, 114 (115b, 67). All these things John Wesley refused to abandon. Perhaps rightly he believed them indispensable to the object of all successful evangelism, the retention of converts once made. Whitefield sadly recognised this when he said of 'brother Wesley' not long before his own death in 1770 that 'the souls that were awakened under his ministry he joined in class, and thus perceived the fruit of his labour: this I neglected, and my people are a rope of sand'.[23] Yet it is easy to see how the organisation of the Wesleyan Methodists would be very hard to absorb into the traditional hierarchical structure of the Church and how it would in itself arouse deep misgivings among many loyal Anglicans, exactly as Presbyterian organisation had done in the late sixteenth and early seventeenth centuries. Nor is it difficult to appreciate the alarm of the Anglican Church at lay preaching and itinerancy. Both struck hard at its clerical tradition; yet both were given the highest priority by Wesley virtually from the start of his mission, for he saw that without his corps of lay preachers, with their 'crude but fervent' message (113b, 9), his movement would never bridge the cultural gap between educated clerics and humble working men; and without itinerant pastors its clerical manpower would be hopelessly inadequate for a nationwide outreach.

Still more repellent to most churchmen were some of the especially flamboyant features of early Methodism, unfortunately most pronounced in the first ten years of the Revival: the stark emotional appeal of the preachers, the hysterical reactions they often provoked from their hearers, and most of all, the seething excitement which accompanied some of the great open-air meetings, which could so easily degenerate into disorders or even full-blown riots. The 1740s were littered with scenes of mob violence, much of it directed against Methodist preachers and preaching-houses by crowds hostile to innovations, enraged no doubt at fearful warnings of damnation but too often egged on by some mischievous local squire, yeoman or even parson (113c, *215ff*; 220, *30–4*). One Methodist preacher was badly injured in Yorkshire in 1741, another killed in Breconshire in 1742, and John Wesley fled from Falmouth by boat in 1745 when his lodgings were under attack. It was the threat to public order which turned Gibson irrevocably against John Wesley and Methodism in 1744–5. Wesley himself he charged with being an 'enthusiast', which for an eighteenth-century clergyman was the rough equivalent of being given the black spot in Flint's pirate crew, and this theme was soon to be taken up publicly in a number of anti-Methodist tracts, the most damaging of which was George Lavington's *The Enthusiasm of Methodists and Papists compared* (1749). Gibson concentrated most of his fire in 1744 against the practice of allowing 'itinerant preachers [to] run up and down from place to place . . . drawing after them confused multitudes of people', and he questioned whether regular church services and attendance 'did not better answer to the true ends of devotion than the sudden agonies, roarings and screamings' which the methods of the field evangelicals produced (108a, *315*).

The most significant of all the bishop's charges came with the warning that the 'same exalted strains and notions' might endanger the state 'by leading the inferiors into whose heads these notions were infused into a disesteem of their superiors' (108a, *316*). Although he did not say so openly, Gibson must have been disturbed by the fact that not only were so many of the itinerant Methodists laymen, they were laymen of humble background. He would have been still more alarmed had he known that in this very year, 1744, Wesley himself was considering 'a scheme of voluntary Christian communism', involving the pooling of incomes by Methodists of all social classes on the model of the first Christian community in Jerusalem (113b, *16–17*). Because the social and political ideology of the Methodist movement is often described as strongly conservative, and both John and Charles Wesley are rightly credited with a profound respect for established lay authority in the state, we must not assume that early Methodism had a sedative effect on the converts it claimed. Historians may or may not be right to argue that during the early Industrial Revolution the success of the Methodists in fixing the eyes of humble folk on future joys rather than present miseries may have made a significant contribution to England's avoidance of a drastic social and political upheaval. But when the first evangelical fervour was at its height it is clear that the emphasis on conversion and 'New Birth', and on the individuality of the Christian's saving relationship with God, was a potent brew for ordinary men and women to imbibe. Like early Quakerism, it was not easy to reconcile at first with traditional concepts of social obligation; later Methodism, like eighteenth- and nineteenth-century Quakerism, was a very different animal (118, *192–7*). It is crucial to remember also that the mid–1740s, when Gibson and other leading Anglicans, once cautiously benevolent towards the Methodists, hardened their attitude, saw the nadir of the Austrian Succession War and the second Jacobite Rebellion. As the Wesleys and their fellow preachers hastened to grasp the 'precious opportunity' of the 'general panic [which] ran through the nation',[24] there was a real fear abroad, among property-owning laity and clergy alike, that Methodism would loosen the bonds of social control, and therefore of political obedience.

John Wesley himself, however, was not to be deterred by the antagonism of the squirearchy or the urban patriciates any more than by the disapproval of his ecclesiastical superiors. To the argument that his itinerancy and field-preaching were poaching on his colleagues' preserves, he replied simply: 'I look upon all the world as my parish.'[25] The unanswerable argument in his eyes – the one which convinced him that his way for the Revival was the right way – was that it was the lost sheep he was gathering in. The crux of the matter he expressed in one unforgettable passage of an open letter he wrote to Gibson in 1747:

> I would fain set this point in a clear light. Here are, in and near Moorfields, ten thousand poor souls for whom Christ died, rushing headlong into Hell. Is Dr Bulkeley, the parochial minister, both willing and able to stop them? If so let it be done, and I have no place in these parts . . . But if, after all he has done . . . they are still in the broad way to destruction, let me see if God will put a word even in my mouth.[26]

The effects of the Evangelical Revival in the closing decades of pre-industrial Britain may be impossible to quantify. But one thing is beyond all question. Without the conviction and courage with which John Wesley clung to *his* way – the way of itinerant mission, open-air preaching and the gathering in of converts into organised 'regenerate groups' – the great numbers of eighteenth-century men and women whose lives were transformed, in content and direction, by the message of the diverse army of evangelists would have been fewer by many tens of thousands.

---

1. N. Curnock, ed., *The Journal of John Wesley* (1938), VI, p. 493.
2. William Law, *A Serious Call to a Devout and Holy Life* (1729) was an immensely influential book in its day, as was Law's *Practical Treatises on Christian Perfection* (1726). For Law, see also Ch. 7 above and N.5.
3. *Mr Whitefield's sermon at Bow Church before the Religious Societies* (1737), and id., *The Nature and Necessity of Society in General and of Religious Societies in Particular* (1737), quoted in Rupp, (99), p. 328.
4. J. Wesley, *A Short History of the People called Methodists* (1781), in *The Works of John Wesley* (14 vols, 1872), XIII, p. 307.
5. Curnock, *Journal of John Wesley*, I, p. 422: 1 Feb. 1738
6. H. Venn, *The Treasure in Earthen Vessels* (1857), p. 23. For Selina Hastings, countess of Huntingdon (1707–91), see Knox (119), pp. 482–9.
7. *The Journals of George Whitefield* (repr. 1960), p. 88.
8. I am grateful to Dr Jeremy Black for a transcript of 'Sur M. Whitefield et les Methodistes d'Angleterre', an anonymous MS account which he discovered in the Quai d'Orsay, Paris: Archives du Ministère des Affaires Etrangères, Memoires et Documents, Angleterre, vol. 8, ff. 209–12.
9. Curnock, *Journal of John Wesley*, I, pp. 475–6: 24 May 1738.
10. J. Wesley, *A Short History*, in *Works*, XIII, p. 307.
11. Curnock, *Journal of John Wesley*, II, p. 167.
12. T. Beynon, ed., *Howell Harris's Visits to London* (1960), quoted in Walsh (113a), p. 134.

13. *The Journals of George Whitefield*, p. 262: 5–6 May 1739.
14. For the extraordinary influence of 'our hymns' (in themselves a rich fund of source material about the first decades of the Revival), see Rupp (99), pp. 409–16; Armstrong (115b), pp. 66–70.
15. *The Causes and Reasons of the Present Declension among the Congregational Churches* (London, 1766), p. 9, quoted in Walsh (113b), p. 7.
16. For Whitefield's many close contacts with the evangelical leaders of the North American Puritan revival, see Watts (95), pp. 394–5, 399.
17. S. Andrews, (115a), p. 67; H. Venn, *The Treasure in Earthen Vessels*, (1857), p. 23.
18. This current was eventually blocked by the secession of the Huntingdon 'connexion' from the Church of England, 1777–83.
19. Venn, *The Treasure,* p. 14.
20. 'Sur M. Whitefield et les Methodistes' (Aug 1739), see n. 8 above.
21. *The Works of the Rev. Thomas Jones* (2nd edn, London, 1763), p. 362.
22. In 1747, for example, on a visit to Gateshead he expelled half of the 800 members of the town's Methodist society there for 'walking disorderly'.
23. W. Sargant, *Battle for the Mind* (1959), p. 197, quoted in Watts (95), p. 404.
24. J. Wesley, *Short History* (1781), in *Works*, XIII, p. 315 (see above, note 4).
25. F. Baker, ed., *The Letters of John Wesley, I: 1721–39* (Oxford, 1980), p. 616: to [?Revd. John Clayton, ?28 Mar 1739].
26. J. Wesley, *A Letter to the Right Reverend the Lord Bishop of London* (1747).

PART TWO

Britain in the eighteenth century

Society and the economy in the eighteenth-century: I – Population and the land, *c*. 1720–*c*. 1780

By the end of the Walpole era Britain was already the richest country in the world *per capita* of her population. Rising agricultural productivity was one cast-iron guarantee that she would grow even wealthier in the last few decades that remained before her Industrial Revolution. The first British Empire, whose accumulation was completed by 1763 (Ch. 16) was another. From the mid–1740s through to the mid–1770s, when Britain – on the very threshold of her first industrial century – was embroiled in the revolt of her American colonies, trade and empire brought bigger profits than ever before into the pockets of the most affluent trading class in Europe. At the same time they continued to pump the life-blood of capital into many industries and to enrich scores of manufacturers, while the two big mid-century wars which secured them gave a fresh boost to the influence of the City of London.

However, as the rich got richer, and as new fortunes were made, so the gap between the 'haves' of Britain's eighteenth-century society and its 'have nots' began to widen in the last few decades of the pre-industrial period. And even before the pace of industrialisation started to gather, the lower storeys of the social fabric (notably stress-free, as we have seen, in the early 1700s) began to look less secure than at any time since the 1650s. In Chapters 9–11, therefore, which offer an overview of British society and the British economy between 1722 and 1783, one central theme will be the antithesis between growing wealth and growing relative poverty and deprivation in the sixty years from the early 1720s, and in particular after 1763. And in Chapter 12 manifestations of a growing social protest by the eighteenth-century poor will be assessed in the wider context of civil disorder and of the reactions of the state and the governing class towards it.

In spite of a rising birth-rate the years of Walpole's supremacy were a period when the recovery of Britain's population from the setbacks of the late seventeenth century was brusquely checked by a resurgence of both epidemic and endemic diseases (*Making of a Great Power*, Ch. 19). By 1741, if we rely on the 'back projection' data of the Cambridge Group (ibid. Ch. 2), the population of England and Wales was still only in the region of 5.96 millions, a mere 220,000 more than in 1721. That of Scotland was probably less than 1.20 millions [B.1, B.3 (ii)][1] Some historians of the Industrial Revolution have seen the remarkable expansion of the domestic consumer market, and therefore a rapidly rising population, as the principal stimulus prompting British manufacturers to achieve strikingly new levels of production and inventiveness late in the century. If we accept their arguments, it is hard to avoid the conclusion that a series of demographic freaks, producing exceptionally high mortality from time to time between 1719 and 1742, set back by some two decades the arrival of the point at which Britain was launched into unprecedented and sustained economic growth. In the event that point was reached, not in the 1760s but (by fairly common consent among those historians who accept that there was such a 'lift-off') in the course of the 1780s.

It was in the mid-1740s that England's population growth began for the first time to achieve an unstoppable momentum.[2] The pace of the advance until 1785, or thereabouts, was steady but none the less remorseless [B.1]. In the fifteen years from 1744 to 1759, despite a fall in births during the Seven Years War when more young Britons were under arms than ever before, England and Wales together acquired over half a million extra inhabitants. After 1783 the rate of growth quickened appreciably, though not quite as quickly as the first official (but defective) Census returns of 1801 suggest. It was 'only in the last 15 years of the eighteenth century that the rate of population growth equalled and then exceeded late-sixteenth-century levels' (152, *212*). The figures for Scotland, such as they are, are less spectacular but still significant [B.3(ii)]. They represent, on the most conservative estimate, an increase of just over 25 per cent in the 46 years down to 1801, compared with over 40 per cent in England and Wales.

There is an obvious risk of trivialising a complex debate by attempting to offer simple explanations for these trends. But it can at least be said with certainty that earlier marriage led to a decisive increase in fertility during the last six decades of the century, and that this was particularly so in those areas, such as South Lancashire, South and West Yorkshire and the central belt of Scotland, where industry and trade were already flourishing before 1750, and where local habits had traditionally differed from national norms. At the same time the death rate declined. The decline was not so marked as to justify regarding it, as historians were often prone to do, as the dominant factor in the growth of 1744–84, but it was far from negligible.[3] Improved living standards, especially among the poorer 50 per cent of English and Scottish families, a better diet, and therefore higher resistance to infection, must have played their part in the fall. But so did the changing pattern of disease itself after 1742 [see B.4]. Professor Smout has written of eighteenth-century Scotland that 'to some extent . . . [she] was fortunate in her epidemiological history' (241, *271*). And it was only in fourteen mostly isolated months between 1744 and 1784 that England was hit by national epidemics of 'crisis' scale.[4] There had been twenty-four such months in the years 1727–30 alone, more horrendous even than the 15 recorded in the three years from 1679 to 1681. Nor was it only epidemic diseases that were losing some of their power to ravage after the early 1740s. Most of the regular child-killers of the past, such as measles and chicken-pox and diphtheria, remained dangerous, but by the middle of George III's reign the battle against smallpox, the biggest endemic scourge in early Hanoverian Britain, was slowly being won both south and north of the Scottish border (122, *52–3*; 131b, *167–73*; 152, *338–9, 533–4*; 241, *266–79*; 151a, *24–50*).

Looking back towards the Restoration era from the early 1780s, it is clear in the light of modern research that however much Britain's pre-industrial society changed over that period, its demographic framework did not expand materially until the final forty years. There is no identi-kit model which can be conveniently used to describe and explain that framework adequately in both England and Scotland. However, the minimal overall growth of the population of Britain between 1660 and the early 1740s – the product in England of a combination of late marriage and low fertility with periodically savage epidemic mortality, and in Scotland of a famine of Malthusian horror (*Making of a Great Power*, Chs. 2, 19) – produced effects in terms of social change and economic progress that over much of Britain were similar in all except timing. It constricted the labour market, with knock-on effects on wages, prices and living standards; it put pressures on landowners and farmers, from the Scottish Lowlands southwards, to improve agricultural methods and to farm for the market, and it provided incentives to manufacturers and traders to seek out new and profitable outlets overseas. The second common demographic experience of fundamental import-ance to Britain as a whole was the renewal of sustained population growth, which had begun before the middle of the century and which by 1783 was about to surge upwards dramatically. Some of the earliest consequences of this experience, for society and the economy, we shall notice later in this chapter and in the chapter which follows.

These consequences can be better understood by appreciating that a most important effect of the demographic trends of the period 1660–1783 was the changes which they, their regional variations and their economic repercussions had wrought during that period in the distribution of Britain's population (cf. ibid., Ch. 2, p. 48). For one thing, they brought about a further reduction of the imbalance of population between countryside and town, a matter to be explored in Chapter 10. But they also produced a redistribution of people between the regions of Britain, a change which had gone a long way by the eve of the Industrial Revolution. Thus Central Scotland, from Ayrshire and Dunbar-tonshire in the west to the Lothians and northward to Dundee in the east, was already gaining population relentlessly at the expense of the north (241, *261, Table I*). In England, the prominence of the South-West and of East Anglia, with Essex, as prime areas of habitation under the later Stuarts, was fading by the 1780s, in spite of the growth of Bristol and a substantial London overspill into Essex, and this was a relative decline that can firmly be linked with the dwindling fortunes of their once-proud cloth industries. The south-east corner of England, including London, had also increased its population in absolute, while declining in relative, terms. The gainers were the very areas which were to push forward even more rapidly as industrialisation gathered speed from the late eighteenth century onwards: the West Riding of Yorkshire, south Lancashire and the West Midlands, above all; and to a lesser extent the North-East of England, West Cumberland, the North and East Midlands and South Wales (but cf. 140, *191*).

By 1783, however, the economic changes which these population shifts reflected, portentous though many of them were, had barely demolished the outworks of that massive bastion of a land-dominated society which pre-industrial Britons had always taken as read. Gregory King had calculated that in 1688 almost 70 per cent of the wealth of England and Wales was land-based or soil-rooted [see B.5]. Without giving unmerited credence either to his figures or to those of his mid- and late-Hanoverian imitators, we can be quite certain that this proportion had shrunk somewhat by the early 1780s: a reasonable estimate[5] would be that by then it was nearer to 60 per cent. But partly because of the continuing, if declining, tendency – especially in the flourishing textile or metal-working regions of the North and Midlands – for families to combine the keeping of a smallholding with weaving, nailing, mining or other industrial occupations (e.g. 145a, *62, 65–6;* 142a, *179*), the pattern of employment remained one in which a great majority of Englishmen earned their livelihoods wholly or in part from agriculture. And notwithstanding the striking expansion of the merchant community and the professions, the vast increase of investment in 'the Funds', and the steady growth of industrial capital and labour between 1690 and 1780, most of the very richest men in the country on the eve of the Industrial Revolution, as in 1690, were still landowners *per se.*

Within the landed sector as a whole, however, some very significant changes had taken place since the 1680s. To begin with, the butter was less evenly spread among owners of land than in the late seventeenth century. Appreciably more of the acreage of England, and probably a more than corresponding share of its landed income, was by 1780 concentrated in the hands of an upper crust of great proprietors, whose numbers could be counted in hundreds rather than in thousands. Changes in the pattern of English landownership in the late seventeenth and early eighteenth centuries have often been attributed (by Sir John Habakkuk, for example) to a combination of special factors (see *Making of a Great Power*, Ch. 18, esp. pp. 280–4). Recent economic historians have viewed with scepticism the effects of certain of these phenomena, and serious reservations have been expressed both about constructing a nationwide stereotype on the basis of them and about over-dramatising one relatively brief period in the course of a long march towards landed oligopoly which probably lasted well over two centuries (201a; 199b; 183). Nevertheless, in most counties which already had a powerfully-established *resident* aristocracy, especially those in a belt between the North and East Midlands and the Thames Valley, the tendency of great estates to grow larger at the expense of smaller properties in late Stuart and early Hanoverian England was quite strongly marked. Likewise it seems difficult to contest that several of the special circumstances to which Habakkuk has drawn attention, such as high direct taxation of land in counties whose estates were realistically assessed or increased opportunities for profitable office-holding, did weight the scales – other things being equal – in favour of 'great lords'.[6] Just as the influence of some developments prior to the 1720s, for instance strict settlement of estates, has been exaggerated as a prime cause of estate aggrandisement, so that of more traditional advantages, such as shrewd estate stewardship and improvement, favourable marriages and fortunate inheritances, has sometimes been underplayed. Nevertheless, carefully re-assessed, the same factors which help to explain the shorter-term, and almost certainly more localised redistribution of land which marked the period of the wars against Louis XIV (194a; 194b; 22), can also tell us much of value about the longer-term, and ultimately more general tilting of the balance in favour of a landowning élite over the whole century from 1680 to 1780.

What they cannot do is wholly account for the persistence of that process almost right through the eighteenth century; for it is clear that the land tax became increasingly fossilised as the century wore on,[7] so that even by the war years of 1739–48 the number of estates which had been put up for sale to ease the embarrassments of overtaxed squires or yeomen and were then gobbled up by great magnates was minimal. Demographic factors were a different matter, certainly more influential than taxation in the process whereby landed wealth continued to be concentrated in fewer hands down to the 1780s, and individual landed fortunes larger than ever before accrued in the process. The exceptionally low fertility of English and Welsh gentry families in the century from 1650 to 1750 led to countless failures of male heirs. It is possible that never before in English history had so much land descended through the female line. This happened to twenty-six out of forty traceable Glamorgan gentry families which died out in the first sixty years or so of the eighteenth century. Not all the land descending to heiresses passed to wealthy aristocrats, of course, but the likelihood is that enough did so (as in Glamorgan) to be of appreciable importance over the century as a whole.[8] We are on even firmer ground with the state of agriculture, the most intelligible single key to long-term shifts in landownership. First, English arable farmers experienced between 1730 and 1750 so many years of plenty that the growers of grain, especially, suffered a crisis of over-production and low prices [K.2]. Modern historians have often labelled this period as one of 'Agricultural Depression'; although, because pastoral farming regions kept largely free of serious problems until the great cattle plague hit England in the late 1740s, the term can be misleading (179a; 180, *41–2*; but cf. 179b). Secondly, this cheap-grain period was swiftly followed by a spectacular upsurge of virtually the whole agrarian economy of England and Wales, which for thirty years after 1750, despite intermittent checks, was still in spate. Both phases worked in favour of the big proprietors, provided they had the prudence to eschew the more lunatic extravagances and the good fortune to escape the worst family disasters.

As the 1680s and 90s had already shown, periods of unusual difficulty for tenants and small owners, whether caused by glut or by crop failures, put an extra high premium on large capital resources, good professional management and the capacity to combine immediate assistance to struggling tenants with improvements and innovations that would be of lasting value. It is significant, for instance, that the biggest enclosure of the eighteenth century on the Leveson Gower estates in Staffordshire and Shropshire took place from 1733–6, and that it probably cost Lord Gower £2,000 – a whole year's income for a very well-to-do squire.[9] Furthermore, with those landowners already in possession of tens of thousands of far-flung acres before the onset of a period of depressed prices and falling rent returns there was always a strong likelihood that losses from one area could be more than counterbalanced by gains from others; it must be emphasised that right through the first half of the eighteenth century – including the years from 1730–50 which ended with record grain exports to the Continent – agricultural output in England and Wales remained strikingly buoyant, reflecting the cumulative advances in productivity and techniques which had begun in the mid-seventeenth century (131b, *13, 17*; 121, *Tables, 118–9*; 176b; 122, *134–5*. See also *Making of a Great Power*, Ch. 2; sources for K.2(i)). Moreover, great landlords disposed to buy in the 1730s and 40s could do so with little fear of competition from well-heeled urban parvenus, for men who had rushed into the market in the years following the South Sea crisis were more selective in a period when land seemed a doubtful bargain economically. When the boom years for agriculture eventually arrived, and then resumed after a temporary interruption for part of the 1760s, the conditions they created pushed up the profits or rental incomes of the great majority of landowners, great and small, more steeply than for generations. If, as seems likely, even well-run yeomen farms increased their profitability by an average of 40–50 per cent between 1750 and 1790, it is not surprising that for many of the very biggest fish in the landed pool these same years saw the achievement of levels of wealth without precedent.

Hence the situation reached by 1790, when contemporary estimates of varying reliability suggest that England by then had an élite of some 400 great landowning families, nobles and commoners, whose incomes ranged from £5,000 to £50,000 a year (197a, *25–6*). It will put these figures in perspective if we recall that the £5,000 which is taken to separate this élite from the 'wealthy gentry', was 80 per cent higher than Gregory King's (admittedly ultra-conservative) estimate for the average income of the 160 peers alone in 1688 [B.5; cf. *Making of a Great Power*, Ch. 4]. Side by side with this may be set the hypothesis put forward by Michael Thompson, speculatively but in conformity with some known trends, that the proportion of the whole acreage of cultivated land in England which was held by 'great landlords' had risen from between 15 and 20 per cent in 1688 to between 20 and 25 per cent in 1790 (183). The process was still, to a marked degree, localised: Devonshire, Cumbria, much of Wales, the North East and the Lindsey division of Lincolnshire being only some of the areas where the gentry profile was just about as high in 1780 as it had been in 1660, and that of the 'great lords' proportionately low (199a; 149; 204b), but that a restructuring did take place can hardly be questioned.

As we know, it can no longer be readily assumed that even in the decades of high taxation before 1720 the lesser gentry were necessarily the chief sufferers from the territorial aggrandisements of their wealthier neighbours. Even in the hard-hit South East the many families which then fell by the wayside were often replenished by other families, often from urban backgrounds, whose arrival did not radically change the basic social and estate structure in their counties (cf. *Making of a Great Power*, Ch. 18). That the redistribution of land in favour of the great owners was achieved mainly through a squeeze on small owners, families with no pretence to even minor gentility, becomes clearer still if we look at the whole century from 1680 to 1780. Over the long haul the shrinkage in the proportion of the country's acreage directly owned and farmed by the yeomen freeholders (or as some historians prefer it, by the 'owner occupiers' or 'peasant proprietors') was big enough to change the social topography of rural England.

To try to quantify the change involves a lot of guesswork. In 1966 Thompson floated the suggestion that the class which was traditionally the backbone of English agrarian society, having owned roughly a third of all cultivated land in 1688, only enjoyed about a fifth a century later. Beckett, for one, has found figures of this scale too dramatic, and indeed Thompson's own subsequent thoughts have been far more cautious (183, *513*; 199b, *16*; 206, *46–7*). Nevertheless, the argument advanced as long ago as 1909 by A.H. Johnson in *The Disappearance of the Small Landowner*, that the years 1688–1785 were probably the most fatal ones since the Middle Ages, has received such broad support from modern authorities that its essence seems unassailable.

There remains, none the less, a need to get the late seventeenth and eighteenth centuries in perspective by thinking of the erosion of the peasant proprietor class as an extremely protracted process, already under way in the sixteenth century (cf. *Making of a Great Power*, Ch. 4) and still a matter for periodic anxiety and enquiry in Victorian and Edwardian England. Furthermore, even in the most damaging years of the eighteenth century for the landowning yeomanry nationally they continued to enjoy far better fortune in some areas than in others. A case in point is the North-West of England, where Marshall's analysis of inventories has uncovered something suspiciously like a golden age for the 'statesmen' farmers of Cumbria (200). Like most of the other counties or areas where either contemporary observers or modern researchers confirm the survival of small landowners in strength down to the end of the eighteenth century – for example, Wales, Lancashire, Devon, Kent, Essex and Northumberland – Cumbria was a region whose farmers were engaged far more in sheep or cattle rearing than in grain-growing. It was also (though in this respect it was unlike Kent and Essex) lightly taxed. Finally, even in arable areas a vital distinction must be drawn between the substantial freeholders, often 20–30 per cent of the whole, who in general maintained their numbers and often increased their incomes, and the bulk of the small owner-occupiers, always far more vulnerable.

So far our concern has been with the *ownership* of land between the late seventeenth and late eighteenth centuries. Going on to enquire, who farmed the land, and how, the picture that emerges is again one of long-term changes of great moment, but changes which left quite large oases of stability little disturbed. Although the aristocracy and the greater squirearchy bought so much land in the eighteenth century, a surprising amount of it in small lots to assuage their passion for 'consolidation' or rounding off their estates, they farmed relatively little land directly, through their own managers and employees. Histories of the Agricultural Revolution are ritually studded with the names of a few celebrated experimenters and improvers among the owners of great patrimonies: Viscount Townshend in Norfolk; the Cokes of Holkham, culminating in the well-publicised activities of Thomas William (1752–1842), later earl of Leicester; the dukes of Bedford at Woburn Abbey; the first marquess of Rockingham in Yorkshire. Especially later in the century, when King George III gave a fashionable lead, such landlordism became highly prestigious. As a matter of sober fact, however, the home farms of most members of the landed élite rarely catered for more than the needs of their own families and servants, only a small proportion produced appreciably for the market, and their farming practices were at least as likely to be conservative as progressive (202a, *Ch. 5*; 197a, *163–71*). The needs of the market in the 1780s were still overwhelmingly met by the same two types of farmers who had catered for them after the Restoration, but in different ratio. Although the more prosperous and viable of the freeholding yeomanry, through buying up large numbers of small holdings as they came up for sale, now had much more expensive and efficient farms than their fathers and grandfathers, it is doubtful whether their class as a whole retained and farmed more than a quarter of the land of England and Wales in 1780. The remaining three-quarters or more, owned by the gentry and aristocracy, was for the most part cultivated by tenant farmers.

The amount of tenant farming increased very significantly during the eight-eenth century, and so too did the size of many tenanted farms. The latter was far from being a blanket development, and there were still numerous parts of the country, particularly in pastoral regions or where farming was combined with industry, where the small tenanted farm survived with notable resilience. In the northern Vale of York and other parts of the North Riding of Yorkshire, for instance, 30 acres represented a large holding, while in the West Riding 20-acre farms were commonplace throughout the century (141, *191*). All the same, most English counties, at least outside the north and the far west and south-west, contained by 1780 substantially more medium-sized and large holdings (80–300 acres) than they had in 1680 or even in 1720. What happened on the Leveson Gower lands in Shropshire and Staffordshire, where only 26 per cent of farms were of 20–100 acres in the years 1759–79, compared with 46 per cent from 1714–20 and where the *average* farm size had risen to well over 100 acres, was probably not untypical of the best-run estates in the rich arable and mixed farming regions of England.[10] In tenant farms, as at every level of landed society, the general tendency was towards greater size and greater resources, and therefore towards an improved capacity to survive bad years and to exact maximum profit from good ones. A good deal of the 44 per cent increase in productivity *per acre* which agricultural England (it is estimated) (135 [E.L. Jones, 'Agriculture 1700–80'], *70*) achieved between 1700 and 1800 was the work of tenant farmers [cf. K.2(i)].

This same propensity throughout the rural economy, reflected among other ways in the atrophy or disappearance of many of the more parochial local markets (172, *Pt. ii, 409–15* [J.A. Chartres. 'Marketing']), undoubtedly maintained the gathering momentum of the Agricultural Revolution, built up by the rapidly rising population, over the second half of the eighteenth century. The two best-known agricultural propagandists of George III's reign, Arthur Young and William Marshall, agreed with the greatest of contemporary economists, Adam Smith, that it was the biggest and best tenant farmers, along with the cream of the substantial freeholders and a progressive section of the gentry, who were in the vanguard of technical and horticultural advance in George III's reign – as they had been, in rather different proportions, under the later Stuarts. Although he and everyone recognised that there were notable exceptions, Adam Smith wrote categorically that the great proprietors were 'seldom great improvers'. Sir

Christopher Sykes and Sir Digby Legard, who did much to reclaim the Yorkshire Wolds by injections of capital and by advanced husbandry, were members of the well-to-do East Riding squirearchy, the former with a long tradition of Hull mercantile enterprise behind him. The 'gentlemen farmers' of the mid- and late eighteenth century on the whole became best known for their breeding experiments, improving the size and weight of livestock. Their star was Robert Bakewell (b. 1725), one of the gentrified Leicestershire graziers for which, as Defoe had noted in Anne's reign (2, *II, 89*), that county was famous. Bakewell produced new breeds of sheep and oxen that were soon in great demand and hired out his rams at astronomical prices (131b, *71*); but among his East Midland neighbours he was but *primus inter pares*. Equally successful, a grade down the social scale, were the Colling brothers, the developers later in the century of the Durham shorthorn cattle: they were admirable representatives of that 'superior class of yeomanry' which Marshall extolled.

An interesting example of cooperation between squire and yeoman produced the popular Rotherham plough, patented in 1730 by Staniforth and Foljambe, and the future model for many of the horse-drawn metal ploughs of the eighteenth century. But in general the agrarian improvements of the pre–1780s cannot remotely be characterised as an implement-led revolution. Jethro Tull's development of horse-hoeing and horse-harrowing in the 1720s and 1730s was as slow to spread initially as his earlier seed 'drill' had been (*Making of a Great Power*, Ch. 19), although by this time 'drilling' was being enthusiastically practised on progressive estates (141, *190*; 173, *581–6*). Metal implements of any sophistication were to be far beyond the pockets of ordinary farmers until industrialisation enabled them to be produced cheaply in the early nineteenth century. Even in farming practice the years 1720–80 were not ones marked by spectacular innovation. Far more influential in making possible the rapid growth of productivity in that period was the wider diffusion of the new crops, grasses and clovers, systems of rotation and methods of fertilisation which had been pioneered under the Later Stuarts (*Making of a Great Power*, Ch. 2). The tide of change moved slowly and jerkily, mostly from the light-soiled east to the west, across England, and in spite of the efforts of two more generations of agricultural publicists in the Houghton tradition, formidable barriers of inertia and conservatism still remained well into George III's reign, especially where small farms abounded and colder, wetter climates prevailed. The turnip is not heard of in Cumbria before the 1750s, and even wheels were still a rarity on Devonshire farms as late as 1790. Where the barriers were broken down, it was enclosure, as often as not, which proved the most powerful engine of destruction and of subsequent change, as it was of increasing landed wealth (p. 143 below).

Even though the majority of big landowners were not great innovators on their home farms, they did make an unsung but essential indirect contribution to the agricultural advances of the eighteenth century. With many of them it became a matter of policy to instruct their stewards, when negotiating agreements with tenant farmers, to stipulate how their land should be farmed. Thus estate policy combined with a growth in both the number and average size of tenant farms to accelerate the pace of agrarian change. By the 1780s England and Wales possessed the most efficient agrarian system in Europe, a profit-based system that had become more and more market-conscious with every decade since 1740, the main stimulus for this being a swiftly-expanding domestic market for food.

It has frequently been urged, however, that the price paid for this progress was a heavy one, and that it was paid preponderantly by the one sector in rural society whose fortunes under the first three Georges we have not as yet touched on – the landless agricultural labourers and the smallholding cottagers. How true is it, therefore, that a great and ever-growing rural poverty trap already existed at the bottom of the structure of landed society in the last fifty–sixty years of pre-industrial England?

First the problem must be reduced to scale. However severe was the pressure on small landowners throughout most of our period to give up the unequal struggle to keep status and to sell out to more prosperous neighbours, it is anachronistic to think in terms of a vast agricultural proletariat already in existence by 1783. As late as the census of 1831 there were still less than 700,000 families of agricultural labourers, a proportion of five labouring families to every two which owned or occupied land. At the end of the seventeenth century the proportion may have been roughly three and a half to two, so the change by 1780 was not cataclysmic but rather one of natural progression. The demand for labour in the eighteenth century was never clamorous. In most pastoral areas the family alone was normally adequate for working the average farm. Even on arable farms, and where acreages were growing, contemporaries observed that a farmer with two teenage or grown-up sons could usually cope with 80 or 90 acres, except at sowing and harvest time when casual labour would be needed, and that a farm as large as 300 acres could be worked with a maximum of five extra hands.

The number of permanent wage-earners on the land in the 1780s, therefore, was probably well under half a million, and there are several good reasons why one should be wary of generalising about their lot. For one thing, there was no such thing as a 'standard' agricultural wage at this time. There were 'high wage' and 'low wage' areas, with the wages of farm labourers undoubtedly benefiting in parts of the North and the Midlands simply from the presence in the neighbourhood of growing towns or manufacturing villages competing with the farmers for labour. Generally speaking, therefore, there was more privation among the rural lower orders of the South of England than in the North, even before the onset of sustained industrialisation, for, quite apart from lack of alternative employment, prices were distinctly higher, year in, year out, in the South (where, in addition, the custom of eating relatively expensive wheaten bread was firmly established long before the mid-eighteenth century). Secondly, despite the fall in real wages which began in 1764, after decades of cheap grain [M.2], the distress caused among agricultural labourers, even in the South, was slight by comparison with the twenty-five years before 1820 when the price of white bread doubled and labourers' wages increased by only 12 per cent. Thirdly, all generalisations about rural poverty must take account of an internal demarcation among the wage-earners, that which divided the relatively privileged 'farm-servants' from the 'day-labourers': the skilled men who were generally hired and paid by the *year*, who 'lived in' with their masters and received their board as a supplement to wages, from those who lived in their own cottages, were normally hired for much shorter periods, and being paid by the *day*, were always vulnerable to being arbitrarily laid off. Except at hay-time and harvest, day-labourers rarely earned more than 6s. [30p.] a week in the middle decades of the century.

Gregory King had surmised that at the bottom of the social heap in 1688 there were 400,000 families of 'cottagers and paupers'. A century later the 'cottager' had by no means disappeared. The numbers of men who occupied a country cottage with a small parcel of cultivable land attached to it, and who subsisted with the aid of casual agricultural labour, family by-employment (for example, their wives' spinning) and the pasturing of a few beasts on common land, were certainly declining, but hardly so much as to justify Massie in 1760 ignoring them almost completely [B.5]. In the favourable conditions of 1730–50 their standard of living had risen; in common with the average farm labourer, they were not only better fed and clothed than their Continental peasant counterparts (as foreigners continued to observe) but better housed. By the 1760s, however, with prices rising and larger families to feed, their brief idyll, like that of the day labourers, was over. It was at this very time of vulnerability that cottagers in many parts of the East and South Midlands, Norfolk, Yorkshire and Lancashire were hit by a renewed burst of enclosure activity which forced thousands to accept unqualified labourer status. These were the cottagers whose families had acquired the customary use of common land over several generations but who had no title to it in law, and their fragile claims were swept aside by a spate of new Enclosure Acts, pushed through Parliament by profit-conscious landlords, stimulated particularly by rising grain prices. Acts of Parliament, of course, tell us only part of the enclosure story. Throughout the eighteenth century both the enclosing of open arable fields and the enclosing of commons and wastes[11] were regularly carried out by local *diktat* or agreement, just as they had been in the seventeenth century (*Making of a Great Power*, Ch. 2, pp. 49–50) (178b). But the rate of increase in enclosures by parliamentary means after 1760 was dramatic [K.3(i)], and we may take it as an index of the growing determination of landowners, regardless of expense, to seek the surest way of overriding all opposition to agrarian improvement. There is little evidence that the enclosures of the mid- and late eighteenth century drove families off the land; indeed the thousands of fresh acres they brought under the plough boosted the demand for labour. On the other hand there is ample evidence that enclosures helped significantly to increase both the numbers and the poverty of the propertyless rural poor.

As farmers grew in prosperity after 1760, so the social gap, as well as the gap in living standards between them and the wage labourers and cottagers in the more fertile regions of England widened appreciably. This was true even of the in-servants; in fact, the practice of living-in itself, though eroded only slowly until the inflationary 1790s, was more and more frowned on by those 'superior yeomanry' and tenants, not to mention their wives and daughters, with social pretensions. But if this was one gap that was widening as the pre-industrial age drew to its close, the gulf between the wealth of the élite of landed society and the poverty of all those whose labour supported that élite had grown to vast proportions. In 1710 only three peers whose wealth was predominantly in land had incomes which topped £30,000 a year (*Making of a Great Power*, Ch. 18). By the 1770s there were probably eight or nine peers with incomes of between £35,000 and £55,000. Magnates such as Bedford, Bridgewater, Devonshire, Derby and Rockingham lived like Continental princes. William Pulteney, earl of Bath, blessed by marriage as well as inheritance, had left an estate valued at more than £1 million in 1764. Although Colquhoun at the start of the nineteenth century was to estimate the *average* income of peers at no more than £8,000 p.a., and it is undeniable that there were always minnows among the whales, incomes of over £15,000 a year were almost commonplace in the English peerage by 1780. A mere baron, the second Lord Foley, left in 1766, in addition to a nest-egg of half a million pounds in the Funds, £21,000 a year in landed rents plus mine revenues worth another £7,000 a year (139, *19*).

Although a number of the *grands seigneurs* of the period, such as the dukes of Bedford (203a, *146*) enjoyed a colossal income from landed rents alone, a high proportion of those who scaled the highest pinnacles of wealth could not have done so without (like the Foleys) exploiting their mineral assets. There was nothing new in this, of course: the Lumleys, earls of Scarborough, would have been very minor aristocrats in the early eighteenth century had they not at that time been reputedly the biggest colliery owners in England, raising coals to the value of nearly £5,000 annually from their Durham pits by the late 1720s and either owning or part-owning 64 coastal ships.[12] What is striking by the eve of the Industrial Revolution is the sheer scale of aristocratic involvement in the extractive industries and the growing efficiency of this commitment. The Dudleys in the West Midlands increased their net income from minerals from £1,941 in 1704 to £17,684 a century later.[13] Sir Hugh Smithson, 1st duke of Northumberland of a new creation, so successfully exploited the mines on the old Percy estates in the North East that between 1766 and 1786 he more than quintupled an income of £8,600 p.a., and throughout the eighteenth century the Lowthers in West Cumberland also showed what spectacular results could be achieved in the long run through a readiness to undertake heavy expenditure in order to improve returns.[14] For every landowner-industrialist, trading in heavy bulk commodities, easy and preferably cheap communications were a vital element in profitability. To the Lumleys and Lowthers this meant iron carriage-ways and ships. To the duke of Bridgewater, concerned to reduce the cost of transporting coal from his Worsley mines to Manchester, it meant building the first English canal: opened in 1761, the product of James Brindley's engineering genius and a capital outlay of £350,000, it inaugurated the canal age in Britain in which landowners were to play a crucial part.

Two notes of caution about the upper reaches of eighteenth-century landed society are called for, in conclusion. In the first place, recent scholarship has tended sharply to play down the accessibility or 'openness' often attributed to the landed élite in pre-industrial England. Certainly the hereditary aristocracy grew more rather than less exclusive and inbred after 1714 than it had been under the Stuarts, a process not decisively checked until the Younger Pitt's creations in the 1790s (195; 203a; 202a, *ch. 3*; 289, *ch. 2*). In the second place, although most aristocratic incomes rose substantially, and some vastly, in the mid- and late eighteenth century so did expenditure and conspicuous consumption. It has been estimated that the average great landlord at this time probably spent on average £5–6,000 a year on taxation and the poor rate, on entertainment, and above all on the manning, maintenance and improvement of his houses, parks, gardens and farms (197a). If he was especially active politically, the cost of borough management and of cultivating the freeholders in county elections might double or even treble normal expenditure. The great rent-rolls of the duke of Newcastle were no proof against his costly fifty-five years in politics (1713–68), and his enforced land sales in the last thirty years of his life cumulatively topped over £200,000.[15] Entertainment was an inescapable obligation on any landowner of status, and could well be a prodigious item in the budgets of the politically involved. Of one of his visits to Walpole's magnificent seat at Houghton Lord Hervey wrote in 1731: 'we used to sit down to dinner a little snug party of about thirty odd, up to the chin in beef, venison, geese, turkeys, etc, and generally over the chin in claret, strong beer and punch. We had lords spiritual and temporal, besides commoners, parsons and freeholders innumerable'.[16] Given all the regular drains on income, and the periodic ravages made by, say, dowries, enclosures, or large-scale building or estate works, it was not only the 'poor lords' or rank-and-file county gentry families who were imperilled by an adverse turn of fortune. A single profligate or gambler (and every family was likely to suffer one bad egg every third or fourth generation); a crop of healthy but not very comely daughters, who wouldn't 'go off'; or a dowager with a handsome jointure living to a ripe old age, like the 3rd duchess of Leeds, who drained the Osborne estates of £190,000 – these or comparable afflictions could shake even the most splendid edifice. To the 'haves' of landed society in the eighteenth century the Lord generally gave more, and often in abundance; but, even from the shining ones, the Lord sometimes took away.

---

1. Scotland, like England, suffered heavy epidemic mortality in the early 1740s. See Wrigley and Schofield, (152), p. 341.
2. Wrigley and Schofield's statistics pinpoint its beginnings precisely in the two years 1744–5 (152), p. 533 (Table A3.3).
3. For example from 1744–59 the annual death rate in a careful sample of *c.* 500 English parishes never once exceeded 28.6 per thousand; cf. 1727–43, when there were only 4 years in which it dropped below that figure and 6 in which it reached danger levels in the range 34.1 to 44.7. For a lucid recent summary of the debate on the causes of population growth in the 18th century, see Lee and Schofield (151c), pp. 31–5.
4. See Wrigley and Schofield (152), pp. 338–9.
5. Based on extrapolations from Joseph Massie's table of social strata, families and incomes for 1760 [B.5], and Colquhoun's table for 1803 (for which see, *inter alia*, H.J. Perkin (139), pp. 20–1).
6. But not invariably. In a few high-tax counties close to the capital most of the smaller gentry properties that came on the market were snapped up, not by the aristocracy but by London-based businessmen and professionals, thereby helping to create a new 'commuter' gentry.

7. See, for example, R.A.C. Parker, *Coke of Norfolk* (1975), p. 3; J.V. Beckett (202a), 198–9; J. Cannon (203a), pp. 145–6.

8. P. Jenkins, 'The Demographic Decline of the Landed Gentry in the Eighteenth Century', *Welsh Hist. Rev.* **11** (1982); J.O. Martin, 'The Landed Estate in Glamorgan, c. 1660 to 1760' (Cambridge University Ph. D. thesis, 1978), cited in Beckett, (199b), p. 20; cf. Jenkins (146).

9. J.R. Wordie, *Estate Management in Eighteenth-Century England: The Building of the Leveson Gower Fortune* (1982), p. 39.

10. Over one-third of the Gowers' tenants farmed more than 200 acres by 1759–79; J.R. Wordie, 'Social Change on the Leveson Gower Estates, 1714–1832', *EcHR*, **27** (1974).

11. The former to secure a better variety and rotation of crops, the latter to ensure either more efficient pasturage or conversion to cultivation.

12. F.W. Beastall, *A North Country Estate: The Lumleys and Saundersons as Landowners, 1600–1900* (1975), pp. 17, 21.

13. T.J. Raybould, *The Economic Emergence of the Black Country* (Newton Abbot, 1972), cited in Beckett (202a), p. 234.

14. J.V. Beckett (147), pp. 77, 218, 230–1.

15. R. Kelch, *Newcastle: A Duke without Money* (1974), p. 191

16. Lord Ilchester, ed., *Lord Hervey and His Friends, 1726–38* (1950), p. 73: Hervey to Prince Frederick, 21 July 1731.

CHAPTER 10

Society and the economy in the eighteenth-century: II – Commerce and the professions, *c.* 1720–*c.* 1780

Although the way was hard, men could still rise within eighteenth-century landed society, starting low down. Labourers or farm servants who were both frugal and exceedingly fortunate, commonly with an auxiliary source of income, were occasionally able to save enough out of their wages to be able to rent, or even buy, small properties. Prospering yeomen continued here and there to make the transition from the owner-occupancy of a large farm to the lower or 'parish' gentry. They did so in nothing like the same numbers as under the Tudors and early Stuarts, and startling changes for the better in family fortunes rarely took place within one generation in eighteenth-century landed society (*Making of a Great Power*, Chs. 2, 18; Ch. 9 above). But we do know that in some regions upward progress from farmer to small gentleman occurred frequently enough for this old pattern still to be regarded as a normal development (204b; 199a).

However, when Harold Perkin characterised English society in the eighteenth century, in a much-quoted phrase, as an 'open aristocracy', with fundamental implications then and later for industrial growth, it was the revitalisation of the landed classes by the *non*-landed wealth which flowed into it, as well as the 'downward flow of their younger sons into the middle ranks', which he chiefly had in mind (139, *56–7, 61*). Over twenty years on, Perkin's celebrated thesis remains resilient but in need of some refinement. For example, although some of the 'new wealth' used to buy land in the period 1720–80 was London business wealth, as it had always been, such City tycoons as Sir Gilbert Heathcote (*Making of a Great Power*, Ch. 17) and Sir Gregory Page, who purchased great estates late in life in the 1720s in the aftermath of the South Sea Bubble, or Samson Gideon and others, who spent equally lavishly on land in the years 1748–55, were very much the exceptions. An analysis of the members of the London aldermanic bench, 'la crème de la crème of the [indigenous] London bourgeoisie' in the mid-eighteenth century,[1] has shown that 'by and large they went in for riverside villas or medium-sized mansions within close proximity of the capital', and were little interested in acquiring substantial landed acreages as such (216a, *448–9*). Great City figures like Sir John Barnard and Micajah Perry never moved further than Clapham, though Horwitz's reappraisal of the traditional aspirations of the businessmen of Augustan London must make us wary of over-generalising on the basis of aldermen alone (12a; 216b. Cf. *Making of a Great Power*, Ch. 18). What is clear is that an increasing proportion of non-landed *provincial* wealth *was* moving into land by the middle of the century. Modern studies have revealed Leeds merchant-clothiers buying big estates in the West Riding, Hull overseas traders setting up as country gentlemen in the East Riding and Lincolnshire, and

Whitehaven merchants and attorneys investing in country properties in Cumberland. Taking the country as a whole, however, the translation into landed assets of fortunes made in trade or industry, or even in the professions (outside the army) occurred less freely in the mid-eighteenth century than it had for two centuries past.

One explanation for this lies in the eighteenth-century land market itself. After the freakish activity of the 1720s was over (ibid., Ch. 17), the market, though far from static, could not match that of 1540–1640 in sheer volatility, particularly in the number of large properties coming up for sale. At the same time the price of land was so inflated – by 1750–70 it was averaging thirty years' purchase, 50 per cent more than the average south of England asking price of the 1680s – that the value of land as a purely economic investment had become more and more questionable (201b; 194a, *201*). Secondly, a place in an *urban* patriciate was increasingly being seen, in Britain as a whole, as a most desirable end in itself, the more so as the quality of urban life was being transformed between 1660 and 1760 (Ch. 14); the obverse of this tendency was that dabbling in land became something to be contemplated only with serious circumspection (199b; 187b; 212a; 213). Thirdly and most compellingly, there remained excellent material reasons why men of non-landed capital should choose to grow even richer by keeping the great bulk of their economic involvement outside land altogether.

We will appreciate these reasons most plainly by briefly examining, in the present chapter and the one that follows, the three most prolific sources of non-landed wealth in mid-Georgian Britain: trade and finance, the professions, and industry. The first, very probably, and the last, self-evidently,[2] were essential in giving Britain that capacity for rapid industrialisation towards the end of the century which otherwise she would not have possessed; even the second, professional wealth and enterprise, contributed to that end in various ways, for example, through the provision of capital to industrialists by rich attorneys or through the work of surveyors and engineers. All three sources had this, too, in common: they ensured that the contribution of *urban* capital to national wealth and to the national product was far higher in 1780, in relation to the contribution of land and agriculture, than it had been in Gregory King's Britain of the late seventeenth century.

Trade and finance

The 'Commercial Revolution' (*Making of a Great Power*, Chs. 3, 19) did not end in 1689. But between then and 1745 the pace of its advance did slacken, with much momentum lost in the early 1690s and in the 1720s, especially, and with only intermittent spurts (ibid., Ch. 19). In fact the progression of British overseas trade in the eighteenth century presents a complicated picture, not only before 1745 but right down to the 1780s, and it would be rash to proceed to any generalisations about trade in this period or to extrapolate from them deductions about Britain's economic growth (e.g. cf. 130a and 159. Cf. Chs 3 and 5 of 135, *I*) without some awareness of these complications [see J.4 *passim*; 135, *Chs. 3, 5*].

In the first place there are statistical complications. The official government trade figures on which historians basically depend (the series inaugurated by William Culliford in 1696) applied only to England and Wales until late in our period,[3] and they are suspect on two major counts: first, because the formal valuation of goods for customs purposes, which is what the figures record, was not revised for seventy-seven years after 1710, and secondly, because of the prevalence of smuggling. The eighteenth century was the golden age of the English and Scottish smuggler, and smuggled goods may periodically have added as much as 15 or 20 per cent to the import account. Both these in-built statistical flaws make it hard to avoid serious undervaluation of overseas trade over the last fifty years or so of our period, so that while we may properly use the figures to construct a rough index of eighteenth-century growth [J.3. B], it is an index which will inevitably undermeasure the scale of that growth. In the second place, the picture is complicated by the irregular trade pattern which the figures reveal. Imports and exports rarely did well simultaneously [J.3.C(i, ii)]; the Spanish and Austrian Succession Wars both saw violent fluctuations; and the final war of the period, that of American Independence, caused a trade slump from 1776–82 – on the very eve of industrial 'take-off' – which Peter Mathias has described as 'disastrous' (131b, *68*; 134). The one extended period when more or less everything clicked together – imports, exports, re-exports, Scottish trade as well as English – was from 1745 until just after the Peace of Paris (1763–4).

These nineteen years were easily the most exciting period for British overseas trade between the late 1680s and the mid-1780s, and they can be seen as the second tidal wave of the Commercial Revolution following half a century of ebb and flow. As under Charles II and James II, the colonies and trading stations were decisive generators. Together with Ireland (trade with which roughly doubled in these years), they revitalised the English re-export trade and induced the biggest commercial boom Scotland had ever known. In addition, the transatlantic colonies were poised by 1763 to replace Southern Europe as the biggest area market for British manufactured exports [J.3.C].[4] Because of rapidly rising population and purchasing power (Ch. 4), the North American market, in particular, proved vital to the recovery of momentum [see J.3.C(ii)] – and not only for *English* exports. By 1764, the sixth year for which there are Scottish export records, total British exports to the colonists had reached £2.63 million. Year by year the Americans took from British manufacturers growing quantities of metal goods, ranging from hundreds of ploughshares to millions of nails. In 1700 West Midland ironmongers were already sending across the Atlantic four-fifths of their total export of nails and almost a half of their exported wrought ironware, mostly agricultural implements and axes. These proportions increased over the next sixty years; so, hugely, did the volume of metal exports, from both the Midlands and South Yorkshire.[5] From around 1750 American demand also had a dynamic effect on the export of woollens and worsteds, giving England's traditionally premier industry a new lease of life just at a time when its traffic with Southern Europe (*Making of a Great Power*, Ch. 3) was beginning to fare badly. In the early 1750s North America took barely 10 per cent of England's exported woollens, but over the years 1772–4 its colonists and the West Indian settlers together took some 30 per cent of the industry's total shipments, with the North Americans now its best customers.

The ultimate, though not the immediate, beneficiary was the West Riding of Yorkshire. The established cloth merchants of Leeds, Wakefield and Halifax clung for a long time to those Continental outlets on which their post-Restoration prosperity had been built. However, a prolonged mid-century textile depression in the Riding [L.3.v(1)] was ended in spectacular style as a new breed of cloth merchant, epitomised by the Elam brothers, attacked the American market with astonishing success through the ports of Hull and Liverpool, exploiting the advantage which dealing both in woollens and in worsteds or mixed cloths gave them over the clothiers of Norfolk. Although there was serious dislocation of the colonial trade from 1772 to 1782, of which John Wesley found stark evidence when he visited Leeds at the time,[6] the solid transatlantic base established before the American crisis got out of hand crucially assisted Yorkshire clothiers and merchants to take a rapid and conclusive lead over all their rivals in the new age of increasing mechanisation after 1783 (155b; 143b, *44, 46–52*; 143a, *277–80*; 141, *230–39*). There is an interesting contrast here with the South Lancashire cotton manufacturers and the Liverpool merchants who now handled most of their products. Their economic interdependence with the United States after 1783 became enormous, yet it was only lightly foreshadowed before the War of Independence. While the transatlantic colonies as a whole took many of the 'fustians' and 'cotton-linens' (since 1750 mostly all-cottons) being produced by a Lancashire experiencing the earliest benefits of new machines (Ch. 11) early in George III's reign, most of the raw cotton the industry absorbed at this stage was still being shipped, not from the plantations of the Deep South but from the Levant or the West Indies (145b, *146, 184, 465–502*).

In the following chapter we shall consider some of the implications for industrial capital of this flourishing colonial trade axis (159, *90–1*; see also J.3.C), as well as of a domestic consumer market which was also expanding rapidly from 1745 onwards [L.1]. It was not until very late in our period, however, that manufacturing wealth in Britain, individual or collective, began even to approach in scale the mercantile wealth generated by the Commercial Revolution. For all their drawbacks, the Board of Trade figures enable us to identify three broad trends in overseas trade over the period 1700–84 (155b; 128a, *48–9*; 128b, *279–80*). One is that in spite of periodic fluctuations and recessions, and the coming and going of wars, there was a striking overall growth in the total volume of English trade – and correspondingly, of English shipping [J.3.A] – between the beginning of the century and the eve of the American Revolution; the average annual value of overseas trade, at official rates, rose from £10.4 million in the decade 1700–09 (it had been £12.3 million in the inter-war years from 1699 to 1701) to £26.8 million from 1765–74 (with peak figures of £28.4 million from 1772 to 1774) [see also J.3.B]. The second clearly discernible trend is that while the rate of trade growth averaged out in the region of 0.5 per cent per annum over the first 45 years of the century, between 1745 and 1771 the rate rose to 2.8 per cent per annum, and over the shorter period 1745–63 it was almost 4 per cent.[7] Thirdly, official figures confirm contemporary accounts of the seriousness of the depression during the American War but also underline the strength of the recovery which began, in anticipation of the peace, in 1782. We may note one eccentricity which the *total* trade figures conceal. Although trade as a whole continued to expand, if more slowly, between 1763 and 1774, the Commercial Revolution would have lost all its impetus in those years but for a recovery of the *re*-export trade and a great surge in imports: by 1771 over twice the value of goods was being imported as in 1746. British manufactured exports had to struggle so hard after 1765 to cope with falling European demand, or with prohibitive duties, that it was to be as late as 1788 before the previous record export figures of 1764 were reached again (128b, *280–1*).

In terms of Britain's mercantile wealth, however, the shifts in the pattern of eighteenth-century trade probably mattered less than the broad consistency of the upward trend. For the greater part of the first three-quarters of the century – at least until the 1760s, when the industrialist began to effect a slight but significant change in the picture – merchant capital steadily increased its share of the whole national capital. Joseph Massie, compiling his statistical summary of English society in 1760 with Gregory King's blueprint as his yardstick, acknowledged this advance [B.5]. Modern scholarship has confirmed that in London, the heart of the country's body commercial, the expectations of the City's numerous mercantile community were appreciably higher by the mid-eighteenth century than they had been in the seventeenth, and that those of the merchant élite – of the men who stocked the aldermanic bench and the company directorships, or ran the London money market[8] – had soared still faster (cf. 216a and 209a). In 1727 Defoe thought a fortune of £25,000 enough to maintain a London merchant and his family in good style and status. But this was small beer among the London aldermen of the period 1738–63, and smaller still when set against the achievements of some of the commercial colossi of George II's reign and George III's. Gilbert Heathcote, the greatest 'monied man' of the reigns of William III and Anne, pursued his long-standing commercial interests as wine merchant and East India trader when the French wars were over and died worth £700,000 in 1733. He was outdone by Sir Samuel Fludyer, a packer and cloth factor with interests in the drugs trade, whose fortune on his death in 1768 was an estimated £900,000, and by William Beckford MP for London (d. 1770), who was the first business millionaire in English history. The Beckford brothers were by no means the only City magnates whose great wealth was founded on sugar. Diversity, however, rather than rigid specialisation, was the normal name of the game for those on their way to 'plums' – City parlance for fortunes of £100,000 – and beyond. Sir John Barnard, who turned down Walpole's offer of the Chancellorship of the Exchequer in 1737, saying he could make £4,000 a year in his own business, and more honestly into the bargain, went on to underscore the point by becoming the leading London marine insurance specialist as well as a successful wine merchant. Sir Joseph Eyles, as well as belonging to the exclusive club of merchants who monopolised the Levant Company trade, also traded with the West Indies, North America and Iberia, and was closely involved with the government as creditor, Bank director and army pay contractor; the last sideline alone bringing him in eventually £2,500 a year (12a, *II, 21–2*; 216a, *439*).

It used to be thought that one of the links between the Commercial and Industrial Revolutions was the substantial amount of mercantile and financial capital in the City of London which was, supposedly, invested in the new industrial ventures of the North and Midlands in the latter half of the eighteenth century. But present-day scholars now accept that most of the financial backing for the manufacturing entrepreneurs of the decades after 1760 came from local sources, and that among them overseas merchants were not particularly prominent. As Eyles's case illustrates, the big money in the City was far more tempted by the stock market and by a financial or contractual relationship with the government than by distant ironworks or cotton mills. Robert Campbell marvelled in 1747 at 'a flagrant instance' a few days earlier 'of the vast influence of commerce, when six millions sterling was subscribed for the use of the government by private merchants in less than four hours'.[9] Not untypical of this exalted company was John Bristow of Bristow, Ward and Co., Portugal merchants, and also a South Sea Company director: he was able to contribute £150,000 to a single government loan in 1744, one of only nine major contractors, all Londoners, who together raised £1.3 million of the whole requirement of £1.8 million (69, *289*; 12a, *I, 487–8*). The monied interest had been closely integrated from the start with the London merchant community (*Making of a Great Power*, Ch. 17). The National Debt, after being reduced and crowned with a halo of respectability by Walpole, rose to £132 million by 1763, having almost trebled since 1739 [G.1]. Bank and East India stock, South Sea annuities and government loans, even at a low 3–4 per cent interest, created an enormous reservoir of investment, and it was one in which the Jewish and immigrant element in the City, prominent from the very start of the Financial Revolution, continued to swim happily. In 1723–4, for instance, Francis Pereira, a Portuguese Jew, and Abraham Craiesteyn, merchant and stockbroker, held over £300,000 of Bank and East India stock between them, while a representative of an old immigrant house, Sir Peter Delmé, personally held £288,000 of these stocks and South Sea annuities simultaneously. Among the public creditors of the 1750s there was more institutional, landed and professional involvement than there had been before 1714; nevertheless, the £8 million war loan of 1758 was wholly underwritten by twenty-two City financiers, led by the Jewish stockbroker and tycoon, Samson Gideon, who had amassed a fortune of £350,000 by the time of his death in 1762 (84, *208*; 18, *393*).

We need a wider focus on eighteenth-century trade and business wealth, however, in order to appreciate its full contribution to the development of the British economy and society. Thereby revealed is a structure far less London-dominated, broader-based and more complex than that of the seventeenth century. A regiment of middlemen, such as corn merchants, wool jobbers and cheese factors, was now in firm possession of the distributive network in England, their prosperity usually in inverse proportion to their popularity (189). In 1716 the first *provincial* private banker made his appearance, in Bristol. Counterparts were slow to follow at first, though they included George Smith of Nottingham, founder of one of the two most successful provincial banking dynasties of the century (the other being Lloyds of Birmingham). Only a dozen 'country banks' were to be found by 1750, but by 1784 there were 120. It has often been claimed that the Industrial Revolution could never have been financed without them.[10] At the same time provincial merchants, in both coastal and overseas trades, gained strikingly in collective wealth as well as in their range of activities and self-confidence, despite the periods of slack business and anxiety which afflicted every port at some stage. The two chief beneficiaries of the boom in transatlantic traffic and in the lucrative slave trade were Liverpool and Bristol; but tidy fortunes were made in Whitehaven during its great years in the mid-eighteenth century, as they were in King's Lynn and Yarmouth out of the grain trade to the Continent. Further up the east coast the burghers of Newcastle prospered on the profits of coal and salt, while West Riding cloth and Sheffield metalware, with the aid of the Aire-Calder and Don navigations, helped to raise Hull to the status of the country's fourth port by the end of our period and to line the pockets of the Crowles, Sykeses, Thorntons and the rest of the twenty-odd merchant houses who controlled the town's commerce.[11] Smaller English ports, such as Lancaster, which edged into the slave trade as well as the tobacco and sugar traffic, flourished on a lesser scale.

To the north, Scotland played her full part in the advance of trade, commerce and finance, particularly after 1740. Scottish banking made impressive strides. The country's overseas trade was still only valued at roughly 5 per cent of England's when her customs officials began to make consistent annual returns in 1755 (155b). But there was already a boom in linen exports to the American colonies – the 92,000 yards sent over in 1744 increasing to 468,000 yards in 1751 and to almost 2 million yards by 1771 – and the breakneck expansion of the Glasgow tobacco trade with Chesapeake Bay (imports shot up six-fold between 1741 and 1771) was bringing great affluence to a group of Glasgow 'tobacco lords' and financiers, for tobacco was now easily Scotland's most profitable export as well as her most valuable import (241, *244*; 246, *258–60, 262–3*. Cf. 251, *471*). By 1771, indeed, they had cornered over half the entire British trade in the commodity, most of it reserved for re-export. It was an extraordinary achievement, and it would not have been possible without a strong corporate spirit, good engineers who dredged the Clyde and transformed it as an anchorage, and the talent and enterprise of the four most successful city merchants, Cunningham, Richie, Spiers and Glassford, each of whom had some 25 ships plying the Atlantic in the 1770s. The east coast merchants were not altogether left out in the cold, however, as Scotland's own Commercial Revolution was launched and set on course. In fact it was an easterner, Sir Lawrence Dundas (though more by army contracting than by trade) who amassed what was possibly the biggest fortune in eighteenth-century Scotland, £900,000 by 1781, and an estate worth £16,000 a year.

Thus, for many decades before 1780 London mercantile and financial wealth, though rising impressively in absolute terms, was declining in relation to the urban business wealth of the English provinces and Scotland. Not only economic but political historians have seen significance in this process; it has even been suggested as a reason why John Wilkes and his causes (Ch. 22) attracted so much malcontent support in the City and its environs during the 1760s and early 1770s.

153

Two features of early and mid-Hanoverian Britain which reflect this gradually changing balance in favour of the outports are shipping and urban population. The shift away from London in the ownership of shipping is very marked. The capital's contribution to the total tonnage of the English merchant fleet was no more in 1763 than it had been 1702, 140,000 tons. Yet during the same period provincially-owned tonnage in England and Wales almost doubled, to reach 357,000 tons [see also J.3.A]. The Liverpool registers show a tonnage of 76,251 tons owned by the town's merchants in 1789, a more than 400 per cent increase over 36 years.[12] During the first quarter of the century the port of Hull was clearing a fairly steady average of 11,000 tons per annum, in and out, but by 1792 this had risen to 135,000 tons. More astonishing is the case of Whitehaven: at the peak of its tobacco and coal boom in 1770 it cleared 192,000 tons of outward-going shipping alone, only 53,000 tons less than the port of London (154).

Of those towns whose populations grew fastest in the half century before 1775, many were ports [B.2 *passim*]. While London's population grew from perhaps 600,000 in 1725 to around 740,000 fifty years later, a far slower rate than in the seventeenth century, its proportion of the total population of England varying little in the process [B.2(i)], that of Bristol, with Clifton, almost doubled in the same period, making it, at 55,000, easily the country's second city in 1775. That of Liverpool and Newcastle upon Tyne, both well past 30,000, were at this same date rapidly overtaking Norwich, earlier in the century the undisputed queen of the provinces [detailed figures are in B.2(ii)]. There was comparable expansion among the smaller emerging ports of the earlier eighteenth century (*Making of a Great Power*, Ch. 19), such as Whitehaven, Sunderland and Hull, and among the dockyard towns [B.2(ii)]. The physical and demographic expansion of Scotland's leading ports had been just as striking. Glasgow's growth, in particular, fully matched its prosperity – only briefly checked by the American War – as it rapidly approached Edinburgh in population [B.3(iii); see also 246, *17–36*].

As the evidence of her commerce and her ports would suggest, Britain south of the Highland Line was an appreciably more urbanised country on the eve of the Industrial Revolution than she had been a century earlier. This was not simply a coastal phenomenon; it was a general trend, wherever there were sound economic, or perhaps even administrative or social, reasons for growth (Ch. 14). Likewise merchants, businessmen and tradesmen were not alone, among the urban 'middling sort', in profiting from it. So too did the members of the professions, already one of the most significant growth sectors in Augustan and early-Georgian society. Their growth, moreover, was less inhibited than that of the commercial classes. For although trade was still, as it had been since the Middle Ages, a regular vehicle of upward social mobility, the merchant community itself was ironically less 'open' by 1760–80 than it had been under the later Stuarts. Apprenticeship premiums, especially in London, had risen to heights that increasingly closed off entries from traditional recruiting grounds such as the minor gentry. Also, where urban trading dynasties were long entrenched (as they were in Hull, for example) it could be very difficult for smaller merchants to penetrate their inbred, oligarchic fastnesses.[13] By contrast, the professions, one of the fastest moving and most capacious upward escalators even in the late seventeenth century, were not only carrying far more traffic in the 1780s than in the 1680s, but were doing so, by and large, with little serious obstruction.

Broad channels of entry were a key factor here. Admission both to the 'lesser degrees' of the legal profession, through an articled clerkship to an attorney or solicitor, and to the swelling ranks of the surgeons, apothecaries and 'surgeon-apothecaries', was still achieved through an apprenticeship system; because of this, the proportion of young men of modest origins who contrived by their own application and brains to achieve social status and some measure of affluence in medicine and the law remained healthy. In addition, over the last fifty years of our period the Edinburgh medical degree, a qualification that could be come by far more cheaply than the standard Oxbridge M.D. or M.B., became a widespread and worthy passport to practice as a physician, at least outside London (187a, *Chs. 5–7*; 186, *9*). The bureaucracy and the army did admittedly become more exclusive during this period, the former through the greater intrusion of patronage and family or political connexion, the latter through the inflation of costs in the purchase system.[14] The Royal Navy, however, continued to offer a hard but fairly clear road of advance through warrant-officer as well as commissioned ranks, which for the man of ability who survived its rigours could end in a place on the captains' list or even in a 'flag' (86, *Chs. 1, 7*); the newer, smaller professions such as architecture, surveying and professional music also afforded unambiguous evidence that a favoured background was not a prerequisite of ultimate success and fortune.

Over and above their relative openness, the ultimate guarantee that the eighteenth-century professions would expand far more rapidly than the population at large was the high level of demand for the services they provided. Part of this demand was generated by the state: by the more complex needs of administration and finance and the requirements of wars of ever-increasing dimensions. But most of it occurred in response to the needs of a society which, from the late seventeenth century so far as England was concerned, 'grew strikingly in material prosperity [and] . . . became more sophisticated, probably more status-conscious, certainly more comfort- and amenity-conscious, and also more cultivated than any which had preceded it' (187b, *316*). The steadily multiplying calls on the services of the attornies, those indispensable factotums of the eighteenth-century propertied classes, and the propensity of Georgian Britons to 'send for the doctor' (or more likely, the 'pothecary) when afflicted by ailments which early generations would more likely have stoically endured, are just two illustrations of this interplay of demand and response. It is difficult to put a valid numerical estimate on the growth of any one profession during the eighteenth century and quite impossible to attach reliable statistics to the expansion of the professional sector as a whole. The contemporary assessments of King, Massie and Colquhoun are not of much help [B.5; cf. 131a, *177*]. For what they are worth, however, Colquhoun's securer estimates for the beginning of the nineteenth century, when compared with King's for the end of the seventeenth, indicate a rise in professional numbers in England and Wales from 55,000 to

122,500 in 115 years, and more significantly, a rise in aggregate family income from £5.77 million to £29.85 million, a more than five-fold increase.

Much of the numerical growth in the older eighteenth-century professions took place at the level of the 'infantry' – attorneys and solicitors, surgeons and apothecaries, clerks and 'revenue men' in the government service, and so on. It was they, and above all the lawyers and medical men among them, who built most of that solid edifice of professional wealth which characterised all towns of any size by the late eighteenth century (187a, *159–65, 227–35*). Manchester (with Salford and Stretford) had 24 sworn attorneys in 1729 and Liverpool, with Prescot, had 26; the numbers recorded for the same towns in Browne's *Law List* of 1790 were 40 and 68, respectively.[15] A local count of Bristol's medical men in 1754 found 29 apothecaries and 19 surgeons there, in addition to 5 resident physicians, which makes it likely that S.F. Simmons missed some names in Bristol when, in the third and best edition of his *Medical Register* in 1783, he listed, as well as 8 physicians, 30 apothecaries, 16 surgeons and 4 surgeon-apothecaries. It is worth noting, nonetheless, that in the whole of England (but not in Wales, for which his figures were manifestly incomplete) Simmons tracked down 3,525 surgeons and apothecaries in domestic practice, including 742 in London, and listed a further 659 serving with the armed forces.[16]

At the apex of most professions, on the other hand, numbers rose more slowly, and existing status hierarchies were not unduly disturbed. By the mid–1780s there were still fewer than 550 graduate physicians in practice in England, some 30 per cent of them based in London or its suburbs, and probably less than 500 active barristers, handling most of the business of the Common Law Courts. In Scotland the members of the Faculty of Advocates – 200 of them in 1714 and nearly 300 by 1810 – monopolised pleading in the Edinburgh courts and constituted a professional and social élite aloof from the rank and file procurators who served the inferior courts of the Scottish provinces.[17] The restricted competition which resulted from the limited numbers in practice at the bars and in 'physic' allowed inflation of fees to set in. As early as 1730 successful advocates at the English bar could command up to double the fees which their Restoration predecessors had charged. In the early decades of the eighteenth century a good practitioner could already hope to earn from £2,000 to £4,000 a year from private practice, which was the main reason why the salaries of judges had to be raised substantially in 1714. Some fashionable London physicians did even better. Richard Mead, for instance, who died in 1754, was able to enjoy an income of £5–6,000 in the fifteen years before his death, in spite of his renowned generosity in waiving fees in cases of hardship. Unlike the top lawyers, few physicians bought landed estates with their profits. Some, like Caleb Cotesworth, stashed away tens of thousands in stocks; Mead invested hugely in his collection of manuscripts, books and paintings, and Dr John Fothergill (d. 1780), as well as being a famous collector, was a princely benefactor. Yet physicians did not wholly monopolise the rewards of eighteenth-century medical practice. The wealthiest London apothecary of Mead's generation, James Sherard, left an estate of £150,000, and the greatest surgeon of the same era, William Cheselden, could ask, and get, £500 per operation from well-to-do patients (187a, *227, 232*).

Even by London standards such incomes were exceptional, of course, and for provincial practitioners they were in the realms of fantasy, but they do give us an insight into the economic possibilities of a seller's market in one major profession.

Disparity of rewards characterised other eighteenth-century professions also. In the civil service, as with the bar, rising fees were a prime cause. The officials who did best financially, especially after 1750, were those who served in departments such as the Treasury, the Exchequer and the Post Office, where remuneration was by fee alone, or by salary supplemented by fees or commissions. The Secretary of the Post Office, for example, had a basic salary of £200 a year, but his income from all sources had soared to £2,000 by the 1780s, roughly double its level in the 1760s.[18] In the Navy it was the prize system which, more than anything, produced distortion and incongruities. It operated on an exaggerated sliding-scale from admirals down to lieutenants. Rear-Admiral Sir Peter Warren netted £125,000 in prize money during the Austrian Succession War. After the fall of Havana in 1762, the naval commander-in-chief and his second-in-command, Pocock and Keppel, received £122,697 and £24,539 respectively; their 42 captains gained £1,600 each; but so many lieutenants were involved in this major operation that their share was fairly negligible (86, *257*). Little wonder that successful single-ship actions were what every hard-up lieutenant dreamed about! Young Anglican curates, on the other hand, on the bottom rungs of a profession as hierarchical as most, but more cursed than any by inequalities of income, could have been forgiven for dreaming of a mitre, for the *average* income of the bishops roughly trebled, to around £4,000 a year, in little more than a century before 1800 (cf. Ch. 7).

While British society, and in particular urban society, was being slowly remoulded, and national wealth redistributed as well as increased, by expanding trade and the advance of the professions, industry too was playing a major part well before the 1780s in changing social structure and a significant one in promoting urbanisation. More ostensible, but no less crucial, was its rôle in strengthening the economic foundations of the eighteenth-century state. The following chapter will examine these processes and then go on to assess their implication for the maintenance of social harmony, as well as for the living standards of Britain's 'industrious poor'.

---

1. Seventy-four citizens were or became aldermen in the years 1738–63.
2. But for counter-arguments in the case of trade, see Floud and McCloskey (135), pp. 87ff.
3. For Scotland central records did not begin until 1755. B.R. Mitchell and P. Deane (128b), p. 275.
4. Ibid., pp. 309–10. In 1759, the first year for which composite *British* figures can be produced, the export total was valued at £2.48m. Though falling back for a while in the unsettled late 1760s, values reached a pre-American War peak of £4.5 millions in 1771.
5. E.R. Schumpeter, *English Overseas Trade Statistics* (1960), Table VIII; M. Rowlands (142b).
6. HMC *Dartmouth MSS* III, f. 220: J. Wesley to [earl of Dartmouth], 23 Aug 1775.

7. Deane and Cole (128b), p. 49. These percentages are based on imports and *domestic exports* only.
8. They included a fair proportion of big wholesalers, factors and bankers as well as overseas traders.
9. R. Campbell [Esq.], *The London Tradesman* (1747), pp. 285–6. But compare P.G.M. Dickson (69), pp. 219ff.
10. L.S. Pressnell, *Country Banking in the Industrial Revolution* (Oxford, 1956).
11. G. Jackson, *Hull in the 18th Century* (Oxford, 1972).
12. F.E. Hyde, *Liverpool and the Mersey* (Newton Abbot, 1971), p. 18.
13. N. Rogers (216a); G. Jackson, op.cit.
14. In the infantry and cavalry, but not (fortunately for Britain's record in eighteenth-century wars) in the artillery and engineers. See I. Roy, 'The Profession of Arms', in (186), pp. 210–15.
15. *Lists of Attornies and Solicitors . . . presented to the House of Commons* (1729[–30]); R. Robson, *The Attorney in 18th-Century England* (Cambridge, 1959), p. 167.
16. Holmes (187a), p. 313; Samuel Foart Simmons, MD, *Medical Register for the Year 1783*.
17. Simmons, op. cit.; D. Duman, 'The English Bar in the Georgian Era', and A. Murdoch, 'The Advocates, the Law and the Nation in Early Modern Scotland' in W.R. Prest, ed., *Lawyers in Early Modern Europe and America* (1981), pp. 89, 150–1; Duman's figures must be scaled up in the light of more recent work by D. Lemmings, *Gentlemen and Barristers: The Inns of Court and the English Bar, 1680–1730* (Oxford, 1990), pp. 123ff.
18. K. Ellis, *The Post Office in the Eighteenth Century* (Oxford, 1958), p. 24.

CHAPTER 11

Society and the economy in the eighteenth-century: III – Industry and labour, *c.* 1720–*c.* 1780

Even in late Stuart Britain the 'manufacturing town' was already a recognisable phenomenon (*Making of a Great Power*, Ch. 19). Between 1720 and 1783 the contribution of both industrial capital and labour to the further growth of such towns, as well as the emergence from economic anonymity of places like Stockport, Burton-on-Trent and Merthyr Tydfil, and the gradual industrial takeover of historic boroughs such as Paisley and Preston, increased significantly, a fact which is too often obscured by histories of modern Britain which begin with 'the Industrial Revolution'. In addition there were the service industries, above all the building industry, possibly the biggest employer of labour outside textiles, which thrived on urban growth itself, much as the professions did. Modern estimates of eighteenth-century urban population, reinforced by contemporary returns, have confirmed that some twenty to thirty towns which were to be prominent centres of industry in the nineteenth century – most of them in the North of England and the Midlands, a few in South Wales and Scotland – were already anticipating that growth strongly before the 1780s. Obvious examples are Birmingham, whose 42,350 inhabitants by 1778 made it more populous by then than Norwich, Wolverhampton (142a, *173*) and Sheffield, Leeds and Manchester, Nottingham, Derby and Leicester (213, *183* and B.2(ii)). Manchester's population grew by 40 per cent between 1758 and 1773 and at much the same rate down to 1783, while Paisley's 6,800 of 1755 probably doubled over the next thirty years.[1] Other towns, from more modest beginnings, also grew briskly in the quarter century after 1760 through a combination of industrial opportunity and vastly improved communications by road, river or canal; they included Bolton, Warrington and Stockport in South Lancashire and Cheshire (the first two being near or over the 10,000 mark by 1785) as well as Dudley in Worcestershire, and Burslem, Hanley and Burton-on Trent in Staffordshire.

In all these places, along with Halifax[2] and other parts of the urban West Riding, or in sundry towns in the North East, Scotland and South Wales, it is clear that industry was rapidly on the move well before the mid–1780s; likewise, the evidence of much slower or stagnant population growth in towns such as Tiverton, Taunton, Colchester and Sudbury, which had buzzed with manufacturing activity under the later Stuarts, betokened the long-term decline of the old weaving centres of the South-West and East Anglia. With the important exception of coalmining, virtually all the industries into which Britain's spectacular economic progress was to be most closely keyed in the first two generations after 1783 were already registering clearly on the barometer of urban growth in the third quarter of the eighteenth century. In the front line stood iron and steel making, metal working, Yorkshire woollens and worsteds and Lancashire cottons; and in the second line, hosiery, pottery, brewing, linen and silk. That same barometer also reflects some of those technical advances, crucial to Britain's future industrial triumph, which made it possible for certain towns to experience quite dramatic changes even in the last so-called 'pre-industrial' decades [L.2]. Merthyr was translated in forty years from remote village status to being the largest town in Wales, following the establishment there of the Crawshays' ironworks in 1757 (215, *44*), right on cue for the wider diffusion of Darby's coke-smelting methods (*Making of a Great Power*, Ch. 19) and at a time when other major technical breakthroughs in puddling and rolling by Peter Onions (a foreman at Merthyr), Hall, Cort and others, were in the offing. Thomas Boulsover's discovery of how to fuse silver and copper and Benjamin Huntsman's epic invention in the 1740s of a method of making cast steel in crucibles, launched the process which began to change Sheffield in the early 1770s from a town of 'little mesters', manufacturing high-quality cutlery, tools and implements, to the world's first steel town with a profitable luxury sideline in 'Sheffield plate'. By 1787, in addition to its innumerable cutlers' workshops, the town contained 20 steel convertors and refiners, 17 manufacturers of silver plate, 5 iron founders and 15 merchant houses, and the population of Sheffield parish had risen to well over 30,000 (141, *228–9*; 169, *303–4*).

The innovations of the mid-eighteenth century in textile manufacture transformed other towns in a short space of time. Paisley began its surging expansion in the 1770s, when many of its former linen weavers switched to the new 'jenny'-spun or roller-spun cotton yarn sent up from the north-west of England; and Stockport sprouted at the same time, when its former silk manufacture was supplemented by its first cotton mills. Burton-on-Trent's future was already assured between 1740 and 1760, when its old brewhouses, specialising in top-quality ale, were converted into about a dozen large and well-equipped breweries, like that of Benjamin Wilson, which began to cater for an international market; that future fruitfully diversified when a former Lancashire calico-spinner, Robert Peel the elder, built one of the new mechanised spinning mills here in 1779 (142a, *220–1*; 169, *379*). New processes in pottery manufacture, which in the view of some historians justify linking that industry with iron and textiles as 'spearheads of technological advance in the eighteenth century' (170, [Heaton], *39*), had been evolved earlier. But to be capitalised on they had to be brought into conjunction with changing social habits (especially mass tea-drinking and the European 'china craze' after 1750), with cheap transport along the widened river Weaver and the Trent and Mersey canal (completed in 1779), and with the revolutionary marketing techniques developed by Josiah Wedgwood (1730–95). It was thus that Burslem, Hanley and later Stoke grew from industrial parishes into towns capable of servicing the needs of potteries whose market in the space of fifty years, up to 1785, had been transformed from a largely local to a world-wide one. 'Do you really think we may . . . conquer France in Burslem?', Wedgwood had written to his partner, Thomas Bentley, in 1769,[3] and yet by 1785 80 per cent of the total annual production of all the Staffordshire potters, worth almost one third of a million pounds, was being sent abroad, not only to France but to a score of eager overseas countries.

Manufacture thus played a part of key importance, along with trade, in that process which in the course of the eighteenth century saw the proportion of England's population living in provincial towns of more than 2,500 inhabitants rise from roughly 7.5 to 20 per cent (213, *Table II, 9*). And as it did so, it began slowly to affect the distribution of wealth in the country. During the last twenty-five years of our period, while Josiah Wedgwood, the twelfth son of a working potter, was well on the way to making the first great pottery fortune of £500,000, many other provincial (as well as some London) industrialists and capitalist entrepreneurs were being counted among the wealthiest men in Britain. In iron, for instance, the once legendary achievements of Sir Ambrose Crowley (d. 1713), Britain's first big unitary ironmaster (*Making of a Great Power* Ch. 19), were no longer unique. Several ironmasters had made great fortunes during or between the Seven Years' and American Wars. Among them was the Quaker Richard Reynolds, whose religious dissent was characteristic of most of the great captains of industry in the second half of the eighteenth century. Reynolds took over the Coalbrookdale works in Shropshire during a minority in the Darby dynasty, and his affluence was achieved despite the strictest business morality and a refusal to take government contracts for cannon (163, *218–20*). No such inhibitions afflicted Samuel Walker of Rotherham, for all his lugubrious Methodism. For sixty years the South Yorkshire iron industry had been dominated by partnerships of gentlemen-ironmasters, headed by the Spencers and Fells, operating a charcoal-fuelled and water-powered industry along conservative lines for limited profit.[4] Walker, originally a nailer and farmer, signalled the end of their era in 1748 when he opened an iron and steel works at Masborough; through coke-smelting and exploiting the Huntsman process, which he learned by trickery, he made himself, well before his death in 1782, the biggest iron and steel master in Yorkshire, living in a princely mansion near Rotherham and bequeathing to his sons plant alone valued at £200,000 in 1796 (163; 169; 141).

Scotland's only major ironworks before the Industrial Revolution (the Carron), founded near Falkirk in 1759–60, was the brainchild of the Sheffield-born physician-turned-industrial entrepreneur, Dr John Roebuck. The Carron Company's original £12,000 capital had been increased by 1773 to £150,000 and two years later its products could be carried by the new Forth-Clyde Canal, which Roebuck had championed, to the outskirts of Glasgow. Although Roebuck himself had to sell out, the unfortunate victim of over-extension in other quarters, the works, whose 'carronades' (perfected in 1778) were sold to armies and navies all over Europe, enriched his leading partners, especially Samuel Garbett, the Birmingham brass-worker who was its co-founder (246, *193–200*). By the end of the American War, however, they and every other ironmaster in Britain had been outstripped, in the armaments field and in much else, by John Wilkinson, the son of a Cumbrian farmer, who controlled a whole complex of works in South Staffordshire, Shropshire and Denbighshire, and at Indret in France. A great innovator, Wilkinson was the first ironmaster to install a Watt steam engine (1775), to erect an iron bridge (1779) and to build an iron boat (1787); it was surely appropriate that when he died he should have been laid to rest in an iron coffin.

In the 1780s, before the widespread application of steam power, most ironworks were still sited outside towns, close to their vital supplies of ironstone, coal and water. Metalworking, however, was a different matter. The Birmingham area, and the Black Country townships to the north-west of it, was now the leading metalworking region in Britain, producing a great range of products in brass, copper and silver as well as in iron and steel. In 1783 Birmingham's historian, William Hutton, estimated that three of the town's 200-odd leading citizens were already worth more than £100,000 and that seven others had accumulated over £50,000. Among the 'plum-men' was Matthew Boulton, whom Wedgwood had called as early as 1768 'the first manufacturer in England', and who nine years earlier, out of the profits of the small-wares workshops of Boulton and Son, had started to build to the north of Birmingham the famous Soho factory: five buildings, housing 600 workmen who turned out a vast range of iron, bronze, copper, silver and tortoiseshell goods – £30,000-worth in one year as early as 1763 – using the most up-to-date water-powered machinery. It was to Soho in 1774 that Boulton lured James Watt from Scotland, to produce, with the aid of cylinders bored with mathematical precision by a new technique patented by Wilkinson, the steam engines that were to project British industry into a future of revolutionary change beyond our period's end (169, *285, 333–4*).

By the years 1785–90 Boulton-Watt engines were being installed to power spinning machinery in cotton mills at Papplewick, Warrington, Manchester, Stockport, Nottingham and Tamworth, and from 1794 dates their introduction into the Yorkshire woollen industry. Yet even before this the biggest textile fortunes had already soared to unprecedented heights, as the most successful Northern businessmen contrived to meet both domestic and overseas demand for cotton and woollen goods. Fine new cloth halls built in Leeds, Huddersfield, Bradford and Wakefield from 1755–75, together with the spectacular Piece Hall at Halifax (1774), were unmistakable monuments to the mid-Georgian prosperity of the West-Riding clothiers and merchants. Robert Denison, head of the largest merchant house in Leeds under the second and third Georges, left over £500,000 at his death in 1782: a triumph not for invention or new organisation but for traditional methods of production and marketing. Twenty years earlier, and also before the advent of the new machines, Samuel Touchet of Manchester and London had accumulated assets of £331,000 in cotton and linen manufacture and overseas trade before 'Icarus-like soaring too high', he plunged into bankruptcy (213, *26–7*; 143b; 145b, *244–8*). The true harbinger among the men of capital of the new age in textiles was the former Bolton barber, Richard Arkwright, who combined a nose for invention and a great gift for organisation with entrepreneurial genius. His 'water frame' (1768) for spinning by rollers and his carding machine of 1775 were shrewd adaptations of the ideas of others, but their key importance both to him and to the future of the textile industries was that, unlike the earlier roller-spinning innovations of Paul and Wyatt (1738) or Hargreaves's 'spinning jenny' [L.2], they needed power (initially water) to drive them and mills to house them. The first of the latter Arkwright built at Cromford, Derbyshire, in 1771, employing between 200 and 300 hands; in 1783 he was able to reinforce it with a second, giving work to 800 more. By 1785, seven years

before his death, Arkwright's clutch of mills in Lancashire, Derbyshire and
Nottinghamshire – now being copied by a score of other manufacturers there and
in Staffordshire, Cheshire and Wales – had already made him a richer man than
his friend Matthew Boulton of Soho. To the north, Scotland's first spinning-mill,
at Penicuik, was in production by 1778, at least six others had followed by the
early 'Eighties, and Arkwright's visit to the Clyde valley in 1783 paved the way
for his Scottish partner, David Dale, to build his remarkable New Lanark
complex from 1785 to 1791 (165, *230*; 246, *170–1*; 245b, *17–18, 38*).

It was not only in iron and cotton, however, that the scale of operations and
the concentration of labour were increasing before the mid-1780s. It has long
been a truism among economic historians that even in the early industrial Britain
of the 1810s and 1820s, rural industry, and the traditional domestic and small
workshop organisation in both town and country, still bulked large in much
British manufacture.[5] Nevertheless, during the first decades of George III's reign
there was already an emphatic tendency for the smaller workshops to become
bigger and the rural elements smaller. We see this process at work, for example,
in the reviving Coventry ribbon industry, and more strikingly in the East Midland
hosiery industry. There as early as 1751, 40 per cent of Nottinghamshire's
stocking-frames were concentrated in the county town, while by the 1780s the
most successful of the one hundred-odd 'merchant stockingers' in Nottingham,
their frame-shops now equipped with the new jennies and their warehouses full,
lived the social lives of country gentlemen. Here, as elsewhere in eighteenth-
century society, 'new riches could [in Roy Porter's words] be manicured into
respectability' (132, *359*; 142a, *241*; 140, *157, 284–5*; 165, *212, 238*). Developments in silk-throwing were more spectacular. Although Sir Thomas Lombe's
patent had expired in 1732 and his pioneering mill at Derby (*Making of a Great
Power*, Ch. 19) fell into disuse (after making £120,000 profit for its owner in
fourteen years), its example was followed in a series of new silk factories built
after 1751. By 1765 there were seven mills of either four or five storeys each in
England throwing organzine on the Lombe principle, including two at Macclesfield, one at Stockport and one at Congleton. There were 2,000 employed at
Stockport and 3,500 at Macclesfield (145b, *305*; 169, *200*; 165, *203*). Sugar-
refining, an urban and capital-intensive industry from the start (*Making of a
Great Power*, Ch. 19), acquired larger concerns during the eighteenth-century and
steam engines were eventually employed to crush the cane. Leading glassmakers
in Newcastle, Bristol and the Stour Valley likewise improved and enlarged their
plant, though none approached the scale of the new Ravenshead plate-glass
works at St. Helen's (1773) (142a, *243*; 136, *126–7*). Finally, we may note the rise
between 1740 and 1790 of the 'big twelve' London and Southwark brewers, who
by vastly expanding both their capital investment and their premises to facilitate
what can only be called 'mass-production', towered over the ordinary common
brewers of the capital by the end of the American War, capable of producing 77
per cent of London's strong ale in 1787.[6] In 1760 Ben Truman's brewery interests
were valued at £92,000 and a single brewery in Spitalfields owned by Truman,
Hanbury and Buxton had assets of £130,000. Samuel Whitbread, starting as an
owner in a small way in 1742, possessed the largest single brewery in London (in

Chiswell Street) by the 1780s. The Barclay family and the Charringtons operated on a comparable scale, with the expectation of anything up to £20,000 clear profit in a good year towards the end of the century. Portentously, too, in the fifty years following their foundation in the 1740s at Burton-on-Trent, the firms of Wilson and Worthington grew appreciably in the image of their bigger London brothers (131b; 125, *308–9*; 142a, *221*).

In the mid- and late 1760s England was afflicted with a rash of industrial disputes and disorders, unprecedented in their severity, which alarmed the authorities, central and local, and focused the worried attention of contemporary observers and writers on the position of labour in their society and on the condition and rights of the working poor. The year 1765, for instance, saw a great miners' strike in Northumberland, which began peaceably but developed violently, with winding ropes cut, machinery smashed and coal stocks fired. Coventry weavers and Holborn builders' labourers also struck for higher wages. In 1767 it was the turn of Spitalfields silk-weavers, protesting against a reduction in earnings. 1768 was startling in its turbulence. Merchant seamen mutinied over pay at Deptford, Newcastle, Tynemouth and Sunderland; for weeks ships lay idle in the port of London owing to action by both seamen and dockers; Southwark hatmakers (in the words of a London newspaper) 'struck and refused to work till their wages had been raised'; coal-heavers were involved in prolonged riots; and Charles Dingley's mechanical saw-mill in Limehouse was attacked and partly destroyed by 500 sawyers – an early instance of proto-Luddism soon to be paralleled by a crop of attacks in Lancashire on spinning jennies between 1768 and 1770. There was further unrest in the 1770s. Virtually every naval dockyard, for example, was brought to a standstill in 1775, and Lancashire erupted again, along with Cheshire, in 1779, in a string of violent protests against the new water-frames. Arkwright put his Cromford mill for a while in a state of siege and the engines at Peel's cotton-printing factory at Altham were thrown into the river Calder (219a; 169, *411–13*; 229, *159–163*).

It has been suggested that these events are portents, that they signal a fundamental change in the social anatomy of the country, foreshadowing the emergence over the next half century of an industrial working class, conscious of its grievances and rights, awakening to its bargaining power, and discovering ways of organising itself (as through 'combinations' and 'clubs') to promote its own interests in opposition to those of a similarly new breed of industrial capitalists (228; on Lancashire, specifically, cf. 145a, *63–4*). Such a hypothesis is not without its value. Like the complex of popular disorders analysed in the next chapter (Ch. 12), it reminds us that real tensions and animosities underlay the surface stability of eighteenth-century society. It recalls many other tokens noted earlier that the structure of that society did undergo significant change in the course of the century, as it had in the late seventeenth, in step with the expansion of trade, the development of industry and the further growth of towns. That the pace of change accelerated in the last quarter-century of our period, and that the lower storeys of the structure felt the repercussions no less than those in the middle, is not in doubt. There is enough of novelty in the protests of 1765–80 to suggest that the apprehensions of contemporaries were not entirely misconceived, and that along with the old pre-factory economy itself, the traditional social framework which encompassed it was at last within sight of a decisive transformation, along with many of the assumptions and relationships which had underpinned it ever since the Restoration.

On the other hand, any hypothesis which bristles with so many misleading or potentially fallacious implications must be met with healthy suspicion. There had after all been an industrial proletariat in England long before the second half of the eighteenth century: not a 'working class' in the sense that early nineteenth-century Britons used the term by the 1820s and 1830s, in a much more rapidly industrialising land, but several hundred thousand families in manufacturing occupations, working either for wages or on piece rates, economically dependent on an employer or on a middleman. Furthermore, there were important gradations among workers in industry, not wholly unlike those in society at large between 1660 and 1760: an 'aristocracy of labour', consisting of superior craftsmen or the possessors of specially sought-after skills; a large 'middling sort', comprising humbler craftsmen, tradesmen and artisans; and the labourers and unskilled workers at the bottom of the heap. The changes that took place, therefore, after 1750 or 1760, important though they were, were changes of degree. The industrial workforce grew in size, not only absolutely but relatively to workers on the land; it became more town-based, or at least located in one of the many constellations of industrial villages or hamlets which now clustered round most of the major manufacturing towns; and it grew more exclusively dependent on industry, as opposed to having one foot in the workshop and the other on the land (e.g. 145a, *63–4*). Its members were also more likely than before to be employed for a wage in an establishment outside the home; for this reason, as well as for the geographical one just mentioned, some of them in particular trades and particular localities grew increasingly group-conscious.

Structural shifts, too, were taking place within this industrial proletariat some decades in advance of the Industrial Revolution. The rôle of the family as an occupational unit was being enhanced. The domestic putting-out system in textiles and hosiery had always involved the family; but the trend towards larger workshops and ultimately the introduction of the new water-powered mills, which were heavily dependent on the labour of women and children in their early years, drew the latter into the system in a more organised way. During the eighteenth century, also, female labour was introduced for the first time into such industries as nailmaking, buttonmaking and pinmaking. Meanwhile, the proportion of unskilled to skilled and semi-skilled workers in industry had been growing for much of the century, and was to do so more rapidly with greater mechanisation and larger units of work, while the status gap, if not the economic gap, between the unskilled worker and the craftsman widened. At the same time work-discipline, 'the tyranny of the clock', as men and women alike undertook to work a fixed-hour day – not infrequently as long as twelve hours – for an agreed wage, gained ground over the self-discipline of the cottage piece-worker and eroded traditional leisure time, including the cherished 'Saint Monday' (230; 122).

Viewing the troubles of the late 1750s and 1760s as portents of a sea-change in industrial relations can also produce a misleading picture of the history of industrial disputes themselves, including the development of labour organisation, as well as a distorting perspective on the evolution of a class structure. A detailed study of labour disputes in the British Isles from 1717 to 1800 has revealed fifty-seven reported disputes in the years 1741–60 and much the same incidence between 1717 and 1740, when sixty were traced. Around three-quarters in both periods are found to concern wages and/or hours of work. There was certainly a deterioration in the next two decades, down to 1780 – an increase to 113 disputes, 80 of them over wages or hours – but that can hardly be called a dramatic change. For the first time in the 1760s and 70s there are the strikes or disorders over the introduction of machinery we noticed earlier, though only eight are recorded all told, and only fifteen from 1781–1800, when the total number of disputes rose to 153. They introduced a new and potentially serious source of violent unrest into the relations between employers and employed in industry, though violence and disorder itself was no novelty in this field, as will be seen (229).

However, the facts behind these bare figures are a good deal less straightforward than the figures themselves. For one thing, the years 1773–83, when the onward march of new industry and new manufacturing methods was growing in pace, was a far quieter period in labour relations than 1762–72 had been. By the early 1780s even the new cotton machines were causing little animosity, at least in the North, where it quickly became apparent that they had improved earnings and cost few jobs; such trouble of that kind as occurred over the next decade came with attempts to bring jennies into the old cloth strongholds of Wiltshire and Somerset and with the first introduction of machine frames in the Midlands hosiery industry (229, *165*). This suggests that some very particular circumstances were at work in the 1760s, the most disorderly period of the whole century until the mid–1790s and indeed there were, as we shall see (below, pp. 167–9). In the second place, the regional distribution of eighteenth-century labour disputes is very striking. London accounted for well over half the cases in England (50 out of 98) from 1761–80 and for nearly 44 per cent over the first 80 years of the century. The South West of England experienced almost as many strikes and disorders as London between 1717 and 1760, overwhelmingly in that region's declining cloth industry. Other regions, except latterly the North West, were little troubled in that period and almost totally unaffected in the 1730s – which again suggests exceptional circumstances. Lancashire's record worsened from the late 1750s to the 70s, as did that of the North East, yet in some of the most rapidly industrialising areas in England and Wales before 1780, the West Riding, North Staffordshire and the West Midlands, and in South Wales, there was a remarkable, sustained industrial peace for sixty years. Analysis of the many London disputes of the same period shows that they took place far more in the clothing and service trades (for example, among tailors, hatters, curriers, wigmakers, coachbuilders and building workers), and among dockworkers, than in large-scale manufactures. Silk weaving was the one major exception.

Equally notable was the number of major industries and important second-line manufactures which were almost entirely trouble-free down to 1780: metalworking in the West Midlands and South Yorkshire, with the noteworthy exception of its most unskilled branch, nailing; iron and steel; West Riding cloth-making; linen manufacture; sugar-refining, brewing, potting, glass and paper-making, and, before the 1770s, the hosiery trade. In the provinces nearly all the trouble throughout the period 1717–80 was confined to a mere handful of occupations: West Country weavers, colliers, riverside workers and merchant seamen were in the forefront, with tailors also obstreperous, as they were in London, and Lancashire textile workers coming into prominence from the late 1750s. Three explanations of these glaring differences would seem to fit the facts. One concerns the vulnerability of some industries and service trades to long-term depression: the woollen and worsted weavers of the South West and later of East Anglia are the classic case, but rivermen and coal-heavers were also sensitive to periodic general declines in trade. Then there is the question of organisation. Miners, weavers, seamen and riverside workers often lived in fairly tight, close-knit communities, even when their habitat was semi-rural, and the early history of workers' combinations and 'clubs' or friendly societies, the seedbed of later trade unionism, can be closely linked with just such areas. The organisation of the Devonshire weavers as early as the 1720s appeared so sinister to the authorities that Parliament legislated against it. But it cannot be overstressed that there is little sign before 1783 of any 'working class' solidarity as opposed to the local solidarity of men in the same trade and the same area. Thirdly, the pattern of eighteenth-century labour disputes raises the whole question of the disparate rewards of labour. Cutlers, men (and for that matter some women) in the Birmingham 'toy' trade, potters in the luxury branch of the industry, furnacemen and forgemen – to give just a few examples – were a whole league better off at most times than weavers, building workers or tailors. Of the skilled craftsmen of Sheffield, the small master cutlers and their journeymen, Arthur Young observed in 1769 that they made 'immense earnings' of between 9 shillings (45p.) and 20 shillings (£1) a week. Not a single dispute is recorded in Sheffield until 1787, when there were complaints that some hard-faced merchants were asking for thirteen knives to the dozen! (141, *229*; 229, *165*).

However, it is unlikely that wage movements in general in the eighteenth century can throw a great deal of light either on industrial relations or on the often extreme oscillations from modest prosperity to demoralising poverty which were the lot of so many of the 'industrious poor' of Hanoverian Britain.[7] In the decade before 1720, broad wage trends had been for the most part upwards [M.2]. The standard study of eighteenth-century wages shows that overall there was a further but only gradual upward movement until 1760, steepest where industry was expanding fast and labour was most in demand (167; see also 168a, *131*). Yet reduced to generalities like these the figures leave so much unexplained. They do not tell us why there was a spectacular deterioration in the relations of capital and labour in the mid-1760s, soon after the long period of relative wage stability had ended – apparently in favour of labour. Nor do they reveal why, of the areas which enjoyed higher than average increases in earnings after 1760, Lancashire should have been prone to strikes and disturbances while South and West Yorkshire and the West Midlands largely escaped them. One key to the problem is the enormous amount of variation and uncertainty which existed at all times within both national and regional wage norms. The second and more important key is the movement of prices, and therefore of '*real* wages' during this period.

As Peter Mathias has explained, pre-industrial Britain had by and large what is called today a 'low-wage economy,' the standard assumption until well after 1750 being that because labour was still, almost universally, the governing factor in production, it was vital to keep labour costs low (especially in the case of textiles, easily Britain's major export commodity and the most vulnerable to undercutting and hostile foreign tariffs). Governments and economists alike looked to the justices of the peace to use their statutory powers to this end in England and Wales. Sir Robert Walpole, in fact, has often been unjustly criticised by historians for taking a hard line on wage demands when his policy was perfectly in step with accepted contemporary wisdom, and indeed rather more pragmatic and flexible than that of some of his predecessors (33b, *63–4*). And yet, as was earlier remarked, there was only minimal industrial strife outside London and the South West in the period 1720–60. The main reason seems plain enough. Except in badly depressed industries or trades, low earnings had little adverse effect on living standards while the *cost* of living was so low. After 1711, a year in which prices temporarily surged to levels not equalled again in the eighteenth century until the 1790s, the cost of consumer goods other than cereals in England remained for fifty-nine years out of the next sixty below, and frequently 10–15 per cent below, their level at the beginning of the century – a level that was about average for the 1690s. Even between 1772, when non-cereal prices for the first time edged above those of 1701, and 1783, the rise was very slight and slow. The conclusion seems inescapable that it was the price of cereals, and fundamentally the cost of bread, which made the great difference to the labouring man's perception of his condition. When a comprehensive price index is constructed which *includes* grain, it follows a roughly similar general pattern to the price of non-cereals until 1757.[8] For the next eight years there was a slow upward trend, but from 1765 – that threshold year when the price of bread in London, having risen by over 50 per cent since 1761, was dearer than at any time since 1709 – Englishmen entered a new age of dearer grain; in the seventeen years from then until 1782 the general cost of living index is an average of 10 per cent up on the level of 1701 (128b, *468–9, 497–8*).

Nevertheless, (and this needs to be emphasised) there is compelling evidence that 'real wages' – always the historian's surest yardstick in making any general assessment of the conditions of 'the industrious poor' – remained remarkably buoyant for virtually the entire eighteenth century, at least between 1711 and the mid-1790s, except for one vital decade. Between 1764–5 and 1774–5 real wages in England, measured on the most sophisticated series now available to us [see M.2], fell to an average level which, though not unprecedentedly low even for the eighteenth-century, was 72 points down on the average for the previous fifteen years, and no less than 128 points down on the nirvana years of the eighteenth century lower orders, in the 1730s. It was the decade of which Adam Smith wrote in 1776: 'the high price of provisions during these ten years past has not in many parts of the kingdom been accompanied with any sensible rise in the money price of labour'.[9] It is hard to resist the conclusion that what contributed most to the unusual ferment of labour relations in the late 1760s was not any absolute state of misery, even in badly-affected trades and regions, but rather the stark contrast with prolonged previous experience. The contrast between the eruptions of 1765–8 and the comparative phlegm with which industrial workers bore far harsher conditions from 1709–11 becomes less striking if we reflect that in the interim the sons and grandsons of those workers had gradually grown used to living standards beyond reasonable expectation sixty years earlier. It was these standards which the exceptional conditions of the 1760s appeared to threaten.

Labouring men and their families were purchasers as well as producers. Enough can be deduced from probate inventories which have survived from the middle and later decades of the eighteenth century to confirm that, in return for their long hours of labour, artisans and unskilled workers in industry, and even the better-off agricultural labourers, expected to be able to buy for their families some of the 'decencies of life' as well as basic necessities. How they achieved these levels of consumption has been a matter for debate, and some wonderment, especially in the light of what is known about levels of the Poor Rate. It has been suggested that an income of at least £50 a year was necessary by the years 1750–80 for a family to become consumers of positive benefit to the economy rather than mere survivors (168b; cf. 122, *212–16*). But that would rule out all but the most skilled craft workers in industry and the entire body of agricultural labourers and domestic servants. Even when grain prices began to rise permanently in the 1760s, a personal or family income of £25–£30 a year would have been enough for modest comfort in much of the North of England, where the cost of living was appreciably lower than in the wheat-dependent south. In the cheap grain years before the middle of the century such an income was adequate, and perhaps rather more than adequate, for a manual worker's household almost everywhere. Subsequently it may be, as Neil McKendrick has argued, that the increasing number of wives and children in industrial employment goes far to explain why habits of 'luxury' went on being attributed to the English lower orders by a stream of observers, domestic and foreign, throughout the early decades of George III's reign. The force of the point can be briefly illustrated from the humblest of the West Midland metal trades. A male nailer in West Bromwich or Walsall in 1780 earned an average of only 7 shillings a week. But if, as often happened, he had a wife and two boys at work in the same trade, the family's income became 17 or 18 shillings (142b, *153*). How much of the purchasing power of ordinary working folk was built on such variables as these it is impossible to say. But it is at least arguable that without the demand for manufactured goods which such folk generated over a century of buoyant real wages, Britain might not have been, near the end of that century, the first nation to experience an Industrial Revolution.[10]

---

1. Paisley had 31,179 inhabitants by 1801. On the rapidity of its expansion, especially after 1770, see Hamilton (246), p. 28 and B.3(iii).

2. See *Making of a Great Power*, Ch. 19 for the earlier growth of Halifax. By 1774 it was ranked by Dean Tucker among 'the richest and most flourishing [towns] in the kingdom'. Ten years earlier the population of the town itself may not have been much more than 6,000 (1,272 families), but including the densely-populated cloth-making villages which covered the hillsides and valleys of Halifax *parish*, the total had risen to at least 40,000 (8,244 families). P. Corfield (213), p. 23; J. Brewer and J. Stiles, eds, *An Ungovernable People* (1980), p. 207.
3. Quoted in N. McKendrick, 'Josiah Wedgwood and the Commercialization of the Potteries', in (191), p. 127.
4. A. Raistrick and E. Allen, 'The South Yorkshire Ironmasters, 1690–1750', *EcHR*, **9** (1939).
5. See J.C.D. Clark (289), pp. 64–7, for a provocative discussion of this question. J.K. Walton (145a), p. 106, underlines the crucial distinction in late eighteenth-century Lancashire between cotton spinning – 'already a factory industry' by the early 1790s – and the still growing army of hand-loom weavers.
6. This was some 35 per cent more than the leading 12 brewers had produced in 1748. In general see P. Mathias, 'The Industrial Revolution in Brewing, 1700–1830', in (131a), pp. 219–27 *passim*.
7. R. W. Malcolmson, *Life and Labour in England 1700–1780* (1981), p. 145 (for shortcomings of general wages evidence). And see Adam Smith, *The Wealth of Nations* [1776], (1874 edn.), Ch. 8 *passim* 'Of the Wages of Labour'.
8. With a few more brief fluctuations, notably, sharp rises in 1720–1 and 1740–1, followed by equally sharp falls.
9. Adam Smith, *The Wealth of Nations* (1874 edn.), p. 57.
10. See also Eversley (168b); N. McKendrick, 'Home Demand and Economic Growth: A New View of the Role of Women and Children in the Industrial Revolution', in (133).

CHAPTER 12

Popular protest and public authority

The fact that the discontents of industrial workers boiled over from time to time into disorder or violence reminds us that strong undercurrents of popular protest were rarely far beneath the bland surface of the eighteenth-century British state. Beginning with the pioneering work of George Rudé (48; 219a), a great deal of scholarly interest has been invested during the past thirty years in a phenomenon which was regarded by contemporary Britons with consternation and by foreigners with astonishment. To the Augustan and Georgian ruling classes it was 'the mob'; historians now prefer to term it, not always advisedly (220, *10–11*), 'the crowd'.

In the place of the myths (mostly of contemporary origin) which once encrusted the subject, considered answers can now be given with varying degrees of confidence to a series of questions about the nature and motives of popular protest in the pre-industrial century, from *circa* 1680 to *circa* 1780, about the composition, objectives and organisation of the crowd, and about the attitudes of authority towards it. This chapter first attempts an overview of these problems, and makes some appraisal of central and local reactions to popular protest. It goes on to consider what institutions existed in eighteenth-century Britain to try to ensure that local communities were adequately governed and the will of the central power given effect, and how far they were capable of exercising social control and, with or without the aid of force, preserving public order.

I

Why did men (and occasionally women, too) riot in the century before 1780? This is the fundamental question and the starting-point for all further analysis. It is a particularly intriguing question in the case of London, whose 450,000 rising to over 750,000 inhabitants – the largest and densest concentration of urban population in Europe, and a potentially horrendous threat to the court and government in its midst – punctuated a record of general quiescence with periodic explosions of alarming ferocity. Such outbreaks occurred five times between the Revolution and the fall of Walpole, in 1688, 1710, 1715, 1733 and 1736, and thereafter in 1753, 1768 and 1780. But the question 'why?' is a very pertinent one also to ask of the English provinces, where disorder was more endemic and its pattern far more kaleidoscopic; it is relevant to Scotland also.

In every notable outburst of rioting in the capital either religious or political passions, or both, were in some degree involved. An undertow of economic unrest is often detectable, however, and on some occasions – as in the riots against the employment of cheap Irish labour in 1736, and above all in the disorders of 1768 already alluded to (Ch. 11) – such unrest could be a powerful force. When the mob took to the streets of London during the Revolution of 1688 Catholic chapels were burned or wrecked in a frightening postscript to the mainly non-violent 'No Popery' demonstrations of the Exclusion Crisis[1], and almost a century later anti-Catholicism horrifyingly reasserted itself in the prolonged mayhem of the Gordon riots, the worst of the entire period. In 1710, the year of the Sacheverell riots (*Making of a Great Power*, Ch. 23), and again in 1715–16, the animus of the crowd was turned against the Protestant dissenters and their meeting-houses, and in 1753 against the Jews (p. 240 below). But in addition to religious prejudice there was also a strong element of popular politics, of disaffection aroused by widely disliked regimes, expressed against the Whigs by the Sacheverell mobs and by the anti-Hanover rioters of 1715–16, as well as by the later protesters against the Excise Bill in 1733 and against the persecutors of John Wilkes in 1768 (Ch. 22).

Not that disorderly political demonstrations, infused more often than not with religious animosity, were a metropolitan preserve. Before 1740, especially, they were the cause of considerable concern in the provinces. Few General Elections down to 1741 passed off without sparking at least a few serious disturbances, usually in the larger boroughs: there was a pitched battle in the streets of Coventry in 1705, a violent affray in Bristol in 1713, and more general 'frenzy', breaking out into disorders in numerous constituencies, at the 'Church in Danger' Election of 1710 and the Excise Election of 1734 (32a, *Ch. 8*). London's anti-Catholic riots of 1688, Sacheverell riots, and the chain of street protests which marked the period between George I's coronation and the suppression of the first Jacobite Rebellion all had their provincial counterparts; indeed, in the summer of 1715, in the course of more than two months of almost unbroken disorders with strong Jacobite undertones, more than forty nonconformist meeting-houses were demolished or sacked, many of them in the West Midlands,[2] and the army was on general alert (222a). In 1746 it was the turn of Roman Catholic chapels to suffer again, notably at Liverpool and Sunderland; as we have seen (Ch. 8) it was in the same decade that Methodists began to offer a fresh target for popular fury. In Scotland, both the Glasgow Malt Tax riots of 1725 (*Making of a Great Power*, Ch. 20) and the tumultuous events in Edinburgh in 1736, when, following the execution of a smuggler, the town guard was ordered to open fire to contain a threatening mob, and its commander, Captain Porteous, was then lynched, had political undercurrents. They should be seen as eruptions of popular dislike for a Union Parliament and a London-based executive which imposed new duties – or enforced old ones – on the Scots, and not simply as protests against the impositions themselves. On the other hand, the 'No Popery' riots of 1779 in Glasgow, Edinburgh and other towns were, like London's Gordon Riots, the expression of a far older prejudice.[3]

Aside from political or religious disorders, it is possible to distinguish three principal nationwide types of popular protest, three categories which embrace virtually all other riots which took place in eighteenth-century Britain before 1790, many hundreds of them in all. Industrial disorders made up by far the smallest of the three. A fair proportion of industrial disputes were in any event solved peacefully. Where rioting did occur it was more likely before 1720 to have been caused by trade depressions or by resentment at 'unfair' competition than by wages or the cost of living (217). From the 1720s to the 1750s industrial relations remained a relatively uncommon cause of serious disorder over Britain as a whole, but there were interludes of dismaying violence in a few particular regions and trades. The discontents of the West Country cloth weavers (Ch. 11) and of that 'set of ungovernable people', the Kingswood coalminers, made Devon, Somerset, Wiltshire and the country west of Bristol a byword for their periodic unruliness between 1717 and 1753. For example, hundreds of injuries were reported from Taunton in 1725 after 500 loom-breaking weavers were confronted by an equally determined force of tradesmen, townsfolk and wool-combers; at Bristol in 1729 seven weavers were shot dead by a besieged clothier and his family, who also accounted fatally for one of a party of soldiers sent to restore order; and four rioters were killed and over fifty seriously injured when the colliers from Kingswood Chase invaded Bristol in 1753 and were fired on by the militia (229, *30–5*; 226, *120–1*). By then, however, the keelmen of the rivers Tyne and Wear and the royal dockyard workers of the South had usurped for a while the colliers' and weavers' special reputation for truculent violence (229, *156–8*; 220, *121–2, 126–7*). Although it is possible, as we have seen, to over-dramatise the change that took place after 1760, it is indisputable that from then on industrial rioting assumed a higher profile in relation to other types of disorder, with violence in the London trades much commoner (there was nowhere worse in the whole century than London in 1768–9), with more provincial regions and industries becoming involved, and a greater propensity for initially peaceful strikes to degenerate into strong-arm confrontations. The employment of troops against rioters of this nature became commoner, and both bloodshed on the streets and hangings afterwards more frequent. At the same time wages figured more prominently as a cause of grievance, along with resentment against new machines (Ch. 11), although traditional aversions continued to obtrude from time to time. Indeed, one of the bloodiest running battles of the whole century, involving the Spitalfields silk-weavers from January to September 1768, was provoked by overseas competition and the over-employment of cheap apprentice labour, as well as by opposition to engine-looms (220, *70–1*; 219a, *73–5*).

In the second half of the eighteenth century, however, as in the first, it was the food riot, or 'grain riot', that remained the quintessential vehicle of popular protest. Rudé traced 275 popular disturbances in the period from 1735 to 1800, and in two-thirds of these cases the source of the trouble was identified as the high price, or scarce supply, of grain (219a, *35–6*). The choice of the date 1735 as a starting-point does, however, distort the picture to some extent, since it falls near the end of a period of fifty–sixty years, marked by long runs of abnormally low cereal prices (Ch. 11), when food rioting was relatively infrequent by normal pre-industrial standards. Beloff, in a precursive study of late Stuart popular unrest published fifty years ago, could find evidence of only thirty-three such riots in England between 1680 and 1714. No fewer than twenty-nine of those were confined to the four dearth years of 1693–5 and 1709, and whole decades passed without a tremor. Because of his work's heavy dependence on central records Beloff's count was not definitive, but there is no reason to doubt the validity of the general message it conveys. A striking fact is that in the entire period 1660–1714 government records reveal not a single food riot north of a line from Shrewsbury to Stamford, or in Wales, and only one further west than Dorset, that is to say, in those parts of the country where coarser grains were still predominant and wheaten bread a relative luxury (217, *169*). By the end of the eighteenth century that situation had altered, along with the economic structure and dietary habits of the population, so that in the 1790s the North West of England had become as combustible as any area in the country. But long before this the intensity as well as the distribution of food riots had begun to change. The unrest of 1746, still more that of 1756–7, and most of all that of 1766–7 – by which time England was locked into the new age of rising prices and declining real wages [M.1, M.2] – was both more widespread and more disturbing than that of, say, 1693 or 1709. In the summer of 1756 the Midlands of England were convulsed from Derbyshire to Northamptonshire and from Staffordshire eastwards to Leicestershire; in the autumn and early winter the trouble spread to the North East, the South West and the Welsh borders. By December two cavalry regiments and nearly 80 companies of foot were detailed for riot duty. During 1757 over 50 towns in 31 counties were affected, though in some of them the Militia Act was the chief cause of disorder (227, *78–93*). 1766 proved an even more alarming year, with grain riots in 68 places in 20 counties, greater destruction and more injuries, at least 13 fatalities, infinitely more arrests, and 24 rioters sentenced to death (219a, *38–43*; 228). Neither then nor at any time in the period, however, was London afflicted. Both the central government and the municipal authority knew well that they were sitting on a powder keg, and Londoners were the first to benefit from emergency measures to increase supplies and keep bread prices within reason. Food riots were in the main a provincial market town or manufacturing town phenomenon, and industrial workers, such as tinners, colliers and weavers, were frequently in the van of protest.

While food riots rarely involved the rural population, two forms of protest which did predominantly do so were those directed against enclosures and turnpikes. The extensive enclosures effected in the second half of the seventeenth century and in the early eighteenth were mainly by local agreement (*Making of a Great Power*, Ch. 2; Ch. 9) and they caused minimal unrest, by contrast with the disorders and even rebellions provoked by agrarian discontent in the sixteenth century. Only two clear cases of an enclosure riot have come to light in the period 1660–1714.[4] As late as William III's reign, when 1,100 countrymen destroyed the drainage works at Deeping Fen in Lincolnshire in a spectacular assertion of their traditional fishing and fowling rights (217, *78–80*), fen reclamation caused more trouble than enclosures. It was not until the great age of *parliamentary* enclosure was under way after 1750 that riotous destruction of hedges and fences became more than an extreme rarity; even then the unrest provoked by the enclosure of commons in Wiltshire and Norfolk (1758), Oxfordshire and Northamptonshire in the 1760s, and Lincolnshire and Worcestershire (1771–2) represents a surprisingly small-scale reaction when set against the 2,000-odd Acts passed by Parliament in the second half of the century (219a, *35*; 220, *40–3*). In relation to their numbers, turnpikes caused greater resentment. After its post-Restoration beginnings the turnpike system for road maintenance took a long time to develop the degree of momentum that was being achieved between 1750 and 1776, when the number of turnpike trusts increased from 143 to 500. Nevertheless, as early as the 1720s forty-six Turnpike Acts had gone through Parliament in a decade and in the 1740s a sudden spurt of twenty-five Acts brought the system from the South and Midlands into the six most northerly English counties.[5] What was welcome to long-suffering travellers, however, was frequently objectionable to local inhabitants, who had to pay the new charges on their horses and waggons and who were likely to view them more as a tax on their produce than as an 'improvement'. The Bristol area seems to have been the scene of the first violent protest, in 1727. From then until 1750 turnpike riots were monopolised by Somerset, Gloucestershire and then Herefordshire, whence in 1735 the Lord Chancellor received such a chilling 'account of a new attempt to demolish the turnpikes near Sedbury, attended with a very outrageous riot', and also with 'the first instance in which I have heard that the country gentlemen opposed themselves against attempts of this nature', that he urged emergency measures on his Cabinet colleagues.[6] Popular opposition to turnpiking spread north to Yorkshire in 1753 when the century's most serious riots of this kind took place near Leeds and Wakefield. Even so, most English regions appear to have escaped, and once again it is the low incidence of violence relative to the widespread nature of change, especially after 1740, which is most notable.

For the historian it makes good sense to consider both enclosure and turnpike riots not as separate local phenomena but as integral parts of a basic syndrome in much eighteenth-century popular protest, in which the crowd was roused from customary passivity to furious anger by what it took to be the violation of traditional rights or of 'liberties' popularly considered part of an Englishman's birthright. When a man's ancestors had pastured their beasts on a piece of common land, or travelled freely to market along a certain road, for generations, one can readily appreciate his sense of outrage when these freedoms were taken away. Manifestations of the same syndrome appear in other disorders which, though in themselves diverse in character, can logically be grouped together. For example, there was a series of riots in the years 1704–09, when Acts of Parliament were in force authorising the conscription of unemployed able-bodied men for the army, but they were as nothing to the effects of the mid-century Militia Acts. First passed in 1757, these provoked alarming disorders during the Seven Years' War, culminating in the most appalling confrontation in 1761 between 5,000 Northumberland colliers, demonstrating against the ballot for recruits, and a force of Yorkshire militia; this Hexham battle was second only to the Gordon riots before 1790 for its 'butcher's bill' of fatal casualties.[7] In between these eruptions, in the early part of 1733, there were mob demonstrations the length and breadth of the country against the Walpole ministry's plans to subject tobacco and wine imports to excise duties and a bonded warehouse system (Ch. 5), causing a storm so intense that, as Paul Langford has said, 'contemporaries . . . could compare [it] only with that of the Sacheverell affair' (32a, *46*).

On the surface, protests against compulsory recruitment in wartime and against excises may seem to have little in common with disturbances over enclosures and turnpikes. But in fact, fear of an army of excisemen extending their statutory rights of search almost indefinitely struck at the Englishman's basic instinct for the sanctity of his private property; while state-imposed conscription was seen (and not by the victims alone) as an unwarrantable violation of personal liberty, all the more unjust because in effect it was only the poor who suffered. These are not the only examples of the way official acts offended against the man-in-the-street's sense of what was customary and proper and stirred him to violence in reaction. There are links here with the rioting against 'the great recoinage' of 1695, and also with riots against the London surgeons in George II's reign, with their message that 'the proper, respectful treatment of the dead was a profound and serious concern to the crowds attending Tyburn hangings' (217, *100–5*; 224a, esp. *116* [P. Linebaugh]). In addition, of course, the 'Wilkes and Liberty' riots of 1768, although considered political disorders in the present context, were in their own way a part of the same syndrome; so too was the food riot, with its roots deep back in the medieval past – in the idea of a 'just price' and in what Edward Thompson has called the traditional 'moral economy' of the English poor (223b).

The implication seems clear, therefore, that the question, 'Why did men riot in eighteenth-century Britain?' cannot be answered simply by detailing and categorising the causes of hundreds of individual disturbances. It must also take account of the underlying instincts and ideas of the rioters and consider how far these amount to a coherent ethos of protest. To penetrate the largely inarticulated ideology of the pre-industrial crowd, however, it is not enough to ask *why* disorders took place: we must also know *who* rioted, and *how*? The social composition of the eighteenth-century crowd and its patterns of behaviour have both been carefully scrutinised by modern students of popular unrest, breaking down the once-impervious anonymity of 'the mobile' by the study of sample members, identified mainly from judicial evidence. If some conclusions have been predictable, others have been quite startling.

Those who engaged in popular street disturbances came in the main, though not exclusively, from what contemporaries called 'the lower sort of people', but under that broad umbrella a profile is revealed that is far from regular. Its components range from small employers, small tradesmen and journeymen craftsmen at one end of the scale to labourers, domestic servants and apprentices (in a wide variety of trades) at the other end. Furthermore, in provincial food riots, and sometimes in other disorders such as the riot of the Tiverton weavers in 1765 (213, *163*), housewives were often participants, and on occasion initiators; though as yet anticipating, rather than justifying, Southey's lofty pronouncement of 1807 that in England 'women are more disposed to be mutinous [than men]; they stand less in fear of law, partly from ignorance, partly because they presume upon the privilege of their sex . . .'[8] It used to be claimed that the bulk of rioting crowds in the towns, and above all in London, was made up of riff-raff, the poorest slum dwellers, probably with a high criminal element incorporated. But modern research has nailed this myth completely. It has shown that rioters were not itinerant trouble-makers; with just a few exceptions they were locally based, operating in their own neighbourhoods and in the case of London, commonly within their own districts. What is more, they usually lived in respectable areas and had fixed and identifiable addresses (only very rarely do we come across a record of a rioter 'of no known abode'); the vast majority were in work, with barely a trace of the endemic unemployed or vagrants. Nicholas Rogers, who describes his early Hanoverian London protestors as 'settled members of society', notes that no less than two-thirds of the rioters he identified in 1715–16 were released on bail after their arrests – in itself a highly significant fact (222b; 219b; *Pt. III*; 221). Even in the latter stages of the Gordon riots, when the release of prisoners from Newgate and other prisons did inject a far more dubious element into the crowd, many of those released were debtors, often of respectable birth, rather than denizens of a criminal underworld.

Men engaged in certain occupations were regarded in the eighteenth century as being unduly riotous, among them tinners, coalminers, silk-weavers, rivermen and, in the West Country at least, woollen cloth workers. Yet in the English provinces, whether in food riots, protests against turnpikes or enclosures, or industrial disorders, the respectable, identifiable working man was as predominant as he was in London. What was generally missing was the *ultra*-respectable element detectable in some of the biggest London disorders of the period. Among those Sacheverell rioters whose status is known the ratio of self-employed to wage-earning employees, for instance, was roughly 1:1, compared with 1:2 in mid- and late eighteenth century London riots; there was a good presence also of the 'lower middle class' (industrial employers in a modest way, craftsmen in prestige trades, bailiffs) and an even more extraordinary white-collar, professional and 'gentlemanly' element, more than a seventh of the whole sample. Similarly, of the 135 anti-Hanover dissidents identified in 1715-16, 30 per cent were made up either of gentlemen and professionals (12–13), workers in 'superior' or 'genteel' trades (16), or yeomen, who were by definition respectable (13). It is also a possibility – if no more than that – that the *apparently* drastic shrinkage of this riotous élite in London between the disorders of 1710–16 and those of 1768 and 1780 is something of an illusion, attributable to the differences in the evidence available for studying the crowd in the two periods, rather than to a basic change of character.[9]

The patterns of behaviour followed by eighteenth-century rioters down to 1780 display several notably consistent traits. Some features, in fact, were almost universal. In the first place, the targets of the crowd's violence invariably reflect its causes; they also pay tribute to the innate restraint of those generally humble but far from disreputable members of society who chose this time-honoured way to make their point, a restraint unhinted at in favourite contemporary sobriquets, like 'the rabble'. The prime, original targets were nearly always *property* rather than persons; the murder of Porteous was the one conspicuous individual exception, and the harrying of Methodist preachers the only general one. The properties attacked were deliberately and discriminatingly selected, as evident symbols of those people or actions which had incurred the crowd's anger. It was also the case, however, that the longer disorders went on, or the greater the delay in redressing the grievances that underlay them, the more likely it was that discipline would break down and that extraneous property, and occasionally unfortunate individuals, would come under attack. But even in London, where the risks were enormous, this happened very rarely, before 1768 at least. Only the Gordon riots, which lasted for a week, got desperately out of hand, and then only with the break-out from the prisons, and after three days' jittery indecision on the part of the military had emboldened the wilder elements (219b, *272–4*; 227, *147–58*).

In food riots the commonest targets were the premises, machinery and stock of millers or corn factors, or sometimes the barns of farmers suspected of hoarding grain – the object being to force down the price to 'just' levels. The fact that bakeries or the shops of small bakers were far less commonly attacked illustrates, along with the timing of the outbreaks, how little the average bread riot was a reflex reaction to hunger and how much an accusing response to local prices that were deemed far too high, even for a time of scarcity; the real villains were seen as those middlemen who were blamed for making unreasonable profits out of the vagaries of Nature (223; 219a). In enclosure and turnpike riots the objects of the crowd's anger were entirely predictable and self-explanatory: fences, hedges, turnpike bars and gates, and toll-collectors' houses. Industrial disorders were characterised sometimes by the smashing of machinery, where that in itself was the principal grievance, sometimes by the destruction of stores or equipment (for example, stocks of coal or winding ropes) or the slashing of thread or cloth on the looms, but occasionally by attacks on the houses of employers. So too with disturbances in which religious passions were unleashed; although places of worship were always the primary targets, the residences of prominent Papists and dissenters, or even of Anglicans believed to be in league with them, might well be in some danger from an overspill of the crowd's wrath.

A further general feature of crowd behaviour which research has identified is the fact that, whether chapels or industrial premises or private houses were under assault, the mobs showed a marked preference for the property of the wealthy. It is doubtful whether a compelling case can be made out for 'class hostility' as a key element in eighteenth-century popular protest, but certainly there is evidence of what Rudé calls 'social discrimination' (219a, *62*). Of the six dissenting meeting-houses sacked in London by the Sacheverell rioters, all but one were in well-to-do areas or had fashionable congregations; the one private mansion in imminent danger that night, before the Grenadiers intervened, belonged to one of the richest of the capital's Presbyterian citizens, Sir Edmund Harrison. In 1780 the mobs left conspicuously untouched the thickly-populated parishes of East London, where the poorer Catholics abounded. They singled out the 'mass-houses', private chapels and town residences of Papists in the West End and Westminster, along with some Catholic-owned business premises, such as the extensive distilleries of Thomas Langdale of Holborn, put to the torch with disastrous consequences for surrounding buildings. Only in the later, anarchic stages of the Gordon riots did the violence spread to the poorer areas of Southwark and Bermondsey (5, *226–47*; 219b, *270–6*). Not surprisingly in a city with a centuries-old tradition of xenophobia, some of the most unpopular men in

London during 'mobbing times' compounded the sin of their wealth with a foreign name. In December 1688, Sir John Reresby took note, the mob did not 'forbear the very chapels and houses of ambassadors and other public ministers'; the Spanish ambassador, for one, claimed to have lost £100,000 in plate and possessions, including a superb library.[10] Seven embassies of Catholic states were either attacked or threatened in 1780, and the Russian and Danish ambassadors, taking no risks, asked for military protection (227, *160*). The Bank of England was also endangered at this time, though less symbolically than in 1710 when it epitomised all the main bugbears of the Augustan High Church mob: indecent wealth; the 'damned Presbyterians', as well as immigrant Huguenots and Dutchmen, who were believed to control its affairs, and an unpopular Continental war which the Bank directors were thought to be supporting for their own further enrichment (221).

Most recent work on the eighteenth-century crowd has stressed its disciplined behaviour and the remarkable degree of organisation it often displayed, in country and urban riots alike (219b; 223b; 221; 228). It was easy enough to 'raise a mob', much less so to control it; although there is ample testimony to the part played by local 'captains' on the ground in directing crowd operations, it is plain that much of the discipline shown was in fact self-discipline, inculcated by clearly-perceived aims and a keen sense of the justice of their cause. Although the bigger riots did develop their own momentum, it is striking how well-defined the targets usually were at the start, and how much care was taken to avoid looting and to protect the wrong property from damage, in particular by keeping fires under control.[11] The low level of *personal* violence in the overwhelming majority of disorders before the 1790s is a further tribute to the discipline of the mobs. There were blood-curdling threats in plenty from rioters, but little serious attempt to carry them out. Even in the attacks on Methodist preachers and worshippers in the 1740s and 50s, Walsh finds 'little doubt . . . that much of the hostility shown by the crowds was intended to terrorise and intimidate rather than to inflict real physical damage' (113c, *215*). And where property was the primary target – as it was in ninety-nine riots out of a hundred in the century before 1783 – the number of *victims* of riot, other than the rioters themselves, was incredibly small. Even in London there was only one possible but unconfirmed fatality in 1710; none in 1715–16, 1733 or 1753; a sailor murdered in 1768; and, amazingly, not one innocent death in the chaos of June 1780, when 210 of the rioters themselves were killed outright by troops, 75 died of their wounds, and 25 more, out of 62 who received the death sentence, were later hanged. Indeed, the restraint shown by protesting crowds is all the more significant when contrasted with the heavy casualties they themselves on occasion suffered, especially after 1750, at the hands of troops, militiamen and civilian 'vigilantes'. They paid a heavy price in blood for their defence of the 'liberties' of 'true-born Englishmen'; if they reacted somewhat vigorously when force was used against them, as they did against the 'mug-house' levies and the duke of Newcastle's Whig bully-boys in 1715–16 (222b) the wonder is that their reactions were not far fiercer.

Discipline, organisation and social respectability do much to explain this restraint, but at root all sprang from the philosophy of the eighteenth-century crowd. This was intensely traditionalist: championing native 'liberties', certainly, but libertarian essentially in a conservative rather than in a radical or reformist sense. (In this respect there is the sharpest contrast between the political rioters of 1680–1780 and those of the 1790s or of 1815–19.) From their traditionalism, as much as anything, the crowd drew its powerful conviction that morality as well as justice was on its side (220, *309–12*; 223b). Only this can adequately explain why the game was so often played only to certain prescribed rules and why physical attacks on persons were considered self-defeating. Two other aspects of the ethos of protest deserve special note, both by-products of the crowd's conservatism and of its instinctive tendency to look backwards to an idealised past rather than forward to a rosy future. One was the protesters' devotion to the Good Old Ways, and consequent resistance to changes made in the name of mere progress, be it new machines, a new coinage, new methods of raising revenue designed to reduce fraud or inefficiency, new organisations and levies for keeping roads in repair, or new methods of marketing corn. The other aspect was its extreme dislike and distrust of nonconformity, in the widest sense of that term – that is to say, of any group, institution or practice which did not conform to the popular notion of established norms. Thus religious prejudice could be detonated, according to the mood of the hour, as easily against Protestant dissenters as against Roman Catholics, as readily against Methodists as against Jews; or racial prejudice stirred as violently against the Catholic Irish (as in 1736 and 1768) as against Protestant Huguenot businessmen or German courtiers (1710, 1715), or against a motley array of Continental diplomats (1688, 1780). Even the excise was hated not just for its authoritarian implications – 'no slavery, no Excise, no wooden shoes', chanted the mobs of 1733 – but also for its association with the Dutch. The new breed of middlemen in the corn trade or the landlords who went to Parliament to enclose common land instead of seeking a negotiated local settlement were nonconformists, no less than the directors of the new-fangled Bank, or parsons who roamed the country preaching in fields or market-places instead of in churches. As common objects of popular suspicion, all were potential foci of popular unrest.

II

There was such a multitude of disorders, great and small, in the Britain of 1660–1783 that it is not easy to keep a sense of proportion about them. Yet the historian must do so. Britons were not the anarchic, ungovernable people that foreigners often loved to caricature in their letters and travel journals. We would do well to remind ourselves that in between the Exclusion Crisis and the heyday of John Wilkes the biggest city in the Western world suffered only two seismic disturbances, in 1688 and 1710, both very brief. As for the rioting provincial crowd, it was only its reputation for occasional eruptions of political and religious disorder that made it more than a seasonal, and regional, visitation; neither food riots, industrial disorders, enclosure riots nor protests against turnpikes became widespread or (with the possible exception of industrial unrest in the South West) unduly serious until the latter part of George II's reign. In short, down virtually to the middle of the century the bonds of social control held reasonably firm, weakening dramatically only in three or four isolated years in England, and in 1725 and 1736 in Scotland.[12] Why was this so?

Late Stuart and Hanoverian Britain did of course offer a variety of outlets for the non-violent emission of popular steam, and in particular of political emotions (Ch. 3). Prominent among them were parliamentary elections (for the unenfranchised as well as for the voters); petitioning of Parliament; and a whole gamut of processions and other ritual displays and demonstrations. It is worth remembering, for example, that most of the street protests in favour of Wilkes in 1768–9 were ritualistic and peaceful, not riotous. Traditionally, one of the strongest of social cements had been the teachings of the Church of England, ceaselessly enjoining obedience to 'higher powers' in the state and to superiors in the social hierarchy (*Making of a Great Power*, Ch. 23). It may not be coincidental that the worst provincial riots in half a century after the Glorious Revolution, those of 1710 and 1715, were in protest against 'the Church in danger', and it is surely significant that the Anglican clergy widely condoned these activities and that some parsons actively encouraged them (221; 222b). By the 1730s and 1740s the Church's social message was becoming diluted and its audience a dwindling one, in common with that of the old dissenting churches (Ch. 7); it was not until the century was almost over that religious restraints on the lower orders were powerfully reactivated, by both evangelical Anglicans and Wesleyan Methodists. This is not to say, however, that habits of social deference lapsed dramatically in the interim. They were too ingrained for that, in custom as well as religious precept; in rural society, at least, they continued to play an essential part in holding together the fabric of public order (289, *67–90*).[13] Arguably, indeed, that contribution was no less important after 1740 than before, and offers one of the most convincing explanations of why agricultural labourers and farm servants are so conspicuous by their absence in virtually all provincial riots in the late seventeenth and eighteenth centuries. By contrast, the force of customary deference, like that of Christian obedience, was becoming less potent in the towns. It is just possible that something of the new political ethic of the urban bourgeoisie in the 1760s, as characterised by Brewer – attitudes intolerant of patrician leadership and with a 'conception of social and political relations [that] was entrepreneurial rather than deferential' (44, *268*) – had begun to seep down to the urban crowd by the last two to three decades of our period. Although very few of the middle-class campaigners for 'Wilkes and Liberty' appeared on the streets in 1768–9, several of the more humble protagonists who did so seem to have imbibed something of their creed; none more than the Southwark rioter who in May 1768 seized a magistrate by his collar and marked the cape of his greatcoat with a large *No. 45*, and who later (and no less symbolically) received the stiffest jail sentence of all for what authority saw as a more subversive act than the destruction of property by his fellows (219b, *236–7*; 44, *182*).

In this last incident, however, the punishment is even more revealing than the crime. For the magistrate was the chief, and the only omnipresent, representative of the king's government beyond the very centre of administration. In town and country alike the justices of the peace *were* the face of public authority. High sheriffs of counties still had honorific status and the power (little considered, in fact) to raise the *posse comitatus*; the lord lieutenants possessed the more important authority to call out the county militias and arm them for action in any emergency (see below). But to the justices fell the unique civil responsibility for maintaining order in the land, as well as for enforcing both common and statute law on the local communities. What is more, since all the deputy lieutenants, who effectively commanded the militia, were themselves prominent members of the commissions of the peace (77, *329*), and since by the Riot Act passed in 1715 JPs acquired new powers to invoke armed assistance (including regular troops) and to authorise its use to suppress 'tumultuous assemblies',[14] theirs was an overarching responsibility for preserving the King's Peace, more complete by the mid- and late eighteenth century than it had ever been. Not least, behind the extraordinary array of local powers which the magistrates wielded stood the authority, not simply of the Crown, but of the whole governing class of the country which they, in a very real sense, represented. Indeed, 'represented' is scarcely an adequate word. For in spite of royal purges in the 1680s, and much partisan pressure from Tories and Whigs over the next half century to produce local benches that were politically acceptable, the increase in the numbers stocking the commissions of the peace was so great between 1680 and 1780 (78a, *Appx., 367–72*) that by 1797 Edward Hasted, the historian of Kent, would write of 'every gentleman of rank and property in a county looking upon himself slighted if his name is not inserted' in its commission.[15] His own county had had only 56 JPs in 1636 and 129 in 1680; by 1791 their number had grown to 280. To cock a snook at a magistrate, therefore – a man who even when dispensing summary justice to a poacher in his private parlour 'exercised the power of the state at one remove', and who embodied in his own person the deification of property and 'degree' by the rules of eighteenth-century British society – was tantamount to *lèse majesté* (77, *372*; see also 78a, *passim*; 78b; 79).

As the inbuilt social controls over the lower orders appeared to many in the governing class to be weakening in the late 1750s and the 1760s, so the pressure on the forces of authority, which in the last resort were required to provide the external restraints on an unruly populace, grew more intense. This is reflected in the increasing severity with which justices of the peace and others in positions of power reacted to popular disorder: a greater readiness to invoke the Riot Act and use *force majeure*, with a particular bias, perhaps, against riotous industrial workers; stiffer penalties in the courts, with more frequent resort to capital punishment; and a tendency for magistrates to take a harder line even with food rioters, with whom a sympathetic, almost pussy-footing approach had been fairly common before 1756. Even so, there is still a world of difference between the climate of the 1760s and that of, say, 1795 or 1819. Not the most reactionary politician nor the most frightened JP saw the seeds of genuine sedition, still less of revolution, in the demonstrations of the Wilkites or the march of the Northumberland miners to Hexham. The first reaction of the majority of magistrates when confronted with a mob (and that of army officers, too, if they found themselves involved) was still likely to be a cautious rather than a fire-eating one (227).

We have referred to the justices as the face of public authority in pre-industrial Britain. But they were not, of course, the entire body; neither were they quite so autonomous within their own shires after the Restoration of 1660 as is often implied (4, *55–6*; 77, *358*; but cf. 79). Above them stood the two (occasionally three) Secretaries of State in their offices in Whitehall, to whom justices were expected to report any local circumstances thought worthy of the notice of central government and from whom they received in return periodic exhortations and instructions. There was also the Privy Council, its palmy days long since past, meeting irregularly but still capable of asserting itself in times of emergency, such as the sudden death of a monarch, the threat of invasion or rebellion, or even a harvest failure, by gingering up the Lord Lieutenants or issuing Orders in Council. Not least there was Parliament itself, its benches replete with men of the justices' own kind and the main generator of their phenomenal and continually-increasing workload.[16] Where there were weaknesses in the chain of authority, it was below rather than above the level of the magistrates that they usually showed themselves. So far as the machinery of public order was concerned there stood very little at ground level but the parish constables, and in some towns the 'watches'. Eighteenth-century Lord Chancellors and their local advisers recognised the growing law-and-order problems of a society becoming steadily urbanised by their appointments to county commissions of the peace. By 1750 it had become common practice for expanding urban parishes to have JPs of their own, resident in or close to the town, and the old criteria of birth and estate were increasingly ignored to make this possible (78a, *315–26*).

There were some awkward hiatuses, however, between their rôle and that of municipal government bodies, as such. An intricate web of dignitaries and officials presided over the affairs of the 200-odd English corporations, both 'closed' and 'open', and the Scottish burghs. Adding to the complexity were the unincorporated towns, including places as important as Manchester, Birmingham and Sheffield, in which considerable authority might be vested in bodies as various as parish vestries, courts leet or town trusts. And the picture was further blurred in the course of the eighteenth century by the creation of scores of special urban authorities, with particular powers (usually conferred by private Acts of Parliament) in such fields as street cleaning and lighting, water supply and workhouse relief (210, *37–41*). Although most of these bodies, from the most ancient corporations to the newest *ad hoc* commissions, had the power to raise their own revenue, employ their own officials and make by-laws, their involvement in the domain of public order was at best a nebulous one. Most towns maintained a 'watch' of some sort, but scarcely anywhere was there anything that remotely resembled a local police force, in the nineteenth- and twentieth-century sense. The nearest approach was in a handful of places where one of the new special statutory authorities was given police powers; the most successful instance was probably the Police Commissioners set up in Manchester in 1765. There was something strangely anomalous in the situation of important towns possessing their own courts and their own legal expertise, in the persons of Recorders,

Deputy Recorders and Town Clerks, yet little if any official responsibility for 'the King's peace'. But it was all part of a wider anomaly. After the outcry caused by the Stuarts' assault on town charters in the 1680s (*Making of a Great Power*, Ch. 11), central government since 1688 had virtually abandoned its right to tamper with municipal independence; in the eighteenth century well-organised and well-heeled corporations – and sometimes unincorporated towns too – could wield considerable clout at Westminster in matters close to their interests, such as the promotion of local bills. And yet urban authorities were rarely seen by Parliament as vehicles to be made use of in the implementation of public legislation (213, *147–65*; 79, *157–8, 164–5*). That, as with so much else, was assumed to be the exclusive province of an overworked magistracy, roughly 50 per cent of whose members by 1750 contributed little except social cachet to the day-to-day work of their commissions.

Alongside the justices, completing the machinery for maintaining civil peace and the authority of the state was a judicial power and a military power. The prerogative courts and councils on which the Tudors and early Stuarts had relied so heavily (*Making of a Great Power*, Ch. 1, pp. 33–4) had gone for good in 1641. Thereafter in England and Wales the twelve Common Law judges in their twice-yearly assizes, the Welsh judges in their 'Grand Sessions', and, in especially serious cases, the judges of the King's Bench at Westminster dealt, along with the juries, with all the criminal cases too weighty for the county Quarter Sessions or the increasingly active divisional Petty Sessions of the local justices (79, *161–2*; 78a, *Pt. III passim*). In Scotland the effectiveness both of justices of the peace and of the sheriff courts had long been compromised by the 'heritable jurisdictions' of the lairds, left untouched by the Treaty of Union; not until these jurisdictions were (with a few exceptions) abolished by Parliament in 1747 could crime and disorder be dealt with, under the stern eye of the high court of judiciary in Edinburgh, without the danger of public good being subordinated to private or clan interest. Other than that, by far the most important change in the instruments for enforcing law and order between 1660 and 1780 was the very significant increase in the military power whose support magistrates could enlist in emergencies. This had both an amateur and a professional arm. On the one hand there were the county militias and the London trained bands. They were made up in the ranks of part-timers, paid only for the brief periods when they were officially mustered, and officered (in the shires) by local country gentlemen of varying experience and competence, stiffened here and there by retired professionals. On the other hand, there was the regular army. This, as we know, was small for much of Charles II's reign and briefly inflated in the 1680s. For a century thereafter it rarely exceeded 20,000 men in peacetime, but *in years of war or rebellion* – and there were nearly fifty such years between 1689 and 1783, a significant fact in the history of pre-industrial popular protest – it rose to treble, sometimes almost quadruple that number. Thus there were long periods when disciplined and seasoned regiments were available for internal security use, especially in the South of England where the heaviest concentrations of troops were generally stationed.

There are two common misunderstandings about the use of armed force to suppress civil disorder between 1660 and 1780. The first concerns the Whig Riot Act of 1715, which did not, as is often believed, inaugurate a new and much harsher era in the quelling of popular unrest by military means. Units of the regular army had been used against rioters before 1715, when the emergency was considered serious enough; the Sacheverell rioters in London, for instance, had been restricted to only one night's havoc by the efficiency and disciplined restraint of a few hundred of Marlborough's veterans (5, *226–47*). After the Act was passed such action did become rather more frequent, particularly in the provinces, but there is little evidence of a trigger-happy attitude on the part of the authorities. Indeed, there remained for decades considerable uncertainty and nervousness about the extent of the legal indemnity which the Riot Act purported to confer. The fate of Captain Porteous, too, was to cast a long shadow (227, *32*), and it was only after 1750, as we have noted (above, pp. 179, 182), that military interventions strikingly increased. The second misunderstanding concerns the militia and its use. It stems from the view, put forward in the standard work on the eighteenth-century militia, that a period of 'eighty years' decay' in England's citizen army, beginning in the 1670s and lasting until the militia reforms of 1757–9, rendered it unfit even for dealing with domestic mobs, let alone for confronting armed rebels or invaders (92, *73 and passim*). It is now clear that, buoyed up by periodic effusions of County and Tory rhetoric, many, though not all county militias, as well as the London bands, retained a passable measure of effectiveness, against civilians at least, until the early eighteenth century.[17] General atrophy only set in with the positive discouragement administered by the Old Corps Whigs from around 1720 onwards. It is also evident that the militias were more acceptable locally than unpopular regulars, and that for this reason some magistrates continued to prefer to use them, when feasible, to deal with serious riots. Militiamen broke up various urban religious disorders between 1662 and 1667, were used against the Spitalfields weavers in 1675, played an important peace-keeping rôle in the disturbed winter of 1688–9, dealt successfully and bloodlessly with corn riots at Worcester (1693) and Bristol (1709), and helped to pacify Kendal in the coinage riot of 1696. In addition, Lord Lieutenants were periodically instructed by the Council to alert their forces as a prophylactic (77, *Ch. 9*; 217, *Ch. 7*).

The Hexham massacre by the Yorkshire militia in 1761 may have been a good advertisement for the fire-power of Pitt's new-model 'home guard' of the Seven Years' War, but it also dramatised its unsuitability for taking over the law-and-order function of the army in a tense political and economic climate. Justices of the Peace still called on the militia from time to time, as at Wigan in 1779. But increasingly over the two decades after the Peace of Paris they turned to professional troops, if these were available; it was in the 1760s and 1770s, especially, that the Secretary-at-War, whose office despatched the orders which moved troops around the country, seems to have virtually usurped the formal responsibilities of the Secretaries of State for domestic peace and to have operated, in Hayter's words, as an unofficial 'chief of police' (227, *4*). But as fatalities became more commonplace in clashes between soldiers and rioters, public uneasiness grew again – even in some government circles – at the higher domestic profile of the military. Burke appealed to a gut English antipathy to standing armies going back 120 years when he argued in the House of Commons in 1768 that nothing short of imminent danger to the constitution could justify the use of military force against civilians. Indeed, such was the dismay caused by the slaughter in Southwark in May 1768 (p. 320 below) that, by frightening the London magistracy and reviving the inhibitions of senior army officers, it almost certainly contributed twelve years later to the fatal delay in deploying troops against the Gordon rioters. In the aftermath of the ensuing disaster, the uneasy equation that had perplexed the British for a century, between popular rights and liberties and the public obligation of governments to maintain order, was partially resolved. A magisterial legal judgement from Lord Mansfield defined the legitimate use of armed force (67, *426–7*), and a new statutory definition was given to the constitutional powers of the Secretary-at-War. The respite was to be brief, however, for in less than a decade revolutionary events across the Channel had plunged nearly all the old norms and assumptions about law and order into a melting-pot from which, like so much else in the traditional scheme of things, they were destined to emerge radically changed.

---

1. W.L. Sachse, 'The Mob in the Revolution of 1688', *JBS* **4** (1964).
2. Twenty in Staffordshire, Worcestershire, Warwickshire and Salop alone, with damage there estimated at £3,694. Dr Williams's Lib., MS. 34.4 (John Evans Papers).
3. H. T. Dickinson and K. J. Logue, 'The Porteous Riot', *History Today*, **22** (1972), pp. 272–81; Smout (241), p. 227.
4. At Chilesmore, near Coventry, 1666, and in Northamptonshire, 1710 – both hard cases which attracted a lot of local sympathy. Beloff (217), pp. 76–8.
5. W. Albert, *The Turnpike Road System of England, 1663–1844* (Cambridge, 1972).
6. Add. MSS 32690, f. 83: Hardwicke to Newcastle, 28 Sept 1735.
7. Many more than the toll of the Porteous Riots (*c.* 30) or the 'Massacre of St. George's Field', London, 1768 (11).
8. Quoted in E.P. Thompson (223b), p. 116.
9. In 1710 we know the identity of those against whom *prima facie* evidence of riot was assembled. The identity of the Wilkite and Gordon rioters, by contrast, is derived from the evidence of those who were actually brought to trial. Few gentlemen in the eighteenth-century were ever *tried* for riot or affray.
10. A. Browning, ed., *Memoirs of Sir John Reresby* (Glasgow, 1936), p. 537.
11. The classic instance is the sacking of Leather Lane meeting-house in 1710. Its contents were carried to the broad thoroughfare of Hatton Garden, and then only burned after the leaders of the assault had insisted on making three small bonfires instead of one huge one. Holmes (221), p. 79–80.
12. The 'Forty-Five rebellion of the Highland clansmen (Ch. 6) was of course of a different genus altogether from the largely spontaneous grassroots demonstrations we have been considering in this chapter.
13. See also I.R. Christie, *Stress and Stability in Late Eighteenth-Century Britain* (Oxford, 1984), Ch. 7, pp. 183–214 *passim*.
14. For the interpretation of the Act in practice, see E.N. Williams (3a), pp. 408–9, 414–17.
15. E. Hasted, *History and Topographical Survey of the County of Kent*, I (2nd edn. Canterbury, 1797–1801), p. 218.
16. Since 1660, the Settlement Act for dealing with poor vagrants, the Game Acts

(1671–1711), the Toleration Act, the Riot Act and the Black Act (*Making of a Great Power*, Ch. 18) were just five major measures which added fresh dimensions to the justices' responsibilities. The lapsing of the Clarendon Code and other Acts against religious disaffection after 1687, on the other hand, was some compensation.

17. As late as 1691 the militias had a combined paper strength of 84,000. Fletcher (77), p. 324.

CHAPTER 13

Literacy, education and the power of the pen

In *Making of a Great Power* (Chs 22–3) reference was made to the voracious appetite of the reading public in post-Revolution England: and in particular to its taste for political propaganda and for religious controversy. Without this appetite and the ceaseless effusions of those who fed it it is hard to believe that the strife of parties, whether in church or state, would have been so passionate and abandoned, or its influence so pervasive, from the Exclusion period down to the 1720s. It is unlikely, too, that in the next decade opposition to the Walpole regime could have been whipped up so effectively (Ch. 5); that extra-parliamentary political life would have grown rather than declined in vigour after the great age of party conflict was over (Chs. 3, 21), or that violent popular passions could have been so readily aroused at street level over such matters as Excise, the Jew Bill or Catholic relief (Ch. 12). With these things in mind two very material questions suggest themselves. How large, roughly, was this English reading public? And what educational provision existed in the later seventeenth and eighteenth centuries for creating it and, subsequently, preparing its members for the diverse rôles they would ultimately play in society and the economy? From these questions a natural next step is to consider briefly those who wrote for this public, and the growth and influence of the press and publishing trade which enabled the writers to communicate with it. It was not, of course, only news, information, comment and propaganda which they purveyed. As well as aiming to inform and proselytise for political or religious ends, they also communicated ideas, at greater depth, or they sought either to entertain or instruct their public – themes to which the next chapter will return.

I

In the introduction to his influential periodical *The Rehearsal* Charles Leslie wrote in 1706 that 'the greatest part of the people do not read books; most of them cannot read at all. But they will gather together about one that can read, and listen to an *Observator* or *Review* (as I have seen them in the streets), where all the principles of rebellion are instilled into them.' As a nonjuring conservative, utterly opposed to Whig ideas of sovereignty, Leslie would have been one of the last knowingly to give credence to the idea that the common people had any realistic claim to political rights. But some of his contemporaries totally disagreed with him about the extent of popular illiteracy, and those recent historians who have found evidence for a vigorous 'plebeian political culture' in pre-industrial Britain (e.g. 33b; 44) have implicitly endorsed their dissent. It is now possible to test these impressionistic generalisations against the work of scholars who have studied either literacy, as such, or popular education in early modern England. What we are not yet able, and may never be able to do, not surprisingly in view of the difficulties presented by the data, is to test them against a clear set of agreed conclusions. V.E. Neuburg has put the case that the heavy output of cheap literature in the eighteenth century, including material, such as chapbooks and printed ballads, self-evidently aimed at 'the poorer sort', points to a wide spread of working-class literacy before the end of the century, the culmination of 'a steady increase' during its course (274b). And his conclusions no longer seem so surprising in view of what is now known about the reading public of the previous century and the eagerness of publishers to cater for its simpler tastes.[1] From the opposite pole, while developing a wider thesis about English literacy and education between the mid-seventeenth and the late nineteenth centuries, Lawrence Stone has sent up a 'trial balloon', part of which contains the tentative conclusion that for at least a century before 1780 the growth of literacy in England was very slow by contrast with the impetus built up during the Elizabethan and early Stuart periods. This, Stone estimates, had produced by 1642 – the year the Protestation Oath was administered by the Long Parliament – an 'average male literacy rate [of] . . . probably not less than 30 per cent', although this was very uneven in its distribution. Progress was possibly sustained (it is suggested) for some time after the Restoration, whereupon there followed a long period of deceleration and stasis.[2] The decisive factor in the change, according to this hypothesis, was a marked alteration in the prevailing attitude towards education, and in particular towards elementary schooling. Primarily this was a reversal in the thinking of the social élite, but the changed views of the governing classes were to some extent mirrored in those of the middling and lower middling orders of urban society, including skilled artisans, craftsmen and tradesmen, for whom education had become a badge of respectability. Whereas in Scotland compulsory primary education, mainly on religious grounds, became theoretically the order of the day, and this policy was reinforced by an Act of 1696 which made the rule of 'one parish, one school' mandatory, at least in the Lowlands (241, *88–9*; 274a), in England (Stone argues) 'between 1660 and 1790 most men were convinced that for the poor a little learning is a dangerous thing' (269b, *85*).

Professor Stone's literacy hypothesis, so far as late Stuart and eighteenth-century England is concerned, was based on signature evidence of acknowledged fragility; but it did dovetail neatly – perhaps rather too neatly – with his earlier theory of an 'educational revolution in England, 1540–1640' and of a post-Restoration and eighteenth-century reaction, producing stagnation and decline at all levels, including those of university and grammar school education (269a). Since 1969 the debate on literacy has been carried much further, especially by Roger Schofield and David Cressy (270c; 270b; 270a). Dr Cressy, for cogent reasons, supports the Stone criterion of literacy, namely, the quantifiable ability to sign one's name (as opposed to the vague yardstick of 'the ability to *read* a book or single sheet printed in English' [274b, *93*]), but he dissents from some of his main conclusions. Although much of his most detailed work on the documentation of literacy has been confined to the seventeenth century, a crucial element in the jigsaw Cressy pieces together (270a, *117, graph 8.1*) is the early evidence of the marriage registers after the passing of Lord Hardwicke's Marriage Act of 1753 – evidence which Schofield has exhaustively analysed. These strongly suggest by *circa* 1760 a literacy level among English males of very close to sixty per cent, and – what is perhaps still more remarkable – a female level by then of nearly forty per cent. To set against these there are now compelling figures for *rural* England, at least, in the early 1640s of around thirty per cent for males and under ten per cent for girls and women. We have to account, therefore, for a remarkable change in the course of 120 years, a change every bit as remarkable as that which apparently took place in the hundred years from 1550 to 1650. Whatever variables further analysis of evidence for the intervening years may finally yield – as between urban and rural country areas, for instance, between North and South, or between social or occupational groups (122, *270*) – such a change cannot be explained away by any hypothesis which postulates an end to rapid improvement at some stage in Charles II's reign. That would defy all logic, even without taking into account the widespread dislocation of educational facilities now known to have occurred from 1640–60. It seems infinitely more likely that the improvement in literacy was strongly sustained well into the eighteenth century and that there was no appreciable deterioration, in percentage terms, among the lower orders until the second decade of George III's reign, *at the very earliest*, when the population was rising steeply again, and industry just beginning to make heavier demands on youthful labour.

This conclusion is wholly consistent with all the evidence scholars have by now marshalled against the long-popular theory that English education 'decayed' between the Restoration and the Industrial Revolution (e.g. 187a, *Ch. 3 and 293–6*; 132, *173–82*; cf. 275, *196–216*). The fact is, at virtually every educational level except the highest, the university level, the provision of educational facilities improved, quantitatively and often qualitatively, for much of that period, and in some respects through the whole of it.[3] Such progress as the endowment of 114 new grammar schools between 1660 and 1714 is the more impressive because for much of that period population growth was, at best, minimal; the undoubted decline under the Hanoverians of many of the older country or market-town grammar schools into 'primary' establishments not offering a classical grounding, was less damaging than is often thought (but see below). The charity school movement, encouraged in some directions by the Anglican Society for the Promotion of Christian Knowledge (cf. Ch. 7); the contribution made by new dissenting schools at both primary and secondary level; the big increase in the provision of private education for girls; and the growing importance attached to the provision of 'technical' instruction to pupils, all were striking features of the development of schooling over the wider period from 1660 to 1780.

The emphasis on technical subjects is particularly revealing, not only in the light it throws on changes in society and in the economy, but because the demand for these subjects was met in three distinct ways, each of which was symptomatic of educational vitality. They were taught either in the crop of specialised establishments (writing schools, mathematical schools), which were part of a notable expansion of private education under the later Stuarts and the first three Georges; or in newly-established general, fee-paying 'secondary' schools or academies, which by their very nature were often able to offer wide and progressive syllabuses, especially in London; or as part of the process whereby 'modern subjects' were being gradually introduced into the curricula of the best of the 'free' grammar schools or 'public' schools, such as Manchester Grammar School, King Edward VI School, Birmingham, or Winchester.

The SPCK schools, one wave of which broke over urban England from the late 1690s to the 1720s, while another subsequently inundated parts of Wales, were in many cases financed by the novel method of public subscription (274a, *19–21, 36–41*). The movement has been much misunderstood and in some respects uncritically maligned. To be sure, the Society's frequently-published statistics were sometimes excessively euphoric. The 1,419 'new' charity schools which it claimed were on its books in 1729, apparently the result of a mere thirty years of endeavour, in fact included scores of establishments founded well before the late 1690s. Nevertheless, over 5,000 pupils, including girls, were attending London's 132 charity schools by 1729 and close to 30,000, those of the country at large (187a, *53–4*). With a turnover of pupils occurring every five years or so, on average,[4] it is probable that the number of children instructed in SPCK-listed schools in the first three decades of the movement alone totalled between 100,000 and 120,000. Although the Society's schools were seen by their founders primarily as instruments for moral and spiritual improvement, a majority of those pupils who stayed the full course learned – contrary to what is often said – to write as well as to read; some mastered elementary arithmetic; and we know that the metropolitan schools, at least, were successful in placing nearly 80 per cent of their children either in apprenticeships or in service down to 1733. Another myth which research has exploded is that the subscription movement absorbed nearly all the effort put into new elementary schools in the early eighteenth century. It was the Victorian charity commissioners who first discovered that no fewer than 625 new schools, teaching the three Rs rather than classical grammar, had been founded by the traditional method of endowment in England between 1698 and 1730, while the foundation of 460 non-classical schools was traced back to before 1698. From 1730–90 such new endowments continued, though at a reduced rate (274a, *351 [Appx. 1]*; 184). In addition, quite outside the ambit of these new or relatively new schools, hundreds of other bequests were made for the purpose of furthering primary education. With the older tradition of parish schools still active, making use of the services of the local curate or, on occasion, the parish clerk as teachers, it is not possible to dismiss as so much moonshine Francis Brokesby's words, written in 1701, 'that there are few country villages where some or other do not get a livelihood by teaching school' (187a, *55*). This was certainly true, for instance, in the North West of England, where scarcely one of the 58 Cumberland parishes was found to be without an elementary school of some kind in 1703, and where for much of the eighteenth century no Cheshire child had to travel more than five miles to get basic instruction in reading and writing. Even in the huge diocese of York it would seem that roughly 60 per cent of parishes possessed a school of some kind in 1743.[5]

We must be careful not to over-react against the 'decline' theory of post-Restoration English education by painting too rosy a picture of this period. Subscriptions as well as endowments, whether for the encouragement of elementary or secondary schooling, both tailed off after the middle decades of the eighteenth century. Furthermore, the rapid increase during the years 1660–1760 in the prevalence of fee-paying and boarding, not only in private schools, but in grammar schools, both old and new, and in the recently-established 'modern schools' such as Sir John Moore's School, Appleby Magna, was not an unmixed blessing. It was necessary to ensure the improvement, and in some cases the very survival, of the secondary education such schools provided, and it undoubtedly helped to produce a more professionalised teaching body. Yet the squeeze on the thousands of traditionally 'free' grammar-school places, which had played such an important part in the educational (and social) mobility of the late sixteenth and early seventeenth centuries, did restrict the opportunities for bright children from poor backgrounds, especially those in once-favoured country areas, to progress beyond the 'petties' to the classics and earn the chance of a university scholarship or exhibition.

Higher education itself was in a parlous state by the middle of the eighteenth century. It is true that the dissenting academies, especially since 1689, had for the most part achieved an excellent reputation, both for quality and range of instruction; but it must be remembered that their intakes were small – even the most successful, such as Findern (1720–54) or Warrington (1757–86), rarely taking in more than 400 students over thirty years. In addition the academies were too often dependent, as individual institutions, on the life and health of a single noted master, as well as being vulnerable to the risk of hostile legislation down to 1714 (*Making of a Great Power*, Ch. 23), and to doctrinal heresy thereafter. Before the 1720s there were never more than thirty of these institutions in existence at any time, and usually far fewer. Nevertheless the best of them, especially after 1730, were at least in the van of curricular reform.[6] By contrast, 'the great depression' in the two ancient universities which Lawrence Stone believes set in after 1670 and persisted until the end of the eighteenth century, may be qualified but cannot be argued away. Its onset was less rapid and its effects less uniform and intense than we are often told. By George II's reign, however, the problems of Oxford, and increasingly of Cambridge too, were beyond disguising. The basic arts curriculum of both universities, even in Restoration England, was time-encrusted and enervating; until the great lawyer Sir William Blackstone in 1759 first perceived a chink in the armour of the Laudian statutes imposed on Oxford University in 1636, hitherto deemed impenetrable, would-be reformers there, at least, thought it futile even to attempt change. Whig ministries occasionally contemplated imposing reforms, for example in 1717 and 1749; but their motives were overwhelmingly political and in the end they produced nothing but angry noises, the Whigs being content, in Porter's words, to 'let sleeping dons lie' (272, *502, 504*; 273, *108, 122–3*; 132, *178*). For at least sixty years after 1660 Cambridge showed itself responsive to some of the main intellectual stimuli of the day. The establishment of the mathematical tripos and the foundation of new Chairs in Astronomy and Experimental

Philosophy illustrate this. And if in Oxford ultra-conservatism and lethargy were creeping on faster, even here by the early eighteenth century new courses were being offered in Chemistry, Newtonian Physics and English Language and Literature, while both Universities had acquired a Regius Professor of Modern History and Languages by 1724. In both, also, some colleges retained a reputation for providing conscientious tutors, and a few, such as Brasenose and Jesus at Oxford, continued even in the eighteenth century to admit *pauperes pueri*, 'poor boys', in quite large numbers (273, *Ch. 12*; 187a, *41*).

Whether more than a small minority of undergraduates were exposed to advanced or distinguished intellectual influences is open to considerable doubt. At Oxford, Lucy Sutherland argues, much that was best in the university's intellectual life 'was carried on . . . largely outside its formal instruction'. In any event, by the middle of the eighteenth century many of the best of the late Stuart and early Hanoverian initiatives, including Oxford's wholly original contribution, under the later Stuarts, to Anglo-Saxon studies, had petered out. The pattern of matriculation tells a similar sad story. Once the artificial admissions boom of the 1660s had ended, student numbers for a long time declined, relatively slowly in both universities; in Oxford, by only 16 per cent between the 1670s and the 1730s. Thereafter, however, things got rapidly worse, and the dismal decade from 1750–59, when Oxford – still a stronghold of Jacobitism – admitted on average only 182 new undergraduates each year, provided disturbingly clear evidence that the English universities were losing all appeal to the serious-minded, except to intending recruits to the Church and to small numbers of students of medicine and civil law, and that they were no longer able to attract even the socialites, whose parents now preferred to invest in private tutors and the Grand Tour (272, *516*; 273, *Ch. 12*; 271a; 187a, *37*).

Fortunately their deficiencies had been at least partially made good in a variety of alternative ways. The dissenting academies obviously played their part, and some Anglicans as well as nonconformists took advantage of their offerings. There was still a rôle of sorts for the Inns of Court (although their former non-professional function was withering fast by 1700). The best of those private schools and academies which spread like a forest fire in the first three-quarters of the eighteenth century provided a high standard of mathematical and technical training. Finally, there is evidence of an increasing recourse by English students – mainly, but not wholly of dissenting families – to the universities of Glasgow, Edinburgh, St Andrews and Aberdeen, and to certain Continental universities, especially, in the early decades of the century, the great medical school at Leyden.

II

It could be argued that by the reigns of William III and Anne, if not earlier, London, and not Oxford or Cambridge, was the true intellectual heart of England. It beat just as strongly in the eager discussions and often heated controversies of the *virtuosi*[7] as in the meetings and publications of the Royal

Society or the closely reasoned arguments of the Boyle Lecturers (*Making of a Great Power*, Ch. 24). But London was also the home by the early years of the eighteenth century of the most vigorous press in the world, and it was the habitat of dense thickets of clubs, coffee-houses and taverns through which the products of that press could find an outlet (280b, *193*, *194*). Thereby were fostered discussions and debate which could reach down to the humblest mug-house as well as up to the most sophisticated drawing-room. During the Spanish Succession War visitors to London could be forgiven for wondering whether the pen was not even mightier in England than the sword; the circumstances of the duke of Marlborough's fall in December 1711 (*Making of a Great Power*, Ch. 14), an event to which Tory propaganda, and especially Swift's *Conduct of the Allies*, made a critical contribution, convinced many Whigs for a while that indeed it was.

It is generally agreed that the great landmark in the post-Restoration fortunes of English writers, journalists, publishers and printers was reached in 1695 with what is usually – though not altogether accurately – called 'the end of press censorship'. Since 1662, with the exception of an interlude of six years after 1679, the press in England had been technically subject to the stringent provisions of the Licensing Act. This legislation had had two effects: first, to create a monopoly for the Stationers' Company of London, which meant that outside the two universities and one licensed printer in York all printing was concentrated in the hands of about twenty master printers of the London livery; second, to suppress the publication of views unacceptable to the civil and religious establishment by means of a system of pre-publication licensing. The main censoring authorities were the government, through the Secretaries of State's official licensers, and the Church of England, through the chaplains of the archbishop of Canterbury and the bishop of London (276). How effective control of the press could be before the Revolution, at times when the political will to exercise control was determined, is well documented (*Making of a Great Power*, Ch. 11); while the state of the printing trade outside London can be judged from the fact that, despite landing in the south-west in 1688, William of Orange had to have his manifesto printed by John White of York (279, 5). Those who were hoping for a dramatic change after the expulsion of James II were soon disappointed. After a brief spree from December 1688 to March 1689, the press once more found its wings severely clipped, not only by an unsympathetic Dutch monarch, a government extremely jittery about the effects of Jacobite propaganda, and a Church very much on the defensive after the passing of the Toleration Act, but by a House of Commons where even the Whigs appeared to have less sympathy with freedom of expression and discussion than their Exclusionist predecessors had shown. Over the next few years illicit, controversial and even inflammatory books and pamphlets did appear, but their authors and printers were liable to considerable harassment. It was not difficult to find reasons for condemning publications as 'seditious', 'heretical', 'schismatical' or simply 'offensive'. In the winter of 1694–5, Robert Stephens, the government's Messenger of the Press, proudly announced that in the previous two years he had seized five private presses, forty-five seditious pamphlets and many heretical books.

There is no simple explanation for Parliament's refusal to renew the Licensing Act in 1695. There does seem to have been a growing impatience among younger MPs with the way censorship had worked in practice. Charges of party bias against the civil licencers were almost as inevitable as the fact that the Church censors would fall foul of anti-clerical or free-thinking sentiments. The majority of reformers would probably have settled for a compromise bill, favoured by Somers, which broke the London printing monopoly but still preserved a fair measure of state and clerical control over new literature. It was only when this was blocked by a combination of vested interests that most members decided – more out of frustration than ideological conviction, it would seem – that, for a period at least, John Locke's solution of no pre-printing restraint at all would be preferable to too much of the wrong kind of restraint.[8]

As things turned out, the first draughts of freedom proved so intoxicating that subsequent attempts in Parliament to revive press licensing all failed. However untidy the causes of the lapsing of the old Act in 1695, its consequences were momentous, and none more so than the establishment of the private-enterprise newspaper as a permanent part of the English scene. Earlier ventures of this kind, whether in the 1640s or during the Exclusion Crisis, had been short-lived. Most of the conservative cavaliers who had passed the 1662 Act had been fully persuaded by recent experience that only gentlemen should aspire to a knowledge of affairs of state. 'For learning has brought disobedience and heresy and sects into the world', as Sir William Berkeley put it, 'and printing has divulged them and libels against the government. God keep us from both' (279, *4*). Mounting concern about Popery in the 1670s did for a while change many attitudes to the free dissemination of news in print, but there were few cries of protest when, under the Stuart reaction, the nine newspapers of March 1681 were reduced to two by 1683, and to one (the official *Gazette*) by 1687. The climate by 1695, however, was very different. Six years of warfare and intense party-political controversy had made not just members of Parliament but virtually all the literate public news-hungry, and their craving could no longer be satisfied by tame government hacks or by subscribing to expensive manuscript newsletters. Three newspapers appeared between May and October 1695, the *Flying Post*, the *Post Boy* and the *Post Man*. All were tri-weeklies; they set the pattern for the next generation by printing more foreign than domestic news; and their instant success had much to do with the defeat of a fresh attempt at restrictive legislation in 1696. All three were still being published at the end of Anne's reign, but by then they had many companions. London alone had acquired eighteen privately-sponsored newspapers as early as 1709, including the first daily, Buckley's *Daily Courant*, and the first evening paper, the *Evening Post*. Most had a strong party bias, as they showed, for example, in their partisan reporting of General Elections; this precedent of emphatic political commitment was to be fully maintained through the years of Walpole's supremacy, and into the reign of George III. In the 1730s, for instance, the *London Evening Post* flamboyantly led the group of papers that were consistently and fiercely critical of the ministry, and the *Daily Courant* (to 1735), the Treasury-subsidised *Daily Gazetteer* and others stolidly defended government policies. Late in our period *The Morning Chronicle* (1769) and, by 1780, the *London Evening Post* were only the two most prominent of the papers which espoused the Rockinghamite, and later Foxite, Whig cause (280b; 278, *16–17*; 15 [O'Gorman], *85*). The best papers had an important provincial, as well as metropolitan, circulation – it was no accident that the tri-weeklies were always published on the three 'post nights' of the week – and some were run by journalists of considerable professionalism and flair, such as Roper, Ridpath, Boyer and de Fonvive in Anne's reign. Finally, thanks in the main to hundreds of tavern and coffee-house sales, most London newspapers enjoyed a readership massively in excess of their formal circulation figures. Thus each of the *Post Boy's* 4,000-odd numbers in the early eighteenth century was probably read by anything from 50,000 to 70,000 readers. Proprietors of the most popular coffee-houses were said in 1728 to be providing 'some two, some three, some four of a sort of the leading papers, every day, besides duplicates of most of the others'.[9] By the 1770s one of the biggest coffee-houses in Birmingham, Overton's, carried ten different London papers (plus the *Utrecht Gazette)*; Knaresborough's only coffee room – perhaps with an eye to patrons of Harrogate spa – was taking four in 1763 (44, *150*).

By the second half of Anne's reign two other developments were under way, running parallel with the galloping growth of the London newspaper press. One was the emergence for the first time of provincial newspapers. The end of licensing gave an important enough stimulus to the printing trade inside the capital city, but outside London its effects were truly remarkable (see below p. 198). No fewer than 55 towns produced their own newspapers at some time between 1700 and 1760, though not, of course, all simultaneously. There were by 1710 already 13 provincial newspapers in business, the pioneering cities (1701–4) being Norwich, Bristol and Exeter; while there were some periods of relative difficulty over the next four decades (especially in the aftermath of wars or taxation) the general trend was emphatically upwards, reaching 24 papers by 1723, falling from 42 to 32, 1746–53, but reaching 50 by 1782. From the beginning provincial newswriters raided the London 'prints' as a matter of course for the overwhelming bulk of their national and international reporting; the same pattern continued into the three decades after 1720, when even the best and most influential papers, such as the *York Courant* and *Newcastle Courant* purveyed to their local readers not only the news items but large chunks of the editorial copy of leading London journalists. A striking feature of the provincial press by the 1730s and the early 1740s was the extent to which, especially in the larger towns, it became politically aligned with the cause of opposition to the Walpole regime, and in the best traditions of metropolitan journalism there was nothing mealy-mouthed about its criticism. The emphasis which recent scholarship has given to the contribution of provincial newspapers to what Dickinson describes as the 'growth of an independent political culture among the urban bourgeoisie and even among the labouring poor' in the towns of early and mid-Hanoverian England, is surely justified (279; 278, *304*; 33b, *64–6*), as well as being fully intelligible in the light of what we now know about the growth of male, and for that matter female, literacy and educational provision. The well-documented electoral defiance towards the Whig oligarchy exhibited by many of the larger boroughs, in addition to London and Westminster (28a, *119–25*; 12a, *I*), was but the tip of a very much larger iceberg which mounting Tory and 'Country' and, increasingly, radical sentiment all combined to build.

The second development fresh to the period after 1695, which lent both greater potency and flexibility to the power of the pen, was the appearance and instant popularity of the 'journal' or periodical. By contrast with the *news*paper, the speciality of this novel type of journalistic enterprise was pithy *commentary* on either current political or religious events, or (when topical) on matters of economic policy or on the social mores of the day. The years 1700–20 saw the birth of a string of successful periodicals, notably the *Observator, Review, Rehearsal, Examiner, Spectator, Tatler, Freeholder* and *Englishman*. No fewer than six of these deployed the talents of four of the giants of Augustan literature, Defoe, Swift, Addison and Steele, while the pen of one of the most brilliant controversialists of the day, Charles Leslie, sustained the *Rehearsal*. Although the *Examiner* at the time Swift was writing it (1710–11) had subscribers at least as far away from London as Scarborough (where the vicar read it to the Tory faithful after evening service each Sunday),[10] circulations at this time were still generally quite small. Even the well-loved *Spectator*, witty brainchild of Addison and Steele, which broke new ground as the first daily periodical, never sold more than 3,000 copies per issue. But the growing taste for such reading matter is illustrated by the great success of the two most famous newcomers of the 1720s and 1730s, the anti-Walpole *Craftsman* and the *Gentleman's Magazine*, the second of which at its peak had a sale of 10,000, while the former at one stage had a print-run as high as 13,000. As 'coffee-house journals', however, they would be read, as most newspapers were, by many times their formal numbers. Addison put the actual readership of an average edition of the *Spectator* in March 1711, 'by a modest computation' at 20, which, if roughly true (which it may have been, since the *Craftsman* was later to claim 40 readers per copy) meant 60,000 readers from a circulation of 3,000 (187a, *Ch. 2*; 193a, *6*; 280a, *8–9*; 280b, *195–6*). Wilkes's weekly, the *North Briton*, is thought to have claimed a readership of more than 100,000 in 1763 (44, *155*).

Newspapers and periodicals were, of course, far from being the only outlets for the busy 'mercenary' pens of post–1695 England. Every long-running political or religious issue or emotive political crisis spawned scores of pamphlets, not infrequently supplemented by printed sermons: the Standing Army controversy, Occasional Conformity, the Sacheverell affair, the Bangorian controversy provoked by Bishop Hoadly, the Excise crisis and the Paris peace negotiations of 1762–3 were among the most striking cases in point. The literature produced by the attack on Henry Sacheverell was so vast that it has justified the production of two substantial bibliographies.[11] Furthermore, every General Election, as we have observed, produced 'hailstorms' of polemics (*Making of a Great Power*, Ch. 21). The quality of the contributors varied enormously, but as with the periodicals, men of great literary talent could involve themselves in pamphleteering: Swift, Defoe and Steele in the early eighteenth century, Fielding and Chesterfield in the 1730s, Edmund Burke, with his masterly *Thoughts on the Present Discontents*, in 1770. Even Dr Samuel Johnson took service before the

General Election of 1774, producing a succinct pro-establishment pamphlet, *The Patriot*.[12] It is important to recognise that all these developments, especially the burgeoning of newspapers and periodicals, were ultimately dependent on demand. Only an eager readership, almost certainly running *in toto* into six figures, could have tempted a whole clutch of London and provincial newspapers and at least six magazines to print or reprint the notorious 'Letters of Junius' over the years 1769–72.[13] Only a ready market would have encouraged London newspapers to persist in, and finally win (1774), their struggle against parliamentary privilege for the right to print Westminster debates.[14] In short, the power of the pen in eighteenth-century England must inevitably have been much diminished without a receptive public, a public with more leisure for reading, as well as more charity or other primary schools, greater literacy and a healthy appetite for reading matter of many kinds.

In the following chapter we shall observe some very different responses to the opportunity to cater for this growing public. Meanwhile, just two further points must be made about the press after the end of licensing in 1695. The first is that, as well as bringing greater freedom and scope – and, for the talented or lucky, higher financial returns – to writers, the lapsing of the old Act also transformed opportunities for the printing and distribution of literature of all kinds. There was such an explosion of printing activity in London after the ending of the Stationers' monopoly that the overspill of trained journeymen, and later masters, inevitably migrated to the provinces: first to Bristol and Shrewsbury, then to Norwich, where Francis Burges set up in 1700 and within six years was clearing nearly £130 a year profit from newspaper business alone. By 1720 there were already about 30 English provincial printing houses, in addition to the 70 in London. By the middle of the century, there was scarcely a town of any significance which lacked its own printer. Newspapers remained a major source of their income. One Northumbrian printer in 1739 was running off around 100,000 copies a year of the *Newcastle Journal*. But the range of a good printer's output was growing more impressive with every decade, and the greater part of it was handled by booksellers. In 1720, in a city now teeming with booksellers, London already had around a hundred who were engaged in publishing as well as distribution; some, like Awnsham Churchill, or Thomas Guy, the founder of Guy's Hospital, had become exceedingly wealthy. By the mid–1740s, 250 provincial booksellers could be found who were willing to put their names on a subscription list for the *Harleian Miscellany* (279, *8, 22, 171*; 277, *40*).

The final point concerns 'the freedom of the press'. Despite its universally-acknowledged influence, the powers of the post-1695 press were by no means absolute. Writers or printers might still, for example, fall foul of the obscenity laws or, later, of the new Copyright Act (1709), aimed – not wholly fruitlessly – against the unbridled piracies which had taken place in the previous fourteen years. More important, the governments of post-Revolution and Georgian England still had two weapons at their disposal by which they could hope to implement a measure of indirect control for *political* ends. These were censorship by prosecution, and what has been called 'censorship by price'. Seditious libel, for example, was a charge which could be stretched to cover a multitude of sins, and Secretaries of State and their messengers, under both Tory and Whig administrations, could be vicious at times in their harassment of those who purveyed political literature of an unacceptable hue.[15] Ultimately this became an emotive popular issue, through the hamfisted attempts in 1763 to stifle *The North Briton* (Ch. 22). Of a more blanket nature were the stamp duties on pamphlets and newspapers, first imposed by a Tory Act of 1712 and later stiffened by Whig Acts in 1725 and 1757 and by Lord North's additional duties of 1776. The first two measures, in particular, had serious short-term consequences for many publications, and the rising cost of an average paper from 1d. to 3d. between 1710 and 1784 must have had a restrictive effect on readership (278, *106–8*). But time showed that neither prosecution nor taxation could effectively stifle criticism from those who were determined to criticise, nor do much more than check intermittently the remarkable capacity of the pen and the press to shape public opinion in the last century of the pre-industrial era.

---

1. M. Spufford, *Small Books and Pleasant Histories: Popular Fiction and its Readership in Seventeenth-century England* (1981).

2. *Where* the turning-point came is a matter which is never clearly resolved. In the course of a long essay the start of the period of regression is variously placed at 1660, 1670, 1675 or 1680, while its end, and the beginning of a renewed upswing, is placed at one point as early as 1765, and at other times at either 1780 or 1790. See L. Stone (269b), pp. 85, 95, 103, 112, 125,136, 138.

3. See for example R.S. Tompson, *Classics or Charity? The Dilemma of the 18th Century Grammar School* (Manchester, 1971); M. Seaborne, *The English School: Its Architecture and Organization 1370–1870* (1971); D. Robson, *Some Aspects of Education in Cheshire in the Eighteenth Century* (Chetham Soc., 1966); J. Simon, 'Post-Restoration Developments: Schools in the County 1660–1700' in B. Simon, ed., *Education in Leicestershire 1540–1640* (Leicester, 1968).

4. Most attended from 7–11; a minority from 7–12 or even 7–14.

5. Bishop William Nicolson, *Miscellany Accounts of the Diocese of Carlisle*, ed. R.S. Ferguson (1877); D. Robson, op.cit., pp. 166–79; 'Archbishop Herring's Visitation Returns [1743]', ed. S.L. Ollard and P.C. Walker, *Yorks Arch. Soc.*, vols. 71–2, 75, 77, 79 (1928–31).

6. H.J. McLachlan, *English Education under the Test Acts*: *being the History of the Nonconformist Academies, 1662–1820* (Manchester, 1931); Watts (95), pp. 465–7.

7. For which see C. Jones and G. Holmes, eds, *The London Diaries of William Nicolson, Bishop of Carlisle, 1702–1718* (Oxford, 1984); J.M. Levine, *Dr Woodward's Shield* (Berkeley and Los Angeles, 1977).

8. R. Astbury, 'The Renewal of the Licensing Act in 1693 and its Lapse in 1695', *Library*, 5th ser., *33* (1978), p. 310 and *passim*.

9. *The Case of the Coffee-Man of London and Westminster*, p. 15, quoted in T. Harris, *London Crowds in the Reign of Charles II: Propaganda and Politics from the Restoration to the Exclusion Crisis* (Cambridge, 1987), p. 193.

10. HMC *Portland MSS*, IV, p. 641.

11. F. Madan, *A Bibliography of Dr Henry Sacheverell* (Oxford, 1884); F. Madan, *A Critical Bibliography of Dr Henry Sacheverell*, ed. W.A. Speck (Lawrence, Kansas, 1978).

12. Reprinted in J. Hart, ed., *Political Writers of Eighteenth-Century England* (New York, 1964), pp. 288–96.

13. For brief accounts of the contents and publication/dispersal of the Junius letters, which

began as a polished but venomous attack on the Grafton ministry, see J.S. Watson, *The Reign of George III, 1760–1815* (Oxford, 1960), pp. 145–6; Brewer (44), pp. 154–5.
14. P.D.G. Thomas, 'The Beginning of Parliamentary Reporting in Newspapers, 1768–74', *EHR.*, **74** (1959).
15. P. Hyland, 'Liberty and Libel: Government and the Press During the Succession Crisis in Britain, 1712–1716', *EHR*, **101** (1986).

CHAPTER 14

Prosperity, culture and the pursuit of leisure

In 1660 Charles II was restored to a country only moderately prosperous. But despite the many drains since the Glorious Revolution on the purses and resources of a relatively small population, Britain was a very much wealthier country in the 1760s than she had been in the 1660s. Virtually all sections of the population of England and Wales, right down to the level of the labouring man, so long as he was *in work* (the vital proviso), had some share in this notable increase of national prosperity. In Scotland the benefits were slower to accrue, but there too they had begun to manifest themselves by 1740. The economic investment of this growing wealth is not difficult to chart (Chs. 10–11, 13, 15). The focus of this chapter, however, is on investment of a quite different nature, sometimes less tangible in form but no less influential in shaping the character of eighteenth-century society: investment in social status and its variety of material symbols, on the one hand, and the pursuit of less concrete – and frequently novel – kinds of social and cultural aspirations, on the other. The social application of the vastly enlarged spending power which accrued from the Commercial and Financial Revolutions, from steady industrial growth, the expansion of the professions and the redistribution of landed wealth has of late intrigued historians of pre-industrial Britain. We shall concentrate here on three of its aspects, in particular: the 'residential revolution' of the period 1680–1780, especially in the towns; the indulgence of artistic and aesthetic tastes by 'a consumer society' (191); and the cult of leisure.

I

The affluence of the great county élites found its most splendid and durable expression in the Baroque and Palladian periods of the English mansion. The sheer amount of building and rebuilding which took place in the countryside, even in the years 1690–1720, when the landed interest insistently trumpeted its sufferings from taxation, has already been noticed; likewise the re-shaping of the landscape which often accompanied it (*Making of a Great Power*, Ch. 18). 'The age of the Baroque' had radical implications for decoration and furnishing as well as for architecture, but it was the conscious seeking after residential scale and grandeur which most awed contemporaries at first, and the gradual marriage of these attributes with a passion for symmetry and simplicity of line which at length enraptured them. Although the palatial rebuilding of Petworth by the duke of Somerset, begun in the years 1688–93, caused a stir,[1] it was Chatsworth House in Derbyshire, planned in the late 1680s when the fourth earl of Devonshire was banished from James II's court (ibid. Ch. 12), and completed in Anne's reign, which probably did most to open up the great baroque highway to the Augustan ruling class. Even Marshal Tallard, whose rigours as a prisoner-of-war after the battle of Blenheim involved a round of country-house visits as the guest of sundry English noblemen, deemed it tactful not to mention to Louis XIV Chatsworth's irresistible combination of the grandiose and the elegant, in case he should imply some disrespect to Versailles! At all events, in the forty years after the peace of 1697 literally scores of temples were raised all over England, and not a few in Scotland, to the aristocratic ideals (overlaying, no doubt, much unvarnished self-importance) which Chatsworth and its owner epitomised.[2] Architects as gifted as Vanbrugh and Talman, Gibbs and Hawksmoor, Thomas Archer and Colen Campbell, and inspired interior decorators of the calibre of Thornhill, Verrio and Louis Laguerre lavished their talents on these magnificences; for good measure, in the soberer intervals of a roisterous eight years, Verrio also created the most spectacular baroque interior in England within the vast Tudor shell of Burghley House, Stamford. Yet the great Augustan architects, along with provincial geniuses, craftsmen such as the Smiths of Warwick, Thomas Thornton of York and William Townesend of Oxford (187a, *24–7*), also found time to design genuine homes, for convenient and graceful living, for successful professional or business men, and not least for local squires – an extraordinary number of whom, even in the war years of 1689–1713, succumbed to the charms of 'the new mode',[3] and damned the cost.

Some of the loveliest country houses still surviving from the first half of the eighteenth century, such as the seat of the Twisdens at Bradbourne in Kent, were the work of unsung and often unknown local master-masons, working from pattern-books. It was in the towns, however, that such craftsmen truly came into their own. For at much the same time as Baroque and Palladianism were taking the county families by storm, an even more significant residential revolution was in progress in urban England and, with some time-lag, in the Scottish Lowlands. In the three types of town which acted as the strongest magnets to both people and wealth (*Making of a Great Power*, Chs. 3, 19; *this vol.*, Chs. *10–11*), it was especially apparent, that is, in the thriving ports of the west and east coasts, the expanding manufacturing centres and dockyard towns, and the leisure and pleasure resorts of the gentry. And it gradually involved every other city or town which enjoyed the functional advantages, of one kind or another, necessary to increase or sustain prosperity: Edinburgh and York, for instance, with their unique metropolitan status; county and assize towns or cathedral cities; places like Northampton, Stamford and Doncaster that were strategically placed on the communications network, or towns which performed a vital market function for a wide region, such as Maidstone or Shrewsbury. In all, there were by 1760 at least seventy towns outside London in which evidence of the material prosperity Britain had then attained was plain for every visitor to see, and not least in the way their successful citizens were housed. As impressive on its own scale as the more grandiloquent testimony of the capital city, or the resplendent rural lifestyles of the aristocracy and greater gentry, it was the visual dimension of that 'urban renaissance' which, as Peter Borsay has reminded us, was one of the most far-reaching cultural developments of the century before the Industrial Revolution (211; 212a; 212c. See also 213, *Ch. 10*; 210, *Intro, 41–9*).

The Great Fire of London, and the equally terrifying, if smaller-scale, conflagrations which destroyed Northampton in the 1670s and a large part of Warwick in 1694, sealed the fate of the vernacular building style which had hallmarked the late medieval and Tudor town. Timber-framing, the use of lath, rubble and thatch, the jettied fronts which made already narrow streets even narrower, and the overall effect of higgledy-piggledy informality and idiosyncracy were for the future out of court, except in the hovels of the urban poor, which only patchily abandoned the vernacular. Safer and more durable materials – brick and stone, ashlar, tile and slate – became the order of the day. Indeed *order*, with symmetry and space, were the watchwords of the new age of classicism in the towns. The uniform rows or terraces of houses, carefully graded according to the status of their potential dwellers, which began to fill the devastated area of London 'within the walls' after 1670, and which dominated the new western, northern and even eastern suburbs of the capital, began (though often slowly) to transform the face of many English provincial towns also: houses with flush façades, and in the better class areas, large and evenly-spaced sash windows, elegant doorways and spacious, airy interiors. The new appeal of *space*, aesthetically and environmentally, governed ideas of lay-out as well as of architecture, as builders and developers alike sought to satisfy an increasingly prosperous clientele in which the professional and mercantile bourgeoisie were at least as demanding as, and increasingly more numerous than, leisured gentry families (211, esp. *62–79*; 212b). Thus old streets were widened, if possible; new streets were made so from the start, with broad pavements enhancing their dimensions, while here and there a handsome new square spoke more eloquently still of the Augustan and Georgian urban ideal.

More perhaps than any other feature of the larger cities and towns of the period 1680–1780, it was the fashionable square which represented physically the apogee of the 'urban renaissance' and most completely captured its ethic. Inigo Jones had first brought the square to the metropolis, in the shape of the Italianate Covent Garden, in the 1630s. Between the Restoration and the death of William III the idea caught on, with St James's, Bloomsbury and Red Lion Squares, for example, providing focal points in the development of the West End, and in the first forty years of the eighteenth century London squares multiplied. Their earliest provincial counterparts had appeared just before 1700 in the new town of Whitehaven – arguably the first 'planned' town in Britain – and in the rebuilt centre of Warwick. Thereafter every traveller's eye was to be caught by fashionable enterprises such as St Anne's Square in Manchester, Queen's and St James's Squares in Bristol, 'Old Square' in Birmingham, and later, the graceful squares of the upper town in Bath.[4] They summed up at one and the same time the prosperity, the civilised taste and the socialising instincts of the new pseudo-gentry, the professionals and the businessmen, of the late Stuart and early-to-mid-Georgian towns, even where (as in Manchester, Birmingham, Liverpool or Sheffield) that gentry was in the main commercially or industrially based. By 1719 nine of the sixteen residences grouped round Birmingham's noble square were owned by master ironmongers, one of whom, John Pemberton, planned the whole project; when the laying-out of a similar though less showy venture began in smoky Sheffield in 1736, its developer, Thomas Broadbent, optimistically named it Paradise Square.⁵

It has to be said that even in some of the wealthiest and fastest-growing towns paradise did not universally reign, especially where space, for one reason or another, was at a premium (215; 212c). In Birmingham hundreds of new dwellings, mostly artisans' houses with workshops, were crammed into existing courts and gardens, while Leeds, despite its garnishing of opulent merchants' mansions, had no entirely new street until 1767 and consequently a severe overcrowding problem even for its better-off citizens (143b, *195–8*; 213, *180*). During the more rapid population growth of 1740–80 other towns – including some, like Nottingham, which had been looked on as models of enlightened modernism fifty years earlier – began to run into serious physical problems, in advance of true industrialisation (215, *114–122*). Nevertheless, across much of the spectrum of towns possessing more than a local market function there had been a notable reflowering of urban pride since the Restoration, the more marked when seen in contrast with the air of crisis which had brooded over much of the urban scene outside London during the sixteenth and early seventeenth centuries (207). Civic pride, *per se*, found many expressions: in a spate of new public buildings – town halls, county halls, market halls, gaols, bridges, assembly rooms, music rooms, churches and, by the mid-eighteenth century, hospitals; in a kind of open competition between towns to provide better and better amenities (cf. above, p. 183; Ch. 12), ranging from piped water, and street drainage and lighting, to 'town walks' or parks;⁶ in the eighteenth-century passion for town histories, maps and 'prospects' (211, *80–5, 371–2*), and towards the very end of our period, in the publication of town directories. But corporate pride was also compounded of the personal pride of the individuals who lived within each town – including the many hundreds who, unable to afford a complete rebuilding of their houses, gave them at least a modern frontage to harmonise with their neighbours (and to preserve face themselves). And in the great inns which graced so many early Georgian towns, and which, like the *Bull* in Stamford (that 'would pass in Italy for a palace')⁷ catered not just for travellers but for the social needs of a whole neighbourhood, the private and the public came prestigiously together.

Apart from its greater severity of style, urban classicism was architecturally more indigenous than aristocratic baroque. Many of the great country houses built between 1690 and 1730 owed much to Continental models and the influence of foreign travel. For the renewal of the English provincial town, as of Glasgow, and later of the 'new town' of Edinburgh, the model was self-evidently London; while doubtless reflecting a cosmopolitan ideal, rooted in the European Renaissance (212b, *5–6*), in the hands of local craftsmen using local materials and sharing common assumptions about order, uniformity and symmetry, this model took on a distinctively English form. The rebuilding of London after the Great Fire and its physical evolution into the city of the Georgian period have been memorably described by Reddaway and Summerson.⁸ It is very striking how eagerly and consciously the provinces adopted the priorities and conventions of a sequence of London architects, developers and builders, from Barbon and Wren to Kent and Adam. Two examples must suffice. One is the general extent to which, first, the Rebuilding Acts of the late 1660s, and then the London Building Acts of 1707–9 and 1774, provided specifications, standards and grades which were adopted as blueprints by provincial builders and planners (213, *176*). The other is a specific case. After a visit to Nottingham, the centre of which had been largely rebuilt since the 1670s, Celia Fiennes wrote in 1697 that it was

> the neatest town I have seen, built of stone and delicate; large and long streets, *much like London*, and the houses lofty and well-built. The market-place is very broad – out of which run two very large streets, *much like Holborn*, but the buildings finer; and there is a piazza all along one side of one of the streets, with stone pillars for walking . . ., which is a mile long.[9]

Many of her contemporaries over the next fifty years were to echo the same theme as they remarked on the small mirror-images of the capital which appeared in the new suburbs or regenerated central areas of provincial towns, in Bristol, Birmingham and Liverpool, for example, or in Whitehaven, Preston and Beverley, and most of all, in Bath. By 1761, the writer of the *Annual Register* could point even to 'many poor country towns' as well as large and prosperous ones that seemed 'to be universally inspired with the ambition of becoming the little *London* of the part of the kingdom wherein they are situated.'[10]

II

A distinctive feature of the urban renaissance outside London, as well as of much domestic building in fashionable areas of the capital itself, is the much wider diffusion of artistic and aesthetic 'taste' into and through the middle ranks of society. The values which filtered down from the social élite through the gentry to the bourgeoisie may not have been unmixed with cruder instincts of social emulation and competition, but the latter alone cannot account for all the ways in which the new wealth of Britain in the century after 1680 found expression. Such is the case with the glorious interiors of so many of the houses whose building that wealth made possible: their plaster work, their fireplaces, their doors and door-frames, their balustrades, and their decorated ceilings and cornices. Only the purses of a few could pay for a Gibbons or a Thornhill. Yet local craftsmen all over Britain created countless interiors of remarkable beauty to satisfy the aesthetic aspirations of their employers. William Francys, master apothecary and mayor of Derby at the beginning of the eighteenth century, even had the painted ceilings of his fine new house in the Corn Market modelled on those at Chatsworth (187a, *228*). Increasingly, however, where space allowed, the Augustans and Georgians sought to create things of beauty outside as well as inside their homes. Never before had the owners of country houses lavished so much care and imagination on their gardens as from the end of the seventeenth century onwards. Fashions, in garden-making as in so much else, changed significantly over the next thirty to forty years, and their influence proved pervasive. The formality and regimentation of the earlier Stuart period went out of favour, as owners sought more scope for individuality. Gardens became places for rest and surcease, and not simply creations that would catch the eye from the drawing-room window; planting became more varied, for example through the growing popularity of evergreens and of nursery-reared 'exotic' species, the import of the tulip from Holland and, under George II, the new craze for hyacinths, which so gripped the Scottish horticulturalist Sir James Justice that by 1755 he had developed 86 varieties (193c).

Within a few decades the environs of London were transformed, and by no means only by the owners of large estates. Defoe thought the riverside villages along the road from Richmond to the capital so full of charming gardens by the 1720s 'that nothing in the world can imitate it' (2, *I, 165*). To the less pretentious east of London, another traveller, passing through the 'large village' of Stratford at the end of Anne's reign, found 'above two hundred little country houses, for the conveniency of the citizens in summer' and thought himself 'in Holland again, the houses having all rows of trees before their doors . . . and little gardens behind'.[11] A consumer society was not backward in catering for this growing passion for horticultural beauty and variety. It did so, for one thing, through the proliferation of seed shops and nurseries, both of which had been rarities in the later seventeenth century (183c, *325*). The book trade, too, addressed itself to the gardening craze among amateurs, as well as to the requirements of the gentry and their professional gardeners; Thomas Fairchild's *The City Gardener* was just one book that found an eager readership, and there was a spate of catalogues (187a, *23–4*; 193a, *10n*). By the 1750s most English towns of any size, and some quite small ones, had their own horticultural or florists' societies, mounting twice-yearly shows and offering prizes; later these spread to Scotland where, for example, the Paisley Florist Society was established in 1782. To such occasions as the Northampton Florists' Feast, gardeners flocked without regard to social barriers (193c, *324–5*; 193a, *8n*; 208b, *117–18*).

According to Daniel Defoe it was the example of William III, after he came to England in 1688, which made 'the love of gardening' socially *de rigeur*, first among English gentlemen, then among 'the middling sort' (2, *I, 165–6*). Be that as it may, the King was indubitably responsible for the mania for collecting paintings which had gripped the English ruling class by the beginning of the eighteenth century. William brought many Old Masters with him into England – the walls of Hampton Court were bedecked with them – and by George I's reign it was being said that 'the love of fine paintings [has] so universally spread itself among . . . persons of figure all over the kingdom that it is incredible what collections have been made . . .; and how all Europe has been rummaged, as we may say, for pictures to bring over hither, where for twenty years they yielded the purchasers, such as collected them for sale, immense profit' (2, *I, 178*). Clearly, the pseudo-gentleman, the cultivated lawyer or doctor and the urban merchant could rarely afford to compete in such an expensive market. But their chance came in the 1720s and 1730s, first with the importation of cleverly-executed copies of many Dutch and Flemish paintings, then with the practice of making skilled engravings and prints of contemporary British masters. Hogarth did especially well out of one of the latter (*The Rake's Progress* sold in tens of thousands) as subsequently did Richardson and Gainsborough; thus, as Plumb has written, 'a middle class who could never afford an original modern or an old master could festoon their drawing rooms with what was modish in the world of art' (193d, *38*).

We saw in an earlier chapter how the picture-collecting craze of the post-Revolution aristocracy was matched by a similar combing of Europe and Asia for costly statuary, Delft ware and fine porcelain (*Making of a Great Power*, Ch. 18). Chinese porcelain, in particular, changed hands for staggering prices. In this case it was not King William but his wife who was widely credited with setting the fashion, 'which increased to a strange degree afterwards, piling their china up on the tops of cabinets, [escri]toires and every chimney-piece, to the tops of the ceilings . . . till it became a grievance in the expense of it, and even injurious to their families and estates' (2, *I, 166*). The technical problems and expense of trying to match porcelain of this quality through domestic production were immense. There were many casualties among those firms which tried, and even the high-class ventures at Worcester and Derby only survived with a struggle. As for the difficulties of producing prestige porcelain for the middling folk, they seemed insuperable until the genius of Wedgwood proved the contrary from the 1750s onwards (Ch. 11) (192b). It was otherwise with fine furniture. The long interruptions of trade between England and France in the late seventeenth and early eighteenth centuries gave native craftsmen the chance to satisfy the ambitions of home consumers, with results that were ultimately spectacular. William Kent designed furniture as well as landscape gardens; the Chippendales, father and son, migrated from Worcester to London in 1727 and became famous; George Hepplewhite, too, was in business as a cabinet-maker before the middle of the century, creating new designs of ravishing beauty, eagerly copied; by the 1780s, when Thomas Sheraton appeared to challenge his artistic supremacy, though not his commercial acumen, Gillows of Lancaster and Seddons of Aldersgate Street had begun mass production of furniture from fashionable designs (193a; 192a, *28*).

The care and money lavished on interior decoration, collecting, the love of fine furniture, even the cultivation of floral beauty, all illustrate the free, almost joyous, rein that was being given to aesthetic taste, scarcely a distinguishing mark of the English down to the mid-seventeenth century, but now, with the decline of the Puritan ethic, as much a natural expression of the prosperity of the age as its craving for houses 'in the new mode'. Music, too, played its part in this cultural florescence, in which art and consumer demand went so happily hand in hand. Indeed that part was vital. In the late seventeenth century Purcell had restimulated pride in the native musical tradition. But in Queen Anne's reign Italian opera also became the rage; in 1710 George Frederick Handel brought with him from Hanover at the age of 25 one of the two greatest musical talents of his generation and spent virtually the whole of his remaining life, down to 1759, in England. Private patronage of music and musicians by the wealthy became both more generous and more widespread; although permanent private orchestras like that of the duke of Chandos were rare, a new breed of entrepreneurs from the

1690s onwards organised professional orchestras *ad hoc* to play at theatres and pleasure gardens as well as to give public concerts (187a, *29–31*).

III

Music, and its contribution to the widening horizons and exuberance of upper- and middle-class culture in eighteenth-century Britain, points us naturally to the third area of social development to be surveyed in this chapter, the cult of leisure. In the long run it was to be the most significant area because it reached further down the social hierarchy than the rest. England had long been a country of natural, spontaneous music-makers. Pepys and his friends in Restoration London, 'making music' to their mutual delight, were inheritors of a tradition stretching back at very least to the early sixteenth century. Yet before the late seventeenth century very little music, apart from sacred music in churches and cathedrals, could be publicly heard. The opening of Britton's music room in Clerkenwell at the end of Charles II's reign, and then of Robert King's concert-hall and Hickford's music rooms, in York Buildings and Piccadilly respectively, between 1689 and 1697 wrought an extraordinary change. Under Anne and George I public music rooms and private music clubs, open to subscribers, sprang up in many places. By the 1720s Roger North, near the end of his life, was writing sorrowfully of the way music had been driven out of the home in his lifetime and delivered into the hands of technically accomplished professionals, performing to passive audiences. Yet those audiences were not invariably exclusive. Thomas Britton hired some of the finest artists of the day to perform the works of Purcell, Correlli, Vivaldi and other masters to quite workaday folk in his converted coal-merchant's loft in Clerkenwell. By the 1720s taverns had entered the serious music business, as they had much else; not even oratorio was beyond the ambition of the largest London inns. The provinces and Scotland were not slow to follow London in providing good music for the middle strata of both town and county communities. The beginning of the Three Choirs Festival early in George I's reign was a landmark in the West Country, and well before 1780 not only most cathedral cities and regional capitals but industrial and trading towns, and even such modest market towns as Dedham or Spalding had their own music societies, subscription concerts and chamber orchestras (187a, *28–31*; 211, *122–7 and App. 4*; 193d, *43–4, 44n*). By then, also, two- or three-day music festivals were being held either regularly or intermittently in Norwich, Bristol, Winchester, Birmingham and Manchester. The growing passion for music had to be assuaged on paper as well as in clubs and in buildings. Before 1688 remarkably little music was printed and there was scarcely a specialist music publisher to be found in England. By the late eighteenth century music was being marketed by more than 400 London publishers, by over 60 in Scotland and by dozens more in the English provinces.

The case of music perfectly illustrates three things about late Stuart and eighteenth-century Britain which have not so far been made explicit. First, that an increasingly prosperous people were also, to a wider extent than ever before, a people who prized leisure; second, that the pleasurable and profitable use of leisure became for the first time something of a cult among them, and third (the point memorably made by Sir John Plumb in his 1973 Stenton Lecture (193a)), that this in turn opened up possibilities hitherto undreamed of for the commercial exploitation of the cult. Clubs and coffee-houses, assemblies, new reading habits and holiday habits, and not least the development of sport, both for participation and spectator interest, further demonstrate how Augustan and Georgian Britons spent a good deal of their time, as well as of their surplus wealth, in the pursuit of leisure activities, and how an enterprising society catered for them.

By 1700 the club and the coffee-house were already pervasive features of the renascent London society of the post-Puritan era. The capital had every kind of club by George I's reign; as well as its music clubs, it had political clubs, dining clubs, drinking clubs, literary clubs and book clubs; even (the Tories darkly alleged) Calves' Head Clubs where ex-republicans could celebrate the martyrdom of Charles I bibulously and ghoulishly. As with so much else, the provinces quickly caught the club habit. Many county towns had clubs for the local gentry, especially well patronised in Assize weeks or during Quarter Sessions; they frequently had a partisan flavour, like the High Tory Royston Club in Hertford which met on the first Thursday in each month in its own specially built 'large, handsome square room, well wainscotted . . . [and] hung with the pictures of King Charles I, Charles II, King James and King William at their full length'.[12] St Cecilia's societies abounded; and in the 'club' which Dr Claver Morris helped to found in Wells early in the eighteenth century, St Cecilia's Day in 1718 was celebrated with the aid of 'Mr Duglass, the blackamoor trumpeter (who is one of the best in England on that instrument) and he sounded two sonatas very finely'.[13] But an equally characteristic feature of the provincial town were those self-improving associations – philosophical societies, natural history and antiquarian societies, and the like – to which educated Britons of the eighteenth century were growing as addicted as they were to courses of public subscription lectures on all manner of mind-stretching subjects (187b, *318 and n. 3*; 210, *32–3*).

Few of the smaller societies boasted their own rooms: most of them met either in taverns or coffee-houses. Every provincial town of any size had at least one coffee-house by George I's reign; the most important centres, such as Bristol, Oxford, Bath and York had four or five, and they became favourite resorts of local businessmen, the more substantial shopkeepers and members of the professions. Claver Morris was a regular visitor to the one in Wells, 'to read the newsletters', and in the intervals between wars half-pay army officers swelled the clientele in many such houses, as they did in Stamford in George I's reign.[14] In the capital, even by 1688 the coffee-house had become the commonest social haunt of gregarious Londoners of almost all degrees above the labouring class. Here peers and members of Parliament might rub shoulders with merchants, small manufacturers, shopkeepers and even artisans, and all 'poring over the same newspapers', the Abbé Prévost was later to marvel, as he extolled the coffee-houses as 'truly . . . the seats of English liberty!'[15] Whether for politics, business, card-playing, news-reading, or simply gossiping in the congenial company of one's fellows, they were a male preserve. Some women, like the formidable Jenny Man, kept coffee-houses, but as a sex they rarely frequented them, even though there were something like 650 such premises open in London and Westminster by 1714.

For the big social occasions of provincial life, such as balls, and for that staple fare of polite leisure in the late seventeenth and eighteenth centuries, the weekly assemblies of the winter season, the great urban inns of the period, like the *Three Cranes* in Leicester or the *George* in Northampton, could often provide suitable venues where town halls could not (208b). Gradually some of the larger 'gentry towns', and even some smaller places, like Warwick and Buckingham, began to acquire purpose-built assembly rooms. Birmingham and several other manufacturing towns followed their example, and by the 1780s assembly rooms were to be found not only in scores of small market towns but even in villages, such as Lamberhurst in Kent, which had little more than 700 inhabitants (208b, *115*). The lofty elegance that the biggest county-town assembly rooms could achieve can still be glimpsed here and there, today. York, whose Burlington Rooms were opened in 1732, and Bath, where Beau Nash ruled supreme until *c.* 1750, were among the fashionable meccas which acquired buildings of striking grandeur.[16] Not everyone approved of the holding of assemblies – Defoe's Puritan instincts, for instance, rebelled against the fast behaviour and unsuitable marriages they were said to encourage among the young, but they enlivened many a drab winter for thousands, and for girls who would otherwise have spent months on end mewed up in draughty manor-houses or parsonages they were a lifesaver. A Whiggish visitor to Chester in 1715, 'when King George's coronation day happened to fall on an assembly day', confessed that 'although that is as Tory a city as any in England, I counted fifty ladies as finely dressed as at an opera in the Haymarket'.[17]

When leisure time was not being devoted to cultural or more extrovert pursuits – among which we must also note the spread of theatre-going (193a, *111–14*) as one of seventeenth-century London's most popular legacies to the eighteenth-century provinces – it was often absorbed in reading. The evidence of a booming newspaper, periodical and pamphlet press (Ch. 13) suggests in itself that the literate Briton of the eighteenth century had become an incurable reader. The further evidence of the book trade and of the contents of libraries, both private and public, leaves no room to doubt it. Gone were the days when the Bible, Foxe's *Book of Martyrs* and *The Whole Duty of Man* constituted the beginning, and not far from the end of the average family's reading. The novel was slow to arrive, even after Defoe had pioneered the way with *Moll Flanders* and *Crusoe*, but when it did so in the 1740s, thanks to Richardson, Fielding and Smollett (above, pp. 8–10), its impact was enormous, particularly on the reading habits of women. One new phenomenon to which it gave a great impetus (for books of any scale were not cheap) was the setting up of circulating libraries. In the West Midlands, to take just one region, it is said that 'every town of any size . . . had at least one circulating library [by 1760], and they would be found flourishing in moderately large villages' (193d, *4*; cf. 211, *132–5*). To gratify the tastes, yet spare the pockets, of a more rarified public there was another new institution, the private book club, while parish, cathedral and some school libraries were built up and more widely used than hitherto. Children's books, too, both for pleasure and instruction, enjoyed a remarkable vogue (193b), and commercially-minded, inventive publishers, like the Newberys, exploited this, along with such novel devices as the 'part-book', which might be sold for as little as 1d. or 2d. an instalment, to penetrate a reading market well below that of 'the middling sort', as usually understood.

If reading habits were changing fast, so too were holiday habits, and like the former they keenly encouraged entrepreneurial enterprise. Visits to inland watering places, to imbibe or bathe in the medicinal waters or simply to socialise, became the great holiday fashion of the first half of the eighteenth century. By 1720 Bath, Tunbridge Wells and Epsom were already flourishing, and Scarborough was quickly catching on, attracting its quota of Scottish as well as northern English visitors. Buxton, too, had its adherents, though still handicapped by poor accommodation and by access roads so hazardous that in 1707 the coach of Sir Richard Pye, lent to some Derby ladies to carry them back home from Buxton, was 'quite unjointed and fell to pieces, past mending'.[18] The spas near London, especially, began to attract distinct social clienteles, and catered accordingly: Tunbridge Wells was for the well-to-do and dashing, Epsom – 'a place adapted wholly to pleasure' – for the solid bourgeois who packed it each July and August, Islington for the humbler 'cits'. Celia Fiennes found Bath well regulated even in the 1690s and it became much more so when its great period began, under Nash's autocratic eye, in the 1730s. But Defoe wrote tartly of Tunbridge Wells that it 'wants nothing . . . that can make a man or woman completely happy, always provided they have money', and primly blacklisted it in his best-selling *Tour* as 'a place in which a lady, however virtuous, yet for want of good conduct may as soon shipwreck her character as in any part of England' (2, *I, 127*).

Sea-bathing was indulged in only by a cranky minority until Dr Richard Russell publicised its therapeutic virtues in the 1750s. Thereafter seaside resorts would mount an increasingly powerful challenge to the spas. Scarborough (inevitably, with its head start), Margate and Brighton led the way, though ironically once Scarborough began attracting the bathers it lost many of its former gentry and aristocratic patrons (213, *Ch. 4*; 214 [J. Barrett]; 212c). In twenty years from 1750 to 1770 Margate was transformed into a fashionable resort which already had, in addition to its bathing facilities, its first square, its assembly rooms and circulating libraries. By 1786, when Booth had opened his theatre there and visitors were flocking to Benson's large new hotel, the place was unrecognisable to those who recalled the small, grubby fishing town of forty years earlier.[19] Despite rival attractions, however, the traditional inland non-spa resorts kept a good deal of their former popularity with the local gentry and professionals, well into the second half of the century. Until, like Nottingham's, its recreational attractions were killed off by industrialisation, Preston boasted a flourishing winter season for the Lancashire squires and their families. So, too, did York for a clientele east of the Pennines. Theatres were added to the former amenities of both places, York's from as early as 1734. Other resorts continued to appeal to summer visitors, Bury St Edmunds with its famous fair, Beverley and Nottingham with their race-meetings. Nottingham's August race week was for decades one of the great social as well as recreational events in the northern calendar.

Horse-racing is one of the prime examples we must note in conclusion of the development of sport in our period, not simply as a private leisure pursuit but as a public spectacle capable of attracting large, and by no means only male, crowds and therefore of generating financial profit. Racing had been popular among the aristocracy and gentry earlier in the seventeenth century. But by the 1680s Charles II, through his patronage of Newmarket, had ensured that, next to fox-hunting, it would become *the* sport of the upper-class Englishman, and, unlike fox-hunting, it became a townsman's as well as a countryman's sport. In the eighteenth century it grew increasingly organised, with the introduction of the Racing Calendar (1727) and the establishment of the Jockey Club (1752), and highly commercialised. Some of the grandees, such as Godolphin and Wharton, were spending thousands on their stables even by Queen Anne's reign, and starting to employ professional jockeys. But every squire with a good horse – and many a townsman too – was eager to match it, and back it, against his neighbour's; so that while Newmarket retained its primacy, inveterate racing men also began to go the rounds of the big local meetings such as those at York, Doncaster, Beverley, Nottingham, Warwick and Epsom. By 1727 there were already 112 recorded courses in England, most of them close to towns, and by 1739, 138. The sport suffered a temporary but serious crisis in the 1740s after the passing of a severe Act of Parliament aimed at eliminating small prizes and, in effect, stopping the proliferation of the smaller meetings. But thereafter prize money and winnings rose steeply and by the 1780s, when the Derby, the Oaks and the St Leger had become a regular part of the calendar, it is clear that 'a complex industry' had come into being (193a, *17*; at length 211, *180–196, 216*).

Racing was above all a gambling sport (a prime concern of the legislators of 1740), and that alone was enough to ensure its success with the English and to attract large and socially cosmopolitan crowds. The same was true of boxing, which became markedly professionalised under the early Hanoverians. And it was true, too, of cricket, which after tentative beginnings in the Restoration period suddenly caught on about the time of the Revolution, originally in the South-East of England, making up its rules as it went along. The earliest cricket matches were between villages or between neighbouring landlords and their respective tenants, but rivalry soon developed between towns – the cricketers of Dartford, for instance, who 'of all the Kentish men . . . lay claim to the greatest excellence', were challenged by the men of Tonbridge in August 1723[20] – and the first known county 'fixture', between Surrey and Kent, took place in 1709. Apart from the inevitably heavy betting it gave rise to (sternly condemned by a judge of the Court of Common Pleas in 1748),[21] a special feature of cricket within the cult of leisure was that not only its spectators but its practitioners were drawn from widely separated rungs of the social ladder; this 'glorious, manly, British game'[22] enslaved yeomen, small tradesmen and shopkeepers, as well as noblemen, squires and their servants, and so acted as something of a social leveller. 'Last Monday your father was at Mr Payn's', wrote Mary Turner of East Hoathly to her son in September 1739, 'and came home pleased enough, for he struck the best ball in the game, and wished he had not anything [else] to do, he would play at cricket all his life.'[23]

In this, as in so much else that has concerned us in this chapter, we see in effect a whole new culture developing in Augustan and early- to-mid-Georgian Britain. And as Plumb has pointed out, it differed from the élitist culture of the nobility and the still vigorous traditional folk culture of the lower orders[24] in its comprehensiveness. It

> was national and poised for growth . . . ; in time it would reach down even to the skilled working class. Books, music, painting were no longer private, and leisure itself had become for the first time in our history an industry (193c, *48*).

Indeed, as a growth industry it has proved to have a longer life and a greater capacity for expansion than the manufacturing industries on which Britain's economic greatness in the late eighteenth and nineteenth centuries was built.

---

1. For one contemporary effusion of superlatives, see John Macky, *A Journey through England*, I (1714), pp. 105–7.
2. For the leading rôle of the post–1714 Whig oligarchs in this process see L. and J.C.F. Stone (195), p. 302.
3. Joseph Clark to his [anon] model-maker, *temp* Anne, on the building of Hill Court, Herefordshire, quoted in J. Lees-Milne, *English Country Houses: Baroque, 1685–1715* (1970), p. 275.
4. For example Defoe (2), II, p. 262 (on Manchester); Macky, *Journey*, II (1722), p. 134 (on Bristol).
5. M. Rowlands (142b), p. 116; J.E. Vickers, *Old Sheffield Town* (Wakefield, 1972), p. 16.
6. See for example M.E. Falkus, 'Lighting in the Dark Ages of English Economic History: Town Streets before the Industrial Revolution', in (126); P.N. Borsay, 'The Rise of the Promenade: The Social and Cultural Use of Space in the English Provincial Town, *c.*1660–1800', *JBS*, **9** (1986).
7. Macky, *Journey*, II, p. 205.
8. T. F. Reddaway, *The Rebuilding of London after the Great Fire* (1940); Sir J. Summerson, *Georgian London* (2nd edn, 1962).
9. C. Morris, ed., *The Journeys of Celia Fiennes* (revised edn, 1949), p. 72. A superb picture by Thomas Sandby of the scene Fiennes describes is reproduced on the jacket of P. Clark (210).
10. *Annual Register* (1761), p. 207, quoted in Falkus, *loc. cit.* p. 259.
11. Macky, *Journey*, I (1714), pp. 24–5.
12. HMC *Portland MSS.*, IV, pp. 153–4: [Defoe] to Robert Harley, N.D. [?1704].
13. E. Hobhouse, ed., *The Diary of a West Country Physician* (1934), pp. 39–43, 65.
14. Ibid. p. 52; Macky, *Journey*, II, p. 205.
15. Prévost, *Adventures of a Man of Quality* (1930 edn.), p. 119, quoted in Porter (132), p. 12.
16. P.N. Borsay (211), pp. 336–49. The present Assembly Rooms in Bath were the city's third, designed by John Wood the Younger and opened in 1771 at the then record cost of £20,000. Its predecessors dated from 1708 and 1730 respectively.
17. Macky, *Journey*, II, p. 214.
18. HMC *Portland MSS.*, IV, p. 429.
19. J. Whyman, 'A Hanoverian Watering-Place: Margate before the Railway', in A. Everitt, ed. (208a).

20. Journal of the Revd. T. Thomas, HMC *Portland MSS.*, VI, p. 76.
21. Jeffreys *versus* Walters (1748). The same judge, however, conceded that cricket was a 'manly' game within the meaning of the statute of 9 Anne c.14.
22. James Love, *Cricket: an Heroic Poem* (1744), p. 1.
23. Neville Cardus, *Autobiography* (1947), p. 196.
24. See, for example, R.W. Malcolmson, *Popular Recreations in English Society 1700–1850* (Cambridge, 1973).

CHAPTER 15

The Scottish revival

Those social implications of the eighteenth century's increasing prosperity, such as residential improvements, urban landscaping, aesthetic and cultural enrichment and leisure provision, examined in the previous chapter, were presented there as *British* phenomena, in which the Scots (though often later and to a lesser degree) were involved along with the English. This is an appropriate point to look at eighteenth-century Scotland, and at that Union of the two countries, the early, somewhat troubled history of which has been outlined in the antecedent volume to this (Ch. 20).

In 1707 Scotland ceased to exist as a separate political entity through mutually agreed fusion with its English neighbour. Technically, both kingdoms' representative assemblies voted themselves into oblivion and a new, British state succeeded them. Actually, the English polity remained completely intact but with a truncated Scottish representation grafted on. In addition, the recrimination and jobbery that had marked the Union's passage (*Making of a Great Power*, Ch. 20) meant the new order had an uphill task to achieve any legitimacy in the eyes of the Scots. Belief in a true, moral union was gradually created, in the course of the eighteenth century, but its creation owed little to official policies and initiatives.

As might have been predicted from the overwhelmingly English dominance of political debate at Westminster, all eighteenth-century governments were totally Anglocentric (64, *85*, *158–9*; 43b). They accordingly pursued two objectives with respect to Scotland: keeping it quiet and running it cheaply. One important consequence of this for Scotland was that it led Westminster, by and large, to rule that country through loyal, but Scottish, agents who intrinsically mediated, and to some extent softened, the impact of metropolitan demands (253, *169–77*). A second effect was that those same loyal Scottish agents, who, very humanly, did not wish to think of themselves as unpatriotic, fostered a myth of 'Britishness' in which support for the Union became a moral act. Scotland's 'revival' (actually more akin to resurrection) in the second half of the eighteenth century rested on her acceptance of ideological, social and economic provincialisation within the new polity. It will be argued later that not even her proud cultural flowering, that 'Scottish Enlightenment' which became the most justly celebrated manifestation of the country's eighteenth-century revival, invalidates this view. A belief in (Scottish) Britishness and an axiomatic assumption of Scotland's significance for the new polity were necessary salves for the wound inflicted on Scots' pride in their separate national identity by Scotland's acceptance of, in effect, provincial status.

The basis for such acceptance had to be built up over a long period of time.

215

Until at least the 1750s Scotland's rulers were a beleaguered native oligarchy, dependent in the final analysis on English arms to keep them in power. The net effect of government control of Scotland resting on the support of such a minority (albeit a growing one) was that for half a century after the Union Scotland was, in the words of Bruce Lenman, a 'client society', administered on semi-colonial lines by a select inner group within the traditional ruling élite (252, *90–3*; 253, *86–7*). Westminster ruled Scotland through a narrow oligarchy of 'reliable' (i.e. Whig) families-cum-connexions. These in turn controlled Scottish society through patronage in the form of government jobs, favourable legal decisions, and so on. The upshot was the demoralisation of Scottish politics and the enervation of Scotland's major institutions, the Kirk, the Convention of Burghs and (to a lesser extent) the legal profession. Furthermore, given the way Scotland was being run, politicians operating within legitimate politics (as opposed to Jacobite conspiracy) were obliged to play to English ministers' prejudices because it was in London that all the crucial decisions were taken. On occasion, this inevitably put Scotland's economic interests in jeopardy at Westminster (253, *43–4*). Within Scotland itself the activities of the Whig oligarchy were restricted to building up cadres of client officials with which to battle against similar opposing groups over who should 'steer the gravy train' (254). Faction became the keystone of Scottish politics, and sterile, parasitic exploitation of its administration's meagre resources virtually their sole objective (252, *82, 85–7, 90–1*).

This degeneration in the tone of Scottish political life was accentuated by the way certain Scottish institutions, such as the Assembly of the Kirk and the Convention of Royal Burghs, had been preserved by the terms of the Union. Most immediately damaging, from the point of view of their functions, was the way these institutions were seized upon by the Scottish Whig oligarchy to do service as pork barrels in their interminable faction fighting. Their upper echelons were soon packed, not with faithful stewards but with reliable adherents of one or other of the Whig factions. More insidiously, subordination to Westminster sapped their vitality. Without their native legislature to lobby, influence and work with, these institutions were effectively emasculated. The new British Parliament, dominated as it was by English MPs and peers, was at best indifferent to their purely Scottish concerns. Consequently, they were left curiously stunted; they still retained some local authority and economic power, but their power and prestige was unrelated to any larger political reality. Inevitably they became introverted and unresponsive to the needs of the society they had been created to serve (253, *95–106*). To take only one example, within five years of the Union even the General Assembly of the Kirk, which for most of the previous century had been a ferocious watchdog of the moral order in Church and State, was reduced to a rubber stamp for the endorsement of government policies and a source of rewards for loyal servants of the new order.[1]

Because it was the key instrument of government control, the Scottish legal system was a partial exception to this decline in Scotland's native institutions. Nonetheless, it too was warped by alien influences and ultimately proved unable to benefit from the eighteenth-century renaissance enjoyed by its former intellectual powerhouses, the Scottish universities, and in particular by the universities of Glasgow and Edinburgh. In spite of the guarantees in the Act of Union, whenever the government at Westminster found Scottish legal traditions a hindrance it simply swept them away. An early manifestation of this tendency appeared after the Franco-Jacobite invasion attempt of 1708, when (despite the well-nigh unanimous objections of Scotland's representatives in Parliament) the Godolphin ministry used its English Whig majority to pass a law aligning Scottish legal practice in treason cases with that current in England, where only one witness was needed to secure a conviction (see *Making of a Great Power*, p. 317 Ch. 20).[2] A more disruptive change was the introduction by the Union of a higher Court of Appeal than the Lords of Session: the House of Lords (ibid. Ch. 20, *loc. cit.*). In 1711 the Episcopalian Scottish Tories (Jacobites almost to a man) used this new avenue to outflank the Presbyterian Whig establishment in Scotland, by appealing successfully to the Lords to reverse the conviction of an Episcopalian clergyman, James Greenshields, under laws upholding the Kirk's position as the established Church of Scotland. In the process the Kirk's ecclesiastical monopoly in Scotland (guaranteed by the Union) was casually breached, and events set in train that were to lead to a major Cameronian schism in 1712 which was not to be healed until 1718.[3] After 1714, because the now Whig-dominated House of Lords could usually be relied on to back up the Whig establishment in Scotland, the erosion of the Scottish judiciary's authority became a dormant rather than an active problem. Nonetheless, the price of continued legal autonomy was clear: the Scottish legal profession had to accept the subordination of their legal system to English Common Law practice. Whenever the two traditions clashed, it was Scotland's that had to give way. Once this bitter pill was swallowed, the Scottish legal profession were able to enjoy what one authority has gone so far as to describe as 'a comfortable, cosy existence as a superior version of a provincial court'.[4]

The customs and mores of everyday life in Scotland were, on the surface, little affected by the existence of the Union. The next two generations of the peerage, lairds and gentry contained large elements that were politically frustrated or even disaffected, but for most of the population, and especially the vast majority who did not live close to Glasgow and its satellite towns, the pace and tenor of life went on relatively unchanged until at least the 1750s. Indeed, the Union was designed to be soothing on precisely that score. Over the century as a whole following the Union Scottish society was changed out of all recognition, but in the short term all that was visible was a slight acceleration of existing social and economic trends.

For over a century before the Union the Scottish peerage had been taking the road southwards to the fount of all patronage: the royal court, in increasing numbers (250a, *4, 23, 53–5, 88*). After 1707, as their hopes and indeed expectations of honourable rewards expanded, the tendency became steadily more pronounced until by the mid-eighteenth century Scotland can fairly be said to have been abandoned by its nobility. The creation of the first British empire, its dismemberment and the conquest of a second, all in the course of the period up to 1815, opened up a plethora of lucrative colonial and military employments suitable for peers in need of a place; whereas the English peerage was, by and large, sufficiently well-to-do to be choosy about the posts it took up, the less affluent Scottish nobility eagerly took advantage of the opportunities offered by Britain's imperial expansion (253, *8–10, 14–15*). Quite apart from seeking their fortunes in England, more and more of the Scottish peerage chose to live in England on a permanent basis and bring up their families there. Once resident, their children were educated at the same schools as their English counterparts and increasingly intermarried with their social equals among the English aristocracy. By the end of the eighteenth century the Scottish, English and Irish peerages were so intertwined that they can fairly be regarded as a single, British, institution, and as such the Scottish aristocracy were a potent force for Scotland's integration into the British polity (203a, *87–8*).

This had considerable repercussions for Scottish society. Scotland's social structure was still intensely hierarchical, each layer of society automatically looking to those above it for protection as well as for social and political direction: labourers to farmers, farmers to lairds, lairds to nobility. The progressive removal of the nobility therefore created a gathering social vacuum. The only alternative source of social authority, given that the Kirk rapidly became discredited by its relationship with the Whig regime, were the lairds. Over the course of the century the lairdly élite's share of Scottish landownership was, however, in decline (ironically, to the profit of the nobility), so that they were never wealthy enough fully to replace their noble superiors.[5] The upshot of all this was that the strong sense of vertical alignment that characterised Scottish social relations in 1700 was rapidly decaying by the end of the century. Only after 1780 did economic criteria (i.e. how much rent they could pay) begin to play a major rôle in the relationship between most landlords and their tenants. Until then putative kinship, prolonged residence and the memory of ancient services rendered was at least as important (256, *53–7*). Nevertheless the pressures pushing the landowning élite in this direction had been steadily building up for two generations before the end of our period. Scottish imitation of English refinement, in terms of mores, dress, manners and social customs became avid and persistent from the 1720s. Every Scottish laird, it seemed, wanted to be able to dress himself and his family according to the latest metropolitan fashions, build a fine house in the latest style (cf. Ch. 14), maintain a suitable separation from his social inferiors, drink tea rather than beer, and so on (241, *266–71*). All this required money. Since landownership (however heavily mortgaged) was the sole criterion of elevated social status in Scotland the lairds were reluctant to sell their estates, and so they looked instead to increase the incomes they yielded. Agricultural improvement on English lines accordingly became more and more fashionable in Scotland from the 1740s, and the general rule from the 1780s, because of the increased rents it offered landowners. It came first in the Lowlands, where local custom, farming practice and landowners' rights most favoured enclosure and improvement, and only later, from the 1760s, in the Highlands. The inevitable consequence of such a profit-seeking approach was the waning of the old social order.

The first casualties were the small farmers in the Lowlands and the middling ranks of the clan gentry in the Highlands. Improvement worked in large part through the amalgamation of smaller landholdings so as to produce economies of scale. Small farmers operating at little more than subsistence level were accordingly eliminated in favour of 'efficient' men (231 [R.A. Dodgshon], *53–7*). The small farmers pushed downwards thereby into the ranks of the landless labourers may well have been better off financially, but they inevitably suffered a loss of status which they could not but resent (241, *294–302*). Likewise the Tacksmen (actually or theoretically kinsmen of the clan chieftains) who traditionally operated as middlemen in the Highlands, subletting to ordinary clansmen in return for a low rent and a pledge of military service if required, were pushed out by the award of tenancies to the highest bidder or the establishment of a direct lease between the clansmen and their chieftains (256, *60–5, 124*). The next stage of agrarian improvement was obviously the economic rationalisation of the landowner-cultivator relationship. In the Lowlands this was an axiomatic part of bringing in, or increasing the holdings of, efficient farmers. In the Highlands, a lingering sense of duty to their clansmen initially led the chieftains to try and increase their rents (as well as cope with overpopulation and poverty) by subdividing tenancies and encouraging domestic industries like kelp-farming and weaving. In the end, though, financial exigency or cupidity led virtually all the clan chieftains to clear out their tenant cultivators in favour of sheep farming. The Highland clearances, with all the bitterness they engendered, were mainly a nineteenth-century phenomenon, but the first scenes in that tragedy were already being enacted in the late eighteenth century. The first wave of clearances began in Perthshire in the 1770s, spread to other Highland regions bordering on improved lowland estates in the 1780s and accelerated to become a continuous process across the whole of the Highlands by the 1790s (256, *124–36, 197–9*).

In any consideration of the eighteenth-century Scottish economy one must always bear in mind that the industrial sector remained very small throughout the period 1707–82. Textile manufactures were the engine of the industrial revolution in England; in 1780 there were only 25,000 full-time weavers of all kinds employed in the whole of Scotland.[6] Until well beyond the end of our period agriculture remained the most important part of the Scottish economy. It employed the majority of the people, provided most of Scotland's exports, and its relative buoyancy set the tone for the rest of the economy. Scotland's most valuable export throughout the eighteenth century remained black cattle for the English market (245a, *34–5*).

For most of the Scottish burghs the first fifty years after the Union were a period of stagnation. The commerce of the east-coast ports with the Continent was restricted by legislation designed to protect English concerns such as the woollen textile industry, and few east-coast Scottish merchants managed to intrude themselves into the English Continental export trade by way of compensation (241, *226*). Glasgow and the Clydeside ports were the one area of the old Scottish burgh system that did well out of free, legal access to England's empire, passing easily from wholesale smuggling to a burgeoning transatlantic trade. Glasgow in particular steadily expanded its trade and population throughout the eighteenth century by acting as an entrepôt for Irish and colonial goods as well as the focus for Scotland's westward exports (245a, *37–9*). One particularly lucrative area of colonial trade cornered by Glasgow merchants was the import of American tobacco. Between 1707 and 1738 the Glasgow 'Tobacco Lords' managed to secure 10 per cent of all America's tobacco exports. By the late 1760s this proportion had risen to nearly half the total produced in the British American colonies. The manufacture of linen, however, remained the leading, and most rapidly expanding sector in Scotland's non-agricultural economy until the establishment of cotton textile mills in the 1780s. When it slumped, as it did in the late 1760s, such widespread economic distress followed that comparisons were soon being drawn with the Darien disaster. Moreover, linen manufacture was, and remained, largely unmechanised and diffused across the whole of the Lowlands, though from the 1750s large concentrations of linen-working began to develop around Glasgow. In Scotland, as elsewhere in the British Isles, the early industrial revolution was not based on mechanisation so much as on the systematic reorganisation of working practices (165, *225–7*). Scottish coal production, too, steadily increased throughout the eighteenth century, serving mainly the English market. Coal-mining was the most heavily mechanised area of the Scottish economy and yet simultaneously the final bastion of its most archaic labour relations. Miners remained enserfed under Scottish law until the 1770s, when the colliery owners belatedly realised that their workforce were quietly exploiting the feudal survivals and the communal solidarity associated with their serfdom to drive up their *de facto*, as opposed to *de jure*, wages.[7] The basis of even greater, and more rapid, industrial expansion was also laid in the 1750s and 60s by heavy investment in canals and road networks close by the coastal centres of industry. In particular, as we know, (Ch. 11), the Forth-Clyde canal (1768–90) opened up Midlothian and previously unexploited areas of Scotland's central belt to investment out of Glasgow.

The substantive economic basis for later eighteenth-century Scottish industrialisation was easy access to English and colonial markets. But it was not until the last decades of the century that the Union began to deliver the full economic dividends hoped for in 1707. Only then did even the Lowlands of Scotland clamber clear of the trough of pre-industrial poverty. The ups and downs of the Carron iron works (see Ch. 11) and the bankruptcy it inflicted on several partners in the enterprise graphically illustrate that it was operating in an economy barely large enough to support it (245a, *55–7*). Significantly, too, it remained a lone swallow until after 1780 when mechanised cotton textile mills began to be established in Glasgow's hinterland. What happened then was that economic circumstances, notably a dynamic trading port and a substantial commercial élite with capital to invest, in and around Glasgow, fostered an industrial boom akin to that occurring around Liverpool and Manchester. Clydeside's initial attraction consisted mainly of the lower wages its workforce would accept (247, *100*). The industrial revolution thus eventually created the prosperity which pro-Unionist Scotsmen yearned for in 1707, and it clearly owed something to the economic provisions of the Union; the length of time it took to arrive, however, leaves the question of *how much* it owed, open to debate (245a, *48*).

Associated with Glasgow's expansion and that of the west-coast ports generally was a steady increase in the urban population. Between 1750 and 1820 the proportion of town- to country-dwellers increased from one Scot in eight to one in three, with the bulk of the increase occurring after 1783. Despite emigration to England and the colonies Scotland's population was booming and Scotland's towns were absorbing most of the increase [B.3 (ii), (iii)]. In addition, those driven off the land by clearances in the Highlands or the loss of their tenancies in the Lowlands tended to drift towards the towns and cities of Scotland's central belt, where there was more non-agricultural employment to be found (241, 240–3). By definition these were masterless men seeking to reforge familiar social relationships. The newly prosperous urban bourgeoisie knew what was expected of them and were pleased to provide it, and so the eighteenth century saw the first stirrings of the emergence of a separate, urban middle-class consciousness, characterised by civic pride and assured social leadership (241, 358–65). This must not be overstressed, because most of Scotland's urban élites remained land- (i.e. traditionally status-) hungry well into the nineteenth century, but the foundations of a non-deferential urban bourgeoisie were being laid in this period (231 [Devine, 'Social Composition'], 164–73).

Increasing economic and social integration with England needed an adjunct if it was to create a 'British' consciousness within which Scotland could find a place: a diminution of English hostility towards, and suspicion of, Scotland and Scotsmen. When James Boswell, as anglicised a Scot as ever there was, witnessed two Scottish officers just returned from the capture of Havana being abused by a crowd at Covent Garden theatre in 1762, he was enraged: 'I hated the English; I wished from my soul that the Union was broke and that we might give them another battle of Bannockburn'.[8] Anti-Scottish prejudice was deeply rooted in the English national psyche and it took a long time to die away. Between 1700 and the 1770s most Englishmen simply regarded the Scots as incorrigible mendicants with alarmingly Jacobite propensities. Hearing a Scotsman defend the beauties of the Scottish landscape at dinner one evening in 1763, Dr Johnson sneeringly riposted 'the noblest prospect a Scotsman ever sees is the road which leads him to England!' – which met with a roar of approval from the other guests.[9] The Jacobite rebellion of 1745–6 duly confirmed English prejudices about Scottish unreliability and excited a torrent of Scotophobia that worked itself out in such channels as Hardwicke's legislative onslaught on Scottish heritable jurisdictions in the 1740s and 50s and John Wilkes's attacks on the earl of Bute in the 1760s. The way back into English good graces and, further, acceptance of Scotland's presence in the new myth of Britishness, came in the course of the wars after 1756. The elder Pitt put a nice gloss on it when he boasted in 1766:

I sought for merit [in the Seven Years War] wherever it was to be found; . . . I was the first minister who looked for it and found it in the mountains of the north. I called it forth, and drew into your service a hardy and intrepid race of men, who, when left by your jealousy, became a prey to the artifice of your enemies, and had gone nigh to have overturned the State in the war before the last. These men in the last war were brought to combat on your side; they served you with fidelity, as they fought with valour, and conquered for you in every part of the world.[10]

Scotland in general, and the Highlands in particular, became a major, disproportionate, source of recruits for Britain's wars.

Scotland, and especially the Highlands, had established a mercenary military
tradition well before her Union with England. Pitt's achievement was the
harnessing of it to the needs of the British Empire during the Seven Years War.
During the late 1750s a few former rebels, like Simon Fraser of Beaufort, were
able to rehabilitate themselves by raising regiments among their clansmen.
During the American war many others, such as Lord MacLeod, heir apparent to
the chieftainship of the Mackenzies, and James Murray, son of Lord George
Murray, followed suit. By the end of the century recruitment had reached such
heights that it was beginning to become a significant drain on the manpower of
the Highlands (256, *147–8*). By at least the 1790s, and probably earlier, it had
also taken on a particularly harsh mien as landlords began to coerce families
holding tenancies on their lands into delivering up their sons for the chieftain's
regiment. In 1794 for example, Alexander Macdonnell of Glengarry ordered the
eviction of all those families among his tenants who had not provided him with a
soldier for his regiment (256, *154–6*). In an abstract economic sense the drain of
young men out of the Highlands and into service as the gendarmerie of the
British empire – from which only a minority returned – may have had some
virtues. It eased the pressure of population in the Highlands to some degree. The
remittances sent home by the soldiers were a valuable input for the ailing
Highland economy. Nonetheless, the one-sidedness of the bargain remains one
of the most striking things about it. The anglicised Highland landowners of
Scotland carved themselves an honourable place in the new British polity on the
backs of their impoverished tenantry, whose eventual reward in the nineteenth
century was to be evicted as an uneconomic form of estate exploitation (256).

The kind of upheavals Scottish society was undergoing in the mid-eighteenth
century do not usually beget an artistic and philosophical renaissance, and
through it, a renaissance of national pride and self-esteem. However, in Hanoverian Scotland for some reason they did. It may have been that there were
precious few other ways for talented Scotsmen to achieve (non-military) social
esteem, fame and fortune untainted by the built-in corruption of Scotland's
institutions. Be that as it may, from the 1740s until the 1820s there was a brief,
explosive interlude of intellectual, literary and artistic activity that is now known
as the Scottish Enlightenment.

The Enlightenment in Scotland, as in the rest of Europe, was an urban
phenomenon. It centred on an axis running from Glasgow to Edinburgh and had
an outpost at Aberdeen. The one thing uniting these disparate locations is that
all three were sites of ancient Scottish universities. And it was the Scottish
universities that gave rise to the Scottish Enlightenment, shaped and nurtured it,
and, not least important, gave it a patina of respectability that made it acceptable
to Scotland's ruling élite. The waning of the universities' support for it, along
with associated conservative reactions in the legal profession and the Kirk after
1800, spelled the end of the Scottish Enlightenment (255, *238–46*). Its foremost

luminaries are now known world-wide, and undoubtedly constitute some of the most influential intellectuals in the history of mankind. Adam Smith wrote the first systematic consideration of the way economic systems work. His best-known book, *The Wealth of Nations*, laid the foundations of modern economic theory. David Hume's considerations on the philosophy of knowledge are *the* seminal philosophical work on epistemology. When the contributions made by various *philosophes* to the Enlightenment are assessed, Hume is in consequence almost invariably listed alongside the likes of Rousseau, Montesquieu and Diderot. Joseph Black's experimental analysis of alkalis, an offshoot of his medical research, laid the foundations of modern chemistry and marked its separation from medicine as a discipline. Robert Burns's brilliance as a poet has no equal in eighteenth-century Scotland, and few anywhere have matched it before or since. Robert Adam almost singlehandedly changed the whole tone and direction in British architecture by building on refined, classical lines that begat a wave of imitators. At the time they did their best work all but Burns were connected with Scottish universities or university towns. Even when they were not actually engaged in university teaching they all inhabited the milieu which surrounded each institution. The taverns, salons and dinners where they associated with interested (and well-educated) laymen, and the conversations they enjoyed in the interstices of every working day with theologians, classicists and mathematicians all contributed to the atmosphere of intellectual inquiry that inspired these great men. None of them, other than Burns, was unique (and even he had competition). Smith, Hume, Black and Adam were all part of a much wider circle peopled with many other intellectuals who were well-known at the time, but have now been forgotten. William Cullen was almost as important in the emergence of modern chemistry as Black; Hugh Blair, who preached weekly to many of the *cognoscenti* at St Giles's Kirk, was at the time a famous Moderate Presbyterian theologian and a profound influence on their treatment of the nature of man; Adam Ferguson wrote one of the most perceptive critiques of Smith's thesis on the beneficial effects of rational economic self-interest ever published (255, *68–9, 114–15*). All of these intellectuals, whether we remember them or not, who participated in the milieu that stimulated the great ones amongst them, also contributed to a renaissance of Scotland's universities that ensured that the Scottish Enlightenment left an enduring legacy. One example may stand for all: medical training at Edinburgh. The medical school was first securely established in the 1720s (cf. Ch. 10). Between the 1750s and 1790s Edinburgh University's medical training was rationalised and modernised and a novel emphasis on practical work introduced. Within a short time such reforms made this medical school the natural successor to Leyden in reputation and achievement, and a model for European medical schools for over a century. This could not have been achieved without a host of teachers and researchers whose work, though important at the time, has long since been forgotten (255).

It was fundamentally a provincial culture that was flowering in these years. All of its leading figures (apart from Robert Burns, who affected a sentimental nationalism) accepted the political *status quo* and indeed many, like David Hume the philosopher and Adam Smith the economist, overtly supported the Union and were proud of their newly discovered Britishness (241, *461*). Their Scottish-ness, like Boswell's, was of the apologetic variety; 'I come from Scotland, but I cannot help it', he told Dr Johnson in 1763.[11] Significantly, in the aftermath of the Scottish Enlightenment even enemies of the established order, like the Scottish Jacobins of the 1790s, had little time for Scottish nationalism; their thoughts were all focused on winning control of the British state.

In part this phenomenon was symptomatic of the increasing prosperity, self-confidence and social leadership of Scotland's urban bourgeoisie and improving landowners. Civic and lairdly patronage played an important part in the Scottish Enlightenment; from one perspective, it can be seen as a form of conspicuous consumption, proving the patrons' social eminence. Certainly, exercising corporate patronage by installing famous Enlightenment figures like Smith as Professor of Moral Philosophy at Glasgow University struck a chord with the traditional Scottish respect for learning, and thus raised a corporation's standing in Scottish society. Being listed as one of those subscribing towards the cost of publication in the preface of one of Burns's books of poetry doubtless achieved the same effect. The subjects that Enlightenment intellectuals were interested in, too, were those that interested (and were fashionable among) the urban bourgeoisie and improving lairds: political economy, scientific improvement, the philosophical basis of rational self-interest, and so on. Likewise the literary and artistic flowering exemplified by men like Burns and Adam came mainly in forms agreeable to the bourgeois and lairdly patrons who were increasingly usurping the rôle of the nobility in that sphere: vernacular poetry and grand civic architecture (241, *456–63*).

Bourgeois involvement in the Scottish Enlightenment profoundly influenced its impact, and with hindsight we can see that the Enlightenment shaped the outlook of the Scottish middle class in the next century, but its effects must not be exaggerated. Though the Kirk was fatally compromised by its association with the Whig regime, its teachings remained the guiding light for the overwhelming majority of ordinary Scotsmen. Noble influence and patronage, though declining in relative importance, were still the most eagerly sought by Enlightenment intellectuals, and aristocratic predilections set off aspects of the Enlightenment, for example in architecture and the decorative arts, that otherwise would have languished. No bourgeois patron was likely to have taken much interest in the brilliant outpouring of Gaelic poetry taking place at the same time as these more 'progressive' developments (241, *465–6*).

The civic pride that lay at the root of the enduring elements of the Scottish Enlightenment in many ways expressed the final stage of the provincialisation of Scotland. If the Enlightenment had a common theme, that theme was the celebration of Britishness, and Scots' regional rather than national pride. In fact as well as in name, Scotland had become, and was to remain for the next century and a half, 'North Britain'.

---

1. HMC *Laing MSS.*, II, pp. 162–3: earl of Oxford to Moderator William Carstares, 9 June 1712.

2. A. Aufrere, ed., *The Lockhart Papers* (2 vols, 1817), I, pp. 300–1.
3. D. Szechi, 'The Politics of "Persecution": Scots Episcopalian Toleration and the Harley Ministry', in W. Sheils, ed., *Toleration and Persecution: Studies in Church History*, 21 (1984).
4. A. Murdoch, 'The Advocates, the Law and the Nation in Early Modern Scotland', in W. Prest, ed., *Lawyers in Early Modern Europe and America* (1981).
5. L. Timperley, 'Landownership in Scotland in the Eighteenth Century', unpublished University of Edinburgh Ph.D thesis (1977), pp. 180, 197, 266.
6. W.H. Fraser, *Conflict and Class: Scottish Workers, 1700–1838* (1988), p. 32.
7. C.A. Whatley, '"The Fettering Bonds of Brotherhood": Combination and Labour Relations in the Scottish Coal-Mining Industry, *c.* 1690–1775', *Social History*, **12** (1987).
8. F.A. Pottle, ed., *Boswell's London Journal, 1762–1763* (1951), p. 72.
9. Ibid., p. 294.
10. Quoted in B. Lenman, *The Jacobite Clans of the Great Glen* (1984), pp. 194–5.
11. *London Journal*, p. 260.

CHAPTER 16

Ireland: from the Williamite settlement to 'Grattan's Parliament'*

On 3 October 1691 the last regular Jacobite forces in the British Isles agreed to surrender their last stronghold, Limerick, on terms designed to facilitate the evacuation of those wishing to carry on the war in France and the return home of those who wanted to remain in Ireland (*Making of a Great Power*, F(iv)). After two years of bloody warfare the Protestant minority, supported by English and Dutch troops, had overcome the Roman Catholic majority (supported by French troops) (236a, *52–257*; see also *Making of a Great Power*, pp. 195–6 and Ch 14). Between 1692 and 1697 the Protestants' precarious military triumph was converted into the Williamite settlement: a colonial ascendancy resting on the twin pillars of English arms and a new, fully sectarian political order (232a, *264*). The economy was in ruins, much of the population had been uprooted, banditry and guerilla warfare were rife, and with the departure of most of the Catholic nobility to France the old social order appeared to have disintegrated. 'Cashel's company gone, its guest-houses and youth; the gabled palace of Brian flooded dark with otters; Ealla left leaderless, lacking royal Munster sons', lamented the poet Aogán Ó Rathaille.[1] The Williamite settlement did not have a happy beginning.

Just over a century later, in 1798, after the suppression of the United Irishmen, the country was in much the same state; nothing, it might seem, ever changed in Ireland. The similarity however, is superficial. The kingdom changed out of all recognition between 1691 and 1782, and to interpret eighteenth-century Ireland solely in the light of its grim inception and its tragic end is utterly to miss the profound changes in Irish society that took place during that period. The eighteenth century was not one long catalogue of vicious resistance overtopped by cruel repression; Ireland was generally peaceful – and that needs to be explained as much as the sectarian confrontations that mark its beginning and its end.

The origins of eighteenth-century Ireland's relative peace lay in the social mores of Irish society. It was deeply stratified. Religious, ethnic, and linguistic divisions sharply marked out different groups, yet their interaction produced reasonably amicable social relations. The sections which follow will outline the basic divisions in Irish society, then illustrate how each group meshed with the others to produce their intriguing harmony.

Ireland's rulers were overwhelmingly Church of Ireland (Anglican) Prot-

---

* I am deeply indebted to Dr David Hayton of the History of Parliament Trust for his invaluable advice on how to approach this subject, and for his effective but courteous criticism of my half-baked ideas. He is, of course, not to be held responsible for what follows.   D.S.

estants. In 1688 they owned nearly 78 per cent of the land; in 1700, nearly 86 per cent; in 1776, almost 95 per cent (237a, *263*). At less than 10 per cent of the total population, they were one of the smallest denominations in Ireland. Nonetheless, as the 'English interest', with (supposedly) roots in the twelfth century, they were the most powerful, not only because they owned most of the country, but also because (from 1704) they enjoyed a legal monopoly of political, municipal and administrative office. The Protestant Ascendancy was the ascendancy of *their* social élite. Noblemen and squires were disproportionately numerous amongst them. They were not, however, the only Anglicans in Ireland. A flourishing Anglican bourgeoisie existed in most of Ireland's ports and towns outside Ulster, with a matching artisanate, especially in Leinster (234b, *34–7*). Until the 1750s Dublin was a predominantly Protestant city and most of its citizens were Church of Ireland. Consequently, the gradations of wealth and poverty applying to every other group in Ireland applied to them too.

Inferior in social and political power, but at about 12 per cent of the population superior in numbers to the Anglicans, were the Presbyterians. Most lived in Ulster, and many were descended from colonists who arrived in the 1600s. Though their numbers had declined as a result of the vicissitudes of the mid-seventeenth century (the Catholic rising of 1641 had been particularly devastating in Ulster) they were augmented in William III's reign by Scottish refugees, fleeing the famine of 1696–9 (*Making of a Great Power*, Ch. 19), and drawn by the favourable leases on offer to Protestant tenants. The majority of Ulster Presbyterians were tenant farmers, though during the eighteenth century a thriving commercial bourgeoisie arose in the linen triangle encompassing Belfast, Armagh and Dungannon (231, *61–5*). As Protestant nonconformists, the Presbyterians suffered almost as much legal circumscription of their civil rights as did the Catholics, and after the Restoration were sometimes seen as an especial threat to the Anglican hegemony (232, *267–9*). In part this was a reaction to their social independence; the number of Presbyterian landowners steadily declined after 1660, and ordinary Presbyterians increasingly looked to their ministers for leadership. Nevertheless, Presbyterian heroism at Londonderry and Enniskillen in 1689–90 convinced most of the Ascendancy that they could be relied on to uphold the 'Protestant interest'. *De facto* they consequently enjoyed virtually complete religious toleration, and even some degree of privilege relative to the Catholics (237a, *110–19*; 234b, *39–40*).

Roman Catholics made up nearly 80 per cent of the population, and were in a majority everywhere except in Ulster and parts of Leinster. Although some Catholic nobility and gentry survived the Williamite confiscation of Catholic lands, notably in Connaught, they were by-and-large a truncated community, with few of their traditional social leaders remaining. The Catholic nobility and gentry were in decline before the Revolution of 1688, and the process gathered pace during the eighteenth century as more and more conformed to the established church or emigrated to evade the penal laws (which were designed, among other things, to break up Catholic landownership). Most Catholics, then, were tenant farmers and landless labourers, though exclusion from politics, the professions and government service fostered the rise of a substantial urban business community by forcing enterprising Catholics into trade. However, because this bourgeoisie almost invariably had lowly origins, it could not fill the social vacuum created in the Catholic community by the disappearance of the old élite. The social mores of native Irish culture – jealously safeguarded by its bards and poets – were heavily élitist, and any attempt by Catholic townsfolk to assume social leadership was bitterly resented. *Faute de mieux*, leadership of the Catholics passed to the priesthood and the occasional exceptional individual.[2] Theoretically, the Catholic church should have died out in the eighteenth century as a result of laws forbidding consecrations by Catholic bishops or entry into Ireland by priests trained in Europe. In reality, the law was tacitly ignored. The established church showed little interest in converting the Catholics, and the Presbyterians were too introverted to try. To leave the mass of the population unchurched was hardly an option, so the Catholic church was generally left in peace.[3]

Alongside these religious divisions a related set of ethnic demarcations further divided Irish society. Among Protestants it was the Anglicans who, because of Catholic conversions and intermarriage going back beyond the sixteenth century, were most nearly related to the native Irish. Consequently, although in the 1690s and for some time afterwards they considered themselves the 'English interest' in Ireland, they simultaneously saw themselves as 'Irish' whenever confronted with English chauvinism (232a, *275–6*). Overall, from 1691 to 1782 their sense of Englishness declined in favour of their Irishness, but the older perception remained vital into the early nineteenth century. Hence the Duke of Wellington's apocryphal apology for his Irish origins, that 'a racehorse does not choose to be born in a stable.' Moreover, apart from the tiny Enlightenment-influenced Catholic intelligentsia, Catholics continued to regard the Ascendancy as 'Saxons', the 'black, horned, foreign, hate-crested crew'.[4] The Ulster Presbyterians emphatically did not consider themselves Irish at the start of the eighteenth century. For many families emigration to Ulster was a recent experience, and their culture, social organisation and agricultural practices remained for some time distinctively Scottish. They saw themselves, and were seen, as the 'Scotch colony', an identity which persisted into the late eighteenth century. Close proximity to, and frequent contact with, Glasgow and Galloway helped to sustain it. Most Irish Presbyterian ministers went to Scotland to be educated, and there were strong bilateral trading links (231, *61–7*).

Not only the Protestants but the Catholics were ethnically divided. The aristocracy's traditional division between 'Old English' descendants of the Anglo-Norman invaders of Ireland and 'Old Irish' native élite still lingered (234a, *lxii*). Further down the scale the same separation remained vital well into the century. As late as the 1750s the fiercely Catholic, but Old English, inhabitants of the baronies of Bargy and Forth in county Wexford still held the native Irish in such contempt that they refused to work alongside them. Mass brawls between feuding 'kinship' groups, or between long-lost political alignments such as the Ormonde and Liberty Boys in Dublin, continued throughout the eighteenth century. Until radical political alignments like the United Irishmen brought them together in the 1790s, the Catholics had very little sense of affinity capable of demolishing or bridging ethnic and factional barriers. Exacerbating the Catholics' other divisions was their own peculiar demarcation: language. In the early seventeenth century Gaelic was the language of the great majority of the population. From the 1690s onwards it began a steep decline everywhere except in Munster and Connaught. By 1800 barely 50 per cent of the population spoke Gaelic, and parents who could afford an education for their children were making them study English, the language of law and government, rather than Gaelic. Bards and poets continued the oral traditions which were the basis of native Irish culture, but their numbers steadily declined; in any event, to preserve Gaelic culture a sustained effort was required (as the nineteenth century was to show) to get as much as possible into print. Instead, publication in Gaelic disappeared even faster than the spoken language. Of the tenantry and labourers who made up most of the Catholic population few had ever been literate in Gaelic, and the surviving Catholic nobility and gentry were increasingly uninterested in Gaelic culture. Most damagingly of all, the Catholic church quietly replaced Gaelic with English as its normal mode of discourse. Only the surge of interest in Gaelic language and culture among Ascendancy literati in the mid-eighteenth century preserved enough to allow for the nineteenth-century revival (234b, *380–91*).

The society composed of these inimical groups worked along much the same lines as its British counterpart. There was a strong 'moral economy' in Ireland, rooted in the traditional relationships between paternalistic landlords and deferential tenants even of different religious persuasions. Landlords who protected, aided and were hospitable to their tenants received their public respect and were consulted and obeyed by them. On Pole Cosby's return from the Continent in 1724 his tenants greeted him at the county boundary with garlands, bonfires and long dances; four years later they welcomed his new bride in the same manner. When, at Clonmel in 1763, Chief Justice Aston passed lenient sentences on the great majority of prisoners convicted for enclosure and tithe riots, the local population signalled their approval by kneeling at the roadside as he departed. There is an Irish cast to these incidents – long dances and respectful kneeling to magistrates were not common elsewhere; nonetheless they reflect the kind of reciprocal, hierarchical relationships still customary in most parts of Europe. We should not be surprised, therefore, by eighteenth-century Ireland's generally harmonious social relations. The Anglican landlords of the Ascendancy probably treated their tenants no worse than their native predecessors had done; the warrior culture of the Gael was traditionally contemptuous of the warriors' social inferiors. Nor was the landowner-tenant divide universally a mirror of the religious one. In parts of Ireland, notably Munster, a substantial Catholic landholding élite persisted through the 'middleman' system. Technically, middlemen were tenants of great, usually Protestant, landowners, subletting to others actual cultivation of the land. Because they took land on leases for multiple lives or as perpetually renewable tenancies, however, the middlemen were the only land-'owners' those actually working it were likely to know (234b, *166–7, 173–7*). The Catholic church's frequent admonitions to obey the powers that be also endorsed the rural population's yearning to return to comfortable, *customary* social relations. As in Wales or in those parts of Scotland where ethnic, cultural and linguistic barriers separated landlord and tenant, there was no accompanying expectation that relations there would always be conducted with an undertow of hostility (cf. 146, *213–16*).

Nevertheless, a general presumption of social harmony should not blind us to outbursts and incidents which suggest eighteenth-century Ireland's rural peace was brittle. Banditry, almost unknown elsewhere in the British Isles, was endemic in the Irish countryside until the 1740s. Moreover, the 'rapparees' were classic 'social' bandits: intelligent, daring peasants, drawn into banditry by dispossession, dissatisfaction or injustice and sustained by the tolerance and admiration of those left on the land. Collective action to enforce the moral economy also took significantly different forms in the Irish countryside from the pattern in England (cf. Ch. 12). In Connaught during Anne's reign protestors 'houghed' (crippled) graziers' animals, and in doing so enjoyed widespread popular support backed by élite connivance. Though all known houghers were Catholics, houghing was non-sectarian, in that Catholic graziers were attacked as much as if not more than Protestants. However, in marked contrast with, say, English and Scottish grain riots or enclosure riots, houghing was organised and directed by rapparees.[5] By 1762, when the 'Whiteboy' protests began in Clare, Limerick and Tipperary, the rapparee element had vanished, replaced by something of lasting significance: secret oath-bound organisation. Again, there was widespread popular, non-sectarian support, as well as encouragement from social superiors for the Whiteboys' attacks on enclosures, and their enforced tithe boycotts. The army eventually suppressed the Whiteboys, whose attacks, processions and dispersals were for two years carried on with paramilitary precision, but they probably only finally disappeared due to hardship caused by the drought that afflicted western Ireland in 1764–5 (239, *21–52 passim*).

The Whiteboy pattern of agrarian protest endured for thirty years, their organisation and techniques becoming standard for protests of all denominational compositions. The Presbyterian-dominated 'Hearts of Oak' (Oakboys) operating in mid-Ulster in the 1760s (234b, *200–1*), and their 'Hearts of Steel' (Steelboy) successors in south Antrim and Armagh in the early 1770s, followed Whiteboy precedents in attacks on enclosures, tithes and tenants who took leases on lands whose former inhabitants had been forced off by higher rents. And although these, like the earlier Whiteboys and the later 'Rightboy' tithe protesters in southern Munster, generally eschewed lethal attacks on malefactors, all contained the potential for sustained agrarian guerilla warfare. Their next stage was the fully underground sectarian secret societies of the 1790s. By the nineteenth century these societies were able to create disorder and violence on a scale unparalleled anywhere else in the British Isles.

These protests were all reactions to the internal and external social and economic pressures enforcing change on Irish society. The Irish economy became commercialised as it developed into a major supplier of foodstuffs for the burgeoning English market. Ireland's population grew rapidly, despite occasional shortages and a famine in 1740–1, and by the 1790s was pressing hard on the available cultivable land. Before Thomas Malthus startled the world with his *Essay on Population* in 1798, an expanding population was taken as a sign of a thriving nation, and a widespread feeling of prosperity encouraged the Ascendancy to regain its self-confidence and rediscover its Irishness. The Williamite settlement, which reinforced Ireland's subordinate status as a colonial satellite whose rulers ultimately depended on English support, could not contain these pressures and finally collapsed between 1778 and 1782 (232a, *264–5*).

Settled cultivation had replaced Gaelic pastoralism during the sixteenth and seventeenth centuries. By the 1690s tenant farming on a semi-subsistence basis was the general rule throughout Ireland. Virtually all those cultivating the land in Ireland were tenants; there was never a free peasantry (231 [Cullen], *252–6*). Nonetheless, the 1690s and the early eighteenth century were a bountiful time for all gradations of the tenantry: farmers, cottiers and labourers (234b, *170–1, 185–6*). Rents were low and leases long. The 31-year/3 lives maximum lease allowed to Catholic tenants, and often cited as an example of the iniquity of the penal laws, was actually a good deal in a period of stagnant or falling rents and relatively buoyant prices. The English market for Irish foodstuffs was expanding, and Irish farmers were quick to take advantage. Moreover, because many leases granted in the 1690s expired in the late 1720s and early 1730s, a period of abundant harvests, low prices and therefore low demand for land, these advantageous terms persisted into the 1750s. Over the same period the Irish linen industry (increasingly centred in Ulster) became more export-orientated, and through busy exploitation of English and Continental markets was booming by the 1750s. British laws designed to inhibit Irish competition with mainland industry seem to have been rendered nugatory by smuggling and evasion (*Making of a Great Power*, Ch. 3; 236).

The long-term effects of the commercialisation of Irish agriculture and the export orientation of the linen industry were not, however, beneficent. When the next great bulge of leases expired in the 1760s and early 1770s, population pressure on land had increased, and landlords could demand substantially higher rents for their renewal. The shock was greater because of the long period of unrealistically low rents preceding it, and the effects were worsened by a prolonged depression in the linen industry beginning in the 1770s and lasting for the rest of the century. Many agrarian disturbances in the 1760s and 1770s stemmed from tenants' attempts to hang on to former advantages at a time when their major supplementary source of income, domestic out-work for the linen industry, was shrinking. Higher rents meant an increased proportion of the area cultivated had to go under cash crops; the poorer cultivators, the cottiers and labourers, sought to solve the problem of how to subsist on the shrunken area remaining to them by going over to intensive potato cultivation. By the 1790s it was rapidly (with hindsight, ominously) becoming the mainstay of their diet (234b, *163–6*).

Irish lore notwithstanding, population pressure was the key factor in the rent rises of the late eighteenth century. The reason for the sudden surge in the population that occurred from the 1750s onward is obscure. The most convincing hypothesis is that Ireland's population always contained the potential for sudden increase because of the relatively high proportion of young adults it contained. Sustained prosperity was liable to trigger rapid expansion by encouraging earlier marriage. The crucial event in the cycle was the series of good harvests and general prosperity between 1746 and the late 1760s. Added to the decline in the mortality rate, which appears to have been a pan-European phenomenon, it set off a baby-boom in Ireland that lasted from the 1760s to the 1800s. Higher rents were met by sub-letting, so though the land initially supported more expanding families, the next generation's demand for land reinforced the pressure, and the process had begun of dividing tenancies down to parts of an acre which was to have horrific results during the potato famine of the 1840s. At the end of the century, however, it was not the emaciation of the population that struck the observer, but the contrast between its youthful good health and its poverty. A diet of potatoes and buttermilk is doubtless boring, but it is also surprisingly healthy, hence the contrast between the rude vitality of most of the population and the rags and hovels that were their only possessions (234b, *161–3, 264*).

Colonists the world over have always had a tendency to identify with their new home, and most eventually generate a separate patriotism linked to that new identity. The first harbinger of the new wave of Protestant Irish patriotism appeared in 1698, when William Molyneux published his tract: *The Case of Ireland Being Bound by Acts of Parliament in England Stated*. Molyneux (MP for Trinity College Dublin) invoked Gaelic legends of pre-Norman legislative assemblies as well as the natural rights of free-born descendants of Englishmen to argue that the Irish Parliament was not subordinate to Westminister and should act independently to safeguard Irish interests (234b, *5–6*). Molyneux was well ahead of his time, and the Irish Parliament repudiated his claims (232a, *267*). Until bitter memories of the triumphal Catholic-Jacobite revanchism of 1685–91 faded, the Ascendancy could only contemplate such ideas, implying separation from England, with horror. Fears that the Catholics would 'cut evry Protestant troat' given half a chance were slow to die. Catholic quiescence and the passage of time, however, inexorably stifled them, and the English dominance that came with the connexion then began to be irksome. It was a slow process. The first signs of a coherent 'Patriot' position emerged only in the 1720s during the popular campaigns first against the British Declaratory Act of 1720, a restatement of Poyning's law reasserting Westminster's right to hear Irish appeals and to legislate for Ireland, if necessary overriding the Irish Parliament, and then from 1722–5 against 'Wood's halfpence', the sale of a patent by the Walpole ministry in England to mint new coins for Ireland (238). At this stage few politicians were consistently 'Patriot'; most took up patriotism when they were 'out' in the game of 'ins' and 'outs' waged by the Undertaker factions.[6] Nevertheless the hard core of Patriots steadily garnered more support, though most of it was outside Parliament. There, Ireland's treatment by Britain's Whig oligarchs as 'a great emerald porkbarrel'[7] caused mounting offence, and the Patriots' rhetoric found a ready hearing. The crucial (non-)event leading to the formation of a Patriot *party*, was the Catholics' reaction to the 'Forty-five rebellion in Scotland; they remained passive throughout, temporarily discrediting the Ascendancy's 'popish conspiracy' theorists. From that point it was a short step to the fashionable, Enlightenment-influenced liberal patriot ideology which eclipsed the conspiracy theorists until the 1790s, when the French Revolution reordered many people's political ideals. By 1748 Charles Lucas, until recently a leading 'No-Popery' polemicist, was publishing selections from Molyneux's *Case of Ireland* in support of his campaign against the oligarchs of Dublin corporation, and arguing that all Ireland's rebellions (even that of 1641 – the touchstone of Protestant fears of Catholic revenge) arose from, 'the oppression, instigation, evil influence, or connivance of the English'.[8]

Ireland's political system was ill-equipped to cope with the rising tide of patriotic feeling. In Anne's reign, David Hayton has written, 'the Dublin Parliament had been infected by English-style "party" politics, as Irishmen fought the battles of Whig and Tory as lustily as their English counterparts' (238, *99*). But with the slow decline of Toryism in Britain after 1714, government and politics in Ireland came to revolve around the apportionment of patronage between the Irish parliamentary factions and the English politicians currently controlling the Lord Lieutenancy. The emergence of the Undertaker factions after 1720 made the bargaining more structured, but correspondingly more cynical. The Undertakers were eminent Irish politicians who built up followings based on kinship, friendship and clientage which they used to get government business through Parliament – provided they and their followers were suitably rewarded (234b, *60–1*). The system was prone to bouts of instability as factions went (or were pushed) into opposition to retrieve their fortunes, but overall it worked tolerably well from an administrative point of view (232a, *272–4*). More important, it also meant the English Lord Lieutenant need only be resident in Ireland during the Irish Parliament's biennial sessions, all the necessary deals and fixing being done in advance for him by his Undertaker *sous-ministre*. The Lord Lieutenant could meanwhile guard his back in London and bolster his English following with his share of Ireland's patronage. The problem with the system at the Westminster end was that it encouraged the rise of overmighty Undertakers. Given sufficient time and access to official patronage the Undertakers could so dominate Ireland's Parliament and administration that they could virtually dictate a government's Irish policy. A climax was reached in 1757–8 when three factions – the Speaker's, the archbishop of Armagh's, and the earl of Shannon's – combined to dictate terms and policy to the Lord Lieutenant, the duke of Bedford.

Even a British government almost wholly indifferent to Irish affairs found this hard to swallow, and in the 1760s the Cabinet several times discussed the possibility of a resident Lord Lieutenant. Nothing came of these ruminations, however, until 1767, when Viscount Townshend was appointed Lord Lieutenant by the Chatham ministry. He had orders to obtain an expansion of the Irish army to help to ease the strain imperial defence expenditure was putting on the British economy. Aware that the Patriots would have a field-day with such a proposal, the Undertakers demanded a popular measure or two to sweeten the pill and that their followers be amply rewarded. Ignoring Townshend's increasing isolation, the British government refused the payment demanded and casually sabotaged a measure designed to allow Irish judges to retain office during good behaviour rather than at the king's pleasure by adding a clause making them dismissable by petition of Lords and Commons at Westminster. The bill was unanimously rejected, and the Undertakers united with the Patriots in opposition to Townshend. Between 1767 and 1771 this unholy alliance harassed the government inside and outside Parliament, and several times succeeded in defeating it outright, most notably in 1768 over the proposed expansion of the Irish army from 12,000 to 15,325 men.[9] It proved a hollow victory for the Undertakers, however. The Cabinet was so exasperated that it gave Townshend its full backing in establishing a resident Lord Lieutenant's interest by a purge of Ireland's administration. Using the places freed, Townshend constructed a new 'Dublin Castle' interest which in 1771 saw off the fading Undertaker challenge. His successor, Earl Harcourt, inherited such a strong position that he was able graciously to readmit Shannon and the duke of Leinster's followers to office in an administration now firmly under his control, and buy off Henry Flood, a leading Patriot (234b, *204–9*).

Superficially it might seem that the Lieutenancy's growing power to control Irish politics was checked only by the imperial crisis attendant on the American Revolution: that England's difficulty was Ireland's opportunity. The American Revolution undoubtedly provided a golden opportunity for the Patriots to extort concessions from Britain, one which they eagerly exploited. Nevertheless, dissatisfaction with the Williamite settlement had reached semi-consensual levels before 1776, and it is hard to see how it could have survived much longer in any event. By the 1770s the Patriots were consistently winning the argument. They had a sophisticated, fashionable ideology, resting on Molyneux (above, p. 232), whereas the government could only offer tired rehearsals of the popish conspiracy theory (240, *119*). The appearance of the eminently respectable Catholic Committee in 1760, a year after the first loyal address was sent up on behalf of the Irish Catholics, rendered the conspiracy argument embarrassing rather than convincing. The Committee's polite lobbying for relaxation of the penal laws was hard to construe as Catholic subversion. The weakness of the government's case was compounded, in an age that prized rhetoric as the supreme form of propaganda, by its defenders having to face Patriot leaders like Henry Grattan and Flood, the best speakers in Parliament. Underpinning the Patriot challenge to the Williamite settlement, moreover, there was the burgeoning pride in their Irishness felt by the Ascendancy. Its symptoms were ephemeral – a flowering of interest in Irish literature and history among Ascendancy literati – but its consequences were profound (240, *101–7*). Before 1771 Undertakers like Ponsonby ('John Bull's pimp' according to one Patriot newspaper) rather than the British were usually blamed for Ireland's problems. The reassertion of their authority by the Lord Lieutenants removed this useful camouflage. Thereafter the Patriots were clearly asserting Ireland's interests against a government party manifestly created to serve Westminster. With the Ascendancy increasingly proud of its Irishness, such a contrast could not fail to sap the establishment's morale.

The downfall of the failing Irish regime was brought about by the Volunteer movement, the product of France's entry into the American war in 1778. Despite their ostentatious loyalism the Volunteers clearly had the same revolutionary potential as the Patriot militias formed in America in the early 1770s. Yet the Irish administration proved incapable of inhibiting the spread of the Volunteers or preventing their movement into politics. The beginning of the end of the

Williamite order was signalled in November 1779 when, to the accompaniment of Volunteer parades and popular demonstrations of support outside the Parliament building in Dublin, Grattan moved that it was inexpedient to grant further taxation – and won by 170 votes to 47 (234b, *222–9*). By deploying all its resources of patronage and persuading Westminster to make huge trade concessions, the administration managed to stagger on for two more years, but it was visibly moribund; even its own supporters were increasingly in agreement with Patriot demands.

Yorktown, in Ireland as in England, precipitated the final crisis. On 15 February 1782 the Dungannon convention of the Ulster Volunteers voted almost unanimously that Poyning's law was 'unconstitutional and a grievance', and that, 'as Christians and as Protestants, we rejoice in the relaxation of the penal laws against our Roman Catholic fellow-subjects.' They went further and gave a strong hint as to what might happen if their demands were not heeded in a 'loyal' address which concluded: 'We know our duty to our sovereign, and are loyal. We know our duty to ourselves, and are resolved to be free. We seek for our rights, and no more than our rights, and, in so just a pursuit, we should doubt the being of a Providence, if we doubted of success' (233, *222*; 9, *130–4*). The twin pillars of the Williamite settlement had given way. Faced with the clear threat of rebellion if Westminster did not concede full legislative independence, the Irish administration was paralysed. The fall of North's administration in Britain and the Rockingham Whigs' acceptance, in defiance of the King's wishes, of virtually all the Patriot demands pitched the new ministry and its successor into an orgy of constitutional concessions. By the end of July 1782 the Williamite constitutional and religious settlement had been almost entirely dismantled and Ireland had entered that brief era of her history, before the Union of 1800, which historians have associated with 'Grattan's Parliament'. Poyning's law, the penal laws (except the disfranchisement of Catholic voters – the basis of much grief in the future), the Test Act, and the perpetual Mutiny Act were all repealed. With hindsight the euphoric excitement of 1782, summarised in Grattan's words: 'Ireland is now a nation; in that new character I hail her, and bowing to her august presence, I say, *Esto perpetua*',[10] seems tragically misplaced. The decay of this bright hopeful morning is, however, a world (and more important a revolution) away from the final collapse of the Williamite order that Grattan was celebrating.

———

1. S. Ó Tuama and T. Kinsella (ed. and translator), *An Duanaire 1600–1900: Poems of the Dispossessed* (Portlaoise, 1981), p. 163.
2. S.J. Connolly, *Priests and People in Pre-Famine Ireland 1780–1845* (1982).
3. Ibid, pp. 6–10; Moody and Vaughan (234b), pp. 375–6.
4. *An Duanaire*, pp. 153, 197, 203.
5. E.J. Hobsbawm, *Bandits* (2nd edn. 1985), pp. 17–29; S. J. Connolly, 'The Houghers', in C.H.E. Philpen, ed., *Nationalism and Popular Protest in Ireland* (Cambridge, 1987).
6. 'Undertakers' were so called because they 'undertook' to get government business through the Irish Parliament with the minimum of effort on the Lord Lieutenant's part.

7. E. Johnson, 'The Bedford Connection. The Fourth Duke of Bedford's Political Influence Between 1732 and 1771', unpublished University of Cambridge Ph.D. thesis (1979), pp. 258–9.
8. S. Murphy, 'Charles Lucas and the Dublin Election of 1748–1749', *Parl. Hist.*, **3** (1983), p. 96.
9. T. Bartlett, 'The Augmentation of the Army in Ireland 1767–9', *EHR*, **96** (1981).
10. Quoted in J.C. Beckett (233), p. 223. See also Christie (9), pp. 141–2.

PART THREE

Power imperial: triumph and disaster, 1746–1783

1747   Tories and Prince of Wales's party begin to move tentatively towards rapprochement (Jan). Naval victory by Anson off Cape Finisterre – all de la Jonquière's men-of-war and many merchantmen captured (Mar). Bill abolishing heritable jurisdictions in Scottish Highlands passes Commons (May); bill abolishing military service as condition of tenancy in Highlands becomes law (June).

       In Carlton House declaration (4 June) Prince Frederick outlines his manifesto, promising measures dear to Tory and Country hearts. George II dissolves Parliament a year prematurely (18 June) to frustrate the Prince's preparations. General Election (Jun–July) produces Tory losses and large ministerial majority [E.1].

       Battle of Lauffeldt: Saxe trounces Cumberland once again; Hawke's victory over French West Indies convoy and escort off La Rochelle (July). Death of Archbishop Potter – succeeded by Thomas Herring (Oct). Meeting of new Parliament (Nov).

       First volumes of Richardson's *Clarissa Harlowe* appear.

1748   Chesterfield resigns as Secretary of State – succeeded by duke of Bedford, quarrelsome leader of the 'Bloomsbury Gang' connection; deal between Prince and Tories finalised (Feb). End of Parliamentary session (May).

       Peace of Aix-la-Chapelle [H(vi)] brings end to Austrian Succession War (Oct).

1749   Jacobite demonstrations in Oxford (March) – government visitation of the University threatened. Parliament prorogued (13 Jan). British base established at Halifax, Nova Scotia and settled with 3,000 government-sponsored emigrants.

       Third session of Parliament opens (Nov); King's Speech urges Commons to 'be watchful to improve any opportunity of putting the National Debt in a method of being reduced'; Pelham proposes to reduce interest on the £57m. of debt carrying 4 per cent charge, first to 3.5 per cent, and after seven years to 3 per cent (Nov); Act embodying proposal passed (Dec).

       The Monthly Review founded; Fielding's *Tom Jones* published; first performance of Handel's oratorio *Solomon*.

1750   Ministerial tensions between Pelham's Old Corps and Bedford faction surface in struggle over Bedford Turnpike Bill – 'the greatest division of any day of the session' (Jan). Session ends (12 Apr). East India Company abandons resistance to Pelham's Debt conversion scheme – latter's success now assured (Apr).

       Commercial Treaty signed with Spain, favourable to Britain. Height of Dupleix's military and diplomatic activity on behalf of French East India Company in India – French puppet rulers installed in Carnatic (1749) and Deccan (1750). Secret visit to London by Young Pretender (Sept).

       Colonial Manufactures Prohibition Bill passed. Baskerville invents papier-mâché. Year of 'the Black Sessions' at the Old Bailey – four judges, four barristers, Lord Mayor and forty jurors contract jail-fever and die.

1751   Parliament reassembles (Jan). Prince Frederick dies, throwing Parliamentary opposition to the Pelhams ('reversionary interest' [A]) into disarray (20 Mar); his son, Prince George, created Prince of Wales; George II recommends Dowager Princess of Wales as Regent in the Regency Bill (Apr); Fox faction and Pitt's Leicester House party dispute over powers of duke of Cumberland's advisory council; Lords accept Commons' amendments to Regency Bill (May). Act abolishing the 'Old-Style' Julian calendar passes (22 May) – change to take effect 1752.

---

* For 1746, see Part I, p. 11 above

Ministerial divisions come to head and settled in favour of the Pelhams (June): Sandwich dismissed from First Lordship of Admiralty, Bedford resigns in protest (12th–13th); Holderness returns as Southern Secretary and Granville appointed Lord President (17th–18th). Parliament prorogued (25th).

In India Robert Clive captures and successfully defends Arcot. Parliament's fifth session begins (Nov). Pitt, ambitious for Secretaryship of State, clashes with Pelhams over Navy Estimates in House of Commons. Bolingbroke dies in France (Dec). Smollett's *Peregrine Pickle* published. The most effective of the eighteenth-century Gin Acts comes into force.

1752   Another somnolent parliamentary session ends (Mar). Lawrence and Clive defeat Jacques-François Law's French and Indian troops at Trichinopoly (June). Last day of old calendar (2 Sept): 3rd September becomes 14th (and by same Act the official and legal year ceases to end on 24 March); widespread public concern and some rioting ('give us back our eleven days!') follows the change. Death of famous surgeon, William Cheselden.

1753   Parliament reassembles (Jan). Jewish Naturalisation Bill passes both Houses (May): over rest of year popular, City and factious political opposition to this moderate measure develops, and becomes clamorous.

'Clandestine Marriages Bill' ('Hardwicke's Marriage Act' – so-called) becomes law: deals successfully with the great abuses of 'Fleet marriages', especially as they affected marriage of minors without consent, and marriage by constraint or trickery of young heirs and heiresses. Parliament prorogued (7 June).

Execution of Dr Archibald Cameron ends last plot by British Jacobites to restore Pretender (June). French forces in North America establish Fort Duquesne on the Ohio river, threatening Virginia. Parliament meets at Westminster (15 Nov). Attempts at truce between warring rival French and English East India companies – conference at Sadras (Dec).

Library of Sir Hans Sloane, physician and collector, and what remains of the Harley collection, acquired for the nation (foundation of 'British Museum').

1754   Death of Henry Pelham (6 Mar); succeeded as First Lord by his brother Newcastle (16th); Newcastle succeeded as Secretary by Sir Thomas Robinson. 'Jew Act' repealed, for fear it might become an election issue. Parliament dissolved under Septennial Act (8 Apr); General Election (Apr–May: see E.1).

New Parliament meets (31 May) but prorogued (5 June) until November. Colonel Washington's Virginia Militia tries, but fails, to expel French from Fort Duquesne (May–July). Representatives of North American colonies, meeting at the Albany Congress, reject Samuel Adams's plan of union and a common policy towards American Indians (June). Parliament meets; 1,000 British regulars under Braddock ordered to North America (Nov).

Dupleix recalled from India by French government (Aug).

1755   End of parliamentary session (Apr); Pitt and the Leicester House party join forces to oppose Newcastle's ministry (May).

Braddock's expedition to attack Fort Duquesne destroyed at Monongahela River (Jul). Anglo-Russian Convention of St Petersburg agreed (Sept) – ratified Feb 1756. George II appoints Lord Bute as Groom of the Stole to Princess of Wales (Oct).

Parliament meets; Henry Fox appointed Southern Secretary of State (Nov); Pitt dismissed from Paymastership after opposing Hessian (mercenary) Treaty in a speech on the Address (20 Nov).

Lisbon earthquake disaster (Nov); Samuel Johnson brings out his *Dictionary*; rebuilding of Eddystone lighthouse completed by John Smeaton.

1756　Britain and Prussia sign the Convention of Westminster (16 Jan: H(vii)). France and Austria conclude the defensive (1st) Treaty of Versailles, completing the 'Diplomatic Revolution' (May). Pitt's Militia Bill passes Commons (10th); Britain declares war on France – start of 'the Seven Years' War' (18th); Parliament prorogued (27 May).

East India Company's station at Calcutta falls to Siraj-ud-Daulah, Nawab of Bengal – British prisoners put in the Black Hole; Admiral Byng fails to prevent French capture of Minorca (June). Frederick II invades Saxony: battle of Lobositz (Aug); British fort and post at Oswego, Lake Ontario, captured and destroyed by General Montcalm (Aug).

Henry Fox commissioned to form a ministry by George II (Oct); both Newcastle and Fox resign (Nov); Devonshire appointed (16th) nominal head of what became (Dec) the Pitt-Devonshire Coalition. Parliament meets (2 Dec); Pitt appointed Secretary of State for the South (4th). Russia joins the Versailles alliance.

The Critical Review founded; Joseph Black discovers carbon dioxide. Great scarcity of grain in England: by autumn widespread and serious food rioting in Midlands and West Country.

1757　Clive retakes Calcutta and captures Hooghly and Chandernagore (Jan–Feb). Austro-Russian Convention (Feb). Death of Archbishop Herring – succeeded by Matthew Hutton; Byng shot after being court-martialled and refused clemency; Fox again tries to form a ministry (Mar); Pitt ordered to resign (6 Apr).

Second Treaty of Versailles, full offensive alliance, made between France and Austria (May). Holderness resigns. Battle of Kolin, Bohemia – Frederick II outnumbered and badly defeated by Austrians under Daun – loses 40 per cent of his troops (18 June); Clive becomes governor of Bengal after great victory at Plassey (23rd); Pitt and Holderness reappointed Secretaries of State (27–9th). Newcastle becomes First Lord of Treasury and parliamentary session ends (July).

Surprise Russian victory over Prussians at Gross-Jägerndorf (29 Aug). Cumberland, after defeat by French army, compelled to sign Convention of Kloster-Zeven; humiliating failure by British land-sea operation against Rochefort (Sept). Frederick II scores major victories over French at Rossbach (Nov) and Austrians at Leuthen (Dec). Parliament meets (1 Dec).

Renewed food rioting in many parts of England and widespread popular protests against Militia Act (June–Dec). Hume's *Natural History of Religion* and Smollett's *History of England* published.

1758　Final Tory motion of George II's reign for shorter Parliaments (Feb) – now opposed by Pittite Whigs and defeated in party vote, 190:87. Thomas Secker, bishop of Oxford, succeeds Hutton (died) at Canterbury (Mar). Second Convention of Westminster concluded with Frederick the Great (Apr). Choiseul becomes French Foreign Minister. Parliament prorogued (June).

Prince Ferdinand of Brunswick's victories over French at Rheinberg and Krefeld; Lally reaches Pondicherry and captures Fort St David (June). Louisburg on Cape Breton Island captured from French by Amherst and Wolfe (July). Capture of Fontenoy and Oswego by Bradstreet and Fort Duquesne by Forbes. Prussian army fails to inflict decisive defeat on Russian general Fermor and suffers terrible losses, at Zorndorf (Aug). British troops capture Cherbourg and destroy its forts (Aug), but are repulsed at St Malo (Sept). Seizure of Fort Duquesne by British forces (Nov).

Sixth session of the Parliament of 1754–61 begins (23 Nov); Pitt breaks last links with Bute and Leicester House (Dec).

Sir William Blackstone delivers his commentaries on the laws of England at Oxford; Jedediah Strutt invents the ribbed stocking-frame machine. Comet predicted for 1758 by Edmund Halley in 1705 appears in the skies on Christmas Day.

1759   Choiseul resumes vigorous pro-Austrian policy – negotiates third Treaty of Versaille [or Paris] (Dec–Mar; ratified May). Bussy's attack on Madras foiled by British fleet under Kempenfeldt (Feb); capture of Masulipatam by Col. Forde (Apr).

Surrender of Guadeloupe by the French (May). Parliament prorogued (June).

Fort Niagara captured from French; Soltikoff defeats Prussians under Wedell at battle of Kay (July). British-German victory over French army at Minden; Boscawen and Brodrick rout France's Toulon fleet off Lagos; Frederick's army annihilated at Kunersdorf by Russians and Austrians; Anglophobe Charles III becomes King of Spain (Aug).

Wolfe-Saunders expedition to Quebec ends in its fall, but also death of Wolfe (Sept). Edward Hawke's victory over Brest fleet at Quiberon Bay guarantees Royal Navy complete command of the sea (Nov). Parliament reassembles in mood of great elation (13 Nov).

Josiah Wedgwood leases a pottery works at Burslem, and Arthur Guinness a brewery in Dublin. Duke of Bridgewater secures passage of first Canal Act. First part of Laurence Sterne's *Tristram Shandy* appears (cf. 1767). Handel dies. British Museum opens.

1760   General Lally decisively defeated by Eyre Coote at Wandewash, South India (Jan). Surrender of French expedition to Ireland at Kinsale (Feb). Parliament prorogued (May).

Battles of Landshut and Glatz – victories by Austrian general Landon over Prussians (June). Morale-lifting victory by Frederick over Landon at Liegnitz, Silesia (Aug). Surrender of French forces in Canada at Montreal (8 Sept). Berlin occupied by Russian troops (Oct). Death of George II and accession of George III, his grandson (25th): at first Privy Council meeting of new reign, reference in King's Speech to a 'bloody and expensive war' altered to 'just and necessary'; short parliamentary session (26–9 Oct).

Battle of Torgau – a bloody victory for Prussians (one-third losses) leads to Austrian evacuation of Saxony (Nov). Parliament begins its ninth and final session (18th).

London's first public exhibition of paintings takes place.

1761   Remains of Lally's army in India finally surrenders at Pondicherry (Jan). 42 out of 5,000 Northumberland miners, marching to Hexham, killed by Yorkshire militia (Mar); Parliament dissolved (20th); Bute appointed Northern Secretary of State following Holderness's resignation (25th). General Election (Mar–Apr; E.1).

British conquest of 'neutral' West Indian island of Dominica; Belle Isle, off Britanny, falls to an expedition led by Keppel and Hodgson (June). Battle of Vellinghausen (July). Bedford, Lord Privy Seal since 1760, appointed peace plenipotentiary to France (Aug); Second Family Compact concluded between France and Spain (Aug). Marriage of George III and Charlotte of Mecklenburg (8 Sept); coronation (12th).

Peace negotiations with France broken off (Sept); resignation of Pitt (5 Oct) – George Grenville becomes ministry's leading spokesman in Commons when new

Parliament meets (Dec). Spain declares war on Britain (19 Dec), reciprocated (4 Jan).

Opening of Bridgewater Canal (Worsley-Manchester), built by James Brindley.

1762   French sugar island of Martinique conquered by Admiral Rodney and General Monckton (Feb) – islands of St Lucia, St. Vincent and Grenada subsequently occupied. Secret peace negotiations re-opened with France (Mar). Spain invades Portugal (Apr).

Newcastle resigns the Treasury – replaced by Bute (25–6 May); Grenville becomes a Secretary of State, *vice* Bute (May). Parliament prorogued (2 June).

Ferdinand of Brunswick and marquess of Granby defeat the French at Wilhelmsthal and Luttenberg (June–July). Havana in Spanish island of Cuba falls to British combined expedition (Aug); Spain suffers defeats in Portugal (Aug–Oct); Manila in Philippines captured from Spain (Oct).

Bedford sent to Paris to conclude final articles of peace (Sept); Fox made leader of Court party in Commons with a view to getting the settlement through (Oct). Peace preliminaries signed at Fontainebleau (3 Nov); approved by Cabinet (10th); meeting of Parliament (25th). Commons debate the Peace of Paris [H(xii)] – Opposition musters only 65 votes against it.

The North Briton, edited by John Wilkes, starts publication. Joseph Black, Scottish physician and chemist, lays foundations of modern thermal science by his investigation of 'latent heat'.

1763   Fox and Bute's slaughter of the 'Pelhamite innocents' draws to a close (Jan). First treaty of Paris signed, ending Seven Years' War (10 Feb). Peace terms laid before Parliament; Pitt attacks them and Grenville, opening way to rapprochement with Newcastle's 'Young Friends' (Mar). Cider tax introduced, leading to popular demonstrations against Bute's continuance in office (Mar). Crescendo of attacks in Parliament and the press leads Bute to resign; Grenville takes over as premier minister (Apr). Parliament prorogued (19 Apr); no. 45 of the *North Briton* published; Wilkes arrested on a General Warrant for attack on Bute and Grenville therein (Apr); released on bail by Chief Justice Pratt (May). Grenville demands George III support his ministry or form an alternative; Pitt's proposals for a new ministry prove unacceptable; King forced to concede to Grenville's demands (Aug). Proclamation establishes new colonies in America and fixes the westward boundaries of older ones (7 Oct). Parliament meets (15 Nov) and votes by 273 to 111 that no. 45 of the *North Briton* is a 'false, scandalous and seditious libel'; Parliamentary privilege then voted not to extend to writing or publishing seditious libel (Nov). Wilkes's arrest on a general warrant declared 'unconstitutional, illegal and absolutely void' by Chief Justice Pratt; upon release Wilkes fights a duel with Buteite Samuel Martin, MP, is wounded and flees to France (Dec).

Oakboy (in Ulster) and Whiteboy (in Munster) agrarian disturbances commence in Ireland (June–July).

Ottawa Indian chief Pontiac raises rebellion on western frontiers of Virginia and Pennsylvania; captures almost every British outpost there and besieges Fort Pitt (May–July). British forces relieve Fort Pitt and begin counter-guerilla operations (July–Dec).

1764   Wilkes expelled from the Commons for co-authorship of pornographic *Essay on Woman* (Jan), and outlawed after failure to appear for trial on charges of seditious libel (Feb). Ministry escapes condemnation in Commons on issue of legality of General Warrants by only 232 to 214 (18 Feb). Grenville outlines plans for a duty on stamps in the colonies to the Commons; postponed for one year to allow time for colonies to submit alternative proposals (Mar). Parliament is prorogued (19 Apr). News arrives of French expulsion of British settlers from the Turks islands (June).

Pontiac rebels slowly ground down by British troops and colonial militia; rebellion finally peters out at end of year.

The Spinning Jenny invented by James Hargreaves. The bolting machine invented by John and Thomas Morris.

1765 Parliament meets (10 Jan). George III falls seriously ill (Feb), but recovers; Stamp Act passed (Mar). American Mutiny Bill introduced; King insists on introduction of unpopular Regency Bill by Grenville while secretly arranging to bring in Cumberland to replace him (Apr). In Lords, Halifax amends Regency Bill to exclude the Princess Dowager; Commons then amends bill to re-include her; King fails to persuade Pitt to serve with Cumberland and is forced to retain Grenville (May). Parliament prorogued (25 May). Virginia Assembly resolves to resist Stamp Act; example soon followed across the 13 colonies (May). Further negotiations with Pitt by King prove fruitless; Cumberland, Rockingham and Newcastle agree to serve without him (June). Grenville administration dismissed and replaced by Cumberland-Newcastle-Rockingham administration (July). Stamp Act riots in Boston trigger attacks on Stamp Act officials throughout the American colonies (Aug). Cumberland dies (31 Oct); Rockingham assumes leadership of ministry. Stamp Act Congress meets in New York; boycott of all British goods instituted (Oct–Nov). London North American Merchants Committee established to clamour for measures to end American trade boycott; Parliament meets (11 Dec).

James Watt invents steam engine condenser.

1766 James, the Old Pretender, dies in Rome (1 Jan); Pope and all other Catholic powers refuse to recognise Charles Edward Stuart as 'Charles III', signalling the virtual demise of the Jacobite cause. Widespread petitioning by British merchants against Stamp Act (Jan). Pitt supports ministerial proposal to repeal Stamp Act, but refuses to join ministry; 'King's Friends' oppose ministry on Scottish election case (Jan). King reluctantly agrees to repeal of Stamp Act; repeal and attendant declaratory bill introduced in Commons (Feb) and easily passed despite Grenville's vocal opposition (Mar). General Warrants declared illegal by Commons; cider tax repealed (Apr). Grafton resigns when Rockingham declares he will not invite Pitt to join ministry again; Bute refuses King's secret suggestions that he should form a ministry (Apr). Rockingham forces Richmond on King as replacement for Grafton (May). King refuses to dismiss sundry King's Friends for voting against the ministry in attempt to speed up transfer of Cumberland inheritance to royal family; Parliament prorogued (3 June). King arranges to bring in Pitt (now Chatham) as head of ministry; Rockingham resigns (July). Old Rockingham-Newcastle connexion disintegrates, leaving only a loyal Rockinghamite rump (Aug–Nov). Widespread food riots by mobs protesting at the price of grain, centred on West Country, Thames Valley, Midlands and East Anglia (Sept). Parliament meets (11 Nov). Townshend duties *de facto* put in effect (Dec).

Oliver Goldsmith's *Vicar of Wakefield* published. Hydrogen discovered by Henry Cavendish.

1767 Initial negotiations to unite the Bedfords and Rockinghams in opposition to the ministry fail; Townshend formally announces to Commons his intention to raise revenue in America by indirect means (Jan). Rockinghams lead independents in forcing reduction in Land Tax from 4s. to 3s. on ministry by 206 votes to 188 (27 Feb). Grenville announces he will not attempt to reintroduce a Stamp Bill;

Bedfords, Rockinghams and Grenvilles consequently able to coordinate joint onslaught against ministry (Mar–Apr). Joint Opposition attack on the ministry's American policy in Lords nearly succeeds, but East India Company Charter Act passes (May). Townshend duties formally and systematically enacted (June). Parliament prorogued (2 July); Opposition coalition collapses in mutual recrimination. Widespread food riots over grain prices, again centred on West Country, Thames Valley, Midlands and East Anglia (Aug). Townshend dies (4 Sep). Rockinghams outmanoeuvred by Bedfords, who are brought into ministry after protracted negotiations (Oct–Nov). Boston promulgates circular letter urging resistance to the Townshend duties; boycott of British goods reimposed (Oct). Parliament meets (24 Nov).

Publication of the last part of Sterne's *Tristam Shandy*, Adam Ferguson's *Essay on the History of Civil Society* and Joseph Priestley's *History and Present State of Electricity*.

1768   Lord North succeeds Conway as the ministry's leading spokesman in the Commons (Jan). Wilkes returns from France and sends letter of apology to George III, which King ignores (Feb). Parliament dissolved (11 Mar); general election March–April [E.1]; Wilkes comes bottom of poll for the City of London (25th Mar), then tops poll for Middlesex (28th Mar); surrenders himself at King's Bench to answer the charges for which he was outlawed, and is imprisoned (Apr). Widespread and persistent rioting in London by mobs protesting against Wilkes's imprisonment, only ended by St George's Fields massacre (10 May). Parliament meets (10 May). Lord Chief Justice Mansfield quashes Wilkes's outlawry but then sentences him to 22-months imprisonment on misdemeanour charges; Parliament prorogued (21 June). Archbishop Secker dies (3 Aug) and is succeeded by Frederick Cornwallis, bishop of Lichfield. Disturbances against Townshend duties in Boston, Massachusetts, provoke occupation of city by regular troops (Sept). Chatham resigns when King and Grafton engineer resignation of Shelburne, but most of his followers remain in office; Grafton accepts premiership (Oct). Parliament meets (8 Nov). Rockingham attack on ministry over French annexation of Corsica easily defeated (Dec).

Lord-Lieutenant Townshend defeated in Irish Parliament over attempt to increase size of Irish army (May).

Joseph Priestley's *An Essay on the First Principles of Government* published.

1769   Wilkes expelled from Commons (3 Feb); elected three times for Middlesex and expelled each time; after third election (13 Apr), electors' decision overturned in Commons and his unsuccessful opponent, Luttrell, declared the winner by 197 to 143 (15 Apr). Parliament prorogued (9 May). Rockinghams and Wilkites organise nationwide petitioning campaign against Middlesex decision (Apr–Oct). Ministry decides to repeal all the Townshend duties except that on tea, which is retained by a vote of 5 to 4 in Cabinet (1 May). Chatham reappears in public for the first time since his resignation (July). Remaining Chathamites resign their offices; Grafton tries to draw in individual Rockinghams, but fails (Nov–Dec).

Last volume of William Blackstone's *Commentaries upon the Laws of England* published. *Letters of Junius* published. The Society of Supporters of the Bill of Rights formed. A new pottery works at Etruria opened by Josiah Wedgwood. Richard Arkwright invents the water frame.

1770   Grafton resigns; North assumes premiership; Parliament meets (9 Jan). Bill ordered in the Commons repealing all colonial duties except that on tea; amendment to repeal the tea duty as well is lost 204–142 (5 Mar). Troops occupying

Boston fire on rioters: the 'Boston Massacre' (5 Mar). Attempt at united opposition by Grenvilles, Chathamites and Rockinghams fails owing to divisions on American issue (Apr–May). Parliament prorogued (19 May). British settlers on Falkland Islands evicted by Spanish forces (June): crisis nearly leads to war (Nov–Dec). Parliament meets (13 Nov). Grenville dies (13 Nov); followers absorbed by ministry (Dec).

Burke's *Thoughts on the Causes of the Present Discontents* published. The first edition of *The Bible* in Welsh published by Peter Williams. Oliver Goldsmith's *The Deserted Village* published. John Wesley denounces Calvinism among Methodists. The Orthodox General Baptists form the General Baptist New Communion. Sulphur dioxide discovered by Joseph Priestley.

1771   War averted when settlement reached with Spain on Falkland Islands (Jan). Printers of parliamentary debates summoned to Commons; protected by Lord Mayor of London and other City JPs, who are in consequence imprisoned for contempt (Feb). Case of the printer John Wheble heard before Alderman John Wilkes; North ministry drops attempt to maintain secrecy of parliamentary debates (Mar). Sawbridge moves the first of his annual motions for shorter parliaments (Apr). Parliament prorogued (8 May). Grafton drawn back into the ministry (June). Wilkes elected High Sheriff of London (July).

Tobias Smollett's novel *Humphrey Clinker* published.

1772   Parliament meets (21 Jan). Royal Marriages Act, making marriages in royal family subject to monarch's approval, passes Commons by 168 to 115 despite strenuous opposition from Rockinghams and Chathamites (Mar). Widespread food riots throughout the summer, by mobs protesting at the price of grain. Parliament prorogued (9 June). Revenue service schooner 'Gaspee' attacked and burned by a mob in America after having run aground while in pursuit of smugglers (9 June). Parliament meets (26 Nov).

Steelboy agrarian disturbances commence in Ulster (Mar).

Morning Post founded. Nitrogen isolated by Daniel Rutherford.

1773   New Corn Laws easily pass Commons (Apr). Ministry rushes through legislation allowing East India Company a monopoly of tea sales in America (May). North ministry's East India Company Regulating Act, giving the ministry greater control over the East India Company's conduct of its affairs, passed; likewise the Spitalfields Act to regulate the wages of silk weavers (June). Parliament prorogued (1 July). Renewed food rioting throughout the summer, in protest at the price of grain. Irish Absentee Landlord tax defeated in London by vigorous Rockingham-led campaign of lobbying and opposition (Oct–Nov). Boston Tea Party (16 Dec).

First performance of Oliver Goldsmith's *She Stoops to Conquer*. Stock Exchange founded.

1774   Parliament meets (13 Jan). Charles James Fox dismissed from the Treasury at King's behest; soon associating with Rockinghams (Feb). Boston Port Act closes Boston harbour until East India Company recompensed for its losses at the Tea Party (Mar). First Continental Congress meets at Philadelphia (Apr). Massachusetts Bay Regulating Act, revoking Massachusetts's charter, passes; also Quebec Act, officially granting Canadian Catholics religious toleration and French forms of law (May). Louis XV dies (May). Parliament dissolved (30 Sept). General Election; ministry returned with a substantial majority (Oct–Nov) [E.1]. Parliament meets (29 Nov). Opposition heavily defeated in attempt to block the traditional loyal address (5 Dec).

James Burgh's *Political Disquisitions* published. Oxygen isolated and ammonia discovered by Joseph Priestley.

1775 Chatham's motion in Lords, proposing reconciliation with the Americans on the basis of the *status quo ante*, is defeated by 68 to 18 (20 Jan). Massachusetts declared to be in rebellion by the ministry; American access to all foreign trade ended, pending suitable submission to Parliament, by New England Trade and Fisheries Act (Feb). Burke's conciliation plan defeated by 270 to 78 (22 Mar). Battle of Lexington-Concord (19 Apr) signals start of the American war. Partial submission by New York rejected by Parliament on North's advice; second Continental Congress meets at Philadelphia (May). Parliament prorogued (26 May). General proclamation of rebellion in America issued (23 Aug). American Congress's 'Olive Branch' petition rejected (Sept). Parliament meets (26 Oct). Grafton speaks against the Address, is dismissed from post as Lord Privy Seal, is reconciled with Rockingham (Nov).

British sortie from Boston badly mauled by Massachusetts militia at battle of Lexington-Concord (19 Apr). Siege of Boston opens (June). British win bloody pyrrhic victory over Massachusetts militia at battle of Bunker Hill (17 June). American Patriot forces invade Canada and capture Montreal (Dec).

Matthew Bolton and James Watt first begin to construct engines in partnership.

1776 Joint Rockingham-Chathamite motions for an end to hostilities conclusively defeated in both Houses (Feb). Wilkes's parliamentary reform bill fails to find a seconder in Commons (Mar). Parliament prorogued (23 May). American Declaration of Independence (4 July) [F(iii)]. Parliament meets (31 Oct). After failing to amend the Address in Reply to protest against the war, most of the Rockinghams secede from Parliament (Nov).

Proclamation imposes embargo on export of provisions from Ireland to anywhere except Britain and its non-rebellious colonies (Feb).

British forces evacuated from Boston to Halifax, Nova Scotia (Mar). Patriot forces abandon Montreal and retreat from Canada (June). British land on Long Island and rout Washington's army at battle of Brooklyn Heights (27 Aug). New York captured by Howe (Sept). Conquest of New Jersey (Oct–Nov). Patriot victories at battles of Trenton (26 Dec) and Princeton (3 Jan. 1777) lead to Patriot reconquest of New Jersey (Dec–Jan. 1777).

Publication of Adam Smith's *The Wealth of Nations* and Thomas Paine's *Common Sense* – a hugely successful bestseller advocating complete American independence from Britain; fundamentally shifts the parameters of debate in America. Publication of John Cartwright's *Take Your Choice*, Jeremy Bentham's *Fragment of Government* and first part of Edward Gibbon's *Decline and Fall of the Roman Empire*. Richard Price publishes *Observation on Civil Liberty*.

1777 Rockinghams return to Parliament to oppose payment of King's Civil List debts, but Commons agree by 137 to 109 to pay debts (18 Apr). Motion in Lords by Grafton (supported by Chatham) calling for an Address for an end to hostilities, fails by 99 to 28 (30 May). Parliament prorogued (6 June), meets again 20 November. Chatham and Rockinghams' joint proposal for the withdrawal of all forces from America defeated (20 Nov), but inaugurates period of joint opposition. News of Saratoga arrives in Britain; ministry sets up Carlisle peace commission (Dec).

Burgoyne commences attack on New England from Canada (May); repulsed in attempt to break through Patriot defences blocking his advance at first battle of Bemis Heights (19 Sept); Howe meanwhile defeats Washington at battle of

Brandywine (11 Sept) and captures Philadelphia (26 Sept). Burgoyne, now surrounded by patriot forces, attempts to break out at second battle of Bemis Heights (7 Oct), but is defeated and forced to surrender after briefly retreating to Saratoga (17 Oct).

1778   France allies with American Patriots; Fox's motion that no more troops be sent to America lost by 259 to 165 (2 Feb). Chatham turns down offer of inclusion in ministry (Mar). Patriot privateer John Paul Jones raids in Irish Sea and attacks Whitehaven (23 Apr). Chatham collapses in Lords while attacking ministry over American war, and subsequently dies (11 May); Shelburne assumes leadership of Chathamites. Rockinghams' terms for fusion with the ministry judged too high by King (May). Savile's Roman Catholic relief bill passes (May–June). Parliament prorogued (3 June). Carlisle Peace Commission arrives in New York; France declares war (17 June). Parliament meets (26 Nov). Carlisle commission reports failure to Parliament (Dec).

First company of Irish Volunteers formed at Belfast (Mar). John Paul Jones's raiding in Irish Sea transforms local, Belfast-based initiative into Ireland-wide movement (Apr–Sept). Irish Parliament passes Catholic Relief Act (Aug).

Washington's army nearly disintegrates through privations suffered while wintering in the open at Valley Forge, Pennsylvania (Jan–Mar). Clinton abandons Philadelphia and retreats to New York, defeating Washington at Monmouth Court House *en route* (27 June). British and French fight indecisive naval battle off Ushant (27 July). Campbell lands in Georgia and subdues entire state within a month (Dec).

1779   Rockinghamite Admiral Keppel's conduct at battle of Ushant vindicated at court-martial (Jan–Feb). Fox's motion condemning ministry's conduct of war draws 174 votes in Commons (8 Mar). Spain declares war (21 June). Bill for regulation of framework-knitting trade rejected; riots and machine-breaking in Nottingham follow, resulting in destruction of Arkwright's mill there (June). Parliament prorogued (3 July). Bedfords resign, hoping to force North out of office and replace him, but fail (Oct–Nov). Parliament meets (25 Nov). Burke announces intention to introduce measures for economical reform; Wyvill's Yorkshire Association formed to petition in support of the measure (Dec). Ministry introduces legislation allowing Ireland to trade direct with colonies (Dec.)

Irish non-importation agreement, boycotting English goods, first promulgated in Galway (Mar). Irish Parliament overwhelmingly agrees to Grattan's motion that further taxation in support of the war would be expedient (24 Nov).

Campbell and Prevost begin conquest of South Carolina (Jan–Mar). Spanish commence siege of Gibraltar (June). Campbell and most of his forces withdrawn to defend West Florida (July). Arrival of D'Estaing's French West Indian squadron off the Carolinas forces Prevost to retreat back to Georgia (Sept). French and Patriot siege of Prevost in Savannah repulsed (Sept–Oct).

Iron bridge built over river Severn at Coalbrookdale. Spinning Mule invented by Samuel Crompton. Dissenting ministers and schoolmasters relieved from subscription to the 39 Articles.

1780   Economical reform petitioning begins on nationwide scale, orchestrated by Rockinghams; Yorkshire Association petitions for parliamentary reform as well as economical reform; Fox comes out in support of parliamentary reform (Feb). Deputies from county associations meet to discuss formation of nationwide association for parliamentary reform; Burke's motion for abolition of office of Secretary of State for America defeated by only 7 votes (8 Mar). Russia announces policy of armed neutrality (1 Apr). Ministry defeats Rockinghams' economical reform package piecemeal, but is itself defeated by 233 to 215 on Dunning's resolution 'that the influence of the crown has increased, is increasing and ought to be diminished' (6 Apr); North tries to resign but dissuaded by King. Richmond unsuccessfully introduces parliamentary reform bill in Lords while Protestant Association demonstration against Savile's Catholic Relief Act simultaneously degenerates into worst riots in British history: Gordon riots (2–9 June). Parliament prorogued (8 July). King sounds Rockinghams about inclusion in ministry, but again baulks at their conditions (July). Russia, Sweden and Denmark inaugurate League of Armed Neutrality (Aug). Parliament dissolved (1 Sept). General election leaves ministry with reduced majority (Sept–Oct) [E.1]. Parliament meets (31 Oct); ministry's candidate for Speaker in new Parliament, Charles Wolfran Cornwall, only elected by 203 to 134. Ministry pre-empts Dutch adherence to the League of Armed Neutrality by declaration of war (20 Dec).

Eighteen Irish counties petition Irish Parliament for repeal of Poyning's law; Ireland admitted to equal trade with colonies (Mar).

Clinton arrives off Georgia with main British army in America (Jan). Besieges and captures Charleston (Apr–May), then returns to New York. South Carolina 'pacified' by Cornwallis (May–July). Outbreak of second Mysore War in India; Hyder Ali invades Carnatic (June). Gates's Patriot army's advance into South Carolina sparks off Patriot uprisings throughout South Carolina, but Gates's force routed at battle of Camden (16 August). Cornwallis 'pacifies' South Carolina again (Aug–Dec). Hyder Ali scatters the only British troops in the Carnatic, under Colonel William Baillie, lays siege to all the British ports there and threatens Madras (Sept). Greene arrives in North Carolina and revitalises the Patriot forces there (Dec).

Jeremy Bentham's *Introduction to the Principles of Morals and Legislation* published. The Society for Promoting Constitutional Information formed.

1781 Burke reintroduces economical reform bill; defeated by 233 to 190 on second reading (26 Feb). Westminster Association and deputies from provincial associations agree on common petition for parliamentary reform, presented to Commons (Apr) but rejected by 212 to 135 (8 May); Hartley's motion for peace with America defeated by only 34 votes (30 May). Parliament prorogued 18 July, meets again 27 November. News of Yorktown prompts Sir James Lowther's motion to end the war in America forthwith; defeated by only 220 to 179 (12 Dec).

Tarleton's defeat by Morgan's Patriots at battle of Cowpens (17 Jan) compromises Cornwallis's prospects of an offensive into North Carolina and Virginia. Sir Eyre Coote outmanoeuvres Hyder Ali in Carnatic and succeeds in raising all the sieges of British ports under way there (Jan–June). Cornwallis's attempt to recoup defeat at Cowpens results in pyrrhic victory at battle of Guildford Court House (15 Mar). Cornwallis retreats to coast to recoup losses, then strikes north for Virginia (May). Coote decisively defeats Hyder Ali at battle of Porto Novo (1 July); despite French reinforcements, Coote then drives him out of Carnatic (July–Dec). Minorca garrison surprised by joint Franco–Spanish invasion; besieged in Fort St Philip (Aug). Cornwallis captures Yorktown (Aug), but surprised and trapped by combined French and Patriot forces; Admiral Graves's failure to break through French naval blockade of Yorktown at indecisive battle of Chesapeake Bay (5 Sept) ends all hope of evacuation by sea; Cornwallis forced to surrender (19 Oct).

Dr Samuel Johnson's *Lives of the English Poets* completed. Countess of Huntingdon's evangelical connexion separates from Church of England.

1782   Ministry initially defeat Opposition motion that war be ended by only 194 to 193 (22 Feb), but Conway's motion that no further attempts be made to subdue the Americans by force passes by 234 to 215 (27 Feb). Ministry defeats two motions of No-Confidence by only 226 to 216 (8 Mar) and 236 to 227 (15 Mar); in consequence, King finally allows North to resign (20 Mar); Rockingham forms new ministry, including Shelburne. William Pitt the Younger's motion to consider parliamentary reform defeated by 161 to 141 (7 May). King secretly woos Shelburne as suitable replacement for Rockingham (May–June). John Crewe's act disfranchising revenue officers, Sir Philip Jennings Clerke's contractors bill, excluding government contractors from Commons, and Burke's Civil Establishment Act all pass: triumph of economical reform movement (June) [F(vi)]. Rockingham dies (1 July); Parliament prorogued (11 July); King chooses Shelburne as premier; Fox and Portland resign in protest. Most of Rockinghams in office resign to follow Fox and Portland (Aug–Sept). Peace preliminaries agreed with Americans; North alienated by Shelburne's abandonment of loyalists (Nov). Parliament meets (5 Dec).

Dungannon convention of Ulster Volunteers calls on Irish Parliament to repeal Poyning's law and implicitly threatens rebellion if demand refused (15 Feb). Lords vote to accept decision of judges overturning Brandon decision of 1711; Scottish peers with British peerages henceforth eligible to sit in Lords (June). Poyning's law and most of rest of Williamite settlement swept away by Irish Parliament with agreement of Lord-Lieutenant Portland (July).

Minorca surrenders to Franco-Spanish besiegers (5 Feb). Admiral Rodney crushingly defeats main French fleet at Battle of the Saints (12 Apr), securing British dominance of West Indies for remainder of war. Naval victory off Negapatam over Admiral Hughes (6 July) allows French Admiral Suffren to take Trincomalee and land De Bussy with reinforcements for Hyder Ali. Final Spanish onslaught against Gibraltar repulsed (Sept–Oct).

Double-acting steam engine patented by Boulton and Watt. Charles Simeon, curate of Trinity College, Cambridge, launches evangelical movement in University.

1783   Peace preliminaries agreed with France and Spain (Jan). Fox and North ally in opposition to terms; preliminaries rejected by 224 to 208 (18 Feb); Shelburne resigns (24 Feb). King tries to persuade Pitt, then North, to head a ministry; both refuse; King forced to accept Fox-North coalition ministry headed by Portland (Apr). Pitt's parliamentary reform bill defeated by 293 to 149 (7 May). Parliament prorogued (16 July). Framework-knitters' protests against wage-cuts in Nottingham lead to riotous attacks on mills of recalcitrant employers; only ended by arrival of regiment of regular troops (July). Peace of Versailles [H(xiv)] marks the official end of the American war (3 Sept). Parliament meets (11 Nov). Coalition easily defeats Pittite attack on Fox's India bill by 229 to 120 (27 Nov); public outcry over powers of patronage it would give any ministry. King's declaration that 'whoever voted for the India Bill were not only not his friends, but he should consider them as his enemies' leads to its defeat in Lords by 87 to 79 (17 Dec); Fox-North ministry dismissed next day and Pitt brought in as premier minister.

Irish Renunciation Act frees Ireland from all *de jure* legislative subordination to Westminster (Mar). National Volunteer convention in Dublin proposes parliamentary reform on basis outlined by Flood (Nov). Irish Parliament rejects Flood's proposal by 157 to 77 (29 Nov).

Coote dies (26 Apr); General James Stuart drives Hyder Ali and De Bussy back to Cuddalore (Apr–May). Stuart defeats Hyder Ali and De Bussy at battle of Cuddalore (13 June), and lays siege to town; Suffren defeats Hughes in naval battle of Cuddalore (20 June), and lands supplies and reinforcements for Hyder Ali and De Bussy. News of peace preliminaries arrives in India (28 June); hostilities cease.

CHAPTER 17

The contest for trade and empire, 1746–1763

In Part One it was suggested that the year 1746 marked a watershed in the history of eighteenth-century Britain. This was not simply because it saw the last serious hopes of the Jacobites dashed and the re-establishment of the Whig Oligarchy after the four years of uncertainty that followed Walpole's fall. In the course of this year it also became clear that Franco-British colonial and commercial ambitions, which had been growing mutually incompatible for years, were now set on a collision course. The French capture of Madras from the British East India Company in 1746 was not a major event in itself. But coming as it did little more than a year after the French had lost their vital Canadian base at Louisburg to the New Englanders and the Royal Navy, it served to confirm that Franco-British rivalry could no longer be confined to Europe and the high seas. It must logically extend to every quarter of the globe in which the two Great Powers had colonies and trading stations, including the West Indies and West Africa as well as North America and the Far East (Ch. 4). Indeed, the conclusion of formal peace in Europe in 1748, with the exchange of Louisburg for Madras, seems to have been regarded almost as an irrelevance by British and French settlers and traders across the oceans. Troops in the pay of the two companies continued their unofficial warfare across the South Indian princedoms of the Deccan and the Carnatic, after as before Aix-la-Chapelle. In Nova Scotia as early as 1749 the English established a new base at Halifax, designed to neutralise Louisburg whenever full-scale hostilities broke out again, while French governors in North America, with a substantial force of regular troops still at their disposal, were already formulating plans to check the expansion of the British colonists westward and to fortify the waterway link between the Great Lakes and Louisiana, along the Upper Ohio River (258, *115–16*). Inside a decade and a half thereafter Britain was to find herself elevated from the status of a European Great Power with an overseas empire to that of the world's most formidable imperial power. And one of the dominant themes of the final part of this book will be the dramatic contrast between the rapid achievement of that position and the almost equally sudden undermining of this first British Empire over the next twenty years, as mounting political weaknesses took their toll. When the treaties of Paris were signed in 1763 it seemed that the fourth great Franco-British war since the Glorious Revolution had ended in an emphatic victory for Great Britain in the contest for trade and empire: a victory tarnished slightly at the last, perhaps (below, pp. 264–5), but nonetheless decisive. At that time few Britons – or Frenchmen either – can have anticipated that disaster would so soon follow triumph and that by 1783 the whole of British North America south of the Canadian border would be lost to the Crown. And yet the sequel to Aix-la-Chapelle, that classic peace of attrition (but cf. Ch. 4) had been to many eyes almost as unexpected as the sequel to Paris. Only the historian, with a good deal of help from hindsight, can confidently claim to detect in some of the later events of the Austrian Succession War clear indicators of the underlying advantages which crucially prepared the way for the great British maritime and colonial successes of 1758–60.

One thing apparent as we look back on the 1740s is that it was not simply a conflict between two major European powers, each with a major economic stake in overseas possessions, that was developing; it was also a contest between two sharply contrasting concepts, or systems, of empire. The British transatlantic empire of the mid-eighteenth century was a loose amalgam of units: eight Caribbean or Atlantic island colonies, and fifteen seaboard or island territories in North America, from Newfoundland down to the most recent acquisition, Georgia [J.2]. Each unit was in essentials independent of the rest and although Parliament legislated from time to time on colonial matters (mostly economic), while the supervisory eye of the responsible department in London, the Board of Trade, grew keener after 1752 under the energetic chairmanship of Lord Halifax,[1] every British colony had a large say in conducting its own affairs. Though differing somewhat in degrees of autonomy, according to whether they were charter colonies, like Connecticut, 'proprietary' colonies, like Pennsylvania, or royal foundations, such as New York and Virginia (263a, *14–16*), the North American colonies – and in particular those of pre-Revolution vintage which had emerged from the trauma of the Stuart reaction in the 1680s – were nearly all as jealous of their local interests as they were of their representative assemblies and other rights. Their truculence towards their own governors was matched by an almost built-in resistance (manifest, for example, in the abortive Albany conference of 1753) (263a, *24*) to ready cooperation with their neighbours. The population of the British colonial empire, its resources, and its whole economic potential were vastly greater than those of France's transatlantic possessions; Massachusetts alone had three times the number of inhabitants of 'New France' (Canada) and Louisiana combined in 1750, and the port of Boston probably boasted more private wealth than all 70,000 French settlers in North America; yet the harnessing of these intrinsic advantages proved very difficult to achieve. The converse of this, however, was that their traditions, combined with the dissident element so common in their personal or family history, had generated among the British colonists themselves fierce pride and self-reliance, and on their behalf at home a protectiveness that went beyond mere economic self-interest.

The contrast with the French colonies, in many respects, could hardly have been more complete. Though sparsely populated, they were subject to rigidly centralised, bureaucratic control from the Ministry of Marine in Paris. That control, and the stereotyped system of civil intendants and military governors which executed power on the spot, offered little scope for local liberties, let alone autonomy. The French governed their colonies, it was once said, like a line of battle ships at permanent anchor. Unlike the administration in London, French governments had an emigration policy, but the feudal system of land settlement on which it was largely based, with a view to encouraging a superior brand of emigrant from France, placed further severe constraints on the rest of the settler population (258, *54*). All in all it is hardly surprising that the average informed Frenchman in Louis XV's reign should have been more indifferent to what was happening in his country's colonies than his British counterpart. The wonder is that a system so stifling to the initiative of French settlers should have continued still to produce intrepid explorers like La Harpe and the Mallet brothers, to carry on the great tradition of René La Salle, whose epic journeys down the Ohio and Mississippi in the late 1680s had taken him to the Gulf of Mexico. Since the French official attitude, post-Utrecht, was that colonies must at all costs be commercially profitable, it was only the sub-tropical territories, producing sugar and other crops of high value which France herself could not grow, which sparked genuine enthusiasm in French government circles. While recognising that Colbert's ewe-lamb, Canada, had to be defended as a matter of dynastic imperative, many at Versailles must have had a sneaking sympathy with Voltaire in wishing it 'at the bottom of the Arctic Sea, together with the reverend Jesuit fathers'. It is significant that at the Paris negotiations of 1762–3, Louis XV's foreign minister, Choiseul, who had shown more concern and ambition over the French empire in the 1750s than any French statesman since Colbert, congratulated himself on a brilliant diplomatic *coup* when he recovered the captured Caribbean sugar islands at the expense of ceding Canada.

Even in India, where commercial priorities on both sides were at their most stark, there was a difference of attitude. In 1750 Britain's trade with the West Indies, the traditional favourite of mercantilist opinion, was still more valuable than her traffic with the Far East, and yet the British East India Company was regarded by Parliament, government and public alike as a gilt-edged national investment. Whenever its situation in India required official support, some support was forthcoming. Not that the London directors of the Company were especially far-sighted. In fact, it was the officials of the *Compagnie des Indes*, prompted by their enterprising representatives in the sub-continent, Bussy and Dupleix, who saw more quickly than their London counterparts that in the chaotic political state of eighteenth-century India, where the writ of the Mogul emperors no longer ran, trade could not be secured in the long run without active involvement in the rivalry of the 'country' princes. In 1750 Dupleix was warmly congratulated by his directors in Paris on 'la glorieuse action de nos troupes', one of a string of military and diplomatic actions which seemed to herald the annexation of a new French empire in the Carnatic and the Deccan. Yet only a few months later the English at Madras were still being warned sternly from Leadenhall Street against 'look[ing] upon yourselves rather as a military colony than the factors and agents of a body of merchants'.[2] When the French recalled Dupleix in disgrace in 1754 it was his financial irresponsibility not his policies they were repudiating; Robert Clive would probably have shared his fate after his victory at Arcot in 1751 if this had not been seen at the time as an isolated, defensive action carried out on a shoe-string budget. The real difference between attitudes to India was at government, rather than at company level. Pelham, Newcastle and Pitt committed both naval squadrons from home, beginning with those of Barnett and Boscawen (1746–8), and later regiments of the regular army, first to the defence of the British East India Company's stations and ultimately to its territorial aggrandisement. Although Clive could call on only 700 British regulars when he fought the battle of Plassey (above, p. 241), Eyre Coote's subsequent control of the Carnatic, secured at Wandewash (p. 264 below), was gained more by regular troops than by Company sepoys. The *Compagnie*, on the other hand, could only call on intermittent naval help from Mauritius (cf. Ch. 4), and the only French soldiers to reach India from France were 4,300 of the rawest recruits, mostly jailbirds, sent out between 1750 and 1754 (258; 259a; 18, *157–8*). It must be added, of course, that in India, as elsewhere, France was at a more fundamental disadvantage, for being the greatest land power on the Continent she could never afford to focus consistently for long on colonial or maritime objectives.

A second long-term advantage which Britain enjoyed in the contest for trade and empire lay in her growing command of the slave trade. The rôle of Africa in the wider struggle is easily overlooked, yet it was vital. Not only the West Indian sugar economy but the tobacco, rice and indigo production of Virginia, Maryland, the Carolinas and Louisiana were entirely dependent on imported slave labour. Even by 1750, by which time they had fourteen forts on the Gold Coast and 150 ships plying the trade, the British were in the driving seat in West Africa. The frightening vulnerability of the French West Indian economy to the drying up of its labour supply in wartime was first demonstrated in 1747–8. It proved conclusive from 1758–62, after the seizure of Gorée (Senegal), when those French sugar islands which were not captured by Britain were economically paralysed. But the slave trade has also a wider relevance to our theme, for it illustrates perfectly that degree of economic interdependence within the British Empire, bringing in India too, which the French simply could not emulate. The slave trade in itself, especially that involving Bristol or Liverpool merchants or shippers by the mid-eighteenth century, was a 'triangular trade'. But in addition the Africans who laboured on the plantations were fed with New England fish and Pennsylvania provisions, and clothed with cheap Indian fabrics; not a little of the rum manufactured in Massachusetts from the sugar cane they grew was traded to the Gold Coast to stupefy yet more Africans and make them ripe for kidnapping and shipment.

As well as revealing the Achilles heel of the French position in the Caribbean, the last two years of the War of the Austrian Succession were a time of humiliation for the naval power of Louis XV. The war at sea had not gone smoothly for Britain between 1739 and 1745, but the work of a reformed and reforming Admiralty Board was finally rewarded in 1747 when a large part of the French Atlantic fleet was destroyed or captured by Anson off Cape Finisterre and by Hawke off La Rochelle (above, p. 239), while over eighty French merchantmen bound for the New World were seized by minor squadrons. Whatever the other advantages or disadvantages of the contestants, the outcome of the struggle for empire turned in the end on the rival navies and the seamen who manned them. Yet although Britain's superiority in naval power was ultimately to prove completely decisive, her advantage at sea was not as clear-cut as is sometimes assumed. In the first place, the legacy of the preponderantly peaceful years from 1713–39 had been a mixed one for the Royal Navy. The alleged 'negligence' of the Walpole era and the direness of its supposed effects both on naval administration and on the sea-service itself have been much exaggerated.[3] In some respects, such as the provision of permanent overseas bases, the Navy was better equipped to fight a worldwide maritime war in 1740 than she had been in Queen Anne's reign. But in general it is true that Britain went into the Austrian Succession War with too many ageing capital ships, and with too many ageing senior officers. In the second place, both the French and the Spaniards had the edge in naval architecture. The master shipwrights of Britain's naval dockyards under the first two Georges were a conservative breed; it was largely because the big ships of the French and Spanish navies handled better in rough weather, and were more effectively armed, gun for gun, that they were able to give such a creditable account of themselves for many years. In the long run, however, most of the naval cards were stacked against them. Britain enjoyed a clear numerical superiority in ships, certainly over France, probably over both Bourbon navies combined by 1760[4], and most of these ships were two-deckers or frigates, which were not by and large inferior in quality to their counterparts. The productivity of her shipyards in wartime was unrivalled (258, *120–1*). All navies had manning problems, especially in the early stages of a new war, but because of the sheer size of her merchant marine Britain had by far the largest pool of trained seamen to tap, whether by the press gang or more reputable methods. Standards of morale and discipline, as well as seamanship, on the lower deck, were the envy of her rivals; Dr Rogers has recently argued vigorously against the view that British ships in the mid-eighteenth century were akin to 'floating concentration-camps' (86). Heavily in Britain's favour, too, was the quality of her naval officers, for in the Royal Navy merit could (though of course it did not always) triumph over birth and influence to an extent no other major navy could match. Anson, Boscawen and, pre-eminently, Hawke were among the finest admirals of the eighteenth century; of the younger men coming through in the 1740s, Rodney, Keppel, Kempenfelt, Howe and Hood all became commanders of very high calibre. Although high birth and political interest did very occasionally raise incompetents to flag rank, a classic example being Newcastle's relative, the Hon. George Clinton, the Admiralty normally had the prudence not to employ them at sea (86; 187a, *Ch. 9*). There was a tragic exception in the case of the squadron sent to Minorca in 1756 (below, p. 258).

Among all the assets which lay behind the resounding naval victories of 1759, and the virtually complete command of the seas which Britain was to enjoy throughout the second half of the Seven Years' War, the expert direction of the Admiralty was not the least important. The Board over which Anson presided as First Lord, for all but seven months of the period from June 1751 to June 1762 [D.6], was the most effective naval high command of the entire eighteenth century. And even more significant, perhaps, than the reforms it instituted was its evolution – not without trial and error – of a comprehensive naval strategy, to which the Elder Pitt ultimately gave his decisive support, a strategy geared to the winning of empire as well as to securing victory in the trade war. Its essentials were three: firstly, to seek out and destroy the enemy's fleets in battle, wherever possible; secondly, to use naval supremacy, once secured, both to cripple French trade and to confine French troops to the Continent by making it too hazardous for them to venture overseas and finally, where enemy ships refused to be drawn out, to bottle them up in their own harbours by organised blockade. It was not until 1747, in the Austrian Succession War, and 1758, in the Seven Years' War, that the British fleet was strong enough, in the context of its many obligations, to maintain a permanent blockading stranglehold on the French Channel ports. When it could do so, the results proved dramatic.

The Seven Years' War, in which Britain was engaged from 1756 to 1763, was the bloodiest Continental war of the eighteenth century as well as being a contest for overseas dominion. Appropriately, therefore, it had two chains of causes, initially separate but increasingly interlinked. On the one hand, two years of unofficial warfare in North America and on the seas led to a series of mounting provocations which by May 1756 had made an overt, major struggle between Britain and France utterly unavoidable. On the other hand, a 'Diplomatic Revolution', so-called, on the Continent in 1755–6, in which the duke of Newcastle (then chief minister) involuntarily played the initiating rôle, took such a succession of bizarre turns that by the autumn of 1756 another war had broken out between Austria and Prussia which by the following year was to involve all the Great Powers except Spain.

The fuse was lit in North America when units from the French army in Canada, renewing their push down the Upper Ohio, built Fort Duquesne in 1753 on territory claimed by Virginia. The Virginian militia, led by Lieutenant-Colonel George Washington, tried to expel the French in 1754 but failed, at heavy cost. General Braddock was ordered from Ireland later that year with the first small force of British regulars (see above, p. 240); but against a reinforced enemy he too failed in 1755 and died in the action. Boscawen was instructed to intercept the next French troop convoy that was sent across the Atlantic. He was thwarted by bad weather, but enough French merchant ships were seized then and over the next few months to serve as a *casus belli* for Louis XV. It was at this stage, late in 1755, that Newcastle's ministry began to exhibit the customary anxiety over the safety of Hanover in the coming Franco-British war. Although the end of the Austrian Succession conflict had left the 'Old System' of Whig alliances in a ruinous state (Ch. 4, p. 71), Newcastle, too old a dog to learn new tricks readily, once again approached Austria for the necessary guarantees of the electorate's security. But Vienna's sights were set on revenge against Prussia and the recovery of Silesia, and von Kaunitz, the Austrian Chancellor, was much more interested in angling for help from the great French army of 200,000 than in patching up an outworn *entente* with a maritime and colonial power. It was this rebuff which led Newcastle to approach St Petersburg for a subsidy treaty with the virulently anti-Prussian Empress Elizabeth. Concluded in September 1755, the agreement committed Russia to defend Hanover with 55,000 troops; it was this treaty which set off the chain reaction of the Diplomatic Revolution. Frederick the Great was so alarmed by the prospect of what Russia might attempt with the £500,000 sterling guaranteed her in a future war that in January 1756 he made his own deal with London for the neutralisation of Germany [H(xi)]. He had no intention of dissolving his former alliance with France, but the French were so unconvinced by his protestations that on the very eve of the outbreak of formal war against Britain in May 1756 they decided finally to accept Kaunitz's overtures. Initially the Austro-French alliance (1st Treaty of Versailles) was a defensive one. But Vienna was determined it should not remain so indefinitely; after Frederick – the spirit of 1740 reincarnated – had hurled his troops into Saxony (above, p. 241), and Russia, who felt cheated of her Prussian prey by Newcastle's subsequent diplomacy, had become a party to the Versailles treaty, the Habsburg court finally gained its objective in May 1757, with an offensive anti-Prussian and anti-British alliance in which France committed huge numbers of men and money to the war on the Continent.

In the long run that commitment was to be a godsend to a beleaguered government in Britain, whose only notable success in the first year of the war had been the diplomatic one of keeping Spain neutral. In the short run, however, it brought no comfort, for the French army's first move was against Hanover, and having defeated Cumberland with his defensive army of mercenaries it forced the duke to accept the humiliating Convention of Kloster-Seven (September), which left the electorate for a while effectively at the enemy's mercy (above, p. 241). Although it predictably reduced George II to gibbering fury, Kloster-Zeven was seen by much of parliamentary and public opinion as far from the worst of the misfortunes suffered in the fifteen months since the official war with France had opened in May 1756. The early loss of the cherished island base of Minorca, held by Britain since 1708, dealt a heavier blow to national pride than any wartime defeat since the Medway catastrophe of 1667 (*Making of a Great Power*, Ch. 6). So great was the outcry that Newcastle and his colleagues, fearing they might suffer the fate of Clarendon, made a scapegoat of Admiral John Byng, who had been guilty of over-caution and inept seamanship rather than cowardice. They insisted on his being court-martialled, and in March 1757, after the King had brushed aside the recommendation for clemency, which was supported by William Pitt, Byng was shot on his own quarterdeck. Throughout the summer of 1756 the threat of invasion was present, as the French once again assembled troops and transports in their Channel ports, and this threat was renewed in the spring of 1757. In North America the French continued to hold the initiative in 1756, as in 1755; under a fine new general, Montcalm, they achieved successes such as the capture of Fort Oswego, and managed, through the gaps in the partial British naval blockade of their ports, to keep their strong Canada-based forces well replenished with reinforcements and supplies. In his first spell as Secretary of State (November 1756–April 1757) Pitt did succeed in getting priority for the despatch of a new military and naval force to America; but for many months it had little to show for its presence, and meanwhile anxiety was growing in the British West Indies because, after capturing Minorca, France was able to spare ships from the Toulon fleet to reinforce her Caribbean squadron. The news from India, too, was hardly cheering before the summer of 1757: four trading posts in the Deccan were lost to Bussy in 1756 and worse still, the East India Company's Calcutta station and fort were seized by a hostile native prince, Suraj-ud-Daula, and many of its garrison and officials subsequently perished in the notorious 'Black Hole'.

Why was Britain so slow in 1756–7 to capitalise on the lessons of the 1740s and on the long-term assets which she possessed? A basic problem, without doubt, was acute political instability at home. There was an urgent need for strong political leadership, directing overall strategy and with sights firmly set on victory, but the onset of war revealed just how serious a loss the Whigs, and the country, had suffered through the death of Henry Pelham in 1754. Even before 1757 it had become transparent that, given the factious state of the ruling oligarchy (Ch. 18), effective leadership could not be provided, either by the duke of Newcastle, or by fellow grandees such as Devonshire, or by Newcastle's ambitious and strident challenger in the House of Commons, Henry Fox. Vastly experienced though he was, as a result of continuous Cabinet service since 1717, Newcastle was as reluctant a war-lord in 1756 as Walpole had been from 1739–42, and he was not altogether unhappy to resign in the autumn after Minorca. The Devonshire-Pitt ministry which then took over displayed a more positive approach to the war during its short life but, lacking the King's confidence, its tenure was always insecure. Following Pitt's dismissal in early April 1757 the administration drifted for almost three months like a rudderless ship, until George II in midsummer was finally chivvied into reluctant acceptance of what, despite many initial uncertainties, was to prove a winning combination. Its key ingredients were Newcastle's return to the Treasury, to guarantee the ministry a parliamentary majority and a generous revenue through the votes of the Old Corps and its backbench friends, and the reappointment of Pitt as Secretary for the South, not entirely on his own terms, but with a better prospect of being able to influence war policy and organisation as well as diplomacy than he had previously enjoyed.

Until comparatively recently students of British policy in the Seven Years' War accepted with only minor qualifications or doubts the view, enshrined in the work of Julian Corbett and Basil Williams, that Pitt the Elder was the master-architect of virtually all Britain's triumphs in the years 1758–61.[5] Of late some dissentient voices have been heard. Newcastle's contribution to what was, by any standards, a notable ministry has been favourably reassessed; his influence in the closet, it has been argued, was considerable, his responsibility for raising supply through his acolytes in the Commons total, and his powers of patronage still formidable. Pitt, on the other hand, has been downgraded. It has even been claimed that his capacity to direct the course of the war did not extend beyond the limits of his own department of state (though it is conceded that this was stretched to include North America and many of the dispositions of the Navy). He has been depicted primarily as a first-class administrator, rather than an 'ideas man', and the orders he signed are said to have 'represented the joint wisdom of the combined administration'.[6] Not all these claims will stand up. Pitt evidently did concern himself – closely at times – with the war in Germany and cultivated a 'special relationship' with Frederick the Great with scant regard for his Northern colleague, Holderness. It is equally clear that he regarded India and Africa as within his province. And if he observed the forms of Cabinet government, as by and large he did, it is hard to imagine that the fiery eloquence and passionate drive which he displayed in the Commons, backed by a popularity 'out of doors' which after his first year in office became more fearsome month by month (40a, *Chs. 4–5*), were wholly bridled in the cabinet room or that he was ever easy to resist there. Nonetheless, any future reappraisal of the conduct of the war in its victorious phase will have to take serious account of the detailed revisionism of Richard Middleton, who has argued strongly that Pitt's influence on events was more circumscribed, both by departmental constraints and by the initiative of the men in the field and on the seas, than the older orthodoxy would concede; and furthermore, that the success even of those policies which were indubitably his owed not a little to a favourable run of the green (91).

There is at least poetic justice in these controversies, for Pitt in his own lifetime was the most controversial of politicians. A manic-depressive, who for much of his life had to fight a protracted battle against acute physical pain as well as neuroses, Pitt had consistently alienated most of the political establishment, from George II downwards, by his egotistical, overbearing manner and blistering tongue, together with his flaunted contempt for the political conventions of his day. Men recognised his genius, but they feared and distrusted it more than they admired it. Before he could storm the closet and the inner citadels of the Whig ruling clique, he had had to wait more than two decades, and for just the right conjunction of events and opinion (the moment when, as Newcastle frankly admitted, Mr Pitt was less to be feared inside the ministry than outside it). And yet, in his few years of glory from 1758 to 1761, after the early disasters of the new administration, such as Kloster-Zeven and Rochefort, had been forgotten, even his enemies had to concede that many of the self-same gifts which in normal times fated Pitt to be an impossible colleague made him an indispensable war minister of more than life-size stature.

Foremost among the assets which Pitt brought to the direction of the war in June 1757 was the arrogant self-belief of a man who was as convinced of his own destiny as he was of his country's.[7] Whether Pitt had long cherished 'a vision of empire', in the sense understood by many nineteenth- and early twentieth-century writers on his life and times, may be open to doubt. That he had since his earliest years in politics consistently advocated policies of aggressive mercantile and commercial expansion and colonial aggrandisement is not. And to the realisation of these ends he now brought a confidence in his own judgement and priorities which after the miseries of 1756 and the anxious summer and autumn of 1757 positively galvanised his colleagues and subordinates. Initially, with his own position still insecure, Pitt was more defensive and traditional in his planning than adulatory biographers have suggested (91; 40b, *75–7*). Even so, month by month he purveyed a growing sense of certainty to a hitherto wavering government. One thing he never doubted from the start, for instance, was that the only sure key to the security of Britain's North American colonies was the expulsion of the French from Canada; by 1759 that aim had come to embrace the outright annexation of the territory to the British crown. He was also certain that to achieve the decisive defeat of the French in North America, as well as to insure against the inevitable invasion hazards at home, the Admiralty's blockade-and-strike policy round the coast of France was the right one, but that to succeed it needed more ships: at least 200, rather than the 130 or so with which the Royal Navy had begun the war. By 1760, with Anson's essential support, all those new ships had been built.

Not perhaps to begin with, but from the end of 1757, after the great Prussian victories of Rossbach and Leuthen (above, p. 241) had first turned the tide of the Seven Years' War in Europe, Pitt also became convinced – and eventually convinced his colleagues, many doubters in Parliament, and public opinion – that Frederick the Great's inspired generalship made him a providential ally for Britain. By 1758 his argument was that now that large French armies were committed to Prussia's destruction, Frederick's survival had become so vital to the accomplishment of Britain's overseas aims that his forces must be kept in the field at all costs. He must therefore be succoured not only by the traditional heavy subsidies and by Hanoverian troops, and by a further series of diversionary raids on the French or German coast, but also by a strong presence of British troops on the Continent (first proposed by Pitt, in a remarkable *volte-face*, in June 1758). The logic of the case has been regarded as suspect by some historians; the extent to which it represented a coherent, integrated 'strategy' has been queried by others. (The expeditions to Rochefort and Cherbourg in 1757–8, for example, have been seen mainly as 'sweeteners' for the sake of Tory and other former 'Patriot' or 'blue-water' supporters of Pitt who would otherwise have found his conversion to 'continental' policies too bitter a pill to swallow (258; 40b, *76*; 40a, *91, 105*)). Yet neither logical flaws (if any) nor evidence of seeming political inconsistency weighed materially with the House of Commons of the late 1750s, which cheerfully footed the vast bills involved, including an annual £670,000 hand-out to Prussia alone.

Particularly revealing about the efficacy of Pitt's distinctive brand of conviction politics in wartime is his, and Parliament's, attitude to Hanover after the summer of 1757. He argued that it had to be protected with the utmost vigour, not simply because George II expected it but lest, if overrun by the French, it should be used by them as a bargaining counter at the peace negotiations, to rob Britain of her overseas gains. Pitt's fellow-politicians were justified in regarding as ironical, if not breathtaking, this extraordinary change of heart by one who had for years castigated the malign influence of the 'despicable electorate'; yet, because Pitt proclaimed his new faith with the fervour of a convert, they too (even in the end the Tories in the House of Commons) succumbed to it. Because well-chosen policies in themselves could not have beaten France without the capacity to execute them, it goes without saying that the government's hold over the Commons during the three most vital years of the war, 1758–60, was of crucial importance. Traditionally Pitt's contribution to this dominance may indeed have been somewhat overvalued, in relation to Newcastle's. Fierce eloquence and pesonal magnetism alone, without 'management', would not for long sway an eighteenth-century Parliament, a fact well illustrated by the ability of the Old Corps in both Houses to obstruct for eighteen months (to June 1758) the militia reform bills, favoured by Pitt and the Townshend brothers but disapproved of by Newcastle and Hardwicke (92, *134–5*). On the positive side, managerial skills of a high order were clearly involved in persuading the Commons in 1758 to approve a war budget of £12.5 million (including £2 million for subsidies) – more than a third of the *total* military and naval expenditure incurred in the war of 1689–97 – and to go on raising the stakes thereafter until the climax was reached in 1760–1 with a supply vote of £19.5 million (82, *152*). This was to keep a British army of over 90,000, some 75,000 naval personnel and scores of thousands of mercenaries in pay [I.2]. A popular view among modern scholars is that, in spite of Pitt's reputation as 'the great commoner', his chief power base in the 1750s was not so much the House of Commons as the City of London: to begin with among the Common Council and a powerful section of the London press, and only later among the wealthiest strata of the merchant community whose pockets his flamboyant brand of imperialism promised to line. And it is plain that in a war in which over 37 per cent of an unprecedented expenditure was met by loans (84, *40, Table 2.2*), Pitt's reputation as well as Newcastle's patient negotiations with the City financiers must have had something to do with the ministry's extraordinary success in raising money at rates as low as 3.5 or 4 per cent. Yet it would be absurd to let the pendulum swing too far. Pitt's reputation as a 'patriot' who would never truckle to connexion and corruption, which had long given him a unique charisma among backbenchers of both parties, survived largely intact down to 1761 (44, *98–101*); it was a very shrewd judge, Lord Chesterfield, who wrote of his near-messianic influence over the Commons at the height of the Seven Years' War: 'Mr Pitt declares only what he would have them do, and they do it *nem.con* . . .'[8]

Modern scholarship and perspectives may have shaken (without destroying) the old certainties about Pitt as the master-strategist of the war. But his organisational genius and his eagle eye for detail, which were legendary at the time, are qualities few historians have ever denied (but cf. 91, *212–13*). Nor is it adequate to see him just as a single-minded administrator, with the capacity to ensure that the ships, the subsidies, the troops all got to the right place at the right time. His close involvement in the planning of some individual operations, such as the capture of Senegal and the sugar island of Guadeloupe in 1759, can be plainly documented. The later fall of Martinique, Grenada and St Lucia (1762) were recognised by many as Pitt's triumphs, as much as those of the commanders involved, even though he was out of office when his plans were belatedly accepted. Above all, it would be hairsplitting to deny that the blueprint for the conquest of Canada – first the recapture of Louisburg (achieved in 1758), then the seizure of Quebec (1759) and finally of Montreal (1760) – was essentially his, drawn up and carried through in the teeth of many gloomy prognostications and some frustrating delays. Of course Pitt sought and listened to advice (from John Cleveland, the experienced Admiralty Secretary, for instance, on Caribbean strategy), but having done so he was ready to back his own judgement.

That judgement was most searchingly tested in the choice of leaders for the many theatres in which British arms were engaged. Little could be done with the army so long as Cumberland, the King's son, was commander-in-chief, but he was disgraced after Kloster-Zeven, and with the King ailing and the septuagenarian, Ligonier, installed at Pitt's insistence instead of the duke, there were more opportunities for the latter to exploit. The old general was no mere cipher, but his personal wishes about appointments could be and sometimes were overridden (91, *103*). In the case of the navy, Pitt had influence with Anson, the First Lord, and was not slow or over-nice about using it. He held to the view – not exactly universal in the eighteenth century – that in the leadership of armies and navies there is no substitute for talent, and was never impressed by the claims of 'experience' alone, still less by the claims of birth. For the expedition given the fiendish task of taking Quebec, the key to Pitt's highest priority, the conquest of Canada, he was able to hand-pick both commanders. Charge of the warships and transports went to Charles Saunders, a protégé of Anson's since he had sailed round the world with him as a junior lieutenant. The 8,600 troops were entrusted to James Wolfe, who had been a captain at the age of seventeen, a brigadier, prominent in the final siege of Louisburg, at thirty-one, and was now, at thirty-two, a major-general. Wolfe was a man very much in Pitt's own mould, self-willed, impatient of obstacles and ferociously energetic; without the calculated heroism he showed in leading his men up the Heights of Abraham, which cost him his life, even this expedition's meticulous preparation would not have been enough.

Pitt was not an unerring talent-spotter. With the army, especially, he made mistakes, and he could be ruthless with those who proved him wrong: Lord George Sackville, for example, the cavalry commander in Germany, was publicly disgraced in 1759 for dereliction of duty. Pitt's nominees, moreover, did not always get the key commands. It was a feather in Newcastle's cap that he successfully pressed the claims of Jeffrey Amherst to replace Abercromby (another of Pitt's less inspired choices) as commander-in-chief in North America late in 1758. As one of the army's youngest major-generals, Amherst had been in command of the force which took Louisburg; subsequently he was to be mainly responsible for completing the reduction of the French forts between the Upper Ohio and the St Lawrence, impressively begun in 1758 by Bradstreet and Forbes, and at length for capturing Montreal (259b, *Ch. 22, 538–40*). Those entrusted with major military or naval responsibilities, whether 'Pitt's men' or not, very rarely had grounds to complain that they were not allowed initiative or that they were denied the tools necessary for the job. This is abundantly clear in the case of Wolfe. We can see it, too, in a smaller way, with commodore Keppel, who led the second expedition to West Africa in 1759, and on a much larger canvas with Boscawen and Hawke, whose naval victories at Lagos and Quiberon Bay (above, p. 242) not only removed the last threat of a French invasion but gave the British navy complete mastery thereafter in the Channel and the Atlantic. No commander repaid Pitt and the ministry more handsomely than Ferdinand of Brunswick, the gifted Prussian-born general, who was given charge of the army of observation after Cumberland's *débâcle*. The prince was amply supplied with money and his army was given successive injections of British regulars, six regiments of whom took part in the famous victory at Minden (August 1759), while 20,000 were in service in Germany by 1760. Ferdinand, for his part, not only preserved Hanover and drove the French, for a while, back across the Rhine, he also took critical pressure off Frederick the Great at a time when Prussia's heavily-outnumbered forces were seriously vulnerable after a number of morale-sapping defeats in 1757–60, Olmütz and Kunersdorf among them, interspersed with victories or indecisive battles, such as Zorndorf, in which the carnage was sickening (above, pp. 241–2)

If even four of the fine French regiments pulverised in the past three years of Continental fighting had been spared for India, the outcome of the contest there might still have been in the balance in 1760, though in view of the disparity in naval strength by then in Far Eastern waters it seems unlikely that they could have done much more than postpone the inevitable. The British East India Company recognised their debt to Pitt (witness their fulsome motion of thanks in 1761), even if some modern historians are reluctant to concede it. Alive to the possibilities opened up by the remarkable victory of Robert Clive over Suraj-ud-Dowla at Plassey (1757), his seizure of Chandernagore from the French and his subsequent overrunning of India's richest province, Bengal, Pitt thereafter kept the Indian theatre supplied with what trained troops and ships could be spared. Indeed it was a typical Pitt selection, a young colonel named Eyre Coote, sent out with two regiments in 1759, who, with the help of a fresh naval squadron, put the coping-stone on Clive's earlier achievements by defeating the French general Lally at Wandewash, in Southern India, and finally taking the *Compagnie's* main trading base at Pondicherry (259a, *Ch. 23*).

Wandewash was fought in January 1760. By the time Montreal capitulated the following September British arms were beginning to seem invincible. Pitt's reputation, now the most formidable in Europe, apart from the desperately embattled Frederick the Great, stood higher even than it had in 1759, that 'year of marvels' when, in Horace Walpole's words, 'our bells are worn threadbare, ringing for victory'. In October 1760, however, the accession of a new King, young, and much influenced both in his morbid suspicion of Pitt and his eagerness for peace by his Leicester House mentor, Lord Bute, swiftly brought about a change of scene. The Secretary of State knew from the start that his position was under threat (44, *101–2*), but his reaction was a characteristically bold one. Since the death of Ferdinand VI (1759) there had always been a likelihood that Spain would eventually be drawn into the war on France's side. When peace talks between Pitt and Choiseul in the spring and summer of 1761 were suddenly torpedoed, Pitt was virtually certain that that intervention was now imminent. He therefore pressed fiercely for a decisive pre-emptive strike against Spain. There was sound logic in his argument that the Spanish fleet should be crippled before it could be put on war footing and that the pickings which had eluded Britain in 1739 would then be there for the taking. But George III was hostile; the Commons were growing uneasy (as was public opinion) about the wisdom of further hefty expenditure [I.2; G.1]; in October 1761 Pitt lost a vote on the Spanish issue in the Cabinet, where stalwarts such as Newcastle were wearying of his overbearing conduct and recent arrivals, notably Bute, resentful of his popularity. He read the signs and decided it was time to go, telling the Council in the course of a predictably histrionic statement 'that he would be responsible for nothing but what he directed'.[9] The old duke and 'the Pelhamite innocents' did not long survive him, and by May 1762 Bute was First Lord of the Treasury

(Ch. 19). Although, as Pitt had forecast, war with Spain (December 1761) had proved unavoidable, and Havana and Manila were captured from her, in addition to the seizure of a clutch of Caribbean islands from France – among them the outstanding prize of Martinique – (above, p. 243), these events took place against the background of new peace negotiations in Paris; the latter caused great uneasiness not only to Pitt and his friends but to Newcastle and others who had served in the great ministry of 1757–61.

The debate on the terms of the Treaty of Paris [H(xii)], negotiated by Bute's ministry, raged furiously at the time and still goes on among historians. Despite the Canada *versus* Guadeloupe controversy which had preceded and accompanied Pitt's abortive negotiations with Choiseul (40a, *166–7, 199–200*), there was little argument now about the retention by Britain of Canada and the British right to expand westward to the banks of the Mississippi: satisfaction was universal that the safety of the American colonies was at last secured. The recovery of Minorca at the price of returning to France Belle Isle (captured by Keppel and Hodgson in 1761) was applauded. The Indian and African terms were almost all acceptable to the British interests involved, though there was some feeling that with the successes of 1762 behind him Bute should have refused to hand back Gorée island. The restoration to Spain of wealthy Havana, a great prize, and of Manila in the Philippines, in return for the swamps of Florida, was much more controversial. But it was the surrender of Guadeloupe and Martinique which was greeted with most outrage by the Pittites, by part (though not all) of the West India interest,[10] and by a vocal section of public and press opinion. Bute's handling of relations with Frederick the Great, who was left with a permanent grievance after discovering that, for once in his life, he had been outdone in political cynicism, was also bitterly criticised.[11] In December 1762 Pitt was carried to Westminster, swathed in bandages, to thunder for three hours on end against this desertion of an ally (which he himself, to his credit, would never have contemplated) and against many other aspects of a treaty which he declared to be 'totally inadmissible'. But he thundered in vain.

There was undoubtedly a case to be made against Bute's ministry on the West Indian as well as the Prussian issue; even with the cession to Britain of the three minor islands of Tobago, St Vincent and Grenada British possessions in the Caribbean still remained strategically, as well as economically vulnerable to French pressure. On the other hand, Choiseul had to be given his half-loaf somewhere, unless a massively expensive and burdensome war was to go on indefinitely; with hindsight some modern authorities have pointed out that, because the prosperity of the sugar trade had been sagging for some time, even on economic grounds it was plausible to argue that Canada would yield the more substantial long-term benefits. It is certainly not inconceivable that tougher bargainers might have held onto not only Gorée but Martinique (which had strategic as well as economic value) (258, *127–8*) and to Havana (as a trade-off against Manila). They might even have pressed for the total exclusion of France from the Newfoundland fisheries – though that was a demand that would very probably have jeopardised the entire negotiations. All the same, taking a view across the world board Britain still seemed by 1763 to have unquestionably won the great contest for trade and empire, and this was the view taken at the time by the bulk of parliamentary opinion. In North America she appeared totally dominant. She had acquired a permanent advantage in, if not yet a stranglehold over, the slave trade. In India French power had been completely broken, militarily and politically as well as economically (the *Compagnie des Indes* was to be wound up within a few years) [H(xii)(2)], and the way was wide open for the British Company, very soon after the Peace, to strike out again along the path of *territorial* conquest which Clive, from 1757–9, had first opened up in Bengal. Whether the French would accept their imperial defeat as final, and whether the first British Empire itself would continue to acquiesce in the future in the rôle it had traditionally been allotted, were questions which only the future could answer. The next twenty years were to answer one of them, at least – and in a startling and almost entirely unforeseen way.

---

1. Among other things this great-nephew of Halifax of the Junto secured for the Board the right to appoint colonial governors.
2. Letters from Paris and London, 15 July, 23 Jan 1750, quoted in J.H. Parry (258), pp. 159–60.
3. For an authoritative corrective, see D.A. Baugh, *Naval Administration 1715–1750* (1977) and *British Naval Administration in the Age of Walpole* (Princeton, 1967), *passim*.
4. An academic point in the Seven Years' War until Spain abandoned her neutrality in January 1762.
5. J.S. Corbett, *England in the Seven Years' War* (2 vols, 1907); B. Williams, *Chatham* (2 vols, 1913). Compare Williams's *The Whig Supremacy* (Oxford, 1939), p. 336, where the success of the war is attributed 'almost entirely . . . to Pitt's torrential energy, to his far-seeing preparations, to his wise choice of commanders on land and sea, and still wiser trust in them when they were chosen, and above all to his strategic insight . . .'
6. For an extreme view see S. B. Baxter, 'The Conduct of the Seven Years' War', in id., ed., *England's Rise to Greatness, 1660–1760* (Los Angeles, 1983), p. 335 and *passim*. For a more restrained anticipation of some of these points, see the views of J.B. Owen and P. Langford, in general works published in 1974 and 1976 (10; 82).
7. That he did indeed tell Devonshire, 'I am sure I can save this country, and no-one else can' seems very much in character, though the words were not quoted by Horace Walpole to redound to his credit. H. Walpole, *Memoirs of the Reign of King George II*, 3 vols (1846–7), III, p. 84.
8. B. Dobrée, ed., *The Letters of Philip . . . 4th Earl of Chesterfield*, V (1932) :2 Feb 1759 (Latin abbreviated).
9. Newcastle's Council minutes, 2 Oct 1761, quoted in Peters (40a), p. 202.
10. Some planters would have welcomed the chance to establish themselves on these two rich sugar islands; others feared the effects on their trade of bringing the French islands into the haven of the Old Colonial System.
11. For an excellent discussion of the merits and fallacies of this criticism, see Langford (82), pp. 145–7.

CHAPTER 18

The Pelhams, public opinion and the last rites of 'party', 1746–1760

The unstable state of British domestic politics in the mid–1750s, which forms the backcloth to the deterioration of Anglo-French overseas relations, the Diplomatic Revolution in Europe and the early failures of the Seven Years' War, had been unforeseeable in the first two months of 1754, while Henry Pelham was still alive. Granville's final defeat at the hands of the Old Corps (Ch. 5) had inaugurated an interlude of relative political peace that was destined to last right down to the unexpected death of Henry Pelham in March 1754. Of the House of Commons in this most placid period of the eighteenth century, Horace Walpole made this often-quoted, caustic remark: 'A bird might build her nest in the Speaker's chair, or in his peruke. There won't be a debate that can disturb her' (10, 72). It was at once the Indian summer of the Robinocracy and the twilight of the first age of party; a period of gentle erosion of former antagonism. The storm of opposition that had assailed and ultimately overwhelmed Walpole, blew itself out in the mid–1740s. The end-product was a ministry firmly based on the Old Corps and its acknowledged leaders, the Pelhams, with the leading lights of the anti-Walpolean Opposition bought off or neutralised. Pulteney had received his coveted peerage and been discredited in the process by his blatant self-interest. Granville (formerly Carteret), twice defeated in confrontations with the Pelhams, was a spent force; so spent that in 1751 the Pelhams brought him into their administration as Lord President of the Privy Council, where he quietly vegetated until his death in 1763. Pitt was Paymaster-General and, with an eye to the future, trying to live down his reputation as an anti-Hanover zealot (a trait the King found hard to forgive). Bolingbroke had retired in despair to France. Only two shrunken centres of opposition remained: the dwindling band of Tories and Frederick Prince of Wales's Leicester House connexion.

The snap election of 1747, timed so as to wrong-foot Frederick, who was preparing an electoral onslaught on the Old Corps' redoubts in the West Country, saw a bare 115 Tories returned to the Commons. In the Lords probably only a score of peers could still be described as Tories. The party's leadership was also wasting away. Following Wyndham's death in 1740 and Gower's departure to the Whigs in 1744, two other Tory stalwarts of the Walpole years, Williams Wynn and Hynde Cotton, died in 1749 and 1752 respectively. Insofar as the Tories still had recognisable leaders, they were weary veterans like the duke of Beaufort and the earl of Oxford (28a; 257). The Jacobite option which so many Tories had toyed with at various times had been bloodily discredited on Culloden moor and at Tyburn tree (Ch. 6). A handful still dabbled in Jacobite conspiracy, and the last significant plot (the 'Elibank' plot) was hatched, and foundered, during 1750–2. However, even this faithful remnant was increasingly disillusioned by the

Young Pretender's dissipation, and by 1754–5, 'the principal of the party . . . gave over all thought of him' (12a, *I, 77*).

The demise of active Jacobitism coincided with a decline in the Tories' political energy. As Earl Waldegrave observed: 'they had lost their ablest leaders; and had neither spirit to make themselves fear'd, nor abilities to give any disturbance'.[1] They were still occasionally capable of isolated efforts, for example in defence of Alexander Murray (a leader of the Tory-inspired Independent Electors of Westminster) in 1750, and in the nationwide campaign to overturn the Oxford University election result in 1754, but the lethargy and absenteeism which otherwise dogged the party mutely points to a fundamental moral crisis. After Frederick's death in 1751 killed any prospect of a renewed opposition offensive in alliance with dissident Whigs, it was virtually impossible to get the Tories up to Westminster in any numbers. Henry Pelham's affability and avoidance of contentious subjects in government legislation offered them little incentive. The Jewish Naturalisation Act of 1753 (above, p. 240) briefly threatened to raise a popular clamour which they could have exploited, in their traditional rôle as the defenders of the Church of England, but Pelham defused the issue by calmly allowing the act to be repealed. Pelham's policy of fiscal retrenchment (see below, p. 271) also intrinsically appealed to Tory sensibilities, leaving them with precious little on which to take a principled stand against the ministry. After all, the Tories had been in the wilderness, defeated time after time, for nearly forty years by the early 1750s, and it would have been remarkable if the cumulative effect of their experiences, especially after their hopes were raised high, only to be dashed following the fall of Walpole, had not been demoralisation.

Moribund, leaderless and spent by the mid–1750s, only the Tory party's distinct social and cultural milieu kept it going at all. Tory kinship and friendship connections, common educational experiences and family traditions remained a cement;[2] but without an injection of real ideological antagonism, this was bound to weaken, so that by 1754 the final disappearance of the Tory party can only have been a question of time.

The only other challenge to the Pelhamite hegemony after 1746 came from the reversionary interest [A.] led by the Prince of Wales. Personally, Frederick was a feeble tool far removed from the 'Patriot King'-in-waiting image he affected. He was prone to fatuous absurdities like ostentatiously wearing a tartan waistcoat, holding intimate *soirées* with Tory leaders publicly compromised by their Jacobite connexions, and employing a sister of the Young Pretender's mistress as maid-of-honour to Princess Amelia. He did, however, have one abiding advantage in the eyes of opponents of the Old Corps: his father George II was in his late sixties. Should Frederick succeed him, he would be entitled to remodel the administration as he chose, and accordingly he spent much of his time fantasising with friends about who would get what when he came to the throne and ousted the Pelhams and their minions. Therein lay Frederick's political allure; as Henry Pelham put it, he 'has as much to give in present as we have, and more in reversion' (12a, *II, 331*). Correspondingly, the dissatisfied, disgruntled and displaced of British politics – about 60 MPs and a few peers by

1750 – gravitated towards the Prince's alternative court. Without Tory support he still could not cut much of a figure against the ministry's legions, but the Tories had nowhere else to go.

Frederick's motives for launching his campaign to oust the Pelhams in 1747 had as much to do with *ennui* as with jealousy and rebelliousness. As he was reported to have told some of his father's ministers: 'there was no way for the Prince of Wales to make a figure here but in war or by opposition. He, being precluded the former, would use the latter'.[3] Frederick had been consistently outmanoeuvred during the power-struggles of 1742–6, and his abandonment by erstwhile followers like Pulteney and Sandys as soon as the King offered them advancement clearly rankled. His brother, the duke of Cumberland, the victor of Culloden, was still the Whigs' 'Conquering Hero'.[4] Only successful Opposition offered Frederick the prospect of immediate significance and the chance to get his own back.

Ironically, however, it was not the existing but the reversionary interest that came to grief; Frederick died, not his father. On his way, vulture-like, to see how the King was faring in March 1751 (George II was reported to be seriously ill), Frederick caught a chill and rapidly expired. Princess Amelia soon agreed to a reconciliation between the junior court and St James's, and the reversionary interest temporarily collapsed as its adherents rushed to work their passage into the Pelhams' good graces. Almost alone, Lord Egmont tried to keep the Opposition going, but even he gave up the unequal fight late in 1751. Thereafter there was no formed Opposition to the Pelhamite hegemony until death removed its keystone, Henry Pelham.

The Pelhams controlled the Lords, Commons and administration, thereby marginalising any prospect of successful opposition. At the heart of their power was the resurgent Old Corps (Ch. 3). This was more than simply a coalition of placemen, clients, kinsmen, friends and admirers of the chief ministers. The Old Corps also had a corporate sense of purpose centred on three principles: moderate Whiggism, service to the crown and personal loyalty to the acknowledged leaders of the Whig party. Old Corps Whiggery was eighteenth-century 'Revolution principles' brought to their irreducible minimum: belief in a sacrosanct Revolution Settlement and fidelity to the House of Hanover (284, *125–59*). By 1746 this creed was profoundly conservative, but it was undeniably Whig and sincerely held to by most of the Old Corps, as demonstrated by the determination with which they raised troops and money and volunteered for service against the Jacobites in 1745. The idea of service to the crown established itself in the Old Corps' ideology during the long years of monopolising office in the Walpole era. Not taken to excess, it was a socially honourable concept, though obviously open to corruption and the abuse of power. Although many Old Corps Whigs were corrupt, we should not assume that the concept of service to the crown was solely there as a camouflage for sleazy venality. Horace Walpole, no friend of Henry Pelham's, noted respectfully that Pelham, 'died poor',[5] despite holding lucrative government offices such as the Treasurership of the Chamber and the Paymaster-Generalship for over thirty years. Likewise, Pelham's half-brother Newcastle spent over £300,000 of his own money supporting the Whig cause, and never received anything like commensurate recompense (10, *78*). Pitt ostentatiously refused to take a penny beyond his official salary as Paymaster-General (a notoriously lucrative office, the perks of which had enriched men such as James Brydges, duke of Chandos, in the past and which Henry Fox was to exploit to the tune of £23,000 a year in the late 1750s) (*Making of a Great Power* Chs. 17, 18; *12a, II, 331*). The Old Corps' corporate loyalty to its acknowledged leaders arose from their leaders' eminence in the party and control of official patronage. In society at large deference was normally returned for leadership and patronage, and in mid-eighteenth-century politics the Old Corps reflected such customary relations in microcosm.[6] No better gauge of the strength of its ties can be found than in the way the Old Corps placemen resigned *en masse* with their leaders in February 1746 when George II tried to replace the Pelhams with Granville and Bath (Ch. 5).

This is not to suggest there were no tensions within the Old Corps. At its apex, Newcastle was a neurotic who was obsessively jealous of his ministerial colleagues. He and Henry Pelham at times complained bitterly of each other to their mutual friend, Lord Chancellor Hardwicke. Both Pelhams had to keep an alert watch on the zealotry of some of the firebrands in the Old Corps, such as Henry Fox. Fox had been one of 'Walpole's Whelps' between 1734 and 1742 and remained a devoted admirer after his fall. He correspondingly saw the Pelhamite hegemony as a golden opportunity for revenge on the New Whigs and other betrayors of his old mentor.[7] Memories of old battles in the 1730s as well as anticipation of future competition fuelled Fox's especially rancorous hostility towards Pitt. None of these antagonisms must be blown out of proportion however; the connexions and factions into which the Old Corps was eventually to dissolve had their origins in this period, but mutual ideological commitment, revitalised by the 'Forty-five, and general acceptance of the Pelhams' leadership overlaid and contained such divisions.

With Granville out of the way, the major problem facing the Pelhams was that of extricating Britain from the grinding attrition of the War of Austrian Succession. There were two schools of thought on the subject. One, headed by Henry Pelham and Fox, argued that Britain should coax some face-saving terms out of the French and then make peace as quickly as possible, specifically taking up the proposals made by France early in 1747. The other, headed by Newcastle and the Captain-General of the army, the duke of Cumberland, argued that making peace without any gains would be disastrous, and therefore that further efforts should be made and the French proposals rejected.[8] Newcastle and Cumberland's policy eventually won over the Cabinet, and the last year of the war, 1747–8, was preoccupied with finding a conquest that could be traded for Madras, seized by the French in 1746, without giving up the captured fortress-base of Louisburg in North America, which was treasured by public opinion at home. All Newcastle's diplomatic schemes and Cumberland's military efforts, however, proved fruitless. The former got no change out of an economically exhausted Dutch Republic, despite prompting the Orangist coup carried out by William IV in 1747. Britain and her allies meanwhile strained every sinew to give Cumberland an army of 100,000 to face the Maréchal de Saxe in Flanders; but

Saxe, true to form, promptly trounced the royal duke and scattered his army at the battle of Laffeldt. The important naval victories gained in the last year of the war (Ch. 17) could not gloss over the fact that Britain ended the campaigning season worse off than when she started. With the Dutch set on peace at all costs, not even Newcastle and Cumberland could face the prospect of shouldering the whole economic burden of keeping the subsidised Continental allies going if the war continued, and they thus gave way to the peace party in Cabinet. The general peace settlement of Aix-la-Chapelle [H(x)] soon followed.

After such prodigious efforts on all sides this was a deeply unsatisfactory result for most of the belligerent powers. The French view of it is summarised by the arrival of a new aphorism in the French language: '*bête comme la paix*'. In Britain it was generally believed the peace was really only a truce while both sides prepared for the next round. Nevertheless, Henry Pelham seized the opportunity offered by the peace and his ascendancy in Cabinet, now that the war-party was subdued, to bring in a policy of swingeing fiscal retrenchment. Pelham's principal ambition as premier minister was to be 'the author of such a plan as might, in time to come, have released this nation from the vast load of debt they now labour under' (12a, *II, 330*). And indeed Pelham's financial achievements were much admired by contemporaries and are his principal claim to fame. George II, by 1752 an experienced judge of financial policy, observed to Newcastle, that 'with regard to money matters, your brother does that, understands that, much better' than Walpole (12a, *II, 331*). Military expenditure was the first target for the Pelham axe. By 1751 the naval establishment had been reduced from 51,550 to 8,000 and the army from 50,000 to 18,850. Government expenditure plummeted from £12 million in 1747–8 to £7 million in 1750. In an exceedingly popular move, the Land Tax was reduced to three shillings in the pound in 1749 and to two shillings in 1752, though not without compensating increases in indirect taxation. Pelham's ultimate target was the national debt [G.1], the servicing of which through interest payments was absorbing by 1748 44 per cent of government expenditure. The Treasury responded by consolidating the funds that made it up and forcing down the rates of interest paid to public creditors. The fourteen national debt funds were reduced to five, and their interest rate went down from 4 per cent to 3 per cent over the nine years to 1758 (73).

In view of the accolades Henry Pelham has received for his fiscal achievements it may seem churlish to point out that the net saving on interest payments in 1755 was less than £300,000, roughly 10 per cent of the debt charge of 1750. Yet this highlights a major weakness in his financial reforms: what point was there in a long-term assault on government debt in the years 1747–54, when the international situation was so manifestly unstable, especially when the only way of retrenching was savagely to cut defence expenditure? Britain paid for the drastic naval cuts made between 1748 and 1750 with the loss of Minorca in 1756 (Ch. 17). However, few of Pelham's colleagues – Pitt was the exception – made any serious criticism of his programme of cutbacks, and given the relative political tranquillity that his reforms fostered, it is easy to see why George II lamented his death.[9]

It was Hardwicke rather than Newcastle who first began the search for a replacement for Pelham. By 1754 it was generally thought impossible to control the Commons from the Lords; hence the ministry required an authoritative spokesman in the Lower House. Hardwicke, and Newcastle when he recovered from his grief, really only had two options: Fox or Pitt. The King detested Pitt, which left Fox the inescapable choice. Newcastle, however, refused to concede to Fox Pelham's status in Cabinet. Accordingly he was offered promotion to the Northern Secretaryship of State and to the leadership of the Commons, the two prizes he most coveted, but stripped of their attendant patronage. He refused, and Newcastle was left trying to control a Commons containing a hostile Pitt and an alienated Fox through second-rate spokesmen such as Bilson-Legge [D.4]. Newcastle's authority within the Old Corps was initially confirmed by a thumping victory in the 1754 election [E.1] for which he got the credit (though the preparations had mostly been Pelham's). Reviewing these results Newcastle sanguinely observed:

> The Parliament is good beyond my expectations, and I believe there are more Whigs in it, and generally well-disposed Whigs, than in any Parliament since the Revolution . . . The great point will be to keep our friends together, and that they should do right when they are chose. For from the enemy we have nothing to fear (39, *90*).

In principle Newcastle was right; in practice keeping the Old Corps together was to prove extremely difficult.

Given the Corps' overwhelming predominance in Parliament in the mid-1750s any struggle for supremacy between rival politicians had to be conducted within it. Because the contest was internal – Old Corps prejudices and values being common currency – it necessarily revolved around personalities, nuances of policy and, above all else, oratory. Whichever politician could convince the infantrymen of the Old Corps that he best represented their interests and ideals would win their support. This is what Pitt and Fox aimed primarily to achieve. In November 1754 Pitt accordingly denounced Oxford University, long a citadel of High Tory loyalism, for 'perpetually breeding up a race of Jacobites'. Fox responded in 1755 with a motion to abolish Parliament's annual day of mourning on the anniversary of Charles I's execution (28a, *268*). Newcastle started to get alarmed early in 1755 when Pitt and Fox began to draw large attentive audiences of Old Corps MPs for their attacks on the ministry's policies. When news arrived of the destruction of Braddock's army in America (Ch. 17), Newcastle reacted with Walpolean aplomb: he stole half the brains out of the opposition by buying Fox (37b, *Ch. 3*).

A recent thesis on Fox has explained how he valued the Secretaryship of State and leadership of the Commons he had extorted from Newcastle more as badges of status and pre-eminence than as sources of real authority.[10] He was therefore happy to let Newcastle take the lead in forming policy, so long as he himself had a seat in Cabinet and the prestige that went with it. Fox had therefore to defend before the Commons decisions and policies not of his own making. Not that this was a problem at first. Despite the eloquence of Pitt's famous Rhône-Saône speech, likening the Fox-Newcastle ministry to an improbable junction of the two rivers, the government's orators brought in a majority of 206 on the division on the Address in reply to the King's Speech in November 1755 that prompted the debate. Newcastle felt sufficiently encouraged by that result to use Pitt's attack as an excuse to dismiss him and his lieutenants (above, p. 240). All Pitt could do now was befriend the newly alienated Leicester House connexion, controlled by the dowager Princess of Wales on behalf of her son, the future George III, and declaim the virtues of a united 'Patriot' Opposition so as to draw in the Tories (37b).

Like Walpole before them, Fox and Newcastle had apparently put together an unassailable combination of forces: overwhelming numbers, convincing rhetoric and the King's confidence. Like Walpole too, however, their vulnerability was exposed in one vital area: competence in waging war. As we know, Frederick the Great's attack on Saxony in August 1756 converted the Franco-British conflict into a pan-European war. The key to British success in European wars throughout the eighteenth century was always the aid of an effective ally (or allies) acting as Britain's Continental 'enforcer', plentifully supplied with British material resources, as well as with some land forces. Britain could then use her navy and the rest of her army to inflict economic damage on the enemy through attacks on coastlines, colonies and sea-going trade. Properly orchestrated, for example under Stanhope from 1718 to 1719 and Pitt from 1757 to 1760, the combination was devastating. It was, however, a tricky policy to handle and Newcastle in 1756 lacked both the self-confidence to manage such an alliance and the strategic sense to grasp the operational constraints it imposed on British war policy. Having for so long slavishly aimed at reconstructing the highly successful Grand Alliance against France, the 'Old System' he remembered from his youth, the duke had no idea what to do with the Prussian alliance Britain was left with in 1756 after the Diplomatic Revolution (Ch. 17; 90, *54–6*).

After the allies' miserable start to the war in Germany, the Mediterranean, North America and India (above, p. 241), the ministry not surprisingly viewed the forthcoming session of Parliament, due to open in November, with apprehension. On the eve of session, doubtful of his own ability to defend the ministry's conduct of the war, Fox 'thought it prudent to avoid the storm'[11] and resigned. Newcastle tried to persuade Pitt to replace Fox, but met a peremptory refusal to serve in any ministry that included himself. Judging himself to have no honourable alternative, Newcastle resigned too. After making an unsuccessful bid to reconcile Fox and Pitt, the King finally commissioned the duke of Devonshire, a widely respected Old Corps veteran, to form a ministry with Pitt, stifling for a while his fears that the man who had once described Hanover as the 'despicable Electorate' could not, or would not, 'do my German business' (37b, *267, 282*).

In the end the Pitt-Devonshire ministry lasted only five months. From the outset it rested on a very narrow base of reliable support, the Leicester House connexion and the Tories, which makes it surprising that it survived so long. Newcastle dutifully instructed the Old Corps to support the ministry, but their continued attendance at his *levées* indicated where their allegiance lay. Meanwhile Fox was playing on the Old Corps' distaste for ministers launched into office by formed Opposition, in the hope of drawing them over to himself, and the King was looking for the first opportunity to be rid of 'these scoundrels' and appoint someone more congenial. As well, the ministry's initial popularity was compromised by Pitt's abandonment of Byng (above, p. 258), who ended up being shot *pour encourager les autres* in Voltaire's immortal words, and his *volte face* over subsidising Frederick the Great. Although Frederick was destined to become the 'Protestant Hero', lauded and admired in the British press, he was as yet still being widely characterised as a bellicose, grasping German princeling, so Pitt's proposals for lavishing British guineas on him were very unpopular. Moreover, even Pitt's administrative energy and strategic perception could not deliver victories immediately, and further defeats tarnished the ministry's reputation. In April 1757, prompted by the refusal of the Captain-General, Cumberland, to serve in Germany while Pitt remained in office, George II ordered the latter to resign.

During the next two months Pitt, Newcastle, Fox, Leicester House and the Tories wheeled and dealed over who was going to be 'in' and who 'out'. Leicester House insensibly found itself cast as Pitt's stepping-stone into office, only to be abandoned once he had secured the Old Corps' allegiance (a betrayal for which the future George III was never to forgive him). The Tories, too, were increasingly marginalised in what was ultimately a battle for the soul of the Old Corps, but were so transfixed by Pitt's patriotic rhetoric that they did not realise it (37b). They were accordingly instrumental in precipitating the 'rain of gold boxes', conferring on the erstwhile Secretary the freedom of various cities, most notably London. These were in essence part of a wider, and in sheer scale a novel, phenomenon: the support of public opinion, marshalled and expressed through an almost unanimous chorus of press and popular as well as constituency approval of Pitt's ostentatious patriotism; and this remarkable show of support unquestionably boosted Pitt's bargaining power. In a very short time the press turned Pitt into a model, patriot minister, politically martyred for his principles by corrupt rivals. In the eyes of the political nation Pitt suddenly became the epitome of political virtue, a reputation he capitalised on to intimidate and wrongfoot his rivals. The public outcry in support of his readmission to office, expressed in the form of petitions, addresses and press uproar, suggested he would be able to deliver popular support for any ministry that included him, which in the volatile political atmosphere produced by Whig feuding and gloomy news from overseas made his inclusion look increasingly politically attractive, despite his lack of a substantial parliamentary following (40a, *75–84*). The upshot was a grand Old Corps compromise engineered by Newcastle: a Newcastle-Pitt ministry with places for Fox and his friends, and yet another St James's-Leicester House reconciliation. Technically the Tories were still 'out', but *de facto* they supported Pitt, and the press and the political nation were vindicated. As well as having fatally compromised the old party system by dazzling the Tories into supporting him, Pitt had achieved a political first in 1757: in Boswell's well-remembered words, he became the first 'minister given by the people to the King' (40a, *265–8*).

The repercussions of the great war triumphs of 1758–9 which followed were far-reaching in terms of domestic politics, as well as in the winning of an empire. The 'patriot' ideology that had so long inspired and sustained Tory separatism became common political currency. The demise of active Jacobitism and the Tories' overarching admiration for Pitt left little to distinguish them now from the independent Whig country gentlemen who had for long been the backbone of Old Corps support. So that by the time George II died in 1760 and a King who, 'rejoiced in the name of Briton' came to the throne, Bolingbroke's premature lament of 1714: 'the grief of my soul is this, I see plainly that the Tory party is gone'[12], at length became an appropriate obituary, not just for the end of a party, but for the passing of Party itself. In the first phase of the new reign, at least, the old order would play little meaningful part in the way politics was structured and functioned. The way Pitt secured his readmission to office in 1757 also irretrievably altered the working of politics. For the first time 'public opinion', primarily though not exclusively expressed in the pages of the press (Chs. 3, 13), had had a decisive impact on political manoeuvring during a ministerial crisis, as opposed to an important contributory effect, as with the fall of the Whigs in 1710. Pitt was propelled into office by his widespread popularity – something he played to (for a while) and exploited, but was never entirely happy with (40a). Because he subsequently neglected his golden asset, and other politicians did not know how to acquire or exploit it, 'popularity' as a political weapon was destined in the 1760s to fall out of the hands of conventional politicians and into the hands of shrewder, more unscrupulous men such as John Wilkes, whose appeal was as much to the *alternative* political nation of the coffee-houses and clubs (cf. Ch. 3) as to that of the existing political classes or even the electorate. Pitt harnessed public opinion to get himself back into office but essentially had no further use for it. It was never for him a power base. Wilkes was to show how public opinion could make a man's entire career (44, *101–11*). The genie unleashed to restore Pitt to power was destined to become, however spasmodically, a major force in future British politics.

---

1. J.C.D. Clark, ed., *The Memoirs and Speeches of James, 2nd Earl Waldegrave, 1742–1763* (1988), p. 158.
2. P. Monod, 'The Politics of Matrimony: Jacobitism and Marriage in Eighteenth-Century England', in E. Cruickshanks and J. Black, eds, *The Jacobite Challenge* (1988).
3. Henry Pelham to Dudley Ryder, 14 Mar 1747, quoted from the Harrowby MSS. in Sedgwick (12a), I, p. 57.
4. Handel's well-known chorus, 'See, the conqu'ring hero comes!' lauding Cumberland, was actually taken from his oratorio *Joshua* and inserted into revivals of *Judas Maccabeus* (written in Cumberland's honour in 1746) after 1748. We are indebted to Dr H. Pitt of St John's College, Oxford for this information.
5. H. Walpole, *Memoirs of King George II*, ed. J. Brooke, 3 vols (1985), I, p. 242.
6. E.P. Thompson, 'Eighteenth-Century English Society: Class Struggle Without Class?', *Social History*, **III** (1978), pp. 150–64; *Waldegrave Memoirs*, pp. 154–5.
7. P. Luff, 'Henry Fox, the Duke of Cumberland, and Pelhamite Politics 1748–1757', unpublished D.Phil. thesis, Oxford, 1981, pp. 9–12, 18–19.
8. Ibid., pp. 3–4.
9. Horace Walpole, *Memoirs* (ed. Brooke), II, p. 4.
10. Luff, 'Henry Fox', pp. 300–1.

11. Clarke, ed., *Waldegrave Memoirs*, p. 184.
12. J. Macpherson, ed., *Original Papers; Containing the Secret History of Great Britain from the Restoration to the Accession of the House of Hannover*, 2 vols, (1775), II, p. 651.

CHAPTER 19

The political system under stress:
George III and the politicians, 1760–1770

The political stability of the later 1750s depended on two wasting assets: success in a war which the political nation would inevitably grow weary of and the ageing King's unflinching support for the Pitt-Newcastle coalition. George II's death, then, made the onset of a fresh bout of political instability highly likely. The new King's approach to politics and to his grandfather's ministers soon precipitated a crisis, but thereafter this crisis rapidly acquired its own momentum. By 1767 unstable government seemed to have become ingrained (above, pp. 242–5); the normal working of politics appeared to deny any ministry the possibility of surviving for more than a couple of parliamentary sessions. That the situation was regarded with grave concern by most politically-conscious Britons may be seen from the way Edmund Burke's *Thoughts on the Present Discontents*, which sold the then exceptional number of 20–30,000 copies, was received in 1770. The quiet, dull competence of Lord North's ministry after 1770 was correspondingly greeted with heartfelt relief by all except his disgruntled opponents. George III certainly never forgot the political maelstrom he created (but soon repented) in the early years of his reign, and thereafter clung limpet-like to any premier minister who showed the least capacity. The period 1760–67 was thus a formative one for the man destined to become England's longest reigning monarch bar Queen Victoria; furthermore, the conservative reaction it provoked among many of his subjects not only consolidated Lord North's hold on power, but also created the kind of political circumstances in which quarrels with colonial legislatures about minor taxation could become the basis of civil war. The breakdown of the old structure of politics is interesting in its own right; the consequences of that breakdown lift it to an entirely new level of importance.

The root cause of the collapse of the old political order was the removal of the Whig–Tory antagonism that had sustained it for so long. As long as a Tory party existed, the conservative interpretation of 'Revolution principles' dominating the ideology of the Whigs by the 1750s could suffice to define their beliefs and keep them (relatively) united. The Whig oligarchs might not be *for* anything beyond the status quo, but they knew what they were *against* (Ch. 18). Once there was no Tory party to define themselves against there was also nothing to keep the Whigs together, and the party rapidly broke down into its basic components: the Court and Treasury group, the Independents, mostly country gentlemen, and aristocratic factions. The key event, therefore, was the disappearance of the Tory party.

The most influential school of thought on the disappearance of the Tory party has its origins in post–1767 Rockinghamite polemic (most coherently expressed by Burke), and sees the event as more apparent than real. According to this interpretation the Tories did not so much disappear as infiltrate. To further his own nefarious designs George III brought the Tories into office under a new label: the 'King's Friends'. Once in place these willing tools of monarchical ambition earned their keep by slavishly following the King's orders on every issue and advancing the royal prerogative as far and as fast as possible at the expense of English liberties. Britain was thus denied the total victory it might have achieved over France and Spain in the Seven Years' War because the King was able to get away with supplanting the architects of victory, Pitt and Newcastle, by deploying the crypto-Tory King's Friends in support of agents of closet government like the earl of Bute. When 'true patriots' (the Rockinghams) came into conflict with the Crown and the King's Friends during the Stamp Act crisis of 1765–6, they appeared in Burke's scenario as defenders of the balanced Revolution constitution locked in mortal combat with the ancestral enemies of all good Whigs. As for the General Warrants affair and John Wilkes's successive expulsions from the House of Commons (Ch. 22), these simply showed how confident the King and his Tory minions were getting, that they should so let the mask slip. Finally, after 1770, the great propagandist of the Rockingham Whigs portrayed Lord North as a renegade, operating a vast engine of corruption manned by secret Tories, designed to keep the natural rulers of Britain out of office while his master's tyrannous ambitions were alienating America, the jewel in England's empire.

No modern historian would go along with the full Burkeian interpretation of the politics of the 1760s and early 1770s. Conspiracy theories are intrinsically unconvincing and rarely outlive the political heats that give birth to them. More or less modified, however, Burke's analysis convinced most nineteenth-century 'Whig' historians and in many of its essentials (at least as far as the Tory party is concerned) has found favour with some scholars down to the present day. A notable recent example is B.W. Hill, who has attempted to rehabilitate the Rockinghamite charge that the 'King's Friends' (or Court and Treasury connexion) were Tories risen phoenix-like from the ashes of their old party (36). If a historian of Dr Hill's calibre finds there is something more to the charge than desperate attempts by the Rockinghamites to explain away their political failure, it must merit serious examination.

The Tory continuity thesis – that there is an unbroken line of succession from the Tory party of the 1680s to that of Pitt the Younger, Peel and Disraeli – rests on three incontrovertible facts. The first is that as late as the 1750s a Tory party directly descended from the first Tory anti-Exclusionists still existed in British politics. The second is that by the mid-1810s there was again a party in British politics that proudly called itself Tory. The third is that the ideology of early nineteenth-century Toryism contained uncanny echoes of that of its early eighteenth-century namesake. It is thus not unreasonable to suggest that the vigorous name-calling of the politics of the 1760s, which still revolved around the epithets 'Whig' and 'Tory' (44, *39–54*), had some basis to it, and that the King's Friends, if not wholly Tory, nonetheless had a substantial Tory input. The question can only be decided by a close scrutiny of the fate of the old Tory party we last encountered in the 1750s.

The Tories were certainly wooed by George III. His appointment of six clear-cut Tories as Lords or Gentlemen of the Bedchamber in 1760, shortly after he came to the throne, caused a political sensation. Likewise his cordiality towards Tory peers and MPs when they ventured to appear at court was a real break with the unchallenged Whig hegemony of the 1750s. Since, in addition, he showed a willingness to allow former Jacobites to return from exile – even to the extent of inviting die-hards like Laurence Oliphant of Gask to do so in the name of the 'Elector of Hanover' because he knew Oliphant would not accept it from him as King of Great Britain[1] – the consternation of the Whig grandees becomes more explicable. Nevertheless their reaction – 'I see we are to expect a Parliament of 1710', wailed Newcastle – was wholly out of proportion. All George III was doing was manifesting an irenic, anti-party (and therefore eminently respectable) approach to politics and to the duties of kingship. One of his first public statements on coming to the throne was that he 'gloried in the name of Briton', which in terms of contemporary political discourse was a clear signal that he intended to model his conduct on the ideal of the 'Patriot King' created by Bolingbroke (above, p. 8). Patriot Kings were supposed to be kings to all their people, not just to Whigs, and George, nothing if not conscientious, was trying to live up to his principles.

The impact of George III's behaviour on the Tory party was devastating. His ostentatious Englishness appealed to their ingrained anti-Hanoverianism. His sincere Anglican piety, taken so far as to upbraid a sycophantically Erastian court preacher: 'I come here to praise God, and not to hear my own praises', struck just the right note with their devotion to the Church of England (28a, *286–7*). And reports of his political rectitude in refusing to allow Newcastle to use secret service funds in securing the return of government candidates in the election of 1761, sent them into paroxysms of loyalty.[2] What proscription, denunciation and the political wilderness had not been able to achieve in forty-six years, kindness achieved in two. By 1762 the Tory party had completely disintegrated.[3] Individual MPs and peers retained some of their old principles, and the party's well-established social nexus naturally survived for considerably longer (friends and kinsfolk do not change in so short a time), but the *party*, as an organised, coherent political force, was dead. Moreover, it died unmourned even by those who had suffered for it. Hearing of the King's first Tory appointments at court, the author William Mason simply observed: 'I am glad at heart to find this annihilation of Toryism' (28a, *286*). More quietly momentous was the attitude of Sir Roger Newdigate, MP for the Tories' spiritual citadel, Oxford University, who abandoned nearly two generations of Tory resistance to the Whig oligarchy. 'I like the King', he wrote to a friend, 'and shall be with his ministers as long as I think an honest man ought' (39, *216*). As we have seen, the Tory party was moribund by the late 1750s, but it could have staggered on in that state for some time; George III's idealistic irenicism ensured that it died instead.

However, ex-Tory MPs and peers did not inexorably gravitate towards the 'King's Friends' as the party disintegrated. Some did end up in royal or government service, but proportionately fewer than might have been expected from their numbers in Parliament. The final blow against the Tory continuity thesis was struck in 1987. By tracing the individual careers of most of the identifiable Tories, I.R. Christie has convincingly shown there was no Tory 'party' worthy of the name by about 1763, and that its former adherents were scattered to the four winds of politics (50a). This is not to say that the spirit of the old Whig-Tory divide entirely vanished. A nascent ideology of service and loyalism existed in the 1760s that was matured and hardened by the American war, and there was unquestionably an ex-Tory input into that (289, *202–10*).

Over the previous three generations the Tories had evolved a comprehensive ideology centred on conservative Anglicanism and a reverence for the established order. The demise of the party dedicated to translating that ideology into action ironically facilitated its diffusion among the political nation. Partly in reaction to the frenetic rise and fall of ministries in the 1760s, and partly through fear of the social radicalism aroused and epitomised by John Wilkes and his supporters, congenial elements of formerly Tory ideology began to be absorbed into the general discourse of the political establishment in Britain. Once the Tory *party* sting was removed, many conservative Whigs (always the bulk of the party) easily adopted hitherto Tory notions of the relationship between church and state, crown and subject, and so on. Nor should we be surprised at this development. From the mid-1760s to the early 1770s the Whigs' old ideology, based on sedate, cautious Lockeianism, was fundamentally challenged by the radical (and profoundly subversive) interpretation of Locke's political thinking advanced by the American Patriots (268, *118–20, 125, 328*). And as the American version was transparently a truer reflection of Locke's argument (cf. *Making of a Great Power* Chs. 9, 13), the old Whig ideology was thrown into disarray. As with so much else, the American and French Revolutions catalysed the process, and the political establishment steadily progressed from conservative Whiggery through loyalism to what was in effect the new Toryism of Burke and his imitators in the 1790s – all the while appropriating useful ideas from the 'defunct' corpus of Tory political thought. Hence the uncanny echo of the ideals of the party of Seymour, Wyndham and Bolingbroke that can be found in that of the later Burke, Pitt the Younger and Lord Liverpool.

The new constellation of politics precipitated by the disappearance of the Tory party contained three main elements: the 'King's Friends', the Independents and the aristocratic factions. The King's Friends played a pivotal rôle on several occasions in the 1760s, but thereafter dropped out of sight until the early 1780s, when the pattern of politics became unstable once again. The 'independent country gentlemen' were an abiding (and massive) presence in every late eighteenth-century House of Commons. The aristocratic factions or 'personal parties' were the movers and shakers of British politics.

The King's Friends grouping was a symptom of the political instability that dogged the 1760s. Between the sweeping purge of Old Corps officeholders loyal to the disgraced Newcastle in late 1762 (see below pp. 283–4), and the fall of the first Rockingham ministry in 1766, brought down by a Crown-inspired revolt of courtiers and civil servants against the repeal of the Stamp Act (above, p. 244), a fundamental change in political orientation took place among the amorphous mass of Court and Treasury MPs and peers (46a, *163–6*; 10, *279*). For the previous two generations the civil servants, placemen and courtiers who did the humdrum work of national and royal administration, but who, for various reasons, also sat in Parliament, had habitually followed the political lead given by the King's premier minister (Chs. 1, 3). They usually achieved, and certainly only continued in, office through a combination of moderate, Old Corps Whiggism and administrative competence, so it was not usually burdensome for them to support the ministry of the day. After 1762, however, they frequently found themselves in a dilemma. The King manifestly detested some of his premier ministers (Newcastle, Grenville and Rockingham for example); they had clearly been imposed on the King against his wishes. Who had the greater call on the Court and Treasury group's loyalty, the First Lord of the Treasury and his political allies or the King? For the vast majority of Court and Treasury men (as would probably have been found to be the case among the majority of the political nation) there was no contest. They looked to the King for a political lead and he duly provided it. In the peculiar circumstances of 1762–7 this development did give the King some additional political leverage in the making and breaking of ministries, but it was a transient phenomenon. George III did not relish the rôle of political manager, and in 1770 gratefully resigned it to the first minister he at length felt he could trust: Lord North (49, *40–6*). Nonetheless, the Court and Treasury group's brief appearance in a pivotal political rôle allowed the Rockinghams to demonstrate to their own satisfaction the working of a pernicious 'secret influence' system, and the economical reform movement eventually sprang from that perception of the King's rôle (Chs 20, 22).

In late eighteenth-century Britain, however, it was not placemen and courtiers but Independents who almost invariably had the final say on the survival or failure of any ministry. The contemporary term, 'independent country gentlemen', is actually a misnomer. There were a good number of country gentlemen among them who were sufficiently well-to-do to be immune to the charms of government patronage, but most were simply gentlemen and provincial bourgeois of modest means whose commitment to the interests of their friends, neighbours and 'country' (i.e. locality) outweighed the lure of office or gain. Every House of Commons returned from 1763 to 1783 contained up to 300 MPs who could, to varying degrees, be described as 'Independents', and if they chose to exercise their disapproval by voting against, or simply refusing to support, a given ministry, such as Grenville's in 1763–4, then its days were numbered. The politics of the 1760s revolved around this group far more crucially than around the King's Friends. Whichever aristocratic faction was in power, its leaders sought to reassure the Independents that they were diligently upholding Britain's interests overseas, were (relatively) honest and frugal and that the King was content to keep them in office. Any aristocratic faction that was out of office sought to convince the Independents that the world was collapsing about their ears, the ministry was rotten with corruption and that the King yearned to be released from the tyrants who had stormed his closet. The factions' successes and failures could be measured by slight shifts in the voting habits of the Independents. Any hint that they might be losing the support of the Independents could compromise a ministry. Even George Grenville, normally a hard-nosed and unbending politician, was reduced to meekly offering amendments to his Cider excise in 1763 (p. 284 below) at the first sign of serious opposition to the tax from the Independent MPs representing the cider counties.[4] Pitt's political significance throughout the period 1762–66 rested on his reputation with the Independents, who for years had been spellbound by his oratory. Fortunately for the governments of the period, however, they were a heterogenous group, prone to absenteeism, never united in opposition, and with an innate inclination to support the King's chosen ministers that usually overbore what Penruddocke Wyndham characterised in 1784 as the 'restless aversion to all government, so prevalent amongst them, and against which the best minister is no more secure than the worst'.[5]

For most of the time, however, the Independents were effectively a sleeping giant. The hereditary leaders of the political nation were the great Whig magnate families, and the ambitions of a select group of these aristocratic chieftains, their kinsmen, clients and friends became – perhaps for the first time since the 1660s – the elemental driving force in British politics (cf. Chs. 2–3). During the 1760s each of these factions or connexions sought to bludgeon its way into office by any means, fair or foul, and then hang on to power as long as possible. Some, like the marquess of Rockingham's following and the Chathamites, especially after the earl of Shelburne took up Pitt's mantle, claimed to be seeking office out of a principled concern for the good of the nation. Others, like the Temple-Grenville connexion, headed by George Grenville and his brother, and the 'Bloomsbury gang' who supported the duke of Bedford, were more transparently concerned with the sweets of power. The Rockingham Whigs, despite their unpromising origins among the Old Corps Whigs purged in 1762–3, were the only connexion with a future, in the sense of outliving the group's progenitors. Over the twenty years following 1762 they gradually emerged from their factional roots and blossomed into a fully ideological political party (46a, *78–81*; see also Ch. 20). The process, however, was a gradual one, and in the 1760s and early 1770s there was not a great deal to distinguish the Rockinghams from the rest of their peers. Only slightly greater coherence, a modicum of sincerity (owed largely to Rockingham himself) and a greater intellectual depth (stemming from Burke) set them apart from the other factions. By contrast, most of the Rockinghams' rivals proved ephemeral, and were closer in spirit to political bandits than political parties.

The Seven Years' War was Britain's greatest military and strategic triumph during the establishment of its first empire. It was also a grinding, exhausting experience. Both faces of the war set the political agenda for the early years of the new reign. The King was determined, and most politicians agreed, that the war must be brought to a close; but on what terms? Once the war was ended the problems of reconstruction and retrenchment had to be faced; there the key question was, who should pay? Success or failure in the struggle for power between the competing political groups hinged on their capacity to tackle these issues.

However critical one may be of George III's political judgement in the early years of his reign, it is undeniable that he was in empathy with his subjects when he tried to insert the description 'bloody and expensive' into a proclamation on the war issued in October 1760. Israel Maudit's pamphlet of that year, *Considerations on the Present German War*, had elicited an enthusiastic public response, and, more ominously, Newcastle was beginning to find it difficult to float further government loans in the City. Britain had already more than achieved her initial war aims, and even Pitt recognised that peace had to come soon, as he revealed in secret talks with Choiseul (Ch. 17). Between Pitt's dark observation of 1759 that, 'Peace will be as hard to make as war', however, and Bute's and the King's determination to have peace at almost any price, there was an unbridgeable gulf (46a, *31, 35*).

The domestic politics of the years 1760–63 were dominated by the struggle over the making of the peace of Paris. As we know George's first preoccupation was to get his 'dearest friend' and mentor, Bute, into the Cabinet by removing the earl of Holderness from the Northern Secretaryship of State. Since the King wanted Bute 'in' so badly, Newcastle was easily prevailed upon to support the change, in the hope that acquiescence would admit him to his new master's good graces. Pitt was inclined to object to such promotion for a relative tyro, but was not ready in March 1761 to press matters to the point of resignation. The circumstances of his ultimate resignation, following two unsuccessful attempts to persuade the Cabinet to agree to a pre-emptive strike against Spain, we are already familiar with (above, p. 264). Newcastle was initially relieved that the Bedford faction chose to stay in the government despite the fact that it now faced a renewal of the war without Pitt to lead it. He was less pleased when he found the 'Gang', aware that the First Lord of the Treasury had been badly compromised by the need to declare war on Spain in January 1762, throwing in their lot with Bute and Grenville (whom the government had brought in to replace Pitt in the Commons) over the question of cutting Frederick the Great's subsidies. Whatever the ministry's financial circumstances, its treatment of Prussia was an appalling act of betrayal which Frederick never forgave; Newcastle saw it in similar terms and resigned (46a, *32–8*).

The way was now clear for Bute and the King to make whatever peace they chose. Bedford was packed off to Paris to negotiate, a mission he mismanaged out of transparent overeagerness,[6] and Fox was brought into the Cabinet to manage the passage of the eventual treaty through the Commons. The outcome of the ministry's diplomacy, the peace of Paris, was greeted with unenthusiastic relief by the vast majority of the political nation, and downright hostility by the architects of victory, Pitt and Newcastle. The two latter, however, failed to concert measures to oppose the settlement in Parliament; and while Pitt stood aloof and Newcastle wavered, a group of the duke's younger followers lost patience and rashly confronted Bute and Fox head-on. Fox's gentle coaxing of the war-weary Independents and his crude threats against government servants duly paid off: the 'young friends of the Duke of Newcastle' were ignominiously defeated by 319 votes to 65 on whether or not to accept the peace preliminaries, and in consequence Bute and the King were emboldened to take one of the most momentous decisions of George III's reign: the decision to order the 'slaughter of the Pelhamite innocents'. Almost all the parliamentary rebels against the peace preliminaries were officeholders. But although the purge initiated in retaliation hit them specifically, it did not stop there. Lords Lieutenant, Justices of the Peace, local revenue collectors, postmasters – anyone felt to be subject to Pelhamite influence was liable to be dismissed. Such a purge had not been seen in two generations. 'But why should Mr Fox turn out all these unhappy men to starve, who have no demerit of their own?' asked a weeping Newcastle (46a, *55*). For Bute, George III and their agent, Fox, it was a cleansing of the Augean stables; for their now inveterate opponents it laid the foundations of a hostility that could only be slaked by revenge. George and Bute sowed the wind; they were to reap the whirlwind.

With the formal ending of hostilities in March 1763 the government's attention turned to the question of how to deal with Britain's war debts. During the Seven Years' War the National Debt had climbed to £140 million [G.1]. When it is borne in mind that over fifty per cent of the government's peacetime revenue was needed simply to pay the interest on this (then) colossal amount, the horror of contemporary British taxpayers at the size of the debt is easily understood. Eighteenth-century British governments knew only two answers to debt, retrenchment and taxation; given the enormous cost of the war it is understandable that the emphasis of the administrations of the early 1760s should have been on the latter rather than the former. It was an awkward dilemma, nonetheless, for the latter way was bound to precipitate political trouble. The Independents would put up with paying taxes during wartime, but in peacetime they needed a lot of convincing, and every new tax was a gift to the Opposition.

In March 1763 the Chancellor of the Exchequer, George Grenville, introduced an increased, effective cider excise. Within a very few months he found himself beset with petitions, lobbying and the manifest coalescence of a nucleus of opposition amongst the Independents. The premier minister, Bute, was shocked to find himself being burned in effigy throughout the cider counties and, as a Scotsman, attacked with all the xenophobic venom the English press could muster (which was considerable). Mortified and weary, Bute insisted on resigning in April, leaving the horrified King to the tender mercies of the delighted Grenville, Bute's natural successor. Though a gifted administrator, Grenville was a dreary, prolix and insensitive human being. Light reading for him consisted of draft parliamentary legislation, and he developed a special passion for lecturing the King on what he considered to be his duty. 'When he has wearied me for two hours', lamented George, 'he looks at his watch to see if he may not tire me for an hour more' (19, *123*). Yet even such a political rhinoceros as Grenville found himself forced to give way before the Independents' gathering hostility to the cider excise, a hostility duly fostered and encouraged by the Rockinghams and Chathamites. He did not rescind the measure, but did tone it down considerably, and one of the first acts of the incoming Rockingham ministry in July 1765, was to be to try and ingratiate themselves with the Independents by signalling that they intended to repeal the duties.[7]

Meanwhile, opposition to a more momentous fiscal measure also brought in by Grenville had been quietly fermenting out of sight of the mainstream of British politics. The American colonists had been getting angry about the Stamp Act.

This was a minor piece of taxation enacted by the ministry in March 1765 with a view to partially offsetting the cost of garrisoning America, which, at well over the estimated £225,000 a year, was a large sum at a time of general retrenchment (47a). Closer acquaintance with the American colonies during the war had convinced many in the political and fiscal establishment that America was easily prosperous enough to pay *part* of the costs of its own defence. The first manifestation of the new appreciation of American resources came in the Sugar and Quartering Acts of 1764. Although these measures converted laws originally designed only to regulate trade into revenue-raising legislation, they technically only tightened up the enforcement of existing laws, and therefore broke no new ground with regard to Westminster's customary practice of not levying internal taxes on the colonies. This did not stop the new regulations proving extremely irksome for the colonists, who found prices being driven up by the increased costs of coastal shipping, which was now obliged to make long detours to get customs clearance on the most mundane items or risk its cargos being seized by naval patrols (263a, *45–9*). Yet neither Act achieved its intended purpose: the Sugar Act failed to raise much extra revenue and the quartering of troops was still fiercely resisted by colonial legislatures. What the two measures did do, however, was predispose colonial opinion to react badly to the Stamp Act, passed a year after Grenville had first floated the scheme before the Commons (above, pp. 243–4).

It is perfectly clear from its uncontested passage at Westminster that in Britain the Stamp Act was initially regarded as an uncontroversial piece of low-level revenue legislation. It was worth no more than £60,000 a year to the ministry. But in an America already irritated by the effects of the 1764 measures it was seen as the sharp end of a long wedge. The colonial legislatures promptly protested, and their agents in London lobbied, against the enforcement of the Act. They met little more than blank incomprehension laced with annoyance (47a, *93–100*). America's grievances were not a live issue in British politics in 1765. The political nation was far more interested in celebrating George III's recovery from the first attack of the malady (possibly porphyria) that would eventually drive him insane, in speculating whether or not he would achieve his dearest ambition at the time and get rid of the insufferable Grenville, or even in the likelihood of renewed conflict between Britain and France (Ch. 21). In any case, British public opinion was not generally sympathetic to the Americans' pleas to be spared taxation Britain had had to put up with for time out of mind. It was generally felt (with some justice) that the Americans had not pulled their weight in the Seven Years' War, and that therefore it was only fair that they should meet some of the increased cost of their own defence. To the British taxpayer, paying on average 26 shillings a year in taxation; making the Americans pay on average one extra shilling a year did not seem unreasonable. To the Americans, however, such a sum represented, at least, a 100 per cent tax increase.[8] And to cap it all, the government and Parliament (though not the King, who *at this stage* favoured conciliation) appeared deaf to their protests.

In May 1765 the Virginia Assembly passed a series of resolutions condemning the Stamp Act on constitutional grounds. Over the next two months, British politicians were absorbed in the Rockinghams' outmanoeuvring of their rivals in the battle to replace Grenville's ministry, a battle they eventually won in July mainly because of Pitt's continuing refusal to serve at this stage (above, p. 244). But in the meantime news of the Virginia resolutions had been broadcast all over the thirteen colonies and imitated by one legislature after another. Frustration with Westminister's lack of response to what the Americans by this time felt was a major constitutional grievance finally exploded into violence in Boston in August when the Massachusetts Stamp Distributor's home was attacked by a mob. In fear of his life, he resigned his position, and a wave of riotous attacks on Stamp Act officials and their property promptly spread across the northern colonies. Confronted by massive popular hostility whipped up by the vigorous American press and connived at by the colonial élite, the imperial administration in America was helpless to prevent the wave of resignations that followed. 'In my present defenceless states, I consider myself only as a prisoner at large, wholly in the power of the people', lamented Governor Bernard of Massachusetts (47a, *132–6*). Colonial militia refused to act against the rioters and the tiny North American garrison (less than 6,000 strong[9]) was all stationed on the western frontiers and in Canada, far from the trouble-centres. Nonplussed by the suddenness of the uprising, the new Rockingham ministry was slow to recognise that it had a major crisis on its hands – and one that threatened to get completely out of control in October when the Stamp Act Congress met in New York, declared 'taxation without representation' unconstitutional, instituted a boycott of all British goods and made ominous noises about the American people arming to defend their liberties. Only in January 1766, after the ministry had successfully covered its back at Westminister by drawing Pitt into outlining his solution to the crisis and then adopting it, was it able to propose a twin solution to the problem, namely, the repeal of the Stamp Act and the passage of the Declaratory Act.

The Declaratory Act, which uncompromisingly asserted Parliament's right to legislate for the American colonies as it saw fit, was a measure designed to sweeten the unpleasant medicine of a British government's retreat in the face of popular protest. Parliamentary opinion was generally hostile to repealing the Stamp Act in the face of American resistance, and royal opinion by now emphatically so: the Declaratory Act was designed to obscure the fact that the ministry was backing down. It thus became a shibboleth subscribed to by the King and most shades of opinion at Westminster (49, *86–7*). Even the Rockinghams theoretically accepted the need to insist on the absolute sovereignty of Parliament, while believing that Parliament's rights should not be insisted on in practice in this case. Out of Parliament's unquestioning belief in its right to absolute authority over the colonies (which, in truth, only mirrored the beliefs of most of the political nation) came the next stage of the American crisis and in the politics of this troubled decade, the stage destined to put Britain and its American colonies on the highroad to war. It was precipitated by the Townshend duties.

The Townshend duties became an issue after Pitt (or Chatham as he now became) had at last accepted the opportunity to take office again. He had spurned all overtures from the inexperienced and panicky Rockingham, but in July 1766 he did accede to the King's (desperately reluctant) appeal to him to rescue the Crown from the tyranny of faction. The Chatham ministry soon identified as one of its priorities, how to find some acceptable way of taxing America in view of the spiralling cost of maintaining the American garrison, even the estimates for which had climbed to over £570,000 by 1767 (47b, *21–2*). Since the Americans had insisted during the Stamp Act crisis that internal taxation was unconstitutional, the Chancellor of the Exchequer, Charles Townshend, declared his intention to exploit customs tariffs to raise the necessary revenue:

> he did not in the least doubt the right of Parliament to tax the colonies internally, and . . . he knew no difference between internal and external taxes, . . . yet since the Americans were pleased to make that distinction he was willing to indulge them, and chose for that reason to confine himself to regulations of trade, by which a sufficient revenue might be raised in America.[10]

What Townshend failed to comprehend was that the ideological furore accompanying the Stamp Act crisis had silently shifted the parameters of acceptable relations between Westminster and the colonies. Whereas at the beginning of the Stamp Act crisis the Americans had distinguished between internal taxation (the Stamp Act), which was totally unacceptable, and trade regulation (the Sugar Act), which was a grievous burden but legitimate, by the end of the crisis the Americans' complaints had risen to a higher plane. The slogan 'No taxation without representation' pithily summarises the essence of the later position. By 1766 the colonies were questioning Britain's right to legislate for them under any circumstances whatsoever. Hence Townshend's duties would have provoked an angry reaction, even without that minister's further exacerbation of the situation by taking advantage of Chatham's frequent absences from Cabinet in 1767 (due to a long bout of mental illness) to alter the purpose of the tariffs from funding the garrison to funding imperial administration in America (47b, *30, 78*). They thus threatened to emancipate colonial governors and other imperial administrators from the control of the colonial legislatures which up till then had paid their salaries.

Their reception therefore was, predictably, violently hostile. As before, Boston took the lead, instituting a general boycott of British goods, and as other New England towns followed Boston's example, the American press shrilly urged general defiance. Unlike Rockingham in 1765–6, however, the ministry was ready and willing to use coercion, ordering, for example, the occupation of Boston by a force of regular soldiers and a small naval squadron. Surprised by Whitehall's resolution – particularly at a time when the administration was embroiled domestically in the Wilkite troubles (Ch. 22) – American resistance was temporarily cowed. Subsequently, the ministry (by then the duke of Grafton's, following Chatham's angry resignation in October 1768 over patronage disputes with the King) offered as a magnanimous gesture to suspend the tariffs, provided the colonial legislatures explicitly accepted Westminster's right to tax, and legislate for, America. This was a bitter pill for the colonial legislatures to swallow, and while they baulked at doing so the more militant elements among the American Patriots began to step up the trade boycott. 'Force alone will not do', Grenville had been warning since the previous summer (265, *298*), and in order to halt the slide towards further confrontation, Grafton on 1 May 1769 proposed in Cabinet the suspension of all the Townshend tariffs. To his chagrin he was defeated 5:4 by a vote of his colleagues led by Lord Hillsborough, the Secretary of State for America, in favour of suspending all the tariffs except the one that produced a revenue significant enough to be of value in funding the administration of America, the duty on tea (47b, *77–141 passim*).

The ground for the final clash between Britain and its American colonies was thereby laid out. In January 1770 Grafton was frightened into resigning by nationwide petitioning, orchestrated by the Rockinghams, against the ministry's 'persecution' of John Wilkes and by a close shave in Parliament over the Middlesex election case (Ch. 22). Lord North, previously Chancellor of the Exchequer and one of Hillsborough's supporters in the Grafton cabinet, became George III's choice to replace him as head of the ministry; it was the King's pathetically earnest hope that his new premier minister could restore some measure of stability to the conduct of his kingdom's – and empire's – affairs. Neither North nor his new cabinet, nor the King, however, would yield the tea duty – the final token of Britain's right to tax and legislate for the colonies. Conversely, most of the colonists, and especially the vociferous Patriot leadership exemplified by men like Samuel Adams, James Otis, Thomas Jefferson and Benjamin Franklin, would not accept the tax, either in principle or because of what came with it: financially independent imperial administration. Moreover, once the government had raised the stakes by using military coercion it was inevitable that without a conscious and determined move towards conciliation, there would be clashes between civilians and the military; after them, as we can now see, a more serious armed confrontation was bound to follow. Some historians indeed discern the first skirmish of the American Revolution as occurring a mere five weeks into North's ministry, when troops occupying Boston fired on rioters in the 'massacre' of 5 March 1770.

Ironically, however, by the time Parliament rose that May, Lord North (who, as the son of the earl of Guilford sat in the Commons) had already begun to offset the disadvantages of an unprepossessing exterior by his debating skills and by shrewd, tactful management, and George III was sensing that, for a while at least, his decade of troubles with the politicians might be giving way to more tranquil and stable times.

---

1. Sir Charles Petrie, *The Jacobite Movement* (1932), p. 260.
2. P. Woodland, 'Political Atomization and Regional Interests in the 1761 Parliament: The Impact of the Cider Debates, 1763–66', *Parl.Hist.*, **8** (1989), p. 81.
3. For a rather more gradualist view, see L. Colley (28a), pp. 286–9. But cf. I.R. Christie (50a).
4. Woodland, *loc.cit.*, pp. 72–5.
5. Quoted by Namier (43a), p. 6, from Wyndham's introduction to *The Diary of the Late George Bubb Dodington* (Salisbury, 1784).

6. E. Johnson, 'The Bedford Connection. The Fourth Duke of Bedford's Political Influence Between 1732 and 1771', University of Cambridge Ph.D. thesis (1979), pp. 278–9, 281–2.
7. Woodland, *loc.cit.*, pp. 79–81.
8. R.R. Palmer, *The Age of the Democratic Revolution*, 2 vols, (1959), I, p. 155.
9. We are indebted to Professor Robin Fabel of Auburn University for this estimate of the British North American garrison in 1765–6.
10. Quoted in P.D.G. Thomas (47b), p. 24.

CHAPTER 20

Lord North, the influence of the crown and the re-birth of 'party', 1770–1783

I

Between 1770, when Lord North became premier minister, and 1774, when the crisis in America began to move towards civil war, Britain appeared to have re-attained a Pelhamite order of stability (Ch. 18). Only with hindsight is it possible to see that Britain was on the edge of a precipice, about to enter its most anguished period of internal turmoil and external retreat before the experience of war and decolonisation in the years 1939–79. There is much to be said for considering the period from the early morning of 18 April 1775, when 'a shot heard round the world' was fired at Lexington Green, Massachusetts, to dawn on 19 June 1815, when it became clear the Emperor Napoleon's last army was irretrievably dispersed after its defeat at Waterloo, as one of prolonged crisis for the British polity. The British state eventually emerged recharged and trium-phant, but at many points between 1775 and 1813, except during the Younger Pitt's 'years of acclaim' and recovery, 1784–92, it seemed doomed to defeat and fragmentation; the nadir of British fortunes was reached in 1781–3, when world-wide military defeats and economic strangulation finally extorted Britain's recognition of America's independence (94, *516–17*). The key to understanding British domestic politics over the period 1775–83 is, then, to grasp the gathering atmosphere of alarm that suffused them as Britain's rebellious subjects defeated royal armies in America and her old enemies, France and Spain, recaptured cherished prizes from former conflicts.

The roots of the most profound political change about to occur, the rebirth of 'party' in an enduring, ideological form, lay in the 1760s. The American Revolution catalysed and gave direction to a process that was already underway. Of crucial importance was the King's emergence as an independent political force. George III was no longer the naïve, eager young man who had followed Bute's every lead and had been cowed by Grenville's bullying. From 1766, when he destroyed Rockingham's first ministry by refusing to express only his ministers' opinion on controversial legislation, George III became a vital element in British politics, making and breaking governments according to the dictates of his conscience (46a, *165–6*). His unexpectedly successful choice of North in 1770 gave credibility to his rôle and stature. George was not acting unconstitutionally, and far from unprecedentedly. What was novel about the King's rôle was its tone, force and purpose. By 1774 George III was an experienced politician with a strong sense of duty and a shrewd understanding of how to get what he wanted.

The practical effects of this more interventionist rôle for the monarchy are most clearly seen after 1778, when it was increasingly the King who kept Lord

North's ministry united so as to carry on the American war. In the summer of 1779, for example, when North was incapacitated with depression following defeats in America and the entry of Spain into the war, and his colleagues were busy intriguing against each other, George simply observed, 'if others will not be active, I must drive', and briskly summoned the Cabinet himself – the first monarch to do so since Queen Anne. The American war became George's own, as befitted 'the spiritual ancestor of Colonel Blimp' (42, *69*), and he was a hawkish proponent of war to the knife right to the bitter end, an attitude inevitably weakening the position of those in the government who favoured peace with America (49, *129*). The King also had no scruples, after North's fall, about destabilising ministries – in particular the Fox-North coalition – which he considered inimical to Britain's best interests (below, p. 299). The monarchy always played a crucial rôle in eighteenth-century politics, but it was rarely as central and dominant as it was under George III from 1774 to 1783.

A more ephemeral legacy of the 1760s, but one casting a long shadow into the 70s and 80s, was the jealousy, suspicion and bitterness left by the rise and fall of the short-lived governments littering the period 1760–8 (Ch. 19). Each faction had scores to settle, and the two main branches of the Opposition to North's ministry, the Rockingham Whigs and the Chathamites, were estranged. Before Chatham died (1778) only coincidental joint opposition was feasible. In the long term only the prospect of British defeat in America brought the two groups into coalition (46a, *344–5, 351, 415*). Given the enormous majorities Lord North could deploy throughout the 1770s, after as well as before his crushing success in the General Election of 1774, on the first occasion his administration faced the electorate, the Opposition's squabbles may seem more like a symptom than a cause of their impotence. All late eighteenth-century governments, however, ultimately depended on the sceptical, detached support of the Independents to give them a majority in the Commons. A concerted, forcefully presented critique of government policy was the only way an Opposition could shake that vital group's inclination to support the King's ministers (50a; see also Ch. 19). By contrast, a divided Opposition heightened the wisdom of backing the King's chosen servants.

Superficially, the factions opposing North's ministry appear nothing more than disgruntled 'outs' as against Northite 'ins'. All of them, however, affected to believe their opposition was a matter of principle, and indeed showed some altruism in their conduct. But with one exception all revolved around the principles and altruism of one man: the faction's leader. The Chathamites, for example, saw themselves as disinterested patriots, but their political agenda was set solely by Chatham (and after him by Shelburne). The only exception was Rockingham's faction; correspondingly, it was the only one with the potential to move beyond connexion-based factional politics to ideologically-based party politics.

Structurally the Rockingham Whigs remained at base a relatively ordinary political faction throughout the period 1770–83, an amalgam of aristocratic connexions personally attached to the marquess. Each connexion supplied a peer or two and a few MPs, depending on wealth, electoral influence and family ties. In 1774 Rockingham himself wielded decisive influence in eight parliamentary seats, all in Yorkshire. In addition, three other MPs were such close friends that they can be counted as part of Rockingham's personal connexion. Allied to this inner core were Rockingham's aristocratic kinsmen and friends: the duke of Portland (who answered for six members); Lord Frederick Cavendish (five or six); the earl of Albemarle (four); the duke of Richmond (two); and Lord Verney (three). But on top of the thirty-two members supplied by these connexions, the Rockinghams also enjoyed in 1774 the committed support of eleven Independents, drawn to Rockingham himself by his charm and, more important, by general sympathy with his views (46a, *222–5, 317–18*). It is this last group, small in 1774 but destined to become the bulk of the Rockingham Whig party, which distinguishes the Rockinghams from the self-interested cousinages that were the sole basis of factions like the earl of Gower's and which substantiates the Rockinghams' claim to be the true heirs of the early eighteenth-century Whig Junto (43b, *203–15*). For the basis of their attachment was primarily ideological.

Factions worked on the basis of charisma and self-interest. What made the Rockinghams different was their ideology. At the heart of that ideology lay a dynamic idea that entirely recast an otherwise ordinary reworking of Country Whig principles: the myth of 'secret influence'. What was 'secret influence'? Primarily a state of mind; Edmund Burke, a devoted follower of Rockingham, summarised it in 1780 as, 'the power of the crown, almost dead and rotten as prerogative, . . . grown up anew, with much more strength, and far less odium, under the name of Influence'[1], and in addition declared:

> the whole of our grievances are owing to the fatal and overgrown influence of the crown; and that influence itself to our enormous prodigality . . . Formerly the operation of the influence of the crown only touched the higher orders of the state. It has now insinuated itself into every creek and cranny in the kingdom . . . (1, *XX, 1297*).

Bolstering this myth (for material crown influence, in terms of Treasury-controlled seats and places in the administration and Household, was actually declining) were bitter memories of George III's using Bute as his secret adviser, 'the minister behind the curtain', after Bute was forced out of office in 1763. Brooding in the political wilderness after their fall from favour in 1766, the Rockinghams convinced themselves that Bute's rôle and the King's hostility to them were all part of a secret plan to subvert the constitution by keeping Britain's natural rulers out of office in favour of mean tools who would slavishly do the King's will (284, *206–7*). Newcastle's fall, the massacre of the Pelhamite innocents, the undermining of the first Rockingham ministry, the Wilkes affair, and successive ministries' determination to extract money from the American colonies were all evidence of the plot's reality. Like most conspiracy theories, once the initial premise, that a conspiracy existed, was accepted, every twist and turn of politics could be interpreted as bearing it out.

The unavoidable, but unvoiceable, inference of the secret influence myth was that the King was malevolent and the system rotten. How then could patriots like the Rockinghams overturn this vast edifice of insidious, creeping corruption? The answer the Rockinghams evolved was momentous: they would have to come into office as a body with an understood, commonly agreed programme of reforms, a conception little different from the modern theory of political parties. Burke's carefully rational, and significantly secular, definition of 'party' stands as well now as then: 'a body of men united for promoting by their joint endeavours the national interest upon some particular principle in which they are all agreed'.[2] The Rockinghams' solution to their dilemma unquestionably involved a real shift in constitutional theory, but we must not get carried away with the affinity between their conception of 'party' and our own. The Rockinghams' views were not generally acceptable. Even some of the marquess's own supporters, for example Robert Gregory, stalwartly resisted the idea that they themselves were attached to a party at all, insisting that they supported his policies only out of the conviction that they were right (39, *284–5*). Then again, the rôle aristocratic connexions played in supplying the Rockinghams with their parliamentary forces is more redolent of eighteenth-century factional, than of twentieth-century party, politics. Indeed the Rockinghams enjoyed a disproportionate share of the creeping accumulation of Commons' seats controlled by aristocratic patrons in Hanoverian Britain (203a). Furthermore, they had a very patronising attitude towards the masses. They came from wholly élite backgrounds and were as indifferent to popular support and disliked mobs as much as any of their peers.

None of these reservations detract, however, from the change in the political system which the emergence of the Rockingham Whig party represented. Richmond's observation to Rockingham after some chastening experiences in 1771, that, 'reduced as we are, we are still the most numerous corps in either House of Parliament and in the nation, indeed we [are] the *only* party now left', is redolent with the pride and sense of corporate purpose that sustained the Rockinghams for so long.[3] This was manifested not only in their impressive average attendance of 80 per cent in all recorded divisions between 1775 and 1780, and in the establishment of a distinct, separate social milieu, based on Brooks's Club, but also in their willingness, on occasion, to dirty their hands with populist politics. The Rockinghams did not shrink from putting out party propaganda aimed at the mass of the political nation. By 1780 three newspapers were directly or indirectly supporting the party, at least one of which, the *Annual Register*, was run by the Rockinghams themselves (46b). In 1780 they worked hard at a local level to elicit county petitions in support of their economical reform programme (see below, p. 298).

The repercussions of the Rockinghams' increasingly hard, doctrinaire approach to all politics are nowhere better demonstrated than by the circumstances of their second departure from office, in July 1782. When the King refused to appoint as First Lord of the Treasury (and hence premier minister) the duke of Portland, who had been accepted as party leader on Rockingham's death, Charles James Fox simply responded by leading a mass resignation of Rockingham Whigs from the ministry. In so doing, Fox was going against all the prevailing constitutional conventions. Nonetheless, within four months he is estimated to have marshalled 90 of his 100 former party colleagues in opposition to the ministry formed by Shelburne (above, p. 250). Bearing in mind that however charismatic Fox may have been, the King plainly detested him, that he had virtually no electoral influence, that those who so promptly returned to the wilderness with him had to relinquish the sweets of office after sixteen years' abstinence, and that by following Fox they were going against accepted practice and the King's express wishes, this was an impressive demonstration of the power of the leaders of the Rockingham Whig party to command the loyalty of its adherents (51, *20–30*). Clearly, as a result of the Rockinghams' travails 'party' as a legitimate, constitutional, non-religious institution was emerging by 1782–3. Equally plainly, given the disapproval their solidarity excited, it still had a long way to go before it was generally acceptable.

For an eighteenth-century political party to be really effective the political nation had to be polarised, as in 1710 or 1715 (*Making of a Great Power*, Ch. 21). By 1774 the North administration, after four years of calm control, on the domestic front at least, was still acceptable, even agreeable to most of the political nation. In order to shake the government's domination of the consensus the Rockinghams needed deeply-felt issues affecting the political nation. Three major issues provided the Rockinghams with the chance to display their wares in the next nine years. The most important was the American Revolution. Of not much less importance was the sudden surge of Irish national self-assertion in the late 1770s (Ch. 16). Finally, the dissatisfaction engendered by Britain's defeats in the American war helped to make the economical reform movement and its thrusting offshoot, the parliamentary reform movement, matters of serious political contention at last.

II

When America became a major issue in British politics in the 1760s, and especially after the colonists forced the withdrawal of the Stamp Act by economic boycotts and riots (Ch. 19), a basic conflict of interests had developed over the extent of imperial authority and colonial autonomy. There was a widespread conviction in Britain that the Americans had not pulled their weight during the Seven Years' War and had been looking to evade their financial responsibilities ever since. The colonists' objection to taxation by Westminster, summarised in the slogan 'No taxation without representation!', was threefold. They resented paying for something they would not control; they feared that even the modest level of taxation proposed would prove the thin end of the wedge; and colonies like Connecticut, New York and (significantly) Massachusetts, which had contributed generously to the war-effort, resented being lumped in with those who had shirked their responsibilities (263a). Each side saw the other as economically exploitative. As the passing of the Declaratory Act by the Rockinghams in 1766 had shown (above, p. 286), even British politicians in general sympathy with the colonists' objections upheld Westminster's constitutional right to tax the colonies. And it was essentially around this same assertion of the principle of imperial authority that the final clash developed from 1773, when Massachusetts Patriots responded to the government's grant of a monopoly of supplying tea to the colonies to the overstocked East India Company by dumping several shiploads of it into Boston harbour. In the first three years of North's ministry colonial resistance, while smouldering generally and occasionally flaring up locally, had at one point (1771) died down low enough to encourage the prime minister to announce: 'the American disputes are settled, and there is nothing to interrupt the peace and prosperity of the nation'. The Boston Tea Party put a decisive end to any such delusions. 'In three short hours on a cold December night . . . a small band of men precipitated a reaction that led with little pause to the Declaration of Independence'.[4]

'In all revolutionary situations', Esmond Wright has written, 'there comes a climax where the pieces form a discernible pattern, where the events . . . suddenly acquire their own momentum. In America, it was provided by the Boston Tea Party and the British decision at this point to be firm . . .' (266, 69). How to deal with colonial waywardness has always been the classic dilemma of imperial government: use force and alienate local opinion, or let miscreants defy imperial authority, thereby undermining it. From 1765 to 1770 insistence on principle but concessions in practice had been the order of the day in Whitehall and Westminster. But confronted with what was seen on nearly all sides as the grotesque outrage of December 1773, North, with overwhelming support at Court (where George III was totally unyielding), in Cabinet and in Parliament, chose 'resolution' (49, *75–6, 80*). Accordingly, the government's response to the Boston tea-party was the 1774 Boston Port Act, closing the harbour until recompense was made, and the Massachusetts Government Act, revoking the colony's charter prior to redrafting it to increase the Governor's power. Such a draconian response, from the American point of view, required retaliation, and British goods were boycotted throughout the colonies. Both sides were now locked into a cycle of action and over-reaction, and a grim ratchet effect started operating as each side's response became more drastic than the action reacted against. From the time a Continental Congress assembled in Philadelphia in autumn 1774 to protest at the treatment Massachusetts was receiving and to coordinate relief for Boston and further resistance, a revolutionary spirit was unmistakably abroad, and on neither side of the Atlantic was there much chance of success for the two eleventh-hour attempts at conciliation – by Chatham (January 1775) and by North himself, shocked at the last by the prevailing bellicosity, in February. That winter Patriot militia began mustering and drilling throughout Massachusetts, and in April 1775 General Gage, the British army commander in Boston, decided to cow them by seizing one of their arms depots, at Concord. On the way there Gage's troops had an exchange of fire with the Lexington militia, and the American Revolutionary war had begun (Ch. 21).

Because the American Revolution was basically a civil war, in which, in the way of these things, initial grievances were quickly overshadowed by the bitterness of atrocity and counter-atrocity, the British soon saw themselves as fighting to suppress anarchy and free the substantial loyalist American population from Patriot oppression; conversely, the American Patriots saw themselves as defending the rights of freeborn Englishmen against brutal military tyranny (Ch. 21). In such circumstances, and in the knowledge that most of the British political nation, and probably the nation at large, supported the government's efforts to re-establish British rule in America, the Rockinghams (who, through Burke, had made their own passionate appeal for conciliation in 1775) seemed to be caught between a rock and a hard place. On what grounds could they oppose the American war? As Rose Fuller put it: 'It is not an error of the ministry, it is an error of the nation. I see it wherever I go' (cited in 49, *77*).

'This country will pay dear for its folly', predicted Rockingham in July 1776, 'but nothing but experience will or can have any effect'.[5] The Opposition to North's ministry was in a quandary. Chathamites and Rockinghams were both horrified at the idea of making war on fellow Englishmen, but neither wanted to see the empire disintegrate and both knew public opinion was overwhelmingly against them. Their visceral rejection of the idea of fighting the colonists meant the only alternative to North's policies they could offer was wholesale concession of the Patriots' demands (46a). This would have yielded *de facto* legislative independence, and was totally unacceptable to the mass of the political nation between 1774 and 1777. Only after July 1776, when the second Continental Congress declared America independent, did the Rockinghams begin to develop a coherent alternative to the government's policies. Even then, it took from July 1776 to early 1778 for them to agree on a new approach, and that only in the aftermath of the British defeat at Saratoga. During 1776–7 all they could do was half-heartedly criticise the conduct of the war and stage a feeble secession from Parliament. The concession of full independence was strong meat for any British political group to digest at this stage. However, it did have the advantage of being a more serious alternative to North's war policy than the Chathamites' unrealistic clinging to the notion that if the Americans were given everything else they would concede their formal independence.

From 1778 to 1781 the Rockinghams pressed their alternative policy with mounting success, as denoted by a creeping erosion of the government's majority. In February 1778 Fox's motion against the despatch of further forces to America secured 165 votes, a big advance on anything achieved in the previous session. In March 1779 a motion censuring conduct of the naval war was defeated by only 34 votes. A year later, when Burke moved the abolition of the third (American) Secretaryship of State, the ministry's majority fell to seven. This so rattled the government that it called a snap election that summer which caught the Opposition unprepared and allowed the government, boosted by successes in the southern colonies, (above, p. 249), partially to rebuild its majority (49). In spite of their indifferent performance in the 1780 General Election, however, [E.1] the Rockinghams remained undaunted, and in May 1781 cut the majority for continuing the war at all to 34 in a thin house. News of the surrender at Yorktown arrived just before the 1781–2 session opened. North's reaction, 'Oh God! It is all over!', came true as full realisation of the finality of the defeat dawned on both Houses (49, *111*). Lord Conway's motion in February 1782 for an end to all attempts to subdue the Americans by force was defeated by one vote in a House of 387. On 15 March the ministry only scraped through a vote of no-confidence and five days later, on the eve of another no-confidence motion, the King finally allowed North to resign with the petulant observation, 'Remember, my Lord, that it is you who desert me, not I you' (46a, *443–4*; 49, *132*).

The secret of the Rockinghams' success between 1778 and 1782 was their ability, as a determined and coherent party, to act as the nucleus of the larger, amorphous opposition. Silently, but inexorably, Independents and disillusioned courtiers drifted over to the Rockingham-led Opposition – the only alternative to carrying on the war indefinitely; of the two the change in allegiance of the Independents was the more important. The fall of Lord North and the forcing of the King's closet that accompanied it was a triumphant vindication of the Rockinghams' resolution and willingness to accept distasteful truths, for all that it was the Chathamite leader, Shelburne, capitalising on the animus between King and Rockinghams, who made best use of the victory.

III

Ireland's recrudescence as an issue in British politics in these same years 1778–82 has been overshadowed in the history books by more dramatic transatlantic events, whereas at the time the Protestant Irish nationalism confronting Westminster's control of Irish affairs seemed to be the forerunner of a calamity every bit as catastrophic as the loss of America. Ominous parallels were drawn on both sides of the Irish Sea between the Irish Volunteer movement, whose arming and drilling also went hand in hand with political petitioning, and the American Patriot militia movement of 1774–5. Ireland's immediate importance was that it allowed the Opposition to attack the ministry on a new front. Speaker after speaker in the Commons in 1779 warned the ministry not to lose Ireland as it had lost America. The ministry responded by granting hitherto unthinkable economic concessions.[6] Yet these only succeeded in slowing, not stopping, the emergence of Irish demands for legislative independence. As early as March 1780 eighteen counties in Ireland sent addresses to the Irish Parliament calling for the repeal of Poyning's law, and the Volunteers began to hold conventions to debate 'Patriotic' issues (see Ch. 16).

For the Rockingham Whigs events in Ireland offered a golden opportunity to roll back the tide of secret influence, as well as evidence at close hand of the havoc the court's 'conspiracy' against the liberties of the people was wreaking on the empire. Their response to events in Ireland also betokens their growing political maturity: it was distinctly less self-interested than their opposition to the proposed Irish absentee landlord tax of 1773, whose only demerit was that it would have hit Rockingham himself in the pocket. By 1779 they were actively supporting the Volunteers and Grattan's patriot party in the Dublin Parliament in their struggle against the ministry. They oversaw the presentation of Wicklow's petition to the King asking for the redress of Ireland's grievances.[7] Appropriately, in 1782 it was the Rockinghamite Lord-Lieutenant of Ireland, Portland, who boldly advocated granting the kingdom virtually complete legislative independence. The Rockinghams gained in votes, of course, by highlighting the ministry's loss of control in Ireland between 1779 and 1782. Nonetheless, they behaved in accord with their principles even when these did not work to their advantage. In power the Rockinghams still went ahead with legislative independence, even though it was bound to involve a substantial diminution of ministerial patronage.

In 1780 the sense of crisis occasioned by the ruinous course of the war in America and the threatened loss of Ireland, and gathering dissatisfaction with the political system that supported the government responsible for these disasters, led to widespread demands first for 'economical', and then for parliamentary, reform. They were part of a backlash affecting both the political nation [A] and the nation at large. Both issues were in many ways ideally suited to an opposition programme, and the former was tailor-made for winning over substantial Independent support. It must be stressed, however, that in terms of the *popular* discontent they generated they were dwarfed by the most terrible domestic event of 1780, the Gordon riots (Ch. 12). The immediate cause of these disorders, the worst in British history, which wracked London for seven days in June, was the presentation by Lord George Gordon of a massive petition against the Catholic Relief Act, brought in by the Rockinghamite Sir George Saville in 1778 (above, p. 248 and Ch. 22). So desperate was the situation at the height of the riots that the ruling élites were frightened into an uncommon degree of solidarity; even the arch-populist John Wilkes shouldered a musket in defence of the Bank of England, and fired on the mob attacking it. In due course main force carried the day, but it is salutary to remember that compared with the massive popular support Gordon's Protestant Association enjoyed, appealing to an atavistic fear of Popery that was more than two centuries old (*Making of a Great Power*, Ch. 8), both the economical reform and parliamentary reform movements were veritable pygmies (289, *339*).

The economical reform movement first began in the 1760s as part of the Rockinghams' campaign against secret influence. The idea was to reduce the Crown's influence in Parliament by abolishing the sinecures and petty offices that were a vital part of government patronage. Theoretically such an initiative had a good old-fashioned 'Country' ring to it which the Independents would find appealing. Yet the issue never caught fire in Parliament until the late 1770s. Dissatisfaction with the American war and unease about Ireland then ensured that Burke's 1780 economical reform bill had a more favourable reception than any previous initiatives of this kind; so much so, that the government decided it would be prudent to destroy the bill piecemeal in committee rather than oppose it wholesale. North and his lieutenants carried this off, to the disgust of many Independents, only for the Opposition to score a resounding moral victory at the end, by passing the Chathamite John Dunning's motion, 'that the influence of the crown has increased, is increasing and ought to be diminished' (49, *123–5*). On this declaration Burke was to capitalise in 1782 when seeing his third, successful, economical reform bill through Parliament, along with two other pieces of anti-influence legislation first sponsored by Rockingham Whigs in 1780, and now revived to good effect – those associated with Sir Philip J. Clerke and John Crewe [F (iv), (v)]; (46a, *457–9, 28ff*; above, pp. 248–50).

The 'Association' movement for parliamentary reform that suddenly blossomed in the wake of the Rockinghams' economical reform initiative in 1780, was a more significant departure in British politics. Though its origins and leadership, exemplified by Christopher Wyvill, the wealthy parson who founded the Yorkshire Association, and by the duke of Richmond, the wealthy, borough-mongering Rockinghamite, were totally respectable, the schemes of some of the later Associations (for example, the Westminister Association) and of Richmond, for equal distribution of constituencies and universal manhood suffrage, were extremely radical. If carried through they would have overturned the existing constitutional and social order in eighteenth-century Britain. Consequently, Rockingham and most of his followers found the focus of their attack (rotten boroughs and magnate influence) pernicious and abhorrent; although in the early 1780s individual Rockinghams, including Charles Fox, took up parliamentary reform (along with some Chathamites like William Pitt the Younger), the movement was hampered by considerable friction, and without full-scale Rockinghamite support the reformers' petitions and attempts at legislation got nowhere (Ch. 22).

The triple blow of the loss of America, retreat in Ireland, and the country-wide unease manifested in the reform movements, each exploited skilfully by the Rockinghams, finally brought down Lord North's administration in March 1782. The King was forced to admit the Rockinghams to power as a party, in the knowledge that they came in – unlike any previous ministry since, perhaps, Harley's in the autumn of 1710 – with a defined programme. For the Rockinghams America, Ireland and the parliamentary reform movement were clear-cut vindications of their theory of secret influence. The traditional, necessary fiction of the good King and the evil ministers was dead; the Rockinghams hated George III and he responded in kind. And therein lay their downfall, for though the King had to take them in in March 1782, he was soon working to separate them from their allies (above, p. 250). Rockingham's death in July 1782 precipitated a struggle between Fox and the King over whether Portland, Rockingham's immediate political heir, or Shelburne, the Chathamite leader who was the King's choice, should replace him. George III won the first round, appointing Shelburne – who brought in the young William Pitt as his Chancellor of the Exchequer – and forcing Fox's resignation, only to be beaten in the second when the formation of the astonishing new Fox-North coalition obliged Shelburne to resign in February 1783 (51). Before the final round went to the King in the autumn of 1783, there was a horrendous interlude in British politics when the King at one stage drafted an abdication speech, and talk of an impending republic was not unknown: when, in fact, the strains placed upon the eighteenth-century constitution by the relations between George III and the politicians seemed at last to have become intolerable. It began with a period (4 February–2 April) when there was in effect no government at all in England, as the King twisted this way and that to evade admitting to office the detested alliance between Fox and North, and Portland, their 'front man'. Having failed, he thereafter made no secret of his loathing for the ministers who had hijacked his administration; near the end of the year he destroyed them by flagrantly undermining Fox's India Bill in the House of Lords (above, p. 250).

When George III in this desperate crisis turned to Pitt the Younger as his next First Lord of the Treasury in December 1783, the new ministry was not expected by the *cognoscenti* to survive even as long as its immediate predecessors; indeed, thinking it would scarcely survive the Christmas recess, the betting men nick-named Pitt's 'the mince-pie administration'. The King, however, totally committed himself to his chosen minister. While Pitt stubbornly refused to resign despite several votes of no-confidence and almost total legislative obstruction by the Opposition, George's naked hostility to Fox and his refusal to accept Commons' addresses calling for Pitt's dismissal wore down their majority in Parliament (51, *160–83*). The April 1784 election, which saw the slaughter of 'Fox's martyrs', and supporters of Pitt and the King returned with a majority of over 100, was a triumphant vindication of George's determination and his tactics. Thus, while the American war and its attendant crises crystallised the re-emergence of 'party' as a major force in British politics, patronage, political tradition and, not least, royal authority, could still be successfully mobilised to stop it in its tracks.

———————————

1. E. Burke, *Thoughts on the Causes of the Present Discontents* (1770), in B.W. Hill, ed., *Edmund Burke on Government, Politics and Society* (1975), p. 82.
2. Burke, *Thoughts . . .*, in Hill, ed., p. 113.
3. M. Bloy, 'Rockingham and Yorkshire: the Political, Economic and Social Role of Charles Watson-Wentworth, the Second Marquis of Rockingham', unpublished University of Sheffield Ph.D thesis, 1986, pp. 271, 274–5. We are grateful to the author for permission to quote from this thesis.
4. B.J. Labaree, *The Boston Tea Party* (1964), p. 256.
5. M. Bloy, p. 39.
6. For example allowing Irish merchants to trade on equal terms with British throughout the empire and sweeping away British anti-Irish protectionist laws.
7. Bloy, p. 375.

CHAPTER 21

The isolation of a great power and the loss of America, 1763–1783*

The American Revolution is one of the most important events in modern history. To name only a few of its most obvious repercussions, it destroyed by far the greater, and most treasured, part of the first British Empire, bankrupted the *ancien régime* in France and led to the formation of a nation-state with the potential – subsequently realised – to become a global superpower. Naturally the origins of an event of such massive significance, laden as they are with implications for modern American national self-esteem, have attracted considerable attention from professional historians. To some extent their debate on the origins of the Revolution has reflected the needs of national mythistories.[1] British contributions, for instance, have often tended to emphasise the reasonableness of Britain's demands on the colonists, and the rectitude of Britain's constitutional stance (e.g. 45a, *202–3*; 45b, *Chs. 1, 2*). By contrast those by Americans have tended, as often as not, to highlight the iniquities of British rule, implicitly justifying the Patriots' rebellion (263b, *192–3*). National biases and subordinate debates apart, however, the historiography of the American Revolution reveals two major and more-or-less consistent preoccupations: one with the question of whether the points at issue between Britain and her colonies were primarily economic or primarily constitutional; and the other, with whether the Revolution was inevitable or avoidable.

Before these questions are briefly reviewed, however, three most necessary caveats must be entered against the hazard of over-facile generalisation about the actions and reactions of *both* sides during the years of mounting crisis from 1763 to 1775. In the first place, though it may be unavoidable occasionally to refer in umbrella terms to 'America', 'the reaction of the American colonists', and so forth, the historian must try to envisage at all times thirteen colonies, all of them with distinctive features and some of them differing vastly from each other. We must be aware that even within the northern colonies and within the southern 'plantation' colonies there were important differences, for example in their civil constitutions, in religion and in their economies and social structures, but that the differences were most striking of all *between* North and South. These complex variations and divisions, which have been expertly dissected by Merrill Jensen (265, *Ch. 1*; see also 266, *3–21*), had prompted a visiting clergyman, Andrew Burnaby, in 1760 to predict that the colonies would be incapable of unification, and as late as 1818 one of the most prominent of the revolutionaries, John

* I am much indebted to Dr Robin Fabel of Auburn University, for kindly reading an early draft of this chapter, and for invaluable advice and insights on the military side of the war, especially. He is not, of course, to be held responsible for what follows. D.S.

Adams, could still look back and marvel that 'in so short a time and by such simple means . . . thirteen clocks were made to strike together' (264, *18*; 265, *33*). The second caveat arises naturally from the first. During the years when disenchantment with the Mother Country and unrest were growing, the thirteen colonies did not all share the same grievances all the time; nor were they or Americans as a whole – even towards the end – equally enthusiastic for confrontation. Indeed the term 'the American Revolution', universal though its usage is, must not obscure the fact that what took place across the North Atlantic between 1775 and 1782 was not only a 'War of Independence' but a civil war as well; and this war situation, compounded of loyalists as well as 'rebels' (though the latter far outnumbered the former) mirrors a comparable one throughout the years leading up to the hostilities. After all, it is hardly conceivable that Parliament or George III would have been prepared to press disagreement with the colonists to the point of open conflict had there been clear evidence that the Americans were absolutely unanimous in their determination to resist it.

The third concealed variable that lurks behind so many of our generalisations on this subject concerns 'British policy' towards the American colonies. With the crucial exceptions of the first and last stages of all, 1764–5 and 1774–5, the policies adopted to deal with the American problem almost invariably met with significant internal opposition: they provoked dissent in Parliament, and among politically-conscious elements outside Parliament, and on occasion they split the government of the day itself. The most notable example of the latter occurred in May 1769. When the Grafton ministry agreed to retain just one duty, that on tea, out of the bitterly unpopular Townshend duties of 1767, it was only by a single vote in the Cabinet, 5 to 4, that this momentous decision was taken. It has often been pointed out – and remains incontestable – that virtually every British politician of any stature was agreed on one thing about the colonial problem, namely, that the Westminster Parliament did have certain sovereign constitutional rights over all the colonies of the Crown, and that *in principle* these did include the right to impose *some* taxation on the overseas territories. But there agreement ended.

That constitutional issues, as such, were of supreme importance in gradually creating a revolutionary climate in North America between 1765 and 1775 is a proposition from which few modern historians of the period would seriously dissent. And yet the contrary notion, that the breach between Britain and her colonies was caused primarily by the economic oppression of the colonists by the mother country, had a long innings, down to the 1950s.[2] It is undoubtedly true that the colonies had been playing an increasingly vital part in the British economy for some decades before the 1770s (Ch. 10), and few contemporary politicians would have challenged the commonly held (but with hindsight, erroneous) belief that Britain would sink to the status of a second-class power without her colonies' markets and resources. Nonetheless, the importance of the colonial sector for the British economy does not mean that the Americans were necessarily subject to severe economic oppression to maintain British economic dominance. We now know that the loopholes in the working of the Navigation laws (*Making of a Great Power*, Ch. 3) were enormous. Dickerson (260) and

Harper[3] have argued that on balance the colonies (and Britain) benefited more than they suffered from the old colonial system, in practice. Since their work was published more recent studies have convincingly shown that at the very most 'the net cost to the colonies was very small' (135, *95–7*). Grenville's unforgivable sin in contemporary American eyes was thus not his institution of new trade restrictions, but that he tried to make the old system work with tolerable efficiency. Even so, nothing he or his successors ever did made much impact on the prodigious quantity of goods smuggled into America. Moreover, it is significant that whereas the colonial agitation of the mid-1760s was initiated by merchants and other traders, that at the end of the decade and subsequently was dominated by other groups, notably lawyers and frontier farmers. Few merchants, even in New England, had any stomach for the non-importation agreements which American popular leaders and agitators pressed on them after 1767, and after 1770 mercantile interests were nearly always prominent among the most moderate and conciliatory opposition groups (265, *354–470*).

Following Lawrence Gipson's magisterial contribution to the debate in the mid–1950s (267), it is non-economic issues which are now generally seen to lie at the heart of the breach between Britain and her colonies. Gipson posited that the British government, having acquired vast new territories in North America in the years 1759–63, was bound to try and devise some general system to administer and defend them in the context of an international situation which remained potentially dangerous (see below, pp. 305–8 and 264, *275*); that its huge war-debts [G.1] made obtaining some form of colonial contribution to the costs of this system imperative; and that attempts to implement such a system and extract a contribution from the colonists occurred just at the point when (after the British conquest of Canada) the Americans felt not at all threatened, and, indeed, inclined to demand the redress of some of their own grievances. Hence Patriot opposition from the Stamp Act to the Revolution was resolutely, and genuinely, constitutional.

What was at stake, in other words, was a conflict of rights. To most British governments, and the majority of the political nation, colonial rights were derivative, as were the colonies. To most Americans (Patriots and later loyalists alike) they were inherent in the colonists' status as free-born Englishmen. Legally and constitutionally, the Patriot slogan 'No taxation without representation!' had no legitimate basis whatsoever: it ignored, for example, the explicit provision for parliamentary taxation in the charter of Pennsylvania; above all it ignored the fact that hundreds of thousands of metropolitan Englishmen were not directly represented in Parliament, but that all were legally required to pay their taxes. Emotionally and practically, however, the Patriots' argument was stronger. Through administrative accretion and the steady evolution of their vigorous colonial legislatures into miniature Parliaments, the Americans had acquired considerable *de facto* control over their own affairs during the course of the eighteenth century; and, whatever the legal rights and wrongs of the matter, a society of some 2.5 million people, enjoying a large measure of religious and press freedom as well as legislative independence, was not going to give up this control simply because Westminster found their newly acquired privileges fiscally inconvenient. (It is worth noting in this connection that the gaining of privileges through custom and accretion has always been the basis of the British constitution.) Moreover, it was starkly apparent that – barring military coercion – metropolitan Britain could not impose its will on the colonists.

Military coercion, as we know (Ch. 19), was the nettle that the Grafton ministry finally grasped, setting America and Britain on the road to civil war. The question remains, however: how far was it inevitable that such a step would be taken, or that the march of events subsequently would prove uncheckable and irreversible? This is a most vexed question, and there has been a long-running debate on the subject and on the associated problem it obviously raises – namely, if the Revolution was not inevitable, who was responsible for it? In a distinguished study in 1975 the Anglo-American team of Ian Christie and B.W. Labaree make skilful and detailed play with the 'if onlys' of the situation which developed after 1764. 'At almost every turn [they argue, with particular reference to 'the chance that brought one man and then another to the place of power in Whitehall'] events might have proceeded differently . . . ', and their unequivocal conclusion is that 'the events of 1775 and 1776 were not inevitable' (264, *277–8*). Many scholars, before and since, have by and large concurred in this conclusion: Esmond Wright, for instance, after castigating a succession of 'vacillating and contradictory' policies pursued by one British ministry after another, wrote of 'a revolution . . . due primarily not to "causes" but to the failure of a government to govern'. (266, *102, 103*). George III has in recent times been held responsible for the continuance of hostilities rather than for their outbreak (Ch. 20). As well as Grafton and the hard-line Secretary for the Colonies, Lord Hillsborough [D.2, 6], Grenville, Townshend and North have all been blamed (and by others exculpated) for the breakdown of relations.[4] Some British historians have singled out the particularly unfortunate circumstances which rendered the pro-American element in the Whig opposition, especially the Rockinghams and Chatham and Shelburne, so ineffectual during the years 1767–74, while in an individualistic thesis Knollenberg has located the main acts of folly of the British much earlier, between 1759 and the Pontiac rising of 1763–4 (above, pp. 243–4), arguing that already after them reconciliation was all but impossible.[5]

It is arguable, nevertheless, that no product of what may be broadly termed the 'accident' school of thought on the origins of the American Revolution has convincingly refuted Tom Paine's simple argument, voiced in his massively influential pamphlet *Common Sense*: 'the distance at which the almighty hath placed England and America, is a strong and natural proof, that the authority of the one, over the other, was never the design of Heaven'.[6] Eighteenth-century communications were not sensitive enough to allow Britain's political institutions to remain in realistic touch with American public opinion, or swift enough to enable them to rule a continent over 3,000 miles away from the metropolitan area if the colonists refused to co-operate. Despite this, the conviction of the majority of the British political nation that they had an inalienable right to dictate what was best for America remained almost unshakeable down to 1775; together with the insistence of successive British ministries – in their fitful and inconsistent way – on exerting that right, it meant that a clash of arms was probably bound to occur sooner or later. Why Britain lost the war she blundered into between 1768 and 1775 is another matter, to which we will now turn.

II

When push finally came to shove in America, Britain found herself woefully ill-prepared. The most convincing counter to the patriotic school of American history, which sees in British policy blunders of the 1760s and 1770s a deep-seated conspiracy to deprive the colonists of their liberty,[7] is Britain's striking inability to do anything about the colonists' rebellion until nearly a year after it started. Within two months of the outbreak of hostilities the only substantial British force in the thirteen colonies was bottled up in Boston, under siege from a combined force of New England militia and George Washington's fledgeling Continental Army. And there it languished until March 1776, while the Patriots busily constructed an *ad hoc* government, trained a regular army, purged and intimidated loyalists and mobilised America's resources for war (268, *275, 301–4*). Not only Britain but the American loyalists paid dearly for the free year vouchsafed by British unpreparedness. It allowed the Patriots to secure their hold on the colonies, promote their regime to that of the *status quo* in the minds of the ignorant or indifferent (always the majority in any civil conflict), and prepare themselves for a full-scale war. Even so, few in Britain or Europe expected the Patriots to defeat what only twelve years earlier had seemed to be an all-conquering military power. How could the Patriots win?

Britain's defeat in the American war stemmed from two closely related problems. One was her diplomatic isolation. The other was the army and navy's inability after 1778 to cope with the strategic difficulties posed by fighting a war across the Atlantic, defending Britain's own shores and trade, and repulsing French and Spanish attacks on British colonies in the East and West Indies. Since diplomatic isolation was a crucial major contributor to military ineffectiveness, we must enquire in the first place why and how it came about.

The American Revolutionary war was the first Britain fought alone in well over a century. For 110 years, except for the brief interlude of 1739–40, before the Anglo-Spanish War merged with the War of the Austrian Succession, Britain always had one or more Continental powers as allies. These performed a vital strategic function. Britain's wars were almost all fought against France and her allies. Britain's Continental partners thus served admirably as either a grand strategic distraction that kept France busy in Europe (as in the Seven Years' war), or as the mainstay of conglomerate armies that could confront the French head-on (as in the War of Spanish Succession). Whichever function her allies were fulfilling, Britain could not hope to win without them, and this George III, his ministers and his generals found out to their cost between 1775 and 1783. The reason was straightforward: unlike France, Britain did not have the human resources to field both a large army and a large navy without dislocating her economy. It was therefore essential for her to have at least one ally who could supply the bulk of the necessary manpower to fight the French on land. Yet, despite the government's best endeavours, Britain went through the entire war without finding a single substantial ally. Indeed, if anything, Britain's isolation was more profound in 1783 than it had been in 1775. The origins of this catastrophe lay ironically in her most decisive victory of the eighteenth century.

Britain ended the Seven Years' War as she had ended the War of Spanish Succession and the War of the Austrian Succession, by selling her allies. Once again British politicians, for perfectly sound domestic political and economic reasons, ended up making a separate peace; although they tried to secure some concessions for the allies they were abandoning, their primary concern was, as in 1711–12 and 1748, to ensure that their own country secured the best terms possible. To Britain's outraged, deserted allies, however, the preferential terms secured by these actions looked like nothing so much as the wages of treachery. The long-term effect of such *realpolitik* was that by 1763 Britain was running out of allies prepared to risk fighting a war alongside her. The Hapsburgs' rapprochement with France in 1756 set the pattern for Imperial foreign policy into the 1790s (83, *137–40*). Frederick the Great decided after 1763 that Russia would be both a more reliable and a more useful ally than Britain. The Dutch Republic by the 1760s could no longer be considered a worthwhile ally. Russia was friendly enough, but had few common interests with Britain and was therefore not interested in making the kind of commitment the British wanted. Sweden was now a third-rate power, and though it recovered some freedom of action after Gustavus III's *coup d'état* of 1772, it was never again an ally worth alienating Russia for (83, *259–61*).

As for the two Bourbon powers, France and Spain, contemporary perceptions on all sides cast them as Britain's inveterate enemies as far as the future was foreseeable after 1763. Although ironically Britain's influence in Europe was probably at its eighteenth-century height in the period of the Franco-British alliance in the late 1710s and 20s, such a daring Stanhopian realignment was inconceivable in the 1760s and 70s. After over a generation of Anglo-French conflict, culminating in the Seven Years' War, it is doubtful if George III's subjects would have tolerated any ministry which sought to align itself with France. As one Secretary of State succinctly put it, if Britain allied with France, the Commons would 'demand the head of the Chancellor who sealed it, and the minister who had signed it' (82, *162*). Nor was the will for reconciliation any more evident on the part of France. After the defeats suffered by French arms (particularly in the later stages of the war), France had done well to excape from the Paris negotiations as lightly as she did (Ch. 17). In retrospect, though, Pitt the Elder's determination to impose an even harsher peace on France might have been better policy. For the fact that the terms of the final settlement were relatively mild made no difference to the revanchist bent of French foreign policy after 1763. Choiseul geared his whole approach to European affairs towards preparing the ground for what he saw as the inevitable French war of revenge. His sucessor, D'Aiguillon, did float the idea of improving Anglo-French relations between 1770 and 1772, only for North's ministry to reject his proposals. One of its motives for doing so was a tendency to play down the French threat at this stage. George III and his ministers were well aware that the French *ancien régime* was in dire financial straits, and ultimately trusted that these would restrain France from launching the war of revenge so ardently desired by many Frenchmen (82). In the event, despite Catherine the Great's anglophilia, the alliance with Russia which North had hoped for failed to materialise after D'Aiguillon's fall in 1774, and the appointment of his subtle, intelligent successor, the Comte de Vergennes, represented the reassertion of the revanchist tendency.

Spain too had scores to settle with Britain. At the Peace of Paris her humiliations in the Seven Years' War were compounded by the loss of Florida and Britain's extortion of extensive trade concessions in Europe and America [H(xii)]. Moreover, Spanish sensibilities continued to be affronted by Britain's retention of Gibraltar and Minorca. On several occasions earlier in the eighteenth century, mostly in the 1720s, British governments had offered to return the two bases annexed at Utrecht, only to break off negotiations when they had evaluated the likely domestic repercussions of such concessions. By the 1770s the anglophobic Charles III and his ministers had reached the conclusion that only force could resolve that particular grievance (82, *298–9*).

The course of Anglo-Bourbon relations down to 1778 reinforced the hostility that already existed in 1763. Choiseul did not dare risk renewed war while France's navy and army were still being rebuilt. He was not averse, however, to probing how determined were the British ministries he was dealing with to hang on to Britain's colonial gains. In May 1764 a French admiral accordingly evicted some British settlers from the Turks islands in the West Indies, and at about the same time French merchants backed up by French soldiers resumed their encroachments on British trade in West Africa. The Grenville ministry's response was belligerent, and Choiseul smoothly backed down (9, *51–2*). On the next occasion he risked war, over the sudden French seizure of Corsica in 1768, the Grafton ministry decided it had too many other problems (Chs. 19, 22) to get involved in hostilities over an island in which Britain had no strategic interest (90, *120–2*); and this emboldened France's foreign minister to foment a full-scale war crisis in 1770 over the Falkland islands. An uninhabited part of Spain's American empire to which Britain had long laid claim, the Falklands were first occupied by a small British force in 1764. In 1770 the Spanish Governor of Buenos Aires despatched an armed expedition which evicted the British settlers. Choiseul enthusiastically backed the Spanish cause in the affair with a view to setting off the war he was now prepared for. As conflict loomed, however, Louis XV intervened. Choiseul was dismissed, and the ageing, cynical king coolly informed his cousin in Madrid that 'my minister would have war, but I will not'.[8] D'Aiguillon's abortive attempts at an Anglo-French rapprochement followed, so that the next occasion for an Anglo-French confrontation came with the outbreak of the American Revolution.

Louis XVI was initially inclined to stand aloof from the American war. His reasons were clear: he disapproved of supporting rebels, and he did not believe the Americans could long resist the full might of Britain exerted against them (83, *64*). Vergennes saw things differently, and by May 1776, by resorting to blatant trickery, he had brought Louis XVI round to allowing secret supplies of French war material to be delivered to the American rebels. When the finance minister, Turgot, objected, Vergennes forced his resignation. The Americans used their French arms (acquired at knockdown prices) (93, *57–62*) well, and as the prospects of an American victory increased, the Vergennes party began to urge direct French involvement. After General Burgoyne's surrender at Saratoga in 1777 King Louis reluctantly accepted their advice. Next Vergennes manoeuvred Spain into demanding the cession of Gibraltar and Minorca as the price of continued Spanish neutrality. When this was refused in 1779 Spain too declared war.

Meanwhile the British had been engaged in a desperate search for allies of their own. The Prussian government returned a frigid response to Britain's overtures, so that after 1776 Britain's efforts focused solely on Russia (93, *71*). Chimerical schemes of utilising Russia's fabled hordes against the American rebels indeed became something of an obsession with the British military and political establishment as the hugeness of the task of reconquering America began to be fully realised. Subsidies, Minorca and a joint war against Turkey were offered as bait, but all hopes were rudely shattered in 1780, when the Russian government announced the formation of a League of Armed Neutrality. High-handed British search and seizure procedures against neutral shipping had by then produced considerable resentment amongst the neutral powers, and the Russian government calculated that it stood to gain more by acting as the protector of smaller countries such as Sweden, Denmark and the Dutch Republic than by allying with the British, who were too transparently eager to fight the Americans to the last drop of Russian blood. By declaring war on the United Provinces before they could join, Britain kept them out of the League and, in due course, captured the Dutch island of St Eustatius as a bargaining counter. Nonetheless, the League effectively broke Britain's attempts to strangle America economically by rigorous naval blockade. When the war with America ended the country was diplomatically more isolated than at any time since the 1680s, and that isolation, compounded by her military defeats, made the peace negotiated at Versailles in 1783 far more unfavourable than it otherwise might have been (90, *65–6*).

III

The course and outcome of the American war was controlled by four factors: geography/topography, the use of militia by the Patriots; considerations of grand strategy; and the rôle of the American loyalists. Each factor imposed certain constraints and enforced particular directions on the way the war was fought by both sides. The eventual outcome was determined by the competition between the two opposing sides as to who could operate most effectively within the constraints and in the direction these factors laid down.

The overtowering geographical reality of the American war was the sheer distance between Britain and America, a factor vividly illuminated in the work of Piers Mackesy (94). It took at least three months, and often as much as six, to get a body of troops and supplies together in Britain and convoy it across the

Atlantic. Moreover, large merchant and transport ships only dared make the Atlantic crossing at certain times of year. It was possible to sail across in winter, but the proportion of ships and men lost in passage increased dramatically, and given that Britain could ill-afford to waste men and *matériel*, winter crossings were generally avoided. Consequently, reinforcements tended to sail for America each spring and arrive in late June or July. The troops convoyed over then needed to recuperate and exercise until they were fit to fight. The upshot was that the British could not usually commence campaigning until August. In north-eastern America, where the most important campaigns were fought, winter sets in about November, by which time the troops had to be established in winter quarters in fortresses and settlements. On average, this gave the British about three months reinforced campaigning a year – a considerable handicap given the size of the task facing them. In addition, the topography of America was calculated to hamper any attempt at swift reconquest. By European standards even the most densely settled parts of America were heavily wooded and criss-crossed with nigh-unfordable rivers. This restricted the movement of substantial bodies of troops and supplies to predictable routes and paths. Correspondingly, guerrilla fighters were provided with excellent opportunities to ply their trade. Ambushes and blockages became commonplace and virtually ineradicable groups of partisans infested woodland and mountain fastnesses in the heart of British-controlled territory. To take only one example of the impact this had on the course of the war, in July 1777 as General Burgoyne's force advanced southward from Canada into upper New York, destroyed bridges and paths blocked by felled trees and boulders combined to slow his army to a snail's pace. It took the British over three weeks to cover less than twenty-five miles. Moreover, every time Burgoyne sent out a scouting or raiding force it was ambushed (268, *376–7*).

The opportunities for irregular warfare inherent in America's terrain were perfectly pitched to maximise a further clear advantage of the Patriots: the number of militia they could mobilise. As Sir Frederick Haldimand observed in 1781, while explaining why an attack from Canada into New England was not feasible,

> It is not the number of troops Mr Washington can spare from his army that is to be apprehended, it is the multitude of militia and men in arms ready to turn out at an hour's notice at the shew of a single regiment of Continental troops that will oppose this attempt (94, *404*).

In many ways the Patriots won the war because of the vast numbers of militia they could deploy. Of the estimated 200,000 Americans who saw service in the war the great bulk served in the militia (268, *547*). Quite apart from giving the Patriots numerical superiority throughout, it also made the Patriot presence ubiquitous and their armies resilient. By contemporary standards militia units were poor soldiers in conventional battles. But when it came to beating up isolated outposts or ambushing detachments or coercing pockets of loyalism or simply occupying settlements and strong points so as to deny them to the British, they were invaluable. The upshot was that the British found they could only hold what they physically occupied, and there were not enough of them to reconquer

America that way. Two examples will illustrate these points. The British force sent to Lexington in 1775 had no trouble dispersing the Lexington militia in a conventional fire-fight. In getting back from Lexington to Concord, however, every copse, bridge and bend in the road had to be fought for, and by the end of the day sniping and ambushes had cost the 800-strong British force 273 casualties as compared with Patriot losses of 95. Six years later, at the battle of Guilford Court House, 1,900 veteran British regulars attacked a 4,500 strong mixed force of militia and Continentals. The militia stayed only long enough to fire two volleys at the British, then ran away, leaving the Continentals to be routed after a hard fight. The final cost was about 500 casualties on each side. Two weeks later, however, the American force was in action again, in South Carolina, militia drafts having brought it back up to a strength of 4,500. Conversely, Cornwallis's British force, unable to replace its casualties, was forced to retreat to the coast (268, *270–3*; 94, *406–7*).

The major strategic problem associated with operations in America was the distances involved, not just between Britain and America, but also within the American theatre of war. To compound the problem, because the Patriots were fighting along interior lines of communication, they could shift their forces to meet British offensives with much greater ease than the British could coordinate their own attacks. The hapless Burgoyne offensive of 1777 (above, pp. 247–8) well illustrates the advantage this gave the Patriots. Whereas Burgoyne was never able to coordinate his advance from Canada with Sir Henry Clinton's offensive out of New York, the Patriots were able to use their superior communications and intelligence to block Clinton's advance with a small force while simultaneously reinforcing Gates and Arnold, who were facing Burgoyne, with every militiaman they could raise in New England. Overwhelmingly outnumbered, Burgoyne was defeated, surrounded and forced to surrender at Saratoga (94).

The basic strategic difficulties associated with British operations in America were massively exacerbated by France's entry into the war in 1778 and the dissipation of her war-effort this forced on Britain. Suddenly troop convoys to America needed substantial protection, naval forces had to be found to defend Britain from invasion, the West Indies had to be defended and reinforcements sent to India to defend British interests there. Spain's entry into the war in 1779 transformed an acute dilemma into a strategic nightmare. Minorca and Gibraltar now required reinforcements and heavily armed supply convoys, and West Florida came under attack (94, *Ch. 21*). It was all too much; even Britain's powerful economy was not up to keeping all these theatres of war going at once. British forces in all theatres of the war were condemned to operate on a shoestring, making a disastrous defeat in one of them increasingly likely. It was perhaps fortunate for Britain that the government fell after the surrender at Yorktown, and that the King was unable to cobble together a ministry willing to carry on the war. Yorktown was probably the least bad of the potential military catastrophes that might have brought the war to an end.

A commonly-held belief among the British political and military establishment for much of the war was that ultimate victory largely depended on how effectively the American loyalists could be mobilised and supported. 'I never had an idea of subduing the Americans', recalled General James Robertson, 'I meant only to assist the good Americans to subdue the bad' (94, *88*). The problem with this assumption was that it ignored two salient facts. One was that the hiatus of over a year following the outbreak of hostilities allowed the Patriots thoroughly to intimidate the loyalists. Sometimes the passage of British troops close by would encourage a few to declare their allegiance, but they were then almost invariably left to shift for themselves shortly afterwards. They then faced the unenviable choice of either fleeing or serving as an object lesson in the penalties of loyalism when Patriot forces moved back in again. The second salient fact ignored by the ministry and its generals was the loyalists' paucity and diffusion: they were a minority scattered over all thirteen colonies. An estimated 19 per cent of the white American population supported the King's cause directly or indirectly between 1775 and 1782, but even where they were not a mere sprinkling of individuals, they were visible minorities. Loyalist groups such as Episcopalians in Massachusetts, Dutch-speakers in Pennsylvania, and Highland Scots in the Carolinas were easily identifiable and hence vulnerable to Patriot coercion (268, *550–1*). The upshot of these two factors was that the loyalists were never able to justify the influence they exerted on British military planning. Howe's *chevauchée* through New Jersey to Philadelphia in 1777–8, the southern campaigns of 1779–80 and Cornwallis's fateful advance into Virginia in 1781 were all launched in the firm conviction that there were considerable numbers of secret loyalists hidden among the general population just waiting for the opportunity to rise. Instead all they collected were loyalist refugees. In effect this total misunderstanding of the limitations of American loyalism meant that for most of the war British strategy in America was based on a mirage.

The course of the war in America fell into two distinct stages. During the years 1775–8, the British attempted to beard the Patriots in their lair: the north-eastern colonies. The second stage, which hinged on a sustained attempt to reconquer the southern colonies, was precipitated by the failure of this strategy and the entry of France into the war. Only the war in the thirteen colonies can be briefly traced here (for a more detailed chronology, see also pp. 347–50 above), but it should not be forgotten that the conflict raged world-wide after 1780. To list only the main theatres of war: British land and sea forces were locked in combat with the French in India, the West Indies, North America and Africa; with the Spanish in the Balearics, Gibraltar, the West Indies, Central America and the Floridas; and with the Dutch in Ceylon, the East Indies, the West Indies and the North Sea. Having also to patrol the waters between four continents as well as the seas round the British Isles themselves, the Royal Navy was stretched near to breaking point.

In the aftermath of Lexington, Gage and his army found themselves ultimately besieged in Boston by hordes of enthusiastic Patriot militia. The only other field engagement of any note before 1776 occurred at Bunker Hill, where General Howe, commanding a sortie out of Boston, stormed a redoubt held by Massachusetts militia. The 'victory', however, cost him nearly 1,000 casualties in a force numbering barely 2,000, and since the total British forces in Boston only amounted to 5,000 men, that spelled the end of any British attempt either to raise the siege or to prevent the Patriots seizing power across all thirteen colonies.

In 1776 Colonel Washington, having forced Howe to pull out of Boston to establish a more viable base at Halifax, Nova Scotia, foolishly decided to put his novice army to the test of battle without further preparation. At Brooklyn Heights on Long Island (August) his 'Continental' army was ignominiously defeated, but because Howe prematurely had his eye set on reconciliation rather than total victory, there was virtually no pursuit (94, *80–8*). Chastened, but unsubdued, Washington retrieved his shattered army, while Howe took New York and then halted. By the time he sallied forth once more (October), Washington had learnt his lesson: henceforth, he ordered, 'We should on all occasions avoid a general action, or put anything to the risk, unless compelled by a necessity into which we ought never to be drawn' (94,*91*). Although in the short term this meant abandoning New Jersey to Howe, in the hands of an intelligent, energetic commander like Washington it was to prove a war-winning strategy; indeed, its possibilities were soon demonstrated by an opportunist Christmas raid against Howe's covering force (after the main British army had retired to winter quarters), which defeated them at Princeton and Trenton and swept the British back to the New Jersey coastline. By contrast, on the British side it was not until the winter of 1776–7 that a coordinated strategy was belatedly hammered out in London. Convinced that New England was the power-house of the Patriot cause, the ministry directed that a two-pronged offensive be launched along the Hudson river so as to cut New England off from the (supposedly) more amenable Middle Colonies. The Canadian-based northern prong was commanded by General John Burgoyne, the southern, New York-based, by Sir Henry Clinton. The fate of this plan has already been adumbrated. A small force of Continentals, supported by large numbers of New England militia, stopped Burgoyne in his tracks, and Clinton did not have sufficient strength to break through to rescue him. And although in a supplementary British offensive Howe fought and won the battle of Brandywine and subsequently captured Philadelphia (above, pp. 247–8), this could not save Burgoyne's army from its traumatic surrender at Saratoga (October) nor rob the Patriot cause of the decisive boost which that spectacular triumph imparted to it.

In March 1778 France declared war. The ministry promptly ordered Clinton, Howe's successor, to abandon Philadelphia and send 8,000 men to the West Indies to ward off the expected French onslaught. It was the death-knell of any remaining hopes the British and loyalists might have had of defeating the Patriots in their north-eastern heartland. Not until December 1778 did a new British strategy materialise: Lieutenant-Colonel Archibald Campbell and 3,000 men landed in Georgia, routed the Patriot forces there and soon subdued the entire colony – auspiciously inaugurating a new southern offensive. The logic behind this offensive lay in the expectation that, while Clinton – by feints, raids and the occasional battle – could hope, at least, to pin Washington's main army down, the southern colonies, reputed hotbeds of loyalism, could be picked off by the small forces Clinton could spare. In early 1779 the strategy looked as if it might work, as Campbell and Prevost fought their way northwards from Georgia into

South Carolina (94, *267–8*). Then in June Spain declared war on Britain. East and West Florida now needed reinforcement against Spanish attacks out of Louisiana; troop withdrawals and summer heat soon forced Campbell and Prevost's offensive back; and by the autumn Savannah in Georgia was under siege from D'Estaing's French West Indies squadron (above, p. 248).

It became clear that if anything further was to be achieved substantial reinforcements would be needed. Clinton invested all his resources in the operation: risking the winter storms, which caused some havoc to his expedition, he committed the entire British field army in America, led by himself. By April he was laying siege to Charleston. It soon surrendered, and with it the entire force of Continentals in the colony; but Washington was by this time stirring out of winter quarters, so Clinton returned to New York, leaving Lord Cornwallis and 4,000 men to finish off the reconquest of South Carolina (94, *340–2*). Cornwallis hoped this would be a swift process, but in fact he was forced to spend the rest of the year in a debilitating *petit guerre* of atrocity, reprisal, raid and counter-raid necessary to shut down guerilla operations in the colony (above, p. 249).

Early in 1781 Cornwallis was reinforced and strategic priority given to his plan to strike north and attack Virginia while Clinton kept Washington occupied in Pennsylvania or Maryland. However, Patriot militia and partisan forces' attacks on British outposts and supply lines, skilfully supported by regular detachments under the able command of one of Washington's subordinates, Nathanael Greene, harried Cornwallis unmercifully; the latter's attempt to retrieve the defeat of one of his colonels at Cowpens led only to the costly battle of Guilford Court House (March), which left him with barely 1,500 battle-worthy troops. With such a depleted army, the odds against subduing Virginia were now heavy, but unwisely Cornwallis pressed on northwards. He could hope to achieve little without support from Clinton, but Clinton, now reduced to a mere 10,000 men to provide reinforcements for the West Indies, did not dare sally forth to take the pressure off him, lest both French and American regulars and the eager hordes of New England militia should descend upon him. When, therefore, Washington and Rochambeau force-marched their troops into Virginia and, linking up with De Grasse and his French West Indian naval squadron, cornered Cornwallis and his men at Yorktown, the last British offensive in North America had come to the end of the line (see above, p. 249). On 17 October 1781 Cornwallis surrendered.

In retrospect the war in the thirteen colonies was probably unwinnable from 1778 onwards, which makes the Yorktown fiasco look like a foregone conclusion. That was not the way it was seen at the time. It took a shock like Cornwallis's surrender to make Parliament accept the unpalatable truth that Britain had lost the war. Technically, there was no real reason for it to have ended even then. There were still over 30,000 British and loyalist troops holding major ports along the coast from Halifax to St Augustine. The reinforced West Indies fleet under Rodney was still capable of inflicting a crushing defeat on D'Estaing at the battle of the Saints (April 1782). The surrender at Yorktown ended the war only because it precipitated a failure of British morale at home, and with it the collapse of North's ministry. That let the Rockinghams in, and they came determined to have peace as soon as possible (Ch. 20).

---

1. W.H. McNeill, 'Mythistory, or Truth, Myth and Historians', *American Hist. Rev.*, **91** (1986).
2. See H.H. Bellot, *American History and American Historians* (1952), pp. 86–7.
3. L.A. Harper, *The English Navigation Laws* (1964).
4. For example J.L. Bullion, *A Great and Necessary Measure* (1982), p. 207; C.P. Foster, *Charles Townshend* (1978), pp. xiii–xiv; A.P. Valentine, *Lord North* (1967), pp. 311–21.
5. B. Knollenberg, *Origin of the American Revolution, 1759–1766* (New York, 1960).
6. T. Paine, *Common Sense* (ed. I. Kramnick, 1987), p. 87.
7. For an example of which, see F. Jennings, *Empire of Fortune* (New York, 1988).
8. M.C. Morison, 'The Duc de Choiseul and the Invasion of England, 1768–1770', *TRHS* 3rd ser., **4** (1910), quoted in (82), pp. 159–60.

CHAPTER 22

Wilkes, 'Liberty' and the stirrings of reform, 1762–1785[1]

Until the late 1760s the idea of Reform, in the sense of a radical overhaul of Britain's social and political institutions, was confined to a handful of intellectuals, mostly obscure figures whose influence, John Cannon has remarked, 'went little beyond persuad[ing] each other' (56, *45*). Various institutions of state, such as the administration of the Customs, and some penal legislation, such as that affecting religious dissenters, were rationalised or otherwise amended between 1689 and the 1760s, but there was no movement towards a general or systematic modernisation of the organs and practices of government – nor, indeed, any widespread conception that such changes might even be necessary (cf. *Making of a Great Power*, Chs. 16–17; Ch. 7). The nineteenth- and twentieth-century concept of 'modernisation', from which stems our assumption that efficiency is more important than antiquity, would have been alien to most eighteenth-century Englishmen and women.[2] Innovation was, by and large, something they distrusted; hence the need for reformers well into the nineteenth century to cloak their ideas in appeals to a mythical past (which many of them may actually have believed in). The emergence, then, of the first signs of a distinct, coherent 'reforming' ideology within a small section of the political nation was a profoundly important watershed in British history. Nevertheless, we must be very careful not to get it out of context. The overwhelming majority of the political nation, and probably the nation at large, were indifferent or hostile to grand schemes of reform; they were sure that tinkering with the existing system would adequately deal with any pressing problems. Hence the significance of the Parliamentary reform movement that first arose in the 1760s, with which much of this chapter will be concerned, lies not in its achievements, which were of little consequence, but simply in its emergence. For all its puny origins it contained the seeds of future greatness and of ultimately epic change.

Political and social conservatism was commonplace, if not axiomatic, throughout the political nation during the half-century before 1768. Its most important locus, however, lay in the mind of the governing élite. The mentality of Britain's aristocratic, Whig rulers was increasingly moulded by two inter-related attitudes which together pushed the leadership of that originally radical party into an entrenched suspicion of reform. One was the gathering complacency of the withering ideology that passed for Whiggery (and dominated government) from the 1720s onwards. The other was the sense of being under siege from its mortal Jacobite-Tory enemy. Given that the Whigs who ruled Britain for nearly fifty years after 1714 necessarily saw themselves as the 'honest' party, critics within or without that party who rocked the boat over the odd bit of corruption or inefficiency came to seem either petty or destructive.

315

By 1760 'Revolution principles' had ossified into a totemic shibboleth. They had become a set of ideas deferred to rather than applied by those politicians who called themselves Whigs. Along with the divine right of freehold property, also derived from the Revolution of 1688, 'Revolution principles' provided the parameters of Whig politics but, except in the matter of full toleration for Protestant dissenters (and even that issue was anaesthetised for half a century before 1788), they very rarely affected their conduct. Since the Whig oligarchy interpreted the events of 1688 as the golden gateway leading to the apogee of human achievement and happiness, subsequently achieved under their benign tutelage, this attitude is hardly surprising (284). For Britain's ruling élite it was inconceivable that there could be anything intrinsically wrong with a state run on Revolution principles; if anything was going awry men, not measures, were to blame. Hence the insistence of even the most ideologically motivated Whig groups, such as the Rockinghams, that there was very little wrong with Britain's government, apart from the woodworm of sinecurists and pensioners, that a thorough change of ministry could not solve (284, *207*).

That the Whig leadership of 1714–60 developed something of a siege mentality is attributable to two salient facts of political life in the period 1714–60. One was that there was an underground Jacobite network working to overthrow the Whig regime. It may have been inefficient, riddled with spies and have posed no real danger, but the Whig leadership was never so foolish as to assume that it could *never* be a threat, particularly after their experiences in the Jacobite rebellions of 1715 and 1745. At the very least the Jacobites represented a potential fifth column that might rise in support of a foreign invasion (Ch. 6). The second aspect was that the Tories commanded a great deal of popular support. The dwindling band of Tory MPs increasingly represented popular constituencies, and the old saw that, 'the majority of the gentry upon a poll will be found Torys', manifestly became applicable to the electorate as a whole between 1714 and 1760. In terms of votes cast the Tories won every election from 1722 to 1741, and the basic message – that their party was unpopular and retained a majority only by exploiting the quirks of the existing constitution – did not fail to impress itself on leading Whigs (28a, *122*). In consequence, for the Whigs to have embraced constitutional reform, involving a wider franchise, would have been tantamount to political suicide. Only the removal of the Tory party could make reform an issue good establishment Whigs could contemplate.

Two developments made possible the emergence of reform as a political rather than an academic issue in the 1760s. One was the demise of the Tory party, which finally broke up in the first years of George III's reign (Ch. 18). The second was the reawakening among certain sections of the Whigs of a fear of creeping royal absolutism. Paranoia on the subject of the tide of 'secret influence' did not automatically lead Whigs to embrace reform – as the case of the marquess of Rockingham conspicuously demonstrated – but it did dispose them to be more sympathetic to the notion. And it was mainly among the ranks of those Whigs who were convinced of the pernicious, stealthy advance of 'secret influence' that the first wave of reformers appeared. Inside Parliament the growing alignment of Rockingham's political heirs, the duke of Richmond and Charles James Fox, with reform, and especially Parliamentary reform, well illustrates the trend. Outside Parliament the formation of reformist organisations like the Society of Supporters of the Bill of Rights, the Yorkshire Association (1779) and the Society for Constitutional Information (1780) suggests that concern was not limited to professional politicians. The SSBR, for instance, was formed in 1769, not to celebrate the Glorious Revolution in convivial fashion, as might have been the case twenty years earlier, but with a view to defending the existing constitution against royal encroachment and raising money to support a popular political martyr: John Wilkes.

At no time in the period 1760–85 was there any coherent reform movement. Rather there were a set of issues that waxed and waned, with which shifting groups of MPs and peers (and sections of the political nation) aligned themselves from time to time. At the chronological and organisational intersections of all these different reform initiatives a handful of individuals gradually emerged who could usually be counted on to support a 'radical' measure. By 1784 the presence of MPs like Sir Joseph Mawbey, Nathaniel Polhill and Frederick Bull generally denoted the radical side in any debate. Yet even their multiple-issue radicalism never fully crystallised into an ideology. When, in 1779, the Rockinghamite Sir George Savile proposed that penal laws directed against Roman Catholics be abolished, two of his most vociferous opponents were Polhill and Bull (39, *296–7*). Radicalism between 1760 and 1785 was primarily a populist approach to politics rather than an inter-related set of ideas. Consequently, a 'reform' platform only haltingly emerged. In the 1760s the rise, fall and rise again of 'that Devil Wilkes' set a prodigious number of constitutional hares running. In the 1770s and early 1780s public reaction to two of them matured into the parliamentary and economical reform movements – thereby giving firmer shape than at any time since 1660 to a distinct 'radical' position.

A syndrome not uncommon with the apostles of late seventeenth- and early eighteenth-century Whiggery was one which progressed from early Puritanism to substantial licence. So it was with John Wilkes. He was a strikingly ugly man, steeped in conventional piety in a strict religious household, then sent off to a dissenting academy to complete his education. Two years at Leyden suitably 'finished' Wilkes, and by the late 1740s he had already married well and was acquiring something of a reputation as a rake and socialite in London. Despite his repellent features he was a brilliant conversationalist (12b, *III, 639*) – 'it takes me only half an hour to talk away my face', he once boasted – and this proved his *entreé* to the highest circles of dissipation in London. At some time in the late 1740s he was inducted into the notorious Hell Fire Club by one of his choicer friends, Sir Francis Dashwood, while another, Thomas Potter, rakehell son of the archbishop of Canterbury, introduced him to the Grenvilles and Pitt. Wilkes became a devoted admirer of Pitt, and, via the Grenville connexion, was first put up for Parliament in 1754 at Berwick with the intention of following his star (48, *17–19*). Given his subsequent reputation as a populist and political innovator, it is ironic that his campaign at Berwick was marked by some very hackneyed eighteenth-century 'dirty tricks', as well as by one ingenious stroke whereby he bribed the captain of a ship bringing up a body of out-voters from London to land them in Norway. Wilkes still lost, but Lord Temple obviously thought he had sufficiently shown his mettle, because he brought him in for the Grenville-dominated borough of Aylesbury in 1757.

Wilkes entered Parliament with the right personal connexions, but heavily burdened with debts accruing from electioneering and high living. He therefore needed employment as rapidly as possible. From 1757 to 1761 he was a loyal follower of the Grenvilles and Pitt, and through them he would probably, in time, have been given the place he so coveted. Unfortunately for Wilkes, in October 1761 the Grenvilles and Pitt resigned their offices (Ch. 17). Left high and dry, in consequence, Wilkes may still have hoped for succour from Bute, but if so, was soon disappointed. By early 1762 he had conceived a special animosity for the king's favourite Scotsman, against whom he unleashed the full force of his literary skills in June in the first issue of his violently xenophobic, pro-Pittite, scandal-sheet, the *North Briton*. Wilkes soon went beyond what was considered decorous in his denunciations of the premier minister, and by October 1762 Temple, who had privately financed the paper, was distancing himself from his creation and its 'daily abominations'. By then, however, the *North Briton* had become a commercial success and Wilkes was less dependent on his patrons' support (48, *19–22*). Bute's resignation in April 1763 looked momentarily as if it might take some of the fire out of the *North Briton*, but after the subject of the Paris peace preliminaries had been broached in the King's Speech at the opening of Parliament, Wilkes in a parting shot exultantly used issue No. 45 to suggest that George III had been tricked into lying by his ministers. This was the final straw, and Bute's successor, George Grenville, and the Secretaries of State began proceedings to have the author of the offending article arrested on a charge of seditious libel.

Although the ministry knew perfectly well that Wilkes had written the offending article they as yet had no legal proof. The earl of Halifax therefore issued, as was established practice in such cases, a General Warrant for the arrest of 'the authors, printers and publishers' of No. 45 of the *North Briton*, and within three days the Secretary of State's messengers had used the warrant to arrest forty-nine individuals, including Wilkes. From his cell in the Tower Wilkes audaciously responded by having his friends apply to the Chief Justice of the Common Pleas, Charles Pratt – a well-known Pittite – for a writ of *Habeas Corpus*. Pratt promptly ruled that Wilkes's imprisonment for any crime other than treason, felony or breach of the peace was an infringement of parliamentary privilege, and to the refrain of 'Wilkes and Liberty' Wilkes was released amidst tumultuous popular applause. With magnificent panache he at once brought a series of legal actions against the messengers, Under-secretaries and others involved in his arrest, which culminated in his winning £4,000 in damages, and the landmark ruling by the Chief Justice that General Warrants were 'illegal and subversive to the liberties of the subject' (48, *24–9*). The affair could have ended here, with the ministry humiliated but politically uncompromised, had not Grenville and his colleagues lost their heads and rushed into trying to use their parliamentary strength as a riposte to their defeat in the courts.

Persuading the Independents to agree that seditious libel should in future constitute a breach of parliamentary privilege was not a problem. Likewise a resolution that No. 45 of the *North Briton* should be burnt by the public hangman as, 'a false, scandalous and seditious libel' sailed through the Commons, and Wilkes was subsequently expelled from the House by a huge majority. Few had any sympathy with a man described by Pitt (in the self-same speech which opposed the motion to remove parliamentary privilege as a defence against seditious libel) as 'the blasphemer of his God and the libeller of his king'. It was early in 1764, when the ministry decided to try to reverse Chief Justice Pratt's decision on General Warrants by a vote in the Commons, that the going became sticky. Now at last the Independents began to heed Pitt's denunciations of ministerial tyranny. The Common Law of England was a sacred institution to the vast majority of them, and the Grenville administration was essentially proposing that it should be set at naught when it conflicted with the needs of the executive. After a heated debate that lasted well into the early hours of the morning, the ministry managed to scrape home by only 14 votes in a House of 450 (46a, *84*). Technically the government had won; actually, they recognised it as a Pyrrhic victory and shortly afterwards allowed the procedure to lapse into abeyance. Wilkes had made his first 'contribution' to the process of reform and 'liberty': General Warrants were henceforth a dead letter.

In the long term, the end of General Warrants was the most important legacy of the *North Briton* affair. At the time, however, its most significant effect was to boost John Wilkes to a level of popularity verging on adulation among the common people of England in general and London in particular. For many (if not most) ordinary Englishmen 'Wilkes' and 'Liberty' became synonymous (44, *169–81*). The ramifications of this conjuncture were only revealed in 1768 when Wilkes decided to stand for Middlesex in the General Election of that year.

He had spent the years 1764–8 in exile in France. Because he had failed to present himself to answer a charge of blasphemy arising from a pornographic poem, the *Essay on Woman*, which he and Thomas Pitt had written years before, Wilkes was outlawed in 1764. Brief trips back to England in 1766 in an attempt to persuade the Rockingham ministry to reverse his outlawry proved fruitless, and by 1768 Wilkes was coming under severe pressure from his French creditors. Characteristically boldly, he seized the initiative, returned to London permanently in February 1768, and histrionically begged for mercy in a letter to the King (which George III ignored). Unwilling to risk refuelling Wilkes's popularity by renewed legal action, however, the ministers studiously ignored his populist denunciations of them as he declared his candidacy for London in the General Election, and initially their softly-softly strategy seemed to work. Possibly due to his late entry to the race, Wilkes came bottom of the poll of seven candidates for London. Nothing dismayed, he promptly announced his candidacy for the county of Middlesex, where he was triumphantly returned amidst riotous celebrations by his supporters.

After nearly fifty years of rising real wages and cheap food, the artisans and labourers of Middlesex, like their counterparts throughout Britain, were facing harder times as the population increase began to match the demand for labour (Ch. 9, 12). This does not explain why such people became enthusiastic Wilkites, but the discontent produced by worsening economic straits does help to account for their dissatisfaction with the established order. A vote for Wilkes was simultaneously an attempt to draw élite attention to the fact that society and the economy were no longer delivering a rising standard of living and a vote for nebulous notions of 'English liberty' that were popularly identified with John Wilkes. As Burke sagely remarked: 'the crowd always want to draw themselves from abstract principles to personal attachments'. Wilkes undoubtedly played to the gallery for all he was worth, but he was very much his electors' creature and was always very deferential to them in public. In return, they gave him unflinching support throughout his travails in the 1760s (48).

The Middlesex election abruptly exhausted the ministry's patience with Wilkes's antics. But while they were still deciding how best to arraign him before the courts, he stole a march on them by ostentatiously surrendering himself to the Court of King's Bench at the end of March 1768. Lord Mansfield duly set aside Wilkes's outlawry, but then remanded him in custody while he awaited trial on various misdemeanour charges. In response, the by then frequent pro-Wilkite celebrations rapidly transformed themselves into almost daily riots against his imprisonment. The authorities, fearful of losing control, moved the 3rd (Scottish) regiment of Foot Guards on to the London streets. Their strong anti-Wilkite sentiments (Scotland was the one area of Britain that was overwhelmingly anti-Wilkes [227, *179–80*]) led them to disperse the rioters at St George's Fields with peculiar ferocity. The resulting 'massacre' (Ch. 12), left seven dead and a minimum of fifteen wounded. The ministry then commended the magistrates for their firmness (48, *53–4*). Nothing could have been better calculated further to inflame the sensibilities of the Wilkite crowd.

Briefly, nonetheless, the death-toll shocked Wilkes's popular following into inactivity, and during this hiatus Wilkes was sentenced to twenty-two months' imprisonment and a £1,000 fine for his various misdemeanours. He hardly suffered during his imprisonment; rather he was deluged with gifts of money and provisions from well-wishers all over the empire, ranging from a female fellow prisoner nicknamed 'Black Bess' who collected £100 from the other prisoners (how is not mentioned) and then publicly offered him such other comforts as she might be able to provide, to the more significant gift of the South Carolina Assembly, £1,500 (44, *177*; cf. Ch. 21). These were tokens of re-gathering support outside. When Parliament expelled Wilkes by 219 votes to 137, on the grounds that he was an outlaw at the time of his election for Middlesex, it was a foregone conclusion that he would be re-elected. Indeed, support for him was so overwhelming that the ministry proved unable even to persuade anyone to contest the election. Re-elected on 16 February 1769, Wilkes was re-expelled on the 17th. That process of re-election (uncontested) and re-expulsion was repeated a month later. Finally, in April 1769 the ministry coaxed Henry Lawes Luttrell, a loyal ministerialist, into standing, and when he was defeated (by 1,143 votes to 296), its supporters overturned the decision of the electorate by a vote in the Commons which blandly declared Luttrell the winner (48, *66–70*). Wilkes's support among the traditional political nation was limited, but many were shocked at such outrageous disregard for the wishes of the electorate. From that disquiet stemmed the beginnings of the parliamentary reform movement.

The Tory party had been touting some measure of parliamentary reform as part of its electoral platform since the 1730s (28a, *115–16*; Ch. 3). Those elements of the party which were genuinely interested in the idea in the 30s and 40s were more concerned with returning the constitution to mythical levels of pristine purity than with altering it. Hence their proposals centred on eliminating corruption by raising the level of the property franchise and barring aristocratic influence from electoral contests (60, *14*). Still, some Tories did appear to be drifting in the direction of franchise reform by the early 1760s. For example, in 1761, on the eve of the party's demise, William Beckford, a wealthy Tory soon to turn radical Pittite, made a speech to his London constituents in which he scathingly criticised the equal representation of 'little pitiful boroughs' and major centres of industry (56, *53*). American protests about taxation without representation kept a low level of interest in the subject going throughout the mid–1760s until it suddenly resurfaced with a vengeance after 1768. The Pittite (but very pro-Wilkes) publisher, John Almon, in March 1768 published in the pages of a popular journal, the *Political Register*, an exhortation to voters in the 1768 General Election in which he urged them only to vote for candidates who agreed to back measures against corruption and for the redistribution of seats. The initial impact of Almon's ideas seems to have been negligible, but when interest in the subject revived in the wake of the ministry's effective disfranchisment of the voters of Middlesex in 1769 the programme he had outlined began to find wider favour. By 1770 pro-Wilkes MPs, Beckford among them, were to be found arguing for parliamentary reform in the most uncompromising terms. Outside the House, Wilkes in 1771 helped to strike another important blow for 'liberty', when as an alderman he backed the Corporation of London's pressure on the Commons to permit freedom of parliamentary reporting in newspapers (17, *336* and *passim*). Enthusiasm for parliamentary reform, however, was still the preserve of a small number of individuals. John Wilkes's massive but uneventful victory at Middlesex in the 1774 General Election (prudently allowed to stand by Lord North) changed that. Wilkes and the dozen or so other members returned on a Wilkite platform were all committed to reform of some kind and their arrival in the Commons potentially offered the possibility of a concerted campaign.

Unfortunately for the reformers, the American war intervened before Wilkes could begin to orchestrate such a campaign. His failure to do so has sometimes been cited as evidence of his lack of commitment to the cause of reform. Alternatively, Wilkes may have recognised that reform measures sponsored by a group of members identified to a man with the pro-American lobby in the Commons were not likely to get much of a hearing in 1775–6. In March 1776 when he moved that the Commons consider measures to provide for a wider franchise (even, he hinted, universal manhood suffrage), Wilkes could not even find a seconder. Outside Parliament his proposals roused little interest in the political nation and scarcely more beyond it; Wilkes and his allies, as was to be the case with the Association movement in the 1780s, were ultimately defeated by public indifference to the reform issue. The reason is plain enough. The unreformed parliamentary system was increasingly open to abuse, but until the early nineteenth century, in the eyes of those who wielded political influence – including those prepared to advocate reform in other areas of government – it served its purpose tolerably well. The number of expanding towns not directly represented had grown between the early eighteenth century and the 1770s; but that does not mean that they were unrepresented (cf. *Making of Great Power*, Ch. 21). As Paul Langford has recently shown (59), if instead of tracing MPs' constituencies on a map of England one superimposes their usual place of residence, a remarkable congruity between the number of MPs living in (and *de facto* serving) regions such as the Home Counties and Midlands and the numbers that would have served those regions had contemporary reform proposals been enacted is found. In short, it appears that the unreformed Parliament was still, overall, representative enough for most of those who then constituted the political nation. And in the end, of course, it was only they or their representatives at Westminster who could change the system legally.

Nonetheless, support for reform was slowly building up and (more important) was becoming self-generating in the period 1760–85. By the 1780s it had become a perennial, if not yet central concern in British politics. For all the reformers' lack of success, their tendency to schism – there was a split in the Bill of Rights Society as early as 1771 – and the diversion of some of them to other reforming causes of these years, such as Catholic relief, anti-slavery or (as with Wilkes himself in his self-styled 'extinct volcano' years) penal reform, the state of the electoral system was an issue that would no longer go away. There were various reasons why this was so, of which the two most important will be considered here. One was a gradual change in popular perception, whereby increasing numbers began to see their unfranchised status as a grievance. Given the decline in the percentage of English males who were able to vote *at some time* in their lives since the heyday of the expanding electorate (1689–1722), many ordinary unfranchised men in the 1760s and 1770s must have had memories of their fathers or grandfathers voting or having voted. The brief flurry of pro-reform activity between 1768 and 1776 served to awaken this section of the general population to the fact that they no longer had a privilege their forbears had enjoyed. The infrequency of General Elections and in particular of county contests aggravated this sense of deprivation (57). The output of pro-reform propaganda never lapsed after 1768, and that may well have acted to rationalise and justify this awakened sense of grievance. This argument can of course only be speculative because the common men who noisily demonstrated their support for parliamentary reform in this period have rarely left us any record of their motives. What is certain, however, is that discontent with indirect representation was beginning to build up, as the city of Birmingham very practically demonstrated in 1774 by its carefully planned and successfully executed campaign to secure one of the Warwickshire county seats for its own chosen representative rather than leaving it to one of the traditional county families (56, 66). The reformers had a long way to go before they could attract a mass following and mount a sustained political campaign, and the unreformed constitution (and the economic condition of the lower orders) had to arouse a lot more public dissatisfaction in order for them to succeed, but the first steps were taken in the 1760s and 1770s. At the same time parliamentary reform attracted, through the work of James Burgh and Richard Price (1774–6), more formidable intellectual and literary backing than it had hitherto known (above, pp. 246–7).

If the outbreak of hostilities between Britain and its American colonists brought the first phase of attempts to achieve the reform of Parliament effectively to an end, it was appropriately Britain's defeat at the hands of the colonists which provoked a revival of reformist agitation. There was always a section of the British population (possibly as many as 30 per cent) who opposed the 'unnatural and cruel conflict of civil war' against 'our brethren', and Britain's defeats gave them a certain intangible political ascendancy.[3] It was on the dismay of this section of the nation that Christopher Wyvill's reformist Yorkshire Association and its imitators fed (61, *68ff*). The intrinsic question the Associations and their supporters posed was: how could Britain have got into, never mind lost, such a bitter civil war unless there was something intrinsically rotten in the State? Their prescription was constitutional reform, and in the atmosphere of war-weary disillusionment pervading Britain in the early 1780s they seemed destined to succeed (94, *516–17*).

The reform movement had two prongs. One was a conventional Opposition campaign to oust the ministry, spearheaded by the Rockinghams, but one with a notably unconventional accompaniment: a genuinely ideological reformist programme centred on economical reform. The other was the parliamentary reform movement stemming from Wyvill's Yorkshire Association. The first was successful on both fronts, as has been seen (Ch. 20). To the twentieth-century eye the second looks much more popular and progressive – and yet it failed utterly.

The Yorkshire gentleman-parson, Christopher Wyvill, launched the first county 'Association' in the winter of 1779–80 as part of the economical reform movement. The Association initially busied itself with securing addresses and petitions in support of the Rockinghams' campaign for the abolition of sinecures and pensions; though both it and several of the other Associations formed in its wake subscribed in general terms to the need for a 'more equal representation' also (61, *110–12*). In March 1780, however, Wyvill and a mixed bag of ex-Wilkite Independents such as James Townsend and Brass Crosby, and Rockinghamite radicals such as Charles James Fox and the duke of Richmond, launched a separate, additional initiative designed to work up petitions and addresses in favour of parliamentary reform. A few Associations, like that of Middlesex and the Westminster Committee, embraced this enthusiastically; a more typical reaction was that of Wiltshire, which quietly backed off (61, *113*). In any case, the radical initiative quickly stalled in the conservative reaction that followed the Gordon riots and when it became apparent that Rockingham himself would not countenance its attachment to the Rockinghamite programme. As a result the two reform streams separated and while the Rockinghams' campaign against the ministry gathered momentum during 1780–1, the Association movement for parliamentary reform stagnated.

However, the fall of North's ministry re-energised Wyvill and his associates, and in May 1782 William Pitt the Younger was persuaded to move for a committee to investigate ways in which Parliament might be reformed. An unholy coalition of moderate Rockinghams and conservative Northites defeated the motion, but the deceptively narrow margin of 161 to 141 encouraged the reformers to introduce a bill actually proposing the abolition of boroughs proven venal and the creation of 100 additional county seats the following year. After a spirited verbal duel between Pitt and North, conducted before a packed house, the bill crashed to ignominious defeat. The reformers were beginning to lose the political edge vouchsafed by the despondency of their opponents in the aftermath of the American war. The final blow to any realistic hope of parliamentary reform in the near future came in 1785, when Pitt, now prime minister and presiding over a remarkable post-war recovery, carried out his pledge to his friend Wyvill and for the last time introduced a reform bill. The remnants of the Association movement had by this time been split by Wyvill's determination to commit it to supporting Pitt in his confrontation with the Fox-North coalition. Consequently, Pitt's very moderate proposal that venal boroughs should be bought out and their seats redistributed to new centres of population was seen by many as a partisan manoeuvre. The bill was accordingly defeated by 248 votes to 174 and Pitt, having assuaged his conscience, entirely abandoned an idea which was inevitably anathema to the king he now loyally served.

By 1785 parliamentary reform was an issue that would periodically subside but would not disappear. The unforeseeable French Revolution initially revived interest in reform of a variety of kinds, and within three years the parliamentary reform movement had for the first time acquired an unambiguously radical working-men's dimension. In order to succeed, however, that movement required MPs returned by venal electorates and peers who owned pocket boroughs to become converted to the still uncongenial idea of a basic constitutional change. And that could not happen until parliamentary reform became a tenet of one of the parties that were beginning to dominate the political landscape at the end of the eighteenth century. Only after the defection of the conservative Portland Whigs to the nascent new Tory party in the 1790s did such a *collective* commitment to parliamentary reform on the part of one of the parties become even possible. Once they took it up, the Foxite Whigs' commitment to a 'more equal' electoral system could, and did, ultimately prove decisive. But it entailed a very long march from 1785 to 1832.

---

1. I am indebted to my colleague Dr R. Rea for his perceptive criticism of an early draft of this chapter. He is not, of course, to be held responsible for what follows. D.S.
2. See Jonathan Swift, *Gulliver's Travels*, ed. P. Dixon and J. Chalker (Penguin Classics, 1987), pp. 219–23.
3. J.E. Bradley, *Popular Politics and the American Revolution in England: Petitions, the Crown and Public Opinion* (Macon, 1986), pp. 209–10, 215.

Conclusion

I

The subsequent volume in this series, covering the period 1783–1870, has been entitled by Eric Evans *The Forging of the Modern State*. It was self-evidently not a 'modern' state which in 1783 signed away its American colonies and had an unprecedentedly youthful prime minister wished on it by its king. The last chapter of the present book, dealing with the painful and mainly abortive birth-pangs of reform, will have made this abundantly clear, as will many of the other chapters in Parts Two and Three.

All the same, Britain in 1783 was a very *different* kind of state – and in many ways a much more *advanced* state – than the 'Britain', or even the more unitary England, of the 1660s had been. In the first place, she was, and had been for three-quarters of a century, a Great Power in Europe and in the wider world; chastened and shocked, admittedly, in the past few years by the bruising experiences of the recent war against the American rebels, France and Spain, but still capable (as the next decade showed) of commanding the respect, provoking the jealousies and arousing the fears of her international neighbours. The War of American Independence had after all been the only major war out of the five she had engaged in since 1689 to end in failure. In the second place, Britain had become in the ninety years before 1783 what John Brewer, in a very recent, and stimulating, study (84) has dubbed 'a fiscal-military state'. We may grimace at the choice of label, one which, if coined in the 1780s, would have had Pitt and Fox, let alone the late Georgian heirs of Sir Roger de Coverly, reaching for the third bottle of port; yet it is an instructive tool for the historian, with which he can chisel away down the years to reveal, in bas relief, the unstable, and at best fitfully-effective, monarchical state of 1660–88.

The militarist republic which had chalked up successes in the wars of the 1650s against the Dutch and against Spain was a forced plant too shallow-rooted and too foreign to the national soil to survive. The Restoration state which succeeded it was woefully under-financed, at least until 1685; its resources were inconsistently and most inadequately tapped by taxation, whether direct or indirect [G.2(iii)]. Despite its on the whole very limited expenditure, the pre-1685 executive was plagued by debt, a debt which was as yet a personal and monarchical, not a national and parliamentary responsibility. Restoration London had its wealthy merchants and bankers; but the infrastructure of City institutions and mechanisms on which a durable and resilient system of public credit could be based – a system capable of financing great wars and defending in peacetime the gains which accrued from them – did not exist before the 1690s. That, too, was the decade when England acquired those other self-evident 'sinews of power' of which Brewer has written [I.2]: an army which, duly reinforced by Scottish fighting men and by large numbers of foreign mercenaries, was to be capable of engaging when necessary in major Continental wars; also a Royal Navy, commanded by the kind of professionalised officer corps of which Pepys had dreamed, a navy which from the 1690s onwards was generally capable of outfacing the combined battle fleets of her enemies, defending the homeland against invasion and, equally crucial, keeping the sea lanes relatively safe[1] for what had become by 1700 the world's largest merchant marine. The eighteenth-century Royal Navy experienced its share of frustrations and setbacks, but the country was never threatened after 1700 with any repeat of the Medway disaster of 1667.

Finally, it was in the 1690s and early 1700s that the British state was equipped with a bureaucracy, and in particular with a corps of revenue officials, in which traditions of skilled, impartial service and insulation from the political spoils system were gradually accepted and cemented (*Making of a Great Power*, Ch. 16). The number of full-time state employees in the fiscal bureaucracy, which had begun to climb towards the 2,000 mark as a result of the historic decision to adopt direct collection of customs and excise duties in the 1670s and 1680s, and which had reached 2,524 by 1690, was to grow by 1782–3 to 8,292, of whom close on 5,000 were excise officers (76; 84, *66–7*). Notwithstanding the unsightly patches of waste and graft rightly detected by the protagonists of 'economical reform' in George III's reign, this eighteenth-century British civil service was the equal and probably the superior in efficiency of any in Europe; without it Lord North's ministry could never have hoped to raise enough money from 1775–82 to pay for a war which cost almost four times as much annually as King William's War and ten times as much as Charles II's Second Dutch War of 1665–6 [I.2].

There need be no doubt in the minds of historians (for indeed there was none in the minds of eighteenth-century Britons) that it was the Glorious Revolution which was the main agent of this transformation of the nature and potential of the British state. It is true, there had been unpalatable evidence available to English, Scots and Anglo-Irish alike in the three years before the autumn of 1688 that James II had begun to lay some sinister foundations of an absolutist, militarised polity (*Making of a Great Power*, Ch. 11). But those were mostly swept away in the backwash from his sudden collapse. And it was the work of the Revolution Settlement to identify the political nation, as represented in Parliament, with government policy and with preservation of the constitution, as never before. After January 1689 a Parliament was to meet every year without fail at Westminster, in startling contrast to its sidelining in the earlier 1680s; it did so in sessions which stretched in duration from the lowest level of three to five months a year, *in toto*, during the relatively somnolent 1720s and 1730s, to as many as nine and a half months in exceptional years such as 1689 and 1715. On average, over the whole period of almost a century from January 1689 to December 1783, the Parliament of England and later of Great Britain sat for under five months in each year [E.2]. And these were Parliaments prepared to authorise, for the protection of 'the Revolution constitution', the Protestant Succession and the commercial and colonial lifelines of the state, the raising of a tax revenue which had climbed to £11.8 million by 1780, by contrast with the £1.3 million scrambled together to fight the Dutch in 1665, or the £3 million extracted to regain Ireland and confront Louis XIV in 1690 [G.2(iii)]. One of the most lightly taxed states in Europe in the 1660s had become by the early 1780s one that was more heavily taxed, *per capita*, even than France. There was, moreover, a further dimension to this change which made it still more momentous, far more at any rate than a plain matter of quantities. For many of the *indirect* taxes which post-Revolution Parliaments voted between 1693 and 1783 were not levied for current revenue purposes, but rather to underwrite and service a 'National Debt'. This was the most striking symbol of the commitment of the political nation to the eighteenth-century British state and of their mutual identification: the debt rose from £14.7 million in 1697 to over £240 million by 1784 [G.1].

But how were the subjects of the last two Stuarts and of the first three Georges, those especially who enjoyed no direct representation in the House of Commons, induced to shoulder such a burden of taxation, with little more than an occasional wince, and even persuaded to come to terms (though with more misgivings) with the massive incubus of the National Debt? It will be obvious that the miracle could not have been worked unaided. It required, for instance, a total reorientation of the attitude of British people to Europe and to their wider extra-insular responsibilities (*Making of a Great Power*, Ch. 15). But the ultimately essential ingredient in the translation of post-Revolution Britain into a fiscally-organised and militarily effective Great Power was the almost consistent rise in the general level of national prosperity which set in barely a decade after 1660. Many aspects of that growth have figured in particular chapters of *Making of a Great Power* and of the present volume. It may best be illustrated here by a few conveniently assembled statistics [G.2(iii); J.4(i); L.1].

It needs to be stressed, first of all, that although between 1670 and 1770 the share of the national income appropriated to taxation did increase very substantially (from 3.4 per cent to 10.5 per cent) during the seven decades from 1710 to 1780, while the British government's total tax income (in each case in wartime) was expanding from £5.3 million to £11.8 million, the percentage rise in the share of national income which this growth represented (9.2–11.7 per cent) was relatively trifling. This becomes intelligible if, secondly, we relate these two sets of figures to W.A. Cole's 1981 table (130a) suggesting a more than doubling of the 'National Product' in real terms in the first ninety years of the century, and a growth (at 1700 prices) from £50 million to £92 million between 1700 and 1780 [J.4] In a subsequent revision of Cole, N.F.R. Crafts (130b) has calculated further that real national output rose remarkably consistently, at the rate of 0.69 per cent per annum from 1700–60 and at 0.70 per cent from 1760–80 [J.4(i), (ii)]. One final statistic of Cole's underlines the extent to which spending power, well down the social scale, kept abreast of rising national output in pre-industrial British society, and ran well ahead of the growth in population during the same period: it concerns domestic consumption of the products of British industry. It can be reliably estimated that this more than doubled (at constant prices) between 1700 and 1785, with consumption per head rising from £2.77 per annum to £3.89. Cole values Britain's total industrial output in 1785 at £42.4 million, and of that figure £30.7 million-worth (he believes) was absorbed by a buoyant home market.

How British governments after 1688 set about tapping this fast-filling reservoir of private wealth is equally instructive. In the first of the great wars against France they began to remodel the antiquated tax system inherited from the Tudor and Stuart past (see *Making of a Great Power*, Ch. 17). But in the course of the next war, 1702–13, and during the mainly peaceful quarter of a century which followed the defeat of the 'Fifteen Rebellion, the main thrust of post-Revolution fiscal policy was diversified. The utterly central initial rôle of the new Land Tax was gradually modified; taxation began to bear increasingly on imported commodities – through many additional customs duties – and more significantly still, on domestic consumer goods of general consumption, through the levying of new excises [G.2(ii)].

Quite apart from its fiscal (and political) significance, this tells us something, too, about how British society itself changed in response to economic progress, to a more settled political climate and to a new set of social priorities – most prominent among the latter being the unprecedented level of private demand for professional services (quite apart from the state's need for greater professionalisation of government and the armed services). In the course of this book and its antecedent volume we have sought to analyse and understand, at various stages throughout our period, both the structural and the qualitative changes that were taking place within pre-industrial British society (See *Making of a Great Power*, Chs. 4, 18–19; Chs. 13–14 and 18–21 above). The decline of the Land Tax from its position of pre-eminence as a source of public revenue did not of course reflect in any *proportionate* way the changing position and relative wealth of the landowning classes, nor indeed changes in the contribution of farming to the national income, over the century following the Glorious Revolution. That such changes did take place, however, is beyond question; they can be clearly identified, if only tentatively measured, in some recent attempts to update the statistical information provided in the 'social tables' of those much-cited contemporaries, Gregory King and Joseph Massie (1688, 1759: see B.5)[2]. These revisionist exercises suggest that 'income clearly attributable to agriculture' shrank, as a proportion of total national income, from 34 per cent in 1688 to 28 per cent in 1759 and, further, to some 25 per cent by 1780; also that, assuming the contribution of 'commerce' remained more or less constant at around 16 or 17 per cent (a highly questionable assumption, it must be said, on grounds of definition alone), the 'individual sector' of English society – from master manufacturers down to craftsmen, artisans and industrial labourers – may have accounted for about 20 per cent of national income in 1688, slightly more in 1759, and 25 per cent by 1780. These figures may well under-estimate the extent of the redistribution of wealth in the eighteenth century between the agricultural and the commercial and industrial sectors of society, in particular, because so many capitalist entrepreneurs engaged in both trade and industry, 1688–1783, also owned landed estates and ranked socially as 'gentlemen' (at least). But in common with the calculations made by Lindert and Williamson, to the effect that the landed classes of England and Wales, from peers down to plain landed 'gentlemen', may have received in 1688 17.8 per cent of the total national income in rents, but in 1759 only 14.8 per cent,[3] they are to be valued as attempts to put *some* statistical flesh on the character and extent of social changes in the late seventeenth and eighteenth century.

Thus, although the British state which attained, and subsequently retained, Great Power status between 1702 and 1763 was in no modern sense 'industrialised', and had come only marginally closer to being so by 1783, she was a commercialised (by contemporary standards highly commercialised) and colonial power, and was already experiencing, to an extent beyond any other European country in the mid-eighteenth century, what is now sometimes called 'proto-industrialisation'. She was a state, too, in which the political dominance still exercised by the landed classes (see Chs. 2–3) was no longer matched by a corresponding economic dominance. For a century, at least, a profound socio-economic metamorphosis had been under way, and one of its most concrete symbols – and symptoms – was the town, a recurring concern of this book. By the last thirty years of the period 1660–1783, Britain was already a far more urbanised land than she had been in the first thirty years after the Restoration; British provincial society was, by the same token, emphatically more town-centred (as opposed to county-centred) in the late eighteenth than in the late seventeenth century. Impressive as is the continuing spectacular growth of the population of London [B.2(i)], still more so are the fortunes of many of those larger English provincial towns and Scottish towns whose expansion prior to the 1780s can plainly be attributed to either increasing trade or industrial growth, or both [B.2(ii), B.3(iii)]. We need remind ourselves here only of cases such as Birmingham, Liverpool, Bristol, Manchester and Glasgow. And it should not be overlooked how far the *physical* landscape of certain parts of England and of the Central Lowlands of Scotland, quite apart from so much else, had altered, even before the mill chimneys began to sprout and the factory workers' dwellings made their scabrous presence seen and felt in the early nineteenth century.

II

It would be easy to assume from the clamour of the reformers in Britain before 1789 that the *political* landscape of the country had changed much less, certainly far less fundamentally, over the years between 1660 and 1780 than the physical, social and economic balance between town and countryside. But that would be an illusion, as easily induced in the historian's perspective as it was in the view of George III's contemporaries, by an excessive focusing on the politics of the recent, mid-Hanoverian past. It must be firmly reiterated, therefore, that the building of a 'fiscal-military state', as depicted by Brewer, along with the many striking successes Britain achieved in the areas of diplomacy and war, and in the aggrandisement of the First British Empire, from 1702 to 1763 would scarcely have been possible if the constitutional tensions and the political instability of the regime of Charles II and James II – together with the bitter religious animosities which had heightened them – had persisted for several more generations after

1688. And here again it is the Glorious Revolution which stands out as the supreme watershed. It was the Revolution which led to a parliamentary settlement of the crown, the succession and the constitution and a resettlement of the relations of Church and Dissent, which was begun in 1689 and was virtually completed, legislatively, by 1706–7 – although not guaranteed permanency in practice until after the Hanoverian Succession.

One of the major themes developed in Part I of the *Making of a Great Power* explained how the many questions left unanswered in the Restoration Settlement combined subsequently with the personal flaws and autocratic instincts of Charles II and his brother to place the ill-defined English constitution under great stress between the 1660s and 1682. It was equally clear that along with constitutional disequilibrium went political instability. With political opposition to the monarch and his ministers denied regular or reliable outlets for peaceful protest and counter-attack, the governing regimes of Restoration England and Scotland were rarely free for long from fear of conspiracies or rebellions; and when opposition was totally proscribed and rendered increasingly desperate after 1681 such fears were quickly shown to have been well-founded. Entirely appropriate to the febrile political atmosphere of Restoration Whitehall and Westminster and the lottery of the political system's working in this period is the fact that the careers of the three most powerful ministers of 1660–88, Clarendon, Danby and Sunderland, ended in either impeachment or enforced exile, or both. The progress made in the last years of William III's reign towards constitutional stability and a more fruitful partnership between the executive and the legislature, and the happy achievement of those objectives under Anne and her successor did not automatically bring political stability in their train. Leading political figures were still from time to time hounded by inveterate former opponents after they fell from office: the Junto lords in 1701, Oxford and Bolingbroke from 1715–17, and even Walpole as late as 1742. Of more basic importance was the unsettling effect of the succession question. As long as the issue first precipitated by the Exclusionists in 1679, the succession to the thrones of England, Scotland and Ireland, Protestant *versus* Catholic, remained *the* burning issue in British politics, attempts to overthrow established political authority by assassination, plot, revolt and invasion were bound to continue. This they did, as we saw, with little abatement down to 1723 (*Making of a Great Power*, Ch. 25; Ch. 6 above); indeed, Jacobite hopes were not finally extinguished, realistically, until they lay amid the carnage on Culloden's field in 1746.

Although the overthrow of James II by revolution and invasion in 1688 created the opportunity for the ultimate achievement of political stability under a parliamentary and responsible, as opposed to an autocratic and arbitrary, monarchy, it for a while increased the threat of further destabilisation from Scotland and Ireland. The great Catholic insurrection in Ireland from 1689 to 1691 was finally quelled by force of arms; the ruthless Williamite settlement which followed, entrenching the supremacy of the small Anglo-Irish Protestant minority, yet at the same time keeping its political wings so severely clipped that its freedom of action *vis-à-vis* England was almost nil, preserved a mainly quiescent, colonialised Ireland until the kingdom's mounting discontents precipitated the campaign for legislative independence from 1778 to 1782 (Chs. 16, 20). But the Scottish case was very different. The Edinburgh Estates received such a fillip from the Revolution Settlement that Scotland's political docility of the 1660s and 1670s had within a decade of 1689 begun to seem irrecoverable, as long as the two ancient kingdoms remained unintegrated either parliamentarily or economically. To this problem a full 'incorporating' Union alone could provide a permanent solution. The Catholic and Episcopalian Highlands and North-East of Scotland would continue to offer hope to a Stuart Pretender, whether outside or inside a united state of Great Britain. But the prospect that the political establishment in Lowland Scotland, too, or an important part of it, might be driven by its various grievances to embrace the Jacobite option – a prospect that had seemed real enough to London politicians for two to three years after the passing of the Act of Security in 1704 (*Making of a Great Power*, Ch. 20) – never seriously returned to haunt British politics once the Union of 1707 had slowly earned grudging acceptance from most Scots, having had its rougher edges smoothed off by the well-oiled patronage wheels of the Whig oligarchy after 1725 (ibid. Ch. 20; Ch. 15).

The ruling families of the Whig Old Corps who governed Britain under the Crown for nearly all the forty years after the election of 1722 did not invariably see eye to eye with the first two Hanoverian monarchs on the interpretation to be placed on the 'Revolution Constitution' they revered. But such differences as there were, over the precise distribution of powers between Parliament, ministry and king (Ch. 2), never seemed likely to unsettle the constitutional relationships forged since 1689. Nor did they seriously threaten to disjoint the political system presided over from the 1720s by Walpole and the Pelhams. This situation was abruptly changed after the accession of George III in 1760, a new broom whose (perfectly legitimate) view of the prerogatives remaining to the monarch, sharpened by personal antipathy towards the remnants of the Walpole-Pelhamite Old Corps, was one of the two main factors contributing to the return of political turbulence to Britain in the 1760s. The second factor was the temporary end of party politics in Britain, with the disappearance of the Tory party (1757–62, Chs. 18–19) and the disintegration of the Whig oligarchy into warring factions, followed by the reincarnation of party through the medium of the Rockinghams and Charles Fox, who can be seen as the natural heirs of the Whig Junto – Old Corps tradition. Parties, parliamentary and national, had been such a continuous and dominant feature of the political landscape of pre-industrial Britain since the birth of the original Whigs and Tories during the Exclusion crisis that their sudden removal from the scene in the 1760s and, up to a point, in the early 1770s, not unnaturally had seismic effects on British politics akin to those of a major geological 'fault' (*Making of a Great Power*, Chs. 8, 9, 21–3; Ch. 3, 18, 20).

In the formative years of the first English parties in Charles II's reign religious differences had played a prominent part in shaping their ideologies and composition. To both the old and the new Cavaliers of 1660–2, the restoration of the Church of England to its former supremacy after the traumas of the Civil Wars and the Interregnum had been almost as potent a symbol of the return of a traditional order as the restoration of the monarchy itself. Over the next two decades that supremacy, which the legislation of 1661–73 (*Making of a Great Power*, Ch. 7; this vol., N.2, N.3) attempted to translate into a civil as well as a religious monopoly, was challenged as much by royal 'indulgence' policies (undertaken with more than half an eye on the future of Roman Catholics) as by the intrinsic strength of post-Restoration Puritanism. The first Whigs accepted almost from the start a commitment to defend and advance the interests of Protestant dissenters, who were so active politically on their behalf; the first Tories became identified as the party of the Church of England, as well as the party of the Crown and of the legitimate, 'divine right' succession. Even the arrival in 1689, after the Revolution, of legal freedom of worship, though not civil equality, for Dissent did not much change these basic dispositions. From 1711–14 the Tories spearheaded a fierce though short-lived counter-attack on the encroaching nonconformists with the Occasional Conformity and Schism Acts (*Making of a Great Power*, Ch. 23), and as late as the 1730s the Whigs in the House of Commons lobbed a whole series of mortar bombs into the remaining fastnesses of the Anglican clergy (Ch. 7) [N.3(ii)]. By contrast, the new Whig party of Rockingham, Fox and Portland which emerged late in our period was more secular in its original ideological thrust (Ch. 20). But it was, nonetheless, a Rockinghamite, Savile, who revived the long moribund cause of Catholic relief in 1778, and in the late 1780s it was appropriately the radical dissenting allies of the Foxites who were to mount, and Fox himself who was to lead, the last charge of the first new campaign against the Test and Corporation Acts for half a century. So it was no surprise that when a new Tory party began to take shape in the 1790s, after Protestant dissenters had begun to figure prominently in the radical parliamentary reform movement, its members should have adopted the defence of the *ancien régime* in Church as well as state as one of its watchwords; indeed, at the end of that decade, in deeply troubled times, the 1689 Toleration Act itself was to come briefly into its sights.

By that juncture there was little but the Anglican monopoly of civil offices left to defend, so much had religious diversity become an integral part of the fabric of eighteenth-century British society. A little-noticed but significant legal change had taken place in 1779 when Parliament agreed to remove from nonconformist ministers the long-standing obligation to accept all the Thirty-Nine Articles of the Anglican faith save those dealing with baptism [N.3.A(iii)]. In spite of the availability, here and there, of formal *membership* figures, as with the Quakers in 1800 and the Wesleyan Methodists after 1767 (in the latter case, a notoriously poor guide to the size of their congregations week by week), reliable figures for the strength of mid- and late eighteenth-century Dissent are impossible to come by.[4] But enough is known, or can reasonably be surmised, for us to be fairly certain that the proportion of Protestant dissenters to the population as a whole in England and Wales in 1783 was no higher, and was very probably lower, than the 7–8 per cent which, on the present author's estimate, they comprised in 1715–16 (*Making of a Great Power*, Ch. 23, N.6). Yet in three ways, at least, the position with regard to religious allegiance had changed very significantly between 1715 and 1783.

In the first place, the Evangelical Awakening in George II's reign had diversified Dissent (Ch. 8). In 1783 John Wesley's titanic presence was still making it impossible for the formal separation of the Wesleyan Methodists and the Established Church to take place, although the issue had been periodically debated in their Annual Conference since 1755. But there were few Anglican parsons in the 1780s who did not regard the Methodists as permanently 'separated' from their communion. In the second place, the traditional dissenting churches, alongside which the Methodist societies had sprung up in the 1740s and 1750s, had themselves come to a crucial parting of the ways in the early years of George III. By 1783 the Congregationalists (the old Independents) and the Particular Baptists had for two decades been experiencing their own evangelical revival, expanding their appeal both by revolutionising their methods and their message in emulation of the Wesleyans, and by directing these to a socially more 'down-market' audience. Already they could justifiably be distinguished, as 'New Dissent', from the declining and increasingly staid, bourgeois-orientated sects of 'Old Dissent': the Presbyterians – once so dominant, now in sorry decline; the General Baptists and the Quakers or 'Friends' (100, *21–61*). Thirdly, the more reliable estimates suggest that the Roman Catholic community in England and Wales had declined between 1720 and 1780, even in absolute terms and still more when measured against a rising population. The expansion of Catholic numbers due to immigration, which was to become so remarkable around the turn of the century, was however just discernible during the 1780s (100, 45–6; 9, *39–40*). This was one of the few points of likeness between the religious situation in England in the late eighteenth century and that in Scotland. Numbers of Scottish Catholics are thought to have increased from a mere 16,000 in 1755 to roughly 30,000 in 1800, but nearly all the increase apparently took place after 1783. At the end of our period adherents of the Roman faith were still heavily outnumbered north of the border by the Episcopalians, of whom there were around 80,000, in spite of the legal proscription of their public worship from 1746–92. Scotland remained an overwhelmingly Presbyterian nation, as she had been at the time of the Union; but Presbyterianism itself had in the meantime, institutionally speaking, disintegrated, as an extraordinary variety of secessionist churches broke away from the established Kirk over both doctrinal and lay patronage issues.

That the established Church of England avoided any comparable schisms in the eighteenth century (for the rise of Methodism had negligible effects on the Church's ministry and none whatever on its structure) might, on a cynical view, be attributed more to its flaccidity than to its strength. Our last view of the Church in the text of this volume was during Secker's primacy (1758–68). It would be unrealistic to claim that the external symptoms of well-being it exhibited thereafter, notably the striking effects of agricultural improvements on its tithe and glebe resources and the (related) higher profile of the Anglican clergy in local affairs with the emergence of a fast-growing clerical magistracy[5], were matched by the degree of internal, pastoral health that would have equipped its ministers to cope with the onset of industrialisation, especially in the urban areas of the North and the Midlands. The 535,000 Anglican Easter communicants recorded in 1801 were only 9.9 per cent of the population of England and Wales aged 15 or over (100, *27–8*), and it is clear from such parish evidence as has been studied for the first two decades of the eighteenth century that those 1801 figures represent a very steep decline in the interim. Not every index of spiritual vigour, however, was as depressing as that. As we have seen (Ch. 8), there had been a few advance beacons as early as 1740–60 pointing to a *Church* evangelical awakening; by the early 1780s the Church Evangelicals, though still very much a minority movement, were increasing alike in numbers, confidence and influence. In particular, they exercised a disproportionate sway over educated, upper-class English laymen, and with and through them formed formidable pressure-groups working for various objectives which can be broadly labelled as movements for 'social and moral reform'. For these the 1780s proved to be a decade of exceptional significance. Some of them – like the great Sunday School movement, first launched through interdenominational cooperation in a few industrial towns from 1783–5 – revealed the common ground that existed among evangelical clergy, and laity, of all churches, English and Scottish; they demonstrate that not all was sectarianism and strife in British religion in the years before the French Revolution arrived to throw it, along with so much else, into turmoil.

III

We recall that it had been concern about the scale of both Protestant and Catholic Dissent, and most of all about its capacity for political subversion, which prompted the first systematic attempt in English history to 'number the people'. The Compton Census of 1676 had limited objectives and its findings were seriously deficient (*Making of a Great Power*, Ch. 2; N.6). Nevertheless, those findings (kept under fairly close wraps for 13 years) were enough to suggest to the few in the know that the various attempts current in Restoration England to arrive at a rough general estimate of the country's population – by applying a crude multiplier to the house data newly available in the Hearth Office – were reaching much exaggerated conclusions. The most celebrated of Britain's pioneer statisticians, Gregory King, through the agency of his friend and publicist, Davenant, put all these efforts into perspective near the end of the seventeenth century by using for 'samplings' the incomplete census returns commissioned by the government for fiscal purposes in 1694–5 (ibid. Ch. 2). Published in summary form at a time when Britain had just struggled with much difficulty up the foothills of her climb to greatness, in the teeth of the mighty power of France, King's (in the circumstances) remarkably accurate revelations showed just how narrow was the demographic platform from which that climb was taking place.

In this volume we have followed the population history of Britain quite closely, in the light of recent research, from the mid seventeenth-century to the very threshold of industrialisation [B.1] (*Making of a Great Power*, Chs. 2, 19; Ch. 9 above). Although the population of England and Wales had increased very rapidly in the first fifty years of the Stuart period, the ensuing demographic decline which was triggered off by the economic depression and heavy epidemic mortality of the late 1650s was to have long-lasting effects, so much so that

Wrigley and Schofield have calculated that it was not until the early 1730s that England again had as many inhabitants as she had had at the peak of the seventeenth-century population rise, in 1657 (with Wales, 5.65 million). In the late seventeenth and eighteenth centuries France had a demographic history not unlike England's in its broad pattern, except that because her people were prey to occasional terrible famines as well as to disease, her mortality crises (1661–2, 1692–3, 1709–10) were the more catastrophic. Nevertheless, careful modern estimates suggest that in the first decade of the eighteenth century, with a population of over 19 million, France could draw on resources of manpower which outnumbered those of her cross-Channel rival, the new United Kingdom of Great Britain, by three to one. When Britain's population began its sharp pre-industrial rise around 1750 – in 1755 England, Wales and Scotland together had an estimated 7.6 million inhabitants – that of France took a similarly steep upward track. By 1776, on Bourgeois-Pichat's figures, the French population had reached 25.6 million, and over the next decade advanced by yet a further million.[6] By the end of the American War of Independence, in other words, France was still maintaining her early eighteenth-century superiority in human resources over Britain of almost three to one.

But human resources in simple *numerical* terms, as the early paragraphs of this Conclusion have emphasised, were in themselves a relatively minor element in the chemistry of Britain's emerging greatness between the 1690s and the early 1760s. Far more active agents were released by four singular experiences in the history of late seventeenth-century England: the political, commercial and financial 'Revolutions' (*Making of a Great Power*, Chs. 3, 13, 17) which left the lives of few of her people untouched at the time, and whose repercussions continued to be felt right through the eighteenth century and beyond; and in addition by 1700, a scientific revolution, part of a process of intellectual enquiry and regeneration which can plausibly be regarded as the harbinger of the Age of Enlightenment in Europe (ibid. Chs. 10, 24). Its influence was not of course confined, even in the eighteenth century, to the rarefied circles which engendered it. As we have seen, it profoundly affected from an early stage the religious thought and practice of the age and can be linked both with the work of the political arithmeticians, not least with that of King, and with the pressure in George III's reign for administrative and institutional (for example, electoral and legal) reform. But what of its contribution, if any, to more material progress, and through that, to 'the sinews of power'? It has seemed unconvincing to some historians to establish any direct connection between the ferment in mathematics, natural science and philosophy in which British *savants* of the late seventeenth and early eighteenth centuries played so conspicuous a part, and that stream of inventions and technological advances which had begun to transform British industry a long time before the onset of sustained industrialisation in the 1780s. To others, however, it seems not at all far-fetched to argue (without in any way exaggerating the cerebral impulses of ingenious artisans such as Kay and Hargreaves [L.2]) that the thought-world of Boyle, Newton, Halley and Locke, with its common currency of belief in the rational empirical method, in untrammelled enquiry, observation and experiment, became the inheritance of many of those eighteenth-century pioneers whose inventive, technological and engineering flair was indispensable to the success of Britain's Industrial Revolution. Innovators such as Wedgwood, Watt, the industrial chemist James Keir, and John Smeaton, the hydraulic and civil engineer who designed and built the Forth-Clyde canal, were well versed in scientific theory and methods – a process in which the universities of Glasgow and Edinburgh came to play an increasingly important part (166, *45–71*; 9, *9–12*).

However, in the many-faceted (and seemingly endless) modern debate about why Britain became the world's first industrial nation, one of the few propositions that would secure a broad consensus of agreement would probably be that early industrialisation in the United Kingdom was primarily a child of demand rather than of invention. And it is surely the case that in the hard struggle to cling on to her status as a front-line European and world power in the three-quarters of a century after 1739, the biggest advantage Britain derived from the long upswing of her demographic pendulum which began during the Austrian Succession War, was the continuing stimulation of her economy (and of its manufacturing sector in particular) by a high and ever-growing level of domestic demand. This was a very different situation from that in the late Stuart period, when in creating the economic and financial springboard for England's first leap on to the Great Power stage it was the commercial and colonial developments of the mid- and late seventeenth century that were decisive, not only as generators of wealth in themselves, but in supplying fresh and profitable markets for domestic industry. Likewise, in the decades of economic consolidation from 1701 to *c*.1745, the link between overseas (now increasingly transoceanic) markets and steady industrial growth in Britain remained of the first importance. But in the 1740s, the terms of the equation began to change very significantly, as the home market (already revivified in the previous two decades by rising real wages) developed into a major engine of industrial growth and, ultimately, modernisation. In the economic chapters of this book and of *Making of a Great Power* there has been discussion of all these matters and of their inter-relationship, along with analysis of those changes in agricultural methods and productivity [K.2(i)] and in the distribution of land, which in their turn interacted beneficially with commerce (through the grain trade) and with industry. In this Conclusion it remains only to sum up statistically the remarkable extent of the economic progress made by this still (so-called) 'pre-industrial' country over the whole of the period between 1660 and 1783. (With the very necessary proviso that for industry especially, figures of *any* kind – let alone reliable figures – are exceedingly difficult to come by before the late 1690s.)

As the architects of the Navigation legislation of 1660–3 had been well aware, shipping was the golden key to the wealth of 'a trading nation' (*Making of a Great Power*, Ch. 3; J.1). It will be remembered that in 1660 the Dutch, despite heavy losses of merchantmen in war, were still the carriers of much of the world's trade, as well as being Europe's leading commercial power *per se*. Before 1700 they had lost both crowns to the English, whose merchant marine by the early eighteenth century had built up a lead over those of the other maritime powers, including France, which was unassailable. It must be doubted whether the total tonnage of the English merchant fleet at the Restoration much exceeded 160,000. By 1786, the first year for which the new General Register of Shipping becomes a source of thoroughly authentic statistics, it had grown to 1,055,000 – not counting the now substantial number of ships which plied from Glasgow and other Scottish ports. Equally striking is the fact that the growth of the English outports, and above all of the biggest provincial ports from Newcastle and Hull in the east round to Bristol, Liverpool and Whitehaven on the west coast, accounted by the mid-1780s for more than three-quarters of all English-owned shipping; their 740,000 tons was well over five times the amount of shipping which the vast port of London had harboured in 1702 and six and a half times the entire English merchant marine of 1629 [*Making of a Great Power*, J.3 (B); this vol., J.3 (A)]

Attempting to measure the increase in the volume of trade passing through English ports which these ships (for the most part) carried, confronts us with the problem posed by the Board of Trade's statistics after 1696, with their misleadingly conservative bias, and still more with the absence of *any* reliable comprehensive data from official sources before this date. With these serious limitations in mind, it is none the less instructive to record Professor D.C. Coleman's estimates that England's total gross overseas commodities trade (imports, domestic exports and re-exports), having grown from around £5.5 million on the eve of the Civil War to an average £7.9 million annually during the years 1663–9, was exceeding £20 million by 1752–4. Twenty years later, just before the trade depression which began in the run-up to the American War of Independence (Ch. 10), that gross total, at official values, had risen to almost £28 million. Figures for the early 1780s still bear some traces of the lingering malaise of the wartime depression, but those for the last two years of the decade, 1789–90, at a gross total of £38.2 million, speak eloquently of the boundless resilience of eighteenth-century entrepreneurs and merchants and the astonishing potential for growth of Britain's commerce and industry, despite the loss of the thirteen North American colonies (121); [J.3].

As for industry specifically, domestic exports and raw material imports offer us possibly the surest guide, in relative terms, to its wider fortunes between William III's reign and George II's. Woollen, worsted and mixed woollen cloth manufacture still reigned supreme on the English industrial scene in 1700 as they had in 1660, and such products massively dominated the domestic export trade during the first boom years of the Commercial Revolution in the 1670s and 1680s, much as tobacco, sugar and East Indian textiles spearheaded the dramatic advance at that time of the re-export or entrepôt trade [*Making of a Great Power*, Ch. 3; J.3. (D, E, F)]. In the first decade after the Restoration, woollens had accounted for almost 75 per cent of London's exports and by the opening years of the eighteenth century they still represented 70 per cent of all Britain's domestic exports. But during the next eighty years that proportion shrank remarkably, down to 63 per cent in the 1730s and to 35 per cent by 1780–9. Nevertheless the industry's supremacy over all other branches of English (though not Scottish [L.3(iv)]) manufacture remained secure throughout this period. This is very evident from the table L.3(v), which shows how the amount of raw wool which the woollen and worsted industry consumed rose from an estimated 40 million to 98 million pounds between 1695 and 1779, as well as pointing to a rise in the gross value of woollen cloth production of more than 270 per cent in the same period. The biggest increase in output took place from 1741–79 and it is plain that the great bulk of it was swallowed up by home consumers.

Pondering the figures we have for retained raw material imports also helps us to understand two other very important eighteenth-century industrial trends. One is the hunger of the metalware trades for foreign bar iron, in spite of a near trebling down to the 1780s of the output of pig iron from Britain's own increasingly coke-fired blast furnaces [L.3(ii) (A), (C)]. The second is the throb of activity in the cotton towns and villages of Lancashire, Cheshire, Derbyshire, and later Scotland, between the 1760s and the early 1780s, as the jenny, the water frame and the mule in turn transformed the spinning capacity of this youthful industry. Retained imports of raw cotton in 1784–6, at 16.1 million pounds a year were nearly five times higher than the annual average for the 1760s [L.3(v)(2)]. Britain's ability to survive the immense challenge of the Revolutionary and Napoleonic Wars between 1793 and 1815 would depend in no small measure on her capacity to produce, and sell, cotton, iron and steel. But at a time when the marriage of steam and machinery had just been sealed (see Ch. 11) that ability would depend no less on the productivity of the country's coal-mines. By dovetailing the careful calculations and estimates of Nef and Flinn, it is possible to reconstruct the pattern of that productivity for at least the near-century from 1680 to 1775 [L.3(i)]. By 1783 total annual output must have comfortably exceeded 9 million tons, a third of it mined in the North-East of England, around one-ninth in Scotland, and at least 35 per cent in the fields of Lancashire, Yorkshire and the West Midlands – a far higher proportion than in 1700, when *total* production in Britain was probably just short of 3 million tons.

The consternation which the mounting quarrel with the American colonists, and the subsequent disasters of the war, caused among Britain's merchants, shippers, and new captains of industry is easily understood. (Roughly three out of every ten ships on Britain's sea-going merchant fleet on the eve of the war had been built in North American yards.) The seemingly crucial importance of the colonies of the First British Empire, and of the Indian and African trading stations, to the eighteenth-century British economy, and above all the key rôle of North America in its growth, has been fully explained in the text of this book (Ch. 10) and is illustrated with great clarity by the statistics in table J.3,C. By 1783 much of that First Empire – and to many traders and manufacturers the most prized part of it – lay in ruins. How swiftly the new United States of America would replace the old thirteen colonies as a keystone of the British economy was unguessable at the time of the Peace of Versailles; in any case, that is a story which the next volume in this series has already told.[7] It would, however, seem appropriate to close this book and conclude one of its recurrent themes, Britain's status as a Great Power, with words written in 1952 by the late Vincent Harlow, in which he propounded what was then a brilliantly novel thesis of prime relevance to historians looking to explain the rapidity of Britain's recovery after 1775–83 and her capacity to withstand the infinitely greater strains which awaited her from 1793–1815:

> The process of founding what may be termed . . . the Second British Empire began some thirty years before the collapse of the First. By the end of the Seven Years' War Britain had attained a commanding position, not only in North America and India, but also on the ocean routes of world trade. Scientific and industrial development at home, and the possession of decisive superiority at sea naturally led a self-confident island people to search the oceans for new markets. The period which followed the Treaty of Paris witnessed a sustained outburst of maritime exploration unparalleled since the days of the Tudor seamen. Indeed, the voyages of the Georgian navigators represented a conscious revival of an ambition to open up new fields of commerce in the Pacific and the South China Seas which had been in the forefront of national policy under Elizabeth. (158, *I, 3*)

'The Second British Empire which began to develop alongside the old colonial system', Harlow continues later, 'was not in fact an empire in the normal sense. Except in India, where the situation was exceptional [for India, 1763–83, see below J.2, *India*; and J.1. for the India Acts and Bills of 1773–83] . . . the expense and friction attending the establishment of [new] territorial jurisdiction was to be avoided. The ideal was a chain of trading posts, protected at strategic points by naval bases' (158, *4*). Yet although it was to be composed in the main of Asians and Africans, this second Empire still had as two of its jewels Eastern Canada [see J.2, *Quebec Act*] and the long-treasured West Indian islands; it is worth recalling that Captain Cook sailed on the first of his famous expeditions, to Australasia, only five years after the Peace of Paris, in the self same year that Grafton's Chancellor of the Exchequer, Charles Townshend, was alienating the Americans with his tea and other duties.

Britain in 1783 was, as Eric Evans has put it, 'the most developed nation on earth'.[8] She was the possessor of the most open society, the most sophisticated financial infrastructure, the most advanced industrial capacity, and – despite the loss of America – still the greatest commmercial potential, in Europe. The materials for rebuilding her dented but by no means demolished greatness in the later 1780s were all to hand as the ink dried on the Treaties of Versailles. And since Britain remained above all a trading power, the facility with which the younger Pitt's ministry could promote the work of reconstruction depended much on the nation's overseas markets and sources of supply. Down to 1792, European markets would play a revivified, essential part in this process. But in the longer term, and particularly during the harsh years of Napoleon's Continental System after 1800,[9] the new imperial trade links (along with the older transatlantic ones in their reincarnated form) would be decisive.

---

1. Of the English Channel, that happy hunting-ground of French privateers, this was true only from about 1708 onwards.
2. Such attempts are full of hazard, because in King's case, especially, (as was pointed out years ago [188]), the base material is often so unreliable.

3. P.H. Lindert and J.G. Williamson, 'Revising England's Social Tables, 1688–1867' (Univ. of Wisconsin, 1981) – mimeo copy, kindly supplied by Peter Lindert; N.F.R. Crafts, (130b), p. 189, n.54 and *passim*.

4. See (100), ch. 2, *passim*. Dr Gilbert is at times rather cavalier in ignoring his own caveats.

5. E.J. Evans, 'Some Reasons for the Growth of English Rural Anti-clericalism, *c*.1750–*c*.1830', *P & P*, 66 (1975); W.R. Ward, *Religion and Society in England, 1790–1850* (1972), pp. 9–10.

6. C.M. Cipolla, *Before the Industrial Revolution* (2nd edn, 1981), p. 4. Some rather higher figures are current (e.g. Louis Henry, 21–22 million [D.V. Glass & D.E.C. Eversley, *Population in History: Essays in Historical Demography* (1965), 455]). But the discrepancies probably arise because of the differences in the boundaries of what is *now* France and what was *then* France. See also Goubert in *ibid*, 458–9. The second suggestion rests on the common but fragile assumption that the population of Scotland at the time of the Union was around 1 million [see B.3(ii)]

7. E.J. Evans, *The Forging of the Modern State: Early Industrial Britain, 1783–1870* (1983), pp. 32–5.

8. Ibid., p. 11

9. Ibid., pp. 83–5

A. GLOSSARY

Armigerous: [of 'gentle'/noble families] having the right to bear coats of arms approved by the College of Heralds.

Assiento: an exclusive contract awarded by the Spanish crown for the supply of slaves [normally Negroes from West Africa] to Spain's New World colonies.

Burgage boroughs: a type of borough represented in Parliament under the unreformed electoral system (pre-1832), distinguished by the limiting of its franchise to either the owners or tenants of ancient pieces of real estate – buildings or plots of land – called 'burgages'.

Deism: a form of 'natural religion' characterised by (1) a rationalist belief in the existence of a Supreme Being, envisaged (on the evidence of the natural world) as a remote and detached Creator, and not as a pervasive, all-powerful judge of men; and (2) rejection of all the elements of mystery and revelation in orthodox Christianity and of the authority of any priesthood.

Erastianism: the belief that the Church was subordinate to the state and should be subject to ultimate control by the lay authorities.

General Warrants: warrants issued by the Secretaries of State which authorised *either* (1) the arrest of an unnamed person or persons, *or* (2) the seizure of unspecified papers belonging to a person or persons. Used only in political cases after 1695; declared injurious to liberty and illegal by Pratt C.J., as regards seizure of papers, after the action brought by John Wilkes in 1763 (Ch. 22); neither type of General Warrant used by British governments again after further hearings in the cases of *Leach v. Money et al.* and *Entick v. Carrington* (1765).

Habeas Corpus: short title of a writ which could be sued out to procure the release (or bail) of persons imprisoned without charge, or charged but not brought to trial. The Habeas Corpus Act of 1679 made the issuing of such a writ obligatory on the Lord Chancellor and all Common Law judges, except in cases of alleged treason.

'Political Nation': as used in this volume, a term signifying that part of the population of Britain which was politically-conscious or aware, either through occupying positions of influence, however modest, in public affairs, central or local; or through ownership of property; or through participation in the election of members of Parliament. (For the 'alternative political nation' of the period – the term coined by John Brewer (44) – see Ch. 3 above.)

Pragmatic Sanction: a house-law of the Habsburg royal family, promulgated by Emperor Charles VI (1711–40) providing that if he had no male issue, the undivided succession to the Habsburg lands should pass, not in order of primogeniture to the daughters of Emperor Joseph I but to his own eldest daughter Maria Theresa. (The product of protracted negotiations down to 1724 in his own dominions, and in particular of a deal with the diet of Hungary: thereafter a vital theme of European diplomacy until 1740.)

Quamdiu se bene gesserint: commissions issued to judges *quamdiu se bene gesserint*, i.e. 'during their good behaviour', meant that they had effective security of tenure, except on evidence of manifest incapacity or corruption, or on the accession of a new monarch.

Queen Anne's Bounty: the supplementation of the incomes of 'poor clergy' of the Church of England (in practice those holding livings of less than £35 p.a. until 1718 and less than £50 p.a. thereafter) from a fund established by Act of Parliament in 1704. Queen Anne's voluntary surrender of the crown's income from first-fruits and tenths formed the basis of the fund, but disbursements from it were much augmented subsequently by private charitable bequests.

'Reversionary Interest': the political influence of the heir to the throne in Hanoverian England and the opposition group or party which centred on the 'rival' court or Household of the Prince and Princess of Wales at Leicester House.

B. POPULATION AND SOCIAL STRUCTURE

B.1: Estimated population of England and Wales at decadal intervals and in some other years of interest, 1721–81

(totals in millions)

	England with Monmouthshire	*England and Wales**
1721	5,350	(5.725)
1727	5.480	(5.864)
1729	5.336	(5.709)[1]
1731	5.263	(5.631)
1737	5.480	(5.864)[2]
1741	5.576	(5.966)
1751	5.772	(6.176)
1761	6.147	(6.577)
1771	6.448	(6.899)
1781	7.042	(7.535)
1783	7.127	(7.626)
1801	8.664	(9.370)[3]

* The estimate for Wales, without Monmouthshire, has been arrived at by following Wrigley and Schofield's recommended method of calculating 7% of the population of England (152, *566*, note 20).

Notes:
1. The last of three years of exceptionally heavy epidemic mortality.
2. The end of the last *decade* of 'massacre by epidemic' in English history.
3. Cf. the official census figure, often said to be inflated, of 9.26 million for England and Wales. It may be that by the late eighteenth century 7% is too high a proportion for the population of Wales.

Source:
E.A. Wrigley and R.S. Schofield (152), Table A3.3, pp. 531–4; estimate reached by back-projection.

B.2: The urban population of England and Wales: estimated growth of some leading towns, 1660–1792

(i) Some recent rough estimates of the population of London

	Wrigley (1967)		*Finlay and Shearer (1986)*
1600	200,000		200,000
1650	400,000		375,000
1700	575,000		490,000
1750	675,000		
1775		[c. 750,000]	
1801 (census)		948,040	

Sources:
1. E.A. Wrigley (144b).
2. R. Finlay and B. Shearer, 'Population growth and suburban expansion', in A.L. Beier and R. Finlay, eds. (144a). Their estimates, based on exhaustive study of all surviving parish register evidence, are the most authoritative yet published.

Year	Bath	Birmingham	Bolton	Bristol	Chester	Coventry	Derby
1792							
1789			11,739*				
1788							8,563*
1786							
1785							
1784							
1781		c.50,000					
1779		42,350*					
1778							
1775	20,500			55,000		c.14,500	
1774					14,713*		
1773			4,568*				
1771							
1762							
1758							
1755							
1752							
1750	9,000	23,688*	c.4,000				
1749						12,817*	
1748							
1740							
1739							
1736							
1730							
1725				c.30,000			
1722					11,000		
1719							
1717							
1713							
1712							4,000
1710							
1700			2–3,000		c.8,000		
1695				19,403*			
1694						6,710*	
1693							
1692							
1690		7,000/9,000‡					
1676		c.4,400					
1673							
1672							
1670							
1665							
1664					c.7,500		
1662							
1660	1,100						

‡ varying estimates
* indicates returns from local censuses
† indicates population of parish (as opposed to township)
$ house-count

Hull	Ipswich	Leeds[2]	Leicester	Liverpool	Manchester (with Salford)	
22,286*						1792
						1789
					c.50,000³	1788
				41,600		1786
			12,784*			1785
						1784
						1781
						1779
						1778
13,500		17,121*				1775
						1774
				34,407*	27,246*	1773
		16,380*				1771
						1762
					19,839*	1758
	12,124*					1755
						1752
		12,000	c.8,000	22,000		1750
						1749
						1748
						1740
						1739
						1736
				c.15,000		1730
		c.10,000				1725
						1722
						1719
					10–12,000$	1717
						1713
			6,450*			1712
				8,186		1710
6,000¹		8,000†		5,145	c.8,000	1700
	7,943*					1695
						1694
						1693
						1692
		6,500		c.4,000		1690
						1676
				c.1,500		1673
						1672
			c.4,800			1670
						1665
						1664
	c.8,000					1662
					c.5,000	1660

Notes to B.2 (ii)
1. The population was 7,500 with Sculcoates
2. In 1775 the parish population figure was 30,400.
3. The population was 42,821 excluding Salford.

(ii) Provincial urban growth (*cont.*)

Year	Newcastle-on-Tyne[4]	Norwich	Nottingham	Plymouth[5]	Portsmouth[6]
1792					
1789					
1788					
1786		41,051			
1785					
1784					
1781					
1779			17,711*		
1778					
1775	33,000		16,510*	25,000	20,000
1774					
1773					
1771					
1762					
1758					
1755					
1752		36,169*			
1750	29,000				
1749					
1748					10,000†
1740				c.12,000	
1739			10,720*		
1736					
1730	20,000†				
1725			9,800		
1722					
1719					
1717					
1713					
1712					
1710					
1700	16,000	31,000*	7,000	8,500	7,500
1695		28,546			
1694					
1693					
1692					
1690					
1676			c.5,500		
1673					
1672					
1670					
1665	c.13,000$				
1664					3,500
1662		c.20,000			
1660					

‡ varying estimates
* indicates returns from local censuses
† indicates population of parish (as opposed to township)
$ house-count

Sheffield[7]	Sunderland	Whitehaven	Wolverhampton	Yarmouth	Year
					1792
					1789
26,538		11,368*			1788
					1786
					1785
			12,608*		1784
					1781
					1779
					1778
	16,000	9,665*			1775
					1774
					1773
					1771
		9,063*			1762
					1758
12,983					1755
					1752
		7,454*			1750
					1749
					1748
					1740
					1739
9,695*					1736
		6,000			1730
					1725
					1722
	6,000				1719
					1717
		4,000			1713
					1712
					1710
3,500				11,000	1700
					1695
					1694
		2,222*			1693
c.2,600					1692
	2,000				1690
					1676
					1673
c.2,100					1672
					1670
					1665
					1664
				c.10,000	1662
		c.200			1660

Notes to B.2 (ii)
4. The 1750 and 1775 figures included Gateshead.
5. The figures include the Dock; in 1740 the population figure was 8,400 excluding the Dock.
6. After 1702 the figures include Southsea.
7. In 1672 the parish population figure was 4,500, in 1736 it was 14,000 and in 1775 it was 27,000.

Note on sources: for B.2 (ii)

The statistics of town growth have to be viewed with some reserve, at least in the first 60–70 years of our period. But with the help of Hearth Tax figures, 1662–88, returns from the Compton census of 1676, returns of population made in response to the Act of 1695 (*Making of a Great Power*, pp. 44–5) and many local censuses and house-counts taken from the early decades of the eighteenth century onwards, urban historians have been able to arrive at figures for most leading towns and cities which are a reliable guide to growth patterns. These patterns can be delineated still more confidently in a few cases with the aid of cartographical evidences and artists' 'prospects' that are precise and valuable. As well as studies of particular towns and counties, the following secondary sources have been used in compiling the above table: C.M. Law, 'Some Notes on the Urban Population of England and Wales in the 18th century', *Local Historian*, **X** (1972); P. J. Corfield, (a) 'Urban Development in England and Wales in the Sixteenth and Seventeenth Centuries', in D.C. Coleman and A.H. John, eds, (126); (b) (213). C.W. Chalklin (215); P.N. Borsay (211).

B.3: Some estimates of the population of Ireland and Scotland, 1678–1801

(i) The population of Ireland, 1678–1791[1] (millions)

1678	2.167	1772	3.584
1712	2.791	1777	3.740
1718	2.894	1781	4.048
1725	3.042	1785	4.019
1726	3.031	1788	4.389
1732	3.018	1790	4.591
1754	3.191	1791	4.753
1767	3.480		

(ii) The population of Scotland, 1700–1801 (millions)[2]

1707	1.048[3]
1755	1.265
1795	1.526
1801	1.608[4]

Estimates of Scotland's population that are based on anything more than guesswork, and solid data on which to base modern demographic 'back projections', are so rare in Scotland before the first (1801) census, that attempts to estimate the size of the population have generally been eschewed by modern Scottish historians. Hence the paucity of figures above. The Alexander Webster 'census' figure for 1755, however, is generally held to be a reliable anchor-point.

(iii) Pointers to Scottish urban population growth, 1691–1801[5]

	Hearth Tax 'Paid Hearths', 1691	c. 1700	Webster[6] 1755	Census 1801
Edinburgh (with Leith)	14,745	30–40,000*	57,000	81,600
Glasgow (with Barony)	4,409	12,766[†]	31,700	83,700
Aberdeen (old & new)	3,580		15,600	27,400
Dundee	2,537		12,400	26,800
Inverness	1,099		9,700	8,700
Perth	984		9,000	14,800
	[town only]			
Dunfermline	(?)		8,500	9,900
Greenock	746		3,800	17,400
	[town only]			
Paisley	(over 500)		6,800	31,200
Kilmarnock	(over 500)		4,400	8,000

* virtually all modern estimates are within this range
† magistrates' enumeration

Notes and Sources:
1. K.H. Connell, *The Population of Ireland 1750–1845* (Oxford, 1950), p. 25.
2. R.H. Campbell and J.B.A. Dow, eds., *Source Book of Scottish Economic and Social History* (New York, 1968), pp. 1, 2 and 8f.
3. T.C. Smout (241), p. 258. But cf. M. Flinn, *et al.*, *Scottish Population History from the 17th century to the 1930s* (Cambridge, 1977), p. 4; 'Estimates by earlier historians of a figure of one million or 1.1 million from the beginning of the eighteenth century are based either on their own or other people's guesses. We must accept therefore that we cannot know what the long-run trends of population were in the seventeenth and eighteenth centuries. We cannot even be sure that the population of Scotland was, say, less in 1690 than it was in 1755, as is commonly assumed.'
4. This is the official census figure, but P. Mathias (131b), p. 166 estimates it to be nearer 1.5 million.
5. Flinn *et al.*, op cit., p. 191; Smout (241), p. 261.
6. Smout (241), p. 259, note 2.

351

B.4: Years of epidemics and heavy mortality in England

		Predominant epidemic disease (where ascertainable)
1657–8	***	influenza
1658–9	**	'the new fever' (regarded by some contemporary physicians as associated with, or a forerunner of, the Plague)
1665–6	***	'The Great Plague'
1670–1	*	
1678–80	* ⎫	influenza in 1679; but in general virulent 'epidemic agues' (including
1680–1	*** ⎭	the 'quartan ague'; 'the New Delight')
1681–3	*	enteric fevers, influenza and agues
1684–5	*	typhus or 'the new fever'; some dysentery
1719–20	*	(?)typhus
1727–30	***	influenza, enteric fever & smallpox; 1729 'relapsing' or 'putrid' fever (probably a new and virulent strain of typhus)
1741–2	***	typhus, in the main; 'spotted fever'
1762–3	**	influenza in 1762
1766–7	*	(?) mainly typhus in 1766; influenza in 1767
1779–80	*	
1781–2	*	influenza; flare-up of smallpox; typhus locally
1783–4	*	probably influenza or 'epidemic agues' in the main; dysentery

Note:
Epidemic years as defined below run from July to June and their severity is graded according to the 'star' system adopted by E.A. Wrigley and R.S. Schofield (152), viz. *** exceptionally severe national mortality crisis ** severe crisis * year of moderately severe, but national, epidemics.

Sources:
Wrigley and Schofield (152), pp. 332—40; J.D. Chambers (150); C. Creighton, *A History of Epidemics in England* (2 vols., Cambridge, 1894; 2nd edn repr., 1965), I. pp. 568–77; II. *passim*; M.W. Flinn (151a).

B.5: Social structure and income distribution in England and Wales, 1688 and 1760: the contemporary views of Gregory King and Joseph Massie*

Rank or occupation	Number of families		Average annual income £		Total income £000	
	1688	*1760*	*1688*	*1760*	*1688*	*1760*
Temporal peers	160		3,200		512	
Bishops	26		1,300		33.8	
Baronets and knights	1,400		780		1,094	
Esquires	3,200		450		1,200	
Gentlemen	12,000		280		2,880	
TOTAL Aristocracy & gentry	16,786	18,000[1]		[1]	5,719	8,720

Rank or occupation	Number of families		Average annual income £		Total income £000	
	1688	1760	1688	1760	1688	1760
Higher clergy	2,000	2,000	72	100	144	200
Inferior clergy	8,000	9,000	50	50	400	450
Lawyers & legal officials	10,000	12,000	154	100	1,540	1,200
'Persons professing liberal arts & sciences'	15,000	18,000	60	60	900	1,080
Civil office-holders	5,000 }	16,000	240 }	60	1,200 }	960
Petty civil officials	5,000 ⌋		120 ⌋		600 ⌋	
Army & Navy officers	9,000	8,000	70	85	640	680
TOTAL Professions	54,000	65,000			5,424	4,570
Prosperous freeholders	40,000	30,000	91	100 }	10,240	9,000
Lesser freeholders	120,000	180,000[2]	55	33.5[2] ⌋		
Tenant farmers	150,000	155,000[3]	42.5	51[3]	6,375	7,950
TOTAL Farming†	310,000	365,000			16,615	16,950
Eminent overseas merchants	2,000	3,000[4]	400	466[4]	800	1,400
Lesser merchants	8,000	10,000	198	200	1,584	2,000
Shopkeepers, innkeepers & domestic tradesmen	50,000	184,500[5]	45	54[5]	2,250	9,900
TOTAL Trade & distribution	60,000	197,500			4,634	13,300
Manufacturers, artisans & craftsmen	60,000[6]	308,000[7]	38	26–7[7]	2,280	9,120
TOTAL Manufacturing	60,000	308,000			2,280	9,120
Husbandmen		200,000				
out-servants and wage-labourers in town & country	364,000	220,000	15	14	5,460	5,950
TOTAL Labouring	364,000	420,000			5,460	5,950
Common seamen & fishermen	50,000	60,000	20	20	1,000	1,200
Common soldiers	35,000	18,000	14	14	490	252
TOTAL Common soldiers & seamen	85,000	78,000			1,490	1,452
Cottagers, small ale-house keepers & paupers	400,000	20,000[8]	6.5	20[8]	2,000	400
TOTAL 'Cottagers and paupers'	400,000	–	–	2,000	–	

* While Massie undoubtedly used King as his model, he was of course writing half a century after the Union and it is not crystal clear that his figures were meant to apply *only* to England and Wales.

† Excl. wage-labourers and outservants.

Notes:

1. In this (largely) landed hierarchy Massie does not distinguish the number of families or average income within each rank. He assumes 10 families with incomes of £20,000 p.a. or more; 20 of £10,000+; 40 of £8,000+, down to 6,400 lesser gentry families of £2–300 p.a. and 4,800 of £3–400 p.a.
2. Subdivided by Massie into 60,000 at av. £50 p.a.; and 120,000 at av. £25 p.a.
3. Subdivided into 5,000 big tenant farmers at av. £150 p.a.; 10,000 at £100 p.a.; 20,000 at £70 p.a. and 120,000 at £40 p.a.
4. Of whom Massie estimated 1,000 formed a merchant élite of av. £600 p.a.
5. Including 2,500 wealthy tradesmen at av. £400 p.a.; and 12,000 at £100 p.a. av.
6. King did not recognise '[master] manufacturers' as a separate occupational or status group.
7. Ranging from the families of 200,000 artisans earning *c*. £20 p.a. av. to an élite of master manufacturers: 2,500 at £250 p.a. av., 5,000 at £100 & 10,000 at £70 p.a. av.
8. The figures for 1760 in the previous three categories, especially those for artisans and wage-labourers, must be read in the light of the fact that, unlike King, Massie subsumed *all* 'paupers' (those in receipt of poor relief at the time), and presumably some 'cottagers' in other working groups.

Sources:

Second revised version [1698/9] of Gregory King's table of 'the income & expense of the several families of England', printed in G. Holmes (188), Appendix, pp. 66–8; Joseph Massie's estimate of the social structure and income, 1759–60, printed in, P. Mathias (131a), pp. 186–9, Tables 9.1 and 9.3. I have partly regrouped and reworked both sets of statistics to make them more comparable and coherent.

C. MONARCHS AND PRETENDERS

C.1: The Houses of Stuart and Hanover [reigning monarchs are given in bold capitals, Stuart Pretenders in italic capitals]

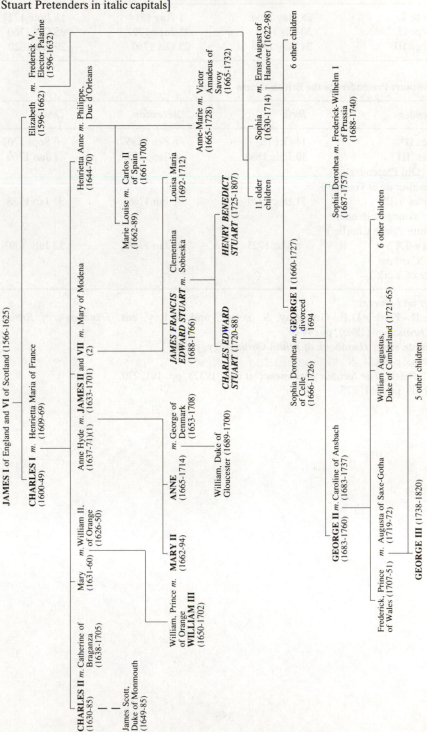

C.2: Reigning monarchs[1]

Monarch	Birth	Accession	Death
George I	28 May 1660	1 Aug 1714	11 June 1727
George II	30 Oct 1683	11 June 1727	25 Oct 1760
George III	24 May 1738	25 Oct 1760	29 Jan 1820

C.3: Stuart Pretenders to the British throne

Pretender	Birth	'Accession'	Death
James II[2]	14 Oct 1633	6 Feb 1685	6 Sept 1701
James 'III'[3] (the 'Old Pretender'; 'Chevalier de St George')	10 June 1688	6 Sept 1701	1 Jan 1766
Charles 'III'[4] (the 'Young Pretender'; 'Bonnie Prince Charlie')	31 Dec 1720	1 Jan 1766	31 Jan 1788
Henry 'IX'[5] (the 'Cardinal Duke of York')	6 Mar 1725	31 Jan 1788	13 July 1807

Notes and sources:

1. E.B. Fryde, D.E. Greenway, S. Porter, and I. Roy, eds, *Handbook of British Chronology* (1986), pp. 44–6.
2. Fryde *et al., Handbook of British Chronology*, p. 44.
3. Ibid., p. 45.
4. C. Petrie, *The Jacobite Movement* (1st edn, 1932), pp. 161, 270.
5. Ibid., pp. 161, 275.

D. LEADING GOVERNMENT OFFICE-HOLDERS, 1722–83

D.1: Heads of the Treasury [First Lord of the Treasury unless otherwise stated]

Note:

Names in capitals indicate acknowledged head or joint heads of ministries/'first ministers'/ 'prime ministers'

George I – George II

ROBERT WALPOLE (SIR ROBERT, 1725)   Apr 1721–Feb 1742

George II

Earl of Wilmington	Feb 1742–Aug 1743
HENRY PELHAM	Aug 1743–d. Mar 1754
Thomas Pelham-Holles,	
DUKE OF NEWCASTLE	Mar 1754–Nov 1756
DUKE OF DEVONSHIRE	
(PITT-DEVONSHIRE Ministry)	Nov 1756–July 1757

George II –George III

DUKE OF NEWCASTLE	
(PITT-NEWCASTLE Ministry, 1757–61)	July 1757–May 1762

George III

EARL OF BUTE	May 1762–Apr 1763
GEORGE GRENVILLE	Apr 1763–July 1765
MARQUESS OF ROCKINGHAM	July 1765–July 1766
DUKE OF GRAFTON	Aug 1766–Feb 1770
(PITT [CHATHAM] Ministry, 1766–8)	
LORD NORTH	Jan 1770–Mar 1782
MARQUESS OF ROCKINGHAM	Mar–d. July 1782
EARL OF SHELBURNE	July 1782–24 Feb 1783
Duke of Portland	2 Apr 1783–Dec 1783
(nominal head of FOX-NORTH Coalition)	
WILLIAM PITT THE YOUNGER	19 Dec 1783–

D.2: Secretaries of State

During the whole of this period there were normally two Secretaries of State in office at any one time, to deal with foreign and domestic affairs. (For the third Secretary appointed from time to time between 1709 and 1746 to deal with affairs in Scotland, see D.5). In a division of duties that was more hard and fast after the Revolution than before it, the Secretary for the Northern Department was responsible for diplomatic contact with the Empire, the United Provinces, Scandinavia and Russia; the brief of the Southern Department embraced France, Switzerland, Italy, the Iberian Peninsula and Turkey. Responsibility for home affairs was shared. In 1782 the old demarcation of duties was abandoned in favour of the modern division between Foreign Secretary and Home Secretary.

George I

Viscount Townshend	Sept 1714–Dec 1716
James Stanhope (Viscount 1717, Earl of Stanhope 1718)	Sept 1714–Apr 1717
Paul Methuen	Dec 1716–Apr 1717
(Whig Schism of 1717)	
3rd Earl of SUNDERLAND	Apr 1717–Mar 1718
Joseph Addison	Apr 1717–Mar 1718
Lord STANHOPE	Mar 1718–d. Feb 1721
James Craggs	Mar 1718–d. Feb 1721
Viscount Townshend	Feb 1721–May 1730
Lord Carteret	Mar 1721–Mar 1724

George I – George II

Duke of Newcastle	Apr 1724–Mar 1754
Lord Harrington	June 1730–Feb 1742
Lord CARTERET[1]	Feb 1742–Nov 1744
Earl of Harrington	Nov 1744–10 Feb 1746
Earl of Granville (Carteret)	10–14 Feb 1746
Earl of Harrington	14 Feb–28 Oct 1746
Earl of Chesterfield	Oct 1746–Feb 1748
Duke of Bedford	Feb 1748–June 1751
Earl of Holderness	June 1751–9 June 1757
Sir Thos Robinson	Mar 1754–Oct 1755
Henry Fox	Nov 1755–Nov 1756
WILLIAM PITT[2]	Dec 1756–Apr 1757

George II – George III

WILLIAM PITT[3]	June 1757–Oct 1761
Earl of Holderness	29 June 1757–Mar 1761
Earl of Bute	Mar 1761–May 1762
Earl of Egremont	Oct 1761–d. Aug 1763
George Grenville	May–Oct 1762
Earl of Halifax	Oct 1762–July 1765
Earl of Sandwich	Sept 1763–July 1765
Henry Seymour Conway	July 1765–Jan 1768
Duke of Grafton	July 1765–May 1766
Duke of Richmond	May–July 1766
Earl of Shelburne	July 1766–Oct 1768
Viscount Weymouth	Jan 1768–Dec 1770
Earl of Rochford	Oct 1768–Nov 1775
Earl of Sandwich	Dec 1770–Jan 1771
Earl of Halifax	Jan–d. June 1771
Viscount Weymouth	Nov 1775–Nov 1779
Earl of Suffolk	June 1771–d. Mar 1779
Viscount Stormont	Mar 1779–Mar 1782
Earl of Hillsborough	Nov 1779–Mar 1782

Foreign Secretary		Home Secretary	
Charles James Fox	Mar–July 1782	Earl of Shelburne	Mar–July 1782
Thos Robinson,			
Lord Grantham	July 1782–Apr 1783	Thos Townsend	July 1782–Apr 1783
CHARLES JAMES FOX[4]	Apr–Dec 1783	LORD NORTH[4]	Apr–Dec 1783
Marquess of Carmarthen	23 Dec 1783	Earl Temple	19–23 Dec 1783
		Lord Sydney	23 Dec 1783

Notes:
1. Premier minister, in terms of influence, until advent of Pelham, 1743 (see D.1).
2. Pitt-Devonshire ministry.
3. Pitt-Newcastle ministry
4. Fox-North coalition.

D.3: Lord Chancellors and Keepers of the Great Seal, 1722–83

Sir Thomas Parker, Lord Macclesfield, earl of Macclesfield (1721)	May 1718–Jan 1725	Lord Chancellor
(Seal in commission, Jan–June 1725)		
Sir Peter King, Lord King	June 1725–Nov 1733	Lord Chancellor
Lord Talbot	1733–d. Feb 1737	Lord Chancellor
Philip Yorke, Lord Hardwick, earl of Hardwicke (1754)	1737–Nov 1756	Lord Chancellor
(Seal in commission until June 1757)		
Sir Robert Henley, Lord Henley (1760), earl of Northington (1764)	June 1757–July 1766	Lord Chancellor (1761)
Charles Pratt, Lord Camden	July 1766–Jan 1770	Lord Chancellor
(Charles Yorke died straight after appointment: Seal in commission until 1771)		
Lord Apsley, earl of Bathurst (1775)	Jan 1771–June 1778	Lord Chancellor
Lord Thurlow	1778–Apr 1783	Lord Chancellor
(Seal in commission Apr–Dec 1783)		
Lord Thurlow	23 Dec 1783–	

D.4: Chancellors of the Exchequer, 1722–1783

Some notable holders of the office who were not at the same time First Lords of the Treasury include:

Samuel Sandys	Feb 1742–Dec 1743
Henry Bilson Legge	1754–55; Nov 1756–1761 (exc. Apr–July 1757)
William Dowdeswell	1765–66 (1st Rockingham ministry)
Charles Townshend	Aug 1766–Sept 1767
Lord North	Oct 1767–1782 (1st Lord, 1770)
Lord John Cavendish	Apr–July 1782 (2) Apr–Dec 1783
William Pitt the Younger	July 1782–Apr 1783

D.5: Scottish Secretaries of State, 1709–46

Duke of Queensberry	1709–d. 1711
Earl of Mar	1713–Sept 1714
Duke of Montrose	1714–Aug 1715
Duke of Roxburgh	1716–Aug 1725
Marquess of Tweeddale	1742–Jan 1746

D.6: Other civil offices held by important politicians, 1722–82

[*Abbreviations*: LHA = Lord High Admiral; 1st Lord Adm. = First Lord of the Admiralty; LL Ireland = Lord Lieutenant of Ireland; L. Pres. = Lord President of the Council; LPS = Lord Privy Seal; Comptroller = Comptroller of the Household]

George I – II

Henry Pelham	Treasury Commr. 1721–4
Henry Boyle, Lord Carleton	L. Pres. 1721–5
Lord Carteret	LL Ireland 1724–30
Henry Pelham	Sec-at-War 1724–30
2nd Duke of Devonshire	L. Pres. 1725–d. 1729
Earl of Wilmington	L. Pres. 1730–42
Henry Pelham	Paymaster-Gen. 1730–43
Sir William Yonge	Sec-at-War 1730–46
3rd Duke of Devonshire	LPS 1731–3
Duke of Devonshire	LL Ireland 1737–45
Lord Hervey	LPS 1740–42
Lord Gower	LPS 1742–3; 1744–d. 1754
Earl of Chesterfield	LL Ireland 1745–6
Duke of Bedford	1st Lord Adm. 1744–8
Duke of Dorset	L. Pres. 1745–51
Earl of Harrington	LL Ireland 1746–7
William Pitt	Paymaster-Gen. 1746–55
Henry Fox	Sec-at-War 1746–55
Earl of Sandwich	1st Lord Adm. 1748–51
Duke of Dorset	LL Ireland 1750–55
Earl Granville	L. Pres. 1751–d. 1760

George II – III

Lord Anson	1st Lord Adm. 1751–6, 1757–d. 1762
Richard Temple-Grenville, 1st Earl Temple	1st Lord Adm. 1756–7
Earl Temple	LPS 1757–61
Duke of Bedford	LL Ireland 1757–61

George III

Charles Townshend	Sec-at-War 1761–2
Duke of Bedford	L. Pres. 1763–5
George Grenville	1st Lord Adm. Jan–Apr 1763
Earl of Sandwich	1st Lord Adm. Apr–Sept 1763
Duke of Newcastle	LPS 1765–66
Viscount Barrington	Sec-at-War 1765–78
William Pitt EARL OF CHATHAM	LPS July 1766–Mar 68
2nd Lord Gower	L. Pres. 1767–79
Lord Hillsborough	Colonial Sec. 1768–72
Duke of Grafton	LPS 1771–5
Earl of Sandwich	1st Lord Adm. 1771–82
Earl of Dartmouth	Colonial Sec 1772–5
Lord George Germain	Colonial Sec 1775–82
Earl of Buckinghamshire	LL Ireland 1776–80
Duke of Portland	LL Ireland 1780–Apr 82
Earl Temple	LL Ireland 1782–87

Principal sources:

1. E.B. Fryde, D.E. Greenway S. Porter and I. Roy, eds, *Handbook of British Chronology*, (3rd edn, 1986), pp. 82–195 *passim*.
2. J.C. Sainty, *Treasury Officials, 1660–1870* (1972); id., *Officials of the Secretaries of State, 1660–1782* (1973), pp. 24–5.

E. PARLIAMENT

E.1: Results of General Elections in Britain, 1715–84

[*Abbreviations*: C = Court/Ministry; O = Opposition; W = Whigs; T = Tories; U = Uncertain; OW = Opposition Whigs; CW = Court/Ministry Whigs

(i) *1715–54*[1]

1715		W:	341	T:	217	(Great Britain)				558
1722	{	W:	379	T:	178					558
	{ *	W:	389	T:	169					
1727	{	W:	424	T:	130					554
	{	*CW:	415	OW:	15	T:	128			558
1734	{	CW:	326	OW:	83	T:	149 }			558
	{	*CW:	330	OW:	83	T:	145 }			
[Eve of dissolution, 1741]		CW:	300	OW:	115	T:	143			558
1741		CW:	286	OW:	131	T:	136			553
[at first meeting Dec 1741]		CW:	276	OW:	124	T:	135			535[2]
1747	{	CW:	338	OW:	97	T:	117			552
	{	CW:	351	OW:	92	T:	115			558
1754		*CW:	368	OW:	42[3]	T:	106	U:	26	542[4]

* after hearing petitions

Principal sources and notes:
1. Sedgwick (12a), I, 33–57. See also Colley (28).
2. 23 seats were vacant at this time, through deaths, double returns, etc.
3. Bedford Whigs.
4. Lord Dupplin's contemporary estimate: J. Brooke (39), p. 89.

(ii) *1761–84*

1761	W: 446	T: 112[1]		

1768   This election took place in a period of political fragmentation and I am not aware of any fully comprehensive analysis of its results in terms of forces in the House of Commons. It has been estimated that the New House contained *c*.140 'party men', i.e. Rockinghamites (57), Chathamites, Grenvillites and Bedford Whigs (*c.* 20?); and that the remaining members consisted of the Court and Treasury group, a great number of Whig Independents, and a rump of Tories (49), of whom only 14 were now genuine independents and *c.* 12 were now ironically subsumed in the Whig aristocratic connexions. It is generally thought that the 'Opposition' (i.e. to the Chatham–Grafton ministry) gained some ground *initially* as a result of this election.[2]

1774   C: 321[3]   O: The number of committed Opposition members returned (including 43 Rockinghams) was almost certainly *lower* than the 170–80 who could be classified as such before the dissolution[4]

1780	C: 260	O: 254	U: 44	558[5]
1784	Pitt: 253	Fox: 123	U: 182	558[6]
		(i.e. committed supporters of both Fox & North)	(of which 116 considered 'hopeful' by Pitt's ministry)	

Notes:
1. L.J. Colley (28a), p. 216.
2. See in general, John Brooke, *The Chatham Administration* (1956); F. O'Gorman (46a); I.R. Christie (9), p. 73.
3. Government estimate after the election.
4. O'Gorman, pp. 320–1
5. John Robinson's contemporary estimates, made retrospectively in Feb 1781, i.e. after more than three months' experience of the first session. See Brooke (39).
6. Robinson's contemporary estimate: See Brooke (39), p. 132. Cf. alternative estimates in E.J. Evans, *The Forging of the Modern State: Early Industrial Britain, 1783–1870* (1985), p. 387.

E.2: Dates of parliamentary sessions, 1722–84

Parliament	Sessions	Date of dissolution	Remarks
George I			
1722–7	(1) Oct 1722–May 1723		
	(2) Jan–Apr 1724		
	(3) Nov 1724–May 1725		
	(4) Jan–May 1726		
	(5) Jan–May 1727		short 6th session called after
	(6) June–Jul 1727		George I's death abroad

George II

1727–34	(1) Jan–May 1728	
	(2) Jan–May 1729	
	(3) Jan–May 1730	
	(4) Jan–May 1731	
	(5) Jan–June 1732	
	(6) Jan–June 1733	
	(7) Jan–Apr 1734	17 Apr 1734
1734–41	(1) Jan–May 1735	
	(2) Jan–May 1736	
	(3) Feb–June 1737	
	(4) Jan–May 1738	
	(5) Feb–June 1739	
	(6) Nov 1739–Apr 1740	
	(7) Nov 1740–Apr 1741	27 Apr 1741
1741–47	(1) Dec 1741–Jul 1742	
	(2) Nov 1742–Apr 1743	
	(3) Dec 1743–May 1744	
	(4) Nov 1744–May 1745	This Parliament was dissolved for
	(5) Oct 1745–Aug 1746	political reasons one year inside
	(6) Nov 1746–June 1747	18 June 1747 maximum term
1747–54	(1) Nov 1747–May 1748	
	(2) Nov 1748–June 1749	
	(3) Nov 1749–Apr 1750	
	(4) Jan–June 1751	
	(5) Nov 1751–Mar 1752	
	(6) Jan–June 1753	
	(7) Nov 1753–Apr 1754	8 Apr 1754
1754–61	(1) May–June 1754	
	(2) Nov 1754–Apr 1755	
	(3) Nov 1755–May 1756	
	(4) Dec 1756–July 1757	
	(5) Dec 1757–June 1758	
	(6) Nov 1758–June 1759	
	(7) Nov 1759–May 1760	
	(8) 26–29 Oct 1760*	* Brief meeting, following George
	(9) 18 Nov 1760–19 Mar 1761	20 Mar 1761 II's death

George III

1761–8	(1) Nov 1761–June 1762	
	(2) Nov 1762–Apr 1763	
	(3) Nov 1763–Apr 1764	
	(4) Jan–May 1765	
	(5) Dec 1765–June 1766	
	(6) Nov 1766–June 1767	
	(7) Nov 1767–Mar 1768	11 Mar 1768

1768–74	(1) May–June 1768	
	(2) Nov 1768–May 1769	
	(3) Jan–May 1770	
	(4) Nov 1770–May 1771	
	(5) Jan–June 1772	
	(6) Nov 1772–Jul 1773	
	(7) Jan–June 1774	30 Sept 1774
1774–80	(1) Nov 1774–May 1775	
	(2) Oct 1775–May 1776	
	(3) Oct 1776–June 1777	
	(4) Nov 1777–June 1778	
	(5) Nov 1778–July 1779	
	(6) Nov 1779–Jul 1780	1 Sept 1780
1780–84	(1) Oct 1780–Jul 1781	Dissolved by George III after 4
	(2) Nov 1781–Jul 1782	sessions, following defeat of Fox–
	(3) Dec 1782–Jul 1783	North coalition and appointment
	(4) Nov 1783–Mar 1784	25 Mar 1784 of Younger Pitt's ministry

Principal source:

Fryde *et al.*, eds, *Handbook of British Chronology* (3rd edn, 1986) pp. 578–80.

F. THE CONSTITUTION: STATUTES, BILLS AND PROPOSALS

(*i*) *The Declaratory Act (Ireland), 1720* (6 George I, c.5)
Sometimes called 'the Dependency of Ireland Act' this Act followed an attempt by the
Irish House of Lords to prevent the execution of a decision of the British House of Lords
on an appeal from Dublin. The Act declared:

> That the said kingdom of Ireland hath been, is, and of right ought to be subordinate unto and
> dependent upon the imperial crown of Great Britain, as being inseparably united and annexed
> thereunto [and that Westminster] had, hath, and of right ought to have full power and authority
> to make laws and statutes of sufficient force and validity, to bind the kingdom and people of
> Ireland.

The House of Lords at Westminster therefore had the right to hear Irish appeals.

Source: D.B. Horn and M. Ransome, eds, *English Historical Documents vol. X 1714–1783*
(1957) p. 683.

(*ii*) *The Declaratory Act (America), 1766* (6 George III, c.12)
Following its preamble: Whereas several of the houses of representatives in his Majesty's
colonies and plantations in America have of late, against law, claimed to themselves 'the
sole and exclusive right of imposing duties and taxes on his Majesty's subjects' [in
America], the Act embodied the claim (following the repeal of the Stamp Act, 1766 [Ch.
21]):

> that the said colonies and plantations in America have been, are, and of right ought to be,
> subordinate unto, and dependent upon the imperial Crown and Parliament of Great Britain;
> and that the King's Majesty . . . had, hath and of right ought to have, full power and authority
> to make laws and statutes of sufficient force and validity to bind the colonies and people of
> America, subjects of the Crown of Great Britain, in all cases whatsoever.

Source: M. Jensen, ed., *English Historical Documents vol. IX: American Colonial
Documents to 1776* (1955), pp. 695–6.

(*iii*) *The American Declaration of Independence, 1776*

> We hold these truths to be self-evident, that all ment are created equal, that they are endowed
> by their Creator with certain unalienable Rights, that among these are Life, Liberty and the
> pursuit of Happiness. That to secure these rights, Governments are instituted among Men,
> deriving their just powers from the consent of the governed, That whenever any form of
> Government becomes destructive of these ends, it is the Right of the People to alter or to
> abolish it, and to institute new Government.

The Declaration then rehearsed the stages by which George III had conspired to try and
steal the Americans' liberty and property, their unavailing attempts to persuade their
British brethren to curtail his 'tyranny' and thence the regretful necessity of their breaking
away from Britain and holding their former kin, 'as we hold the rest of mankind, Enemies
in War, in Peace Friends.'

Source: M. Jensen, ed., op. cit, pp. 877–80.

The following three Acts are the first important legislative achievements of the movement
for economical reform.

(*iv*) *Crewe's Act, 1782* (22 George III, c.41)
'An Act for better securing the freedom of elections . . .' (disfranchisement of revenue officers)
Main groups of officers disfranchised:

(1) Excise officials;   (2) Customs officials;   (3) Stamp officers;   (4) Salt officers;
(5) Window duty officers;   (6) Post Office employees.

Source: E.N. Williams (3a), pp. 198–9.

(*v*) *Contractors'* [Sir P.J. Clerke's] *Act, 1782* (22 George III, c.45)
'for further securing the freedom and independence of parliament'.
Debarred from election to the House of Commons 'any person concerned in any contract, commission, or agreement, made for the public service'.

Source: E.N. Williams (3a), pp. 200.

(*vi*) *Civil Establishment Act, 1782* [Burke's Act] (22 George III, c.82)
Centre-piece of economical reform programme, passed at the third attempt, after rejections 1780 and 1781.
The nominal purpose of the Act was to prevent the Civil List from falling into debt in future: 'a new and oeconomical plan is intended to be adopted . . .'

Summary provisions
(a) Various offices (mainly though not entirely sinecures) to be 'utterly suppressed, abolished and taken away', e.g. Secretary of State for the Colonies; Commissioners of Trade and Plantations; principal officers of the great wardrobe; principal officers of the jewel office; Treasurer of the Chamber; Cofferer of the Household; the six clerks of the board of green cloth; paymaster of the pensions; master of the harriers and fox hounds;
(b) regulations laid down for control of pensions; no pension exceeding £300 p.a. to be granted to any individual; total of pensions granted in any one year not to exceed £600; names to be laid before Parliament, etc.
(c) 'For preventing as much as may be all abuses in the disposal of . . . secret service money, or money for special service': the total annual expenditure under this head not to exceed £10,000.

Source: E.N. Williams (3a), pp. 200–6.

Compendium of information

G. PUBLIC FINANCE

G.1: War and the growth of the National Debt, 1739–84

Year	Size of Debt £ (to nearest 100,000)
1739	46,900,000
1748	76,100,000
1756	74,600,000
1763	132,600,000
1775	127,300,000
1784	242,900,000

Sources:
1. *British Parliamentary Papers*, **35** (1868–9). *British Parliamentary Papers*, **52** (1898).
2. J. Brewer (84), Table 2.1.
3. P.G.M. Dickson (69), Tables 7 & 9.

G.2: Taxation, 1722–83

(i) *The Land Tax, 1693–1783*:
levied at 4s. in the £: 1693–7, 1701–12, 1716, 1727, 1740–9, 1755–65, 1770, 1775–83
levied at 3s. in the £: 1698–9, 1717–21, 1728–9, 1750–1, 1766–9, 1771–4
levied at 2s. in the £: 1700, 1713–15, 1722–6, 1730–1, 1734–9, 1752–4
levied at 1s. in the £: 1732–3 (2 years)

(ii) *Major changes in indirect taxation, 1721–83*:
1721–2   Walpole's comprehensive *customs reforms* (8 George I, c. 15, c. 16):

(1) Drawback allowed on wide range of exported silk goods;
(2) import duties repealed on dyestuffs, raw silk and raw materials used in paper and linen manufacture;
(3) additional 20% import duty on drugs abolished; duties on pepper and spices reduced and greatly simplified;
(4) NB all *British* goods and merchandise to be *exported duty free*, except alum, lead, tin, copper and some other minerals; tanned leather and hides; white woollen cloth; raw materials for hats.

1723   *Bonded warehousing* for tea, coffee and cocoa nuts: compulsory warehousing of these imports after payment of small duty; could be taken out for re-export without further duty; full tax payable as excise only if taken out for home consumption.
1730–32 *Salt Duty* briefly discontinued (see pp. 5, 6).
1743   New duties on *spirits* (16 George II, c.8).
1745   Additional duties on wines and vinegar (double rate for French); reduction of tea duty.
1746   Additional duties on wines and on manufactured glass.
1748   *Standard duty* level on imports raised to 20%
1756–63 Repeal of duties on foreign raw linen yarn; new stamp duties; *standard duty level* on imports raised to 25% (1759); additional duty on coffee; increased malt, beer and spirits duties; further duties on wines and vinegar (double rate for France).

1779–82 Further *general rise* of 5% in import duties and excises, except on beer, soap, candles and leather; malt duty up by 15% (1779 Impost); *general excise* duties raised by an additional 5%, with above exceptions (1781); further specific duties on beer, spirits, wines and salt (1780); also on tobacco and soap (1782); a third additional 5% on *general port and excise* duties, except those on beer, malt, soap, candles and leather.

Sources:
1. J.V. Beckett (72).
3. S. Dowell, *A History of Taxation and Taxes in England*, 4 vols, (2nd edn., 1888); *The Statutes at Large*, vols 3–14.

(iii) *Changing levels and incidence of taxation, 1720–80*

Year (5-year average centred on)	Share of national income appropriated to taxation	Excises and stamps		Customs		Direct taxes		Total tax income
	%	£m	%	£m	%	£m	%	£m
1720	10.8	2.8	(46)	1.7	(28)	1.6	(26)	6.1
1730	10.7							
1735		3.2	(55)	1.6	(28)	1.0	(17)	5.8
1745		3.1	(48)	1.3	(20)	2.1	(32)	6.5
1750	10.5	3.5	(51)	1.4	(20)	2.0	(29)	6.9
1760	11.5	4.1	(49)	1.9	(23)	2.3	(28)	8.3
1770	10.5	6.0	(57)	2.6	(25)	1.9	(18)	10.5
1780	11.7	6.6	(56)	2.6	(22)	2.6	(22)	11.8

Source:
N.P.K. O'Brien (73), pp. 1–32, Tables 2 and 4.

H. FOREIGN POLICY

Treaties of alliance and peace, 1713–83

(i) 1713 Treaty of Utrecht
[a] Britain and France: (April 1713)
  (1) France recognised the order of succession in Britain laid down by Parliament. Louis XIV undertook for himself and his successors never to acknowledge the Stuart claim to that succession. Pretender never to be allowed to return to France.
  (2) Louis renounced any prospect of the French and Spanish crowns being united, and promised to seek no special commercial favours from Spain.
  (3) Fortifications of Dunkirk [privateering base] to be rased and the harbour filled in.
  (4) France ceded to Britain St Kitts, Newfoundland, Nova Scotia and her pretensions to the Hudson's Bay settlement, but retained Cape Breton and other islands commanding the St Lawrence.
  (5) Britain's allies promised 'just and reasonable' satisfaction * by France.
  (6) By separate Commerce treaty signed on same day each country granted the other 'most favoured nation' treatment in trade.
(But 8th and 9th articles, dealing with the necessary tariff changes, were rejected by House of Commons.)

1713 Tready of Utrecht
[b] Britain and Spain: (July 1713)
  (1) Philip V of Spain renounced his claim to French throne and promised not to transfer to France any Spanish-held land or lordship in America (which Philip retained, along with the mother Kingdoms).
  (2) Spain recognised the Hanoverian succession in Britain.
  (3) Gibraltar and Minorca ceded to Britain; also the *Assiento* contract for 30 years and the right to send an 'annual ship' to 3 specified harbours in Central America.
  (4) Catalans (supporters of 'Charles III') to have amnesty and equal rights with Castilians (there was no possibility of enforcing this provision).

[* The Dutch received in 1713 a limited fortress barrier (Second Barrier Treaty – January 1713): only about half the fortresses promised to them in 1709, including Ypres, Namur and Tournai, but excluding Lille, Condé and Valenciennes. The Spanish Netherlands, Milanese, Naples and Sardinia allocated to the Emperor (who delayed his consent until Rastadt, 1714); Sicily to duke of Savoy; and Prussia secured international recognition of the kingly title of Frederick I (pre-1701, Elector of Brandenburg-Prussia) along with Upper Guelderland and the principality of Neuchâtel; Portugal drew a blank.]

(ii) 1715 Third Barrier Treaty: Austria and UP (Britain guarantor) (4 November O.S.)
  (1) Dutch to hold 7 fortresses, as a Barrier in the (now) Austrian Netherlands and garrison 35,000 troops there and in the jointly-garrisoned Dendermonde. Vienna to pay three-fifths of their cost.
  (2) Britain, as guarantor, to furnish 10,000 men and 20 warships in case the Barrier was attacked.

[*Note*: In the Second Barrier Treaty, 1713, Dutch had renewed their promise of 6,000 troops to assist Britain against attack from Pretender.]

(*iii*) *1717* (N.S.) *The Triple Alliance*: France, Britain, U.P. (24 December/4 January 1716–17)
1. France confirmed previous engagements made about the British Succession and the Pretender.
2. France reaffirmed destruction of Dunkirk, except new canal and port at Mardyke.
3. All powers reaffirmed the settlement of Utrecht. If one attacked, and mediation failed, the other two would come to her assistance: France and Britain with 8,000 foot and 2,000 horse, States-General with 4,000 foot and 1,000 horse.
4. Each power promised to assist the other two in the event of internal rebellion.

(*iv*) *1718 The Quadruple Alliance*: France, Britain, Emperor and UP*
1. Emperor to give up Sardinia [to duke of Savoy] in return for Sicily.
2. Charles VI to renounce the Spanish Crown unequivocally.
3. Philip V to renounce reconquest of Spain's former Italian possessions.
4. Don Carlos's [son of Queen Elizabeth Farnese] right to the Farnese succession (Parma and Piacenza) and the Medici succession (Tuscany) to be recognised and secured by neutral garrisons.
5. Problems arising from settlement to be dealt with by congresses.
6. Secret articles committed signatories to use force against Philip V of Spain if he refused to accept terms.

[*Intended and expected to sign; but never did so.]

(*v*) *1725 Treaty [Alliance] of Hanover:* Britain, France, Prussia (23 Aug O.S)
1. Mutual guarantee of possessions against the Vienna Alliance powers, Spain and Austria, and of Balance of Power in light of supposed engagement of Maria Theresa and Don Carlos.
2. Spanish attacks on Gibraltar and Minorca and encroachments of Ostend East India Company to be resisted.
3. Frederick William I of Prussia's succession to duchy of Julich-Berg guaranteed.

(*vi*) *1729 Treaty of Seville:* Britain, France, Spain (29 Oct O.S.)
1. Spain entered into defensive alliance with Britain and France.
2. Britain and Spain restored wartime captures; Britain restored to its trading privileges in Spain and Spanish Empire, including *Assiento*.
3. Emperor to be forced to admit Spanish garrisons in Parma and Tuscany as surety for Don Carlos's claims to the succession to the duchies, which Britain and France guaranteed.
4. Spanish claims on Gibraltar tacitly suspended.

(vii) *1731 2nd Treaty of Vienna:* Britain, Emperor Charles VI (5 March O.S.)
In return for British guarantee of Pragmatic Sanction [A.], in which the Dutch joined, Charles accepted the terms of the Seville settlement, agreeing to dissolve Ostend Company and admit Spanish trooops into the Parman and Tuscan fortresses.

(*viii*) *1739 Convention of El Pardo:* Britain, Spain (3 Jan O.S.)
  (1) The balance of rival claims for compensation for destruction and seizure of ships and cargoes since Passaro (1718) agreed at £95,000 in Britain's favour (but what could be got in practice reduced to £27,000 by a counter-claim against South Sea Company).
  (2) Disputes over right of search and boundaries of Florida and Georgia deferred to a separate conference.

(*ix*) *1743 Treaty of Worms:* Britain, Austria, Sardinia (2 Sept O.S.)
  (1) Britain to subsidise Sardinia with £200,000 and keep a fleet in Mediterranean.
  (2) Maria Theresa agreed to some territorial concessions to Sardinia in return for £300,000 British subsidy.
  (3) Sardinia to reject French offer of alliance and assist Maria Theresa with 45,000 troops.

(*x*) *1748 Treaty of Aix-la-Chapelle* (11 Oct O.S.)
  (1) Britain to give up Louisburg in exchange for Madras.
  (2) Sea defences of Dunkirk to be rased; land defences to be left standing.
  (3) France recognised right of House of Hanover in Britain and repudiated the Pretender.
  (4) South Sea Company's annual ship concession from Spain, and *Assiento*, renewed for four years.
  (5) Spain to obtain Parma and Piacenza for the Infante Don Philip.
  (6) France to evacuate and restore captured territories and barrier fortresses in Low Countries to the Dutch.
  (7) Sardinia to recover Savoy and Nice and most of the territories promised at Worms (*q.v.*).
  (8) [Silesia remained in Prussian hands.]

(*xi*) *1756 Convention of Westminster:* Britain and Prussia (16 Jan 1756)
  (1) Frederick II guaranteed neutrality of Hanover and both powers would seek to restrain their allies from hostile attempts against it.
  (2) Both to join in resisting by force any attempt by a foreign power to invade Germany. Treaty not to extend to Austrian Netherlands.

(*xii*) *1763 Treaty of Paris* (10 Feb 1763)
  (1) Preliminary articles 3 November 1762:– Britain confirmed in possession of her conquests: Canada [see J.2], Cape Breton, St Vincent, Tobago, Dominica, Grenada and the Grenadines; Senegal in Africa; regained Minorca in exchange for Belle Isle.
  (2) In India, France allowed to retain only those trading factories held in 1749 and could station no troops there. Britain annexed Clive's conquests in Bengal.
  (3) France restored to the possession of Gorée in Africa, Guadeloupe, Martinique, Marie Galante and St Lucia in the West Indies. Her rights in the Newfoundland fisheries recognised by Britain as were St Pierre and Miquelon in the St Lawrence as French territory.
  (4) Havana and Manila restored to Spain by Britain who received Florida in exchange.
  (5) [No stipulations made at Paris about Prussia; but at Hubertusburg, 1763, Prussia and Austria agreed that the former would lose none of the territory she had held in 1756 at the start of the war.]

(*xiii*) *1783 Treaty of Paris:* Britain, America (3 Sept)

    (1) American independence formally recognised.

    (2) Boundaries of the new 'United States' fixed.

    (3) Rights of British merchants in the USA defined, and debts due to Britain prior to 1775 acknowledged.

(*xiv*) *1783 Treaties of Versailles*: France, Spain, United Provinces (Sept)

    (1) France given Tobago and recovered St Lucia. Britain regained French conquests of Grenada, Dominica, St Kitts, Nevis and Monserrat.

    (2) France granted fishing rights along the west coast of Newfoundland.

    (3) In Africa France allotted the Senegal river as a base for the slave trade, Britain, the river Gambia. In India France restored to trading ports round Pondicherry.

    (4) Britain gave up East and West Florida and Minorca to Spain, but retained Gibraltar; recovered her island possessions in the Bahamas.

    (5) Conquests made from Dutch restored, including Trincomalee in Ceylon.

    (6) (May 1784) Britain obtained the former Dutch station of Negapatam near Madras and the freedom of navigation among the Dutch spice islands.

Principal sources:

1. C. Parry and C. Hopkins, *An Index to British Treaties, 1101–1968*, 3 vols (1970).
2. C. Parry, ed., *The Consolidated Treaty Series* (New York, 1969), vols 6–49.
3. C. Jenkinson, *A Collection of all the Treaties of Peace, Alliance and Commerce, between Great Britain and other Powers from . . . 1648 to . . . 1783*, 3 vols (1785).

I. BRITAIN'S MAJOR WARS, 1722–83

I.1: Britain's principal allies

War	Allies
The War of Jenkins's Ear, 1739–[43]	(none)
The War of Austrian Succession 1740–8	United Provinces[1]; Habsburg[2]; Savoy[3]
The Seven Years' War, 1756–63	Prussia[2]
The War of American Independence, 1775–83	(none)

Notes:
1. Ally forced out of war by catastrophic defeats.
2. Ally deserted when Britain made a separate peace.
3. Ally changed sides during the course of the war.

I.2: The armed forces and the cost of war, 1689–1783

		Average annual personnel			Average annual expenditure (£m.)	Government expenditure on forces (%)	Government expenditure on interest payments (%)*
		Navy	Army	Total			
War	1689–97	40,262	76,404	116,666	5.46	79	6
War	1702–13	42,938	92,708	135,646	7.06	72	19
Peace	1714–39					39	44
War	1739–48	50,313	62,373	112,686	8.78	65	25
Peace	1750–55					41	44
War	1756–63	74,800	92,676	167,476	18.04	70	22
Peace	1764–75					37	43
War	1776–83	82,022	108,484	190,506	20.27	62	30

* Balance of expenditure spent on civil government.

Sources:
1. J. Brewer (84), Table 2.1, p. 30.
2. N.P.K. O'Brien (73), Table 1, p. 2.

J. OVERSEAS TRADE AND THE COLONIES

J.1: Legislation

(*i*) *1733 Molasses Act* (George II, c.13)
Imposed duties on all molasses (at 6d. a gallon), sugar and rum imported into American colonies from foreign [overwhelmingly French] plantations.

Note: The molasses import from French islands into the colonies was vast (an estimated 9 million gallons per annum by 1763–4) and evasion of the duty became almost universal between 1733 and 63.

Source: M. Jensen, ed., *English Historical Documents vol. IX: American Colonial Documents to 1776* (1955), pp. 354–6.

(*ii*) *1764 'Sugar Act'* [American Revenue Act] (4 George III, c.15)
This revised the Act of 1733.
  (1) The rate of 6d. a gallon on foreign molasses was *reduced* to 3d. But
  (2) duty on sugar imported into colonies from French or Spanish colonies *increased* more than five-fold and heavy new duties were laid upon imports of foreign wines, coffee, indigo and East India goods.
  (3) It was intended both for trade regulation and to raise £45,000 for colonial defence.

Source: Jensen, op. cit. pp. 643–8.

(*iii*) *1765 Stamp Act* (5 George III, c.12)
  (1) It imposed a basic stamp duty of 3d. on legal documents within North America *and the West Indies,* plus duties on newspapers and newspaper advertisements; duties of 10s. and £2 on appointment to public office or presentation to benefice, and £1 for licence to sell liquors.
  (2) The proceeds were to contribute (an estimated one-seventh of whole) towards cost of keeping an army in the colonies.

Source: Jensen, op. cit. pp. 655–6.

(*iv*) *1766 Declaratory Act* [see F (i)]
Source: Jensen, op. cit. pp. 695–6.

(*v*) *1767 American Import Duties Act* ('Townshend Duties') (7 George III, c.46)
  (1) The Act imposed duties on tea, paper, glass and lead entering American ports.
  (2) The proceeds were to go to an American Civil List; surplus, if any, was for the maintenance of the army.

Note: All except tea duty were repealed in 1770.

Source: Jensen, op. cit. pp. 701–2.

(*vi*) *1773 Tea Act* (13 George III, c. 44)
This was Parliament's response to the financial difficulties of the East India Company in the trade recession of 1772–3.
  (1) Tea duty of 3d. per lb., imposed in 1767, was *not* repealed, despite wishes of East India interest.
  (2) The company was to be allowed to sell surplus tea from its London warehouses, through its agents in America, and was entitled to receive the 'drawback' (refund of duty payable).

Source: Jensen, op. cit. pp. 769–70.

(*vii*) *1773 Regulating Act* (for India) (13 George III, c. 63)

Note: This remodelled the constitution of the East India Company both at home and in India, in response to scandals in the administration of Bengal and irresponsible/corrupt conduct of the Company's finances by the proprietors in the general court of the Company in London; the aim was to subject the Company to closer supervision by the government in Bengal [Calcutta]).

(1) The membership of the Court of Proprietors was controlled by raising voting qualifications from £500 to £1,000 of stock and stipulating that stock must have been held for twelve months (*c*. 1,600 proprietors disfranchised).

(2) Splitting of stock to multiply votes was illegalised.

(3) Directors elected by the Court of Proprietors were to have 4-year instead of one-year tenure of office, one-quarter to retire annually.

(4) Copies of correspondence from India were to be shown to the government.

(5) Bengal to be under a governor-general holding office for five years, nominated by the Crown [Warren Hastings–£25,000 p.a.], assisted by four councillors (also nominated by Crown), with power to supervise presidencies of Madras and Bombay in making war and peace with native states.

(6) The Crown was to appoint by charter a Chief Justice and three other judges to make up a Supreme Court.

Source: D.B. Horn and M. Ransome, eds, *English Historical Documents* vol. X (1957), pp. 811–16.

(*viii*) *April 1783 First India Bill* (Dundas)

(1) The Crown was to have the power to recall principal servants of East India Company (EIC) without prior representation from directors.

(2) The Governor-General was to have the power to take unilateral decisons against majority opinion of Council.

Source: H.H. Dodwell, ed., *The Cambridge History of India vol. V: British India 1497–1858* (Cambridge, 1929) p. 194.

(*ix*) *November 1783 Second India Bill* (Fox)

(1) A Board of Commissioners, to be named in the Act, was to administer the revenues and territories of India and to appoint/dismiss all persons in EIC's service; it was irremovable except on address from either House of Parliament.

The Board was to sit in London, with minutes open to parliamentary scrutiny.

(2) Vacancies were to be filled by Crown.

(3) Nine assistant directors were to be nominated by Parliament from proprietors with largest holdings and to hold office for five years; vacancies were to be filled by Court of Proprietors.

Source: Dodwell, op. cit. p. 195.

J.2: The foundation and annexation of colonies: the first British Empire, 1606–1774

(i) North America

	Date	Colony	Remarks
(1)	1606–7	Virginia	
	1620	New Plymouth	(later embodied in Massachusetts)
(2)	1628–9	Massachusetts	
(3)	1629	New Hampshire	
(4)	1632	Maryland	
(5)	1636–47	Rhode Island	
(6)	1637–51	Maine	(later embodied in Massachusetts)
(7)	1663	Carolina	(see below, 1713)
(8)	1664	New York	captured from United Provinces; retained 1667 (Peace of Breda) with rest of 'New Netherlands'
(9)	1665	New Jersey	captured from United Provinces; retained at Peace of Breda
(10)	1681	Pennsylvania	
(11)	1682	Delaware	settled from 1664
(12)	1713	North and South Carolina	Carolina split into 2 colonies (see above, 1663)
	1713	Newfoundland, Nova Scotia (Acadia), and Hudsons Bay Territory	annexed at Peace of Utrecht All partly settled and disputed with France since 17th century
(13)	1732	Georgia	

1763 Peace of Paris and Proclamation of October 1763:

	Date	Colony	Remarks
	1763	East and West Florida	annexed from Spain: divided into two provinces; lost 1783
	1763	Quebec	new colony founded out of captured France's Canadian territories, centering in Quebec and Montreal, annexed at the Peace
	1763	Mississippi–Ohio valleys	ceded by France. Western boundaries of British colonies fixed 'for the present' at the Appalachian mountain range (the 'Proclamation Line'). Intervening land intended by Britain as an Indian Reserve
	1774	*Quebec Act*	Quebec's boundaries extended southwards to cover the forest wilderness south of the Great Lakes

(ii) India*

Date	Colony	Remarks
1661	Bombay	acquired from Portugal (part of Catherine of Braganza's dowry)
1753–63	Madras Presidency	captured from France
1765	The Northern Circars	(Eastern seaboard; between Orissa and the Carnatic)
1765	Calcutta region	overlordship and effective government of Bengal, Bihar and Orissa (Clive's conquests: 7 Years' War and after)

* administered by East India Co.; but see J.1(vii) for Act of 1773

(iii) West Indies

Date	Colony	Remarks
1624	St Kitts	(part – see below, 1713)
1625	Barbados	
1628–36	Nevis, Montserrat and Antigua (in Leeward Islands)	
1655	Jamaica	captured from Spain
1655–70	Cayman Islands	
1666	Virgin Islands	
1670	The Bahamas	
1713	Remaining part of St Kitts	(see above, 1624) from France
1763	Dominica	from France
1763	St Vincent, Grenada and Tobago	in Windward Is; from France

J.3: The eighteenth-century commercial revolution

A *Merchant shipping*

Total tonnage English-owned merchant shipping:
London and the Outports (tons)

	London	Outports	Total
		183,000	323,000
1732	178,000*	c. 240,000	418,000
1770	150,000[†]	440,000	over 590,000[†]
1786[‡]	315,000	740,000	1,055,000

Note: Captured foreign prize ships were added to the merchant fleet as a result of the wars of 1689–1763 as follows: *1689–97* 1,279; *1702–13* 2,203; *1739–48* 1,499; *1756–63* 1,855. Britain was a net loser in the first war, but a considerable net gainer as a result of the other three. R. Davis (154), pp. 51, 68.

Sources:
R. Davis (154), p. 27.
* W. Maitland, *History of London*, 2 vols II (1756).
[†] The figure for London, 1770 (from BL Add. MSS. 11256), and therefore the total for that year, is almost certainly far too low. See Davis (154), Appx. A.
[‡] The first year for which authentic figures are available from the General Register of Shipping.

B *Total English trade (imports, exports and re-exports), 1699–1784*

(av. annual value: £million)			
1699–1701	12.3	1700–09	10.4
1710–19	12.1	1722–4	14.5
1745–54	18.9	1752–4	20.1
1765–74	26.8	1772–4	28.4
1775–84	24.2	1778–80	22.9

Sources:
R. Davis (155b), Appx.
P. Deane and W.A. Cole (128a), p. 48.
B.R. Mitchell and P. Deane (128b), pp. 279–80.

C *Growth and Geography of Eighteenth-Century Trade: at Stages*

	1700–1 England	1750–1 England	1772–3 England (£ million)	1772–3 Britain	1789–90 Britain
(i) Retained imports from:					
Ireland*	0.285	0.695	1.303	1.437	2.563
N. & W. Europe	1.928	2.204	2.532	2.849	4.413
S. Europe†	1.650	1.445	1.769	1.793	2.573
N. America	0.372	0.877	1.442	1.977	1.351
W. Indies	0.785	1.484	3.080	3.222	4.045
East India	0.775	1.101	2.203	2.203	3.256
Africa, etc.‡	0.024	0.050	0.101	0.107	0.275
Value total imports	5.819	7.855	12.432	13.595	18.476

* plus Channel Isles & Isle of Man
† incl. Turkey
‡ incl. Fisheries

(ii) Domestic exports to:					
Ireland	0.144	0.275	0.912	1.008	1.377
N. & W. Europe	2.182	2.872	1.751	1.853	3.148
S. Europe	1.478	3.562	2.132	2.143	2.229
N. America	0.256	0.971	2.460	2.649	3.295
W. Indies	0.205	0.449	1.168	1.226	1.630
East India	0.114	0.585	0.824	0.824	2.096
Africa, etc.	0.081	0.089	0.492	0.492	0.517
Value total domestic exports	4.461	9.125	9.739	10.196	14.350

(iii) Re-exports to					
Ireland	0.159	0.609	1.102	1.262	1.056
N. & W. Europe	1.419	1.880	3.196	3.871	3.010
S. Europe	0.233	0.248	0.459	0.464	0.292
N. America	0.106	0.384	0.522	0.605	0.468
W. Indies	0.131	0.140	0.169	0.176	0.202
East India	0.011	0.068	0.069	0.069	0.077
Africa, etc.	0.064	0.099	0.285	0.285	0.282
Value total re-exports	2.136	3.428	5.800	6.930	5.380

Source:
Adapted from P. Deane and W.A. Cole (128a), Table 22: official Customs House valuations.

D *London and the outports in the eighteenth century*

(i) London's percentage share of English overseas trade, 1700–1770

	1700	1710*	1730	1750	1770
Imports	80	72	80	71	73
Exports	69	71	69	62	63
Re-exports	86	80	83	70	69

*At the height of the Spanish Succession War

Source:

T.S. Ashton, Introduction to E.B. Schumpeter, *English Overseas Trade Statistics, 1697–1808* (Oxford, 1960), p. 9.

(ii) Ships entering Bristol, Liverpool and Hull, 1687–1772
(those from America and W. Indies in brackets)

	1687	1728	1764	1772
Bristol	324 (73)		322 (143)	
Liverpool	172 (21)		762 (188)	
Hull	154 (1)	219 (1)		286 (15)

Source:
R. Davis (154), pp. 36–9.

(iii) Outward clearances from the five leading English ports, 1750 and 1770
(tonnage – English and foreign ships)

	All English Ports Tonnage cleared	London	Whitehaven	Liverpool	Newcastle	Bristol
1750	[1751: 694,000]	179,860	100,778	42,662	45,336	27,636
1770	[1772: 888,000]	212,876	189,445	76,578	54,264	24,839

Source:
W.E. Minchinton (153), pp. 35, 61.

J.4: National output in the eighteenth century: commerce, industry, agriculture

(i) The national product of England and Wales in the eighteenth century (Cole)*

	Industry & Commerce £m	(%)	Agriculture £m	(%)	Rents & Services: Government & Defence £	(%)	Total £m
			A. at 1700 prices				
1700	16.5	33	20.0	40	13.5	27	50.0
1710	17.2	32	20.6	38	16.2	30	53.9
1720	19.6	34	24.1	42	13.9	24	57.5
1730	21.1	36	23.6	40	14.0	24	58.7
1740	21.6	34	26.1	41	16.4	26	64.1
1750	24.6	35	28.1	40	17.7	25	70.4
1760	29.6	36	28.9	35	23.4	29	81.9
1770	33.0	41	29.0	36	18.3	23	80.3
1780	32.2	35	31.5	34	28.3	31	92.0
1790	46.2	44	33.4	32	24.4	23	104.1
			B. at current prices				
1700	16.5	33	20.0	40	13.5	27	50.0
1710	16.2	31	20.4	39	15.3	29	51.9
1720	17.1	36	18.2	38	12.2	26	47.4
1730	18.0	37	18.2	38	12.0	25	48.2
1740	18.1	36	18.4	37	13.8	27	50.3
1750	20.6	37	20.7	37	14.9	26	56.2
1760	27.1	37	25.1	34	21.4	29	73.6
1770	30.5	38	33.5	41	16.9	21	80.9
1780	33.1	34	34.1	35	29.1	30	96.4
1790	49.8	43	40.6	35	26.2	22	116.6

Notes:
(1) The index figure of £50m. for 1700 is a crude estimate, broadly derived from Gregory King.
(2) A very different picture of the pattern of expansion of commercial and industrial output, and its relationship to agricultural growth, *especially from the years 1760–80,* is offered by N. F. R. Crafts in the table below.

* *Source*:
W.A. Cole (130a), p. 64.

(ii) Growth in real national output (% per annum) [Crafts]
[Cole's estimates in brackets for comparison]

	Industry	Commerce	Industry & Commerce	Agriculture	National Output incl. Rents, Services etc.
1700–60	0.71	0.69	0.70 (0.98)	0.60 (0.64)	0.69 (0.84)
1760–80	1.51	0.70	1.05 (0.43)	0.13 (0.440	0.70 (0.60)
1780–1801	2.11	1.32	1.81 (3.24)	0.75 (0.710	1.32 (1.98)

Source:
N.F.R. Crafts (130b), pp. 185, 187.

K. AGRICULTURE

K.1: The English Harvest, 1660–1783

(i) The wheat harvest: years of scarcity, 1660–1759

1657–61	(5)	4 bad or deficient harvests, followed by dearth in 1661
1692–8	(7)	'the seven lean years'; only 1694 average, the rest bad or deficient or, as in 1693 and 1697, years of dearth
1708–11 } 1713 }	(4)	bad in 1708; 1709 – the worst dearth since 1596; 1710–11 deficient; 1713 bad
1725–8	(4)	a deficient and an average harvest, followed by 2 bad ones
1739–40	(2)	deficient 1739; dearth 1740
1756–7	(2)	dearth 1756; deficient 1757

(ii) The wheat harvest: years of plenty, 1660–1759

1665–72	(8)	7 harvests either good or (1666–7) abundant; only 1668 'average'
1683–90	(8)	7 harvests either good or (1687–8) abundant; 1684 average
1700–07	(8)	4 abundant harvests, 3 good; 1703 average
1721–3	(3)	all good
1730–33	(4)	4 good harvests in a row
1741–4	(4)	3 good; 1743 abundant
1754–5 } 1758–9 }		4 good harvests, punctuated by the bad years 1756–7 (above)

Source and method of classification:
W.G. Hoskins (175) esp. pp. 15, 28–31.

(iii) 1760–1800

Hoskins notes 12 poor, 16 good and 13 average harvests in the last four decades of the century (ibid. pp. 15–16), but does not specify. Over the years down to 1783 it would seem from the evidence of wheat prices that the best harvests were those of 1760, 1761, 1769, 1775 and 1778–9, and that the harvests of 1766–8, 1772–4 and 1780–3 (especially 1783) were deficient or bad. But because the 'harvest year' ran from August–August and the *worst* effects of a poor harvest one year were sometimes not reflected until the prices of the next, the above dates for 1760–83 must be treated with a certain caution.

Source:
Mitchell and Deane (128b), p. 48

K.2: Output

(i) English agricultural productivity in the eighteenth century

(a) *Estimated net output of corn (million quarters)*		(b) *Agricultural output: rates of growth (average % p.a.)*	
1700	13.29	1710–40	0.9[2]
1750	14.82	1740–80	0.5[1]
1770	16.70	1780–1800	0.6[1]
1790	18.99		

Sources:

(a) P. Deane and W.A. Cole (128a), p. 65.

(b) 1. P. Deane and W.A. Cole (128a), p. 78.

    2. N.F.R. Crafts and R.D. Lee, in R.C. Floud and D.H. McCloskey (135), p. 2, revising Deane and Cole's estimated NIL rate of growth, 1710–40.

(ii) Grain prices and exports

(a) *Index of grain prices, 1660–1749 (1641–55 = 100)*		(b) *Prices of wheat at Cambridge, 1750–83 (shillings per quarter)*	
Decade		1740–9	29.6
1660–9	107	1750–9	37.7
1670–9	101	1760–9	41.9
1680–9	89	1770–83	49.7
1690–9	104		
1700–09	84		
1710–19	104		
1720–9	89		
1730–9	73		
1740–9	77		

Sources:

(a) D.C. Coleman (121), p. 112.

(b) calculated from T.S. Ashton, *An Economic History of England: the Eighteenth Century* (1972 edn), Table I, p. 239.

(c) *Grain exports (wheat, rye, barley, malt),*
1692–1764: annual average, in quarters

1692–1700	80–100,000

Decade	
1700–9	283,000
1710–19	369,000
1720–9	426,000
1730–9	531,000
1740–9	661,000
1750–9	650,000
1760–4	373,000

As a % of all domestic exports
(best year per decade)

1703	9.6
1713	12.2
1722	13.1
1734	18.2
1749	14.8
1750	19.2
1761	10.6
[1765	5.4][†]

[†] Year of prohibition of grain shipments, dwindling and intermittent trade only thereafter.

Source:
A.H. John (477), pp. 48–9, 64.

K.3: Enclosures

(i) Enclosure Acts passed

1604–99	20+
1700–60	208
1760–80	1068

Sources:
1. J.R. Wordie (178), p. 486.
2. W.E. Tate, *The English Village Community and the Enclosure Movement* (1967).

(ii) Enclosure Rate in England: total surface area enclosed (%)

already enclosed by 1600	c. 47
enclosed 1600–99	
(overwhelmingly by private agreement)	*c.* 24
enclosed 1700–99	
(by agreement and over 1800	
parliamentary Acts)	c. 13

Source:
Proportions calculated by J.R. Wordie (178) p. 502.

L. INDUSTRY

L.1: Industrial output, exports and home consumption in England and Wales, 1700–1785*

	Industrial output (£m)	of which: exports (£m)	(%)	Home consumption (£m)	Consumption per capita (£)
1700	18.5	3.8	20.6	14.6	2.77
1705	19.3	4.2	22.0	15.0	2.79
1710	19.2	4.9	25.3	14.4	2.61
1715	20.4	5.1	24.8	15.3	2.75
1720	21.9	5.0	23.1	16.8	2.97
1725	22.6	5.6	22.6	17.4	3.10
1730	23.5	5.4	23.1	18.1	3.24
1735	24.8	6.0	24.2	18.8	3.26
1740	24.2	6.3	26.1	17.9	3.01
1745	24.3	6.7	27.7	17.5	2.89
1750	27.5	8.0	29.0	19.5	3.14
1755	30.4	9.2	30.1	21.2	3.31
1760	33.2	10.3	31.0	22.9	3.46
1765	35.5	10.9	30.8	24.6	3.62
1770	36.9	11.2	30.3	25.7	3.69
1775	36.5	10.6	29.1	25.9	3.56
1780	36.0	9.9	27.6	26.1	3.45
1785	42.4	11.7	27.6	30.7	3.89

* At *c*. 1697–1704 prices.

Source:

Estimates of W.A. Cole (130a), Table 3.1, p. 40 and Note on Sources.

For a markedly different pattern of expansion for industrial output, positing a somewhat slower build-up to 1760 and a far more spectacular spurt from 1760–80 see J.4 (ii).

L.2: Inventions and other industrial landmarks

c. 1660–70	'Dutch loom' (engine loom) introduced in Manchester area for ribbon and tape manufacture (Manchester 'smallwares')
1676	Robert Hook: universal joint
1683	William Palin and William Luggins: mill-powered machine for manufacturing ironware
1698	Thomas Savery: steam pump for draining land and mines; supplying water; but many practical problems
1709	Abraham Darby: coke-fired blast furnace for iron smelting
1712	Thomas Newcomen: steam engine (piston) – the first practical pumping engine
1717–18	John Lombe } began construction of first genuine silk mill (Derby) Sir Thomas Lombe } with water-powered throwing-machines
1730	Nottingham workmen produced first mechanically-made pair of *cotton* hose (from Indian yarn) on a stocking-frame (*woollen* hose manufactured on frames in Vale of Trent since 1660s)

1733	John Kay: Flying Shuttle: hand-operated machine, enabling broader cloths to be woven more quickly
1733	John Wyatt and Lewis Paul: spinning machine (inventor Wyatt; marketed Paul)
1742	Benjamin Huntsman: invented 'crucible steel' technique – smelting metal at very high temperatures in sealed fireclay crucibles
1743	David Bourne: carding machine, using wire-toothed revolving cylinder
1743	Thomas Boulsover: first produced 'Sheffield Plate'
1760	Job and William Wyatt: screw manufacturing machine
1761	Robert Hinchcliffe: high quantity production of scissors and shears in cast steel
1764	John Hargreaves: Spinning Jenny
1765	James Watt: invented the steam engine condenser (originally a Newcomen engine with a separate condensation chamber)
1768–9	Richard Arkwright: Water Frame (though his first spinning-frame mill [Nottingham, 1771] was in fact horse-powered not water-powered – as subsequently at Cromford, etc.)
1770	Jesse Ramsden: Ramsden's Lathe
1776	Andrew Meikle: threshing machine
1779	'Ironbridge' – cast-iron bridge spanning River Severn at Coalbrookdale
1779	Samuel Crompton: Spinning 'Mule' – combined principle of jenny and frame spinning
1779	James Keir: patented an early version of 'Muntz metal' – capable of being forged or wrought when red-hot or cold
c. 1780	Keir discovered distinction between carbonic acid gas and atmospheric air
1783	Thomas Bell: cylindrical roller process for cotton printing
1784	Henry Cort: puddling furnace (iron)
1785	Edmund Cartwright: power loom

Sources:

1. P. Mantoux (169).
2. K. Desmond, ed., *The Harwin Chronology of Inventions* (1986).

L.3: Industrial production and expansion

(i) Coal

Estimated annual production of main coalfields (000s of tons)

Fields	1651–60[1]	1681–90[1]	1700[2]	1750[2]	1775[2]
North-East	65	1,225	1,290	1,955	2,990
Scotland	40	475	450	715	1,000
S. Wales	20		80	140	650
Yorkshire			300	500	850
Lancashire			80	350	900
W. Midlands	65	850	510	820	1,400
E. Midlands			75	140	250
South-West	14	132	150	180	250
Cumberland	6	(?)		350	400
TOTAL OUTPUT: ENGLAND, WALES AND SCOTLAND	210	c. 2,900	2,985	5,230	8,850

TOTAL OUTPUT BY 1783: well over 9m. tons p.a.

Notes and sources:

By 1775 the Northumberland and Durham field accounted for less than 34% of total output (cf. 43% in 1700). The contribution of Lancashire and Yorkshire increased in the same period from 12.8 to 19.8% and that of South Wales from 2.7 to 7.3%

1. J.U.Nef (164a), I, pp 19–20.
2. M.W.Flinn (164b), II (2 vols, 1984), pp. 26–7.

(ii) Iron

(a) *Estimated output of pig iron in Britain, 1720–88 (tons)*

	Total		Shropshire	Staffs	Yorks	S. Wales	Scotland
1720	25,000	of	2,100	3,100	1,400	4,850	–
1788	68,000	which	24,900	4,800	5,100	12,500	7,000
1796	125,000		32,970	15,170	10,390	34,100	16,000

(b) *Number of blast furnaces in Britain*

	charcoal	coke
1717	61	(1?)
1760		17
1774		31
1798	25	81

(c) *Imports of bar iron*

(for metal working)	(tons)
1700	16,900
1750	35,100
1783	44,000

Sources:

B.P. Mitchell and P. Deane (128b), pp. 131, 141.

H.R. Schubert, *History of the British Iron and Steel Industry* (1957), p. 175.

(iii) Paper

Paper charged with duty in England and Wales rose from 2,583 tons in 1713 to 4,115 tons in 1750, to 9,223 tons in 1783 (Mitchell and Deane [128b], pp. 263–4)

(iv) Scottish Linen

(a) *Flax imports into Scotland*		(b) *Linen stamped for sale*		
	(cwts)		(million yds)	£000
av. 1740–9	686	1728	2.2	103
av. 1760–9	3,325	1748	7.4	294
av. 1780–9	4,777	1768	11.8	600
		1783	17.1	867

(v) Cotton and Woollen/Worsted Industries: England and Wales

(1) *Expansion of West Riding woollen cloth production, 1727–85*
'An account of the number of [broad or narrow] cloths milled at the several fulling mills in the West Riding of the County of York'
(from contemporary registers compiled under the Act of 11 George I, c.24)

Broad Cloths			Narrow Cloths	
No. of Pieces	Yards	Year	No. of Pieces	Yards
28,990		1727	–	
41,441		1740	58,620	
50,453		1745	63,423	
60,477		1750	78,115	
49,362		1760	69,573	
54,660		1765	77,419	
93,075	2,717,105	1770	85,376	2,255,625
110,942	3,427,150	1779	93,143	2,659,659
157,275	4,844,855	1785	116,036	3,409,278

Source:
Printed in H. Heaton (143a), p. 278

(2) *Growth of textile industries measured by raw material, export and production figures, 1695–1789*

Years	Raw wool consumed (incl. imports)	Gross value final product: wool	Exports of woollens and worsteds (official value)	Domestic exports	Retained imports: raw cotton	Gross value final cotton products	Exports of cotton goods (official value)
	lbs m	£m	£m	%	lbs m	£m	£000
1695	40	5.0					
1695–1704					1.14		
1700–09			3.09	70			13
1730–9			3.58	63			15
1741	57	5.1					
1740–9			3.45	53	2.06		11
1760					3.4	0.6	
1760–9			4.49	44			227
1772	85	10.2					
1772–4					4.2	0.9	
1770–9			3.99	43			248
1779	98	13.8					
1781–3					8.7	(c. 2.0)	
1784–6					16.1		
1780–9			3.53	35			756
(1790–9)			(5.23)	(30)			(2,631)
(1798–1800)					(41.8)	(11.1)	

Note:

In the first 9 decades of the 18th century total textile exports increased from an average £3,190 million (official value), 1700–09 to £5.340 million, 1760–9, and then fell back to £4.921 million, 1780–9, before a massive expansion in the 1790s. But the percentage of *total domestic exports* which these values represented declined over the same stages from 72% to 53% (1760–9) and to 48% (1780–9).

Sources:

1. P. Deane and W.A. Cole (128a), pp. 59, 185.
2. B.R. Mitchell and P. Deane (128b), pp. 177. 190–1.
3. M. Berg (165), p. 32.

M. LIVING STANDARDS

M.1: Prices in England, 1661–1783

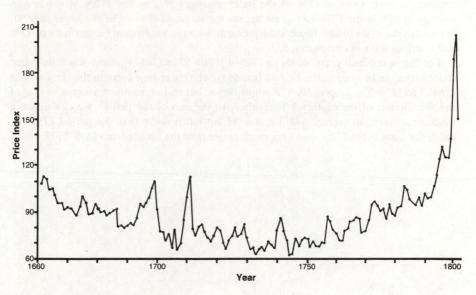

The Schumpeter-Gilboy Price Index

Sources:

Constructed from Indices in B.R. Mitchell and P. Deane (176b) and printed in J.M. Beattie, *Crime and the Courts in England, 1660–1800* (Oxford, 1986), p. 206, Fig. 5.3.

M.2: The trend of real wages (England), 1660–1783

The most detailed and up-to-date guide to the trend of real wages in our period, year by year, is provided by E.A. Wrigley and R.S. Schofield (152), p. 643: it is the appropriate section of the authors' *Real wage index for England 1500–1912* (Table A9.2). The following are the more important extrapolations and conclusions to be noted.

In the opening seven years of the period (1659–60 to 1665–6) – characterised by the last of the hard late-republican years, the economic depression which spilled over into the early 1660s (*Making of a Great Power*, Ch. 5), and in conclusion by the Great Plague and the Fire of London – the index averages *447*. This figure throws a cold light on the 'Merrie England' image popularly associated with the aftermath of the Restoration, for it is actually lower (by almost 20 points) than that for the years of the Civil Wars and the Interregnum. It does, however, represent a considerably higher average level of real wages than was achieved in the earlier Stuart period (it was surpassed in only four isolated years between 1607–8 and 1638–9).

After 1665–6, however, the trend of real wages ran steadily upwards, with only a few slight and brief dips, notably in 1674–5 and 1684–5, to average *541* on the index in the 1680s (1679–80 to 1688–9) – making that the best whole decade in the seventeenth century for the ordinary man's living standards. Better still was to come briefly in the opening years of William III's reign, when over the three years 1688–9 to 1691–2 the Wrigley-Schofield real wage index rises to an average of *614*.

In any case, in the long-term experience of four generations of wage labourers from the mid-1660s to the mid-1760s, the tightened belts of the middle to late 1690s proved no more than a brief hiatus. Thus for the first decade of the new century (which included the appalling harvest years of 1708–9) the index averages *591*; by the 1720s, it reaches an average of *636*; in the 1730s (*the* great decade for standard of living of the lower orders), *719* and in the 1740s (which began inauspiciously with the widespread hunger riots of 1740 and a serious wave of epidemics), *673*.

For the next fifteen years, down to 1763–4 [1749–50 to 1763–4], there was little major change, despite two bad years, 1756–8 (av. *663*). The big change came in the eleven years 1764–5 to 1774–5, a drop to *591* (72 points down, but still an identical average to that of the first decade of the century.) Thereafter, to the end of the period, we can detect a modest recovery: an average *640*, i.e. a level not much worse than the period 1739–64, much the same as the 1720s, and very much better than the decade from 1699–1709.

N. RELIGION

N. 1: Leading Dignitaries of the church of England, 1691–1783

Archbishops of Canterbury		Archbishops of York		Bishops of London	
John Tillotson	1691–4	John Sharp	1691–1714	Henry Compton	1675–1713
Thomas Tenison	1694–1715	Sir William Dawes	1714–24	John Robinson	1713–23
William Wake	1715–37	Lancelot Blackburn	1724–43	Edmund Gibson	1723–48
John Potter	1737–47	Thomas Herring	1743–7	Thomas Sherlock	1748–61
Thomas Herring	1747–57	Matthew Hutton	1747–57	Thomas Hayter	1761–2
Matthew Hutton	1757–8	John Gilbert	1757–61	Richard Osbaldeston	1762–4
Thomas Secker	1758–68	R. Hay Drummond	1761–76	Richard Herrick	1764–77
Fred. Cornwallis	1768–83	William Markham	1776–1807	Robert Lowth	1777–87

N.2: The Anglican Bishops and their annual incomes, 1660–1762

See	pre-Revolution (£)	post-Revolution (£)	1762 ('reputed yearly value') (£)
Canterbury	4,317 (1681–2)	4,775 + fines etc. (1711–14)	7,000
York	–	2,524 + fines (1692–1704)	4,500
Bath and Wells	850 (c. 1688)	1,400 + (c. 1710)	2,000
Bristol	350 (c. 1688)	400 (c. 1710)	450
(with Residentiary of St Paul's and rectory of Bow *in commendam*,* TOTAL 1,550)			
Chester	744 (c. 1680)	1,000 (c. 1710)	900
(with rectory of Stanhope *in commendam**)			TOTAL 1,500)
Carlisle	713 (1688)	800 (c. 1710)	1,300
Chichester	800 (c. 1680)	1,000 (c. 1710)	1,400
Durham	3,500 (1664)	–	6,000
Exeter	584 (c. 1670)	500 (c. 1710)	1,500
Ely	1,106 (1684)	2,300 + fines (1707–8)	3,400
Gloucester	–	600 (c. 1710)	900
(with prebend of Durham *in commendam**)			TOTAL ?1400)†
Hereford	–	1,000 (c. 1710)	1,200
Lichfield & Coventry	1,200 (c. 1660)	1,400+ (c. 1710)	1,400
Lincoln	1,193 (1660)	1,100 (1715)	1,500
London	3,000 + fines (1679)	–	4,000
Norwich	–	1,529 (1692–1706)	2,000
Oxford	–	600 (c. 1710)	500
(with deanery of St Paul's *in commendam**)			TOTAL 2,300)
Peterborough	630 (1688)	800 (c. 1710)	1,000
(with vicarage of Twickenham *in commendam**)			TOTAL [not known])
Rochester	500 (1663)	600 (c. 1710)	600
(with deanery of Westminster *in commendam**)			TOTAL 1,500)

See	pre-Revolution	post-Revolution	1762 ('reputed yearly value')
	(£)	(£)	(£)
Salisbury	1,920 + fines (1675)	–	3,000
Winchester	3,563 gross (*c.* 1670)	–	5,000
Worcester	–	–	3,000
St Asaph	800 max (1685)	800 (*c.* 1710)	1,400
	(an archdeaconry and 3 sinecures normally attached)		
Bangor	150 (*c.* 1680)	400 (*c.* 1710)	1,400
St. David's	*c.* 500 (1684)	700 (*c.* 1710	900
Llandaff	344 + *commendam** (1680)	300 (*c.* 1710)	500

* *In commendam*: literally, 'in trust'; used of a benefice which a bishop or other dignitary was permitted to hold along with his own preferment. Usually, in effect, a convenient supplementary source of income for poorly endowed bishoprics.
† my estimate.

Sources:
1. D.R. Hirschberg, 'Episcopal Incomes and Expenses, 1660–*c.* 1760', in R. O'Day and E. Heal, eds (98), pp. 213–16.
2. Sir J. Fortescue, ed., *The Correspondence of King George III* (1927), I, pp. 33–44: 'A list of Archbishops, Bishops, Deans, and Prebendaries in England and Wales . . . with the reputed yearly value of their respective dignities' (1762).

N.3: Parliament, the Church and Dissent, 1689–1779

A 'The Toleration', 1689–1779
(*i*)*Toleration Act* (1 William & Mary, c.18)
This 'Act for exempting their Majesties' Protestant subjects, dissenting from the Church of England, from the penalties of certain laws' had as its original, very limited purpose to grant 'some ease to scrupulous consciences in the exercise of religion' as 'an effectual means to unite their Majesties' Protestant subjects in interest and affection'.
The main provisions were:

(1) [penal statutes repealed].
(2) *Protestant* dissenters relieved of the penalties laid down in certain earlier statutes, notably in the Elizabethan Act of Uniformity (1559), making parish church attendance obligatory, and in the Conventicles Act of 1670 (see *Making of a Great Power*, N.2).
(3) Such dissenters could worship without penalty in their own meeting-houses, provided latter were licensed (by church authorities or JPs) and doors left unlocked during services.
(4) Dissenting ministers who took the oaths of allegiance and supremacy and made declaration against transubstantiation were relieved of penalties of Act of Uniformity, Five Mile Act and Conventicles Act (ibid., N.2), provided they also subscribed to 35 of the 39 Articles of Religion of the Church of England (the doctrinal articles); *except* that
(5) Baptists were not obliged to accede to the article relating to infant baptism, and Quakers were not required to swear any of the oaths, but rather make declarations

acknowledging allegiance to William and Mary, belief in the Trinity and the authority of Bible.

(6) Papists and Unitarians were explicitly excluded from the Act's benefits.

Source: Williams (3a), pp. 42–6.

(ii) [Annual] *Indemnity Acts 1727 et seq.* (1 George II, c. 23)

In the first year of George II's reign an Act was passed 'indemnifying persons who have omitted to qualify themselves for offices and employments [by taking the sacrament and oaths] within the time limited by law, and for allowing further time for that purpose'. Time allowed was one year, until 28 November 1728; it is sometimes said that by passing such acts annually thereafter the Parliaments of the Walpole period and their successors down to 1828 for practical purposes extended the scope of the 1689 Toleration Act by, in effect, suspending the civil disabilities of the Protestant dissenters under the unrepealed Test and Corporation Acts. But *note*:

(1) The Acts were *not*, for many years, an annual event. No fresh indemnity was granted in seven of the 29 years from 1728–57, including 1730, 1732 and 1745. Only from 1756 onwards did these Acts become regular.

(2) The indemnity was not total. The original Act of 1727 temporarily nullified the penal effects on individuals of the 1673 Test Act and of the Act for Further Securing the King's Person and Government (1715), but did not – contrary to common belief – cover the Corporation Act of 1661 as well.

Source: Williams (3a), pp. 341–3.

(iii) Dissenters' Relief Act 1779 (19 George III, c. 44)

Dissenting ministers (and teachers in schools and academies) required only to take the oaths and make a new declaration 'that I am a Christian and a Protestant, and as such, that I believe that the Scriptures of the Old and New Testament, as commonly received among the Protestant churches, do contain the revealed Will of God; and that I do receive the same as the rule of my doctrine and practice'. (This relieved them of the necessity, by law under the Toleration Act, of subscribing to the 35 specified Articles of Religion).

[*Note*: Previous bills to this effect had failed in 1772 and 1773.]

Source: Williams (3a), pp. 345–6.

B The anti-clerical campaign of 1725–36

1725	Fifty new Churches project for London (Tory Act of 1711) abandoned long before completion
1730	Bill to prevent suits for tithes
1730	Bill to prevent translation of bishops
1733	Bill to reform ecclesiastical courts
1733	Church Rates Bill
1735–6	Attempt to repeal Test and Corporation Acts; defeated in House of Commons, 251:123
	Note: all the attempted measures of 1730–5 failed – in the end; all lacked Walpole's support
1736	Mortmain Bill, impeding charitable bequests to the Church: received government backing and passed
1736	Quaker Relief Bill (government measure): defeated in the Lords

N.4: The growth of Methodism, 1740–c.90

The official total membership of the societies of Wesleyan (Arminian) Methodists at the first English count in 1767 was 25,911 (Davies and Rupp [114] *405*). The total for the whole of Britain in 1791 had increased to 72,000. These figures (the latter, especially) have often struck students as astonishingly small. It is essential to bear in mind, however, that the statistics available before 1770 take no account of the membership of Whitefield's Societies or, more significant numerically, of the fact that in Wales – Howell Harris's stamping ground and the most successful region of all for the Evangelical Revival *per capita* of the population – it was the Calvinistic Methodists who held sway throughout.

N.5: Religious controversy: the debates on the Trinity, Deism and Freethinking: some landmarks, 1680–1736

1685	George Bull	*Defensio Fidei Nicaenae*
1687	Stephen Nye	*Brief History of the Unitarians, called also Socinians* (in fact, an apologia for Socinianism)
1690	Arthur Bury	*The Naked Gospel*
1690	William Sherlock	*A Vindication of the Doctrine of the Holy . . . Trinity*
1692	John Wallis	*Three Sermons concerning the Sacred Trinity*
1692	anon	*The Unreasonableness of the Doctrine of the Trinity*
1692	Stephen Nye	*An Accurate Examination of . . . the Divinity of our Saviour*
*1693	Charles Blount	*The Oracles of Reason*
1695	John Locke	*The Reasonableness of Christianity*
*1696	John Toland	*Christianity not Mysterious*
1698	Stephen Nye	*Considerations of the Explications of the Doctrine of the Trinity*
*1706	Matthew Tindal	*Rights of the Christian Church*
1708	William Whiston	*Apostolic Constitutions*
1711	William Whiston	*Primitive Christianity Revived*
1712	Samuel Clarke	*The Scripture Doctrine of the Trinity*
*1713	Anthony Collins	*A Discourse of Free Thinking*
1718	Thomas Chubb	*The Supremacy of the Father Asserted*
*1724	Anthony Collins	*A Discourse of the Grounds and Reasons of the Christian Religion*
*1730	Matthew Tindal	*Christianity as Old as the Creation*

The Attack on the Deists, 1731–6

1731	William Law	*The Case of Reason*
1732	George Berkeley	*Alciphron*
1736	Joseph Butler	*The Analogy of Religion*

* Signifies works of leading Deists or Freethinkers

O. MAPS

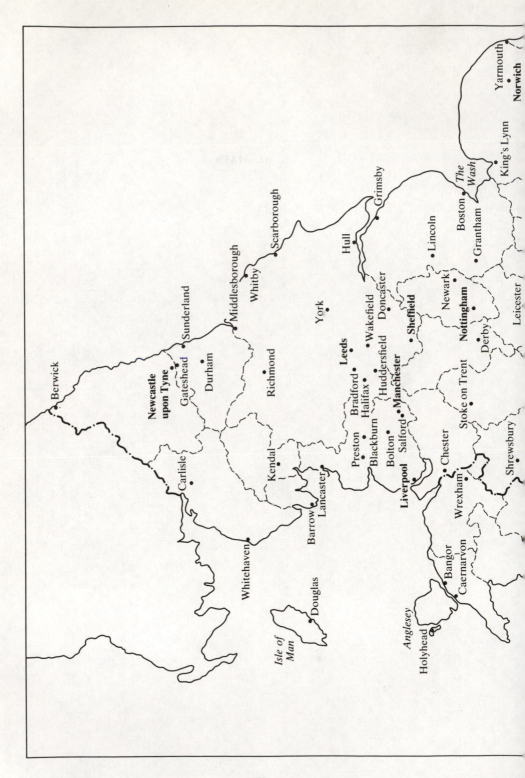

Newcastle
upon Tyne

Gateshead

Sunderland

Durham

Berwick

Carlisle

Kendal

Whitehaven

Barrow

Lancaster

Isle of
Man

Douglas

Middlesborough

Whitby

Scarborough

Richmond

York

Hull

Grimsby

Leeds

Bradford

Halifax

Preston

Blackburn

Bolton

Salford

Manchester

Liverpool

Huddersfield

Wakefield

Doncaster

Sheffield

Chester

Wrexham

Bangor

Caernarvon

Anglesey

Holyhead

Lincoln

Boston

Grantham

Newark

Nottingham

Derby

Stoke on Trent

Shrewsbury

Leicester

The
Wash

King's Lynn

Yarmouth
Norwich

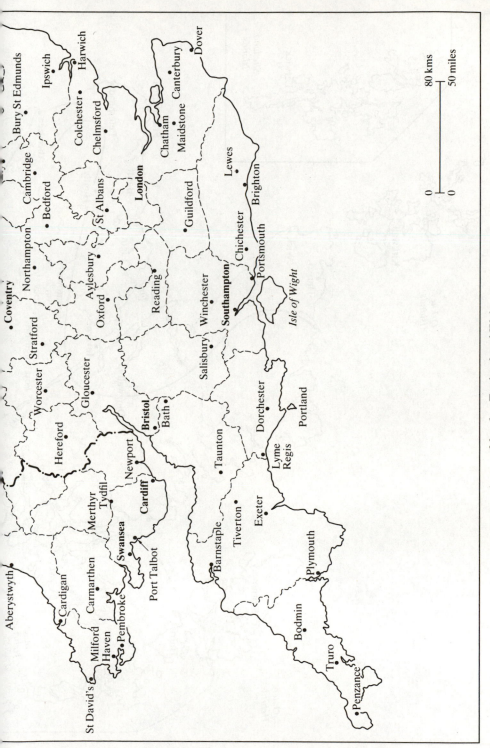

Map 1. England and Wales

401

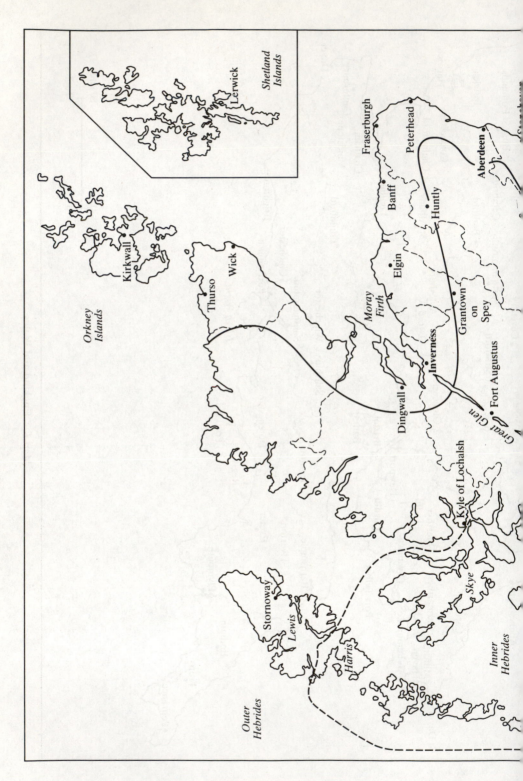

Shetland Islands

Lerwick

Orkney Islands

Kirkwall

Thurso
Wick

Fraserburgh
Peterhead
Banff
Aberdeen
Huntly

Elgin

Moray Firth

Grantown on Spey

Inverness

Dingwall

Fort Augustus

Great Glen

Kyle of Lochalsh

Skye

Stornoway

Lewis

Harris

Inner Hebrides

Outer Hebrides

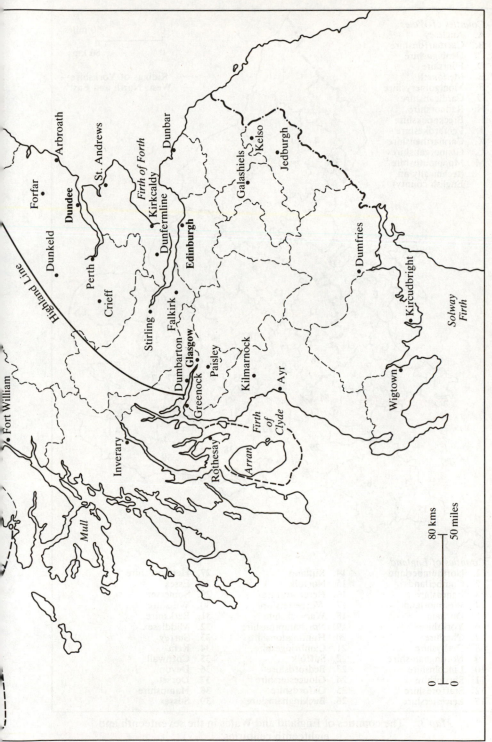

Arbroath

Forfar

Dundee

St. Andrews

Firth of Forth

Dunbar

Dunkeld

Kirkcaldy

Dunfermline

Galashiels

Kelso

Perth

Edinburgh

Jedburgh

Crieff

Falkirk

Stirling

Dumfries

Highland Line

Dumbarton

Glasgow

Kircudbright

Greenock

Paisley

Solway
Firth

Kilmarnock

Fort William

Ayr

Wigtown

Inverary

Firth
of
Clyde

Rothesay

Arran

Mull

80 kms

50 miles

0

0

Map 2. Scotland

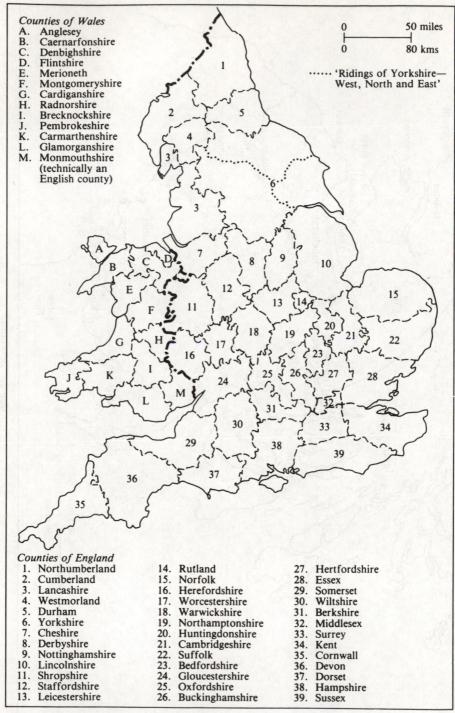

Counties of Wales
A. Anglesey
B. Caernarfonshire
C. Denbighshire
D. Flintshire
E. Merioneth
F. Montgomeryshire
G. Cardiganshire
H. Radnorshire
I. Brecknockshire
J. Pembrokeshire
K. Carmarthenshire
L. Glamorganshire
M. Monmouthshire
(technically an English county)

0   50 miles

0   80 kms

······· 'Ridings of Yorkshire—
West, North and East'

Counties of England
1. Northumberland
2. Cumberland
3. Lancashire
4. Westmorland
5. Durham
6. Yorkshire
7. Cheshire
8. Derbyshire
9. Nottinghamshire
10. Lincolnshire
11. Shropshire
12. Staffordshire
13. Leicestershire
14. Rutland
15. Norfolk
16. Herefordshire
17. Worcestershire
18. Warwickshire
19. Northamptonshire
20. Huntingdonshire
21. Cambridgeshire
22. Suffolk
23. Bedfordshire
24. Gloucestershire
25. Oxfordshire
26. Buckinghamshire
27. Hertfordshire
28. Essex
29. Somerset
30. Wiltshire
31. Berkshire
32. Middlesex
33. Surrey
34. Kent
35. Cornwall
36. Devon
37. Dorset
38. Hampshire
39. Sussex

Map 3. The counties of England and Wales in the seventeenth and eighteenth centuries

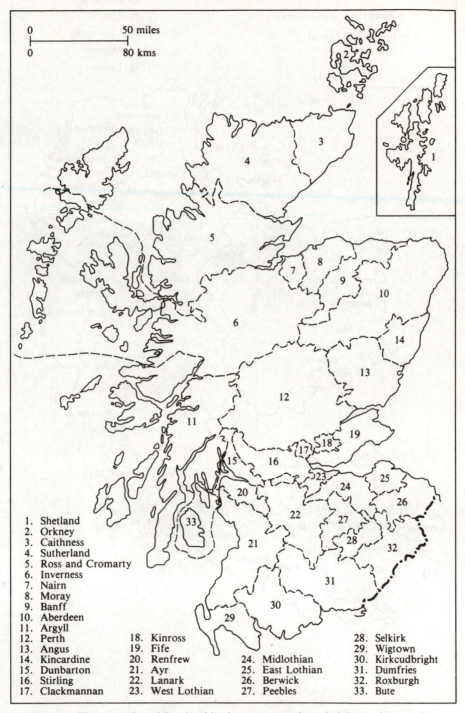

0   50 miles

0   80 kms

1. Shetland
2. Orkney
3. Caithness
4. Sutherland
5. Ross and Cromarty
6. Inverness
7. Nairn
8. Moray
9. Banff
10. Aberdeen
11. Argyll
12. Perth
13. Angus
14. Kincardine
15. Dunbarton
16. Stirling
17. Clackmannan

18. Kinross
19. Fife
20. Renfrew
21. Ayr
22. Lanark
23. West Lothian

24. Midlothian
25. East Lothian
26. Berwick
27. Peebles

28. Selkirk
29. Wigtown
30. Kirkcudbright
31. Dumfries
32. Roxburgh
33. Bute

Map 4.   The counties of Scotland in the seventeenth and eighteenth centuries

Map 5. Ireland in the seventeenth and eighteenth centuries

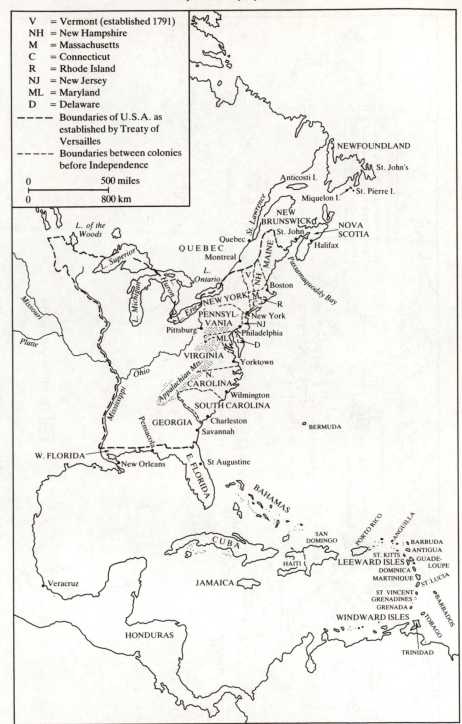

Legend:

V = Vermont (established 1791)
NH = New Hampshire
M = Massachusetts
C = Connecticut
R = Rhode Island
NJ = New Jersey
ML = Maryland
D = Delaware
– – – – Boundaries of U.S.A. as established by Treaty of Versailles
– – – – – Boundaries between colonies before Independence

0   500 miles
0   800 km

NEWFOUNDLAND
St. John's
Anticosti I.
Miquelon I.
St. Pierre I.
NEW BRUNSWICK
St. John
NOVA SCOTIA
Quebec
Halifax
QUEBEC
Montreal
MAINE
Passamaquoddy Bay
St. Lawrence
L. of the Woods
L. Superior
L. Michigan
L. Huron
L. Ontario
L. Erie
Missouri
Platte
NEW YORK
V
NH
C
M
R
Boston
New York
NJ
Philadelphia
PENNSYL-VANIA
Pittsburg
ML
D
VIRGINIA
Yorktown
Ohio
Mississippi
Appalachian Mts.
N. CAROLINA
Wilmington
SOUTH CAROLINA
GEORGIA
Charleston
Savannah
BERMUDA
W. FLORIDA
Pensacola
New Orleans
E. FLORIDA
St Augustine
BAHAMAS
Veracruz
CUBA
SAN DOMINGO
HAITI
JAMAICA
HONDURAS
PORTO RICO
ANGUILLA
BARBUDA
ST. KITTS
ANTIGUA
LEEWARD ISLES
GUADE-LOUPE
DOMINICA
MARTINIQUE
ST. LUCIA
ST. VINCENT
GRENADINES
GRENADA
WINDWARD ISLES
BARBADOS
TOBAGO
TRINIDAD

Map 6.   North America and the West Indies
After: I. Christie, *Wars and Revolutions* (1982)

407

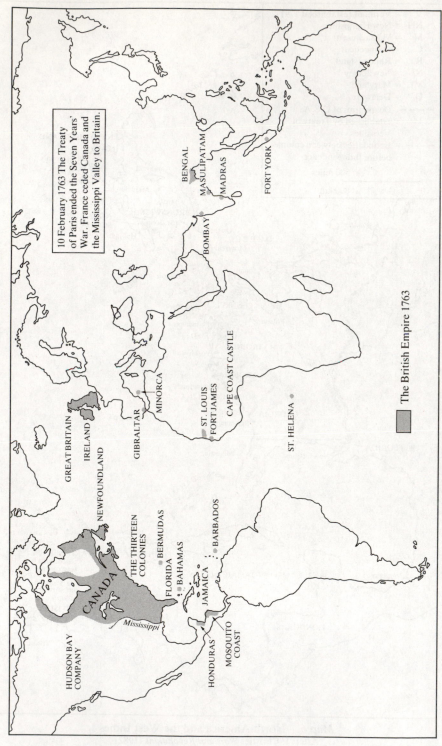

10 February 1763 The Treaty of Paris ended the Seven Years' War. France ceded Canada and the Mississippi Valley to Britain.

BENGAL
MASULIPATAM
MADRAS
FORT YORK
BOMBAY

CAPE COAST CASTLE
MINORCA
ST. LOUIS
FORT JAMES
GIBRALTAR
ST. HELENA

GREAT BRITAIN
IRELAND
NEWFOUNDLAND

THE THIRTEEN COLONIES
BERMUDAS
CANADA
FLORIDA
BAHAMAS
BARBADOS
JAMAICA
Mississippi
HONDURAS
MOSQUITO COAST
HUDSON BAY COMPANY

The British Empire 1763

Map 7. The British Empire in 1763

Bibliography

The standard bibliography for the early Hanoverian period though now showing its age, is M. Pargellis and D.J. Medley, eds, *Bibliography of British History: the Eighteenth Century, 1714–1789* (Oxford, 1951). A welcome, more up-to-date addition, containing helpful assessments, is R.A. Smith, *Late Georgian and Regency England, 1760–1837* (Cambridge, 1984). The Historical Association also publishes an *Annual Bulletin of Historical Literature*, which is very useful for keeping in touch with important new work in all fields.

The bibliography which follows is considerably longer than that of most other volumes in this series. From the multitude of books available for studying the period and supplying the essential groundwork for the writing of this volume, we have tried single-mindedly to select (except in the brief section 1) only those which a conscientious honours student could reasonably be expected to read in preparing for an essay or seminar on any of the main topics which the book deals with. That our attempted rigour has fallen short in the end of the ruthless hatchet-work and decimation that would have been necessary to slim the bibliography much further is attributable in the main to the almost sinful outpouring of secondary work on the eighteenth century during the present decade, i.e. since the first drafts of the earliest chapters of the book were begun. In addition to the items listed below there were, of course, many other more specialised or recondite works which the present authors themselves found it necessary to consult; since a zealous, enquiring reader will find these of interest and value, they have been – in accordance with series policy – siphoned off, along with the bulk of the primary source material used and quoted from, into the end-notes which follow each chapter.

To assist the compilation of purpose-designed reading lists the bibliography has been organised into ten subject categories and into further sub-categories, and within each sub-category readers will find entries made in a broadly chronological way.

1. Source material (1–3)
2. General: Textbooks, survey histories and collective studies (4–11)
3. Politics and Parliament; political biographies (12–66)
4. Finance, central and local government, and the law (67–80)
5. Foreign policy and war (81–94)
6. Religion (95–119)
7. The economy and society (120–230)
8. Ireland and Scotland (231–256)
9. Overseas territories (257–268)
10. Education and the printed word; science and ideas (269–289)

Note: Place of publication is London, unless otherwise stated.

1. SOURCE MATERIAL

1 W. Cobbett, ed., *The Parliamentary History of England* [debates], 36 vols [to 1803], (1806–20)

2 D. Defoe, *A Tour through England and Wales* (1724–6); refs cited from Everyman edn, ed. G.D.M. Cole, 2 vols (1927). But note also Defoe's *A Tour through the Whole Island of Great Britain* (ed. P. Rogers, Penguin edn, abridged [but sensitively so], 1971)

3 (a) E.N. Williams, ed., *The Eighteenth Century Constitution* (Cambridge, 1960); (b) W.C. Costin and J.S. Watson, eds, *The Law and Working of the Constitution: Documents 1660–1914*, I, *1660–1783* (1952)

The meaty volume of *English Historical Documents, vol. X: 1714–1783* (1957) eds. D.B. Horn and M. Ransome, remains of enduring usefulness

2. GENERAL: TEXTBOOKS, SURVEY HISTORIES AND COLLECTIVE STUDIES

4 J.R. Jones, *Country and Court: England 1658–1714* (1978).

5 G. Holmes, *Politics, Religion and Society in England, 1679–1742* (1986) – collected essays, pamphlets, etc.

6 J. Black, ed., *Britain in the Age of Walpole* (1984). 'Problems in Focus' series

7 C. Jones, ed., *Britain in the First Age of Party 1680–1750: Essays presented to Geoffrey Holmes* (1987). Wide-ranging collection covering politics, government, religion, society, the press etc.

8 W.A. Speck, *Stability and Strife: England 1714–1760* (1977). Companion vol. of (9)

9 I.R. Christie, *Wars and Revolutions: Britain, 1760–1815* (1982)

10 J.B. Owen, *The Eighteenth Century 1714–1815* (1974)

11 (a) J.S. Bromley, ed., *New Cambridge Modern History*, VI, *1688–1725* (Cambridge, 1970); (b) J.O. Lindsay, ed., *New Cambridge Modern History*, VII, *1713–63* (Cambridge, 1957)

3. POLITICS AND PARLIAMENT; POLITICAL BIOGRAPHIES

12 (a) R. Sedgwick, ed., *The History of Parliament: The House of Commons 1715–1754*, 2 vols, (1970); (b) L.B. Namier and J. Brooke, eds, *The History of Parliament: The House of Commons, 1754–1790*, 3 vols (1962)

13 C. Jones, ed., *Party and Management in Parliament, 1660–1784* (Leicester, 1984)

14 J.H. Plumb, *The Growth of Political Stability in England, 1675–1725* (1967)

15 J. Cannon, ed., *The Whig Ascendancy: Colloquies on Hanoverian England* (1981) – first class collection of essays and discussions on politics 1689–1832

16 J.C.D. Clark, 'A General Theory of Party, Opposition and Government, 1688–1832', *HJ*, **23** (1980)

17 P.D.G. Thomas, *The House of Commons in the Eighteenth Century* (Oxford, 1971) – admirable study of the way parliamentary business was conducted

18 L.S. Sutherland (ed. A.N. Newman), *Politics and Finance in the Eighteenth Century* (1984) – collected essays

19 H. Van Thal, ed., *The Prime Ministers*, I (1974) – biographies from Walpole to Portland

20 B.W. Hill, *The Growth of Parliamentary Parties 1689–1742* (1976)

21 C. Jones, 'The House of Lords and the Growth of Parliamentary Stability, 1701–1742' in (7)

22 G. Holmes, *British Politics in the Age of Anne* (revised edn, 1987)

23 H.T. Dickinson, *Bolingbroke* (1970)

24 R. Hatton, (a) *George I: Elector and King* (1978); (b) 'New Light on George I of Great Britain' in S.B. Baxter, ed., *England's Rise to Greatness, 1660–1760* (Berkeley, 1983)

25 J.M. Beattie, *The English Court in the Reign of George I* (Cambridge, 1967)

26 J.H. Plumb, (a) *Sir Robert Walpole*, I: *The Making of a Statesman* (1956); (b) *Sir Robert Walpole*, II: *The King's Minister* (1960)

27 H.T. Dickinson, (a) *Walpole and the Whig Supremacy* (1973); (b) 'Whiggism in the 18th Century', in (15)

28 (a) L. Colley, *In Defiance of Oligarchy: The Tory Party, 1714–60* (Cambridge, 1982); (b) L. Colley and M. Goldie, 'The Principles and Practice of Eighteenth-Century Party', *HJ*, **22** (1979)

29 J.C.D. Clark, 'The Politics of the Excluded: Tories, Jacobites and Whig Patriots, 1715–60', *Parl. Hist.*, **2** (1983)

30 G. Holmes, 'Sir Robert Walpole', in (5)

31 E. Cruickshanks, 'The Political Management of Sir Robert Walpole 1720–42', in (**6**)

32 (a) P. Langford, *The Excise Crisis: Society and Politics in the Age of Walpole* (Oxford, 1975); (b) J.M. Price, 'The Excise Affair Revisited', in S.B. Baxter, ed., *England's Rise to Greatness 1660–1763* (Berkeley, 1983) – valuable reappraisal marred by an implausible final hypothesis re. Walpole (p. 306)

33 (a) H.T. Dickinson, 'The Precursors of Political Radicalism in Augustan Britain', in (**7**); (b) H.T. Dickinson, 'Popular Politics in the Age of Walpole' in (6)

34 J.B. Owen, 'George II Reconsidered', in A. Whiteman, J.S. Bromley and P.G.M. Dickson, eds, *Statesmen, Scholars and Merchants: Essays in Eighteenth-Century History Presented to Dame Lucy Sutherland* (Oxford, 1973)

35 L.B. Namier, (a) 'Monarchy and the Party System'; (b) 'Country Gentlemen in Parliament', in *Personalities and Powers* (1955); (c) W.A. Speck, 'Whigs and Tories Dim their Glories: English Political Parties under the First Two Georges', in (15)

36 B.W. Hill, *British Parliamentary Parties, 1742–1832: From the Fall of Walpole to the First Reform Act* (1985).

37 J.C.D. Clark, (a) 'The Decline of Party, 1740–1760', *EHR*, **93** (1978); (b) *The Dynamics of Change: The Crisis of the 1750s and English Party Systems* (Cambridge, 1982)

38 J.B. Owen, (a) *The Rise of the Pelhams* (1957); (b) *The Pattern of Politics in Eighteenth-Century England* (1962)

39 J. Brooke, *The House of Commons 1754–1790: Introductory Survey* (1968)

40 (a) M. Peters, *Pitt and Popularity: The Patriot Minister and London Opinion during the Seven Years War* (Oxford, 1980); (b) P. Langford, 'William Pitt and Pubic Opinion, 1757', *EHR*, **88** (1973)

41 J. Brooke, *King George III* (1972)

42 R. Pares, *King George III and the Politicians* (Oxford, 1953)

43 Sir L.B. Namier, (a) *The Structure of Politics at the Accession of George III* (2nd edn, 1982); (b) *England in the Age of the American Revolution* (2nd edn, 1961)

44 J. Brewer, *Party Ideology and Popular Politics at the Accession of George III* (Cambridge 1976)

45 (a) P. Lawson, *George Grenville, a Political Life* (Oxford, 1984); (b) J. Derry, *British Politics and the American Revolution* (1976)

46 F. O'Gorman, (a) *The Rise of Party in England: The Rockingham Whigs 1760–82* (1975); (b) 'Party in the Later Eighteenth Century', in (15)

47 P.D.G. Thomas, (a) *British Politics and the Stamp Act Crisis: The First Phase of the American Revolution 1763–1767* (Oxford, 1975); (b) *The Townshend Duties Crisis: The Second Phase of the American Revolution 1767–1773* (Oxford, 1987)

48 G. Rudé, *Wilkes and Liberty* (Oxford, 1965)

49 P.D.G. Thomas, *Lord North* (1976)

50 I.R. Christie, (a) 'Party in Politics in the Age of Lord North's Administration', *Parl. Hist.*, **6** (1987); (b) *Myth and Reality in Late Eighteenth Century British Politics* (1970)

51 J. Cannon, *The Fox–North Coalition: Crisis of the Constitution 1782–4* (Cambridge, 1969)

London politics

52 G.S. de Krey, *A Fractured Society: The Politics of London in the First Age of Party 1688–1715* (Oxford, 1985)

53 H. Horwitz, 'Party in a Civic Context: London from the Exclusion Crisis to the Fall of Walpole', in (7); see also A.J. Henderson, *London and the National Government, 1721–1742* (Durham N.C., 1945)

54 N. Rogers, 'Resistance to Oligarchy: the City Opposition to Walpole and his Successors, 1725–47' in J. Stevenson, ed., *London in the Age of Reform* (Oxford, 1977)

55 L.S. Sutherland, 'The City of London in Eighteenth-Century Politics', in (18); first published 1956 in R. Pares and A.J.P. Taylor, *Essays presented to Sir Lewis Namier* (1956)

The electorate and parliamentary reform

56 J. Cannon, *Parliamentary Reform, 1640–1832* (Cambridge, 1973)

57 G. Holmes, *The Electorate and the National Will in the First Age of Party* (Lancaster, 1976), repr. (5)

58 J.E. Bradley, 'Nonconformity and the Electorate in Eighteenth-Century England', *Parl. Hist.*, **6** (1987)

59 P. Langford, 'Property and "Virtual Representation" in Eighteenth-Century England', *HJ*, **31** (1988)

60 L. Colley, 'Eighteenth-Century English Radicalism before Wilkes', *TRHS*, **31** (1981)

61 I.R. Christie, *Wilkes, Wyvill and Reform: The Parliamentary Reform Movement in British Politics 1760–1785* (1962)

Jacobitism

62 G.V. Bennett, (a) see (106); (b) 'Jacobitism and the Rise of Walpole', in N. McKendrick, ed., *Historical Perspectives: Studies in English Thought and Society in Honour of J.H. Plumb* (1974)

63 B. Lenman, *The Jacobite Risings in Britain 1689–1746* (1980)

64 D. Szechi, *Jacobitism and Tory Politics 1710–1714* (Edinburgh, 1984)

65 (a) E. Cruickshanks, *Political Untouchables: The Tories and the '45* (1979); (b) E. Cruickshanks, ed., *Ideology and Conspiracy: Aspects of Jacobitism 1689–1759* (Edinburgh, 1982)

66 F.J. McLynn, *The Jacobites* (1985)

4. FINANCE, CENTRAL AND LOCAL GOVERNMENT, AND THE LAW

67 M.A. Thomson, *A Constitutional History of England, 1642–1801* (1938) – still the most wide-ranging and best general survey of its kind on this period, but note (3) above

68 H. Roseveare, *The Treasury, 1660–1870* (1973)

69 P.G.M. Dickson, *The Financial Revolution in England: A Study in the Development of Public Credit, 1688–1756* (1967)

70 R. Davis, 'The Rise of Protection in England, 1689–1786', *EcHR,* **19** (1966) – links closely with war finance

71 W.R. Ward, *The Land Tax in the Eighteenth Century* (Oxford, 1953)

72 J.V. Beckett, 'Land Tax or Excise: the Levying of Taxation in Seventeenth- and Eighteenth-Century England', *EHR,* **100** (1985)

73 N.P.K. O'Brien, 'The Political Economy of British Taxation, 1660–1815', *EcHR,* **41** (1988)

74 E. Hughes, *Studies in Administration and Finance 1558–1825* (Manchester, 1934) – valuable on 1670s–1730s

75 J.H. Plumb, 'The Organization of the Cabinet in the Reign of Queen Anne', *THRS,* **7** (1957)

76 G. Holmes, 'The New Men of Government' [Chap. 8 of 187a] – deals with growth of bureaucracy 1680s onwards

77 A. Fletcher, *Reform in the Provinces: The Government of Stuart England* (New Haven and London, 1986)

78 (a) N. Landau, *The Justices of the Peace, 1679–1760* (Berkeley, 1984); (b) L.K.J. Glassey, *Politics and the Appointment of Justices of the Peace 1675–1725* (Oxford, 1979)

79 L.K.J. Glassey, 'Local Government', in (7)

80 Sir L. Radzinowicz, *History of English Criminal Law,* I, 1948

5. FOREIGN POLICY AND WAR

General surveys

81 J.R. Jones, *Britain and the World 1649–1815* (1980)

82 P. Langford, *The Eighteenth Century 1688–1815* [Foreign Policy] (1976)

83 D.B. Horn, *Great Britain and Europe in the Eighteenth Century* (Oxford, 1967)

84 J. Brewer, *The Sinews of Power: War, Money and the English State 1688–1783* (1989)

Periods and topics

85 M. Sheehan, 'The Development of British Theory and Practice of the Balance of Power before 1714', *History,* **73** (1988)

86 N.A.M. Roger, *The Wooden World: An Anatomy of the Georgian Navy* (1986)

87 G.C. Gibbs, 'Parliament and Foreign Policy in the Age of Stanhope and Walpole', *EHR* , **77** (1962)

88 G.C. Gibbs, (a) 'Parliament and the Treaty of Quadruple Alliance', in R.M. Hatton and J.S. Bromley, eds, *William III and Louis XIV: Essays 1680–1720 by and for Mark A. Thomson* (Liverpool, 1968); (b) 'Great Britain and the Alliance of Hanover', *EHR*, **73** (1958)

89 J. Black, (a) *British Foreign Policy in the Age of Walpole* (Edinburgh, 1985); (b) 'Foreign Policy in the Age of Walpole', in (6).

90 J. Black, *Natural and Necessary Enemies: Anglo-French Relations in the Eighteenth Century* (1986)

91 R. Middleton, *The Bells of Victory: the Pitt-Newcastle Ministry and the Conduct of the Seven Years' War* (Cambridge, 1985) – revisionist study, rich in archival research but short on psychological insight; important, but not the last word

92 J.R. Western, *The English Militia in the Eighteenth Century: The Story of a Political Issue 1660–1802* (1965)

93 J.R. Dull, *A Diplomatic History of the American Revolution* (1985)

94 P. Mackesy, *The War for America 1775–1783* (1965) – the outstanding work on the subject

6. RELIGION

95 W.R. Watts, *The Dissenters: from the Reformation to the French Revolution* (Oxford, 1978)

96 J. Bossy, *The English Catholic Community 1570–1850* (1975)

97 N. Sykes, *From Sheldon to Secker: Aspects of English Church History 1660–1768* (Cambridge, 1959)

98 R. O'Day and F. Heal, eds, *Princes and Paupers in the English Church, 1500–1800* (Leicester, 1981)

99 E.G. Rupp, *Religion in England 1688–1791* (Oxford, 1986)

100 A.D. Gilbert, *Religion and Society in Industrial England: Church, Chapel and Social Change 1740–1914* (1976)

101 N. Sykes, *Church and State in England in the 18th Century* (Cambridge, 1934)

102 D.R. Hirschberg, 'The Government and Church Patronage in England, 1660–1760', *JBS*, **20** (1980–1)

103 R. O'Day, 'The Anatomy of a Profession: the Clergy of the Church of England', in (186)

104 (a) J.H. Pruett, *The Parish Clergy under the Later Stuarts: The Leicestershire Experience* (Urbana, Illinois, 1978); (b) E.J. Evans, 'Anglican Clergy of the North of England', in (7)

105 G.F. Nuttall and O. Chadwick, eds, *From Uniformity to Unity 1662–1962* (1962) – especially for 1661–89

106 G.V. Bennett, *The Tory Crisis in Church and State: The Career of Francis Atterbury, Bishop of Rochester* (Oxford, 1975)

107 G.M. Townsend, 'Religious Radicalism and Conservatism in the Whig Party under George I: The Repeal of the Occasional Conformity and Schism Acts', *Parl. Hist.*, **7** (1988)

108 N. Sykes, (a) *Edmund Gibson, Bishop of London* (Oxford 1926); (b) *William Wake, Archbishop of Canterbury* (Cambridge, 1957)

109 (a) S. Taylor, 'Sir Robert Walpole, the Church of England and the Quaker Tithe Bill of 1736', *HJ*, **28** (1985); (b) T.F.J. Kendrick, 'Sir Robert Walpole, the Old Whigs and the Bishops, 1733–36', *HJ*, **11** (1968); (c) N.C. Hunt, *Two Early Political Associations: The Quakers and the Dissenting Deputies in the Age of Sir Robert Walpole* (Oxford, 1961)

110 E.J. Evans, *The Contentious Tithe* (1976)

111 (a) G.F.A. Best, *Temporal Pillars: Queen Anne's Bounty, the Ecclesiastical Commissioners and the Church of England* (Cambridge, 1964); (b) I.M. Green, 'The First Years of Queen Anne's Bounty', in (98)

112 F.C. Mather, 'Georgian Churchmanship Reconsidered: Some Variations in Anglican Public Worship 1714–1830', *JEH*, **36** (1985)

113 J.D. Walsh, (a) 'The Origins of the Evangelical Revival', in G.V. Bennett and J.D. Walsh, eds, *Essays in Modern English Church History* (1966); (b) 'Elie Halévy and the Birth of Methodism', *TRHS*, **25** (1975); (c) 'Methodism and the Mob', in G.J. Cuming and D. Black, eds, *Popular Belief and Practice* (Cambridge, 1972)

114 R. Davies and E.G. Rupp, eds, *A History of the Methodist Church in Great Britain*, I (1965)

115 (a) S. Andrews, *Methodism and Society* (1970) – includes documents; (b) A. Armstrong, *The Church of England, the Methodists and Society* (1973). Uncritical of the Church of England, adequate introduction to Methodism

116 M. Edwards, 'John Wesley', in (114)

117 A. Everitt, 'Philip Doddridge of Northampton and the Evangelical Tradition', in *idem, Landscape and Community in England* (1985)

118 B. Semmel, *The Methodist Revolution* (1974)

119 R.A. Knox, *Enthusiasm: A Chapter in the History of Religion with Special Reference to the XVII and XVIII Centuries* (Oxford, 1950)

7. THE ECONOMY AND SOCIETY

General surveys or articles and collected essays

120 F.M. Carus-Wilson, ed., *Essays in Economic History*, II (1962)

121 D.C. Coleman, *The Economy of England, 1450–1750* (Oxford, 1977)

122 J. Sharpe, *Early Modern England: A Social History 1550–1750* (1987)

123 (a) C.G.A. Clay, *Economic Expansion and Social Change: England 1500–1700*, I: *People, Land and Towns*; (b) II: *Industry, Trade and Government* (Cambridge, 1984)

124 B.A. Holderness, *Pre-Industrial England: Economy and Society from 1500 to 1750* (1976)

125 C. Wilson, *England's Apprenticeship: 1603–1763* (2nd edn, 1984)

126 D.C. Coleman and A.H. John, eds, *Trade, Government and Economy in Pre-industrial England: Essays presented to F.J. Fisher* (1976)

127 J. Thirsk, *Economic Policy and Projects* (Oxford, 1978)

128 *For statistics*: (a) P. Deane and W.A. Cole, *British Economic Growth, 1688–1959* (2nd edn, Cambridge, 1967); (b) B.R. Mitchell and P. Deane, *Abstract of British Historical Statistics* (Cambridge, 1962)

129 P. Clark, 'Migration in England during the Late Seventeenth and Eighteenth Centuries', *P & P*, **83** (1979)

130 (a) W.A. Cole, 'Factors in Demand, 1700–1800', in (135); (b) N.F.R. Crafts, 'British Economic Growth 1700–1831: A Review of the Evidence', *EcHR*, **36** (1983)

131 P. Mathias, (a) *The Transformation of England: Essays in the Economic and Social History of England in the Eighteenth Century* (1979); (b) *The First Industrial Nation* (2nd edn, 1983)

132 R. Porter, *English Society in the Eighteenth Century* (1982)

133 N. McKendrick, ed., *Historical Perspectives: Studies in English Thought and Society in Honour of J.H. Plumb* (1974)

134 T.S. Ashton, *Economic Fluctuations in England 1700–1800* (Oxford, 1959)

135 R.C. Floud and D.N. McCloskey, eds, *The Economic History of Britain since 1700:* I, *1700–1860* (Cambridge, 1981)

136 H.A. Pawson, *The Early Industrial Revolution: Britain in the Eighteenth Century* (1979)

137 A.H. John, (a) 'Aspects of English Economic Growth in the First Half of the Eighteenth Century' in W.E. Minchinton, ed., *The Growth of English Overseas Trade in the 17th and 18th Centuries* (1969); (b) 'War and the English Economy, 1700–1763', *EcHR*, **7** (1955)

138 M. Jubb, 'Economic Policy and Economic Development', in (6)

139 H.J. Perkin, *Origins of Modern English Society, 1780–1880* (1969)

Local studies

140 J.V. Beckett, *The East Midlands from AD 1000* (1988)

141 D. Hey, *Yorkshire from AD 1000* (1986)

142 M. Rowlands, (a) *The West Midlands from AD 1000* (1987); (b) *Masters and Men in the West Midland Metalware Trades before the Industrial Revolution* (Manchester, 1975)

143 (a) H. Heaton, *Yorkshire Woollen and Worsted Industries from the Earliest Times up to the Industrial Revolution* (2nd edn, Oxford, 1965); (b) R.G. Wilson, *Gentlemen Merchants: The Merchant Community in Leeds, 1700–1830* (Manchester, 1971)

144 (a) A.L. Beier and R. Finlay, eds, *The Making of the Metropolis: London 1500–1700* (1986); (b) E.A. Wrigley, 'A Simple Model of London's Importance in Changing England's Society and Economy, 1650–1750', *P&P*, **37** (1967)

145 (a) J.K. Walton, *Lancashire: A Social History, 1558–1939* (Manchester, 1987); (b) A.P. Wadsworth and J. de L. Mann, *The Cotton Trade and Industrial Lancashire 1600–1780* (Manchester, 1931)

146 J.P. Jenkins, *The Making of a Ruling Class: The Glamorgan Gentry, 1640–1790* (1983) – comprehensive study, far wider than socio-economic in range

147 J.V. Beckett, *Coal and Tobacco: The Lowthers and the Economic Development of West Cumberland, 1660–1760* (1981)

148 J.D. Chambers, *Vale of Trent 1670–1800: A Regional Study of Economic Change* (Cambridge, 1958)

149 E. Hughes, *North Country Life in the Eighteenth Century: The North-East 1700–1750* (Oxford 1952)

Demography
(see also end-notes to Ch. 9)

150 J.D. Chambers, *Population, Economy and Society in Pre-Industrial England* (Oxford, 1972)

151 (a) M.W. Flinn, *British Population Growth 1700–1850* (1970); (b) E.A. Wrigley, 'The

Growth of Population in Eighteenth-Century England: A Conundrum Resolved?', *P&P*, **98** (1983), p. 220; (c) R.D. Lee and R.S. Schofield, 'British Population in the Eighteenth Century', in (135)

152 E.A. Wrigley and R.S. Schofield, *The Population History of England 1541–1871: A Reconstruction* (1981)

Overseas trade (and Empire)

153 W.E. Minchinton, ed., *The Growth of English Overseas Trade in the Seventeenth and Eighteenth Centuries* (1969)

154 R. Davis, *The Rise of the English Shipping Industry in the Seventeenth and Eighteenth Centuries* (1962)

155 (a) R. Davis, 'English Foreign Trade, 1660–1700', *EcHR* **7** (1954); (b) 'English Foreign Trade 1700–1774', *EcHR*, **15** (1962). Reprinted in (153)

156 C. Wilson, *Mercantilism* (HA 1958) – helpful introduction for the uninitiated

157 R.S. Dunn, *Sugar and Slaves: the Rise of the Planter Class in the English West Indies* (1973)

158 V.T. Harlow, *The Founding of the Second British Empire, 1763–1793*, I (1952)

159 R.F. Thomas and D.N. McCloskey, 'Overseas Trade and Empire, 1700–1860', in (135)

See also section 9 below, especially (258) and Section 4 above (70)

Industry

160 D.C. Coleman, *Industry in Tudor and Stuart England* (1975)

161 J. Thirsk, 'Industries in the Countryside', in F.J. Fisher, ed., *Essays in the Economic and Social History of Tudor and Stuart England* (1961)

162 G. Hammersley, 'The Charcoal Iron Industry and its Fuel', *EcHR*, **26** (1973)

163 T.S. Ashton, *Iron and Steel in the Industrial Revolution* (4th edn, Manchester, 1968)

164 (a) J.U. Nef, *The Rise of the British Coal Industry* (1932); (b) M.W. Flinn, *History of the British Coal Industry*, 2 vols (1984)

165 M. Berg, *The Age of Manufactures 1700–1820* (1985)

166 P. Mathias, 'Who unbound Prometheus? Science and Technical Change, 1600–1800', in (131a)

167 E.W. Gilboy, *Wages in 18th Century England* (1934)

168 (a) E.W. Gilboy, 'Demand as a Factor in the Industrial Revolution', in (170); (b) D.E.C. Eversley, 'The Home Market and Home Demand, 1750–1850', in E.L. Jones and G.E. Mingay, eds, *Land, Labour and Population in the Industrial Revolution* (1967)

169 P. Mantoux, *The Industrial Revolution in the Eighteenth Century* (1928)

170 R. Hartwell, ed., *The Causes of the Industrial Revolution in England* (1967)

Agriculture and communications

171 E. Kerridge, *The Agricultural Revolution* (1967) – makes, but heavily overstates, a case for considering the 'Revolution' as primarily a 16th and 17th century phenomenon

172 J. Thirsk, ed., *Agricultural History of England and Wales*, V: *1640–1750* (1984)

173 J. Thirsk, 'Agricultural Innovations and their Diffusion', in (172)

174 C.G.A. Clay, 'Landlords and Estate Management', in (172)

175 W.G. Hoskins, 'Harvest Fluctuations and English Economic History 1620–1759', *AgHR* **16** (1968)

176 (a) E.L. Jones, 'Agriculture and Economic Growth in England 1660–1750: Agricultural Change'; (b) A.H. John, 'Agricultural Productivity and Economic Growth in England', both in E.L. Jones, ed., *Agriculture and Economic Growth in England 1650–1815* (1967)

177 A.H. John, (a) 'The Course of Agricultural Change, 1660–1760', in L.S. Pressnell, ed., *Studies in the Industrial Revolution*, (1960); (b) 'English Agricultural Improvements and Grain Exports, 1660–1765', in (126)

178 (a) J.R. Wordie, 'The Chronology of English Enclosure, 1500–1914', in *EcHR*, **36**, (1983); (b) R.A.C. Parker, *Enclosures in the Eighteenth Century* (1960)

179 (a) G.E. Mingay, 'The Agricultural Depression, 1730–1750', *EcHR*, **8** (1956); (b) J.V. Beckett, 'Regional Variations and the Agricultural Depression, 1730–50', *EcHR*, **35** (1982)

180 J.D. Chambers and G.E. Mingay, *The Agricultural Revolution, 1750–1880* (1966)

181 T.S. Willan, (a) *River Navigation in England 1600–1750* (1964); (b) *The English Coasting Trade 1600–1750* (1967)

Society: landed and urban

182 P. Laslett, *The World We Have Lost* (2nd edn, 1971)

183 F.M.L. Thompson, 'The Social Distribution of Landed Property in England since the 16th Century', *EcHR*, **19** (1966)

184 D. Owen, *English Philanthropy 1660–1960* (1965)

185 (a) D.A. Baugh, 'Poverty, Protestantism and Political Economy: English Attitudes Towards the Poor, 1660–1800', in S.B. Baxter, ed., *England's Rise to Greatness 1660–1760* (1983); (b) C. Wilson, 'The Other Face of Mercantilism', *TRHS*, **9** (1959)

186 W. Prest, ed., *The Professions in Early Modern England* (Beckenham, 1989)

187 G. Holmes, (a) *Augustan England: Professions, State and Society 1680–1730* (1982); (b) 'The Professions and Social Change in England, 1680–1730', in (5)

188 G. Holmes, 'Gregory King and the Social Structure of Pre-Industrial England', *TRHS*, **27** (1977), repr. (5)

189 R.B. Westerfield, *Middlemen in English Business, Particularly Between 1660 and 1760* (New Haven, 1915)

190 A. McInnes, 'The Revolution and the People', in G. Holmes, ed., *Britain after the Glorious Revolution 1689–1714* (1969)

191 N. McKendrick, J. Brewer and J.H. Plumb, *The Birth of a Consumer Society: The Commercialization of Eighteenth-century England* (1982)

192 N. McKendrick, (a) 'The Consumer Revolution of 18th-Century England'; (b) 'Josiah Wedgwood and the Commercialization of the Potteries' – both in (191)

193 J.H. Plumb, (a) *The Commercialization of Leisure in Eighteenth-Century England* (Reading, 1973); (b) 'The New World of Children in Eighteenth-Century England', *P&P*, **67** (1975); (c) 'The Acceptance of Modernity', in (191); (d) 'The Public, Literature and the Arts in the 18th Century' in P. Fritz and D. Williams, eds, *The Triumph of Culture: Eighteenth-Century Perspectives* (Toronto, 1972)

194 H.J. Habakkuk, (a) 'The Rise and Fall of English Landed Families 1600–1800: I', *TRHS*, **29** (1979); 'The Rise and Fall of English Landed Families 1600–1800: II',

TRHS, **30** (1980); (c) 'The Rise and Fall of English Landed Families, 1600–1800: III', *TRHS* **31** (1981)

195 L. and J.F.C. Stone, *An Open Elite? England 1540–1880* (Oxford, 1984)

196 (a) H.J. Habakkuk, 'The Land Settlement and the Restoration of Charles II', *TRHS,* **28** (1978); (b) J. Thirsk, 'The Restoration Land Settlement', *Journal of Modern History,* **26** (1954); (c) idem, *The Restoration* (1976) – prints documents

197 G.E. Mingay, (a) *English Landed Society in the 18th Century* (1963); (b) *The Gentry* (1976)

198 H.J. Habakkuk, 'English Landownership, 1680–1740', *EcHR,* **10** (1939–40)

199 J.V. Beckett, (a) 'English Landownership in the Later Seventeenth and Eighteenth Centuries', *EcHR,* **30** (1977); (b) 'The Pattern of Landownership in England and Wales, 1660–1880', *EcHR,* **37** (1984)

200 J.D. Marshall, 'Agrarian Wealth and Social Structure in Pre-industrial Cumbria', *EcHR,* **33** (1980)

201 C.G.A. Clay, (a) 'Marriage, Inheritance and the Rise of Large Estates in England, 1660–1815', *EcHR,* **21** (1968); (b) 'The Price of Freehold Land in the Later Seventeenth and Eighteenth Centuries', *EcHR,* **27** (1974)

202 J.V. Beckett, (a) *The Aristocracy in England, 1660–1914* (Oxford, 1986); (b) 'The English Aristocracy', *Parl. Hist.,* **5** (1986)

203 J. Cannon, (a) *Aristocratic Century: The Peerage of Eighteenth-century England* (Cambridge, 1984); (b) 'The Isthmus Repaired. The Resurgence of the English Aristocracy 1660–1716', *Proceedings of the British Academy,* **68** (1982)

204 (a) P. Roebuck, *Yorkshire Baronets 1640–1760* (Oxford, 1980); (b) B.A. Holderness, 'The English Land Market in the Eighteenth Century: The Case of Lincolnshire', *EcHR,* **27** (1974)

205 J.V. Beckett, 'The Decline of the Small Landowner in Eighteenth- and Nineteenth-Century England: Some Regional Considerations', *AgHR,* **30** (1982)

206 F.M.L. Thompson 'Landownership and Economic Growth in England in the Eighteenth Century', in E.L. Jones and S.J. Woolf, eds, *Agrarian Change and Economic Development* (1969)

207 P. Clark and P. Slack, eds, *Crisis and Order in English Towns: Essays in Urban History* (1972)

208 A. Everitt, (a) ed., *Perspectives in English Urban History* (1973); (b) 'The English Urban Inn, 1560–1760', in (208a)

209 R. Grassby, 'The Personal Wealth of the Business Community in Seventeenth-Century England, *EcHR,* **23** (1970)

210 P. Clark, ed., *The Transformation of English Provincial Towns, 1600–1800* (1984)

211 P.N. Borsay, *The English Urban Renaissance: Culture and Society in the Provincial Town, 1660–1770* (Oxford, 1989)

212 P.N. Borsay, (a) 'The English Urban Renaissance: the Development of Provincial Urban Culture, *c.* 1680–*c.* 1760', *Social History,* **5** (1977); (b) 'Culture, Status and the English Urban Landscape', *History,* **67** (1982); (c) 'Urban Development in the Age of Defoe', in (7)

213 P. Corfield, *Impact of English Towns, 1700–1800* (1982)

214 P. Corfield, *et al.,* eds, *Rise of the New Urban Society* (1975)

215 C.W. Chalkin, *The Provincial Towns of Georgian England: A Study of Eighteenth-Century England* (Cambridge, 1984)

216 (a) N. Rogers, 'Money, Land and Lineage: the Big Bourgeoisie of Hanoverian London', *Social History,* **4** (1979); (b) H. Horwitz, '"The mess of the middle class"

revisited: the case of the "big bourgeoisie" of Hanoverian London', *Continuity and Change*, **2** (1987)

Disorder and crime

217 M. Beloff, *Public Order and Popular Disturbances, 1660–1714* (Oxford, 1938)
218 J.A. Sharpe, *Crime in Early Modern England 1550–1750* (1984)
219 G. Rudé, (a) *The Crowd in History, 1730–1848* (1964); (b) *Paris and London in the 18th Century* (1970) – collected essays
220 J. Stevenson, *Popular Disturbances in England 1700–1870* (1979)
221 G. Holmes, 'The Sacheverell Riots: The Church and the Crowd in Early Eighteenth-Century London', *P&P*, **72** (1976), repr. (5)
222 N. Rogers, (a) 'Riot and Popular Jacobitism in Early Hanoverian England', in (65b); (b) 'Popular Protest in Early Hanoverian London', *P&P*, **79** (1978)
223 E.P. Thompson, (a) *Whigs and Hunters: The Origin of the Black Act* (1975); (b) 'The Moral Economy of the English Crowd in the Eighteenth Century', *P&P*, **50** (1971)
224 (a) D. Hay, P. Linebaugh and E.P. Thompson, *Albion's Fatal Tree: Crime and Society in Eighteenth-Century England* (1975); (b) D. Hay, 'Property, Authority and the Criminal Law', in (224a)
225 J.H. Langbein, 'Albion's Fatal Flaws', *P&P*, **98** (1983)
226 J. Brewer and J. Styles, *An Ungovernable People: The English and their Law in the Seventeenth and Eighteenth Centuries* (1980)
227 A.J. Hayter, *The Army and the Crowd in Mid-Georgian England* (1978)
228 W.J. Shelton, *English Hunger and Industrial Disorders: A Study of Social Conflict during the First Decade of George III's Reign* (1973)
229 C.R. Dobson, *Masters and Journeymen: A Pre-History of Industrial Relations, 1717–1800* (1980) – violent disputes only a part of its brief
230 E.P. Thompson, 'Time, Work Discipline and Industrial Capitalism', *P&P*, **38** (1967)

8. IRELAND AND SCOTLAND

231 T.M. Devine and D. Dickson, eds, *Ireland and Scotland 1600–1850: Parallels and Contrasts in Economic and Social Development* (Edinburgh, 1983)
232 (a) D. Hayton, 'John Bull's other Kingdoms: Ireland', in (7); (b) D. Szechi, 'John Bull's other Kingdoms: Scotland', in (7). These form two halves of a joint essay on 'Scotland and Ireland'
233 J.C. Beckett, *The Making of Modern Ireland 1603–1923* (1966)
234 (a) T.W. Moody, F.X. Martin and F.J. Byrne, eds, *A New History of Ireland*, III: *Early Modern Ireland, 1534–1691* (Oxford, 1986); (b) T.W. Moody and W.E. Vaughan, eds, *A New History of Ireland*, IV: *Eighteenth-Century Ireland, 1692–1800* (Oxford 1986)
235 J. Miller, 'The Earl of Tyrconnel and James II's Irish Policy, 1685–1688', *HJ*, **20** (1977)
236 L.M. Cullen, *Anglo-Irish Trade 1600–1801* (Manchester, 1968)
237 J.G. Simms, (a) *Jacobite Ireland 1685–91* (1969); (b) *The Williamite Confiscation in Ireland 1690–1703* (1956)
238 D. Hayton, 'Walpole and Ireland', in (6)
239 J.S. Donnelly, 'The Whiteboy Movement', *Irish Historical Studies*, **21** (1978)
240 J. Hill, 'The Disputed Lessons of Irish History', *P&P*, **118** (1988)

241 C. Smout, *A History of the Scottish People 1560–1830* (1970)

242 G. Donaldson, *Scotland: James V – James VIII* (Edinburgh, 1965)

243 R. Mitchison, *Lordship to Patronage: Scotland 1603–1745* (1983)

244 W. Ferguson, (a) *Scotland: 1689 to the Present* (Edinburgh and London, 1968); (b) *Scotland's Relations with England to 1707* (Edinburgh, 1977)

245 R.H. Campbell, (a) *Scotland since 1707: The Rise of an Industrial Society* (2nd edn, Edinburgh, 1985); (b) *The Rise and Fall of Scottish Industries* (Edinburgh, 1980)

246 H. Hamilton, *An Economic History of Scotland in the Eighteenth Century* (Oxford, 1963)

247 B. Lenman, *An Economic History of Modern Scotland, 1660–1976* (1977)

248 J. Buckroyd, *Church and State in Scotland, 1660–1681* (Edinburgh, 1980)

249 T.C. Smout, *Scottish Trade on the Eve of Union, 1660–1707* (Edinburgh, 1963)

250 P.J. Riley, (a) *King William and the Scottish Politicians* (Edinburgh, 1979); (b) *The Union of England and Scotland: A Study in Anglo-Scottish Politics of the Eighteenth Century* (Manchester, 1978); (c) *The English Ministers and Scotland 1707–1727* (1964)

251 R.H. Campbell, 'The Anglo-Scottish Union of 1707: II. The Economic Consequences', *EcHR*, **16** (1964)

252 B. Lenman, 'A Client Society: Scotland Between the '15 and the '45', in (6)

253 J.S. Shaw, *The Management of Scottish Society 1707–64: Power, Nobles, Lawyers, Edinburgh Agents and English Influences* (Edinburgh, 1983)

254 J.M. Simpson, 'Who Steered the Gravy Train, 1707–1766?', in N.T. Phillipson and R. Mitchison, eds, *Scotland in the Age of Improvement: Essays in Scottish History in the Eighteenth Century* (Edinburgh, 1970)

255 A.C. Chitnis, *The Scottish Enlightenment: A Social History* (1976)

256 E. Richards, *A History of the Highland Clearances: Agrarian Transformation and the Evictions 1746–1886* (1982)

9. OVERSEAS TERRITORIES

257 J.H. Rose, A.P. Newton and E.A. Benians eds, *The Cambridge History of the British Empire*, I: *to 1783* (Cambridge, 1929)

258 J.H. Parry, *Trade and Dominion: The European Overseas Empires in the Eighteenth Century* (1971)

259 (a) C.C. Davies, 'Rivalries in India', in (11b) – an informative sketch; (b) J.H. Parry and F. Thistlethwaite, 'Rivalries in America', in (11b)

260 C.M. Dickerson, *The Navigation Acts and the American Revolution* (1951)

261 C.L. Ver Steeg, *The Formative Years, 1607– 1763* (1965) ['The Making of America', vol I]

262 P. Haffenden, 'The Crown and the Colonial Charters, 1675–1688', *William and Mary Quarterly*, **23** (1958)

263 I.R. Christie, (a) *Crisis of Empire: Great Britain and the American Colonies 1754–1783* (1984); (b) 'The Historian's Quest for the American Revolution', in *Essays . . .* (34)

264 I.R. Christie and B.W. Labaree, *Empire or Independence 1760–1776* (Oxford, 1976)

265 M. Jensen, *The Founding of a Nation: A History of the American Revolution, 1763–1776* (Oxford, 1968)

266 E. Wright, *Fabric of Freedom, 1763–1800* (1965) ['The Making of America', vol II]

267 L.H. Gipson, *The Coming of the Revolution 1763–1775* (1956)

268 R. Middlekauf, *The Glorious Cause: The American Revolution, 1763–1789* (1985)

See also in Section 7: 157, 158

10. EDUCATION AND THE PRINTED WORD; SCIENCE AND IDEAS

269 L. Stone, (a) 'The Educational Revolution in England, 1560–1640', *P&P*, **28** (1964); (b) 'Literacy and Education in England, 1640–1900', *P&P*, **42** (1969)

270 D. Cressy, (a) *Literacy and the Social Order: Reading and Writing in Tudor and Stuart England* (Cambridge, 1980); (b) 'Levels of Illiteracy in England, 1530–1730', *HJ*, **20** (1977); (c) R. Schofield, 'Dimensions of Illiteracy, 1750–1850', *Explorations in Economic History*, **10** (1973)

271 L. Stone, 'The Size and Composition of the Oxford Student Body 1580–1909', in *idem*, ed., *The University in Society*, I (Princeton, 1974)

272 L.S. Sutherland, 'The University of Oxford in the Eighteenth Century', in (18)

273 L.S. Sutherland and L.G. Mitchell, eds, *The History of the University of Oxford,* V: *The Eighteenth Century* (Oxford, 1986)

274 (a) M.G. Jones, *The Charity School Movement*, 1938; (b) V.E. Neuburg, *Popular Education in Eighteenth Century England* (1971)

275 R.O'Day, *Education and Society, 1500–1800* (1982)

276 F.S. Siebert, *Freedom of the Press in England, 1476–1776* (Urbana, Illinois, 1965)

277 P. Rogers, 'The Writer and Society', in *idem*, ed., *The Eighteenth Century* (1978)

278 J. Black, *The English Press in the Eighteenth Century* (1987)

279 G.A. Cranfield, *The Development of the Provincial Newspaper 1700–1760* (Oxford, 1962)

280 (a) J.A. Downie, *Robert Harley and the Press* (Cambridge, 1979); (b) M. Harris, 'Print and Politics in the Age of Walpole', in (6)

281 P. Hyland, 'Liberty and Libel: Government and the Press during the Succession Crisis in Britain 1712–16', *EHR*, **101** (1986)

282 M.C. Jacob, *The Newtonians and the English Revolution, 1689–1720* (1976)

283 A.C. Crombie and M. Hoskin, 'The Scientific Movement and the Diffusion of Scientific Ideas, 1688–1751', in (11a)

284 H.T. Dickinson, *Liberty and Property: Political Ideology in Eighteenth-Century Britain* (1977)

285 (a) R. Porter, 'The Enlightenment in England', in R. Porter and M. Teich, eds, *The Enlightenment in National Context* (Cambridge, 1981); (b) A.M. Wilson, 'The Enlightenment Came First to England', in S.B. Baxter, ed., *England's Rise to Greatness, 1660–1760* (Berkeley, 1983)

286 J. Redwood, *Reason, Ridicule and Religion: The Age of Enlightenment in England, 1660–1750* (1976)

287 G.R. Cragg, *Reason and Authority in the Eighteenth Century* (Cambridge, 1964)

288 J.G.A. Pococke, 'Machiavelli, Harrington and English Political Ideologies in the Eighteenth Century', in *Politics, Language and Time* (1972)

289 J.C.D. Clark, *English Society 1688–1832: Ideology, Social Structure and Political Practice during the Ancien Regime* (Cambridge, 1985)

Bibliography addenda

1. P. Virgin, *The Church in an Age of Negligence: Ecclesiastical Structure and Problems of Church Reform 1700–1840* (Cambridge, 1989)
2. C. Jones, ed., *A Pillar of the Constitution: The House of Lords in British Politics, 1640–1784* (1989)
3. P. Earle, *The Making of the English Middle Class: Business, Society and Family Life in London 1660–1730* (1991)
4. B.L. Wykes, 'Religious Dissent and the Penal Laws: An Explanation of Business Success?, *History*, **75** (1990)
5. P. Langford, *A Polite and Commercial People: England 1727–1783* (Oxford, 1989)
6. E. Cruickshanks and J. Black, eds, *The Jacobite Challenge* (Edinburgh, 1988)
7. F. McLynn, *Charles Edward Stuart: A Tragedy in Many Acts* (1988)

Index

Note: Page references in italics indicate entries in the Compendium of Information; those in **bold** type indicate entries in the Glossary. Subentries are arranged in alphabetical, rather than chronological order, for ease of reference.